BASIC
ENGLISH
DICTIONARY

for elementary and pre-intermediate students

PETER COLLIN PUBLISHING

First published in Great Britain in October 2001

Published by Peter Collin Publishing Ltd
32-34 Great Peter Street, London, SW1P 2DB

© Copyright PH Collin, F Collin, SMH Collin 2001

British Library Cataloguing-in-Publication Data

A catalogue record for this book is available from the British Library

ISBN 1-901659-96-8

Text processing and computer typesetting by PCP
Printed and bound in Finland by WS Bookwell
cover design by Gary Weston

General editor

PH Collin

Preface

This dictionary has been written for elementary and pre-intermediate students of all ages who are learning English and need a basic-level dictionary of English; it would also be an ideal reference book for children who have progressed beyond their first picture dictionary. This dictionary provides a compact reference book for any student working towards an elementary level English examination such as KET or PET *(managed by UCLES)*.

The vocabulary of over 5,000 main entry words covers the basic language of children, young learners and adults but also includes common terms from fashion, sports and games, money and business, etc., which students are likely to come across.

Each entry includes the pronunciation in the international phonetic alphabet, the part of speech and clear definitions in simple English, using only a small defining vocabulary.

All words have example sentences to show how the word is used in practice, and for the commonest words we give many examples, all set in contexts which are easy to understand. Common expressions are highlighted and explained, and examples are also given. Throughout the book, notes give irregular forms, constructions, words which can be confused, etc.

Phonetics

The following symbols have been used to show the pronunciation of the main words in the dictionary.

Stress has been indicated by a main stress mark ('), but these are only guides as the stress of the word may change according to its position in the sentence.

Vowels		*Consonants*	
æ	ba**ck**	b	**b**uck
ɑ:	**h**arm	d	**d**ead
ɒ	**st**op	ð	o**th**er
aɪ	**t**ype	dʒ	**j**ump
aʊ	**h**ow	f	**f**are
aɪɪ	**hire**	g	**g**old
aʊɪ	**hour**	h	**h**ead
ɔ:	**cour**se	j	**y**ellow
ɔɪ	**p**oint	k	**c**ab
e	**h**ead	l	**l**eave
eə	**fair**	m	**m**ix
eɪ	**m**ake	n	**n**il
ə	a**br**oad	ŋ	**br**ing
əʊ	**fl**oat	p	**p**ost
əʊə	**lower**	r	**r**ule
ɜ:	**w**ord	s	**s**ave
iː	**k**eep	ʃ	**sh**op
ɪ	**f**it	t	**t**ake
ɪə	**near**	tʃ	**ch**ange
uù	**p**ool	θ	**th**eme
ʊ	**b**ook	v	**v**alue
ʌ	**sh**ut	w	**w**ork
		z	**z**one
		ʒ	mea**s**ure

Aa

A, a [eɪ] first letter of the alphabet, followed by B; **the A to Z** = street guide for a town, especially one for London; *you can find our road in the A to Z*

a, an [eɪ or æn] *article* **(a)** one; *I want a cup of tea*; *the bomb left an enormous hole*; *we had to wait an hour for the bus*; *a useful guidebook* **(b)** for each or to each; *apples cost 50p a kilo*; *the car was travelling at 50 kilometres an hour*; *he earns £100 a day*

abandon [ə'bændən] *verb* **(a)** to leave; *the crew abandoned the sinking boat* **(b)** to give up, to stop doing something; *we abandoned the idea of going to India on holiday*

abbreviation [əbriːvɪ'eɪʃn] *noun* short form of a word; *'Ltd' is the abbreviation for 'Limited'*

ability [ə'bɪlɪti] *noun* being able to do something; **I'll do it to the best of my ability** = I'll do it as well as I can

able ['eɪbl] *adjective* **to be able to do something** = to have the power or chance to do something; *she wasn't able to breathe*; *will you be able to come to the party?*

about [ə'baʊt] **1** *preposition* **(a)** referring to; *he told me all about his holiday*; *what do you want to speak to the doctor about?*; *he wrote a book about the kings and queens of England* **(b) to be about to do something** = to be just going to do something; *we were about to go home when you arrived* **(c)** *(informal)* **how about** *or* **what about** = what do you think of; *we can't find a new secretary for the club - what about Sarah?*; **how about a cup of tea?** = would you like a cup of tea? **2** *adverb* **(a)** more or less; *the table is about two*

metres long; *she's only about fifteen years old* **(b)** in various places; *there were papers lying about on the floor*

above [ə'bʌv] *preposition* **(a)** higher than; *the plane was flying above the clouds* **(b)** older than; *if you are above 18, you have to pay the full fare* **(c)** louder than; *I couldn't hear the telephone above the noise of the children playing*

abroad [ə'brɔːd] *adverb* in another country; to another country; *they've gone abroad on holiday*; *holidays abroad are more and more popular*

absent ['æbsənt] *adjective* not there; *ten of the staff are absent with flu*

absolutely ['æbsəluːtli] *adverb* completely; *I am absolutely sure I left the keys in my coat pocket*; *you're absolutely right - 'Twelfth Night' was written by Shakespeare, not Marlowe*

absorb [əb'zɔːb] *verb* **(a)** to take in (a liquid, etc.); *salt absorbs moisture from the air* **(b)** to reduce a shock; *the car's springs are supposed to absorb shocks from the road surface*

absurd [əb'sɜːd] *adjective* ridiculous; *it's absurd to expect you will win the lottery if you only buy one ticket*

abuse [ə'bjuːs] *noun* **(a)** very bad treatment; *she suffered physical abuse in prison* **(b)** rude words; *the strikers shouted abuse at the police*

accelerate [æk'seləreɪt] *verb* to make a car go faster; *don't accelerate when you get to traffic lights*

accent ['æksənt] *noun* **(a)** particular way of saying words; *she has an Irish accent*; *he speaks with an American accent* **(b)** sign over a printed letter; **an acute accent** = sign sloping forwards over a vowel, such as é; *'résumé' has two acute accents*

accept [ək'sept] *verb* **(a)** to take a present; *we hope you will accept this little gift* **(b)** to say 'yes' or to agree to something; *we invited* *her to come with us and she accepted* (NOTE: do not confuse with **except)**

acceptable [əkˈseptəbl] *adjective* easily accepted; *a small gift of flowers would be very acceptable*

accident [ˈæksɪdənt] *noun* **(a)** unpleasant thing which happens and causes damage; *she was hurt in a car accident and had to go to hospital*; *thirty people were killed in the rail accident* **(b)** something which happens by chance; *he discovered the missing papers by accident*

accidentally [æksɪˈdentəli] *adverb* by chance; *he discovered the missing papers accidentally*

accommodation [əkɒməˈdeɪʃən] *noun* place to live; *visitors have difficulty in finding hotel accommodation during the summer*

accompany [əˈkʌmpni] *verb* **(a)** to go with; *he accompanied his sister to the hospital*; *turkey is served accompanied by roast potatoes* **(b)** to play a musical instrument, when someone else plays or sings; *she sang and was accompanied on the piano by her father*

according to [əˈkɔːdɪŋ tu] *adverb* **(a)** as someone says or writes; *according to John, there are buses to town every fifteen minutes* **(b)** in relation to; *the teachers have separated the children into classes according to their ages*

account [əˈkaʊnt] **1** *noun* **(a) bank account** = arrangement which you make with a bank to keep your money safely; *I put all my savings into my bank account* **(b) on account of** = because of, due to; *the trains are late on account of the fog* **(c) to take something into account** *or* **to take account of something** = to consider something; *we have to take the weather into account* **(d)** story of what has happened; *they were amused by his account of the journey* **(e) accounts department** = department in a company which deals with money paid, received, borrowed or owed **2**

verb **to account for** = to explain; *he was asked to account for all the money he had spent*

accurate [ˈækjʊrət] *adjective* correct in all details; *are these figures accurate?*

accurately [ˈækjʊrətli] *adverb* correctly; *the weather forecast accurately predicted the storm*

accuse [əˈkjuːz] *verb* to say that someone has done something wrong; *she was accused of stealing from the shop where she worked*

achieve [əˈtʃiːv] *verb* to succeed in doing something; *he achieved his dream when he saw the Great Wall of China*

achievement [əˈtʃiːvmənt] *noun* thing which has been done in a successful way; *coming sixth was a great achievement, since he had never raced before*

acid [ˈæsɪd] *noun* liquid chemical substance containing hydrogen, which burns; *the robbers threw acid in her face*; *vinegar is a sort of acid*

acorn [ˈeɪkɔːn] *noun* fruit of an oak tree; *if you plant an acorn in front of your house, it will take years to grow into an oak tree*

acrobat [ˈækrəbæt] *noun* **circus acrobats** = people who perform exercises as part of a circus show; *the children watched as the acrobats swung on trapezes high above their heads*

across [əˈkrɒs] **1** *preposition* **(a)** from one side to the other; *don't run across the road without looking to see if there are any cars coming* **(b)** on the other side; *he called to her from across the street*; *their house is across the street from ours* = it is just opposite our house **2** *adverb* from one side to the other; *the stream is very narrow - you can easily jump across*

act [ækt] **1** *noun* **(a)** thing which is done; *we caught him in the act* = we caught him as he was doing it **(b)** part of a play, of a show; *Act II of the play takes place in the garden* **(c)** law passed by Parliament; *an act to ban the* *sale of weapons* **2** *verb* **(a)** to take part in a film, play, etc.; *he acted the part of Hamlet in the film* **(b)** to do something; *you have to act quickly if you want to stop a fire*; **to act on behalf of** = to act for someone; *the lawyer is acting on behalf of the old lady's family*; **to act as** = to do the work of; *the thick curtain acts as a screen to cut out noise from the street* **(c)** to behave; *he's started acting in a very strange way*

action ['ækʃən] *noun* **(a)** doing something; *what action are you going to take to prevent any more accidents?*; **out of action** = not working; *the car has been out of action for a week*; *the goalkeeper broke his leg and will be out of action for some time* **(b)** what happens in a play, film, etc.; *the action of the film takes place in London* **(c)** case in a law court where someone asks someone else to appear; *he is going to bring an action for damages against the hospital*

active ['æktɪv] *adjective* **(a)** energetic; *my grandmother is still very active at the age of 88* **(b)** *(volcano)* which is erupting; *scientists think the volcano is no longer active* **(c)** form of a verb which shows that the subject is doing something; *if you say 'the car hit him' the verb is active, but 'he was hit by the car' is passive*

activity [æk'tɪvɪti] *noun* **(a)** being active; *there was a lot of activity on the building site* **(b)** occupation, thing you do to amuse yourself; *children are offered various holiday activities - sailing, skating, skiing, etc.*; **activity holiday** = planned holiday where you do certain things (such as painting, climbing rocks, etc.) (NOTE: plural is **activities)**

actor *or* **actress** ['æktə or 'æktrəs] *noun* person who acts in the theatre, in films, on television; *a famous TV actor* (NOTE: the plural of **actress** is **actresses)**

actual ['æktjʊəl] *adjective* real; *the hut looks quite small but its actual size is nine square metres*; **in actual fact** = really; *in spite of what the newspapers said, in actual fact he*

did win first prize

actually ['æktjʊəli] *adverb* really; *is he actually going to sell the house where his mother is still living?*

ad [æd] *noun (informal)* = ADVERTISEMENT *if you want to sell your car quickly, put an ad in the paper*

adapt [ə'dæpt] *verb* **(a)** to change something so that it fits; *she adapted the story for TV*; *the car has been adapted for a disabled driver* **(b)** to change to become more suitable; *the children adapted easily to life in a tropical country*

adaptable [ə'dæptəbl] *adjective* able to change to deal with a new situation; *she's very adaptable, I'm sure that she won't mind teaching another subject*

add [æd] *verb* **(a)** to make a total of numbers; *if you add all these numbers together it should make fifty*; *adding is usually shown by the plus sign + : 10 + 4 = 14 (say 'ten add four equals fourteen')* **(b)** to put something with something else; *put a tea bag into the pot and add boiling water*; *add a few touches of green to the picture* **(c)** to say or to write something more; *she added that we still owed her some money for work she had done last year*

add up ['æd 'ʌp] *verb* to put several figures together to make a total; *she quickly added up the invoices*

add up to ['æd 'ʌp 'tʊ] *verb* to make a final total; *the money we spent on holiday adds up to over £1000*

addition [ə'dɪʃn] *noun* **(a)** action of adding figures to make a total; *you don't need a calculator to do a simple addition* **(b)** thing or person added; *baby John is the latest addition to the family* **(c) in addition** = also, as well as; *there are twelve registered letters to be sent in addition to this parcel*

additional [ə'dɪʃənəl] *adjective* more; *an additional charge will have to be paid because the suitcase is very heavy*

address [ə'dres] **1** *noun* details of the number of a house, the name of a street and the town where someone lives or works; *what is the doctor's address?*; *our address is: 15 High Street, Teddington, Middlesex*; **address book** = special notebook, with columns printed in such a way that names, addresses and phone numbers can be written in (NOTE: plural is **addresses**) **2** *verb* **(a)** to write the details of name, street, town, etc., on a letter or parcel; *that letter is addressed to me - don't open it!* **(b)** to speak to, to write to; *please address your inquiries to the information office* **(c)** to make a formal speech; *the Member of Parliament addressed the meeting*

adhesive [əd'hiːzɪv] **1** *adjective* which sticks; *she sealed the parcel with adhesive tape*; **self-adhesive** = which sticks to itself; *self-adhesive envelopes are easy to use* **2** *noun* glue; *she bought a tube of adhesive*

adjective ['ædʒektɪv] *noun* word which describes a noun; *in the phrase 'a big black cloud', 'big' and 'black' are both adjectives*

adjust [ə'dʒʌst] *verb* **(a)** to make a slight change to something; *if the trousers are too tight, we can easily adjust the fitting* **(b)** to **adjust to** = to change and adapt to; *it's difficult adjusting to life in a tropical climate*

admiration [ædmə'reɪʃn] *noun* respect for; *everyone watched in admiration as she showed how to toss pancakes*

admire [əd'maɪə] *verb* to look at someone or something with respect; *he's admired for his skill as a rally driver*; *we admired the view from the balcony*

admission [əd'mɪʃn] *noun* **(a)** being allowed to go in; *admission to the exhibition is free on Sundays*; *my friend was refused admission to the restaurant because he was not wearing a tie* **(b)** statement saying that something is true; *her admission that she had taken the money led to her arrest*

admit [əd'mɪt] *verb* **(a)** to allow someone to go in; *children are admitted free, but adults*

have to pay (b) to say that something is true; *he admitted stealing the car*; *she admitted she had taken the watch* (NOTE: admitting - admitted)

adopt [ə'dɒpt] *verb* **(a)** to take a child by law as your son or daughter; *they have adopted a little boy* **(b)** to tell all students to use; *the book has been adopted for use in all English classes*

adore [ə'dɔː] *verb* to like very much; *she adores Italian food*

adult ['ædʌlt] **1** *adjective* **(a)** completely grown; *an adult lion* **(b)** referring to people who are older than children; **adult education** = teaching people over the age of 20 **2** *noun* person who is older than a youth; *children are admitted free, but adults have to pay*

advance [əd'vɑːns] **1** *noun* **(a)** movement forwards; *the team made an advance into their opponents' half* **(b)** money paid as a loan or as a part of a payment to be made later; *can I have an advance of £50 against next month's wages?* **2** *verb* **(a)** to go forward; *the police slowly advanced across the square* **(b)** to pay as a loan; *he advanced me £100*

in advance *phrase* early; *if you want to get good seats for the play, you need to book three weeks in advance*; *they asked us to pay £200 in advance*

advanced [əd'vɑːnst] *adjective* which is studied after several years' of study; *he is taking advanced mathematics*; **advanced level examination (A level)** = examination taken at about 18, at the end of secondary school, which is used as a basis for entry to university or college

advantage [əd'vɑːntɪdʒ] *noun* thing which will help you to be successful; *being able to drive a car is an advantage*; *knowledge of two foreign languages is an advantage in this job*; **to take advantage of** = to profit from; *they took advantage of the cheap fares on offer*; **to take advantage of someone** = to cheat someone; *he took advantage of the old lady*

adventure [əd'ventʃə] *noun* new, exciting and dangerous experience; *I must tell you about our adventures in the Sahara desert*

adverb ['ædvɜːb] *noun* word which describes a verb, an adjective, another adverb or a whole sentence; *in the phrase 'he walked slowly, because the snow was very thick', 'slowly' and 'very' are both adverbs*

adverse ['ædvɜːs] *adjective (conditions)* which do not help, which go against you; *will the plan for the set of new traffic lights have any adverse effects on traffic in the village?*

advertise ['ædvətaɪz] *verb* to make sure that people know that something is for sale, that something is going to happen, that a show is on; *there are posters all over the town advertising the circus*; *did you see that the restaurant is advertising cheap meals on Sundays?*

advertisement [əd'vɜːtɪzmənt] *noun* announcement which tries to make sure that people know that something is for sale, that something is going to happen, that a show is on; *he put an advertisement in the paper*; *she got her job through an advertisement in the newspaper*

advice [əd'vaɪs] *noun* saying what should be done; *my grandfather gave me a very useful piece of advice*; *my mother's advice was to stay in bed*

advise [əd'vaɪz] *verb* to suggest what should be done; *he advised her to put all her money into a bank account*

advise against [əd'vaɪz ə'genst] *verb* to suggest that something should not be done; *he advised against buying the car*

aerial ['eəriəl] *noun* device for receiving radio or TV signals; *we have fixed a TV aerial on the roof*

aeroplane ['eərəpleɪn] *noun* plane or aircraft, a machine which flies in the air, carrying passengers or cargo; *we all got into the little aeroplane and it took off*

aerosol ['eərəsɒl] *noun* can which sends out a liquid such as an insect spray, medicine, etc., in the form of tiny drops; *it's much easier to use an aerosol to spray the kitchen*

affair [ə'feə] *noun* (a) thing which concerns someone; *that's his affair - it's nothing to do with me*; *she's always sticking her nose into other people's affairs* (b) state of affairs = general situation; *the present state of affairs is very serious*

affect [ə'fekt] *verb* to have an influence on, to change; *train services have been seriously affected by the strike*

affection [ə'fekʃn] *noun* love; *she felt great affection for her youngest grandson*

afford [ə'fɔːd] *verb* to have enough money to pay for; *we can't afford to run a large car these days*; *how can they afford two holidays a year?*

afraid [ə'freɪd] *adjective* (a) to be afraid of something = to be frightened of something; *I am afraid of snakes*; *she is afraid of going out alone* (b) to be afraid (that) = to be sorry to say; *you can't see the boss - I'm afraid he's ill*; *have you got a mobile phone? - no, I'm afraid not*

Africa ['æfrɪkə] *noun* large continent, to the south of the Mediterranean, between the Atlantic Ocean and the Indian Ocean; *they want to go to Africa on holiday*; *after ten days at sea, they saw the coast of North Africa in the distance*

African ['æfrɪkən] **1** *adjective* referring to Africa; **African elephant** = largest type of elephant with large ears (the other type is the Indian elephant) **2** *noun* person from Africa; *the head of the United Nations is an African*

after ['ɑːftə] **1** *preposition* (a) following or next in order; *what's the letter after Q in the alphabet?*; *if today is Tuesday, the day after tomorrow is Thursday*; **after you** = you go first; **after you with the milk** = pass me the milk when you have finished with it (b) later than; *we arrived after six o'clock*; *we don't let the children go out alone after dark* (c) to be

after someone = (i) to be looking for someone; (ii) to be angry with someone; *the police are after him*; *if you leave mud all over the kitchen floor, your mother will be after you* **2** *conjunction* later than a time; *after the snow fell, the motorways were blocked*; *phone me after you get home*

after all ['ɑːftə 'ɔːl] *adverb* **(a)** in spite of everything; *she changed her mind and decided to come with us after all* **(b)** the fact is; *I think I'll go out shopping - after all, it's a fine day and I've finished my work*

afternoon [ɑːftə'nuːn] *noun* time between 12 o'clock midday and the evening; *he always has a little sleep in the afternoon*; *the shop is closed on Wednesday afternoons*; *I'm playing tennis tomorrow afternoon*

afterwards *US* **afterward** ['ɑːftəwədz or 'ɑːftəwərd] *adverb* later; *we'll have lunch first and go shopping afterwards*; *she felt fine before dinner but was ill afterwards*

again [ə'gen] *adverb* **(a)** another time, once more; *we'd love to come to see you again*; *he had to take his driving test again* **(b)** back as you were before; *although I like going on holiday, I'm always glad to be home again*

once again ['wʌns ə'geɪn] another time; *once again, the train was late*

yet again ['jet ə'geɪn] once more after many times; *she's taking her driving test yet again*

against [ə'genst] *preposition* **(a)** touching; *he was leaning against the wall*; *she hit her head against the low door* **(b)** not as someone suggests; *it's against the rules* or *against the law* = it's not as the rules say, not as the law says; *it's against the law to drive in the dark without lights*; *you mustn't hold the football in your hands - it's against the rules* **(c)** opposite; *England is playing against South Africa tomorrow*

age [eɪdʒ] *noun* **(a)** the number of years which you have lived; *she is thirty years of age*; *he looks younger than his age*; *old age* = period when you are old **(b)** *ages* = a very long time; *I've been waiting here for ages*; *it took us ages to get served*

agency ['eɪdʒənsi] *noun* office which acts for another firm; *we have the agency for Ford cars*; *estate agency* = office which arranges for the sale of houses, flats, etc. (NOTE: plural is agencies)

agent ['eɪdʒənt] *noun* person who works for or represents someone else; *our head office is in London but we have an agent in Paris*

ago [ə'gəu] *adverb* in the past; *he phoned a few minutes ago*; *she came to England two years ago*

agree [ə'griː] *verb* **(a)** to say 'yes', to say that you will do something; *we asked her to come with us and she agreed*; *most of the group agreed with her suggestion*; *she agreed to look after the baby for us* **(b)** to agree with someone = to think the same way as someone; *I agree with you that most people drive too fast* **(c)** not to agree with someone = to make someone ill; *all this rich food does not agree with me*

agreement [ə'griːmənt] *noun* **(a)** thinking the same; *any agreement between the two sides is still a long way off*; *they are in agreement with our plan* = they agree with our plan **(b)** contract; *we signed an agreement with the Italian company*

ah [ɑː] *interjection showing surprise*; *Ah! John, how nice to see you!*; *the circus audience let out 'oohs' and 'ahs' as they watched the lions in the ring*

ahead [ə'hed] *adverb* in front; *our team was losing, but now we are ahead again*; *you need to go straight ahead, and then turn left*

ahead of [ə'hed 'ɒv] *preposition* **(a)** in front of; *ahead of us was a steep hill*; *you have a mass of work ahead of you* **(b)** *(informal)* before; *they drafted in extra police ahead of the international rugby match*

aid [eɪd] *noun* **(a)** help; *aid to Third World countries* **(b)** in aid of = to help; *they are collecting money in aid of refugees*

aim [eɪm] **1** *noun* what you are trying to do;

his aim is to do well at school and then go to university **2** *verb* **(a)** to plan to do something; *we aim to go on holiday in June* **(b)** to point a gun at someone or something; *he was aiming at the policeman*

air   [eə] **1** *noun* **(a)** mixture of gases which cannot be seen, but which is all around us and which every animal breathes; *the mountain air feels cold*; *he threw the ball up into the air* **(b)** method of travelling (or sending goods) using aircraft; **air fares** = different types of fares charged for travel on aircraft **2** *verb* to make (a room, clothes, etc.) fresher; *let's open the windows to air the bedroom*

by air   ['baɪ 'eə] in an aircraft; *we are going to France by ferry, not by air*; *send the letter by air if you want it to arrive before Christmas*

aircraft   ['eəkrɑːft] *noun* machine which flies in the air; *the passengers got into the aircraft*; *the president came down the aircraft steps*

air force   ['eə 'fɔːs] *noun* a country's military air organization; *American Air Force planes attacked the enemy*

airline   ['eəlaɪn] *noun* company which runs air services; *he's an airline pilot*; *the airline has been voted the most popular with travellers*

airmail   ['eəmeɪl] *noun* way of sending letters or parcels by air; *we sent the package by airmail*; **airmail envelope** = very light envelope for sending airmail letters; **airmail sticker** = blue sticker with the words 'by air mail' which can be stuck to an envelope or packet to show it is being sent by air

airplane   ['eərpleɪn] *noun US* aircraft; *the president came down the steps of the airplane*

airport   ['eəpɔːt] *noun* place where aircraft land and take off; *you can take the underground to London Airport*; *we are due to arrive at London Airport at 6 p.m.*; **airport bus** = bus which takes passengers to and from an airport; *there is an airport bus which takes passengers to the centre of town*

ajar   [ə'dʒɑː] *adjective* slightly open; *leave the*

door ajar to let in some air

alarm   [ə'lɑːm] **1** *noun* **(a)** loud warning; *an alarm will sound if someone touches the wire*; *it was only a false alarm* = it was a warning of danger when there wasn't any **(b)** **fire alarm** = bell which rings if there is a fire; **alarm bell** = bell which rings to warn people; **alarm (clock)** = clock which can be set to ring a bell at a certain time to wake you up; *I set my alarm for 5.30 because I had to catch the 7 o'clock train* **(c)** being afraid; *there's no cause for alarm, the injection won't hurt at all* **2** *verb* to warn or frighten; *I don't want to alarm you, but the police say a dangerous criminal has been seen in the village*

album   ['ælbəm] *noun* **(a)** large book; *he showed me his stamp album* **(b)** collections of songs on a CD, cassette, etc.; *this is her latest album*

alcohol   ['ælkəhɒl] *noun* liquid, such as beer, wine, etc., which can make you drunk; *pubs will not serve alcohol to anyone under the age of 18*

A Level   ['eɪ 'levəl] = ADVANCED LEVEL examination taken at about 18, at the end of secondary school; *if you pass your A Levels, you can go on to university*

alien   ['eɪliən] *noun* **(a)** a person who is not a citizen of the country; *when you arrive at the airport, you must go through the door marked 'aliens'* **(b)** creature coming from outer space; *in the film, the earth is attacked by aliens from Mars*

alight   [ə'laɪt] **1** *verb (formal)* to get off a bus, etc.; *alight here for the Post Office* **2** *adjective* on fire; *after pouring petrol on the heap of rubbish he set it alight*

alike   [ə'laɪk] *adjective* very similar; *the two sisters are very alike*

alive   [ə'laɪv] *adjective* **(a)** not dead; *he was still alive when he was rescued, even though he had been in the sea for hours*; *TV did not exist when my grandfather was alive* **(b)** lively; *the Greek village is rather dead during* *the day time, but it really comes alive at night*

all [ɔːl] **1** *adjective & pronoun* everything or everyone; *did you pick all (of) the tomatoes?*; *where are all the children?*; *they all like coffee* or *all of them like coffee* **2** *adverb* **(a)** completely; *the ground was all white after the snow fell*; *I forgot all about her birthday* **(b) all by yourself** = all alone; *you can't do it all by yourself*; *I'm all by myself this evening - my girlfriend's gone out*

not at all ['nɒt ət 'ɔːl] certainly not; *do you mind waiting for a few minutes? - not at all!*

all along ['ɔːl ə'lɒŋ] *adverb* **(a)** along the whole length of; *policemen were standing all along the route of the procession* **(b)** right from the beginning; *we suspected all along that something was wrong*

all at once ['ɔːl ət 'wɒns] *phrase* suddenly; *all at once the telephone rang*

all in ['ɔːl 'ɪn] *adjective* **(a)** including everything; *they quoted us an all-in price of £250* **(b)** *(informal)* tired out; *after moving all my stuff to my new flat I was all in*

all over ['ɔːl 'əʊvə] *phrase* **(a)** everywhere; *his trousers were dirty all over* **(b)** finished; *the show was all over by nine o'clock*

all right ['ɔːl 'raɪt] **1** *adjective* well, not sick; *she was ill yesterday but is all right now* **2** *interjection; (meaning 'yes')* **all right, here's your money**; *will you answer the telephone for me? - all right!*

all the same ['ɔːl ðə 'seɪm] *phrase* **(a)** in spite of this; *I'm not really keen on horror films, but I'll go with you all the same* **(b)** it's **all the same** = it makes no difference; *if it's all the same to you, I won't come to the party*

allergic [ə'lɜːdʒɪk] *adjective* **to be allergic to** = to react badly to; *she is allergic to cats*; *he showed an allergic reaction to peanuts*

allergy ['ælədʒi] *noun* bad reaction to a substance; *she has an allergy to household dust*; *the baby has a tomato allergy*

allow [ə'laʊ] *verb* to let someone do something; *smoking is not allowed in the restaurant*; *you are allowed to borrow two*

library books

allowance [ə'laʊəns] *noun* **(a)** money paid at regular intervals; *she gets an allowance from her father every week* **(b)** amount of money which you are allowed to earn without paying tax; *allowances for married couples have been increased in the budget* **(c) to make allowances for** = to take something into account; *you must make allowances for his age*

ally ['ælaɪ] *noun* person or country which is on the same side; *when one of our allies is attacked, we have to come to their defence* (NOTE: plural is **allies**)

almost ['ɒlməʊst] *adverb* nearly; *London is almost as far from here as Paris*; *she's almost as tall as I am*; *hurry up, it's almost time for the film to start*

alone [ə'ləʊn] **1** *adjective* with no one else; *she lives alone with her cats*; *she was all alone in the shop when three men walked in*; *we don't let the children go out alone after dark* **2** *adverb* **(a) to leave someone alone** = not to bother someone; *leave that cat alone and come and have your tea* **(b) let alone** = and certainly not; *he can't even ride a bike let alone drive a car*

along [ə'lɒŋ] **1** *preposition* **(a)** by the side of; *the river runs along one side of the castle* **(b)** from one end to the other; *walk along the street until you come to the post office* **2** *adverb (with verbs)* **(a) to get along with someone** = to agree with or to work well with someone; *she doesn't get along very well with her new boss* **(b)** to go with, to come with, etc.; *after the accident, the driver was taken along to the police station*

alongside [əlɒŋ'saɪd] *preposition & adverb* beside; *we had stopped at a red light when a police car pulled up alongside*

aloud [ə'laʊd] *adverb* in a voice which can be heard; *he insists on reading the football scores out aloud*

alphabet ['ælfəbet] *noun* series of letters in

order, A, B, C, etc.; *A is the first letter of the alphabet, and B is the second*; *if you're going to Greece on holiday, you ought to learn the Greek alphabet*

alphabetical [ælfə'betɪkl] *adjective* referring to the alphabet; **in alphabetical order** = in order of the first letter of each word; *the words in the dictionary are in alphabetical order*

already [ɔːl'redi] *adverb* before now, before a certain time; *it's only nine o'clock, I've already done all my shopping*; **I have seen that film already** = I've seen that film before

also ['ɔːlsəʊ] *adverb* too, as well as; *she sings well and can also play the piano*

alter ['ɒltə] *verb* to change; *he has altered so much I didn't recognize him*

alteration [ɒltə'reɪʃn] *noun* change; *she made some alterations to the design*

alternate 1 *adjective* [ɔːl'tɜːnət] every other one; *we see each other on alternate Sundays* 2 *verb* ['ɔːltəneɪt] to put in place of something, then switch them round; *fill the pot with alternating slices of potato and onion*

although [ɔːl'ðəʊ] *conjunction* in spite of the fact that; *although it was freezing, she didn't put a coat on*; *I've never been into that shop although I've often walked past it*

altogether [ɔːltə'geðə] *adverb* taking everything together; *the food was £10 and the drinks £5, so that makes £15 altogether*

aluminium *US* **aluminum** [æljʊ'mɪnjəm or ə'luːmɪnəm] *noun* metal coloured like silver, which is extremely light; *cover the meat in a sheet of aluminium foil*

always ['ɔːlweɪz] *adverb* **(a)** every time; *she is always late for work*; *why does it always rain when we want to go for a walk?* **(b)** all the time; *it's always hot in tropical countries* **(c)** again and again; *she's always asking me to lend her money*

am [æm] *see* BE

a.m. *US* **A.M.** ['eɪ 'em] *adverb* in the morning, before 12 o'clock; *I have to catch the 7 a.m. train to work every day*; *the TV breakfast news starts at 6.30 a.m.*

amazement [ə'meɪzmənt] *noun* great surprise; *to his amazement he won first prize*

amazing [ə'meɪzɪŋ] *adjective* **(a)** which surprises you very much; *it was amazing that she never suspected anything* **(b)** extremely interesting and unusual; *it was an amazing experience, sailing down the Nile*

ambulance ['æmbjʊləns] *noun* van which carries sick or injured people; *when she fell down the stairs, her father called an ambulance*

America [ə'merɪkə] *noun* **(a)** one of two large continents between the Atlantic and Pacific Oceans; *in the year 1492 Columbus discovered America* **(b)** the United States; *she spent all her savings on a holiday in America*

American [ə'merɪkən] **1** *adjective* referring to America or to the United States of America; *we are stying with an American family for the summer*; *her mother is American* **2** *noun* person from the United States of America; *the Americans won several gold medals at the Olympics*

among *or* **amongst** [ə'mʌŋ or ə'mʌŋst] *preposition* **(a)** surrounded by, in the middle of; *to make a camp, we put up tents among the trees*; *he was standing amongst a crowd of tourists* **(b)** between various people in a group; *the Christmas cake was divided among the class of children*

amount [ə'maʊnt] *noun* quantity of something, such as money; *the amount in my bank account has reached £1,000*; **a certain amount** = some; *the storm did a certain amount of damage*

amount to [ə'maʊnt tʊ] *verb* to make a total of; *the total bill amounts to over £100*

amuse [ə'mjuːz] *verb* **(a)** to make someone laugh; *the story about the Prime Minister's cat will amuse you*; *I was amused to hear that you and Jim are sharing a flat* **(b)** to make the time pass in a pleasant way; **to amuse yourself** = to play, to get pleasure from what you are doing; *the children amused themselves quietly while their parents talked*

amusement [əˈmjuːzmənt] *noun* **(a)** pleasure; **amusement park** = outdoor park with various types of entertainment, such as roundabouts, shooting galleries, etc. **(b) to someone's amusement** = making someone laugh; *much to her amusement, the band played 'Happy Birthday to you!'*

an [æn or ən] *see* A

ancient [ˈeɪnʃənt] *adjective* very old; *he was riding an ancient bicycle*

and [ænd or nd] *conjunction; (used to join two words or phrases)* *all my uncles and aunts live in the country*; *use a knife and fork to eat your meat*; *come and sit down next to me*

and so on [nd ˈsəʊ ɒn] *adverb* with other things; *he talked about plants: flowers, vegetables, and so on*

angel [ˈeɪndʒl] *noun* **(a)** being that lives in heaven; *a grave with a statue of an angel* **(b)** *(informal)* sweet, kind person; *be an angel and get me my slippers*

anger [ˈæŋɡə] *noun* strong feeling of being annoyed with someone, and wanting to hurt them; *the anger of the crowd was obvious as they tried to attack the referee*

angle [ˈæŋɡl] *noun* corner between two lines; *she planted the tree in the angle of the two walls*; **acute angle** = angle less than 90°; **right angle** = 90° angle; **at an angle** = not straight; *the shop front is at an angle to the road*

angrily [ˈæŋɡrɪli] *adverb* in an angry way; *he shouted angrily when the children climbed over his fence*

angry [ˈæŋɡri] *adjective* upset and annoyed, and sometimes wanting to harm someone; *the shopkeeper is angry with the schoolchildren because they broke his window*; *when the taxi still hadn't arrived by 3 o'clock she got angrier and angrier* (NOTE: **angrier - angriest**)

animal [ˈænɪməl] *noun* living and moving thing (but usually not people); *I like to have animals about the house, so we have two dogs and three cats*

ankle [ˈæŋkəl] *noun* part of the body, where your leg joins your foot; *I couldn't swim, the water only came up to my ankles*; *she twisted her ankle when she slipped on the stairs*; **ankle socks** = short socks

anniversary [ænɪˈvɜːsəri] *noun* the same date as an important event in the past; *1966 was the nine-hundredth anniversary of the Battle of Hastings*; **wedding anniversary** = date which is the day when two people were married (NOTE: plural is **anniversaries**)

announce [əˈnaʊns] *verb* to say officially or in public; *the judges announced the results of the competition*

announcement [əˈnaʊnsmənt] *noun* statement made in public; *the airline made several announcements about flight changes*

annoy [əˈnɔɪ] *verb* to make someone angry; *we play loud music to annoy our neighbours*

annoyed [əˈnɔɪd] *adjective* angry; *he was annoyed with his neighbours who had cut down one of his trees*; *you can tell he's annoyed by the way his ears go red*; *I was annoyed to find someone had stolen my car*

annoying [əˈnɔɪɪŋ] *adjective* which makes you angry; *I find it very annoying that the post doesn't come before 10 o'clock*; *how annoying! - I've got to go back to the supermarket because I forgot to buy some milk*

annual [ˈænjʊəl] **1** *adjective* happening once a year; *I get annual interest of 6% on my savings account* **2** *noun* book which comes out each year; *have you got the new 'Star Wars Annual'?*

anorak [ˈænəræk] *noun* warm waterproof jacket, sometimes with a hood; *you need a thick anorak when climbing mountains in winter*

another [əˈnʌðə] *adjective and pronoun* **(a)**

one more (like others); *I'd like another one of those cakes, please* (b) a different (one); *he's bought another car*; *can I have another plate, please, this one's dirty?*

answer [ˈɑːnsə] 1 *noun* reply, letter or conversation after someone has written or spoken to you, asking you a question; *have you had an answer to your letter yet?*; **in answer to** = as a reply to; *I am writing in answer to your letter of October 6th* 2 *verb* (a) to reply, to speak or write words when someone has spoken to you or asked you a question; *when he asked us if we had enjoyed the meal we all answered 'yes'* (b) **to answer the phone** = to lift the telephone when it rings and listen to what the caller is saying; *when I called, it was his mother who answered the phone*; **to answer the door** = to open the door when someone knocks or rings; *he jumped out of the bath and answered the door with a towel round his waist*

ant [ænt] *noun* small insect which lives in large groups of thousands together; *I found an ants' nest outside the kitchen door*

antenna [ænˈtenə] *noun* (a) tube on the head of an insect, used to feel things; *a butterfly has two antennae which it uses to sense things* (NOTE: plural is **antennae** [ænˈteniː]) (b) device for receiving radio or TV signals; *a bigger TV antenna should give better reception* (NOTE: plural is **antennas**)

antibiotic [æntibaɪˈɒtɪk] *noun* substance which kills germs; *he was given a course of antibiotics*

anticlockwise [æntɪˈklɒkwaɪz] *adverb & adjective* in the opposite direction to the hands of a clock; *he was driving anticlockwise round the ring road when the accident took place* (NOTE: the opposite is **clockwise**)

antique [ænˈtiːk] 1 *adjective* old and valuable; *he collects antique Chinese bowls* 2 *noun* valuable old object; *their house is full of antiques*; **antique shop** = shop which sells antiques

antiseptic [æntiˈseptɪk] 1 *adjective* which prevents germs spreading; *she washed her mouth out with an antiseptic solution* 2 *noun* substance which prevents germs growing or spreading; *the nurse put antiseptic on his knee*

anxious [ˈæŋkʃəs] *adjective* (a) nervous and very worried about something; *she's anxious about the baby* (b) eager to do something; *the shopkeeper is always anxious to please his customers*

anxiously [ˈæŋkʃəsli] *adverb* in a nervous worried way; *they are waiting anxiously for the results of the exam*

any [ˈeni] 1 *adjective and pronoun* (a) it doesn't matter which; *take any book you like*; *I'm free any day next week except Tuesday* (b) a quantity; *have you any money left?*; *is there any food for me?* (c) **not...any** = none; *there isn't any food left - the children have eaten it all* 2 *adverb (used for stress in comparatives)* **not...any** = not even a little (more); *can't you sing any louder?*; *he can't pedal any faster*

any more [eniˈmɔː] *adverb* (a) a certain number more; *do you have any more books on bees?* (b) **not ... any more** = no longer; *we don't go there any more*

anyone *or* **anybody** [ˈeniwʌn or ˈenibɒdi] *pronoun* (a) it doesn't matter who; *anyone can learn to ride a bike*; **anyone else** = any other person; *is there anyone else who can't see the screen?*; *did you see anyone else apart from Uncle Richard?* (b) *(after questions, negatives)* some person; *can anybody lend me some money?*; *did anyone telephone while I was out?*; **we didn't meet anybody we knew** = we met no one we knew; **hardly anybody came to the meeting** = very few people came to the meeting

anything [ˈeniθɪŋ] *pronoun* (a) it doesn't matter what; *our dog will bite anything that moves* (b) *(in questions, negatives)* something; *did you do anything interesting during the weekend?*; *has anything happened to their* plans for a long holiday?; he didn't eat anything

anything else [ˈenɪθɪŋ ˈels] *pronoun* any other thing; *do you want anything else to drink?*; *is there anything else you don't like eating?*; *is there anything else you would like to know about?*

anyway [ˈenɪweɪ] *adverb* in any case; *I think it's time to leave - anyway, the last bus is at 11.40*

anywhere [ˈenɪweə] *adverb* **(a)** it doesn't matter where; *put the chair anywhere* **(b)** *(in questions, negatives)* somewhere; *is there anywhere where I can sit down?*; *I can't see your wallet anywhere*

apart [əˈpɑːt] *adverb* **(a)** separated; *the two villages are about six miles apart* **(b)** in separate pieces; **the watch came apart** = the watch came to pieces; **to tell something** *or* **someone apart** = to identify two things or people that are similar; *the twins are very alike - how can you tell them apart?*

apart from [əˈpɑːt frɒm] *phrase* except, other than; *I'm feeling fine, apart from a slight cold*

apartment [əˈpɑːtmənt] *noun* separate set of rooms for living in (British English is usually 'flat'); *she has an apartment in central New York*; **an apartment block** *or* **a block of apartments** = large building divided into many apartments; **a studio apartment** = apartment with one main room, plus kitchen and bathroom

ape [eɪp] *noun* large monkey, such as a chimpanzee; *does man really come from the apes?*

apologize [əˈpɒlədʒaɪz] *verb* to say you are sorry; *did you apologize to your mother for what you said?*; *he shouted at her and then apologized*

apology [əˈpɒlədʒi] *noun* saying sorry; *my apologies for being so late*; *I expect we will receive an apology in due course* (NOTE: plural is **apologies**)

apostrophe [əˈpɒstrəfi] *noun* printing sign ('); *an apostrophe either shows that a letter has been left out (weren't) or is used with 's' to show possession: before an 's' with singular words, after the 's' with plural words (a boy's coat, the girls' team)*

apparatus [æpəˈreɪtəs] *noun* scientific or medical equipment; *the firemen had to wear breathing apparatus to enter the burning building*

apparently [əˈpærəntli] *adverb* as it seems; *apparently she took the last train home and then disappeared*

appeal [əˈpiːl] **1** *noun* **(a)** asking for help; *the police have made an appeal for witnesses*; *the hospital is launching an appeal to raise £50,000* **(b)** attraction; *the appeal of Greece as a holiday destination* **2** *verb* **(a)** to appeal for = to ask for; *they appealed for money to continue their work* **(b)** to appeal against a decision = to ask a court to look again at a decision; *he has appealed against the sentence* **(c)** to appeal to = to attract; *the idea of working in Australia for six months appealed to her*

appear [əˈpiːə] *verb* **(a)** to start to be seen; *a ship appeared through the fog* **(b)** to seem; *there appears to be a mistake*; *he appears to have forgotten the time* **(c)** to play a part in a film or play; *his dream is to appear on TV*

appearance [əˈpiːərəns] *noun* **(a)** look; *you could tell from his appearance that he had slept badly*; **to keep up appearances** = to try to show that you are still as rich or important as you were before **(b)** being present, being there; *this is her second appearance in a film*; **to put in an appearance** = to come to a meeting, etc.

appetite [ˈæpɪtaɪt] *noun* wanting to eat; *going for a long walk has given me an appetite*; *he's not feeling well and has lost his appetite*; **good appetite** = interest in eating food; *the baby has a good appetite*

applause [əˈplɔːz] *noun* clapping; *at the end*

of the concert there was a storm of applause

apple ['æpl] *noun* common hard round sweet fruit, growing on a tree; *don't eat those green apples - they'll make you ill*; **apple tree** = tree which apples grow on; *there's an old apple tree behind our house*

application [æplɪ'keɪʃn] *noun* action of applying for a job, etc.; *we've received dozens of applications for the job of van driver*; **application form** = form to be filled in when applying; *she filled in an application form*

apply [ə'plaɪ] *verb* **(a) to apply for a job** = to ask for a job; *she applied for a job in the supermarket*; **to apply to take a course** = to ask to be admitted to a course; *it's encouraging to see that so many students have applied to take the course* **(b)** to put on (paint); *wait until the first coat of paint is dry before you apply the second* **(c) to apply to** = to affect or to link with; *this rule only applies to people coming from outside the European Union*

appoint [ə'pɔɪnt] *verb* to give (a job) to someone; *he was appointed as manager*; *we want to appoint someone to manage our sales department*

appointment [ə'pɔɪntmənt] *noun* **(a)** being given a job; **on her appointment as manager** = when she was made manager **(b)** agreed time for a meeting; *I want to make an appointment to see the doctor*; *I have an appointment with Dr Jones*

appreciate [ə'priːʃɪeɪt] *verb* to recognize that something is worth a lot; *most people appreciate shops which give good value*

approach [ə'prəʊtʃ] **1** *noun* **(a)** coming closer; *with the approach of winter we need to get the central heating serviced* **(b)** way which leads to; *the approaches to the city were crowded with buses* **(c)** way of dealing with a situation; *his approach to the question was different from hers* (NOTE: plural is **approaches**) **2** *verb* to come near; *the plane was approaching London airport when the*

lights went out

approval [ə'pruːvəl] *noun* **(a)** agreeing with; *does the choice of colour have your approval or meet with your approval?* **(b) on approval** = (goods) taken by a customer to use and see if he or she likes them; *the shop let us have the washing machine for two weeks on approval*

approve [ə'pruːv] *verb* **(a) to approve of** = to think something is good; *the staff don't approve of people using mobile phones in the library* **(b)** to agree to something officially; *the committee approved the scheme*

approximately [ə'prɒksɪmətli] *adverb* roughly; *it takes approximately 35 minutes to get to central London from here*

apricot ['eɪprɪkɒt] *noun* stone fruit with yellow flesh, like a small peach, but not as juicy; *you have a choice of marmalade or apricot jam for breakfast*

April ['eɪprəl] *noun* the fourth month of the year, the month after March and before May; *her birthday is in April*; *we went on holiday last April*

April Fools' Day ['eɪprəl 'fuːlz deɪ] *noun* April 1st, the day when you play tricks on people

apron ['eɪprən] *noun* cloth worn over your clothes when cooking or doing housework; *the chef wore an apron with blue stripes*

aquarium [ə'kweərɪəm] *noun* **(a)** tank for keeping tropical fish; *he keeps an aquarium with little blue fish in the kitchen* **(b)** building with an exhibition of fish; *we went to the London Aquarium on Saturday afternoon*

arch [ɑːtʃ] *noun* curved part of a building, forming a roof or door; *the church roof is formed of tall stone arches* (NOTE: plural is arches)

architect ['ɑːkɪtekt] *noun* person who designs buildings; *we've asked a local architect to draw up plans for a new town hall*

architecture ['ɑːkɪtektʃə] *noun* design of buildings; *she is studying architecture or* *she's an architecture student*

are [ɑ:] *see* BE

area [ˈeərɪə] *noun* **(a)** space; *we always sit in the 'no smoking' area* **(b)** measurement of the space taken up by something (calculated by multiplying how long it is by how wide it is); *the area of the room is four square metres* **(c)** district, part of a town or country; *the house is in a very good area for getting to the motorways and airports*; **the London area** = the part of England round London; *houses in the London area are more expensive than in other parts of the country*

area code [ˈeərɪə ˈkəʊd] *noun* special telephone number which is given to a particular area; *the area code for central London is 0207*

aren't [ɑ:nt] *see* BE

argue [ˈɑ:gju:] *verb* to discuss without agreeing; *they argued over the prices*; *she argued with the waiter about the bill*

argument [ˈɑ:gju:mənt] *noun* quarrel; **to get into an argument with someone** = to start to argue with someone; *he got into an argument with the taxi driver*

arithmetic [əˈrɪθmetɪk] *noun* calculations with figures; *children must concentrate on reading, writing and arithmetic*

arm [ɑ:m] **1** *noun* **(a)** part of your body which goes from your shoulder to your hand; *he held the parcel under his arm*; *lift your arms up above your head*; **arm in arm** = with their arms linked; *they walked down the street arm in arm* **(b)** part of a chair which you can rest your arms on; *he put his coffee cup on the arm of his chair* **2** *verb* to give weapons to someone; *the government armed the police and sent them to arrest the strikers*

armchair [ˈɑ:mtʃeə] *noun* comfortable chair with arms; *each room in the hotel has two armchairs and a TV*

armed [ɑ:md] *adjective (person)* carrying weapons; *most British policemen are not armed*; *(informal)* **armed to the teeth** = carrying lots of weapons; *the robbers were armed to the teeth*

armour *US* **armor** [ˈɑ:mə] *noun* metal clothing worn by soldiers in the Middle Ages; *you can see suits of armour in the museum*

arms [ɑ:mz] *noun* **(a)** weapons, such as guns or bombs; *they were selling arms to African countries* **(b) up in arms about** = very annoyed about; *they are up in arms about the new bus timetable*

army [ˈɑ:mi] *noun* all the soldiers of a country, trained for fighting on land; *he left school and joined the army* (NOTE: plural is **armies**)

around [əˈraʊnd] **1** *preposition* **(a)** going all round something; *she had a gold chain around her neck*; *the police car drove around the town* **(b)** close to, nearby; *a few boys were hanging around the bus stop* **(c)** in various places; *we have lots of computers scattered around the office* **(d)** more or less; *it will cost around £200* **2** *adverb* **(a)** in various places; *papers were lying around all over the floor* **(b)** close to, nearby; *the children stood around waiting for the bus*; *it's the only swimming pool for miles around* **(c)** in existence; *the new coins have been around for some weeks now*

arrange [əˈreɪndʒ] *verb* **(a)** to put in order; *the chairs are arranged in rows*; *the books are arranged in alphabetical order* **(b)** to organize; *let's arrange to meet somewhere before we go to the cinema*; *she arranged for a taxi to meet him at the airport*; *I've arranged with my mother that she will feed the cat while we're away*

arrangement [əˈreɪndʒmənt] *noun* **(a)** putting into an order; *the arrangement of the pictures in a book* **(b)** organizing; *all the arrangements for the wedding were left to the bride's mother*

arrest [əˈrest] **1** *noun* holding someone for breaking the law; *the police made several arrests at the demonstration*; **under arrest** =

held by the police; *after the fight three people were under arrest* **2** *verb* to hold someone for breaking the law; *the police arrested two men and took them to the police station*; *if you are arrested you must try to get in touch with your lawyer*

arrival [əˈraɪvl] *noun* **(a)** action of reaching a place; *we announce the arrival of flight AB 987 from New York*; *we apologize for the late arrival of the 14.25 express from Edinburgh*; **on arrival** = when you arrive; *on arrival at the hotel, members of the group will be given a programme of events* **(b)** person who has arrived; *he's a new arrival on our staff* **(c) arrivals** = part of an airport that deals with passengers who are arriving; *I'll wait for you in arrivals*

arrive [əˈraɪv] *verb* to reach a place; *the train from Paris arrives in London at 5 p.m.*; *when we arrived at the cinema we found it was full*

arrow [ˈærəʊ] *noun* **(a)** piece of wood with a sharp point, shot into the air with a bow; *King Harold was killed by an arrow at the Battle of Hastings* **(b)** printed sign (➜) which points to something; *follow the arrows to the exhibition*

art [ɑːt] *noun* painting, drawing, etc.; *she is taking art lessons*; *he went to an exhibition at the local art college*; **art gallery** = museum of paintings, sculptures, etc.

artery [ˈɑːtəri] *noun* tube carrying blood from the heart round the body (as opposed to a vein which takes blood back to the heart); *a main artery runs down the side of the neck* (NOTE: plural is **arteries**)

article [ˈɑːtɪkl] *noun* **(a)** report in a newspaper; *did you read the article on skiing holidays in yesterday's paper?* **(b)** object, thing; *several articles of clothing were found near the road* **(c)** one of the parts of speech; *'the' is the definite article; 'a' is the indefinite article*

artificial [ɑːtɪˈfɪʃl] *adjective* not real; *they're not real flowers on the restaurant tables - they're artificial*

artist [ˈɑːtɪst] *noun* person who paints, draws, etc.; *he collects paintings by local artists*; **pavement artist** = artist who draws pictures on the pavement with coloured chalks

arts [ɑːts] *noun* **(a)** all work connected with art; *she's the arts director of the local council* **(b)** subject taught which is not a science; *she has an arts degree*

as [æz] **1** *conjunction* **(a)** because; *as you can't drive, you'll have to go by bus* **(b)** at the same time as; *as he was getting into the bath, the telephone rang* **(c)** in this way; *leave everything as it is* **2** *preposition* **(a)** in a certain job; *he had a job as a bus driver* **(b)** because you are; *as a doctor, he has to know the symptoms of all the common diseases* **(c)** like; *she was dressed as a nurse*

as...as [æz] *(making comparative)* like; *she is as tall as I am*; *I can't run as fast as you*

as from [ˈæz ˈfrɒm] *preposition* from a time; **as from next Friday** = starting from next Friday

as if *or* **as though** [əz ˈɪf *or* əz ˈðəʊ] in the same way as; *it looks as if it is going to be fine for the cricket match*

as well [ˈæz ˈwel] *phrase* in addition, also; *she came to the party and brought her little sister as well*

as well as [əz ˈwel æz] *phrase* in addition to, together with; *as well as being a maths teacher, he delivers newspapers in his spare time*

ascend [əˈsend] *verb (formal)* to go up; *the balloon rapidly ascended to 3000m*

ash [æʃ] *noun* **(a)** grey dust left after a fire, from a volcano, etc.; *there was a pile of black ash left after we burnt the rubbish*; *Pompeii was covered with a thick layer of ash from the volcano* **(b)** tree growing in the northern part of Europe; *ash trees have black buds and are the last trees to have leaves in spring*

ashamed [əˈʃeɪmd] *adjective* embarrassed and sorry (for what you have done or not done); *I am ashamed to say that I have never been to the Tate Gallery*; *being proud of your* *family is nothing to be ashamed of*

Asia ['eɪʒə] *noun* large continent running from the east of Europe to China and Japan; *the Trans-Siberian Railway crosses the deserts of central Asia*

Asian ['eɪʒən] **1** *adjective* referring to Asia; *we went to a concert of Asian music* **2** *noun* person coming from one of the countries of Asia; *more than half the children in the class are Asians*

aside [ə'saɪd] *adverb* **(a)** to one side; *he took me aside and whispered in my ear*; **to put aside** *or* **to set aside** = to save money; *he is putting £50 aside each week to pay for his car* **(b)** *(usually US)* **aside from** = apart from; *aside from asthma attacks, his health is remarkably good*

ask [ɑːsk] *verb* **(a)** to put a question to get information; *she asked a policeman the way to the hospital*; *ask her how much her shoes cost* **(b)** to put a question to get someone to do something; *ask your father to teach you how to drive*; *I asked them not to make so much noise* **(c)** to invite; *we asked them round for dinner*; **to ask someone out** = to ask someone to go out to a restaurant, to a film, etc., with you; *don't ask her out - she always orders the most expensive things on the menu*

ask for ['ɑːsk 'fɔː] *verb* to say that you want something; *he asked Father Christmas for a new bike*; *someone came into the shop and asked for the manager*

asleep [ə'sliːp] *adjective* sleeping; *he was asleep and didn't hear the fire alarm*; *the cat was asleep on top of the kitchen boiler*; **to fall asleep** = to begin to sleep; *she fell asleep in front of the TV*

aspirin ['æsprɪn] *noun* **(a)** common drug, used to stop the symptoms of flu, colds, headaches, etc.; *she always keeps a bottle of aspirin in her bag* **(b)** one tablet of aspirin; *take a couple of aspirins and lie down*

ass [æs] *noun* **(a)** *(informal)* stupid person; *he's an ass - he should have accepted straight*

away **(b)** donkey, grey farm animal with long ears; used for riding or pulling; *the men were riding asses* (NOTE: plural is **asses**)

assemble [ə'sembl] *verb* **(a)** to come together; *the fans assembled at the gates of the football ground* **(b)** to put various pieces together; *the cars are assembled in Scotland*

assembly [ə'sembli] *noun* **(a)** meeting; **school assembly** = meeting of all the children and teachers in a school, usually at the beginning of the morning, when prayers are said, and notices read out (NOTE: plural in this meaning is **assemblies**) **(b)** putting together; *the parts are shipped to Scotland for assembly*; **assembly line** = moving line in a factory, where the product moves slowly past workers who add pieces to it as it goes past; *he works on an assembly line* *or* *he is an assembly line worker*

assist [ə'sɪst] *verb (formal)* to help; *I will be assisted in my work by Miss Smith*; *grandmother will need someone to assist her with her luggage*; *you should not assist the students during their exams*

assistance [ə'sɪstəns] *noun* help; *she was trying to change the wheel, when a truck drew up and the driver offered his assistance*; *grandmother will need assistance with her luggage*

assistant [ə'sɪstənt] *noun* person who helps; *his assistant works in the office next door*; **assistant manager** = person who is second, after a manager; **shop assistant** = person who serves the customers in a shop

asthma ['æsmə] *noun* disease where you find breathing is difficult, often caused by a reaction to something; *she has suffered from asthma since she was a little girl*

astonish [ə'stɒnɪʃ] *verb* to surprise someone a lot; *his success in maths astonished the teacher - he never came to any of her classes*

astonished [ə'stɒnɪʃt] *adjective* very surprised; *we were astonished to learn that the head teacher had left*

astonishing [ə'stɒnɪʃɪŋ] *adjective* which surprises you very much; *they spent an astonishing amount of money buying Christmas presents*

astronomer [ə'strɒnəmə] *noun* person who studies the stars; *astronomers around the world observed the new comet*

at [æt] *preposition* **(a)** *(showing time)* *we'll meet at eleven o'clock*; *at the weekend, we went to see my mother* **(b)** *(showing place) meet me at the post office*; *she's got a job at the supermarket* **(c)** *(showing speed) the train was travelling at 200 kilometres an hour* **(d)** *(showing direction) they threw tomatoes at the MP who was speaking*

at least ['æt 'liːst] *phrase* **(a)** *(mentioning one good thing in a bad situation) it rained all day but at least we brought our umbrellas* **(b)** *(to correct a statement) she lives in Liverpool - at least, she used to* **(c)** as the smallest thing possible; *try to tidy yourself up, at least comb your hair* **(d)** not less than; *at least a third of the children are ill*

at once ['æt 'wɒns] *adverb* **(a)** immediately; *the ambulance came at once* **(b)** at the same time; *don't all speak at once!* **(c)** **all at once** = suddenly; *all at once the phone rang*

at sign ['æt 'saɪn] sign (@) used in email addresses; *my email address is peter@petercollin.com (say 'peter at petercollin dot com')*

ate [eɪt] *see* **eat**

athlete ['æθliːt] *noun* sportsman who competes in races, etc.; *the Olympic athletes marched round the stadium*

athletics [æθ'letɪks] *noun* organized sports; *at school I hated athletics*; *we spent the afternoon watching athletics on TV*

Atlantic (Ocean) [ət'læntɪk 'əʊʃən] *noun* ocean between America and Europe and Africa; *he's planning to sail across the Atlantic in a small boat*

atlas ['ætləs] *noun* book of maps; *can you find Mexico in the Atlas?* (NOTE: plural is **atlases**)

atmosphere ['ætməsfɪə] *noun* **(a)** air around the earth; *the atmosphere surrounds the earth to a height of several hundred kilometres* **(b)** general feeling; *I like the friendly atmosphere in our school*

atom ['ætəm] *noun* smallest basic bit of matter; *all substances are composed of atoms*

attach [ə'tætʃ] *verb* **(a)** to fasten; *the seat belts are attached to the floor of the car* **(b)** to **attach importance to something** = to consider that something is particularly important; *she attaches great importance to food safety*

attached [ə'tætʃt] *adjective* fond of; *he's very attached to his old car, and won't get a new one*

attack [ə'tæk] **1** *noun* **(a)** trying to hurt someone or something; *the enemy made an attack on the town* **(b)** criticism; *he launched an attack on the government* **(c)** sudden illness; *she had a heart attack* **2** *verb* to try to hurt someone or something; *three boys attacked her and stole her watch*

attempt [ə'tempt] **1** *noun* try; *he failed in his attempt to climb Mount Everest*; *she passed her driving test at the second attempt* **2** *verb* to try; *she attempted to climb into the flat through a bedroom window*

attend [ə'tend] *verb* **(a)** to be present at; *twenty-five people attended the wedding* **(b)** to listen carefully; *students should attend carefully to the teacher's instructions*

attendant [ə'tendənt] *noun* person on duty; *ask the lavatory attendant if he found your wallet*; *as she went into the museum, the attendant asked her to open her bag*

attention [ə'tenʃən] *noun* **(a)** careful thinking; *don't distract the driver's attention*; **for the attention of** = words written on a letter to show that a certain person must see it and deal with it; *mark your letter 'for the attention of Mr Jones', because it might go to* *the wrong house*; **to pay attention to** = to listen to something carefully; *don't pay any attention to what she tells you!* **(b)** position of a soldier, standing straight, with heels together and looking straight ahead; *the guards stood to attention at the entrance of the palace*

attic ['ætɪk] *noun* room at the top of a house under a roof (also called a 'loft'); *he slowly climbed up the stairs to the attic*

attorney [ə'tɜːni] *noun* **(a)** *(especially US)* lawyer; *after his arrest he tried to call his attorney* **(b) power of attorney** = written document, which gives you the power to act on behalf of someone else; *she's going to the solicitor's today to sign the power of attorney so that she can deal with her mother's affairs*

attract [ə'trækt] *verb* to make someone come near; *the shops are lowering their prices to attract more customers*; *the exhibition attracted hundreds of visitors*; **to attract attention** = to make someone notice what you are doing; *she waved her umbrella in the air to attract the policeman's attention*

attraction [ə'trækʃn] *noun* **(a)** the ability to attract; *what is the attraction of cricket?* **(b)** something which attracts people; *the Tower of London is a great tourist attraction*

attractive [ə'træktɪv] *adjective* **(a)** who or which looks pleasant; *she's an attractive young girl* **(b)** which attracts; *the rival firm made him a very attractive job offer*

audience ['ɔːdiəns] *noun* people at a theatre, cinema, concert hall, or watching TV or listening to the radio; *there was a huge audience on the first night of the TV series*

August ['ɔːgəst] *noun* eighth month of the year, the month after July and before September; *my birthday is in August*; *I left my job last August*

aunt [ɑːnt] *noun* sister of your mother or father; wife of an uncle; *say goodbye to Aunt Anne*; *she lives next door to my aunt*

auntie ['ɑːnti] *noun* child's name for an aunt; *show me the present Auntie Vic gave you*

Australia [ɒs'treɪliə] *noun* large country, covering a whole continent in the south west of the Pacific Ocean; *she spent all her savings on a holiday in Australia* (NOTE: capital: **Canberra**; people: **Australians**; language: **English**)

Australian [ɒs'treɪliən] **1** *adjective* referring to Australia; *I'm letting my house to an Australian family for the summer*; *his wife is Australian* **2** *noun* person who lives in or comes from Australia; *we beat the Australians at cricket last year*

Austria ['ɒstriə] *noun* country in central Europe, south of Germany and east of Switzerland; *we often go skiing in Austria* (NOTE: capital: **Vienna**; people: **Austrians**; language: **German**)

Austrian ['ɒstriən] **1** *adjective* referring to Austria; *you can get Austrian wine in some supermarkets* **2** *noun* person from Austria; *the group was made up mainly of Germans and Austrians*

author ['ɔːθə] *noun* person who writes books; *she is the author of a popular series of children's books*

authority [ɔː'θɒrɪti] *noun* **(a)** power to do something; *he has no authority to act on our behalf* **(b)** ruling organization; *the education authority pays teachers' salaries*; **local authority** = council which runs a town or country area (NOTE: plural is **authorities**)

autograph ['ɔːtəgrɑːf] *noun* signature of a famous person; *he asked the footballer for his autograph*

automatic [ɔːtə'mætɪk] *adjective* which works by itself; *there is an automatic device which cuts off the electric current*

automatically [ɔːtə'mætɪkli] *adverb* working by itself; *the doors open automatically when someone comes near them*

automobile ['ɔːtəməbiːl] *noun (especially US)* car; *Ford is one of the main companies in the automobile industry*

autumn ['ɔːtəm] *noun* season of the year

between summer and winter (in American English this is 'the fall'); *in autumn, the leaves turn brown and fall off the trees*; *they say the building will be finished next autumn*; *I'll be starting my new job in the autumn*

available [ə'veɪləbl] *adjective* **(a)** which can be obtained; *the tablets are available from most chemists* **(b)** to make yourself available = to arrange to be free to do something; *the manager is never available when customers want to complain*

avalanche ['ævəlɑːnʃ] *noun* fall of masses of snow down the side of a mountain; *two climbers were killed by an avalanche in the Alps*

avenue ['ævənjuː] *noun* wide street in a town, often with trees along the side (in names of streets, usually written as 'Ave': 15 Laurel Ave); *they live in an avenue in the suburbs lined with trees*; **Fifth Avenue** = famous shopping street in New York; *we went into the stores on Fifth Avenue*

average ['ævərɪdʒ] **1** *noun* **(a)** number calculated by adding several figures and dividing by the number of figures added; *the temperature has been above the average for the time of year* **(b) on average** = as a rule; *on average, £150 worth of goods are stolen from the shop every day* **2** *adjective* **(a)** ordinary; *it was an average working day at the office*; *the little girl's of average height for her age* **(b)** calculated by dividing the total by the number of quantities; *his average speed was 30 miles per hour* **3** *verb* to work out as an average; *price increases have averaged 10% per year*

avocado [ævə'kɑːdəu] *noun* dark green tropical fruit with yellow flesh and a very large stone, eaten as a salad or vegetable; *add slices of avocado to your salad* (NOTE: plural is avocados)

avoid [ə'vɔɪd] *verb* **(a)** to keep away from; *aircraft fly high to avoid storms*; *travel early to avoid traffic jams* **(b)** to try not to do something; *he's always trying to avoid taking a decision*

awake [ə'weɪk] **1** *verb* **(a)** to stop somebody sleeping; *he was awoken by the sound of the telephone* **(b)** to wake up; *he awoke when he heard them knocking on the door* (NOTE: awaking - awoke [ə'wəuk] - has awoken) **2** *adjective* not asleep; *I can't get to sleep - it's 2 o'clock and I'm still awake*; **wide awake** = completely awake

award [ə'wɔːd] **1** *noun* prize; *the school has been proposed for an award* **2** *verb* to give money, a prize, etc., to someone; *he was awarded first prize*

aware [ə'weə] *adjective* knowing; *is he aware that we have to decide quickly?*; *I am not aware of any problem*; **not that I am aware of** = not as far as I know; *has there ever been an accident here before? - not that I am aware of*

away [ə'weɪ] **1** *adverb* **(a)** at a distance; *they've gone away on holiday*; *the nearest shop is three kilometres away*; *the flood washed away most of the village* **(b)** (to stress, after verbs) without stopping; *the birds were singing away in the garden* **(c)** not here, somewhere else; *the managing director is away on business* **(d)** (in sports) at your opponents' sports ground (the opposite is 'at home'); *our team is playing away next Saturday* **2** *adjective* **away game** = game played at your opponents' sports ground

awful ['ɔːfəl] *adjective* very bad, very unpleasant; *turn off the television - that programme's awful!*; *he's got an awful cold*

awfully ['ɔːflɪ] *adverb* (informal) very; *I'm awfully sorry to have to disturb you*; *it was awfully cold in Russia*

awkward ['ɔːkwəd] *adjective* **(a)** difficult to do; *I couldn't reach the handle - it's in a very awkward position* **(b)** difficult and embarrassing; *when he asked for the loan the bank started to ask some very awkward questions* **(c)** not convenient; *next Thursday is awkward for me - what about Friday?*

awoke, awoken [ə'wəuk or ə'wəukn] *see*

AWAKE

axe *US* **ax** [æks] *noun* tool with a heavy sharp metal head for chopping; *he chopped the tree down with an axe*

Bb

B, b [biː] second letter of the alphabet, between A and C; *he wrote his initials on the document with a large 'BB' for Ben Brown*

B & B *or* **b. & b.** [ˈbiː ənd ˈbiː] *noun* = BED AND BREAKFAST *we want to find a B & B away from the main road* (NOTE: plural is **B & Bs**)

baby [ˈbeɪbi] *noun* **(a)** very young child; *most babies start to walk when they are about a year old*; **to have a baby** = to give birth to a baby; *she's going into hospital to have her baby* **(b)** very young animal; *a baby rabbit* (NOTE: plural is **babies)**

back [bæk] **1** *noun* **(a)** part of your body from your neck down to your behind, which is not in front; *she went to sleep lying on her back*; *don't lift that heavy box, you might hurt your back*; **he did it behind my back** = he did it without telling me; **we were glad to see the back of him** = we were glad to see him leave **(b)** the opposite part to the front; *he wrote his address on the back of the envelope*; *she sat in the back of the bus and went to sleep*; **he knows London like the back of his hand** = he knows London very

well; **he put his trousers on back to front** = he put them on the wrong way round **(c)** in football, a person who defends the goal area; *the backs should stay behind to defend the goal* **2** *adjective* **(a)** on the opposite side to the front; *he knocked at the back door of the house* **(b)** referring to the past; **back pay** = salary which has not been paid; *I am owed £500 in back pay* **3** *adverb* **(a)** towards the back; *he stepped back from the edge of the platform*; *can you please sit back, I can't see the screen* **(b)** in the state where things were before; *put the telephone back on the table*; *they only came back home at 10 o'clock* **(c)** in the past; *back in the 1950s, life was much less complicated than it is today* **4** *verb* **(a)** to go backwards; to make something go backwards; *he backed (his car) down the drive*; **to back away from** = to go backwards from something frightening; *the little girl backed away from the dog* **(b)** to support with money; *she is backing her son's restaurant*

back up [ˈbæk ˈʌp] *verb* **(a)** to help someone; *nobody would back her up when she complained about the service* **(b)** *US* to make a car go backwards; *can you back up, please - I want to get out of the parking lot*

background [ˈbækgraʊnd] *noun* **(a)** part of a picture which seems farther away; *the photograph is of a house with mountains in the background* **(b)** **background music** = music played quietly in a film, restaurant, etc.; *the background music was very loud, so we asked for it to be turned down* **(c)** past life or experience; *do you know anything about her background?*

backward [ˈbækwəd] **1** *adjective* **(a)** not as advanced as is normal; *he is backward for his age* **(b)** not having much industry; *poor and backward countries* **2** *adverb US* = BACKWARDS

backwards *US also* **backward** [ˈbækwədz] *adverb* from the front towards the back; *don't step backwards when you're standing on the edge of the pool*; *'tab' is 'bat'* *spelt backwards*; **backwards and forwards** = in one direction, then in the opposite direction; *the policeman was walking backwards and forwards in front of the bank*

bacon ['beɪkən] *noun* salted or smoked meat from a pig, cut in thin slices; **bacon and eggs** = fried bacon and fried eggs (served at breakfast)

bacteria [bæk'tɪərɪə] *noun* tiny things which can cause disease; *the cleaning liquid will kill any bacteria in the toilet*

bad [bæd] *adjective* **(a)** not good; *I think it would be a bad idea to go on holiday in November* **(b)** of poor quality; *she's good at singing but bad at playing the piano* **(c)** unpleasant; *he's got a bad cold*; *the weather was bad when we were on holiday in August* **(d)** serious; *she had a bad accident on the motorway* (NOTE: **bad - worse** [wɜːs] - **worst** [wɜːst])

not bad ['nɒt 'bæd] quite good; *the food in this restaurant isn't bad*; *what did you think of his video? - not bad!*

badge [bædʒ] *noun* small sign pinned to someone's clothes (to show who he or she is, what club or company he or she belongs to, etc.); *all the hotel staff must wear badges*

badly ['bædlɪ] *adverb* **(a)** not well; *she did badly in her driving test* **(b)** seriously; *he was badly injured in the motorway accident* **(c)** very much; *his hair badly needs cutting* (NOTE: **badly - worse** [wɜːs] - **worst** [wɜːst])

bag [bæg] **1** *noun* **(a)** container made of paper, plastic, etc., in which you can carry things; *he put the apples in a paper bag*; **carrier bag** = large paper or plastic bag with handles, for carrying shopping, often given by a shop with the shop's name on it; *have you got a carrier bag for all this shopping?*; **shoulder bag** = bag which you carry on a strap over your shoulder; **string bag** = bag made of string like a net **(b)** what is contained in a bag; *he bought a bag of potatoes*; *(informal)* **bags of** = a large amount of; *let him pay the bill if he wants to - he's got bags*

of money **(c)** handbag; *my keys are in my bag* **(d)** suitcase, piece of luggage; *I always pack my bags at the last minute* **2** *verb (informal)* **bags I go first** = let me go first

baggage ['bægɪdʒ] *noun* luggage, cases and bags which you take with you when travelling; *she brought a huge amount of baggage with her*; **baggage allowance** = weight of baggage which a passenger is allowed to take free when he or she travels on a plane

bait [beɪt] **1** *noun* something used to attract fish or animals so that you can catch them; *we must put down some more bait to try to get rid of the mice* **2** *verb* to attach bait (to a hook); *he baited his fishing line with a worm*

bake [beɪk] *verb* to cook in an oven; *Mum's baking a cake for my birthday*; *do you like baked potatoes?*

baked beans ['beɪkt 'biːnz] *noun* dried white beans cooked in tomato sauce; *we had baked beans on toast for supper*

baker ['beɪkə] *noun* person who makes bread and cakes; *bakers start work very early in the morning*; **the baker's** = shop where you can buy bread and cakes; *can you go to the baker's and get me a loaf of brown bread?*

balance ['bæləns] **1** *noun* **(a)** staying steady; *the cat needs a good sense of balance to walk along the top of a fence*; **to keep your balance** = not to fall over; **to lose your balance** = to fall down; *as he was walking along the log across the stream he lost his balance and fell in* **(b)** money left in an account; *I have a balance of £25 in my bank account* **(c)** money which still has to be paid; *you can pay £100 down and the balance in three instalments* **2** *verb* **(a)** to stand without falling; *the cat balanced on the top of the fence* **(b)** to make something stand without falling; *the waiter balanced a pile of dirty plates on his arm*

balcony ['bælkənɪ] *noun* **(a)** small floor sticking out from the upper level of a building; *the flat has a balcony which looks out over the harbour* **(b)** upstairs rows of seats in a theatre or cinema; *we booked seats at the front of the balcony* (NOTE: plural is **balconies**)

bald [bɔːld] *adjective* who has no hair; *his grandfather is quite bald*

ball [bɔːl] *noun* **(a)** round thing for throwing, kicking, playing games, etc.; *he kicked the ball into the goal*; **I'll start the ball rolling** = I'll start things going; **they won't play ball** = they won't work with us **(b)** any round thing; *he crushed the paper up into a ball* **(c)** formal dance; *Cinderella lost her shoe at the ball*; *(informal)* **to have a ball** = to enjoy yourself; *the children don't want to go home - they're having a ball*

ballet [ˈbæleɪ *US* bæˈleɪ] *noun* **(a)** type of dance, given as a public entertainment, where people perform a story to music; *she's taking ballet lessons* **(b)** a performance of this type of dance; *we went to Tchaikovsky's ballet 'Swan Lake' last night*

balloon [bəˈluːn] *noun* large ball which is blown up with air or gas; *he was blowing up balloons for the party*; **hot-air balloon** = very large balloon which rises into the air as the air inside it is heated, with people travelling in a basket attached underneath; *we went for a ride in a hot-air balloon*

bamboo [bæmˈbuː] *noun* tropical plant, which grows very tall and of which the stems are used as supports or in making furniture; *we bought some bamboo chairs for the living room*; **bamboo shoots** = young shoots of bamboo, eaten especially in Chinese cooking; *she fried some chicken and bamboo shoots*

ban [bæn] **1** *noun* order which forbids something; *the council has put a ban on cycling in the park* **2** *verb* to forbid; *children have been banned from playing football in the park* (NOTE: **banning - banned**)

banana [bəˈnɑːnə] *noun* long yellow, slightly curved fruit which grows in hot countries; *she was peeling a banana*; **banana split** = dessert made of a banana cut in half, whipped cream, ice cream, chocolate sauce and nuts, usually served in a long dish

band [bænd] *noun* **(a) elastic band** *or* **rubber band** = thin circle of rubber for holding things together; *the roll of papers was held together with a rubber band* **(b)** group of people; *bands of football fans wandered around the streets* **(c)** group of people who play music together; *the dance band played all night*

bandage [ˈbændɪdʒ] **1** *noun* cloth for putting round a wound, an injured leg, etc.; *the nurse put a bandage round his knee* **2** *verb* to put a cloth round a wound, an injured leg, etc.; *his mother took him to the hospital and the nurse bandaged his knee*

BandAid [ˈbændeɪd] *noun US (trademark)* small strip of cloth which can be stuck to the skin to cover a wound (British English is 'sticking plaster'); *let me put a BandAid on your finger*

bang [bæŋ] **1** *noun* sudden noise like the noise made by a gun; *the door went bang when the wind blew it shut* **2** *verb* to hit hard, so as to make a loud noise; *he banged (on) the table with his hand* **3** *interjection (showing the something makes a sudden noise) a firework suddenly went bang*; **bang in the middle** = right in the middle; *bang in the middle of the film, someone's mobile phone started to ring*

banger [ˈbæŋə] *noun* **(a)** type of firework which makes a bang; *keep the dog indoors on November 5th - she doesn't like bangers* **(b)** *(informal)* sausage; **bangers and mash** = fried sausages and mashed potatoes

banisters [ˈbænɪstəz] *noun* rail on top of a series of poles along the side of stairs; *the children love sliding down the banisters*

bank [bæŋk] **1** *noun* **(a)** place where you can leave your money safely, business which lends money to people for interest; *how much money do you have in the bank?*; *she took all her money out of the bank and bought a car* **(b)** land along the side of a river; *there is a*

path along the bank of the canal **(c)** long heap of earth, sand, snow, etc.; *the road was blocked by banks of snow blown by the wind* **2** *verb* **(a)** to put money away into a bank; *have you banked the money yet?* **(b)** to pile up in a long heap; *the snow was banked up along both sides of the road*
bank account [ˈbæŋk əˈkaʊnt] *noun* arrangement which you make with a bank to keep your money safely; *I put all my savings into my bank account*; **to open a bank account** = to start keeping money in a bank; *he opened a bank account when he started his first job*
bank holiday [ˈbæŋk ˈhɒlɪdeɪ] *noun* special day when most people do not go to work and the banks are closed; *Christmas Day is a bank holiday*
banner [ˈbænə] *noun* **(a)** long flag; *they hung banners from the tops of buildings for the festival* **(b)** large piece of cloth with words written on it; *the demonstrators carried banners with the words 'Down with the Government'*
bar [bɑː] **1** *noun* **(a)** solid piece of something; *put a new bar of soap by the bath*; *she was eating a bar of chocolate* **(b)** long piece of wood or metal which closes a door or window; **bars** = pieces of metal in front of a prison window; *the prisoners escaped by sawing through the bars*; **behind bars** = in prison; *he spent several years behind bars* **(c)** long metal or plastic key on a typewriter or computer keyboard; **space bar** = long bar at the bottom of the keyboard on a typewriter or computer which inserts a single space into text **(d)** place in a hotel or pub where you can buy and drink alcohol; *let's meet in the bar before dinner* **(e)** small shop where you can buy food; **coffee bar** = small restaurant which sells coffee, cakes and sandwiches **2** *verb* **(a)** to block; *the road was barred by the police* **(b)** **to bar someone from doing something** = to prevent someone doing something; *she was barred from entering the building* (NOTE:

barring - barred)
bar code [ˈbɑː ˈkəʊd] *noun* printed lines which can be read by a computer; *there doesn't seem to be a price on the packet - just a bar code*
barbecue [ˈbɑːbɪkjuː] **1** *noun* **(a)** meal or party where food is cooked out of doors on a metal grill; *they've been invited to a barbecue* **(b)** metal grill for cooking out of doors; *light the barbecue at least half an hour before you start cooking* **2** *verb* to cook on a metal grill; *she was barbecuing sausages for lunch when it started to rain*
barber [ˈbɑːbə] *noun* person who cuts men's hair; **barber's** *US* **barber shop** = shop where men have their hair cut; *I'm just going to the barber's to have my hair cut*; *barber's shops usually have poles outside with red and white stripes*
bare [ˈbeə] *adjective* **(a)** with no clothes on; *he walked on the beach in his bare feet* **(b)** with no leaves on, no furniture inside, etc.; *in winter, the trees are all bare*; *they slept on the bare boards* (NOTE: do not confuse with **bear**)
barely [ˈbeəli] *adverb* almost not enough; *she barely had enough money to pay for her ticket*
bargain [ˈbɑːgɪn] **1** *noun* **(a)** an agreed deal; **to make** *or* **to strike a bargain** = to agree terms; *let's make a bargain - you do the washing up and I'll clean the car* **(b)** **into the bargain** = as well as other things; *the plane was late and they lost my suitcase into the bargain* **(c)** something bought more cheaply than usual; *the car was a real bargain at £500*; **bargain offer** *or* **bargain sale** = sale at an especially low price **2** *verb* **(a)** to discuss terms; *after bargaining with the man at the door, we managed to get into the club* **(b)** to discuss a price; *if you bargain with the man in the carpet shop, you'll probably get him to reduce the price* **(c)** **to bargain for something** = to expect something to happen; *I hadn't bargained for him being away and leaving me to do all the work*

barge [bɑːdʒ] **1** *noun* cargo boat on a river or canal; *we watched the barges go past along the river*; *barges on English canals are also called 'narrow boats' because they are long and narrow* **2** *verb* **to barge in** = to interrupt; *we were having a quiet chat when he came barging in*

bark [bɑːk] **1** *noun* **(a)** hard outside layer of a tree; *the rough bark of an oak tree* **(b)** sound made by a dog; *the dog gave a bark to greet us as we came into the house*; *his bark is worse than his bite* = he is not as frightening as he seems; *don't be afraid of Aunt Bessie - her bark is much worse than her bite* **2** *verb* to make a sound like a dog; *the dog barks every time he hears the postman*

barn [bɑːn] *noun* large farm building for storing cereals; *the barn is full of wheat*

barrel [ˈbærəl] *noun* **(a)** round wooden container for liquids; *they sell wine by the barrel* **(b)** amount contained in a barrel; *the price of oil has reached $30 a barrel* **(c)** tube of a gun in which the bullet is fired; *you need to clean the barrel of your gun very carefully*

barrier [ˈbæriə] *noun* bar which blocks the way; *the guard lifted the barrier and we drove across the border*; **crush barriers** = metal fences which are put up to control crowds; *the fans simply climbed over the crush barriers to get at the pop group's car*

base [beis] **1** *noun* **(a)** bottom part; *the table lamp has a flat base* **(b)** place where you work from; *he lives in London but uses Paris as his base when travelling in France*; **a military base** = a camp for soldiers; *he was posted to an air base in East Anglia* **(c)** **to touch base with someone** = to get in touch with someone again; *I'm calling because I wanted to touch base with you* **2** *verb* to use as a base; *the company is based in Paris*

baseball [ˈbeisbɔːl] *noun* **(a)** American game for two teams of nine players using a bat and a hard ball; *we went to the baseball game last Saturday*; *he's playing in the school baseball team*; **baseball cap** = soft cotton cap with a large peak; *she was wearing a baseball cap back to front* **(b)** the hard ball used in playing baseball; *we lost yet another baseball in the river*

basement [ˈbeismənt] *noun* floor in a building below the ground level; *we keep the washing machine in the basement*

basic [ˈbeisik] *adjective* very simple, at the first level; *knowledge of basic Spanish will be enough for the job*

basically [beisikli] *adverb (used when stating the simplest fact)* at the simplest level; *basically, he's fed up with his job*

basin [ˈbeisən] *noun* large bowl; *mix the flour and butter in a basin*

basket [ˈbɑːskit] *noun* container made of thin pieces of wood, wire, grass, etc.; *if you're going shopping, don't forget your shopping basket*; *he threw the letter into the waste paper basket*

basketball [ˈbɑːskitbɔːl] *noun* game played by two teams of five players, where you have to throw a ball into a basket placed high on a wall; *he plays in the college basketball team*

bat [bæt] **1** *noun* **(a)** piece of wood used for hitting a ball; *he did it off his own bat* = he decided to do it himself without asking anyone **(b)** little animal, similar to a mouse, which can fly; *bats were flying all round the trees in the garden* **2** *verb* to be one of the players or to be the team which is hitting the ball; *Atherton is batting*; *England batted all day*; *I watched him batting on TV this afternoon* (NOTE: batting - batted)

bath [bɑːθ] **1** *noun* **(a)** large container in which you can sit and wash your whole body; *the bath has not been cleaned properly* **(b)** washing your whole body; *after a game of football you need to have a bath* **(c)** **public baths** = large building belonging to a local council, with an indoor swimming pool; **swimming baths** = large building with a swimming pool; *she goes to the local swimming baths every day before breakfast* **2**

verb to wash all over; *Mum's bathing the baby* (NOTE: do not confuse with **bathe**)

bathe [beɪð] **1** *noun* act of swimming in a pool, a river, the sea, etc.; *we all went for a bathe before breakfast* **2** *verb* **(a)** to wash a wound carefully; *the nurse bathed his wound before applying a dressing* **(b)** *US* to have a bath; *I just have enough time to bathe before my dinner guests arrive* **(c)** *(formal)* to go swimming in a pool, lake, the sea, etc.; *on summer evenings, we like to bathe in the lake behind our house*

bathroom ['bɑːθruːm] *noun* **(a)** room in a house with a bath, a washbasin and usually a toilet; *the bathroom scales must be wrong - I'm heavier than I was yesterday* **(b)** *(said instead of 'toilet')*; *can I use your bathroom, please?*; *does anyone want to go to the bathroom before the coach leaves?*

ꞇery ['bætəri] *noun* little device for storing electricity; *the battery has given out so I can't use my mobile phone*; *does your radio use a battery or the mains?* (NOTE: plural is **batteries**)

ꞇ ['bætl] **1** *noun* **(a)** important fight between armed forces; *Napoleon was beaten at the Battle of Waterloo*; *Nelson was killed at the Battle of Trafalgar* **(b)** fight against something; *the government's constant battle against drugs* **2** *verb* **to battle against** = to fight against; *his last years were spent battling against cancer*

bay [beɪ] *noun* **(a)** place where a coast bends away inland in a large curve; *the ferry to Spain crosses the Bay of Biscay* **(b) bay window** = window which sticks out from a flat wall; *can we sit at that table in the bay window?* **(c) parking bay** = place for one car in a car park; *you can park in the visitors' parking bay* **(d)** bush with leaves used in cooking; *add a bay leaf to the soup*

BBC [biːbiː'siː] = BRITISH BROADCASTING CORPORATION a British national radio and TV company; *we were listening to the BBC news* or *to the news on the BBC*; *a BBC reporter wanted to interview her*

be [biː] **1** *verb* **(a)** *(describing a person or thing)* *she is bigger than her brother*; *lemons are yellow*; *the soup is hot*; *I'm cold after standing waiting for the bus* **(b)** *(showing age or time)* *she will be two next month*; *it is nearly ten o'clock*; *today is Thursday, so tomorrow will be Friday* **(c)** *(showing price)* *onions are 80p a kilo*; *the cakes are 50p each* **(d)** *(showing a job)* *his father is a bus driver*; *she wants to be a teacher* **(e)** *(showing size, weight, height, etc.)* *he's 1.70m tall*; *our house is ten miles from the nearest station* **(f)** *(meaning to add up to)* *two and two are four* **(g)** *(showing that something exists)* *there's your hat on the chair over there!*; *there were only two people left on the bus* **(h)** *(meaning to go or visit)* *have you ever been to Spain?*; *we have been to see the film three times* **2** *(making part of a verb)* **(a)** *(making a present tense)* *don't make a noise when he's watching the football on TV*; *we are hoping to go on holiday in June* **(b)** *(making a past tense)* *he was singing in the bath* **(c)** *(making a future tense)* *we will be going to Germany next week* **(d)** *(showing a passive)* *she was knocked down by a bus*; *the children were sent home by the teacher* (NOTE: present: **I am, you are, he/she/it is, we are, they are**; short forms: **I'm, you're, he's, she's, it's, we're, they're**; past: **I was, you were, he/she/it was, we were, they were**)

beach [biːtʃ] *noun* area of sand or little stones by the edge of the sea ; *many of the beaches are covered with oil from the tanker*; *we walked along the beach and looked for shells*; **beach umbrella** = large coloured umbrella to use on a beach to protect you from the sun (NOTE: plural is **beaches**)

beak [biːk] *noun* hard part of a bird's mouth; *the bird was carrying the worm in its beak*

beam [biːm] **1 (a)** long block of wood or metal which supports a structure, especially a roof; *you can see the old oak beams in the ceiling* **(b)** ray of light; *the beam from the car's lights shone into the room* **2** *verb* to give a wide smile; *the little girl beamed at him*

bean [biːn] *noun* **(a)** long thin green vegetable, of which you eat the outside or the seeds; *we had fish with chips and French beans* **(b)** seed of other plants; *we ground some coffee beans to make the coffee*; *soya sauce is made from soya beans*

bear [beə] **1** *noun* large wild animal covered with fur; *they say that bears like honey* **2** *verb* **(a) not to bear** = not to like; *I can't bear the smell of cooking fish* **(b)** to turn slightly; *bear right at the next set of traffic lights* (NOTE: **bearing - bore** [bɔː] **- has borne** [bɔːn])

beard [ˈbiːəd] *noun* hair growing on a man's chin; *Father Christmas has a long white beard*

beat [biːt] **1** *noun* **(a)** regular sound; *the patient's heart has a beat which is not regular*; *they danced to the beat of the steel band* **(b)** area patrolled by a policeman on foot; *here policemen on the beat have to go round in pairs* **2** *verb* **(a)** to do better than someone else, than another team in a game; *our football team beat France 2 - 0*; *we beat the Australians at cricket last year* **(b)** to make a regular sound; *his heart was still beating when the ambulance arrived* **(c)** to stir a food mixture hard; *beat the eggs until they are solid* **(d)** *(informal)* **beat it!** = go away! (NOTE: **beating - beat - has beaten**)

beat up [ˈbiːt ˈʌp] *verb* to attack someone; *three young men beat him up and stole his credit cards*

beautiful [ˈbjuːtɪfʊl] *adjective* very nice, especially to look at; *what beautiful weather!*; *they have a beautiful house in the country*

beautifully [ˈbjuːtɪfʊli] *adverb* in a very pleasing way; *she sang the song beautifully*

beauty [ˈbjuːti] *noun* **(a)** being beautiful; *the beauty of the autumn trees against the background of the blue lake* **(b)** beautiful person or thing; *his motorbike is a beauty - I wish I had one like it*

became [bɪˈkeɪm] *see* BECOME

because [bɪˈkɒz] *conjunction* for this reason; *I was late because I missed the train*; *the dog's wet because he's been in the river*; *she's fat because she eats too much*

because of [bɪˈkɒz ɒv] *preposition* on account of, due to; *the trains are late because of the fog*

beckon [ˈbekən] *verb* **to beckon to someone** = to make a sign with your hand telling someone to come; *the nurse beckoned to her to come into the room*

become [bɪˈkʌm] *verb* **(a)** to change to something different; *the sky became dark and it started to rain* **(b)** to start to work as; *he wants to become a doctor* **(c) to become of** = to happen to; *I never saw her brother again, I wonder what became of him* (NOTE: **becoming - became** [bɪˈkeɪm] **- has become**)

bed [bed] *noun* **(a)** piece of furniture for sleeping on; *lie down on my bed if you're tired*; **double bed** = bed for two people; **single bed** = bed for one person; **to go to bed** = to get into your bed for the night; *she always goes to bed at 9 o'clock*; **to be in bed** = to be sitting or lying in bed; *she's in bed with a cold*; **to make a bed** = to make it tidy or change the sheets after someone has slept in it; *you can't go into your hotel room because the beds haven't been made* **(b)** piece of ground, especially for certain plants; *there's a strawberry bed at the bottom of the garden* **(c)** ground at the bottom of water; *the bed of the river is made of sand and small stones*

bed and breakfast (b. & b. *or* **B & B)** [ˈbed n ˈbrekfəst] *noun* **(a)** private house offering a bed for the night and breakfast; *we got a list of bed and breakfasts from the tourist office* **(b)** staying for a night in a hotel, etc., and having breakfast but no other meals; *I only want to have bed and breakfast*

bedroom [ˈbedruːm] *noun* room where you sleep; *my bedroom is on the first floor*; *the hotel has twenty-five bedrooms*

bedtime ['bedtaɪm] *noun* time when you go to bed; *10 o'clock is my bedtime*; **go to bed - it's past your bedtime** = it's later than the time when you usually go to bed

bee [bi:] *noun* little insect which makes honey, and can sting you if it is annoyed; *the bee moved from flower to flower*

beech [bi:tʃ] *noun* **(a) beech (tree)** = common large tree; *beeches are common on the chalk hills in the south of England* **(b)** wood from this tree; *the floor is made of beech* (NOTE: do not confuse with **beach**)

beef [bi:f] *noun* meat from a cow or bull; *a plate of roast beef and vegetables*; *would you like another slice of beef?*

beehive ['bi:haɪv] *noun* box for bees to make a nest in; *he took the honey carefully out of the beehive*

been [bi:n] *see* BE

beer [bɪə] *noun* **(a)** alcohol made from cereals and water; *can I have a glass of beer?* **(b)** a glass of beer; *three beers, please*

beetle ['bi:tl] *noun* insect with hard covers on its wings; *ladybirds are types of beetles*

beetroot ['bi:tru:t] *noun* vegetable with a dark red root, eaten cooked with vinegar to make a salad; **as red as a beetroot** = very red in the face; *he went as red as a beetroot when we asked him about his girlfriend*

before [bɪ'fɔ:] **1** *adverb* earlier; *why didn't you tell me before?* **2** *preposition* earlier than; *you must be home before 9 o'clock*; *G comes before H in the alphabet* **3** *conjunction* earlier than; *the police got there before I did*; *think carefully before you start to answer the exam questions*

beg [beg] *verb* **(a)** to ask for money, food, clothes, etc.; *children were begging outside the railway station* **(b)** to ask someone in an emotional way to do something; *his mother begged him not to go* **(c)** **to beg a favour of someone** = to ask someone to do something for you **(d) I beg your pardon!** = excuse me, forgive me; *I beg your pardon, I didn't hear*

what you said; *I do beg your pardon - I didn't know you were busy* (NOTE: **begging - begged**)

began [bɪ'gæn] *see* BEGIN

begin [bɪ'gɪn] *verb* to start; *the children began to cry*; *she has begun to knit a red pullover for her father*; *his surname begins with an S*; **to begin again** = to start a second time; *she played a wrong note and had to begin all over again* (NOTE: **beginning - began** [bɪ'gæn] - **has begun** [bɪ'gʌn])

beginner [bɪ'gɪnə] *noun* person who is starting; *he can't paint well, he's only a beginner*

beginning [bɪ'gɪnɪŋ] *noun* first part; *hurry up if you want to see the beginning of the film*

begun [bɪ'gʌn] *see* BEGIN

behalf [bɪ'hɑ:f] *noun* **on behalf of someone** = for someone, to help someone; *we are protesting on behalf of the victims of the civil war*; *the lawyer is acting on behalf of the old lady's family*

behave [bɪ'heɪv] *verb* to act in a certain way with someone; *he behaved very badly towards the other children*; *(of children)* **to behave (yourself)** = to be good; *if you don't behave (yourselves) you won't have any ice cream*

behaviour *US* **behavior** [bɪ'heɪvjə] *noun* way of doing things; *his behaviour was very odd*; *local people complained about the behaviour of the football fans*

behind [bɪ'haɪnd] **1** *preposition* **(a)** at the back of; *they hid behind the door*; *I dropped my pen behind the sofa* **(b)** responsible for; *the police believe they know who is behind the bombing campaign* **(c)** supporting; *we're behind you!* **2** *adverb* **(a)** at the back; *he was first, the rest of the runners were a long way behind*; **he left his umbrella behind** = he forgot to take his umbrella with him; **when the others went out, he stayed behind to watch TV** = he stayed at home when the others went out **(b)** later than you should be; *I am behind with writing my Christmas cards* **3** *noun* (informal) part of the body which you sit on; *there was some water on the chair and my behind's all wet*

being ['biːɪŋ] *noun* **(a)** action of existing; **for the time being** = for a short time; *I'm staying with my mother for the time being until I can find a room in town* **(b) human being** = a person; *the first human beings came to the British Isles thousands of years ago*

Belgian ['beldʒən] **1** *adjective* referring to Belgium; *Belgian chocolates are very popular here* **2** *noun* person from Belgium; *there were ten people at the meeting, and two of them were Belgians*

Belgium ['beldʒəm] *noun* country on the North Sea, between France and Holland; *if you're driving to Denmark, it is quicker to drive through Belgium into Germany* (NOTE: capital: **Brussels**; people: **Belgians**; languages: **Flemish, French**)

belief [bɪ'liːf] *noun* feeling sure that something is true; **to the best of my belief** = as far as I know; *to the best of my belief, no one else has seen this letter*

believe [bɪ'liːv] *verb* **(a)** to be sure that something is true, although you can't prove it; *people used to believe that the earth was flat* **(b)** not to be absolutely sure; *I believe I have been here before* **(c) to believe in** = to be sure that something exists; *some people believe in miracles* **(d) can't** *or* **couldn't believe your eyes** *or* **ears** = be very surprised to see or hear something; *I couldn't believe my ears when I heard my name read out as the winner*; *she couldn't believe her eyes when she saw the car he had bought her*

bell [bel] *noun* metal object, like a cup, which makes a ringing noise when hit; electric device which makes a ringing noise if you push a button; *the alarm bell rings if you touch the door*; *the postman rang the door bell*; *you ought to have a bell on your bicycle*; **that rings a bell** = that reminds me of something; *does the name Forsyth ring a bell?*

belly ['beli] *noun (informal)* stomach and the front part of your body below the chest; *the little boy lay on his belly and screamed* (NOTE: plural is **bellies**)

belong [bɪ'lɒŋ] *verb* **(a) to belong to someone** = to be the property of someone; *does the car really belong to you?* **(b) to belong to a group or club** = to be a member of a group or club; *which tennis club do you belong to?* **(c) to belong with** = to be part of, to be stored with; *these plates belong with the big dinner service*

below [bɪ'ləʊ] **1** *adverb* lower down; *standing on the bridge we looked at the river below* **2** *preposition* lower down than; *in Singapore, the temperature never goes below 25°C*; *do not write anything below this line*

belt [belt] *noun* **(a)** long piece of leather or cloth which goes round your waist (to hold up a skirt or trousers); *she wore a bright red belt* **(b) seat belt** *or* **safety belt** = belt which you wear in a car or a plane to stop you being hurt if there is an accident; *please fasten your seat belts as we are preparing to land*

bench [bentʃ] *noun* **(a)** long wooden seat; *we sat down on one of the park benches and ate our sandwiches* **(b)** table in a workshop at which someone works; *he was standing at his work bench* (NOTE: plural is **benches**)

bend [bend] **1** *noun* **(a)** curve (in a road, line, etc.); *don't drive too fast, there's a sudden bend in the road*; *the pipe under the sink has an awkward S-bend* **(b)** *(informal)* **round the bend** = mad; *he's completely round the bend*; *that music is driving me round the bend* **2** *verb* **(a)** to make something curved; *you will have to bend the pipe to fit round the corner* **(b)** to curve; *the road bends suddenly after the bridge* (NOTE: **bending - bent** [bent])

bend down *or* **bend over** ['bend 'daʊn *or* 'əʊvə] *verb* **(a)** to bend your body so that your head is lower than your waist; *he bent down to tie up his shoe*; *she was bending over the desk* **(b) to bend over backwards to do something** = to do everything you can to help; *social* services bent over backwards to help the family

beneath [bɪˈniːθ] **1** *adverb* underneath; *from the bridge we watched the river flowing beneath* **2** *preposition* under; *the river flows very fast beneath the bridge*; *in the woods the ground was soft beneath our feet*

bent [bent] *adjective* **(a)** curved; *these nails are bent so we can't use them*; *see also* BEND **(b) to be bent on** = to be very keen on doing something; *he is bent on buying the car even if he can't afford it*

berry [ˈberi] *noun* small fruit; *they spent the afternoon picking berries in the woods* (NOTE: plural is **berries**; do not confuse with **bury**)

beside [bɪˈsaɪd] *preposition* at the side of someone or something; *come and sit down beside me*; *put the teapot down beside the milk jug*

besides [bɪˈsaɪdz] **1** *preposition* as well as; *they have two other cars besides the big Ford*; *besides managing the shop, he also teaches in the evening* **2** *adverb* in any case; *I don't want to go for a picnic - besides, it's starting to rain*

best [best] **1** *adjective* very good, better than anything else; *what is the best way of getting to London from here?*; *he put on his best suit to go to the interview* **2** *noun* **(a)** thing which is better than anything else; **to do your best** = to do as well as you can; *she did her best, but only came third* **(b) to make the best of something** = to take any advantage you can from something; *they say it will rain this afternoon, so we'd better make the best of the sunshine while it's here*; **to make the best of a bad job** = to do something in spite of terrible conditions; *it was raining when we stopped for a picnic, so we made the best of a bad job and had our sandwiches in the car* **3** *adverb* in the best way; *which of you knows London best?*; *oranges grow best in hot countries*

best man [ˈbest ˈmæn] *noun* man who helps the bridegroom at a wedding; *the best man gave a speech and told some funny stories about the bridegroom when he was a student*

best wishes [ˈbest ˈwɪʃɪz] *noun* greetings sent to someone; *give my best wishes to your father*

bet [bet] **1** *noun* money which is risked by trying to say which horse will come first in a race, which side will win a competition, etc.; *I've got a bet on England to win the next World Cup*; **safe bet** = bet which you are not likely to lose; *it's a safe bet that if we decide to go camping it will rain* **2** *verb* **(a)** to risk money by saying which horse you think will come first in a race, which team will win, etc. **(b)** to be sure of something; *I bet you she's going to be late* (NOTE: **betting - bet**)

better [ˈbetə] **1** *adjective* **(a)** good when compared to something else; *the weather is better today than it was yesterday*; *she's better at maths than English* **(b)** healthy again; *I had a cold last week but I'm better now* **2** *adverb* well as compared to something else; *my old knife cuts better than the new one* **3** *noun* **for the better** = which makes the situation better; **he took a turn for the better** = his health began to improve

had better *or* **would be better** [ˈhæd ˈbetə or wʊd bi ˈbetə] *phrase* it would be a sensible thing if; *you had better wear a coat - I think it's starting to snow*; *she'd better go to bed if she's got flu*; *it would be better if you phoned your father now*

between [bɪˈtwiːn] *preposition* **(a)** placed with things on both sides; *there's only a thin wall between his bedroom and mine, so I hear everything he says on the phone* **(b)** connecting two places; *the bus goes between Oxford and London* **(c)** in the interval separating two times; *can you come to see me between now and next Monday?* **(d)** in the space separating two amounts; *the parcel weighs between four and five kilos* **(e)** showing a difference; *she can't tell the difference between red and green* **(f)** among; *we only had £10 between the three of us*; *she* *could choose between courses in German, Chinese or Russian* (g) between you and me = speaking in private; *between you and me, I don't think he's very good at his job*

in between [ɪn bɪˈtwiːn] in the middle, with things on both sides; *the hotel looks over the river, with a railway line in between*

beware [bɪˈweə] *verb* watch out for; *beware of the dog!*

beyond [bɪˈjɒnd] *preposition* further away than; *the post office is beyond the bank*

Bible [ˈbaɪbl] *noun* (a) Christian and Jewish book of holy writing; *he reads from the Bible every evening* (b) important and useful reference book; *I keep my mother's old recipe book in the kitchen - it's my bible*

bicycle [ˈbaɪsɪkl] *noun* vehicle with two wheels which is ridden by one person who makes it go by pushing on pedals (also called a 'bike'); *he goes to school by bicycle every day*; *she's learning to ride a bicycle*; *it's odd - he can drive but he can't ride a bicycle*; **bicycle pump** = small hand pump for blowing up bicycle tyres

bid [bɪd] 1 *noun* offer to buy at a sale; *his bid for the painting was too low* 2 *verb* to make an offer to buy something at a sale; *he bid £500 for the car* (NOTE: bidding - bid)

big [bɪg] *adjective* of a large size; *his father has the biggest restaurant in town*; *I'm not afraid of him - I'm bigger than he is*; **big toe** = the largest of your five toes (NOTE: bigger - biggest)

Big Ben [ˈbɪg ˈben] *noun* clock and bell at the top of the tower of the Houses of Parliament in London; *Big Ben strikes the hours for the TV news*

bike [baɪk] *noun* (*informal*) = BICYCLE; *he goes to school by bike*; *she was knocked off her bike by a car*; **mountain bike** = strong bicycle with wider tyres, used for country cycling; *she rode her mountain bike along the hill paths*; **push bike** = ordinary bicycle (used to show the difference with a motorcycle)

bill [bɪl] *noun* (a) piece of paper showing the amount of money you have to pay (in a restaurant, for repairs, etc.); *does the bill include VAT ?*; *he invited her for a meal, and then asked her to pay the bill*; *don't forget to pay the gas bill* (b) hard part of a bird's mouth; *the bird was picking up food with its bill* (c) *US* piece of paper money; *a 10-dollar bill* (d) proposal for an act of parliament which, if passed by parliament, becomes law; *Parliament will consider two bills this week*

bin [bɪn] 1 *noun* (a) metal box for keeping things; **bread bin** = metal box for keeping bread in (b) container for putting rubbish; *don't throw your litter on the floor - pick it up and put it in the bin*; **pedal bin** = container for rubbish which opens with a pedal 2 *verb* (*informal*) to throw away into a rubbish bin; *he just binned the letter* (NOTE: binning - binned)

bind [baɪnd] *verb* (a) to tie with tight knots; *the burglar bound her hands and feet together with string* (b) to force someone to do something; *the contract binds us to make regular payments* (c) to put a cover on a book; *the book is bound in a blue cover* (NOTE: binding - bound [baʊnd])

biologist [baɪˈɒlədʒɪst] *noun* scientist who specializes in the study of living things; *Darwin was a famous biologist*

biology [baɪˈɒlədʒi] *noun* study of living things; *she took biology and chemistry as exam subjects*

birch [bɜːtʃ] *noun* **silver birch** = northern tree, with small leaves and white bark which peels off in strips; *the birch forests of Russia* (NOTE: plural is **birches**)

bird [bɜːd] *noun* animal with wings and feathers; *most birds can fly, but some, such as penguins, can't*

birth [bɜːθ] *noun* being born; *he was a big baby at birth*; **to give birth to** = to have a baby; *she gave birth to a boy last week*; **birth**

certificate = official document which says when and where someone was born; **date of birth** = day, month and year when a person was born; *he put his date of birth as 15th June 1985*

birthday ['bɜ:θdeɪ] *noun* date on which you were born; *April 23rd is Shakespeare's birthday*; *my birthday is on 25th June*; *what do you want for your birthday?*; **birthday cake** = cake made especially for a birthday and decorated with icing, candles, etc.; **birthday card** = card sent to someone to wish him or her good luck on their birthday; *remind me to send her a birthday card, it's her birthday next Tuesday*; **birthday party** = party held for a birthday; **birthday presents** = presents given to someone for his or her birthday; *the watch was a birthday present from my father*

Happy Birthday ['hæpi 'bɜ:θdeɪ] greetings said to someone on their birthday; **'Happy Birthday to you!'** = song sung at a birthday party; *we all sang 'Happy Birthday to you' and then she blew out the candles on her cake*

biscuit ['bɪskɪt] *noun* small flat hard cake, usually sweet; *a packet of chocolate biscuits*; **cheese and biscuits** = cheese served with biscuits (which are not sweet); *they had cheese and biscuits after the meal*

bishop ['bɪʃəp] *noun* (a) Christian church leader; *the Bishop of London* (b) piece in chess, which looks like a bishop's hat; *she took both his bishops in three moves*

bit [bɪt] *noun* (a) little piece; *would you like another bit of cake?*; **to come to bits** = to fall apart; *the chair has come to bits*; **to take something to bits** = to put something in pieces to mend it; *he's taking my old clock to bits* (b) **a bit** = a little; *the painting is a bit too dark*; *have you got a piece of wood a bit bigger than this one?* (c) tool which fits into a drill, used for making holes; *have you seen the big bit for the drill anywhere?* (d) metal rod which is in a horse's mouth, and which the

person riding uses to control the horse (e) *see also* BITE

bit by bit ['bɪt baɪ 'bɪt] *phrase* not all at the same time, little by little; *he paid back the money he owed, bit by bit*

bite [baɪt] **1** *noun* (a) amount you have in your mouth when you have chewed something; *she took a big bite out of the sandwich* (b) place where someone has been bitten; **insect bite** = sting caused by an insect which goes through the skin and hurts; *her arms were covered with mosquito bites* **2** *verb* (a) to cut with your teeth; *the dog tried to bite the postman* (b) *(of an insect)* to sting; *she's been bitten by a mosquito* (NOTE: **biting - bit** [bɪt] - **has bitten** ['bɪtn])

bitten ['bɪtn] *see* BITE

bitter ['bɪtə] *adjective* (a) not sweet; *this black coffee is too bitter* (b) angry and annoyed; *she was very bitter about the way the boss treated her* (c) very cold; *it was a bitter December night*

bitterly ['bɪtəli] *adverb* (a) deeply; *he bitterly regrets what he said* (b) **bitterly cold** = very cold; *it was bitterly cold in the tent*

black [blæk] *adjective* (a) with a very dark colour, the opposite to white; *an old black and white photograph*; **black coffee** = coffee with no milk in it; *do you want your coffee black or white?* (b) with a dark-coloured skin (NOTE: **blacker - blackest**)

blackberry ['blækbəri] *noun* small black fruit that grows on a bush; *for dessert we're having blackberry and apple pie*; *we had to struggle through blackberry bushes which had grown over the path*

blackbird ['blækbɜ:d] *noun* common garden bird with black feathers and a yellow bill; *listen to the blackbird singing*

blackboard ['blækbɔ:d] *noun* dark board on the wall of a classroom, in a restaurant, etc., which you can write on with chalk; *he wrote the instructions for the exam on the blackboard*; *some dishes are not on the* *menu, but are written on a blackboard*

blackcurrant [blæk'kʌrənt] *noun* little black berry which is usually eaten cooked; *a jar of blackcurrant jam*

blade [bleɪd] *noun* **(a)** sharp cutting part; *be careful - that knife has a very sharp blade* **(b) shoulder blade** = one of two large flat bones covering the top part of your back; *he fell when skiing and broke his shoulder blade* **(c)** thin leaf of grass; *she sat in the shade of an apple tree, chewing a blade of grass* **(d)** one of the parts of a propeller; *don't go near the helicopter when the blades are still turning*

blame [bleɪm] **1** *noun* criticism for having done something (even if you did not do it); *I'm not going to take the blame for something I didn't do*; **to get the blame for** = to be accused of; *who got the blame for breaking the window? - me, of course!* **2** *verb* **to blame someone for something** *or* **to blame something on someone** = to say that someone is responsible for something; *he blamed the accident on the bad weather*; **I don't blame you** = I think you're right to do that; *I don't blame you for being annoyed, when everyone else got a present and you didn't*; **to be to blame for** = to be responsible for; *the driver was to blame for the accident*

blank [blæŋk] **1** *adjective* **(a)** (paper) with no writing on it; *she took a blank piece of paper and drew a map* **(b) he looked blank** = he didn't seem to know anything about it; *when she mentioned the money he owed, he just looked blank* **2** *noun* empty space (on a piece of paper); *just fill in the blanks on the form*

blanket ['blæŋkɪt] *noun* **(a)** thick cover which you put over you to keep warm; *he woke up when the blankets fell off the bed*; **wet blanket** = miserable person who spoils a party, etc.; *don't ask her to your birthday - she's such a wet blanket* **(b)** thick layer; *the motorway was covered in a blanket of fog*

blankly ['blæŋkli] *adverb* not showing any reaction; *when the teacher asked him about his homework he just stared at her blankly*

blast [blɑːst] **1** *noun* **(a)** explosion; *windows were broken by the blast* **(b)** strong wind; *a cold blast from the north* **(c)** sharp blow on a signal or whistle; *three blasts of the alarm means that passengers should go on deck* **2** *verb* to destroy with an explosive or bullets; *the burglars blasted their way into the safe*

blaze [bleɪz] **1** *noun* large bright fire; *five fire engines were called to the blaze* **2** *verb* to burn fiercely; *the camp fire was blazing and everyone sang songs*

blazer ['bleɪzə] *noun* jacket, often with a club badge; *she was wearing a blue blazer with brass buttons*; **school blazer** = blazer of a special colour with the badge of the school on it; *a crowd of boys and girls in school blazers got onto the bus*

bled [bled] *see* BLEED

bleed [bliːd] *verb* to lose blood; *she punched him on the nose and it bled*; *he was bleeding from his wound* (NOTE: **bleeding - bled** ['bled])

blend [blend] *verb* to mix; *blend the eggs, milk and flour together*

bless [bles] *verb* **(a)** to make holy by prayers, etc.; *the church was blessed by the bishop* **(b)** *(informal) (said when someone sneezes)* **bless you!** (NOTE: **blessing - blessed** [blest])

blew [bluː] *see* BLOW

blind [blaɪnd] **1** *adjective* not able to see; *a blind man with a white stick got onto the bus* **2** *noun* **(a)** covering over a window that can be pulled up and down; *he pulled down the blind to keep out the sun* **(b) the blind** = people who cannot see; *the library has recorded books for the blind* **3** *verb* to make someone unable to see; *she was blinded by the bright lights of the cars coming towards her*

blindfold ['blaɪndfəʊld] **1** *noun* cloth put over someone's eyes to prevent him or her seeing; *the people who kidnapped her did not let her take off the blindfold* **2** *verb* to put a piece of cloth over someone's eyes to prevent him or her seeing; *he was blindfolded and* *pushed into the back of a car* **3** *adverb* wearing a blindfold; *I could find my way round London blindfold*

blink [blɪŋk] *verb* **(a)** to close your eyelids very quickly; *he blinked when the light was switched on* **(b)** *(of lights)* to go on and off; *the alarm light is blinking*

blister [ˈblɪstə] *noun* swelling on your skin where the skin has been rubbed; *I can't run - I've got a blister on my heel*

block [blɒk] **1** *noun* **(a)** large building; *they live in a block of flats* **(b)** group of buildings surrounded by streets; *he lives two blocks away*; *let's go for a walk round the block* **(c)** large piece; *blocks of ice were floating in the river* **2** *verb* to prevent something passing along something; *the pipe is blocked with dead leaves*; *the crash blocked the motorway for hours*

blockage [ˈblɒkɪdʒ] *noun* something which blocks; *there was a blockage in the pipe*

blond *or* **blonde** [blɒnd] *adjective* fair, or with fair hair; *two little blond children*; *she has lovely long blonde hair*

blood [blʌd] *noun* red liquid in your body; *blood was pouring out of the cut on his leg*; *the doctor's going to do a blood test*; *blood goes from the heart and lungs round the body and back again*

blood pressure [ˈblʌd ˈpreʃə] *noun* pressure at which the heart pumps blood round the body; *he has to take pills for his high blood pressure*

blossom [ˈblɒsəm] **1** *noun* mass of flowers on trees; *the hedges are covered with white blossom* **2** *verb* to flower; *the roses were blossoming round the cottage door*

blot [blɒt] **1** *noun* drop of ink; *the boy with blots of ink on his shirt is my kid brother* **2** *verb* **to blot something out** = to hide something completely; *the thick fog blotted out the details of the landscape* (NOTE: **blotting - blotted**)

blow [bləʊ] **1** *noun* knock or punch; *he*

received a blow to the head in the fight **2** *verb* to make air move; *the wind had been blowing hard all day*; *blow on your soup if it's too hot*; **to blow your nose** = to clear a blocked nose by blowing down it into a handkerchief; *she has a cold and keeps sneezing and blowing her nose* (NOTE: **blowing - blew** [bluː] - **has blown** [bləʊn])

blow away [ˈbləʊ əˈweɪ] *verb* **(a)** to go away by blowing; *his hat blew away* **(b)** to make something go away by blowing; *the wind will blow the fog away*

blow down [ˈbləʊ ˈdaʊn] *verb* **(a)** to make something fall down by blowing; *six trees were blown down in the storm* **(b)** to fall down by blowing; *the school fence has blown down*

blow off [ˈbləʊ ˈɒf] *verb* **(a)** to make something go away by blowing; *the wind has blown all the leaves off the trees* **(b)** to go away by blowing; *my hat blew off*

blow out [ˈbləʊ ˈaʊt] *verb* to make something go out by blowing; *she blew out the candles on her birthday cake*

blow up [ˈbləʊ ˈʌp] *verb* **(a)** to make something get bigger by blowing into it; *he blew up balloons for the party* **(b)** to destroy something in an explosion; *the soldiers blew up the railway bridge* **(c)** to make a photograph bigger; *can you blow up the picture so that we can see the details better?*

blue [bluː] **1** *adjective* coloured like the colour of the sky; *they live in the house with the dark blue door*; *all their children have got blue eyes* (NOTE: **bluer - bluest**) **2** *noun* **(a)** the colour of the sky; *she was dressed all in blue*; *(informal)* **the boys in blue** = the police **(b) out of the blue** = suddenly; *out of the blue came an offer of a job in Australia*

bluebell [ˈbluːbel] *noun* wild plant with blue flowers like a string of little bells; *we went into the woods to see if there were any bluebells out*

bluebird [ˈbluːbɜːd] *noun US* little bird with blue feathers; *a pair of bluebirds are nesting* *in the yard*

blunt [blʌnt] *adjective* **(a)** not sharp; *that knife is so blunt it won't cut butter*; **blunt instrument** = something used as a weapon, such as a piece of wood or a hammer, which is not sharp; *the doctor says the wounds were caused by a blunt instrument* **(b)** almost rude (way of speaking); *he replied with a blunt 'No!'* (NOTE: **blunter - bluntest**)

bluntly [ˈblʌntli] *adverb* quite rudely; *he told her bluntly that she had failed her exam*; *to put it bluntly, you're just no good at your job*

blurred [blɜːd] *adjective* not clear; *the paper printed a blurred photograph of the suspect*

blush [blʌʃ] *verb* to go red in the face because you are ashamed or embarrassed; *she blushed when he spoke to her*

board [bɔːd] **1** *noun* **(a)** long flat piece of wood, etc.; *the floor of the bedroom was just bare boards*; **ironing board** = long narrow table for ironing; **board games** = games (like chess) which are played on a flat piece of wood **(b)** blackboard; *the teacher wrote on the board* **(c)** food; **board and lodging** = meals and accommodation **(d) to go on board** = to go on to a ship, train, plane, etc.; *we went on board at 9.30 and the ship sailed at 12.00* **2** *verb* to go on to a ship, train, plane, etc.; *police boarded the ship in the harbour*; *the 16.50 train to Paris is now ready for boarding at platform 5*

boast [bəʊst] *verb* **(a) to boast of** *or* **about something** = to say how good, etc., you are; *she's always boasting about her boyfriends* **(b)** to have something good; *the school boasts three tennis courts*

boat [bəʊt] *noun* small ship; *they sailed their boat across the lake*; *they went to Spain by boat*

the Boat Race [ðə ˈbəʊt ˈreɪs] *noun* the annual race on the Thames between rowing boats from Oxford and Cambridge universities; *we watched the Boat Race on TV*; *the Boat Race is rowed each year on the Thames between Putney and Mortlake*

body [ˈbɒdi] *noun* **(a)** the whole of a person or of an animal; *he had pains all over his body*; *the dead man's body was found in the river* **(b)** the main part of an animal or person, but not the head and arms and legs; *she was burned on her arms and the upper part of her body* **(c)** the main part of a car, plane, etc.; *the car has an all-steel body* (NOTE: plural is **bodies**)

bodyguard [ˈbɒdigɑːd] *noun* **(a)** person who guards someone; *the demonstrators were grabbed by the president's bodyguards* **(b)** group of people who guard someone; *he has a bodyguard of six people* or *a six-man bodyguard*

boil [bɔɪl] **1** *noun* swelling on your skin which hurts; *he has a boil on the back of his neck* **2** *verb* **(a)** *(of water or other liquid)* to bubble and change into steam or gas because of being very hot; *put the egg in when you see that the water's boiling*; **the kettle's boiling** = the water in the kettle is boiling **(b)** to heat water (or another liquid) until it changes into steam; *can you boil some water so we can make tea?*; *in some parts of Africa, it's best to boil the water before you drink it* **(c)** to cook (vegetables, eggs, etc.) in boiling water; *small potatoes do not take long to boil*; *would you like a boiled egg for breakfast?*; **soft-boiled egg** = egg cooked by boiling in water until it is hot, but with the yellow part still more or less liquid; **hard-boiled egg** = egg that has been boiled until it is hard; *I need two hard-boiled eggs for the salad*

boil over [ˈbɔɪl ˈəʊvə] *verb (of liquid)* to rise up when boiling and run over the side of the pan; *the milk boiled over and made a mess on the cooker*

boiler [ˈbɔɪlə] *noun* machine that heats water for central heating and the hot water supply; *of course our boiler had to break down just before Christmas*

boiling [ˈbɔɪlɪŋ] **1** *noun* action of heating a liquid to the point where it becomes steam or gas; *boiling water for five minutes will kill germs in it* **2** *adjective* **(a)** which has started to boil (i.e., for water, at 100°); *put the potatoes in a pan of boiling water*; **boiling point** = temperature at which a liquid boils, i.e. when it turns into steam or gas; *100°C is the boiling point of water* **(b)** very hot; *it is boiling in this room - can't you open a window?* **3** *adverb* **boiling hot** = very hot; *it's boiling hot in our office*; *a pan of boiling hot oil fell on her foot*

bolt [bəʊlt] **1** *noun* **(a)** long metal rod with a screw which is fastened with a nut; *the legs of the table are fastened to the top with bolts* **(b)** long metal rod which is pushed into a hole to fasten a door; *she looked through the window and then pulled back the bolt* **(c)** **to make a bolt for** = to rush towards; *at the end of the show everyone made a bolt for the door*; **to make a bolt for it** = to run away; *when the guards weren't looking two prisoners tried to make a bolt for it* **2** *verb* **(a)** to run fast, to escape; *the horse bolted* **(b)** to fasten with a bolt; *he bolted the door when he went to bed*; *the tables are bolted to the floor* **3** *adverb* **sitting bolt upright** = sitting with your back very straight

bomb [bɒm] **1** *noun* **(a)** weapon that explodes, dropped from an aircraft or placed by hand; *the bomb was left in a suitcase in the middle of the station*; *enemy aircraft dropped bombs on the army base* **(b)** *(informal)* **it went like a bomb** = it went very well indeed; **it costs a bomb** = it costs a lot of money **2** *verb* to drop bombs on something; *enemy aircraft bombed the power station*

bone [bəʊn] *noun* one of the solid pieces in the body, which make up the skeleton; *he fell over and broke a bone in his leg*; *be careful when you're eating fish - they have lots of little bones*

bonfire [ˈbɒnfaɪə] *noun* large fire made outdoors; *he put the dead leaves on the bonfire*; *they sat around the bonfire singing songs*; **Bonfire Night** = 5th November, when the attempt by Guy Fawkes to blow up the

Houses of Parliament in 1605 is remembered, when bonfires are burnt with a figure of a man on top (called a 'guy') and fireworks are set off

bonnet [ˈbɒnɪt] *noun* metal cover for the front part of a car, covering the engine (American English for this is 'hood'); *he lifted up the bonnet and looked at the steam pouring out of the engine*

bonus [ˈbəʊnəs] *noun* **(a)** extra money; *the sales people earn a bonus if they sell more than their target* **(b)** advantage; *it was an added bonus that the bus arrived early, as we could get back home in time for tea* (NOTE: plural is **bonuses**)

bony [ˈbəʊni] *adjective* **(a)** thin, with bones which you can see easily; *he grabbed her arm with his bony hand* **(b)** with many bones; *I don't like smoked fish - they're usually too bony* (NOTE: **bonier - boniest**)

book [bʊk] **1** *noun* **(a)** sheets of printed paper attached together, usually with a stiff cover; *I'm reading a book on the history of London*; *he wrote a book about butterflies* **(b)** sheets of paper attached together; **account book** = book in which you record sales and purchases; **a book of stamps** = several stamps attached inside a little paper cover; **a book of matches** = set of cardboard matches attached together in a paper cover; *he collects books of matches* **2** *verb* to reserve a place, a seat, a table in a restaurant or a room in a hotel; *we have booked a table for tomorrow evening*; *I want to book two seats for Friday evening*

book up [ˈbʊk ˈʌp] *verb* to book everything; **the hotel is booked up** = all the rooms have been reserved in advance

booking [ˈbʊkɪŋ] *noun* reserving seats, places, etc.; *we had to cancel our booking and travel the next day*; **to make a booking** = to reserve a room, a seat, a table, etc.; *we tried to make a booking for the week beginning May 1st, but the camp site was full*

booking office [ˈbʊkɪŋ ˈɒfɪs] *noun* office in a cinema, theatre, etc., where you can buy tickets in advance; *phone the booking office to see if there are any seats left for tonight*

boom [buːm] **1** *noun* **(a)** loud noise, like a deep bang; *there was a loud boom and everyone jumped* **(b)** increase in money for everyone; *everyone is forecasting a boom for next year* **2** *verb* **(a)** to increase; *sales to Europe are booming* **(b)** to make a loud deep noise; *the ship's horn boomed through the fog*

boot [buːt] *noun* **(a)** strong shoe which goes above your ankle; *put on your boots if you're going to dig the garden*; *bring walking boots with you as we will be climbing in the hills*; **football boots** = boots to wear when playing football; **ski boots** = boots to wear when skiing **(b)** the space at the back of a car where luggage is put (American English for this is the 'trunk'); *put the cases in the boot*

border ['bɔːdə] **1** *noun* **(a)** line marking the edge between countries; *they managed to cross the border into Switzerland*; *he was killed by the border guards* **(b)** edge; **flower border** = flower bed by the side of a path or lawn **2** *verb* to be along the edge of something; *the path is bordered with rose bushes*

bore [bɔː] *verb* **(a)** to make a round hole in something; *bore three holes two centimetres apart* **(b)** to make someone fed up with what you are saying or doing; *I won't bore you with the details of my operation* **(c)** *see also* BEAR

bored [bɔːd] *adjective* fed up, not interested in what is happening; *I'm bored - let's go out to the disco*; **bored with** = fed up with; *I'm bored with this programme, can't we change to another channel?*; *(informal)* **bored stiff** = very bored; *can't we switch on the TV? - I'm bored stiff waiting for the rain to stop* (NOTE: do not confuse with **board**)

boring ['bɔːrɪŋ] *adjective* dull, not interesting; *I don't want to watch that boring TV programme*

born [bɔːn] *verb* **to be born** = to come out of your mother's body and begin to live; *he was*

born in Scotland; *she was born in 1989*; *the baby was born last week*

borne [bɔːn] *see* BEAR

borrow ['bɒrəʊ] *verb* **(a)** to take something for a short time, usually with the permission of the owner; *can I borrow your car to go to the shops?*; *she borrowed three books from the school library* **(b)** to take money for a time, usually paying interest; *he borrowed £10 from me and never paid it back*

boss [bɒs] **1** *noun (informal)* person in charge, owner (of a business); *if you want a day off, ask the boss*; *I left because I didn't get on with my boss* (NOTE: plural is **bosses**) **2** *verb* **to boss someone about** *or* **around** = to tell someone what to do all the time; *she's always bossing her little brother about*

both [bəʊθ] *adjective & pronoun* two people together, two things together; *hold on to the handle with both hands*; *both her brothers are very tall*; *she and her brother both go to the same school*

bother ['bɒðə] **1** *noun* trouble or worry; *we found the shop without any bother*; *it was such a bother getting the tickets that we nearly didn't go on holiday* **2** *verb* **(a)** to annoy, to cause trouble; *stop bothering me, I'm trying to read*; **to be hot and bothered** = to be annoyed and nervous about something **(b)** **to bother to do something** = to take the time or trouble to do something; *don't bother to come with me to the station - I can find my way easily*; **can't be bothered to** = don't have the time to, don't have the energy to; *he couldn't be bothered to answer my letters* **3** *interjection (informal) (used to show you are annoyed)* **bother!** *I've left my umbrella on the train*

bottle ['bɒtl] **1** *noun* **(a)** tall plastic or glass container for liquids; *he bought two bottles of milk*; *she drank the water straight out of the bottle* **(b)** **hot water bottle** = rubber bottle filled with hot water, used to warm a bed **(c)** *(informal)* courage; *he hasn't got the bottle to do it* **2** *verb* to put in bottles; *only bottled* water is safe to drink

bottle bank ['bɒtəl 'bæŋk] *noun* place where you can throw away empty bottles to be recycled; *there's a box of bottles in the kitchen ready to be taken to the bottle bank*

bottom ['bɒtəm] **1** *noun* **(a)** lowest point; *is there any honey left in the bottom of the jar?*; *turn left at the bottom of the hill*; **he's bottom of his class** = he gets the worst marks **(b)** far end; *go down to the bottom of the street and you will see the post office on your left*; *the greenhouse is at the bottom of the garden* **(c)** part of the body on which you sit; *if you are naughty again, you will get a smack on your bottom* **(d)** lower part of a piece of clothing; *he was wearing just his track suit bottom*; *I can't find the bottom of my swimming costume* **2** *adjective* lowest; *the jam is on the bottom shelf*; *he was standing on the bottom rung of the ladder*

bough [baʊ] *noun* branch of a tree; *a bough broke off the old oak tree in the storm* (NOTE: do not confuse with **bow**)

bought [bɔːt] *see* BUY

bounce [baʊns] **1** *noun* **(a)** springing movement up and down; *he hit the ball on the second bounce* **(b)** energy; *she's always full of bounce* **2** *verb* to spring up and down or off a surface; *the ball bounced down the stairs*; *he kicked the ball but it bounced off the post*

bound [baʊnd] **1** *noun* great jump; **in leaps and bounds** = very rapidly; *the new college building is going up in leaps and bounds* **2** *adjective* **(a)** **bound for** = on the way to; *a ship bound for the Gulf* **(b)** tied up; *the boy was left bound to a tree*; *the burglars left him bound hand and foot* **3** *verb* **(a)** to leap; to run fast; *she bounded into the room*; *the dog bounded into the bushes* **(b)** *see also* BIND

bound to *phrase* very likely; *they are bound to be late*

boundary ['baʊndri] *noun* line marking the edge of property, knowledge, etc.; *the white fence marks the boundary between our farm*

and his; **the boundaries of knowledge** *or* **of science** = the furthest point that anyone knows (NOTE: plural is **boundaries**)

bow 1 ['bəʊ] *noun* **(a)** ribbon tied in a shape like a butterfly; *the parcel was tied up with red bows*; **bow tie** = tie which is tied in the shape of a butterfly; *he always wears a bow tie* **(b)** piece of wood with strong hairs attached to it, used for playing a string instrument; *he slowly drew the bow across the strings of his violin* **(c)** weapon used for shooting arrows; *at the Battle of Hastings, the Norman soldiers drew their bows and shot arrows into the air* **2** [baʊ] *noun* **(a)** bending the body forward as a mark of respect; *he made a deep bow to the queen*; **to take a bow** = to step forward on a stage and bow to the audience to thank them for their applause; *the actors took their bows one after the other* **(b)** front part of a ship; *a sailor stood in the bows to look out for rocks*; **bow wave** = big wave which forms at the front of a boat **(c)** the person rowing who sits nearest to the bow of a boat; *he rowed bow for Cambridge* **3** [baʊ] *verb* to bend forward in salute; *he bowed to the queen*

bowl [bəʊl] **1** *noun* **(a)** wide container for food, water, etc.; *put the egg whites in a bowl and beat them*; **salad bowl** = special bowl for salad; **soup bowl** = special bowl for soup **(b)** the food or liquid contained in a bowl; *he was eating a bowl of rice*; *give the dog a bowl of water* **2** *verb (especially in cricket)* to send a ball (to a batsman); *it's your turn to bowl*

bowler ['bəʊlə] *noun (in cricket)* person who sends the ball to the batsman; *he's one of the England fast bowlers*

bowls [bəʊlz] *noun* game played on grass, where teams of players roll large balls towards a small ball thrown as a target; *their team are the bowls champions*

box [bɒks] **1** *noun* **(a)** container made of wood, plastic, metal, etc., with a lid; *she put the cakes into a cardboard box*; **cash box** = metal box for keeping cash in **(b)** a container and its contents; *he took a box of matches* *from his pocket*; *he gave her a box of chocolates for her birthday* **(c)** **letter box** or **pillar box** = container for posting letters; *she posted her cards in the letter box on the corner of the street*; **PO box number** = address with a number at a post office **(d)** small separate section in a theatre; *they took a box for the performance of the 'Marriage of Figaro'* (NOTE: plural is **boxes**) **(e)** tree with very small leaves, used to make hedges; *the beds of flowers are edged with box* **2** *verb* to fight by punching; *he learnt to box at a gym in the East End*

boxing ['bɒksɪŋ] *noun* sport in which two men fight each other in a ring by punching each other with thick gloves; **boxing gloves** = thick padded gloves, tied at the wrist, worn for boxing; **boxing ring** = square area, surrounded with a rope fence, in which boxing matches take place; *in boxing, a fight lasts for 10 or 15 rounds*

Boxing Day ['bɒksɪŋ 'deɪ] 26th December, the day after Christmas Day; *we're going to see my grandparents on Boxing Day*

boy [bɔɪ] *noun* **(a)** male child; *a boy from our school won the tennis match*; *I knew him when he was a boy*; **paper boy** = boy who delivers newspapers to your house; *the paper boy comes every morning at seven o'clock*; *a boys' school* = a school for boys only **(b)** a son; *her three boys are all at university*

boyfriend ['bɔɪfrend] *noun* young man that a girl is very friendly with; *she brought her boyfriend to the party*

bracelet ['breɪslət] *noun* chain or other ornament worn round the wrist; *she had a blue bracelet for her birthday*

braces ['breɪsɪz] *noun* straps over your shoulders to hold up your trousers; *he wore bright red braces with his jeans*

bracing ['breɪsɪŋ] *adjective* cool and healthy; *the bracing climate of the east coast*

brain [breɪn] *noun* **(a)** nerve centre in the head, which controls all the body; *the brain is* the most important part of the body **(b)** being intelligent; **use your brain** = think hard; **she's got brains** or **she's got a good brain** = she's intelligent

brake [breɪk] **1** *noun* device for stopping a vehicle or making it go slower; *put the brake on when you go down a hill*; *help, the brakes aren't working!*; **hand brake** or **foot brake** = brake which is worked by hand or by foot; **brake lights** = red lights at the back of a car which light up when you put the brakes on; *do you know that one of your brake lights isn't working?*; **brake pedal** = pedal in a car which you press with your foot to make the brakes work **2** *verb* to slow down by pressing the brakes; *the driver of the little white van braked hard* (NOTE: do not confuse with **break**)

branch [brɑːnʃ] **1** *noun* **(a)** thick part of a tree, growing out of the trunk; *he hit his head against a low branch* **(b)** local office of an organization; *he's the manager of our local branch of Lloyds Bank*; *the store has branches in most towns in the south of the country* (NOTE: plural is **branches**) **2** *verb* to **branch off** = to split off from a main road; *drive along for about a mile and you will see a small road branching off on the left*

brand [brænd] *noun* product with a name; *a famous brand of soap*

brand-new [brænd'njuː] *adjective* completely new; *these shoes are brand-new - I bought them for the wedding*

brandish ['brændɪʃ] *verb* to wave something about; *the cook ran out of the kitchen brandishing a knife*; *she burst into the room brandishing a letter*

brass [brɑːs] *noun* **(a)** yellow mixture of metals; *the doctor has a brass name plate on his door* **(b)** musical instruments made of brass; *a brass band led the parade*

brave [breɪv] *adjective* full of courage; *it was very brave of him to dive into the river to try to save the little girl* (NOTE: **braver - bravest**)

bravely ['breɪvli] *adverb* in a brave way; *she*

bravely volunteered to go back into the burning house

bread [bred] *noun* food made from flour and water, baked in an oven; *can you get a loaf of bread from the supermarket?*; *she cut thin slices of bread for sandwiches*; **bread and butter** = slices of bread covered with butter; *they passed round a plate of bread and butter*; **brown bread** = bread made from brown flour; **white bread** = bread made from white flour; **French bread** = bread in the form of a long thin stick (NOTE: do not confuse with bred)

breadth [bredθ] *noun* **(a)** *(formal)* measurement of how broad something is; *the breadth of the plot of land is over 300m* **(b)** how wide your knowledge is; *his answers show the breadth of his knowledge of the subject*

break [breɪk] **1** *noun* **(a)** short rest; *there will be a 15-minute break in the middle of the meeting*; **they worked for three hours without a break** = they worked without stopping; **to take a break** = to have a short rest; *we'll take a break now, and start again in fifteen minutes*; **coffee break** *or* **tea break** = short rest in the middle of work when you drink coffee or tea; *let's have our coffee break now* **(b)** *(in schools)* **morning break** *or* **afternoon break** = short period for rest and play in the middle of the morning and afternoon; *we couldn't go out during the morning break because it was raining* **(c)** short holiday; *we took a few days' break and went to Spain* **(d)** short period between TV programmes or parts of programmes when advertisements are shown; *we will continue with the news after this break* **2** *verb* **(a)** to make something come to pieces; *he dropped the plate on the floor and broke it*; *she broke her leg when she was skiing* **(b)** to come apart; *the clock fell on the floor and broke* **(c)** **to break a record** = to do better than a previous record; *he broke the record for the 2000 metres* **(d)** **to break your journey** = to

stop for a while before going on; *we'll break our journey in Edinburgh* **(e)** not to do what you should do; *you're breaking the law if you park on a double yellow line*; **to break a promise** = not to do what you had promised to do; *he broke his promise and wrote to her again* **(f)** **to break it to someone** *or* **to break the news to someone** = to tell someone bad news; *we will have to break it to her as gently as possible* (NOTE: do not confuse with **brake**; note also **breaking - broke** [brəʊk] **- has broken** [ˈbrəʊkn])

break down [ˈbreɪk ˈdaʊn] *verb (of machine)* to stop working; *the lift has broken down again*; *the car broke down and we had to push it*

break into [ˈbreɪk ˈɪntʊ] *verb* to use force to get into a building; *burglars broke into the office during the night*; *the police caught him breaking into the house*

break off [ˈbreɪk ˈɒf] *verb* **(a)** to make something come apart by breaking; to come apart; *he broke a piece off the bar of chocolate*; *several branches broke off in the wind* **(b)** to stop something suddenly; *they were going to get married, but she broke it off*

break up [ˈbreɪk ˈʌp] *verb* **(a)** to come to pieces; *the oil tanker was breaking up on the rocks* **(b)** to stop being in a group; *the meeting broke up at 3 p.m.*; *the group broke up when the lead singer left* **(c)** **school breaks up next week** = the school holidays start next week **(d)** **come on, break it up!** = stop fighting!

breakdown [ˈbreɪkdaʊn] *noun* **(a)** collapse of the body or mind; **nervous breakdown** = state of being severely depressed; *he had a breakdown after he was sacked* **(b)** *(of machine)* stopping working; *we had a breakdown on the motorway*

breakfast [ˈbrekfəst] *noun* first meal of the day; *I had a boiled egg for breakfast*; *she didn't have any breakfast because she was in a hurry*; *the hotel serves breakfast from 7.30 to 9.30 every day*; **breakfast TV** = TV show at breakfast time

breast [brest] *noun* **(a)** one of two parts on a woman's chest which produce milk; **breast stroke** = swimming stroke where you face downwards, pushing your arms out in front and bringing them back together while your feet are kicking; *she won the 200m breast stroke* **(b)** white meat from the front part of a bird; *do you want a wing or a slice of breast?*

breath [breθ] *noun* **(a)** air which goes into and out of the body through the nose or mouth; *you should smell his breath - he must have been eating onions*; **out of breath** *or* **gasping for breath** = having difficulty in breathing; *he ran all the way to the school and got there out of breath*; **to get your breath back** = to breathe normally again, after exercise; *first get your breath back, then tell me all about it*; **to take a deep breath** = to breathe in as much air as you can; *take a deep breath for the X-ray*; **to take someone's breath away** = to make someone very surprised; *the view of the mountains took my breath away*; **under your breath** = quietly; *he said something under his breath* **(b) a breath of wind** = very slight wind; *there wasn't a breath of wind all day*

breathe [briːð] *verb* to take air into your lungs or let it out; *take your hand off my mouth, I can't breathe*; *I want to listen to your chest, so breathe in and then out when I tell you to*; **to breathe deeply** = to take in a lot of air; **he's breathing down my neck all the time** = he's always watching how I'm working

breathless ['breθləs] *adjective* out of breath; finding it difficult to breathe; *she was breathless after running upstairs*

bred [bred] *see* BREED (NOTE: do not confuse with **bread**)

breed [briːd] **1** *noun* race of animal or plant; *Alsatians and other large breeds of dog* **2** *verb* **(a)** to produce young (animals); *rabbits breed very rapidly* **(b) I was born and bred in the country** = I was born and grew up in the country (NOTE: **breeding - bred** [bred])

breeze [briːz] **1** *noun* slight wind; *a cool breeze is welcome on a hot day like this*; a

stiff breeze = a strong wind; *there was a stiff breeze blowing from the south* **2** *verb* to walk around looking very pleased with yourself; *he breezed into the room carrying a cup of coffee*

brew [bruː] *verb* **(a)** to make beer; *they've been brewing beer in this town for over two hundred years* **(b)** to make tea or coffee; *let's brew some tea before we sit down and talk* **(c) there's trouble brewing** = there will soon be trouble; *the police moved in when they sensed trouble brewing in the crowd*

brick [brɪk] *noun* hard block of baked clay used for building; *he bought some bricks to build a wall*; *the children threw a brick through the window*

bride [braɪd] *noun* woman who is getting married; *the bride was given away by her father*; *it is usual for the bride to arrive a few minutes late for her wedding*

bridegroom ['braɪdgruːm] *noun* man who is getting married; *the bridegroom and best man waited anxiously in the church*

bridesmaid ['braɪdzmeɪd] *noun* girl who is one of the bride's attendants at a wedding (a boy who does the same is a 'page'); *three bridesmaids followed the bride into the church*

bridge [brɪdʒ] *noun* **(a)** construction built over a road, river, etc., so that you can walk or drive from one side to the other; *there are a dozen bridges across the River Thames in London*; **railway bridge** = bridge which carries railway lines **(b)** part of a ship where the captain and crew can keep watch and steer; *the captain was on the bridge when the accident occurred*

brief [briːf] *adjective* short; *he wrote a brief note of thanks*; *the meeting was very brief*

briefcase ['briːfkeɪs] *noun* thin case for carrying papers, documents, etc.; *he put all the files into his briefcase*

briefly ['briːfli] *adverb* for a short time; *she spoke briefly about the work of the hospital*

brigade [brɪ'geɪd] *noun* **fire brigade** =

group of fire fighters; *she called the fire brigade when she saw smoke coming out of the windows*

bright [braɪt] *adjective* **(a)** shining with a strong light; *they left the church and stepped out into bright sunshine* **(b)** with a very strong colour; *they have painted their front door bright orange* **(c)** intelligent; *he's a bright little boy*; **bright idea** = clever thought; *I've had a bright idea - let's all go to the beach!* **(d)** clear and sunny; *there will be bright periods during the afternoon* **(e)** cheerful; *she gave me a bright smile* (NOTE: **brighter - brightest**)

brightly [ˈbraɪtli] *adverb* **(a)** in a bright way; *a children's book with brightly painted pictures*; *the streets were brightly lit for Christmas* **(b)** in a cheerful way; *she smiled brightly as she went into the hospital*

brilliant [ˈbrɪljənt] *adjective* **(a)** extremely clever; *he's the most brilliant student of his year* **(b)** (*informal*) very good; *the graphics on this computer package are brilliant* **(c)** shining brightly; *she stepped out of the shop into the brilliant sunshine*

bring [brɪŋ] *verb* to come with someone or something to this place; *she brought the books to school with her*; *are you bringing any friends to the party?* (NOTE: **bringIng - brought** [brɔːt])

bring back [ˈbrɪŋ ˈbæk] *verb* to carry something back; *you must bring the book back to the library by Monday*; *he brought back presents for all his family from Germany*

bring in [ˈbrɪŋ ˈɪn] *verb* to come with something or somebody in here; *the dog's all wet - don't bring him into the kitchen*

bring up [ˈbrɪŋ ˈʌp] *verb* **(a)** to look after and educate a child; *he was born in the USA but brought up in England* **(b)** to mention a problem; *he brought up the question of the noise from the next flat*

brink [brɪŋk] *noun* edge; **on the brink of** = very close to; *she was on the brink of a*

nervous breakdown

brisk [brɪsk] *adjective* rapid; *we went for a brisk walk along the beach* (NOTE: **brisker - briskest**)

Britain [ˈbrɪtən] *noun* **(Great) Britain** = country formed of England, Scotland and Wales (which with Northern Ireland makes up the United Kingdom); *we sometimes go abroad for our holidays, but usually we stay in Britain*; *in 1814 Britain was at war with France* or *Britain and France were at war*; *in Britain, cars drive on the left hand side of the road*; *'England' is often used instead of Britain, and this is a mistake, as England is only one part of Britain* (NOTE: the capital: **London**; people: **British**; language: **English**)

British [ˈbrɪtɪʃ] **1** *adjective* referring to Great Britain; *he's a British citizen*; *the British press reported a plane crash in Africa*; *the word 'English' is often used instead of 'British', and this is a mistake, as England is only one part of Great Britain*; **the British government** = the government of the United Kingdom; **the British Isles** = the islands which make up Great Britain and Ireland **2** *noun* **the British** = the people of Great Britain

British Broadcasting Corporation (BBC) [ˈbrɪtɪʃ ˈbrɔːdkɑːstɪŋ kɔːpəˈreɪʃn] *see* BBC

broad [brɔːd] *adjective* **(a)** very wide; *a broad staircase led to the next floor* **(b)** (*to stress*) **in broad daylight** = when it is light during the day; *the gang attacked the bank in broad daylight*; **a broad Irish accent** = a strong Irish accent **(c) broad beans** = large flat pale green beans (NOTE: **broader - broadest**)

broadcast [ˈbrɔːdkɑːst] **1** *noun* radio or TV programme; *the broadcast came live from Buckingham Palace*; **outside broadcast** = programme not done in the studio **2** *verb* to send out on radio or TV; *the police broadcast an appeal for information* (NOTE: **broadcasting - broadcast**)

broke [brəʊk] *adjective* (*informal*) with no money; *it's the end of the month and, as* usual, *I'm broke*; **to be flat broke** = to have no money at all; *see also* BREAK

broken ['brəʊkən] *adjective* **(a)** in pieces; *she tried to mend the broken cup* **(b)** not working; *they came to mend the broken TV*; *we can't use the lift because it's broken* **(c)** *see also* BREAK

brooch [brəʊtʃ] *noun* woman's ornament with a pin; *she wore her favourite brooch to the wedding* (NOTE: plural is **brooches**)

brook [brʊk] *noun* small stream; *they jumped over the brook and walked on up the hill*

brother ['brʌðə] *noun* boy or man who has the same mother and father as someone else; *my brother John is three years older than me*; *she came with her three brothers*

brought [brɔːt] *see* BRING

brown [braʊn] *adjective* with a colour like the earth or wood; *she has brown hair and blue eyes*; *it's autumn and the leaves are turning brown*; *he's very brown - he must have been sitting in the sun*; *brown bread is better for you than white* (NOTE: **browner - brownest**)

bruise [bruːz] **1** *noun* dark, painful area on the skin, after someone has hit you; *the little girl had bruises all over her arms* **2** *verb* to make a bruise; *she bruised her knee on the corner of the table*

brush [brʌʃ] **1** *noun* **(a)** tool made of a handle and hairs or wire, used for cleaning, painting, etc.; *you need a stiff brush to get the mud off your shoes*; *she used a very fine brush to paint the details* **(b)** act of cleaning with a brush; *she gave the coat a good brush* **(c)** short argument or fight with someone; *he's had several brushes with the police recently* (NOTE: plural is **brushes**) **2** *verb* **(a)** to clean with a brush; *always remember to brush your teeth before you go to bed* **(b)** to go past something touching it gently; *she brushed against the door which had just been painted*

brush off ['brʌʃ 'ɒf] *verb* to clean something off with a brush; *he brushed the mud off his boots*

brush up ['brʌʃ 'ʌp] *verb* to make your knowledge better; *you must brush up your Spanish if you are going to work in Spain*

bubble ['bʌbl] **1** *noun* **(a)** ball of air or gas trapped in liquid; *he blew bubbles in his drink*; **bubble bath** = bath with special liquid soap which makes lots of bubbles; *she relaxed in a hot bubble bath* **(b)** *(informal)* **bubble and squeak** = fried potatoes and cabbage **2** *verb* to make bubbles, to have bubbles inside; *the soup was bubbling in the pan*

buck [bʌk] **1** *noun* **(a)** *US (informal)* dollar; *it'll cost you ten bucks*; **to make a quick buck** = to get rich quickly; *all he wants is to make a quick buck* **(b)** *(informal)* **to pass the buck** = to pass responsibility to someone else; **the buck stops here** = I am the person who is responsible **2** *verb* **to buck the trend** = to go against the trend; *sales of holidays abroad have bucked the trend and risen while sales of holidays in Britain have fallen*

bucket ['bʌkɪt] **1** *noun* **(a)** round container with a handle but no lid, used mainly for liquids; *the children made castles on the sand with their buckets*; *throw the water on the fire and pass the empty bucket back to me* **(b)** the contents of a bucket; *they threw buckets of water on the fire* **2** *verb (informal)* to pour with rain; *it's bucketing down outside*

buckle ['bʌkl] **1** *noun* metal fastener for a strap; *she wore a black leather belt with a big gold buckle* **2** *verb* **(a)** to attach with a buckle; *he buckled on his seat belt* **(b)** to bend and collapse, to become bent; *the whole bridge buckled under the weight of the traffic*; *the front wheel of my bicycle has buckled*

bud [bʌd] *noun* place where a new shoot comes on a plant; *in the spring the buds on the trees begin to open*; **in bud** = flower which has not yet opened; *the roses are in bud*

Buddhist ['bʊdɪst] **1** *adjective* referring to the teaching of Buddha; *a Buddhist temple* **2** *noun* person who follows the teaching of Buddha; *life in Nepal suits him so much that* *he's become a Buddhist*

budget ['bʌdʒɪt] **1** *noun* proposal of how money is to be spent; **the Budget** = the government's plans for spending and tax **2** *adjective* cheap; **budget prices** = low prices; **budget travel** = cheap travel **3** *verb* to plan how you will spend money in the future; *we will have to budget carefully if we're going to buy a flat*

buffalo ['bʌfələu] *noun* **(a)** *(in the Far East)* **water buffalo** = animal of the cow family, used for ploughing and pulling carts; *the plough was pulled by a pair of buffaloes* **(b)** *(in North America)* large wild animal with long hair, like a large bull, which used to be common in North America but is now much less common; *buffalo used to roam the plains of the Mid West* (NOTE: the plural is **buffaloes** *or* **buffalo**)

buggy ['bʌgi] *noun* **(a)** pushchair, light folding carriage for pushing a baby in; *she pushed the buggy across the busy road*; **double buggy** = buggy for two children **(b)** a little car for one or two people; *beach buggies have very large tyres so that they can drive on sand* (NOTE: the plural is **buggies**)

build [bɪld] *verb* to make something by putting things together, by putting bricks, etc., on top of each other; *the house was only built last year*; *they are planning to build a motorway across the fields*; *the children built sand castles on the beach* (NOTE: building - built [bɪlt])

builder ['bɪldə] *noun* person who builds houses, blocks of flats, etc.; *the builders are starting work on the kitchen today*

building ['bɪldɪŋ] *noun* something which has been built, such as a house, railway station, factory, etc.; *the flood washed away several buildings*; *his office is on the top floor of the building*

built [bɪlt] *see* BUILD

bulb [bʌlb] *noun* **(a)** glass ball which gives electric light; *you'll need a ladder to change*

the bulb (b) fat underground part of a plant, from which leaves and flowers grow; *she planted bulbs all round the house*

bulge [bʌldʒ] *verb* **to bulge with** = to be fat with; *her pockets were bulging with pieces of paper*

bull [bʊl] *noun* male animal of the cow family; *be careful when you cross the field - there's a bull in it*

bulldozer ['bʊldəuzə] *noun* large powerful tractor with a curved plate in front for pushing or moving earth, sand, etc.; *they hired bulldozers to clear the site*

bullet ['bʊlɪt] *noun* little piece of metal fired from a gun; *the police said that two bullets had been fired*

bully ['bʊli] **1** *noun* person who hurts or is unkind to weak people; *he's a bully and is always trying to make smaller children frightened* (NOTE: plural is **bullies**) **2** *verb* to hurt or to be unkind to someone who is weaker than you are; *she said she was bullied by the other children in school* (NOTE: bullying - bullied)

bump [bʌmp] **1** *noun* **(a)** slight knock against something; *the plane landed with a bump* **(b)** raised place; *drive slowly, the road is full of bumps* **(c)** raised place on your body, where something has hit it; *he has a bump on the back of his head* **2** *verb* to hit; *he's crying because he bumped his head on the door*

bump into ['bʌmp 'ɪntʊ] *verb* **(a)** to hit slightly; *he kept bumping into furniture because the lights were switched off* **(b)** **to bump into someone** = to meet someone by chance; *I bumped into him at the station*

bumper ['bʌmpə] *noun* bar on the front and rear of a car which protects against damage; *he backed into a lamp-post and dented the rear bumper*

bun [bʌn] *noun* little round bread or cake; *hamburgers are made of minced beef fried and served in a bun*

bunch [bʌntʃ] *noun* **(a)** group of things taken

together; *he carries a bunch of keys attached to his belt*; *he brought her a bunch of flowers* **(b)** cluster of fruit on the same stem; *a bunch of grapes*; *a bunch of bananas* (NOTE: plural is **bunches)**

bundle [ˈbʌndl] **1** *noun* group of things wrapped up or tied up together; *he produced a bundle of papers tied up with string*; *she left her clothes in a bundle on the floor* **2** *verb* to put people or things somewhere roughly; *she bundled the children off to school*; *the police bundled him into the back of their van*

bungalow [ˈbʌngələʊ] *noun* house with only a ground floor; *my grandparents have bought a bungalow by the sea*

bunk [bʌŋk] *noun* bed attached to a wall, as in a ship, etc.; *he climbed up into his bunk and fell asleep*; *do you want the top bunk or the bottom one?*; **bunk beds** = two beds one on top of the other, with a ladder to climb to the top one

burden [ˈbɜːdn] *noun* heavy load; something hard to bear; **to make someone's life a burden** = to make someone's life difficult

burger [ˈbɜːgə] *noun* minced beef, fried and served in a bun (also called a 'hamburger'); *the children want burgers and French fries for lunch*

burglar [ˈbɜːglə] *noun* person who tries to get into a building to steal; *burglars broke in during the night*; **burglar alarm** = device which rings a loud bell if someone enters a building

burn [bɜːn] **1** *noun* burnt area of the skin or a surface; *she had burns on her face and hands* **2** *verb* **(a)** to damage or destroy by fire; *all our clothes were burnt in the hotel fire*; *she burnt her finger on the hot frying pan*; *look, you've burnt the toast* = you've cooked it too much, so that it is black **(b)** to be on fire; *the firemen were called to the burning school* **(c)** to use as a fuel; *the cooker burns gas* (NOTE: **burning - burnt** [bɜːnt] *or* **burned)**

burn down [ˈbɜːn ˈdaʊn] *verb* to destroy

completely by fire; *they were playing with matches and burnt the house down*

burnt [bɜːnt] *adjective* black with fire; *the kitchen smells of burnt toast*; *all that remained of the roof were some burnt beams*

burst [bɜːst] **1** *noun* **(a)** sudden loud sound; *bursts of laughter came from the office* **(b)** sudden effort; *he put on a burst of speed* **2** *verb* **(a)** to explode suddenly; *when she picked up the balloon it burst* **(b) she burst into tears** = she suddenly started crying; **he burst out laughing** = he suddenly started to laugh; **he was bursting to tell everyone the news** = he was eager to tell the news (NOTE: **bursting - burst)**

bury [ˈberi] *verb* to put into the ground; *he is buried in the local cemetery*; *they buried the gold somewhere on the island*; *(informal)* **to bury your head in the sand** = to pretend that a danger or problem doesn't exist (NOTE: do not confuse with **berry)**

bus [bʌs] *noun* large motor vehicle which carries passengers; *she takes the 8 o'clock bus to school every morning*; *we missed the last bus and had to walk home*; *the number 6 bus goes to Oxford Street* (NOTE: plural is **buses)**
bus stop [ˈbʌs ˈstɒp] *noun* place where a bus stops and passengers can get on or off; *there were ten people waiting at the bus stop*

bush [bʊʃ] *noun* **(a)** small tree; *a holly bush with red berries* (NOTE: plural is **bushes) (b)** *(in Africa, India, etc.)* **the bush** = land covered with bushes or low trees; *they walked through the bush for several days before finding a village*

business [ˈbɪznəs] *noun* **(a)** the work of buying or selling things; *they do a lot of business with European countries*; **business college** *or* **business school** = place where people learn to work in business; *he's going to a business school in September*; **business letter** = letter about business matters; **on business** = on commercial work; *the director is in Holland on business* **(b)** commercial company, office, shop, etc.; *she runs a house* *cleaning business*; **business address** = details of number, street and town where a company is based; **business card** = card showing a person's name and the name and address of the company he works for; **business hours** = time (usually 9 a.m. to 5.30 p.m.) when a business is open (NOTE: plural is **businesses**) **(c)** affair, matter; **it's none of your business** = it's nothing to do with you

busy ['bɪzi] *adjective* **(a)** working on something, doing something; *he was busy mending the car*; *the busiest time for shops is the week before Christmas* **(b)** very active; *Oxford Street is very busy at lunchtime* (NOTE: **busier - busiest**)

but [bʌt] **1** *conjunction (coming before a contrast) he is very tall, but his wife is quite short*; *we would like to come to your party, but we're doing something else that evening* **2** *preposition* except; *everyone but me is going to the cinema*

butcher ['bʊtʃə] *noun* man who prepares and sells meat; *ask the butcher for some lamb chops*; **the butcher's** = shop where you can buy meat; *can you get me some sausages from the butcher's?*

butter ['bʌtə] **1** *noun* yellow fat made from cream, used on bread or for cooking; *could you pass the butter, please?*; *fry the mushrooms in butter* **2** *verb* to spread butter on something; *she was busy buttering slices of bread for the sandwiches*

buttercup ['bʌtəkʌp] *noun* common yellow flower found in fields; *she picked buttercups in the field*

butterfly ['bʌtəflaɪ] *noun* insect with large brightly coloured wings which comes out in daylight; *butterflies were flying around in the sunshine* (NOTE: plural is **butterflies**)

button ['bʌtən] **1** *noun* **(a)** little round disc for fastening clothes; *the wind is cold - do up the buttons on your coat*; *a button's come off my shirt* **(b)** little round disc which you push to ring a bell, etc.; *press the 'up' button to call*

the lift; *push the red button to set off the alarm*; *push the button marked 'black' if you want coffee without milk* **2** *verb* to fasten with buttons; *he buttoned (up) his coat because it was cold*

buy [baɪ] *verb* to get something by paying money; *I bought a newspaper on my way to the station*; *she bought herself a pair of ski boots*; *what did you buy your mother for her birthday?* (NOTE: **buying - bought** [bɔːt])

buzz [bʌz] **1** *noun* **(a)** noise like the noise made by a bee; *I can hear a buzz but I can't see the bee* **(b)** *(informal)* telephone call; *give me a buzz tomorrow* (NOTE: plural is **buzzes**) **2** *verb* to make a noise like a bee; *wasps were buzzing round the jam*

by [baɪ] **1** *preposition* **(a)** near; *the house is just by the bus stop* **(b)** before, not later than; *they should have arrived by now*; *you must be home by eleven o'clock* **(c)** *(showing means or way)* send the parcel by airmail; *you can get in touch with the office by phone*; *they came by car*; *she paid by cheque, not by credit card* **(d)** *(showing the person or thing that did something) 'Hamlet' is a play by Shakespeare*; *the postman was bitten by the dog*; *she was knocked down by a car* **(e)** **by yourself** = alone; *don't sit at home all by yourself*; *she made the hat all by herself*; *can he find his way to the station by himself?* **(f)** *(showing how much) prices have been increased by 5%*; *they won by 4 goals to 2* **(g)** *(showing size) the table is 60cm long by 25 wide* **2** *adverb (used with verbs to mean 'past') she drove by without seeing us*

by and large ['baɪ n 'lɑːʒ] in general; *by and large, the trains run on time*

by the way ['baɪ ðə 'weɪ] *(used to mention something not very important) by the way, did you see the TV programme on cars yesterday?*

bye *or* **bye-bye** [baɪ *or* 'baɪbaɪ] *interjection* goodbye; *bye! see you next week!*

Cc

C, c [siː] third letter of the alphabet, between B and D; *remember the rhyme: I before E except after C: so write 'receive' and not 'recieve'*

cab [kæb] *noun* **(a)** taxi, a car which takes people from one place to another for money; *he took a cab to the airport*; **black cab** = London taxi (which is higher than an ordinary car) **(b)** separate section for a driver in a large vehicle, such as a truck; *the truck driver climbed into his cab and started the engine*

cabbage ['kæbɪdʒ] *noun* vegetable with large leaves which you eat; *the school always smells of boiled cabbage*; *he was planting cabbages in his garden*

cabin ['kæbɪn] *noun* **(a)** small room on a ship; *she felt sick and went to lie down in her cabin* **(b)** small hut; *he has a cabin by a lake where he goes fishing* **(c)** inside section of an aircraft; *the first-class cabin is in the front of the plane*

cabinet ['kæbɪnət] *noun* **(a)** piece of furniture with shelves; **filing cabinet** = piece of office furniture with drawers for storing files **(b)** committee formed of the most important members of a government; *there's a cabinet meeting every Tuesday morning*

cable ['keɪbl] *noun* **(a)** thick electric wire; *he ran a cable out into the garden so that he could use his electric saw* **(b)** thick rope or wire; *the cable snapped and the ship was carried by the currents out to sea* **(c)** wire for sending messages underground or under the sea; *they've been digging up the pavements to lay cables*; **cable TV** = TV where the programmes are sent along underground wires

cable car ['keɪbl 'kɑː] *noun* **(a)** vehicle which goes up a mountain, hanging on a wire cable; *ten people were killed when the cable car fell to the floor of the valley* **(b)** US *(in San Francisco)* type of tram which is pulled by a metal cable set in a channel in the road; *we took the cable car down to Fisherman's Wharf*

cactus ['kæktəs] *noun* plant with thorns which grows in the desert; *cacti don't need much water* (NOTE: plural is **cactuses** *or* **cacti** ['kæktaɪ])

café ['kæfeɪ] *noun* small restaurant selling snacks or light meals; *we had a snack in the station café*

cafeteria [kæfɪ'tɪərɪə] *noun* restaurant where you serve yourself; *we'll meet for lunch in the cafeteria on the top floor of the book shop*

cage [keɪdʒ] *noun* box made of wire or with metal bars for keeping birds or animals so they cannot get out; *the rabbit managed to get out of its cage*

cake [keɪk] *noun* **(a)** food made by mixing flour, eggs, sugar, etc., and baking it in an oven; *she had six candles on her birthday cake*; *(slang)* **it's a piece of cake** = it's very easy; *the exam was a piece of cake - I finished it in half an hour!*; **you can't have your cake and eat it** = you can't take advantage of two things which are opposites **(b)** small round or square piece of something; *a cake of soap* **(c)** food made by mixing ingredients together into small round pieces which are then fried; *a meal of fish cakes and chips*

calculate ['kælkjuːleɪt] *verb* to find the answer to a problem using numbers; *the bank clerk calculated the rate of exchange for the dollar*; *I calculate that it will take us six hours to finish the job*

calculation [kælkjʊ'leɪʃn] *noun* act of calculating; *according to my calculations, we have enough fuel left to do only twenty kilometres*; **rough calculation** = not very accurate answer to a problem using numbers; *I made some rough calculations on the back of an envelope*

calculator ['kælkjʊleɪtə] *noun* little machine for doing sums; *he worked out the price on his calculator*

calendar ['kæləndə] *noun* paper showing the days and months of the year, which can be pinned on a wall; *turn over to the next page of the calendar - today is November 1st*

calf [kɑːf] *noun* **(a)** young cow or bull; young (of elephant, etc.); *the cow stood in a corner of the field with her two calves* **(b)** back part of your leg between the ankle and the knee; *he's strained his calf muscle and won't be able to play on Saturday* (NOTE: plural is **calves** [kɑːvz])

call [kɔːl] **1** *noun* **(a)** telephone conversation; trying to get in touch with someone by telephone; *were there any calls for me while I was out?*; **to make a call** = to dial and speak to someone on the telephone; **to take a call** = to answer the telephone **(b)** telephone call or shout to wake someone; *I want a call at 7 o'clock* = I want someone to wake me at 7 o'clock **(c)** visit; *the doctor made three calls on patients this morning*; **on call** = available for duty **2** *verb* **(a)** to say something loudly to someone who is some distance away, to tell someone to come; *call the children when it's time for tea*; **call me at 7 o'clock** = wake me up at 7 **(b)** to give someone or something a name; *they're going to call the baby Sam*; *his name is John but everyone calls him Jack*; *our cat's called Felix* **(c)** to telephone; *Mr Smith is out - shall I ask him to call you back?*; *call the police - there's a burglar downstairs!* **(d)** to visit; *the whole family called round to see if she was better*

call for ['kɔːl 'fɔː] *verb* **(a)** **to call for someone** = to fetch someone before going somewhere; *he called for me to take me to the cinema* **(b)** **to call for help** = to shout to ask for help; *we could hear people calling for help from under the ruins*

call off ['kɔːl 'ɒf] *verb* to decide not to do something which had been planned; *the picnic has been called off because of the weather*

call on ['kɔːl 'ɒn] *verb* **(a)** to visit someone; *she called on her mother to see how she was* **(b)** to ask someone to do something; *the police have called on everyone to watch out for bombs*

call up ['kɔːl 'ʌp] *verb* to tell someone to join the army, navy or air force; *thousands of men were called up at the beginning of the war*

callbox ['kɔːlbɒks] *noun* public telephone box; *I'm phoning from the callbox outside the post office* (NOTE: plural is **callboxes)**

calm [kɑːm] *adjective* quiet, not rough or excited; *the sea was perfectly calm and no one was sick*; *keep calm, everything will be all right* (NOTE: **calmer - calmest**)

calmly ['kɑːmli] *adverb* quietly, not in an excited way; *the doctor explained calmly what would happen during the operation*

calves [kɑːvz] *see* CALF

came [keɪm] *see* COME

camel ['kæml] *noun* desert animal with long legs and one or two humps; *when we were on holiday in Kuwait we went to camel races in the desert*

camera ['kæmrə] *noun* piece of equipment for taking photographs; *they went on holiday and forgot to take their camera*; *did you remember to put a film in your camera?*

camp [kæmp] **1** *noun* place where people live in tents in the open air; *we set up our camp halfway up the mountain*; **camp fire** = small bonfire at a camp **2** *verb* to spend a holiday or a period of time in a tent; *we go camping in Sweden every summer*; *they had camped by the side of the lake*

campaign [kæm'peɪn] **1** *noun* **(a)** organized attack by the army; *Napoleon's Russian campaign of 1812* **(b)** organized attempt to achieve something; *he's organizing a campaign against the new motorway*; *the* government's campaign to stop people smoking isn't working **2** *verb* to work in an organized way to achieve something; *they are campaigning for a new ring road round the town*

camping site *or* **campsite** [ˈkæmpɪŋ saɪt or ˈkæmpsaɪt] *noun* area especially arranged for camping, with special places for tents and caravans, washing and toilets, etc.; *there are several campsites near the lake that are equipped with everything you need*

can [kæn] **1** *noun* round metal container for food or drink (also called a 'tin'); *there were empty beer cans all over the pavement* **2** *verb* used with other verbs **(a)** *(to mean 'be able')* **he can swim well but he can't ride a bike (b)** *(to mean 'be allowed')* **the policeman says we can't park here (c)** *(asking in a polite way)* **can we come in, please?** (NOTE: negative is **cannot** or **can't**)

can opener [ˈkæn ˈəʊpnə] *noun US* device for opening cans (the British English is 'tin opener'); *there's a can opener in the kitchen*

Canada [ˈkænədə] *noun* very large country in North America, to the north of the United States; *they live in Canada, though his family comes from France* (NOTE: capital: **Ottawa**; people: **Canadians**; languages: **English, French)**

Canadian [kəˈneɪdjən] **1** *adjective* referring to Canada; *his mother is Canadian and so is he*; *the ticket costs 250 Canadian dollars* **2** *noun* person from Canada; *how many Canadians are there living in London?*

canal [kəˈnæl] *noun* artificial river made to allow boats to go from one place to another; *you can take a boat trip round the canals of Amsterdam*

cancel [ˈkænsl] *verb* to stop something which has been planned; *the star was ill, so the show had to be cancelled*

cancer [ˈkænsə] *noun* disease in which cells in the body grow in a wrong way; *she developed skin cancer*; *he died of lung cancer*

candidate [ˈkændɪdət] *noun* **(a)** person who applies for a job, who stands for election; *we have asked three candidates to come for an interview* **(b)** person who has entered for an examination; *all candidates should answer three questions*

candle [ˈkændl] *noun* stick of wax with a thread in the centre, which you light to make a flame; *he blew out all the candles on his birthday cake*

candy [ˈkændi] *noun US* **(a)** sweet food, made with sugar (British English for this is 'sweets'); *eating candy is bad for your teeth* **(b)** one piece of this food; *she bought a box of candies* (NOTE: plural is **candies**)

cane [keɪn] **1** *noun* **(a)** strong stem of a plant, especially of tall thin plants like bamboo; *a field of sugar cane* **(b)** thin walking stick; *she walks with a cane because of her hip* **2** *verb* to beat someone with a stick as a punishment; *he was often caned when he was at school*

cannon [ˈkænən] *noun* **(a)** large gun; *the sailors hauled a cannon across the ship's deck* **(b)** **water cannon** = machine for spraying water against demonstrators, etc.; *the police turned the water cannon on the group of students*

cannot [ˈkænɒt] *see* CAN

canoe [kəˈnuː] **1** *noun* boat with two pointed ends, which is moved forward by one or more people using paddles; *she paddled her canoe across the lake* **2** *verb* to travel in a canoe; *they canoed down the river*

can't [kɑːnt] *see* CANNOT

canvas [ˈkænvəs] *noun* thick cloth for making tents, sails, etc.; *he was wearing a pair of old canvas shoes*

cap [kæp] **1** *noun* **(a)** flat hat with a flat hard piece in front; *the bus driver was wearing an old black cap*; **England cap** = cap worn by a sportsman who has played for England in an international match **(b)** top which covers something; *screw the cap back on the medicine bottle* **2** *verb* to name someone to play for his country in an international match; *he has been capped five times for Wales* (NOTE: **capping - capped**)

capable ['keɪpəbl] *adjective* able to work well; **capable of** = able to do something; *the car is capable of very high speeds*

capacity [kə'pæsɪti] *noun* (**a**) amount which something can hold; **seating capacity** = number of seats in a bus, cinema, etc.; **to work at full capacity** = to do as much work as possible (**b**) position; **acting in his capacity as manager** = acting as a manager; **speaking in an official capacity** = speaking officially

capital ['kæpɪtəl] **1** *noun* (**a**) main city of a country, usually where the government is based; *Madrid is the capital of Spain* (**b**) money which is used by a company to work with; *company with a capital of £10,000* (**c**) (**block**) **capitals** = letters written as A, B, C, D, etc., and not a, b, c, d; *Rome begins with a capital R*; *write your name in block capitals at the top of the form* **2** *adjective* **capital letters** = letters written as A, B, C, D, etc., and not a, b, c, d; *write your name in capital letters at the top of the form*

capping, capped ['kæpɪŋ or kæpt] *see* CAP

capsule ['kæpsjuːl] *noun* (**a**) small hollow case, filled with a medicine, which you can swallow; *she swallowed three capsules of the drug* (**b**) **space capsule** = front section of a space rocket

captain ['kæptən] *noun* (**a**) person in charge of a team; *the two captains shook hands at the beginning of the match* (**b**) person in charge of a ship or of an aircraft; *go and see the captain if you want to use the radio phone* (**c**) rank in the army below a major; *a captain has to report to his major*

caption ['kæpʃn] *noun* phrase printed beneath a picture; *the caption read 'England manager to resign'*

capture ['kæptʃə] *verb* to take someone or something as a prisoner; *they captured the enemy capital very quickly*

car [kɑː] *noun* (**a**) small private vehicle for carrying people; *he goes to his office every morning by car*; **car ferry** = boat which carries vehicles and passengers from one place to another (**b**) wagon which is part of a train; *is there a restaurant car on the train?*

car park ['kɑː pɑːk] *noun* special place where you can leave a car when you are not using it (in American English, this is a 'parking lot'); *there's a free car park next to our office*

caravan ['kærəvæn] *noun* van with beds, table, washbasin, etc., which can be pulled by a car; *we got stuck behind a caravan on a narrow mountain road*

card [kɑːd] *noun* (**a**) postcard, a flat piece of stiff paper (often with a picture on one side) which you send to someone with a message on it; *they sent us a card from Italy* (**b**) piece of stiff paper, folded in two, so that a message can be written inside it; **birthday card** = card which you send someone to wish them a happy birthday (**c**) piece of stiff paper with a picture or pattern on it, used to play games; *would you like a game of cards?* (**d**) piece of stiff paper with your name and address printed on it; *he gave me his business card* (**e**) piece of stiff plastic used when paying; *do you want to pay cash or with a credit card?*

cardboard ['kɑːdbɔːd] *noun* thick stiff paper used to make boxes; *we put the glasses into cardboard boxes*

cardigan ['kɑːdɪgən] *noun* woollen jacket which buttons at the front; *take a cardigan with you in case it gets cold*

care [keə] **1** *noun* (**a**) serious attention; *they handled the antiques with great care*; **to take care** = to be very careful; *take care when you cross the road* (**b**) looking after someone; *the local authority is responsible for the care of old people*; *the council has several children in care*; **to take care of someone** = to look after someone; *who will take care of mother while I'm away?* **2** *verb* to be worried; *she cares a lot about the environment*; *he*

couldn't care less = he doesn't worry at all about it

care for   ['keə 'fɔ:] *verb* **(a)** to like; *would you care for another cup of coffee?* **(b)** to look after; *nurses cared for the injured people after the accident*

career   [kə'rɪə] *noun* life of professional work; *go and see the school careers officer - she will give you advice on how to become a dentist*

careful   ['keəfʊl] *adjective* taking care; *be careful not to make any noise, the baby is asleep*

carefully   ['keəfəli] *adverb* with great care; *carry the box of eggs carefully!*

careless   ['keələs] *adjective* without taking care; *he made several careless mistakes when he took his driving test*

carelessly   ['keələs] *adverb* without taking care; *he carelessly dropped his bag of shopping and broke the eggs*

caretaker   ['keəteɪkə] *noun* person who looks after a building; *go and ask the caretaker to put a new light bulb on the staircase*

cargo   ['ka:gəʊ] *noun* goods carried (especially on a ship); *a cargo of coal was loaded in Scotland* (NOTE: plural is **cargoes**)

caring   ['keərɪŋ] *adjective* loving and helping; *she's a very caring person*

carnival   ['ka:nɪvl] *noun* festival, often with music, dancing and eating in the open air; **Notting Hill Carnival** = big carnival held every year in August in Notting Hill, in the west of London; *thousands of people take part in the Notting Hill Carnival every year*

carol   ['kærəl] *noun* **Christmas carol** = special song sung at Christmas; *we went to a carol service at our local church*

carpenter   ['ka:pəntə] *noun* person who works with wood, especially in building; *the carpenter has arrived to fit shelves in the children's bedroom*

carpet   ['ka:pɪt] *noun* thick material for covering the floor, stairs, etc.; *he spilt his coffee on our new white dining-room carpet*

carriage   ['kærɪdʒ] *noun* **(a) railway carriage** = railway wagon for passengers; *the first three carriages were full* **(b) horse-drawn carriage** = open vehicle pulled by a horse; *the queen rode in an open carriage* **(c)** cost of carrying goods; action of carrying goods; *how much did they charge you for carriage?*

carried, carries   ['kærɪd or 'kærɪz] *see* CARRY

carrier bag   ['kærɪə 'bæg] *noun* large paper or plastic bag with handles, for carrying shopping; *her carrier bag split and all her shopping fell onto the pavement*

carrot   ['kærət] *noun* vegetable with a long orange root which can be eaten; *we had boiled carrots with our meat*

carry   ['kæri] *verb* **(a)** to take something and move it to another place; *there was no lift, so they had to carry the beds up the stairs*; *that suitcase is too heavy for me to carry* **(b)** to be heard at a distance; *the sound of the bells carried across the fields*

carry on   ['kæri 'ɒn] *verb* to go on doing something; *when the police came into the restaurant, everyone carried on talking as if nothing had happened*

carry out   [kæri 'aʊt] *verb* to do something which has been planned; *doctors carried out tests on the patients*

cart   [ka:t] **1** *noun* vehicle pulled by a horse; *the refugees pushed carts piled high with furniture* **2** *verb* to carry a big or heavy thing; *they carted all their equipment up three flights of stairs*

carton   ['ka:tən] *noun* container made of cardboard; *a carton of yoghurt*; *a milk carton*

cartoon   [ka:'tu:n] *noun* **(a)** funny, often political, drawing in a newspaper; *he draws a cartoon for the 'Evening Standard'* **(b)** film made of moving drawings; *I like watching Tom and Jerry cartoons*

carve   [ka:v] *verb* **(a)** to cut up a large piece

of meat; *Father sat at the end of the table, carving a chicken* (b) to cut stone or wood to make a shape; *he carved a bird out of wood*

case [keɪs] *noun* (a) suitcase, a box with a handle for carrying your clothes, etc., in when travelling; *my plane went to Chicago, but my case went to New York by mistake* (b) special box for something; *I've lost my red spectacles case* (c) large wooden box for goods; **a packing case** = large wooden box for carrying items which can be easily broken; *the removal men are bringing the packing cases tomorrow* (d) situation, way in which something happens; *your case is very similar to mine* (e) **court case** = legal action or trial; **the case is being heard next week** = the case is coming to court next week

in any case [ɪn 'eni 'keɪs] anyway, whatever may happen; *she missed the bus but in any case it didn't matter because the film started late*

in case [ɪn 'keɪs] because something might happen; *take your gloves in case it's cold on the mountain*; **just in case** = because something might happen; *it's still sunny, but I'll take my umbrella just in case*

in that case [ɪn 'ðæt 'keɪs] if that happens or if that is the situation; *there is a bus strike - in that case, you'll have to take the train*

cash [kæʃ] **1** *noun* money in coins and notes, not in cheques; *we don't keep much cash in the house*; **cash machine** = machine which gives out money when a special card is inserted and instructions given **2** *verb* **to cash a cheque** = to change a cheque into cash; *he tried to cash a cheque for seven hundred pounds*

cash desk ['kæʃ 'desk] *noun* place in a store where you pay for the goods you are buying; *take your purchases to the nearest cash desk*

cash in on ['kæʃ ɪn 'ɒn] *verb* to profit from something; *ice cream men are cashing in on the fine weather*

cassette [kə'set] *noun* magnetic tape in a plastic case which can fit directly into a playing or recording machine; *he bought a cassette of folk songs*; **cassette player** = machine which plays cassettes

cast [kɑːst] **1** *noun* (a) all the actors in a play or film; *after the first night the cast went to celebrate in a restaurant* (b) **plaster cast** = shape made by pouring liquid plaster into a mould **2** *verb* to choose actors for a play or film; *he was cast as a soldier in 'Henry V'* (NOTE: **casting - cast**)

castle ['kɑːsl] *noun* (a) large building with strong walls; *the Queen is spending the week at Windsor Castle* (b) one of two pieces used in chess, shaped like a little castle tower; *she took my last castle*

cat [kæt] *noun* animal with soft fur and a long tail, kept as a pet; *she asked her neighbours to feed her cat when she went on holiday*; *don't forget to get some tins of cat food*; *cats are often called 'Puss' or 'Pussy'*

catalogue *US* **catalog** ['kætəlɒg] *noun* list of things for sale, or in a library or museum; *look up the book you want in the library catalogue*; *we got the latest catalogue of computer equipment*

catch [kætʃ] **1** *noun* (a) thing which has been taken; *the boat brought back a huge catch of fish* (b) action of grabbing a ball in the air; *he dropped an easy catch* (c) something hidden which makes a deal less good; *it seems such a bargain, there must be a catch in it somewhere*; **catch 22** = circle of events which you cannot escape from (NOTE: plural is **catches**) **2** *verb* (a) to grab hold of something moving in the air; *can you catch a ball with your left hand?*; *he knocked a glass off the table but managed to catch it before it hit the floor* (b) to grab hold of something; *as he slipped, he caught the rail to stop himself falling* (c) to get hold of an animal, especially to kill it; *he sat by the river all day but didn't catch anything*; *our cat is no good at catching mice* (d) to get on a bus, plane, train, etc., before it leaves; *you will have to run if* *you want to catch the last bus*; *he caught the 10 o'clock train to Paris* (e) to get an illness; *he caught a cold from standing in the rain watching the rugby match*; *the baby has caught measles* (f) to find someone doing something wrong; *the police caught the burglar as he was climbing out of the window* (g) to hear; *I didn't quite catch what she said* (NOTE: **catching - caught** [kɔːt] **- has caught**)

catch up [ˈkætʃ ˈʌp] *verb* to move to be level with someone who is in front of you; *she walked so slowly that he soon caught up with her*

catching [ˈkætʃɪŋ] *adjective* (disease) which is infectious; *don't come near me - your cough may be catching*

category [ˈkætɪɡəri] *noun* way of classifying people or things which have the same qualities; *don't expect luxury in the cheapest category of hotels* (NOTE: plural is **categories**)

caterpillar [ˈkætəpɪlə] *noun* insect worm with many legs, which turns into a moth or butterfly; *caterpillars have eaten most of the leaves on our trees*

cathedral [kəˈθiːdrəl] *noun* large church where a bishop takes services; *you can see the tower of Ely cathedral from miles away*

Catholic [ˈkæθlɪk] **1** *adjective* referring to the Roman Catholic Church; *the main Catholic daily service is called a mass*; *there's a French Catholic church near Leicester Square* **2** *noun* a **Catholic** = a member of the Roman Catholic Church; *she became a Catholic when she married*

catkin [ˈkætkɪn] *noun* long flower which hangs down from the branches of some types of tree; *she picked some branches of catkins*

cattle [ˈkætl] *noun* animals of the cow family; *the cattle are brought inside for the winter*

caught [kɔːt] *see* CATCH

cauliflower [ˈkɒlɪflaʊə] *noun* vegetable with hard white flowers, which are cooked; *would you like some more cauliflower?*; **cauliflower cheese** = cauliflower cooked in the oven with

a white sauce and cheese on top

cause [kɔːz] **1** *noun* **(a)** thing which makes something happen; *the police are trying to find the cause of the fire* **(b)** organization which people support; **in a good cause** = in order to support something which is good and useful; *give as much as you can - it's all in a good cause* **2** *verb* to make something happen; *the accident caused a traffic jam on the motorway*

cautious [ˈkɔːʃəs] *adjective* careful, not taking any risks; *we were warned to be cautious when driving through the safari park*

cavalry [ˈkævəlri] *noun* soldiers on horses; *the cavalry did not attack in time*

cave [keɪv] *noun* large hole in rock or earth; *when the tide goes out we can explore the cave*; **cave paintings** = paintings done by ancient peoples on the walls of caves

CD [ˈsiː ˈdiː] *abbreviation for* compact disc; *I don't like his new CD - do you?*

cease [siːs] *verb* to stop; **to cease to exist** = to stop being there; *the shop on the corner ceased to exist some time ago*

ceiling [ˈsiːlɪŋ] *noun* inside roof over a room; *he's so tall, he can easily touch the ceiling*; *she painted the kitchen ceiling white*

celebrate [ˈselɪbreɪt] *verb* to have a party or do special things because something good has taken place, or because of something that happened in the past; *our team won, so we're all going out to celebrate*; *they celebrated their wedding anniversary quietly at home with their children and grandchildren*

celebration [selɪˈbreɪʃn] *noun* action of celebrating something; *after our team won, the celebrations went on all night*

celery [ˈseləri] *noun* plant with a white or green stem, eaten as a vegetable or raw as a salad; **a stick of celery** = a piece of the stem of the celery plant (often served raw with cheese)

cell [sel] *noun* **(a)** room in a prison; *he was arrested in the centre of town and spent the night in the police cells* **(b)** basic unit forming an animal or plant; *you can see the cancer cells under a microscope* (NOTE: do not confuse with **sell**)

cellar ['selə] *noun* underground room beneath a house; *we keep our wine in the cellar*

cello ['tʃeləʊ] *noun* large stringed musical instrument; *a group made up of two violins and two cellos* (NOTE: plural is **cellos**)

Celsius ['selsiəs] *adjective & noun* scale of temperature where the freezing point of water is 0° and the boiling point is 100°; *the temperature outside is only 6°C (say 'six degrees Celsius'); what is 75° Fahrenheit in Celsius?; Celsius is used in many countries, but not in the USA, where the Fahrenheit system is still preferred*

cement [sɪ'ment] *noun* **(a)** powder made from lime and clay, which is mixed with water and dries hard; *he was mixing cement to make a path round the house* **(b)** strong glue; *she used china cement to stick the handle back on the cup*

cemetery ['semətri] *noun* place where people are buried; *he is buried in the cemetery next to the church* (NOTE: plural is **cemeteries**)

cent [sent] *noun* small coin, one hundredth part of a dollar; *they are selling oranges at 99 cents each* (NOTE: do not confuse with **sent**, **scent**)

center ['sentə] *see* CENTRE

centigrade ['sentɪɡreɪd] *noun* scale of temperature where the freezing point of water is 0° and the boiling point is 100°

centimetre *US* **centimeter** ['sentɪmiːtə] *noun* measure of length, one hundredth part of a metre; *I need a short piece of string - about 25 centimetres (25cm) long*

central ['sentrl] *adjective* in the centre; **central heating** = heating of a whole house from one main boiler and several radiators; *the house has gas central heating*

centre *US* **center** ['sentə] *noun* **(a)** middle; *they planted a rose bush in the centre of the lawn* **(b)** large building containing several different sections; **health centre** *or* **medical centre** = building with various doctors and specialized medical people; **sports centre** = place where several different sports can be played; **shopping centre** = several shops in one big building

century ['sentʃəri] *noun* **(a)** one hundred years; *the number of a century is always one more than the date number: so the period from 1900 to 1999 is the 20th century*; **the seventeenth century** = the period from 1600 to 1699 **(b)** score of 100, especially in cricket; *he scored a century, including four fours and two sixes* (NOTE: plural is **centuries**)

cereal ['siːriəl] *noun* **(a)** (breakfast) **cereal** = food made from corn, oats, etc., eaten with milk for breakfast; *would you like some cereal for breakfast?* **(b)** plant similar to grass, such as corn or oats, which produces seeds which can be cooked; *production of cereals is important to the USA* (NOTE: do not confuse with **serial**)

ceremony ['serɪməni] *noun* important official occasion when something special is done in public; *they held a ceremony to remember the victims of the train crash* (NOTE: plural is **ceremonies**)

certain ['sɜːtən] *adjective* **(a)** sure; *are you certain that you locked the door?* **(b)** without any doubt; *our team is certain to win the prize* **(c)** which you don't know or are not sure about; *certain mushrooms can make you ill if you eat them*

certainly ['sɜːtənli] *adverb* **(a)** *(after a question or order)* of course; *can you give me a lift to the station? - certainly; give me a kiss - certainly not!* **(b)** definitely; *he certainly knows how to score goals*

certificate [sɜː'tɪfɪkət] *noun* official document which proves or shows something; **death certificate** = paper signed by a doctor which shows that someone has died and what was the cause of death

chain [tʃeɪn] **1** *noun* **(a)** series of metal rings joined together; *she wore a gold chain round her neck*; *he stopped when the chain came off his bike* **(b)** series of stores, restaurants, pubs, hotels, etc., belonging to the same company; *she runs a chain of shoe shops* **2** *verb* to attach with a chain; *I chained my bike to the fence*

chair [tʃeə] **1** *noun* piece of furniture which you can sit on, with a back; *'someone has been sitting in my chair,' said Father Bear* **2** *verb* to sit in the main chair and run a meeting; *the meeting was chaired by Mrs Smith*

chalk [tʃɔːk] *noun* **(a)** type of soft white rock; *the white cliffs of Dover are formed of chalk* **(b)** stick of white or coloured material for writing on a blackboard; *he wrote the dates on the board in coloured chalk*

challenge ['tʃæləndʒ] **1** *noun* test of skill, strength, etc.; **to pose a challenge to someone** = to be a difficult task; *getting the piano up the stairs will pose a challenge to the removal men* **2** *verb* to ask someone to show that he is better than you; **to challenge someone to a fight** = to ask someone to fight you

champion ['tʃæmpiən] *noun* best in a particular competition; *he's the world champion in the 100 metres*

championship ['tʃæmpjənʃɪp] *noun* contest to find who is the champion; *the schools' tennis championship was won by a boy from Leeds*

chance [tʃɑːns] *noun* **(a)** being possible, something which is likely to happen; *has our team any chance of winning? - yes, I think they have a good chance*; *is there any chance of our getting home tonight?* **(b)** time when you can do something; *I wish I had the chance to visit South Africa* **(c)** luck; *it was pure chance that we were travelling on the same bus*

by chance *phrase* by luck; *it was quite by chance that we were travelling on the same bus*

by any chance *phrase* perhaps; *have you by any chance seen my glasses?*

chancellor ['tʃɑːnsələ] *noun* **(a)** important official; *he became chancellor of the university in 1996* **(b) Chancellor (of the Exchequer)** = chief finance minister in the British government; *newspapers always carry pictures of the Chancellor on Budget day*

change [tʃeɪndʒ] **1** *noun* **(a)** making something different or becoming different; *there was a change of plan at the last minute* **(b)** something different; *we usually go on holiday in summer, but this year we're taking a winter holiday for a change* **(c)** money in coins or notes; *I need some change for the parking meter* **(d)** money which you get back when you have given more than the correct price; *the book is £3.50, so if you give me £5, you should get £1.50 change* **2** *verb* **(a)** to make something different; to become different; *London has changed a lot since we used to live there*; *he's changed so much since I last saw him that I hardly recognized him* **(b)** to put on different clothes; *I'm just going upstairs to change or to get changed*; **changing room** = room where you can change into or out of sports clothes **(c)** to use or have something in place of something else; *can we change our room for one with a view of the sea?*; **to change trains** *or* **to change buses** = to get off one train or bus and onto another to continue your journey **(d)** to give smaller coins or notes for a large note; *can you change a £20 note?* **(e)** to give one type of currency for another; *I had to change £1,000 into dollars*; *we want to change some traveller's cheques*

channel ['tʃænl] *noun* **(a)** narrow piece of water; **the (English) Channel** = the sea between England and France; *many people use the Channel Tunnel to get to France*; *the boat only takes 50 minutes to cross the Channel* **(b)** TV station using a range of radio signals; *we're watching Channel 4*; *can you* *switch to Channel 1 for the news?*

chaos ['keɪɒs] *noun* state of confusion; *there was total chaos when the electricity failed*

chap [tʃæp] *noun (informal)* man; *I bought my bike from a chap at work*

chapel ['tʃæpl] *noun* small church; separate small part of a large church; *we visited a little chapel in the mountains*

chapter ['tʃæptə] *noun* section of a book; *don't tell me how the story ends - I'm only up to chapter three*

character ['kærəktə] *noun* **(a)** the part of a person which makes him or her different from everyone else; *she has a very strong character* **(b)** person in a play or novel; *the leading character in the film is an old blind man*

charge [tʃɑːdʒ] **1** *noun* **(a)** money which you have to pay; *there is no charge for delivery*; **admission charge** *or* **entry charge** = price to be paid before going into an exhibition, etc. **(b)** claim by the police that someone has done something wrong; *he was kept in prison on a charge of trying to blow up the Houses of Parliament* **(c) to take charge of something** = to start to be responsible for something; *he took charge of the class while the teacher was out of the room* **2** *verb* **(a)** to ask someone to pay; *the restaurant charged me £10 for two glasses of water*; *how much did the garage charge for mending the car?* **(b)** *(of the police)* to say that someone has done something wrong; *he was charged with stealing the jewels* **(c)** to run making a lot of noise; *the children charged into the kitchen* **(d)** to put electricity into a battery; *my mobile phone doesn't work - the battery probably needs charging*

in charge *phrase* being in control of; *he is in charge of the sales department*

charity ['tʃærɪti] *noun* organization which collects money to help the poor or to support some good cause; **charity shop** = shop run by a charity, where you can take old clothes,

china, etc., which are then sold and the money given to the charity (NOTE: plural is **charities**)

charm [tʃɑːm] **1** *noun* **(a)** being attractive; *the charm of the English countryside* **(b)** magic object; *she wears a lucky charm round her neck* **2** *verb* to attract someone, to make someone pleased; *I was charmed by their tiny cottage in the country*

chart [tʃɑːt] **1** *noun* **(a)** diagram showing figures; *a chart showing the increase in cases of lung cancer* **(b) the charts** = list of the most popular records; *his latest record is going up in the charts* **(c)** map of the sea, a river or a lake; *you will need an accurate chart if you're planning to sail along the coast* **2** *verb* to make a map of the sea, a river or lake; *he charted the coast of southern Australia in the 18th century*

charter ['tʃɑːtə] **1** *noun* **charter flight** = flight in an aircraft which has been hired by the airline for a special occasion; *our charter flight for Marbella was ten hours late* **2** *verb* to hire an aircraft, bus or boat for a particular trip; *we chartered a boat for a day trip to the island*

chase [tʃeɪs] **1** *noun* running after someone to try to catch him; *he was caught after a three-hour chase along the motorway* **2** *verb* to run after someone to try to catch him; *the policeman chased the burglars down the street*

chat [tʃæt] **1** *noun* informal friendly talk; *I'd like to have a chat with you about your work* **2** *verb* to talk in an informal and friendly way; *they were chatting about their holidays when the bus arrived* (NOTE: **chatting - chatted**)

cheap [tʃiːp] **1** *adjective* which does not cost a lot of money; *buses are by far the cheapest way to travel* (NOTE: **cheaper - cheapest**) **2** *adverb* at a low price; *I bought them cheap in the local market*

cheaply ['tʃiːpli] *adverb* without paying much money; *you can live quite cheaply if you don't go out much*

cheat [tʃiːt] **1** *noun* person who lies or acts in an unfair way in order to win; *I won't play with you again, you're a cheat* **2** *verb* to act in an unfair way in order to be successful; *the teachers are sure he cheated in his exam, but can't find out how he did it*

check [tʃek] **1** *noun* **(a)** examination or test; *the police are carrying out checks on all cars* **(b)** US *(in a restaurant)* bill; *I'll ask for the check* **(c)** pattern made of small squares; *the restaurant has red check tablecloths* **2** *verb* to make sure; to examine; *I'd better check with my girlfriend if there have been any messages for me*; *did you lock the door? - I'll go and check*

check in ['tʃek 'ɪn] *verb* **(a)** *(at a hotel)* to arrive at a hotel and sign to show you are taking a room; *he checked in at 12.15* **(b)** *(at an airport)* to give in your ticket to show you are ready to take the flight; *please check in two hours before your departure time*

check-in ['tʃekɪn] *noun* place where passengers give in their tickets and baggage for a flight; *the check-in is on the first floor*

check out ['tʃek 'aʊt] *verb* **(a)** *(at a hotel)* to leave and pay for a room; *we will check out after breakfast* **(b)** US to see if something is all right; *I thought I heard a noise in a kitchen - I'll just go and check it out*

checkbook ['tʃekbʊk] *see* CHEQUEBOOK

checkout ['tʃekaʊt] *noun* cash desk in a store, where you pay for the goods you have bought; *there were huge queues at the checkouts*

cheek [tʃiːk] *noun* **(a)** fat part of your face on either side of the nose and below the eyes; *a baby with red cheeks* **(b)** *(informal)* being rude and unpleasant; *he had the cheek to ask for more money*

cheer ['tʃɪə] **1** *noun* shout which praises or encourages; *when he scored the goal a great cheer went up* **2** *verb* to shout and encourage; *the crowd cheered when the first cyclists appeared*

cheer up ['tʃɪə 'ʌp] *verb* to become

happier; **cheer up!** = don't be miserable!

cheerful ['tʃiːəfʊl] *adjective* happy; *she's always cheerful, even when things are difficult at home*

cheers! ['tʃɪəz] *interjection (informal)* **(a)** thank you!; *can I help you with your bag? - cheers, mate!* **(b)** *(when drinking)* good health!; *they all lifted their glasses and said 'cheers!'*

cheese [tʃiːz] *noun* solid food made from milk; *at the end of the meal we'll have biscuits and cheese*; *(informal)* **'say cheese!'** = asking people to smile when their photo is being taken; *Uncle Charles got us all in a line and then told us to say 'cheese!'*

chef [ʃef] *noun* cook in a restaurant; *they've got a new chef at the 'King's Head' and the food is much better*; **chef's special** = special dish, sometimes one which the chef is famous for, which is listed in a separate section on the menu

chemical ['kemɪkl] **1** *adjective* referring to chemistry; *if you add acid it sets off a chemical reaction* **2** *noun* substance which is formed by reactions between substances; *chemicals are used a lot in farming*

chemist ['kemɪst] *noun* **(a)** person who sells medicines and also prepares them; *ask the chemist to give you something for your cough*; **the chemist's** = shop where you can buy medicine, toothpaste, soap, etc.; *go to the chemist's and get me some cough medicine* **(b)** scientist who studies chemical substances; *he works as a chemist in a government laboratory*

chemistry ['kemɪstri] *noun* science of chemical substances and their reactions; *she's studying chemistry at university*

cheque *US* **check** [tʃek] *noun* note to a bank asking for money to be paid from your account to another; *I paid for the jacket by cheque*; *he made out the cheque to Mr Smith*

chequebook *US* **checkbook** ['tʃekbʊk] *noun* set of blank cheques attached together in a cover; *I need a new chequebook*

cherry ['tʃeri] *noun* small sweet red fruit, which grows on a tree; *a pot of cherry yoghurt*; **cherry tree** = the tree which grows this fruit; *we have a beautiful cherry tree in the middle of the lawn* (NOTE: plural is **cherries)**

chess [tʃes] *noun* game for two people played on a board with sixteen pieces on each side; *would you like a game of chess?*

chest [tʃest] *noun* **(a)** the top front part of the body, where the heart and lungs are; *the doctor listened to the boy's chest* **(b)** large box; *he keeps his old clothes in a chest under his bed*; **chest of drawers** = piece of furniture with several drawers for clothes

chestnut ['tʃesnʌt] *noun* **(a)** large tree, with large shiny red-brown seeds; *there is an avenue of chestnuts in the middle of the park* **(b)** large shiny nut from a horse chestnut tree which cannot be eaten; *little boys were picking up chestnuts in the road*; **sweet chestnut** = chestnut from a sweet chestnut tree which can be eaten; *in winter, men stand at street corners selling roasted chestnuts; see also* CONKER

chew [tʃuː] *verb* to make something soft with your teeth; *the dog was lying on the kitchen floor chewing a bone*

chewing gum ['tʃuːɪŋ gʌm] *noun* sweet substance which you chew for a time but do not swallow; *would you like a piece of chewing gum?*

chick [tʃɪk] *noun* baby bird; *the chicks came running along behind the mother hen*

chicken ['tʃɪkɪn] *noun* **(a)** young hen; *chickens were running everywhere in front of the farm* **(b)** meat from a hen; *we're having roast chicken for lunch*; *we bought some chicken salad sandwiches*

chickenpox ['tʃɪkɪnpɒks] *noun* infectious disease of children, with fever and red spots that itch; *he got chickenpox and couldn't go to school*

chief [tʃiːf] **1** *adjective* most important; *what is the chief cause of air accidents?* **2** *noun* person in charge in a group of people or in a business; *the fire chief warned that the building was dangerous*

chiefly ['tʃiːfli] *adverb* mainly; *our town is famous chiefly for its pork pies*

child [tʃaɪld] *noun* **(a)** young boy or girl; *there was no TV when my mother was a child*; *a group of children were playing on the beach* **(b)** son or daughter; *they have six children - two boys and four girls* (NOTE: plural is **children** ['tʃɪldrən])

childhood ['tʃaɪldhʊd] *noun* time when someone is a child; *he spent his childhood in the country*

childish ['tʃaɪldɪʃ] *adjective* like a child; *it was a bit childish of her to start to cry when the boss told her off*

children ['tʃɪldrən] *see* CHILD

chill [tʃɪl] **1** *noun* illness caused by cold; *you'll catch a chill if you don't wear a coat* **2** *verb* to make something cool; *he asked for a glass of chilled orange juice*

chilly ['tʃɪli] *adjective* quite cold; *even summer evenings can be chilly in the mountains* (NOTE: **chillier - chilliest)**

chime [tʃaɪm] **1** *noun* ringing of bells; *the chimes of Big Ben start the BBC News* **2** *verb* (of bells) to ring; *the church clock has just chimed four*

chimney ['tʃɪmni] *noun* tall brick tube for taking smoke away; *the house has two tall chimneys*

chimpanzee *(informal)* **chimp** [tʃɪmpæn'ziː or tʃɪmp] *noun* type of African ape; *children love watching the chimps at the zoo*

chin [tʃɪn] *noun* front part of your bottom jaw; *she suddenly stood up and hit him on the chin*

china ['tʃaɪnə] *noun* fine thin white cups, plates, etc.; *all our china was broken when we moved house*

China [ˈtʃaɪnə] *noun* very large country in Asia; *visitors to China always go to see the Great Wall* (NOTE: capital: **Beijing**; people: **the Chinese**; language: **Chinese**)

Chinese [tʃaɪˈniːz] **1** *adjective* referring to China; *we often go to a Chinese restaurant in the evening* **2** *noun* **(a)** person from China; *the Chinese are very good at mathematics* **(b)** language spoken in China; *my book has been translated into Chinese*

chip [tʃɪp] **1** *noun* **(a)** long thin piece of potato fried in oil (in American English called 'French fries'); *he ordered chicken and chips*; **fish and chips** = traditional British food, obtained from special shops, where pieces of fried fish are sold with chips; *we're having fish and chips for dinner* **(b)** *US* thin slice of potato, fried till crisp and eaten cold as a snack (in British English, called 'crisps'); *he ordered a beer and a bowl of chips* **(c)** small piece of something hard, such as wood or stone; **chocolate chip** = small piece of hard chocolate; *a packet of chocolate chip biscuits* **(d) a computer chip** = a small piece of a substance which can store data, used in a computer **2** *verb* to break a small piece off something hard; *he banged the cup down on the plate and chipped it* (NOTE: **chipping - chipped**)

chipmunk [ˈtʃɪpmʌŋk] *noun US* little animal with stripes along its back; *a chipmunk popped his head out of a hole in the ground*

chisel [ˈtʃɪzl] *noun* metal tool which you hit with a hammer to cut small pieces of wood or stone; *he tapped the chisel very carefully with his hammer*

chocolate [ˈtʃɒklət] *noun* **(a)** sweet brown food made from the crushed seeds of a tropical tree; *her mother made a chocolate cake* **(b)** a single sweet made from chocolate; *John ate a whole box of chocolates and then felt ill* **(c)** drink made from chocolate powder and milk; *I always have a cup of hot chocolate before I go to bed*

choice [tʃɔɪs] *noun* **(a)** thing which is chosen; *Paris was our first choice for our holiday* **(b)** act of choosing something; *you must give the customer time to make his choice* **(c)** range of things to choose from; *the store has a huge choice of furniture*

choir [ˈkwaɪə] *noun* group of people who sing together; *he sings in the church choir*

choke [tʃəʊk] *verb* **(a)** to block a pipe, etc.; *the river was choked with weeds* **(b)** to stop breathing because you have swallowed something which blocks your throat; *he choked on a piece of bread*

choose [tʃuːz] *verb* **(a)** to pick something which you like best; *have you chosen what you want to eat?*; *they chose him as team leader* **(b)** to decide to do one thing when there are several things you could do; *in the end, they chose to go to the cinema* (NOTE: **choosing - chose** [tʃəʊz] **- has chosen** [ˈtʃəʊzn])

chop [tʃɒp] **1** *noun* piece of meat with a rib bone attached; *we had lamb chops for dinner* **2** *verb* to cut into small pieces; *he spent the afternoon chopping wood for the fire* (NOTE: **chopping - chopped**)

chop down [ˈtʃɒp ˈdaʊn] *verb* to cut down a tree, etc.; *they chopped down hundreds of trees to make the motorway*

chop off [ˈtʃɒp ˈɒf] *verb* to cut off; *he chopped off the dead branch*

chop up [ˈtʃɒp ˈʌp] *verb* to cut into pieces; *chop the vegetables up into little cubes*

chopsticks [ˈtʃɒpstɪks] *noun* pair of small sticks used in China, Japan, etc., to eat food or to stir food when cooking; *he said he didn't know how to use chopsticks and asked for a knife and fork instead*

chorus [ˈkɔːrəs] *noun* part of a song which is repeated later in the song; *I'll sing the verses and everyone can join in the chorus* (NOTE: plural is **choruses**)

chose, chosen [tʃəʊz or ˈtʃəʊzən] *see* CHOOSE

Christ [kraɪst] *noun* Jesus Christ, the person on whose life and teachings the Christian religion is based

christen ['krɪsn] *verb* to give a name to a Christian baby in church; *she was christened Natasha*

Christian ['krɪstʃn] *noun* person who believes in the teaching of Christ and follows the Christian religion; *the early Christians were victims of the Roman rulers*

Christian name ['krɪstʃn 'neɪm] *noun* a person's first name, the special name given to someone as a child; *I know his surname's Smith, but what's his Christian name?*

Christmas ['krɪsməs] *noun* Christian festival on December 25th, the birthday of Jesus Christ; *have you opened your Christmas presents yet?*; **Christmas cake** = special fruit cake eaten at Christmas time; **Christmas card** = special card sent to friends at Christmas to wish them a happy time; **Christmas pudding** = special pudding eaten at Christmas time; **Christmas stockings** = large coloured stockings, which children hang up by their beds or under the Christmas tree, and which are filled with presents by Father Christmas; **Christmas tree** = green tree which is brought into the house at Christmas and decorated with coloured lights

Christmas Eve ['krɪsməs 'iːv] *noun* 24th December, the day before Christmas Day; *the office is closed on Christmas Eve*; *we've been invited to a Christmas Eve party*

chuckle ['tʃʌkl] *verb* to give a quiet laugh; *he chuckled when she said she wanted a good steady job*

church [tʃɜːtʃ] *noun* building where Christians go to pray to God; *we usually go to church on Sunday mornings* (NOTE: plural is **churches**)

cigar [sɪ'gɑː] *noun* tight roll of dried tobacco leaves which you can light and smoke; *I like the smell of cigar smoke*

cigarette [sɪgə'ret] *noun* chopped dried tobacco rolled in very thin paper which you can light and smoke; *she was smoking a cigarette*;

he's trying to cut down on cigarettes

cinema ['sɪnəmə] *noun* place where you go to watch films; *we went to the cinema on Friday night*; *what's on at the cinema this week?*

circle ['sɜːkl] *noun* **(a)** line forming a round shape; *he drew a circle on the blackboard*; *the children sat on the floor in a circle round the teacher* **(b)** row of seats above the stalls in a theatre; *we got tickets for the upper circle*

circuit ['sɜːkɪt] *noun* path along which electricity flows; *he's designed a circuit for a burglar alarm*

circular ['sɜːkjʊlə] **1** *adjective* round in shape; *Chinese restaurants often have circular tables* **2** *noun* leaflet which advertises something; *the new restaurant sent out circulars offering 10% off all prices*

circumference [sə'kʌmfərəns] *noun* distance round the outside edge of a circle; *you can calculate the circumference of a circle by multiplying the radius by* 2π

circus ['sɜːkəs] *noun* **(a)** travelling show, often given in a large tent, with animals and other entertainments; *we went to the circus last night* **(b)** busy road junction in the centre of a large town; *Oxford Circus is where Oxford Street crosses Regent Street* (NOTE: plural is **circuses**)

citizen ['sɪtɪzən] *noun* person who comes from a certain country or city; *all Australian citizens have a duty to vote*; **senior citizen** = old retired person

city ['sɪti] *noun* large town; *traffic is a problem in big cities*; **city break** = short holiday in a large and famous town; *we took a city break in Prague*; **the city centre** = the central part of a town; *he has an office in the city centre* (NOTE: plural is **cities**)

civil ['sɪvɪl] *adjective* referring to the ordinary people of a state; **civil law** = laws relating to people's rights and agreements (the opposite, laws relating to crimes against the law of the land punished by the state, is 'criminal law'); **civil rights** = rights of an ordinary citizen; *she campaigned for civil rights in the 1980s*; **civil war** = situation inside a country where groups of armed people fight against each other or against the government

civil servant ['sɪvɪl 'sɜːvənt] *noun* person who works in a government department; *she is a civil servant in the Department of the Environment*

civil service [sɪvɪl 'sɜːvɪs] *noun* the organization which runs a country, and its staff; *you have to pass an examination to get a job in the civil service*

civilization [sɪvɪlaɪ'zeɪʃn] *noun* society or way of organizing society; *she is studying Chinese art and civilization*

claim [kleɪm] **1** *noun* **(a)** asking for money; *his claim for a pay rise was turned down* **(b)** statement; *his claim that the car belonged to him was correct* **2** *verb* **(a)** to demand as a right; *if they charged you too much you must claim a refund* **(b)** to state, but without any proof; *she claims that the umbrella belongs to her*

claim back ['kleɪm 'bæk] *verb* to claim something which you owned before; *his car was towed away and he had to go to the police station to claim it back*

clap [klæp] *verb* to beat your hands together to show you are pleased; *at the end of her speech the audience stood up and clapped* (NOTE: **clapping - clapped**)

class [klɑːs] *noun* **(a)** group of people (usually children) who go to school or college together; *there are 30 children in my son's class* **(b)** lesson; **evening classes** = lessons given in the evening (usually to adults); *I am going to evening classes to learn German* **(c)** people of the same group in society; *people from different social classes mixed at the reception* **(d)** certain level of quality; *these peaches are Class 1*; **first-class** = very good; *he is a first-class tennis player* (NOTE: plural is **classes**)

classified ['klæsɪfaɪd] *adjective* which has been put into a category; **classified ads** *or* **classified advertisements** = newspaper advertisements which are listed under special categories, such as 'jobs wanted' or 'household goods for sale'; *look in the classified ads if you want a cheap cooker*

classify ['klæsɪfaɪ] *verb* to arrange things into groups; *the hotels are classified according to a star system*

classroom ['klɑːsrʊm] *noun* room in a school where children are taught; *when the teacher came into the classroom all the children were shouting and throwing things at each other*

clause [klɔːz] *noun* part of a sentence containing a subject and a verb; *the sentence 'the bus came, and all the people waiting got on it' has two clauses, separated by the conjunction 'and'*

claw [klɔː] *noun* nail on the foot of an animal or bird; *our cat scratches the furniture with its claws*

clay [kleɪ] *noun* stiff soil used for making bricks or china; *he put a lump of clay onto his wheel and started to make a pot*

clean [kliːn] **1** *adjective* not dirty; *wipe your glasses with a clean handkerchief*; *the girl forgot to put clean towels in the bathroom* (NOTE: **cleaner - cleanest**) **2** *verb* to make clean, by taking away dirt; *she was cleaning the kitchen when the telephone rang*; *he cleans his car every Saturday morning*

clean up ['kliːn 'ʌp] *verb* to make everything clean and tidy; *it took us three hours to clean up after her birthday party*

cleaner ['kliːnə] *noun* **(a)** machine which removes dirt; **vacuum cleaner** = machine which sucks up dirt from floors **(b)** person who cleans (a house, office, etc.); *the cleaners didn't empty my waste paper basket* **(c)** the **cleaner's** = shop where you take clothes to be cleaned; *when I got my suit back from the cleaner's there was a button missing*

clear [klɪə] **1** *adjective* **(a)** with nothing in the way; *from her bedroom window, she had a clear view of the street*; *on a clear day, you can see the other side of the lake* **(b)** easily understood; *she made it clear that she wanted us to go*; *will you give me a clear answer - yes or no?* (NOTE: **clearer - clearest**) **2** *verb* to remove something which is blocking a way; *snow ploughs cleared the snow from the railway line*; *we'll get a plumber to clear the blocked pipe in the bathroom*; **to clear the table** = to take away knives, forks, plates, etc., after a meal **3** *adverb* not near; *stand clear of the doors, please*

clear away [ˈklɪə əˈweɪ] *verb* to take something away completely; *can you help to clear the rubbish away from the pavement?*

clear off [ˈklɪə ˈɒf] *verb (informal)* to go away; *clear off! I don't want you here*

clear out [ˈklɪə ˈaʊt] *verb* to empty completely; *can you clear out your bedroom cupboard?*

clear up [ˈklɪə ˈʌp] *verb* **(a)** to tidy and clean completely; *the cleaners refused to clear up the mess after the party* **(b)** to get better; *I hope the weather clears up because we're going on holiday tomorrow*

clearly [ˈklɪəli] *adverb* **(a)** in a way which is easily understood or heard; *he didn't speak very clearly* **(b)** in an obvious way; *he clearly didn't like being told he was too fat*

clench [klentʃ] *verb* to close tightly; *he clenched his fists ready for a fight*

clerk [klɑːk *US* klɜːk] *noun* person who works in an office; *he has started his new job as a bank clerk*

clever [ˈklevə] *adjective* intelligent, able to learn quickly; *she's the cleverest person in the family* (NOTE: **cleverer - cleverest**)

cleverly [ˈklevəli] *adverb* in a clever way; *the cat had cleverly worked out how to open the door*

click [klɪk] **1** *noun* short sharp sound; *she heard a click and saw the door start to open* **2** *verb* **(a)** to make a short sharp sound; *the cameras clicked as she came out of the church* **(b)** to press the button on a mouse quickly to start a computer program; *click twice on the mouse to start the program*

cliff [klɪf] *noun* steep face of rocks, usually by the sea; *their first view of England was the white cliffs of Dover*

climate [ˈklaɪmət] *noun* general weather conditions in a certain place; *the climate in the south of the country is milder than in the north*

climb [klaɪm] *verb* **(a)** to go up (or down) using your arms and legs; *the cat climbed up the apple tree*; *he escaped by climbing out of the window* **(b)** to go up; *the road climbs up to 500m above sea level*

cling [klɪŋ] *verb* **to cling onto something** = to hold tight to something; *she survived by clinging onto a piece of wood* (NOTE: **clinging - clung** [klʌŋ])

clinic [ˈklɪnɪk] *noun* specialized medical centre or hospital; *she had treatment in a drugs clinic*

clip [klɪp] **1** *noun* **paper clip** = piece of bent wire for attaching papers, etc., together; *he attached the cheque to the letter with a paper clip* **2** *verb* **(a)** to attach things together with a clip; *she clipped the invoice and the cheque together and put them in an envelope* **(b)** to cut with scissors or shears; *she was clipping the hedge*; *he carefully clipped the article out of the newspaper* (NOTE: **clipping - clipped**)

cloak [kləʊk] *noun* long outer coat which hangs from your shoulders and has no sleeves; *she wore a long cloak of black velvet*

cloakroom [ˈkləʊkrʊm] *noun* **(a)** *(informal)* public toilet (i.e. room with lavatories, washbasins, etc.); *the ladies cloakroom is on the first floor* **(b)** place where you leave your coat in a restaurant, theatre, etc.; *I left my coat and briefcase in the cloakroom*

clock [klɒk] *noun* large machine which shows the time; *the station clock is always* *right*; **alarm clock** = clock which rings a bell at a certain time to wake you up

clockwise ['klɒkwaɪz] *adjective & adverb* in the same direction as the hands of a clock; *turn the lid clockwise to tighten it* (NOTE: the opposite is **anticlockwise)**

clockwork ['klɒkwɜːk] *noun* machine such as a toy, clock, etc., which works using a spring which is wound up with a key; *he invented the clockwork radio*

close 1 [kləʊs] *adjective* very near, just next to something; *our house is close to the railway station* 2 [kləʊs] *adverb* very near; *keep close by me if you don't want to get lost* (NOTE: **closer - closest)** 3 [kləʊz] *verb* **(a)** to shut; *he closed his book and turned on the TV* **(b)** to come to an end; *the meeting closed with a couple of songs* 4 *noun* **(a)** [kləʊz] end, final part; *the century was drawing to a close* **(b)** [kləʊs] small street of houses which is open only at one end; *they live in Holly Close*

closed [kləʊzd] *adjective* shut; *the shop is closed on Sundays*

close down ['kləʊz 'daʊn] *verb* to shut a business; *they're going to close down the factory because they haven't enough work*

closely ['kləʊsli] *adverb* with a lot of attention; *she studied the timetable very closely*

close-up ['kləʊsʌp] *noun* photograph taken very close to the subject; *use a zoom lens to give you a close-up of lions from a safe distance*

cloth [klɒθ] *noun* **(a)** material; *her dress is made of cheap blue cloth* **(b)** piece of material for cleaning; *he wiped up the spill with a damp cloth* **(c)** tablecloth, piece of material which you put on a table to cover it; *the waiter spread pink cloths over the tables*

clothes [kləʊðz] *noun* things (such as shirts, trousers, dresses, etc.) which you wear to cover your body and keep you warm; *he walked down the street with no clothes on*

clothing ['kləʊðɪŋ] *noun* clothes; *take plenty of warm clothing on your trip to the mountains*

cloud [klaʊd] *noun* **(a)** mass of white or grey mist floating in the air; *do you think it's going to rain? - yes, look at those black clouds* **(b)** similar mass of smoke; *clouds of smoke poured out of the burning shop*

cloudy ['klaʊdi] *adjective* with clouds in the sky; *the weather was cloudy in the morning, but cleared up in the afternoon* (NOTE: **cloudier - cloudiest)**

clown [klaʊn] *noun* man who makes people laugh in a circus; *the clown had a big red nose*

club [klʌb] *noun* **(a)** group of people who have the same interest or form a team; *she belongs to our local swimming club*; *our town has one of the top football clubs in the country* **(b) clubs** = one of the black suits in a pack of cards, shaped like a leaf with three parts (the other black suit is spades; hearts and diamonds are the red suits); *he had the five of clubs in his hand* **(c)** large heavy stick; *a golf club* = stick with a heavy end for playing golf

clue [kluː] *noun* information which helps you solve a mystery or puzzle; *the detective had missed a vital clue*; **I haven't a clue** = I don't know at all

clumsy ['klʌmzi] *adjective* who frequently breaks things or knocks things over; *don't let Ben set the table - he's so clumsy, he's bound to break something* (NOTE: **clumsier - clumsiest)**

clung [klʌŋ] *verb see* CLING

cluster ['klʌstə] 1 *noun* group of things close together; *can you see that cluster of houses in the distance?* 2 *verb* **to cluster together** = to form a group; *they clustered round the notice board to read their exam results*

clutch [klʌtʃ] 1 *noun* device for changing the gears in a car; **clutch pedal** = pedal which works the clutch and allows the driver to change gear 2 *verb* to grab hold of; *she clutched my arm as we stood on the edge of the cliff*

cm ['sentɪmiːtəz] *see* CENTIMETRE; *yesterday we had 3cm of rain*; *25cm of snow had fallen during the night*

co. [kəʊ or 'kʌmpəni] *abbreviation for* COMPANY; *J. Smith & Co.*

coach [kəʊtʃ] **1** *noun* **(a)** large comfortable bus for travelling long distances; *there's a coach service from here to Oxford which leaves every hour*; *they went on a coach tour of southern Spain* **(b)** passenger wagon on a train; *the first four coaches are for Waterloo* **(c)** person who trains sports players, etc.; *the coach told them that they needed to spend more time practising* (NOTE: plural is **coaches**) **2** *verb* **(a)** to train sports players, etc.; *she was coached by a runner who won a gold medal in the Mexico Olympics* **(b)** to give private lessons to someone; *some of the children were coached in small groups*

coal [kəʊl] *noun* black rock which is dug out of the ground and which you can burn to make heat; *it's getting cold in here - put some more coal on the fire*

coarse [kɔːs] *adjective* rough, not fine; *coarse grains of sand*; *coarse cloth is used to make sacks* (NOTE: **coarser - coarsest**; do not confuse with **course**)

coast [kəʊst] *noun* land by the sea; *after ten weeks at sea, Columbus saw the coast of America*; *the south coast is the warmest part of the country*

coat [kəʊt] *noun* **(a)** piece of clothing which you wear on top of other clothes; *you'll need to put your winter coat on - it's just started to snow* **(b) coat of paint** = layer of paint; *that window needs a coat of paint*

cobweb ['kɒbweb] *noun* net made by a spider to catch flies; *the bedroom hadn't been cleaned and everything was covered with cobwebs*

cock *or* **cockerel** [kɒk or 'kɒkrəl] *noun* male chicken (American English is a 'rooster'); *we were woken by the cocks on our neighbour's farm*

cocoa ['kəʊkəʊ] *noun* **(a)** brown chocolate powder, used for making a drink; *there's a tin of cocoa on the top shelf* **(b)** drink made with cocoa powder and hot water or milk; *he always has a cup of cocoa before going to bed*

coconut ['kəʊkənʌt] *noun* large nut from a type of palm tree, with white flesh inside; *I bought a packet of coconut biscuits*

code [kəʊd] **1** *noun* **(a)** set of laws, rules of behaviour; **the Highway Code** = rules for driving on the road **(b)** secret words or system for sending messages; *we're trying to break the enemy's code*; **code word** = secret word which allows you to do something **(c)** system of numbers or letters which mean something; *the code for Heathrow Airport is LHR*; **area code** = numbers which refer to an area for telephoning; *what's the international code for France?*

coffee ['kɒfi] *noun* **(a)** hot drink made from the seeds of a tropical plant; *would you like a cup of coffee?*; *I always take sugar with my coffee* **(b)** a cup of coffee; *three coffees and two teas, please*

coffee shop ['kɒfi 'ʃɒp] *noun* small restaurant (often in a hotel) serving tea, coffee and snacks; *it will be quicker to have lunch in the coffee shop*

coffin ['kɒfin] *noun* long wooden box in which a dead person is buried; *they watched in silence as the coffin was lowered into the ground*

coil [kɔɪl] **1** *noun* one ring in something twisted round and round; *they surrounded the camp with coils of wire* **2** *verb* to twist round something to form a ring; *the sailors coiled the ropes on the deck*

coin [kɔɪn] *noun* piece of metal money; *I found a 50p coin in the street*; *this machine takes only 10p coins*

coke [kəʊk] *noun* fuel processed from coal, which produces a very strong heat; *the steel is produced in coke ovens*

cold [kəʊld] **1** *adjective* not hot, with a low

temperature; *they say that cold showers are good for you*; *the weather turned colder after Christmas*; *start eating, or your soup will get cold* (NOTE: **colder - coldest**) **2** *noun* **(a)** illness, when you sneeze and cough; *don't come near me - I've got a cold* **(b)** cold weather outdoors; *he got ill from standing in the cold waiting for a bus*

coldly ['kəʊldli] *adverb* in an unfriendly way; *she greeted him coldly*

collapse [kə'læps] *verb* to fall down suddenly; *the roof collapsed under the weight of the snow*; *she turned pale and collapsed on the floor*

collar ['kɒlə] *noun* **(a)** part of a shirt, coat, dress, etc., which goes round your neck; *I can't do up the top button on my shirt - the collar's too tight*; *she turned up her coat collar because the wind was cold* **(b)** leather ring round the neck of a dog or cat; *the cat has a collar with her name and address on it*

collect [kə'lekt] *verb* **(a)** to fetch something or bring things together; *your coat is ready for you to collect from the cleaner's*; *I must collect the children from school* **(b)** to buy things or bring things together as a hobby; *he collects stamps and old coins* **(c)** to gather money for charity; *they're collecting for Oxfam*

collection [kə'lekʃən] *noun* **(a)** group of things brought together as a hobby; *he showed me his stamp collection* **(b)** money which has been gathered; *we're making a collection for Oxfam*

college ['kɒlɪdʒ] *noun* place where adults and young people (but not children) study; *she's going on holiday with some friends from college*; *he's studying at the local college*

collide [kə'laɪd] *verb* **to collide with something** = to bump into something; *he lost control of the car and collided with a bus*

collision [kə'lɪʒən] *noun* bumping into something; *two people were injured in the collision between a lorry and a bus*

colon ['kəʊlən] *noun* printing sign (:); *use a colon before starting a list*

colour *US* **color** ['kʌlə] **1** *noun* **(a)** shade which an object has in light (red, blue, yellow, etc.); *what colour is your bathroom?*; *his socks are the same colour as his pullover* **(b)** not black or white; *the book has pages of colour pictures* **2** *verb* to add colour to something; *the children were given felt pens and told to colour the trees green and the earth brown*; **colouring book** = children's book with black and white drawings which you can then colour with paint or crayons

column ['kɒləm] *noun* **(a)** tall pillar; *Nelson's Column is in Trafalgar Square* **(b)** block of printing going down a page; *the article ran to three columns on the first page of the newspaper* **(c)** series of numbers, one under the other; *add up the figures and put the total at the bottom of the column* **(d)** regular article in a newspaper; *she writes a food column for the local newspaper*

comb [kəʊm] **1** *noun* instrument with long teeth used to make your hair straight; *her hair is in such a mess that you can't get a comb through it* **2** *verb* **(a)** to smooth your hair with a comb; *she was combing her hair in front of the mirror* **(b)** to search; *police combed the woods for the missing girl*

combine 1 [kəm'baɪn] *verb* **to combine with** = to join together with; *the snow combined with high winds made driving difficult* **2** ['kɒmbaɪn] large farm machine which cuts corn, takes out and keeps the seeds and throws away the straw; *a row of combines moved across the huge field*

come [kʌm] *verb* **(a)** to move to this place; *come and see us when you're in London*; *the doctor came to see him yesterday* **(b)** to happen; *how did the door come to be open?*; *(informal)* **how come?** = why?; *how come the front door was left open?* **(c)** to be placed; *what comes after R in the alphabet?*; *what comes after the news on TV?* (NOTE: **coming -**

came [keɪm] - **has come**)

come across [ˈkʌm əˈkrɒs] *verb* to find by chance; *we came across this little bottle on the beach*

come along [ˈkʌm əˈlɒŋ] *verb* to go with someone; *the children can come along with us in the car*

come back [ˈkʌm ˈbæk] *verb* to move back to this place; *he started to walk away, but the policeman shouted at him to come back*

come in [ˈkʌn ˈɪn] *verb* to enter; *come in, and make yourself comfortable*

come off [ˈkʌm ˈɒf] *verb* **(a)** to stop being attached; *the button has come off my shirt* **(b)** to be removed; *the ink won't come off the tablecloth*

come on [ˈkʌm ˈɒn] *verb* to hurry; *come on, or we'll miss the start of the film*

come out [ˈkʌm ˈaʊt] *verb* **(a)** to move outside; *come out into the garden, it's beautifully hot* **(b)** to be removed; *those ink marks won't come out*

come to [ˈkʌm ˈtuː] *verb* **(a)** to add up to; *the bill comes to £10* **(b)** to become conscious again; *when he came to, he was in hospital*

comedy [ˈkɒmədi] *noun* play or film which makes you laugh; *'A Midsummer Night's Dream' is one of Shakespeare's comedies* (NOTE: plural is **comedies**)

comet [ˈkɒmɪt] *noun* body which moves in space, which you can see at night because of its bright tail; *Halley's Comet returns every 76 years*

comfort [ˈkʌmfət] **1** *noun* being comfortable; *she complained about the lack of comfort on the coach* **2** *verb* to make someone who is miserable happier; *she tried to comfort the little girl*

comfortable [ˈkʌftəbl] *adjective* **(a)** soft and relaxing; *there are comfortable chairs in the lounge* **(b)** to make yourself comfortable = to relax; *she made herself comfortable in the chair by the fire*

comfortably [ˈkʌmftəbli] *adverb* in a comfortable or relaxing way; *if you're sitting comfortably, I'll explain to you what we have to do*

comic [ˈkɒmɪk] *noun* children's paper with funny cartoon stories; *he spends his pocket money on comics and sweets*

coming [ˈkʌmɪŋ] *adjective* which is approaching; *the newspaper tells you what's on TV in the coming week*

comma [ˈkɒmə] *noun* punctuation mark (,) showing a break in the meaning of a sentence; *use a comma between each item listed*; **inverted commas** = printing signs (« «), which are put round words which are being quoted or round titles; *the title Pickwick Papers should be in inverted commas*

command [kəˈmɑːnd] **1** *noun* **(a)** order; *the general gave the command to attack* **(b)** **in command** = in charge; *who's in command here?* **2** *verb* **(a)** to order; *the general commanded the troops to move forward* **(b)** to be in charge of; *he commands a group of soldiers*

commercial [kəˈmɜːʃl] **1** *adjective* **(a)** referring to business; **commercial college** = college which teaches business studies **(b)** used for business purposes; *commercial vehicles such as trucks, taxis and buses* **2** *noun* advertisement on television; *the TV commercial attracted a lot of interest*

commit [kəˈmɪt] *verb* **(a)** to carry out a crime; *the gang committed six attacks on banks before they were caught* **(b)** **to commit suicide** = to kill yourself **(c)** **to commit yourself** = to promise to do something; *I can't commit myself to anything until I have more details*

commitment [kəˈmɪtmənt] *noun* agreement to do something; *she made a firm commitment to arrive for work on time in future*

committee [kəˈmɪtiː] *noun* official group of people who organize things for a larger group; *committee members will be asked to vote on* *the proposal*

common ['kɒmən] **1** *adjective* which happens often, which you find everywhere; *it's very common for people to get colds in winter* (NOTE: **commoner - commonest**) **2** *noun* public land which local people can use; *we went walking on Wimbledon Common*

common sense ['kɒmən 'sens] *noun* ordinary good sense; *it's common sense to lock your car at night*

commonly ['kɒmənli] *adverb* often; *mobile phones are commonly used in restaurants*

commotion [kə'məʊʃən] *noun* confusion or trouble; *there was a sudden commotion in the playground and the head teacher went to see what was the matter*

communicate [kə'mjuːnɪkeɪt] *verb* to send or give information to someone; *she tried to communicate with her local MP*

communication [kəmjuːnɪ'keɪʃn] *noun* **(a)** sending of information; *email is the most rapid means of communication* **(b)** message sent; *we had a communication from the local council*

community [kə'mjuːnɪti] *noun* group of people living in one area; *the local community is worried about the level of violence in the streets*; **community centre** = building which provides a place for sports or arts in a community; *flood victims are being housed in the local community centre* (NOTE: plural is **communities**)

compact disc (CD) ['kɒmpækt 'dɪsk] *noun* metal disc, which can hold a large amount of data, pictures or music, and which is read by a laser in a special player; *the sound quality on CDs is better than on old records*

companion [kəm'pænjən] *noun* person or animal who lives or travels with someone; *his constant companion was his old white dog*

company ['kʌmpni] *noun* **(a)** commercial firm; *the company has taken on three secretaries*; *she works for a computer company* **(b)** being together with other people;

I enjoy the company of young people; **to keep someone company** = to be with someone to prevent them from feeling lonely; *would you like to come with me to keep me company?* **(c)** group of people who work together; **a ship's company** = the crew of a ship; **a theatre company** = the actors and directors of a theatre

comparative [kəm'pærətɪv] *noun* form of an adjective or adverb which compares; *'happier', 'better' and 'more often' are the comparatives of 'happy', 'good' and 'often'*

compare [kəm'peə] *verb* **to compare something with** *or* **to something** = to look at two things side by side to see how they are different; *compared to his father he's not very tall*

compared [kəm'peəd] *adjective* **compared to** *or* **with** = when you compare it to; *compared to last year, this summer was cold*

compass ['kʌmpəs] *noun* **(a)** device with a floating needle which points to the north; **the points of the compass** = the different directions, north, south, east and west **(b)** a **pair of compasses** = device for drawing a circle; *set your compasses to 10mm and draw a circle with a diameter of 20mm*

compete [kəm'piːt] *verb* to try to beat someone in sport, trade, etc.; *he is competing in both the 100 and 200 metres*; *we have to compete with cheap goods from the Far East*

competition [kɒmpə'tɪʃn] *noun* **(a)** sport or game where several teams or people try to win; *he won first prize in the piano competition* **(b)** trying to do better than someone in business; *our main competition comes from the big supermarkets*

complain [kəm'pleɪn] *verb* to say that something is no good or does not work properly; *the shop is so cold the staff have started complaining*

complaint [kəm'pleɪnt] *noun* **(a)** saying that something is wrong; *she sent a letter of complaint to the head of the college*;

complaints department = department in a company which deals with complaints from customers **(b)** illness; *he was admitted to hospital with a kidney complaint*

complete [kəm'pli:t] **1** *adjective* with all its parts; *he has a complete set of the new stamps*; *we have to study the complete plays of Shakespeare* **2** *verb* to finish; *the builders completed the whole job in two days*

completely [kʌm'pli:tli] *adverb* totally; *I completely forgot about my mother's birthday*

complicated ['kɒmplɪkeɪtɪd] *adjective* with many small details; difficult to understand; *chess has quite complicated rules*; *the route to get to our house is rather complicated, so I'll draw you a map*

compliment 1 *noun* ['kɒmplɪmənt] **(a)** remark which praises someone or something; *she turned red when she read his compliments on her dancing* **(b) compliments** = good wishes; *we each got a box of chocolates with the compliments of the manager* **2** *verb* ['kɒmplɪment] to praise; *I want to compliment the cook on an excellent meal*

compose [kəm'pəuz] *verb* to write something, especially a piece of music; *it took Mozart only a few days to compose the opera*

composition [kɒmpə'zɪʃn] *noun* **(a)** something which has been composed, a poem, piece of music, etc.; *we will now play a famous composition by Beethoven* **(b)** essay, piece of writing on a special subject; *we had three hours to write a composition on 'pollution'*

compound ['kɒmpaund] **1** *adjective* made up of several parts; **compound interest** = interest calculated on the original total plus any previous interest (as opposed to 'simple interest') **2** *noun* **(a)** chemical made up of two or more substances; *water is a compound of hydrogen and oxygen* **(b)** buildings and land surrounded by a fence; *guard dogs patrol the compound at night*

computer [kəm'pju:tə] *noun* electronic machine which calculates and keeps information automatically; *he wrote his book on his home computer*; *the boys spent the weekend playing computer games*

conceal [kən'si:l] *verb* to hide something, to put something where it cannot be seen; *he tried to conceal the camera by putting it under his coat*

concentrate ['kɒnsəntreɪt] *verb* to pay a lot of attention to; *the exam candidates were all concentrating hard when someone started to giggle*; *don't talk - he's trying to concentrate on his homework*

concern [kən'sɜ:n] *verb* **(a)** to have as the subject; **that does not concern him** = it has nothing to do with him; **as far as money is concerned** = referring to money **(b)** to worry; *it concerns me that he is always pale and tired*

concerned [kən'sɜ:nd] *adjective* worried; *her parents are concerned about her health*

concerning [kən'sɜ:nɪŋ] *preposition* about, dealing with; *can you answer some questions concerning holidays?*

concert ['kɒnsət] *noun* public performance of music; *I couldn't go to the concert, so I gave my ticket to a friend*

conclusion [kən'klu:ʒn] *noun* **(a)** opinion which you reach after careful thought; *she came to the conclusion that he had found another girlfriend* **(b)** end; *at the conclusion of the trial all the people accused were found guilty*

concrete ['kɒŋkri:t] *noun* mixture of cement and sand, used in building; *the pavement is made of blocks of concrete*; **concrete mixer** = machine which turns to mix cement, sand and water to make concrete

condition [kən'dɪʃn] *noun* **(a)** state that something is in; *the car is in very good condition considering it is over thirty years old* **(b)** something which has to be agreed before something else is done; *one of conditions of the deal is that the company pays all my travel costs*; **on condition that** = only if; *I will come on condition that you pay my fare*

conduct 1 *noun* ['kɒndʌkt] (a) way you behave; *his conduct in class is becoming worse; she got a prize for good conduct* 2 *verb* [kən'dʌkt] (a) to guide; **conducted tour** = tour led by a guide (b) to direct an orchestra; *the orchestra will be conducted by a Russian conductor* (c) to allow electricity, heat, etc., to pass through; *copper conducts electricity very well*

conductor [kən'dʌktə] *noun* (a) metal, or other substance which conducts heat or electricity; *copper is a good conductor but plastic is not* (b) person who directs an orchestra; *the orchestra will be conducted by a Russian conductor* (c) **bus conductor** = person who sells tickets on a bus

cone [kəʊn] *noun* (a) shape which is round at the base, rising to a point; **ice cream cone** = cone-shaped biscuit with ice cream in it (b) brightly coloured plastic cone, used to warn drivers not to park; *the police put cones along one side of the street* (c) **fir cone** = the fruit of a fir tree

conference ['kɒnfərəns] *noun* discussion, meeting; **press conference** = meeting where newspaper, radio and TV reporters are invited to hear news of something or to talk to a famous person; *he gave a press conference on the steps of Number Ten*

confess [kən'fes] *verb* to admit that you have done something wrong; *he confessed to six raids on supermarkets*

confident ['kɒnfɪdənt] *adjective* sure that you or something will be successful; *I am confident the show will go off well; she's confident of doing well in the exam*

confuse [kən'fjuːz] *verb* (a) to muddle; *she was confused by all the journalists' questions* (b) to mix up; *the twins are so alike I am*

always confusing them

confused [kən'fjuːzd] *adjective* not clear in your mind; *I'm a bit confused - did we say 8.00 p.m. or 8.30?*

confusing [kən'fjuːzɪŋ] *adjective* which is difficult to make clear; *she found the instructions on the computer very confusing*

congratulate [kən'grætjʊleɪt] *verb* to give someone good wishes on a special occasion or for having done something; *I want to congratulate you on winning first prize*

congratulations [kəngrætjuː'leɪʃnz] *noun* good wishes to someone who has done well; *congratulations on passing your exam!*

Congress ['kɒngres] *noun* part of the government of the USA, formed of the House of Representatives and the Senate; *the President sends Bills to Congress for discussion*

conjunction [kən'dʒʌŋkʃn] *noun* word which links different words together to make phrases or sentences; *'and' and 'but' are conjunctions*

conjuror ['kʌndʒərə] *noun* person who does tricks with cards, rabbits, etc.; *they hired a conjuror for the children's party*

conker ['kɒŋkə] *noun* the nut of the chestnut tree, used in children's games; *the children were playing conkers in the school yard; to play conkers, you put a piece of string through a chestnut and hold it up in front of you, your opponent tries to hit it with his chestnut, and the one whose conker breaks into pieces first loses the game*

connect [kə'nekt] *verb* (a) to join things together; *the computer should be connected to the printer* (b) to link up with a bus, plane, train, etc.; **the flight from New York connects with a flight to Athens** = the plane from New York arrives in time for passengers to catch the plane to Athens

connection [kə'nekʃn] *noun* (a) link; *there is a definite connection between smoking and lung cancer* (b) train, plane, etc., which you catch after getting off another train or plane; *my train was late and I missed my connection to Birmingham*

conquer ['kɒŋkə] *verb* to defeat by force; *England was conquered by the Normans in 1066*

conscious ['kɒnʃəs] *adjective* aware of things happening around you; *she was conscious during the whole operation*

consecutive [kən'sekjʊtɪv] *adjective* one after the other; *he got letters from the tax office on two consecutive days*

conservation [kɒnsə'veɪʃn] *noun* saving of energy, natural resources, old buildings, etc.; *we are very keen on energy conservation*

conservative [kən'sɜːvətɪv] *adjective* (a) not wanting to change; *he has very conservative views* (b) *(politics)* the **Conservative party** = political party which is in favour of only gradual change in society and does not want the government to be too involved in society and welfare

consider [kən'sɪdə] *verb* to think carefully about something; *please consider seriously the offer which we are making*

considerable [kən'sɪdrəbl] *adjective* quite large; *he lost a considerable amount of money at the horse races*

considerably [kən'sɪdrəbli] *adverb* quite a lot; *the weather is considerably hotter than it was last week*

considering [kən'sɪdrɪŋ] *conjunction & preposition* when you think (of); *he plays the piano extremely well, considering he's only five*

consist of [kən'sɪst] *verb* to be formed of; *the English class consists of twenty girls and only two boys*

consonant ['kɒnsənənt] *noun* letter representing a sound which is made using the teeth, tongue or lips (as opposed to a 'vowel'); *'b' and 't' are consonants, while 'e' and 'i' are vowels; the five vowels are 'a', 'e', 'i', 'o'*

and 'u': all the other letters of the alphabet are consonants*

constable ['kʌnstəbl] *noun* ordinary member of the police; *the inspector was accompanied by a sergeant and three constables*

constant ['kɒnstənt] **1** *adjective* not changing or stopping; *the constant noise of music from the flat next door is driving me mad*

constantly ['kɒnstəntli] *adverb* all the time; *he is constantly changing his mind*

construct [kən'strʌkt] *verb* to build; *the plane's wings are constructed of light steel*

construction [kən'strʌkʃn] *noun* the act of building; *the construction of the new stadium took three years*; **under construction** = being built; *the airport is under construction*

consultant [kən'sʌltənt] *noun* doctor who specializes in a particular type of medicine, attached to a hospital; *we'll make an appointment for you to see a consultant*

consume [kən'sjuːm] *verb* (a) to eat or drink; *the guests consumed over 100 hamburgers* (b) to use up; *the new car consumes about half the amount of petrol of an ordinary car*

consumer [kən'sjuːmə] *noun* person or company that buys goods or services; *gas consumers are protesting at the increase in prices*

contact ['kɒntækt] **1** *noun* (a) touch; **contact lenses** = tiny lenses worn on your eyes (b) act of communicating with someone; **to get in contact with someone** = to communicate with someone you have not spoken to or written to **2** *verb* to get into communication with someone; *he tried to contact his family by phone*

contain [kən'teɪn] *verb* to hold, to have inside; *the envelope contained a cheque for £1000*

container [kən'teɪnə] *noun* box or bottle,

etc., which holds something else; *the gas is shipped in strong metal containers*

content [kən'tent] *adjective* **content to** = happy to; *she was content to sit in the sun and wait for him to come back*

contents ['kɒntents] *noun* things which are inside something, which are in a container; *the burglars took the entire contents of the safe*; **table of contents** = list of chapters in a book, usually printed at the beginning of the text

contest *noun* ['kɒntest] fight, competition; *only two people entered the contest*

continent ['kɒntɪnənt] *noun* **(a)** one of the main land areas in the world (Africa, North America, South America, Asia, Australia, Europe, etc.) **(b)** *(in Britain)* **the Continent** = the rest of Europe, as opposed to Britain itself, which is an island; *when you drive on the Continent remember to drive on the right*

continual [kən'tɪnjuəl] *adjective* which happens again and again; *I am getting fed up with her continual complaints*

continue [kən'tɪnjuː] *verb* to go on doing something or go on happening; *he continued working, even though the house was on fire*

continuous [kən'tɪnjuəs] *adjective* with no break; *she has been in continuous pain for three days*

contract **1** ['kɒntrækt] *noun* legal agreement; *I don't agree with some of the conditions of the contract* **2** [kən'trækt] *verb* **(a)** to agree to do some work under a binding contract; *they contracted to supply us with spare parts* **(b)** to become smaller; *metal contracts when it gets cold*

contradict [kɒntrə'dɪkt] *verb* to say that what someone else says is not true; to be different from what has been said before; *what you have just said contradicts what you said yesterday*

contrary ['kɒntrəri] *noun* **the contrary** = the opposite; **on the contrary** = just the opposite; *I'm not annoyed with her - on the contrary, I think she has done the right thing*

contrast *noun* ['kɒntrɑːst] sharp difference between two things; *there's a very sharp contrast in weather between the north and the south of the country*; **in contrast to** = as opposed to; *he is quite short, in contrast to his sister who is very tall*

contribute [kən'trɪbjuːt] *verb* to give money to; *everyone was asked to contribute to the secretary's leaving present*

contribution [kɒntrɪ'bjuːʃn] *noun* money, etc., given to help something; **National Insurance contributions** = money paid each month to the government by a worker and the company he or she works for, to go towards the costs of looking after the sick, poor and unemployed

control [kən'trəʊl] **1** *noun* keeping in order, being able to direct something; *the teacher has no control over the class*; **control button** = on a TV, radio, etc., the button which switches it on, changes channel, increases volume, etc.; **under control** = controlled; *we try to keep our spending under tight control*; *the firemen quickly brought the fire under control*; **out of control** = not controlled; *the fire started in the roof and quickly got out of control* **2** *verb* to keep in order, to direct; *the police couldn't control the crowds*; *there was nobody there to control the traffic*; *we must try to control our spending on holiday* (NOTE: controlling - controlled)

convenient [kən'viːniənt] *adjective* easy to use, which does not cause any problems; *the house is convenient for the shops*; *6.30 in the morning is not a very convenient time for the first lesson*

conveniently [kən'viːniəntli] *adverb* in a useful way; *the hotel is conveniently placed next to the railway station*

conversation [kɒnvə'seɪʃn] *noun* talk; *she had a long conversation with her mother*

convict **1** *noun* ['kɒnvɪkt] criminal who has been sent to prison; *the police are searching for two escaped convicts* **2** *verb* [kən'vɪkt] to find someone guilty; *she was convicted of stealing goods from the local supermarket*

convince [kən'vɪns] *verb* **to convince someone of something** = to persuade someone that something is true; *at an interview, you have to convince the employer that you are the right person for the job*

convinced [kən'vɪnst] *adjective* very certain; *the police are convinced that she knows something about the stolen car*

cook [kʊk] **1** *noun* person who gets food ready; *she worked as a cook in a pub during the summer* **2** *verb* **(a)** to get food ready for eating, especially by heating it; *don't bother your mother when she's cooking the dinner*; **a cooked breakfast** = a breakfast of eggs, bacon, etc. (and not just coffee and toast) **(b)** *(of food)* to be got ready by heating; *the chicken is cooking in the oven*; *how long do these vegetables take to cook?*

cooker ['kʊkə] *noun* stove, a machine which runs on gas, electricity, coal, etc., used for cooking food; *we have a fridge, a dishwasher and a gas cooker in the kitchen*

cookie ['kʊki] *noun (usually US)* biscuit, a small flat hard sweet cake; **chocolate chip cookie** = cookie made with little pieces of hard chocolate inside

cool [kuːl] *adjective* **(a)** quite cold; *blow on your soup to make it cool*; *it gets cool in the evenings in September* **(b)** calm; *the nurses remained cool while they dealt with all the accident victims* (NOTE: **cooler - coolest**)

cope [kəʊp] *verb* **to cope with something** = to manage to deal with something; *we are trying to cope with a sudden mass of orders*

copier ['kɒpjə] *noun* machine which makes copies; **copier paper** = special paper used in photocopiers

copper ['kɒpə] *noun* **(a)** red metal which turns green in the air; *copper is a good conductor of electricity* **(b)** small coin made of copper or other brown metal; *it only costs a few coppers*

copy ['kɒpi] **1** *noun* **(a)** something made to look the same as something else; *this is an exact copy of the painting by Picasso* **(b)** one book; one newspaper; *where's my copy of today's 'Times'?*; *I lent my old copy of Shakespeare to my brother and he never gave it back* (NOTE: plural is **copies**) **2** *verb* **(a)** to make something which looks like something else; *he stole a credit card and copied the signature*; **copying machine** = a machine which copies **(b)** **to copy someone** = to do what someone else does; *I get very annoyed because he copies everything I do*

core [kɔː] *noun* central part; **apple core** = hard part in the middle of an apple, containing the seeds; *when he had finished his apple he threw the core into the lake*

cork [kɔːk] *noun* **(a)** piece of light wood from the bark of a tree, used for closing wine bottles; *he pulled the cork out of the bottle* **(b)** material made from the very light bark of a type of oak tree; *we put cork mats on the table to stop the hot plates marking it*

corn [kɔːn] *noun* **(a)** cereal plants such as wheat, etc.; *a field of corn* **(b)** in particular, a very tall cereal crop; **sweet corn** = sweet variety of corn, which you can eat as a vegetable; **corn on the cob** = a piece of corn, with seeds on it, boiled and served hot, with butter and salt

corner ['kɔːnə] *noun* place where two walls, sides or streets meet; *the bank is on the corner of London Road and New Street*; *the number is in the top right-hand corner of the page*; **to turn a corner** = to go round a corner; *the motorbike tried to turn the corner too fast*

cornflakes ['kɔːnfleɪks] *noun* breakfast cereal of crisp pieces of roasted corn; *I'll just have a bowl of cornflakes and a cup of coffee for breakfast*

correct [kə'rekt] **1** *adjective* right; without any mistakes; *can you tell me the correct time?*; *you have to give correct answers to all the questions if you want to win first prize* **2** *verb* to mark the mistakes in something; *the* *teacher is correcting our homework*

correctly [kəˈrektli] *adverb* in a correct way; *you must answer all the questions correctly if you want to win first prize*

corridor [ˈkɒrɪdɔː] *noun* long, narrow passage; *the ladies' room is straight ahead at the end of the corridor*

cost [kɒst] **1** *noun* price which you have to pay for something; *what is the cost of a return ticket to London?* **2** *verb* to have a price; *potatoes cost 20p a kilo*; **what does it cost?** = how much is it? (NOTE: **costing - cost - has cost**)

cost of living [ˈkɒst əv ˈlɪvɪŋ] *noun* money which has to be paid for food, heating, rent, etc.; **cost-of- living increase** = increase in pay to allow it to keep up with the increased cost of living

costume [ˈkɒstjuːm] *noun* **(a)** **bathing costume** *or* **swimming costume** = clothing worn by women or children when swimming; *bother! we forgot to bring our swimming costumes* **(b)** set of clothes worn by an actor or actress in a play or film or on TV; *the costumes for 'Henry V' are magnificent* **(c)** **national costume** = special clothes worn by people of a certain country; *they all came to the wedding in national costume*

cosy [ˈkəʊzi] *adjective* comfortable and warm; *she wrapped herself up in a blanket and made herself cosy on the sofa* (NOTE: **cosier - cosiest)**

cot [kɒt] *noun* child's bed with sides; *the baby was fast asleep in her cot*

cottage [ˈkɒtɪdʒ] *noun* little house in the country; *my grandmother lives in the little cottage next to the post office*; **cottage pie** = minced meat cooked in a dish with a layer of mashed potatoes on top (also called 'shepherd's pie')

cotton [ˈkɒtən] *noun* **(a)** thread from the soft fibres from a tropical plant; *she put a new reel of cotton on the sewing machine* **(b)** cloth made of cotton; *he was wearing a pair of* *cotton trousers*

cotton wool [ˈkɒtən ˈwʊl] *noun* soft cotton fibres used to clean wounds, to clean the skin, to apply cream, etc.; *the nurse cleaned the cut with cotton wool*

cough [kɒf] **1** *noun* sending the air out of your lungs suddenly, for example when you are ill; *take some cough medicine if your cough is bad*; **cough sweet** = sweet with medicine in it against coughs; *she always carries a tube of cough sweets in her bag* **2** *verb* to send air out of your lungs suddenly because your throat hurts; *the smoke from the fire made everyone cough*; *people with flu go around coughing and sneezing*

could [kʊd] *verb used with other verbs* **(a)** *(meaning 'was' or 'would be able')* *the old lady fell down and couldn't get up* **(b)** *(meaning 'was allowed')* *the policeman said we could go into the house* **(c)** *(in asking)* *could you pass me the salt, please?* **(d)** *(meaning 'might happen')* *the new shopping centre could be finished by Christmas*

couldn't [ˈkʊdnt] = COULD NOT

council [ˈkaʊnsəl] *noun* **town council** = elected committee which runs a town; *the town council has decided to sell off the old swimming pool*; **council flat** *or* **council house** = flat or house belonging to a town council which is let to at a low rent to someone; *they live in a council house, but are hoping to save up enough money to buy a flat*

count [kaʊnt] **1** *noun* **(a)** action of counting or of adding; **to lose count** = to no longer have any idea of how many there are; *I tried to add up all the figures but lost count and had to start again*; *I've lost count of the number of times he's left his umbrella on the train* **(b)** large amount of something, calculated in a scientific way; *today there is a high pollution count* **2** *verb* **(a)** to say numbers in order (1, 2, 3, 4, etc.); *she's only two and she can count up to ten*; *count to five and then start running*; **to count backwards** = to say numbers in the opposite order (9, 8, 7, 6, etc.)

(b) to find out a total; *did you count how many books there are in the library?*; *there were sixty people in the boat if you count the children*

count on ['kaʊnt 'ɒn] *verb* to be sure that someone will do something; *don't count on having fine weather for the school sports day*

counter ['kaʊntə] *noun* **(a)** long flat surface in a shop for displaying goods, or in a bank for placing money; *she put her bag down on the counter and took out her purse*; *the cheese counter is over there* **(b)** small round disc used in games; *you've thrown a six - you can move your counter six places*

country ['kʌntri] *noun* **(a)** land which is separate and governs itself; *some African countries voted against the plan* **(b)** land which is not the town; *he lives in the country*; *road travel is difficult in country areas* (NOTE: plural is **countries)**

countryside ['kʌntrɪsaɪd] *noun* land away from towns, with fields, woods, etc.; *the countryside is in danger of being covered in new houses*

county ['kaʊnti] *noun* large district which is part of the system of local government; *the southern counties of England* (NOTE: plural is **counties)**

couple ['kʌpl] *noun* **(a)** two things together; **a couple of** = (i) two; (ii) a few; *I have a couple of jobs for you to do*; *do you mind waiting a couple of minutes while I make a phone call?* **(b)** two people together; *several couples strolled past hand in hand*

coupon ['kuːpɒn] *noun* piece of paper which is used in place of money or in place of a ticket; *collect all seven coupons and cross the Channel for £1!*; **gift coupon** = coupon from a store which is given as a gift and which must be exchanged in that store

courage ['kʌrɪdʒ] *noun* being brave when in a dangerous situation; *she showed great courage in attacking the burglar*

course [kɔːs] *noun* **(a)** **in the course of** =

during; *in the course of the evening he must have eaten six or seven sausages* **(b)** series of lessons; *I'm taking a maths course* **(c)** series of treatments, medicines, etc; *he's taking a course of antibiotics* **(d)** separate part of a meal; *the first course is soup, and then you can have either fish or roast lamb*

in due course [ɪn 'djuː 'kɔːs] after a certain amount of time; *if you study for several years at college, in due course you will get a degree*

of course [ɒf 'kɔːs] *(used to stress 'yes' or 'no')* *are you coming with us? - of course I am!*; *do you want to lose all your money? - of course not!*

court [kɔːt] *noun* **(a)** place where a judge tries criminals; *the court was packed for the opening of the murder trial*; *please tell the court what you saw when you opened the door* **(b)** area where a game of tennis, basketball, etc., is played; *the tennis courts are next to the school*; **Centre Court** = the main tennis court at Wimbledon **(c)** group of people living round a king or queen; *it was dangerous to be a pretty young girl at the court of Henry VIII*

courtyard ['kɔːtjɑːd] *noun* small square yard surrounded by buildings; *the hotel is built round a courtyard with fountains and palm trees*

cousin ['kʌzɪn] *noun* son or daughter of your uncle or aunt; *our cousins from Canada are coming to stay with us for Christmas*

cover ['kʌvə] **1** *noun* **(a)** thing put over something to keep it clean, etc.; *put a cover over the meat to keep the flies off* **(b)** front and back of a book, magazine, etc.; *she read the book from cover to cover* **(c)** place where you can hide or shelter; *they ran for cover when it started to rain*; **under cover** = under a roof, not in the open air; *if it rains the meal will be served under cover* **2** *verb* **(a)** to put something over something to keep it clean, etc.; *you should cover the furniture with sheets before you start painting the ceiling* **(b)** to hide something; *he covered the hole in* the ground with leaves **(c)** to travel a certain distance; *they covered twenty miles in the first day*

cow [kaʊ] *noun* large female farm animal, kept to give milk; *the farmer was milking a cow*

coward ['kaʊəd] *noun* person who is not brave; *when it comes to going to the dentist, I'm a coward*

cowboy ['kaʊbɔɪ] *noun* man who looks after cows in the west of the USA; *a cowboy film* = film about the west of the USA in the late 19th century

crab [kræb] *noun* **(a)** sea animal with eight legs and two large pincers, which walks sideways; *they caught several little crabs in the rock pool* **(b)** meat of this animal, used as food; *he ate a crab salad sandwich*

crack [kræk] **1** *noun* **(a)** sharp sound; *the crack of a branch behind her made her turn round* **(b)** long thin break in something hard; *a crack appeared in the ceiling* **2** *verb* **(a)** to make a sharp sound; *a piece of wood cracked as he stepped on it* **(b)** to make a long thin break in something; *the stone cracked the windscreen*

cracker ['krækə] *noun* **(a)** dry biscuit made of flour and water; *after the main course they served cheese and crackers* **(b)** **(Christmas) cracker** = colourful paper tube which makes a little bang when it is pulled, given at Christmas parties (crackers have little presents inside them; usually folded paper hats, small plastic toys, and pieces of paper with bad jokes written on them); *what did you get in your cracker? - a paper hat and a puzzle*

crafty ['krɑːfti] *adjective* planning something in secret; *I have a crafty plan for making a lot of money* (NOTE: **craftier - craftiest**)

cramped [kræmt] *adjective* too small; *on some planes, the seats in tourist class can be very cramped*

crane [kreɪn] *noun* tall machine for lifting heavy weights; *they had to hire a crane to get*

the piano into the upstairs room

crash [kræʃ] **1** *noun* **(a)** accident where cars, planes, etc., are damaged; *none of the passengers were hurt in the coach crash*; **crash helmet** = hard hat worn by people riding bicycles, motorbikes, etc.; *it is against the law to ride a motorbike without a crash helmet* **(b)** loud noise when something falls over; *he said he would go and do the washing up, and then there was a crash in the kitchen* (NOTE: plural is **crashes**) **2** *verb* **(a)** *(of vehicles)* to hit something and be damaged; *the bus crashed into a wall* **(b)** to move, making a loud noise; *the wall came crashing down*

crate [kreɪt] *noun* **(a)** large rough wooden box; *the china arrived safely, carefully packed in a wooden crate* **(b)** container for bottles; *the school orders a crate of milk every day*

crawl [krɔːl] **1** *noun* **(a)** very slow speed; *the traffic on the motorway was reduced to a crawl* **(b)** swimming style where each arm goes over your head in turn; *he won the 100m crawl* (NOTE: no plural) **2** *verb* **(a)** to move around on your hands and knees; *the baby has just started to crawl* **(b)** to go along slowly; *the traffic was crawling along*

crayon ['kreɪɒn] *noun* coloured pencil; *the children had a box of crayons and coloured the pictures in the colouring book*

crazy ['kreɪzi] *adjective* mad; *it was a crazy idea to go mountain climbing in beach shoes*; **to drive someone crazy** = to make someone very annoyed; *the noise is driving me crazy*; **crazy about** = very enthusiastic about; *she's crazy about Indian films* (NOTE: **crazier - craziest**)

creak [kriːk] **1** *noun* noise like a little squeak; *she heard a creak on the stairs and sat up in bed* **2** *verb* to make a little noise; *the shed door creaked and banged all night in the high wind*

cream [kriːm] **1** *noun* **(a)** top part of milk, full of fat; *I like strawberries and cream* **(b)** soft stuff for cleaning, oiling, etc.; *face cream*; *shoe cream* **2** *adjective* coloured like cream, a very pale brown; *do you like our new cream carpet?*

crease [kriːs] **1** *noun* **(a)** fold made by ironing; *trousers should have a crease in front* **(b)** fold made accidentally; *she ironed his shirts to remove the creases* **2** *verb* to make folds accidentally in something; *after two hours in the car, my skirt was badly creased*

create [krɪˈeɪt] *verb* to make, to invent; *there's a government scheme which aims at creating new jobs for young people*

creature [ˈkriːtʃə] *noun (formal)* animal; *some sea creatures live in holes in the sand*

credit [ˈkredɪt] *noun* **(a)** time given to pay; *we give customers six months' credit* **(b)** account showing money which is owed to you; **credit note** = note showing that money is owed; *she took the jumper back to the shop and got a credit note*

credit card [ˈkredɪt ˈkɑːd] *noun* plastic card which allows you to buy goods without paying for them immediately; *how do you want to pay - cash, cheque or credit card?*

creek [kriːk] *noun* little stream leading into the sea; *we sailed along the coast exploring all the little creeks*; *(informal)* **up the creek** = in a difficult situation; *if we don't get any money by tomorrow evening we'll all be up the creek*

creep [kriːp] *verb* **(a)** to move around quietly; *they crept down the stairs as quietly as possible*; **to creep up on someone** = to come up close behind someone without making any noise; *he crept up behind the policeman and hit him with a stick* **(b)** to go along slowly; *the traffic was creeping along the motorway because of the fog* (NOTE: **creeping - crept** [krept])

crept [krept] *see* CREEP

cress [kres] *noun* little plant used for salads, especially together with small mustard plants;

the egg sandwiches were served with mustard and cress

crew [kruː] *noun* people who work on a boat, aircraft, bus, etc.; *the plane was carrying 125 passengers and a crew of 6*

cricket [ˈkrɪkɪt] *noun* **(a)** game played between two teams of eleven players using bats and a hard ball; *we haven't played much cricket this year - the weather has been too bad*; *we are going to a cricket match this afternoon* **(b)** little insect which makes a singing noise

cried, cries [kraɪd or kraɪz] *see* CRY

crime [kraɪm] *noun* act or acts which are against the law; *we must try to reduce the levels of crime in the inner cities*; *more crimes are committed at night than during the day*

criminal [ˈkrɪmɪnəl] **1** *adjective* referring to acts that are against the law; *stealing is a criminal act*; **criminal law** = laws which deal with crimes against the law of the land, which are punished by the state (as opposed to laws dealing with actions between people or which refer to people's rights, which is 'civil law') **2** *noun* person who commits a crime; *the police think two Russian criminals did it*

crisis [ˈkraɪsɪs] *noun* serious situation where decisions have to be taken quickly; *the government had to take crisis measures to stop the the currency collapsing* (NOTE: plural is **crises** [ˈkraɪsiːz])

crisp [krɪsp] **1** *adjective* **(a)** hard, which can be broken into pieces easily; *these biscuits are not crisp any more, they have gone soft* **(b)** sharp and cold; *it was a beautiful crisp morning, with snow on the mountains* (NOTE: **crisper - crispest**) **2** *noun* **crisps** = slices of potato fried until they are dry and break easily (American English for these is 'chips'); *we always take packets of crisps with us on picnics*

criticism [ˈkrɪtɪsɪzm] *noun* talk or writing that criticizes; *there was a lot of criticism of* *the plan*

criticize [ˈkrɪtɪsaɪz] *verb* to say that something or someone is bad or wrong; *she criticized the sales assistant for not being polite*

crocodile [ˈkrɒkədaɪl] *noun* large reptile which lives in or near rivers and lakes and eats other animals; *don't go swimming in a river full of crocodiles*

crocus [ˈkrəʊkəs] *noun* spring flower, in various colours, especially yellow and blue or purple; *crocuses are one of the first flowers to come out in spring* (NOTE: plural is **crocuses**)

crooked [ˈkrʊkɪd] *adjective* bent, not straight; *I don't think that mirror is straight - it looks crooked to me*

crop [krɒp] *noun* plants, such as vegetables or cereals, grown for food; *we had a wonderful crop of potatoes this year*

crop up [ˈkrɒp ˈʌp] *verb* to happen suddenly; *phone me if any problem crops up*

cross [krɒs] **1** *adjective* angry, annoyed; *the teacher will be cross with you for missing school* **2** *noun* shape made where one line goes straight across another; *write your name where I have put a cross*; **the Red Cross** = international organization which provides medical help; *Red Cross officials have been allowed into the war zone* (NOTE: plural is **crosses**) **3** *verb* **(a)** to go across to the other side; *she just crossed the road without looking to see if there was any traffic coming*; *the road crosses the railway line about 10km from here* **(b)** to put one thing across another; *she sat down and crossed her legs*

cross off *or* **cross out** [ˈkrɒs ˈɒf or ˈkrɒs ˈaʊt] *verb* to draw a line through something which has been written to show that it should not be there; *he's ill, so you can cross him off the list for the party*

crossing [ˈkrɒsɪŋ] *noun* **(a)** action of going across to the other side of an area of water; *how long is the crossing from England to Germany?*; *they had a rough crossing* = the

sea was rough when they travelled **(b)** place where you go across safely; **zebra crossing** = place marked with black and white lines where you can walk across a road; *it's safer to use a zebra crossing when you're going across a main road*

crossword [ˈkrɒswɜːd] *noun* puzzle where small squares have to be filled with letters to spell words; *I can't do today's crossword - it's too hard*

crouch [kraʊtʃ] *verb* to bend down low; *she sat crouched down in the bottom of the boat*

crowd [kraʊd] *noun* mass of people; *if you travel early, you will avoid the crowds of people doing their Christmas shopping*

crowded [ˈkraʊdɪd] *adjective* with a large number of people; *the train was crowded and I had to stand all the way*

crown [kraʊn] **1** *noun* **(a)** gold or silver ring, decorated with jewels, worn on the head by a king, queen, etc.; *the bishop placed the crown on the head of the young king* **(b)** false top attached to a broken tooth; *I'm going to the dentist to have a crown fitted* **2** *verb* **(a)** to make someone king, queen, etc., by placing a crown on his or her head; *the Queen was crowned in Westminster Abbey* **(b)** to attach a false top to a broken tooth; *the dentist said that the tooth was so badly broken that he would have to crown it*

cruel [ˈkruːəl] *adjective* who causes pain, who makes a person or animal suffer; *you must not be cruel to your little puppy* (NOTE: crueller - cruellest)

cruise [kruːz] **1** *noun* long voyage in a ship stopping at different places; *when he retired they went on a cruise round the Mediterranean* **2** *verb* **(a)** to go in a boat from place to place; *they went cruising from island to island* **(b)** to travel at an even speed; *the car cruises very comfortably at 100 kilometres an hour*

crumb [krʌm] *noun* small piece of bread, cake, etc.; *they left crumbs all over the table*

crumble ['krʌmbl] **1** *noun* hot cooked dessert made of fruit covered with a mixture of flour, fat and sugar; *we are having apple crumble for pudding* **2** *verb* to break up into small pieces; *he picked up a lump of dry earth and crumbled it between his fingers*

crunch [krʌntʃ] *verb* to chew something hard which makes a noise when you are eating; *she was crunching an apple when the phone rang*

crush [krʌʃ] *verb* to press flat; *she was crushed against the wall by the car;* **crush barriers** = metal fences which are put up to control crowds; *the fans simply climbed over the crush barriers to get at the pop group's car*

crust [krʌst] *noun* hard outside layer on a loaf of bread, the earth, etc.; *you can cut the crusts off the sandwiches*

cry [kraɪ] **1** *noun* loud shout; *no one heard her cries for help* (NOTE: plural is **cries**) **2** *verb* **(a)** to have tears coming out of your eyes; *the baby cried when her mother took away her toys; cutting up onions makes me cry* **(b)** *(formal)* to shout; *'hello there', she cried*

crystal ['krɪstl] *noun* solid chemical substance with a regular shape; *the salt formed crystals at the bottom of the jar;* **crystal clear** = very clear and simple to understand

cub [kʌb] *noun* young animal, especially a bear or fox; *the bear led her cubs down to the river*

cube [kjuːb] *noun* **(a)** shape where all six sides are square and join each other at right angles; *the design for the library is nothing more than a series of cubes* **(b)** piece of something shaped like a cube; *he put two cubes of sugar in his tea; put the ice cubes in the glasses and then add orange juice* **(c)** *(mathematics)* the result when a number is multiplied by itself twice; *27 is the cube of 3*

cuckoo ['kʊkuː] *noun* common bird which comes to Britain in summer only; *the cuckoo lays its eggs in the nests of other birds;*

cuckoo clock = wooden clock where a small bird comes out at each hour and makes a noise like a cuckoo

cucumber ['kjuːkʌmbə] *noun* long dark green vegetable used in salads; *we had cucumber sandwiches for tea*

cuddle ['kʌdl] **1** *noun* a hug; *she picked up her daughter and gave her a cuddle* **2** *verb* to hug someone; *the little girl was cuddling her teddy bear*

culprit ['kʌlprɪt] *noun* person who has done something wrong; *the police say that they have not yet caught the culprits*

cunning ['kʌnɪŋ] *adjective* clever and full of tricks; *they had a cunning plan to get into the exhibition free*

cup [kʌp] *noun* **(a)** small bowl with a handle, used for drinking tea, coffee, etc.; *she put out a cup and saucer for everyone* **(b)** liquid in a cup; *he drank two cups of coffee; can I have a cup of tea?* **(c)** tall silver bowl given as a prize for winning a competition; *he has won three cups for golf;* **cup final** = last game in a football or rugby competition, where the winning side is given a silver cup

cupboard ['kʌbəd] *noun* piece of furniture with shelves and doors; *put the jam in the kitchen cupboard; she painted the cupboard doors white*

cure [kjuːə] **1** *noun* something which makes a disease better; *doctors are still trying to find a cure for colds* **2** *verb* to make a patient or a disease better; *I don't know what was in the medicine, but it cured my cough very fast*

curious ['kjʊəriəs] *adjective* **(a)** strange; *she has a curious high voice that squeaks* **(b)** wanting to know; *I'm curious to know if anything happened at the party*

curl [kɜːl] **1** *noun* piece of hair which twists; *the little girl looked so sweet with her golden curls* **2** *verb* **to curl up** = to bend your body into a round shape; *she curled up on the sofa and went to sleep*

curly ['kɜːli] *adjective* **curly hair** = hair with

natural waves in it; *she has naturally curly hair* (NOTE: curlier - curliest)

currant ['kʌrənt] *noun* **(a)** small dried black grape; *currants are smaller and blacker than raisins or sultanas, but they are all sorts of dried grapes* **(a)** small black or red soft fruit, such as a blackcurrant; *I have planted some currant bushes* (NOTE: do not confuse with current)

currency ['kʌrənsi] *noun* money used in a certain country; *I want to change my pounds into French currency*; **foreign currency** = the money of other countries; *the bank will change your foreign currency for you*

current ['kʌrənt] **1** *noun* **(a)** flow of water or air; *don't go swimming in the river - the current is very strong* **(b)** flow of electricity; *switch the current off at the mains* **2** *adjective* referring to the present time; *who is the current Prime Minister of Japan?*

current account ['kʌrənt ə'kaʊnt] *noun* bank account from which you can take money at any time; *her salary is paid directly into her current account*; *current accounts often do not pay any interest, but you can write cheques on them*

currently ['kʌrəntli] *adverb* at the present time; *we are currently in the process of buying a flat*

curriculum [kə'rɪkjʊləm] *noun* subjects studied in a school, etc.; *the National Curriculum is followed by all British schools*

curriculum vitae (CV) [kə'rɪkjʊləm 'viːtaɪ] *noun* summary of the details of a person's life, especially details of education and previous jobs (the American English for this is 'résumé'); *please apply in writing, with a current curriculum vitae* (NOTE: plural is curriculums or curricula vitae)

curry ['kʌri] *noun* Indian food prepared with spices; *we ordered chicken curry and rice* (NOTE: plural is curries)

cursor ['kɜːsə] *noun* little arrow or a bright spot on a screen which shows where the next

character will appear; *to print your text, point your cursor at 'print' and click twice*

curtain ['kɜːtən] *noun* **(a)** long piece of cloth hanging in front of a window, etc.; *can you close the curtains, please?* **(b)** long piece of cloth hanging in front of the stage at a theatre; **the curtain will go up at 8.30** = the play begins at 8.30

curve [kɜːv] **1** *noun* round shape like part of a circle; *the road makes a sharp curve to the left* **2** *verb* to make a rounded shape; *the road curves round the side of the mountain*

curved [kɜːvd] *adjective* with a rounded shape (not straight); *a chair with curved legs*

cushion ['kʊʃən] *noun* bag filled with feathers, etc., for sitting or leaning on; *if you find your chair is too hard put a cushion behind your back*

custom ['kʌstəm] *noun* habit, thing which is usually done; *it's a local custom in this part of the world*

customer ['kʌstəmə] *noun* **(a)** person who buys something in a shop; *she was locking up the shop when a customer came in* **(b)** person who uses a service, such as a train passenger; *we apologize to customers waiting on Platform 5 for the late arrival of their train*

cut [kʌt] **1** *verb* **(a)** to make an opening using a knife, scissors, etc.; *he needs to get his hair cut*; *there were six children, so she cut the cake into six pieces* **(b)** to hurt yourself by making a wound in the skin; *she cut her finger on the broken glass* **(c)** to reduce the size of something; *accidents have been cut by 10%* (NOTE: cutting - cut - has cut) **2** *noun* **(a)** place which bleeds when your skin has been broken; *she had a bad cut on her leg* **(b)** **short cut** = shorter way; *he took a short cut through the park* **(c)** *(computers)* **cut and paste** = taking a section of text from one point and putting it in at another

cut back ['kʌt 'bæk] *verb* to reduce spending; *we are having to cut back on staff costs*

cut down ['kʌt 'daʊn] *verb* **(a)** to make a tree fall down with a saw, etc.; *he cut the tree down* **(b)** to cut down (on) = to reduce; *she's trying to cut down on chocolates*

cut off ['kʌt 'ɒf] *verb* **(a)** to take away a small part of something using a knife, etc.; *he cut off two slices of ham* **(b)** to stop someone from being with someone or reaching a place; *the village was cut off by the snow; the tide came in and cut off a party of children*

cut out ['kʌt 'aʊt] *verb* to remove a small piece by cutting it from a large piece (of paper, etc.); *he used a pair of scissors to cut out the picture*

cut up ['kʌt 'ʌp] *verb* to make into small pieces by cutting; *can you cut up the meat for the children?*

cutlery ['kʌtləri] *noun* knives, forks, spoons; *put the cutlery out on the tables, please*

CV *or* **cv** [si:'vi:] *noun* = CURRICULUM VITAE; *please send a CV with your application form*

cycle ['saɪkl] **1** *noun* bicycle; *if your bike's got a flat tyre, take it to the cycle shop*; **cycle path** = special path for cyclists; *there are thousands of cycle paths in Holland* **2** *verb* to go on a bicycle; *he thinks nothing of cycling ten miles to work every day*

cyclist ['saɪklɪst] *noun* person who rides a bicycle; *the police told the crowds to stand back as the cyclists were passing*

cylinder ['sɪlɪndə] *noun* object shaped like a round tube closed at both ends; **gas cylinder** = metal tube containing gas; *the divers carried oxygen cylinders on their backs*

Dd

D, d [di:] fourth letter of the alphabet, between C and E; *you don't spell 'riding' with two Ds*

dad *or* **daddy** [dæd or 'dædi] *noun* child's name for father; *Daddy! look at my exam results!*; *my dad has bought me a new bike*

daffodil ['dæfədɪl] *noun* bright yellow spring flower; *he brought his mother a bunch of daffodils*

daily ['deɪli] **1** *adjective* happening every day; *in England there are several daily newspapers such as 'The Times' and 'Daily Mail'*; *she does her daily keep fit exercises* **2** *adverb* every day; **twice daily** = two times a day; *take the pills twice daily*

dairy ['deəri] *noun* place where milk, cream and butter are sold; *you can buy butter and cheese from the dairy*; **dairy farm** = farm which produces milk, cheese, etc. (NOTE: plural is **dairies)**

daisy ['deɪzi] *noun* small white and yellow flower; *the lawn was covered with daisies* (NOTE: plural is **daisies)**

dam [dæm] **1** *noun* wall of earth or concrete which blocks a river to make a lake; *after the thunderstorm people were afraid the dam would burst* **2** *verb* to block a river with a wall of earth or concrete; *when they built the power station, the river had to be dammed* (NOTE: **damming - dammed)**

damage ['dæmɪdʒ] **1** *noun* harm (done to things not to people); *the storm did a lot of damage*; *the fire caused damage estimated at £100,000* **2** *verb* to harm something; *a large number of shops were damaged in the fire*

damp [dæmp] *adjective* rather wet; *she'd just had a shower and her hair was still damp* (NOTE: damper - dampest)

dance [dɑːns] **1** *noun* **(a)** way of moving in time to music; *Scottish dances are very lively* **(b)** evening entertainment for a group of people where you can dance; *the club is holding a New Year's Eve dance* **2** *verb* **(a)** to move in time to music; *there he is - he's dancing with that tall girl* **(b)** to move or jump around happily; *football fans were dancing in the streets*

Dane [deɪn] *noun* person from Denmark; *Danes often speak very good English*

danger [ˈdeɪndʒə] *noun* chance of damage, getting hurt, etc.; *when it rains, there's a danger of flooding*; *nobody warned us of the dangers of travelling alone in the desert*

in danger [ˈɪn ˈdeɪndʒə] *phrase* likely to be harmed; *the whole building was in danger of catching fire*

out of danger [ˈaʊt əv ˈdeɪndʒə] *phrase* no longer likely to be harmed, not likely to die; *she's out of danger now*

dangerous [ˈdeɪndʒərəs] *adjective* which can cause injury or damage; *be careful - those old stairs are dangerous!*

dangerously [ˈdeɪndʒərəsli] *adverb* in a dangerous way; *she was standing dangerously close to the edge of the cliff*

Danish [ˈdeɪnɪʃ] **1** *adjective* referring to Denmark; **Danish pastries** = sweet pastry cakes with jam or fruit folded inside **2** *noun* language spoken in Denmark; *if you're going to Copenhagen on holiday, you'll need a Danish phrase book*

dare [ˈdeə] *verb* **(a)** to be brave enough to do something; *I bet you wouldn't dare put your hand into the cage and stroke that tiger*; *how dare you!* = you are very rude to do that; *how dare you borrow my bike without asking!* **(b)** *(negative)* *I daren't go out into the street while that man is standing there* **(c)** to challenge someone to do something by

suggesting he is too afraid to do it; *I dared him to go to school in his pyjamas*

dark [dɑːk] **1** *adjective* **(a)** with little or no light; *the sky turned dark and it started to rain*; *can you switch the light on - it's getting too dark to see* **(b)** not a light colour; *she was wearing a dark blue coat* **(c)** to keep something dark = to keep something a secret; *they kept their plans dark from the rest of the family* (NOTE: darker - darkest) **2** *noun* when there is no light; *little children are afraid of the dark*; *they say cats can see in the dark*; *after dark* = during the night time; *you must put on your car lights after dark*

darkness [ˈdɑːknəs] *noun* **the building was in total darkness** = there were no electric lights on in the building

darling [ˈdɑːlɪŋ] *noun* **(a)** name used to talk to someone you love; *Darling! I'm back from the shops* **(b)** person who is very nice; *be a darling and fetch me the newspaper*

dart [dɑːt] **1** *noun* **(a)** **darts** = game for two or more people, played by each player throwing three darts in turn at a round target; *they had a game of darts* **(b)** small heavy arrow with plastic feathers, used for playing the game of darts; *each player takes turn to throw his three darts* **2** *verb* to rush; *the little boy darted across the street*

dash [dæʃ] **1** *noun* **(a)** little written line (-); *the reference number is one four six dash seven (146-7)* **(b)** sudden rush; *while the policeman wasn't looking she made a dash for the door* (NOTE: plural is dashes) **2** *verb* to rush; *I dashed home to watch the football on television*

data [ˈdeɪtə] *noun* information in the form of figures; *the data is stored in our main computer*

database [ˈdeɪtəbeɪs] *noun* data stored in a computer, which can be used to provide information of various kinds; *I'll just add your details to our customer database*

date [deɪt] **1** *noun* **(a)** number of a day in a

month or year (when something happens or happened); *what's the date next Wednesday?*; *do you remember the date of your girlfriend's birthday?*; **date of birth** = date on which someone was born; *please write your date and place of birth on the application form* **(b)** small sweet brown fruit of the date palm; *there was a bowl of dates and dried apricots on the table* **2** *verb* **(a)** to write the date on something; *the cheque was dated the 15th of June*; *you forgot to date the cheque* **(b) to date from** = to exist since; *this house dates from or dates back to the seventeenth century*

out of date ['aʊt əv 'deɪt] not containing recent information; *this guidebook is out of date*

daughter ['dɔːtə] *noun* girl child of a mother or father; *they have two sons and one daughter*; *our daughter Mary goes to the local school*

dawn [dɔːn] **1** *noun* beginning of a day, when the sun rises; *we must set off up the mountain at dawn, so you'll have to get up very early* **2** *verb* **it dawned on him that** = he began to realize that; *it gradually dawned on him that someone else was opening his letters*

day [deɪ] *noun* **(a)** period of time which lasts for 24 hours; *there are 365 days in a year and 366 in a leap year*; *New Year's Day is January 1st* **(b) the day before yesterday** = two days ago; *I spoke to him on the phone the day before yesterday*; **the day after tomorrow** = two days from now; *we are planning to meet the day after tomorrow*; **the other day** = quite recently; *the other day I went for a walk by the river* **(c)** period from morning until night, when it is light; *it took the workmen four days to build the wall*; **day tour** *or* **day trip** = tour which leaves in the morning and returns the same day in the evening **(d)** work period from morning to night; **she took two days off** = she did not come to work for two days

a day [ə 'deɪ] every day; *an apple a day keeps the doctor away*

all day ['ɔːl 'deɪ] the whole day; *it's been raining hard all day*

daylight ['deɪlaɪt] *noun* light from the sun during the day; **in broad daylight** = in the middle of the day; *three men robbed the bank in broad daylight*

daytime ['deɪtaɪm] *noun* period of light between morning and night; *he sleeps during the daytime because he works at night*

dazzle ['dæzl] *verb* to make someone blind for a moment; *she was dazzled by the lights of the cars coming towards her*

dead [ded] **1** *adjective* **(a)** not alive any more; *his parents are both dead*; *he brushed the dead leaves into piles* **(b)** complete; *there was dead silence in the exam room*; *the train came to a dead stop* **(c)** not working; **the line went dead** = the telephone line suddenly stopped working **(d)** not lively, not exciting; *seaside towns can be quite dead in winter* **2** *adverb* **(a)** completely; *he was dead tired after his long walk* **(b)** exactly; *the train arrived dead on time*

deaf [def] *adjective* (person) who cannot hear, who has difficulty in hearing; *you have to shout when you talk to my grandmother because she's deaf* (NOTE: **deafer - deafest**)

deal [diːl] **1** *noun* **(a) a good deal** *or* **a great deal** = much; *he's feeling a good deal better after two days off work*; *she didn't say a great deal*; **a good deal of** *or* **a great deal of** = a lot of; *there's a great deal of work still to be done* **(b)** business affair, agreement, contract; *we've signed a deal with a German firm* **2** *verb* **(a) to deal in** = to buy and sell; *she deals in carpets and rugs imported from India* **(b)** to hand out cards to people playing a game of cards; *he dealt me two kings* (NOTE: **dealing - dealt** [delt])

deal with ['diːl 'wɪθ] *verb* to organize things, to handle something; *the job involves dealing with the public*; *don't worry about getting the tickets - I'll deal with them*

dealt [delt] *see* DEAL

dear [dɪə] **1** *adjective* **(a)** well liked, loved; *she's a very dear friend of mine*; *we had a letter from dear old Mrs Smith* **(b)** *(used at the beginning of a letter)* **Dear Sir** *or* **Dear Madam** = addressing a man or woman whom you do not know, or addressing a company; **Dear Mr Smith** *or* **Dear Mrs Smith** *or* **Dear Miss Smith** = addressing a man or woman whom you know **(c)** costing a lot of money; *that restaurant is too dear for me* (NOTE: **dearer - dearest**) **2** *interjection (meaning how annoying)* *oh dear! it's started to rain* **3** *noun (way of referring to someone you like)* *be a dear, and pass me my glasses*; *did you have a good day at the office, dear?* (NOTE: do not confuse with **deer**)

death [deθ] *noun* **(a)** act of dying, the end of a life; *road accidents caused over 1,000 deaths last year*; **death rate** = number of deaths per thousand of population **(b)** *(informal)* **to death** = completely; *he was bored to death watching football on television*

debt [det] *noun* money which is owed to someone; *parents can be made liable for their children's debts*; **to be in debt** = to owe money

decay [dɪ'keɪ] **1** *noun* rotting, falling into ruin; *tooth decay is serious in children who eat sweets* **2** *verb* to rot, to fall into ruin; *sugar makes your teeth decay*

deceive [dɪ'siːv] *verb* to trick someone, to make someone believe something which is not true; *he deceived everyone into thinking that he was a policeman*

December [dɪ'sembə] *noun* twelfth and last month of the year, after November and before January; *his birthday is December 25th - Christmas Day!*; *they always go skiing in December*

decide [dɪ'saɪd] *verb* to make up your mind to do something; *have you decided which restaurant to go to?*; *they decided to stay at home and watch TV*

decide against [dɪ'saɪd ə'genst] *verb* to make up your mind not to do something; *we've decided against going to Spain again this year*

decimal ['desɪml] *noun* fraction expressed as tenths, hundredths and thousandths; *three-quarters is 0.75 in decimals*; **decimal system** = system of counting based on the number 10; **decimal point** = dot used to show the division between whole numbers and parts of numbers in decimals, such as 2.05; *the decimal point is used in the USA and Britain, but not in most European countries where a comma is used instead: so 4,75% in Germany is written 4.75% in Britain*

decision [dɪ'sɪʃn] *noun* act of making up your mind to do something; **to come to a decision** *or* **to reach a decision** *or* **to take a decision** = to decide to do something; *they talked for hours but didn't come to any decision*

deck [dek] *noun* floor of a ship, bus, etc.; *I'll stay on deck because I feel sick*; *let's go up to the top deck of the bus - you can see better from there*

deckchair ['dektʃeə] *noun* folding wood and canvas chair (for sitting in the sun); *he spent the afternoon sitting in a deckchair trying to do the crossword*

declare [dɪ'kleə] *verb* to state officially; *he was declared dead on arrival at hospital*; *it was declared that Mrs Broom had been elected president of the tennis club by 46 votes*

decorate ['dekəreɪt] *verb* **(a)** to paint (a room or a building); *she can't come to the phone - she's decorating the kitchen* **(b)** to cover something with pretty or colourful things to make it look attractive, or to celebrate an occasion; *the streets were decorated with flags*

decoration [dekə'reɪʃn] *noun* **(a)** action of decorating; *she is charge of the decoration of the church for the wedding* **(b)** action of painting a room, etc.; *the decoration of the town hall took over a year* **(c)** **decorations** =

flags or lights, etc., used to celebrate an occasion; *we put up the Christmas decorations at the beginning of the holidays*

decrease 1 *noun* ['di:kri:s] falling, becoming less; *there is no sign of a decrease in traffic*; *there has been a decrease of 20% in applications to join the class* **2** *verb* [di:'kri:s] to fall, to become less; *the number of road accidents is decreasing*

deed [di:d] *noun* legal document; **the title deeds** *or* **the deeds of a house** = legal documents showing who owns a house

deep [di:p] **1** *adjective* **(a)** which goes a long way down; *the water is very deep in the middle of the river*; *in the shallow end of the pool, the water is only a few centimetres deep* **(b)** low (voice); *who's been sitting on my chair, said Father Bear in his deep voice* (NOTE: **deeper - deepest**) **2** *adverb* a long way down; *the mine goes deep under the sea*

deeply ['di:pli] *adverb* **to sleep deeply** = to sleep without waking; *after taking the drug she slept deeply for ten hours*

deer [dɪə] *noun* wild animal of which the male has long horns, often hunted; *there is a herd of red deer in the park* (NOTE: do not confuse with **dear**; the plural is **deer**)

defeat [dɪ'fi:t] **1** *noun* losing a fight, a vote, a game; *it was the team's first defeat for two years* **2** *verb* to beat someone in a fight, game or vote; *our team has not been defeated so far this season*; *she was defeated in the election*

defence *US* **defense** [dɪ'fens] *noun* **(a)** protection against attack, infectious diseases, etc.; *several people ran to her defence when she was attacked by robbers* **(b)** protection provided by the armed forces; *some countries spend more on defence than on education*

defend [dɪ'fend] *verb* to protect someone who is being attacked; *they tried to defend themselves against the robbers*

defense [dɪ'fens] *US* = DEFENCE

define [dɪ'faɪn] *verb* to explain clearly, to give the meaning of something; *how would*

you define 'environment'?

definite ['defɪnət] *adjective* **(a)** very clear, very sure; *he was quite definite that he had seen the girl at the bus stop* **(b) definite article** = 'the' (as opposed to the indefinite article 'a' or 'an')

definitely ['defɪnətli] *adverb* certainly, for sure; *I'll definitely be there by 7 o'clock*

definition [defɪ'nɪʃn] *noun* clear explanation (of a word); *look up the definition of 'mischievous' in the dictionary*

degree [dɪ'gri:] *noun* **(a)** division of a scale of measurements; *the temperature of the water is above 20 degrees*; *with figures, degree is usually written as a little circle: 25°* **(b)** diploma from a university; *she has a degree in mathematics from Oxford*

delay [dɪ'leɪ] **1** *noun* length of time that something is late; *we are sorry for the delay in replying to your letter* **2** *verb* **(a)** to make late; *the train has been delayed by fog* **(b)** to put something off until later; *we will delay making a decision until we see hear the weather forecast*

deliberate [dɪ'lɪbərət] *adjective* done on purpose; *it was a deliberate attempt to spoil her birthday party*; *the fans came with the deliberate aim of creating trouble*

deliberately [dɪ'lɪbərətli] *adverb* on purpose; *the police think that the fire was started deliberately*

delicate ['delɪkət] *adjective* **(a)** easily damaged; *a delicate china vase* **(b)** liable to get illnesses; *little babies are very delicate*

delicious [dɪ'lɪʃəs] *adjective* which tastes or smells very good; *can I have another piece of that delicious cake?*

delight [dɪ'laɪt] *noun* pleasure; *the news was greeted with delight by the waiting crowd*

delighted [dɪ'laɪtɪd] *adjective* very pleased; *she's delighted with her present*; *we are delighted that you were able to come*

delightful [dɪ'laɪtfʊl] *adjective* very pleasant;

we had a delightful picnic by the river

deliver [dɪ'lɪvə] *verb* to bring something to someone; *they promised to deliver the sofa this morning*; *he delivered the letter himself so as to save buying a stamp*

delivery [dɪ'lɪvri] *noun* bringing something to someone; *there is no charge for delivery within the London area*; **delivery van** = goods van for delivering goods to customers

demand [dɪ'mɑːnd] **1** *noun* **(a)** asking for something; **final demand** = last letter from a company, after which they will take you to court to get payment or cut off supplies; *we had a final demand from the gas company* **(b)** need for goods or services at a certain price; **to meet a demand** *or* **to fill a demand** = to supply what is needed **2** *verb* to ask for something in a firm way; *she demanded to see the manager*; *I demand my money back*

demonstrate ['demənstreɪt] *verb* **(a)** to show; *he demonstrated how the machine worked* **(b)** **to demonstrate against something** = to protest against something in public; *a group were demonstrating against the new motorway*

demonstration [demən'streɪʃn] *noun* **(a)** showing how something works; *can you give me a demonstration of how the machine works?* **(b)** crowd of people who are protesting against something; *they staged demonstrations against the government*

demonstrator ['demənstreɪtə] *noun* person who marches, or who forms part of a crowd protesting against something; *the police used tear gas to clear demonstrators from the square*

den [den] *noun* **(a)** place where an animal hides away; *a lion's den* **(b)** *(informal)* small room where you can hide away to work; *Father's in his den, so don't disturb him*

Denmark ['denmɑːk] *noun* country in northern Europe, south of Sweden and Norway, and north of Germany; *Legoland is one of the tourist attractions of Denmark*

(NOTE: capital: **Copenhagen**; people: **the Danes**; language: **Danish**)

dense [dens] *adjective* **(a)** very thick; *dense fog closed the airport* **(b)** crowded together; *they tried to find their way through dense forest* (NOTE: **denser - densest**)

dent [dent] **1** *noun* slight hollow made by hitting something; *someone has made a dent in my car door* **2** *verb* to make a slight hollow mark in something; *he backed into a tree and dented the bumper*

dentist ['dentɪst] *noun* person who looks after your teeth; *she had to wait for an hour at the dentist's*; *the dentist filled two of my teeth*

deny [dɪ'naɪ] *verb* to state that something is not correct; *he denied stealing the car*

depart [dɪ'pɑːt] *verb* to go away, to leave; *the coach departs from Victoria Coach Station at 0900*

department [dɪ'pɑːtmənt] *noun* **(a)** specialized section of a large company; *write to the complaints department about the service*; **accounts department** = section in a company which deals with money **(b)** one of the sections of the government; *the Department for Education and Skills* **(c)** part of a large shop; *if you want cheese you must go to the food department*

department store [dɪ'pɑːtmənt 'stɔː] *noun* a large shop with many departments; *Selfridges is one of the largest department stores in London*

departure [dɪ'pɑːtʃə] *noun* **(a)** leaving; *the plane's departure was delayed by two hours* **(b)** **departures** = part of an airport terminal which deals with passengers who are leaving

depend (on) [dɪ'pend] *verb* **(a)** to happen because of something or someone; *(informal)* **it (all) depends** = it is not certain; *we may go to France on holiday, or Spain, it all depends* **(b)** **to depend on someone or something** = to rely on someone or something, to be sure of someone or something; *you can depend on her to do her best*

deposit [dɪˈpɒzɪt] **1** *noun* **(a)** money placed (in a bank); **deposit account** = bank account which pays an interest if you leave money in it for some time **(b)** money given in advance so that the thing which you want to buy will not be sold to someone else; *she had to leave £50 as deposit on the watch* **2** *verb* to put money into a bank account; *he deposited £100 in his current account*

depressed [dɪˈprest] *adjective* sad, miserable; *she's been feeling depressed since the accident*

depressing dɪˈpresɪŋ] *adjective* gloomy; *a depressing November day*

dept. = DEPARTMENT

depth [depθ] *noun* how deep something is; *the pool is three metres in depth*; *the submarine dived to a depth of 200m*
out of your depth *phrase* to be in deep water and not be able to touch the bottom; *she got out of her depth and had to be rescued by the beach guards*

describe [dɪˈskraɪb] *verb* to say or write what something or someone is like; *can you describe the car which hit the old lady?*; *she described how the bus suddenly left the road*

description [dɪˈskrɪpʃn] *noun* saying or writing what something or someone is like; *she gave the police a clear description of the car*

desert [ˈdezət] *noun* very dry area of the world; *we watched a TV programme on desert animals* (NOTE: do not confuse with **dessert)**

deserted [dɪˈzɜːtɪd] *adjective* with no one in, with no people; *the restaurant was completely deserted*; *the centre of town is quite deserted on Sunday afternoons*

deserve [dɪˈzɜːv] *verb* to earn something because of what you have done; *I've been working all day - I think I deserve a rest*

design [dɪˈzaɪn] **1** *noun* plan or drawing of something, before it is made or built; *the architect has produced the designs for the*

new town hall **2** *verb* to draw plans for the shape or appearance of something before it is made or built; *he designed the new college library*

designer [dɪˈzaɪnə] *noun* artist who plans the shape or appearance of goods, clothes, rooms, etc.; **designer clothes** = clothes designed by a famous designer; *she was wearing a pair of designer jeans*; **designer label** = label attached to clothes made by a famous designer

desk [desk] *noun* table for writing (often with drawers); *he put the papers away in his desk drawer*; *she was sitting at her desk when the telephone rang*

despair [dɪˈspeə] **1** *noun* lack of hope; *when he lost his job and his girlfriend left him, he was filled with despair* **2** *verb* **to despair of something** = to give up all hope of something; *after two months in the jungle, he despaired of ever being rescued*

desperate [ˈdesprət] *adjective* **(a)** hopeless; *food ran out and the situation on the ship was becoming desperate* **(b)** urgent; *there is a desperate need of medical supplies*

dessert [dɪˈzɜːt] *noun* sweet course at the end of a meal; *the meal will end with a dessert of strawberries and cream* (NOTE: do not confuse with **desert)**

destination [destɪˈneɪʃn] *noun* place to which a person or vehicle is going; *we reached our destination at eight o'clock*; *the destination is shown on the front of the bus*

destroy [dɪˈstrɔɪ] *verb* to ruin completely; *the earthquake destroyed many buildings*

destruction [dɪˈstrʌkʃn] *noun* action of ruining completely, of causing a lot of damage; *the volcano caused enormous destruction*

detached [dɪˈtætʃt] *adjective* **detached house** = house which stands alone, not attached to another; *they live in a pleasant detached house with a large garden*

detail [ˈdiːteɪl] *noun* small item of information; *send in your CV including full* *details of your work experience*; **in detail** = with plenty of details; *the catalogue lists all the furniture in detail*

detailed ['diːteɪld] *adjective* in detail, giving a lot of details; *the police gave out detailed descriptions of the two men*

detective [dɪ'tektɪv] *noun* policeman who investigates crimes; *detectives have interviewed four suspects*

determined [dɪ'tɜːmɪnd] *adjective* having made up your mind; *she is determined to win the prize*

develop [dɪ'veləp] *verb* **(a)** to grow and change; *eventually, that little acorn will develop into a giant oak* **(b)** to make larger; *she does exercises to develop her leg muscles* **(c)** to start a disease, etc.; *she developed a cold from standing in the rain* **(d)** to plan and build; *they are planning to develop the site as an estate of new houses*

device [dɪ'vaɪs] *noun* small useful machine; *he invented a device for screwing tops on bottles*

dew [djuː] *noun* water which forms at night on objects in the open air; *the grass was wet with dew* (NOTE: do not confuse with **due)**

diagonal [daɪ'ægənl] *adjective* going from one corner to another opposite; *he drew a diagonal line on the floor, running from one corner of the room to the other*

diagram ['daɪəgræm] *noun* sketch, plan or drawing; *she drew a diagram to show how to get to her house*

dial ['daɪəl] **1** *noun* round face of a clock, meter, telephone, etc.; *modern telephones don't have dials - just buttons* **2** *verb* to call a telephone number; *to call the police you must dial 999*; *dial 9 to get an outside line*

diameter [daɪ'æmɪtə] *noun* distance across the centre of a circle; *each pipe is one centimetre in diameter*

diamond ['daɪəmənd] *noun* **(a)** very hard precious stone; *he gave her a diamond ring*; **diamond wedding** = 60th anniversary of a

wedding day **(b)** one of the red suits in a pack of cards (the other red suit is hearts; clubs and spades are the black suits); *he held the ten of diamonds*

diaper ['daɪəpə] *noun* US cloth which is wrapped round a baby's bottom (British English for this is 'nappy'); *she changed the baby's diaper*

diary ['daɪəri] *noun* **(a)** description of what has happened in your life day by day; *she kept a diary of the places she visited on holiday* **(b)** small book in which you write notes or make appointments for each day of the week; *I've noted the appointment in my diary* (NOTE: plural is **diaries)**

dice [daɪs] *noun* small cubes with one to six dots on each side, used for playing games; *he lost hundreds of pounds playing dice* (NOTE: plural is **dice)**

dictionary ['dɪkʃənri] *noun* book which lists words in alphabetical order, giving their meanings or translations into other languages; *look up the word in the dictionary if you don't know what it means*; **a French dictionary** = book which gives English words with their French translations, and French words with their English translations (NOTE: plural is **dictionaries)**

did, didn't [dɪd or dɪdnt] *see* DO

die [daɪ] *verb* to stop living; *his mother died in 1995*; *if you don't water the plants they'll die* (NOTE: do not confuse with **dye**; note also **dies - dying)**

die away ['daɪ ə'weɪ] *verb* to become fainter; *the sound of footsteps died away*

die down ['daɪ 'daʊn] *verb* to get less strong; *the wind began to die down*

die out ['daɪ 'aʊt] *verb* to disappear gradually, to become extinct; *this butterfly is likely to die out unless measures are taken to protect it*

diesel ['diːzl] *noun* engine fuel which is thicker than petrol; *London taxis have diesel engines*

diet ['daɪət] **1** *noun* **(a)** the kind of food you usually eat; *during the war, people were much healthier than now because their diet was simpler* **(b)** eating only certain types of food, either to become thinner or to cure an illness; *because she is pregnant she has to follow a diet*; **to be on a diet** = to eat only certain types of food, especially in order to become thin or to deal with an illness; *he's been on a diet for some weeks, but still hasn't lost enough weight* **2** *verb* to eat less food or only one sort of food; *she dieted for two weeks before going on holiday*

difference ['dɪfrəns] *noun* way in which two things are not the same; *can you tell the difference between an apple and a pear with your eyes shut?*; **it doesn't make any difference** = it's not important

different ['dɪfrənt] *adjective* not the same; *I went to three different clothes shops but I couldn't find anything in my size*; *he looks different now that he has a beard*

difficult ['dɪfɪkʌlt] *adjective* not easy; which is hard to do; *the German examination was very difficult*; *finding a parking space is difficult on Saturday mornings*

difficulty ['dɪfɪkʌlti] *noun* **(a) to have difficulty with something** *or* **in doing something** = to find it hard to do something; *he has difficulty in getting up in the morning*; **with difficulty** = not easily; *she climbed out of the hole with difficulty* **(b)** problem, awkward situation; *she went swimming in the rough sea and got into difficulties* (NOTE: plural is **difficulties**)

dig [dɪg] *verb* to make a hole in the ground (with a spade); *she's been digging in the garden all morning*; *the prisoners dug a tunnel to try to escape* (NOTE: digging - dug [dʌg] - has dug)

dig up ['dɪg 'ʌp] *verb* **(a)** to find by digging; *we dug up a Roman coin in the garden* **(b)** to break a solid surface by digging; *the workmen had to dig the road up to mend the gas pipe*

digest [daɪ'dʒest] *verb* to break down food in your stomach so that it can be absorbed by the body; *I find cabbage salad difficult to digest*

digestion [dɪ'dʒestʃən] *noun* process by which food is broken down in the body; *brown bread helps the digestion*

digital ['dɪdʒɪtəl] *adjective* **(a)** which involves figures; **digital clock** = clock where the time is shown by figures, such as 11:52:02, and not by hands on a dial **(b) digital TV** = TV where the picture has been changed into a form which a computer can process

dim [dɪm] **1** *adjective* weak (light); *the lights grew dimmer* (NOTE: dimmer - dimmest) **2** *verb* to make a light less bright; *they dimmed the cabin lights before the plane took off* (NOTE: dimming - dimmed)

dime [daɪm] *noun* US coin worth ten cents; *they only cost a dime each*

dimension [daɪ'menʃn] *noun* **dimensions** = measurements of length, height, etc.; *what are the dimensions of the kitchen?*

din [dɪn] *noun* loud noise; *the children are making such a din I didn't hear the phone ring*

dining room ['daɪnɪŋ 'ruːm] *noun* room in a house or hotel where you usually eat; *we were sitting in the dining room having supper*; *he was doing his homework on the dining room table*

dinner ['dɪnə] *noun* **(a)** main meal of the day (usually eaten in the evening); *we were having dinner when the telephone rang*; *what are we having for dinner?* or *what's for dinner?* **(b)** formal evening meal; *the club is organizing a dinner and dance on Saturday* **(c)** meal eaten in the middle of the day (especially at school); *school dinners are awful*

dinnertime ['dɪnətaɪm] *noun* time when you usually have dinner; *hurry up, it's almost dinnertime*

dinosaur ['daɪnəsɔː] *noun* large animal that lived many millions of years ago, and whose bones are found in rock; *at the time when dinosaurs lived, England was covered with* *tropical forests*

dip [dɪp] **1** *noun* **(a)** sudden drop of a road, of land; *watch out - there's a dip in the road* **(b)** soft food into which biscuits, etc., can be dipped as snacks; *a bowl of smoked salmon dip* **2** *verb* to dip something into = to put something quickly into a liquid; *she dipped the biscuit into her coffee* (NOTE: **dipping - dipped**)

diploma [dɪ'pləʊmə] *noun* document which shows that someone has finished a specialized course; *at the end of the course she got a diploma in tropical medicine*

direct [daɪ'rekt] **1** *adjective* straight, without any stops; **direct flight** = flight without any stops; *there are direct flights every day to London* **2** *verb* **(a)** to manage or to organize; *the policeman was directing the traffic* **(b)** to aim towards a point; *can you direct me to the nearest post office?* **3** *adverb* straight, without stopping; *the plane flies direct to Miami*

direction [dɪ'rekʃn] *noun* **(a)** point towards which you are going; *you are going in the wrong direction if you want to get to the station* **(b)** **directions** = instructions how to do something; *we couldn't find the railway station, so we asked a policeman for directions*; *I can't use the washing machine because there are no directions as to how to switch it on*

directly [daɪ'rektli] *adverb* **(a)** straight, without anything or anyone between; *this door opens directly into the kitchen* **(b)** soon; *I'll be with you directly*

director [daɪ'rektə] *noun* **(a)** person who is appointed to run a firm; *the sales director gave a report on sales*; **managing director** = director in charge of a company **(b)** person in charge of making a film or a play; *who was the director of 'Vertigo'?*

dirt [dɜːt] *noun* mud; earth; *children were playing in the dirt*

dirty ['dɜːti] *adjective* not clean; *playing rugby gets your clothes dirty*; *after the party,*

someone has to wash all the dirty plates (NOTE: **dirtier - dirtiest**)

disabled [dɪs'eɪbld] **1** *adjective* not physically able to do things; *the car crash left him permanently disabled* **2** *noun* **the disabled** = people with physical handicaps; *the library has a special entry for the disabled*

disagree [dɪsə'griː] *verb* **(a)** not to agree, to say that you do not think the same way as someone; *they all disagreed about what to do next* **(b)** **to disagree with someone** = to make someone feel ill; *raw onions disagree with me*

disappear [dɪsə'pɪə] *verb* to vanish, not to be seen any more; *he hit the ball hard and it disappeared into the bushes*; *there was a bottle of orange juice in the fridge this morning and now it's disappeared*

disappointed [dɪsə'pɔɪntɪd] *adjective* sad, because things did not turn out as expected; *she is disappointed with her exam results*; *he was disappointed because his ticket didn't win a prize*

disapprove [dɪsə'pruːv] *verb* **to disapprove of something** = to show that you do not approve of something, that you do not think something is good; *the head teacher disapproves of children wearing jeans in school*

disaster [dɪ'zɑːstə] *noun* very bad accident; *ten people died in the air disaster*

disastrous [dɪ'zɑːstrəs] *adjective* very bad, as in a disaster; *it would be disastrous if the car didn't start*

disc [dɪsk] *noun* round flat object, such as a music record; **disc jockey (DJ)** = person who plays recorded music at a night club; *the DJ played another track from the album*

disco ['dɪskəʊ] *noun* (informal) place where people dance to recorded music; *you can't have a conversation in the disco because the music is too loud* (NOTE: plural is **discos**)

discover [dɪ'skʌvə] *verb* to find something new; *in the year 1492 Columbus discovered America*; *she discovered that someone had* *been using her credit card*

discovery [dɪˈskʌvəri] *noun* **(a)** act of finding something new; *they congratulated him on his discovery of a new planet* **(b)** new thing which has been found; *look at his latest discovery - an old oak table which he found in a shed*

discuss [dɪˈskʌs] *verb* to talk about a serious matter or problem; *we were just discussing how to get to Scotland*

discussion [dɪˈskʌʃn] *noun* talking about a serious matter or problem; *the next programme will be a discussion between pollution experts*

disease [dɪˈziːz] *noun* serious illness (of people, animals, plants, etc.); *hundreds of people caught the disease*

disgraceful [dɪsˈgreɪsful] *adjective* which you should be ashamed of; *people living near the football stadium complained about the disgraceful behaviour of the fans*; *it's disgraceful that you have to pay £1 for a cup of tea in the museum café*

disguise [dɪsˈgaɪz] **1** *noun* clothes, false hair, etc., to make a person look like someone else; **in disguise** = dressed to look like someone else; *the burglar turned out to be a policeman in disguise* **2** *verb* to dress so as to look like someone else; *he entered the country disguised as a French fisherman*

disgust [dɪsˈgʌst] **1** *noun* strong feeling of disliking something and being annoyed by it; *to my disgust, my girlfriend passed her driving test and I failed*; **in disgust** = because you are upset and annoyed; *she walked out of the interview in disgust* **2** *verb* to give you a very strong feeling because you dislike or disapprove of something; *the smell of cooking fish disgusted her*

dish [dɪʃ] *noun* **(a)** large plate for serving food; *put the vegetables in a vegetable dish* **(b) to wash the dishes** *or* **to do the dishes** = to wash plates, glasses, knives and forks, etc., after a meal **(c)** part of a meal; plate of prepared food; *she is trying to make a new Mexican dish* **(d)** round device, shaped like a plate, used to get signals from satellites; *almost every house in the street has a satellite dish on the roof* (NOTE: plural is **dishes**)

dish out [ˈdɪʃ ˈaʊt] *verb (informal)* to hand out roughly and in large quantities; *they were dishing out free tickets for the concert*

dishonest [dɪsˈɒnɪst] *adjective* not honest; *he has a record of dishonest business deals*

dishwasher [ˈdɪʃwɒʃə] *noun* machine for washing dishes, knives, forks, spoons, etc.; *I never put saucepans in the dishwasher*

disk [dɪsk] *noun* any round flat object, especially a piece of plastic used in computers to record information; *all the data is on two disks*

dislike [dɪsˈlaɪk] **1** *noun* not liking something or someone; **to take a dislike to** = to hate; *their dog took a sudden dislike to the postman* **2** *verb* not to like; *I dislike it when the people behind me at the cinema start whispering*

dismay [dɪsˈmeɪ] *verb* to strike someone with horror; *she was dismayed to find that her car had been towed away*

dismiss [dɪsˈmɪs] *verb* **(a)** to send someone away; *the teacher dismissed the class at the end of the lesson*; **to dismiss an employee** = to remove an employee from a job; *he was dismissed for being late* **(b)** to refuse something that someone asks for; *they dismissed my application for a loan*

disobey [dɪsəˈbeɪ] *verb* not to obey; *he disobeyed the instructor and did not attach his seat belt*

display [dɪˈspleɪ] **1** *noun* show, exhibition; *a display of Scottish dancing*; **on display** = shown in an exhibition or for sale; *the shop has various computer models on display* **2** *verb* to put something on show; *she is displaying her collection of dolls at the antique fair*; *make sure your parking ticket is clearly displayed on the windscreen*

dissolve [dɪˈzɒlv] *verb* to make a solid substance become part of a liquid; *dissolve the sugar in half a litre of boiling water*; *stir the water until the tablet has dissolved completely*

distance [ˈdɪstəns] *noun* (a) space from one point to another; *what is the distance from London to Paris?*; *within walking distance* = near enough to walk to; *the hotel is within walking distance of the town centre* (b) in the distance = a long way away; *can you see that white house in the distance?*

distant [ˈdɪstənt] *adjective* far away, not at all close; *we could hear the sound of distant guns*; *in the not too distant future* = quite soon; *we expect to move house in the not too distant future*

distinct [dɪˈstɪŋkt] *adjective* (a) separate; *there are two distinct varieties of this plant* (b) clear; *you could hear a distinct sound of scratching from under the floor*

distinctly [dɪˈstɪŋktli] *adverb* clearly; *I distinctly heard him say that she was his sister*

distress [dɪˈstres] 1 *noun* great sad or painful feeling; *I don't want to cause the family any distress* 2 *verb* to make someone very sad and worried; *the news of her grandmother's death distressed her very much*

distribute [dɪˈstrɪbjuːt] *verb* to give to several people; *the girls stood outside the hairdresser's, distributing leaflets*

district [ˈdɪstrɪkt] *noun* area or region; *the shop is well placed right in the main business district of the town*

disturb [dɪˈstɜːb] *verb* to interrupt someone; *sorry to disturb you, but the bank manager wants to speak to you*; *'do not disturb'* = notice placed on a hotel room door, asking the hotel staff not to come into the room

disturbance [dɪˈstɜːbəns] *noun* fighting by a crowd of people; *there are always disturbances after a football match between the two local teams*

ditch [dɪtʃ] *noun* long hole in the ground for taking away water; *after the storm, the ditches were full of water* (NOTE: plural is **ditches)**

dive [daɪv] *verb* to go down into water head first; *he dived in and swam across the pool under water* (NOTE: diving - dived US also **dove** [dəʊv])

diver [ˈdaɪvə] *noun* (a) person who plunges head first into water; *an Australian Olympic diver* (b) person who swims and works under water; *police divers searched the canal*

divide [dɪˈvaɪd] *verb* (a) to split or cut into parts; *the cake was divided among the children* (b) to calculate how many of one number there are in another; *'divide' is usually shown by the sign ÷ : 10 ÷ 2 = 5: (say 'ten divided by two equals five')*

division [dɪˈvɪʒn] *noun* (a) important part of a large organization; *the sales division employs twenty people* (b) calculation, where one figure is divided by another; *my little sister is just learning how to do division*

divorce [dɪˈvɔːs] 1 *noun* legal ending of a marriage, where the husband and wife are each free to marry again; *her parents are getting a divorce* 2 *verb* to end a marriage; *they divorced last year*

Diwali [dɪˈwɑːli] *noun* important Hindu festival of light, celebrated in the autumn

dizzy [ˈdɪzi] *adjective* feeling when everything seems to turn round; *can we stop the car, please, I feel dizzy*; *she has started having dizzy spells* (NOTE: dizzier - dizziest)

DJ [ˈdiːdʒeɪ] = DISC JOCKEY

do [duː] *verb* (a) *(used with other verbs to make questions) does this train go to London?*; *where do they live?* (b) *(used with other verbs and 'not' to make the negative) it doesn't matter any more*; *his parents don't live in London* (c) *(used to make a verb stronger) why don't you work harder? - I do work hard!*; *why didn't you tell me? - I did tell you!* (d) *(used instead of another verb with* so *and* **neither***) we don't smoke - neither do I*; *he likes jam sandwiches and so does she*

(e) *(used instead of another verb in short answers to questions using the word 'do')* **do you live in London? - yes I do; but your parents don't live there, do they? - no they don't (f)** *(used instead of another verb at the end of a question or statement)* **it looks very nice, doesn't it?; it doesn't rain much in Spain, does it? (g)** *(used instead of another verb)* **can you run as fast as he does?; he speaks German better than I do (h)** *(telling someone not to do something)* **don't throw away that letter!; don't put your coffee cups on the computer! (i)** *(with nouns ending in -ing)* **he always does the washing up; she was doing the ironing (j)** *(used when greeting someone)* **how do you do? (k)** *(followed by a noun)* to work at something or to arrange something or to clean something; **she's doing her hair; have you done the dishes yet? (l)** to succeed, to continue; **she's doing very well in her new job; well done!** = congratulations **(m)** to finish being cooked; **the carrots aren't done yet (n)** to be satisfactory; **will this size do?; that will do** = that's enough **(o) to make do with** = to accept something which is not as good as you wanted; **the ordinary plates are all dirty, so we will have to make do with paper ones** (NOTE: **do - does** [dʌz] **doing - did** [dɪd] **- has done** [dʌn])

do away with [ˈduː əˈweɪ wɪθ] *verb* to get rid of something; **the government did away with passport controls**

do up [ˈduː ˈʌp] *verb* **(a)** to attach; **can you do up the zip at the back of my dress? (b)** to repair and make like new; **they bought an old cottage and did it up**

do with [ˈduː ˈwɪθ] *verb* **(a)** to concern; **it has nothing to do with me (b)** to put somewhere; **what have you done with the newspaper? (c)** *(informal)* to need; **after that long walk I could do with a cup of tea**

do without [ˈduː wɪðˈaʊt] *verb* not to have something, to manage without something; **if you live in the country can you do without a car?**

dock [dɒk] **1** *noun* **(a) the docks** = a harbour where cargo is put on or taken off ships; **cars should arrive at the docks 45 minutes before sailing time; the ship is in dock** = the ship is being repaired **(b)** section of a law court, where the prisoner sits; **she was in the dock, facing a charge of murder 2** *verb (of ship)* to arrive in harbour; **the ship docked at 17.00**

doctor [ˈdɒktə] *noun* person who looks after people who are ill; **if you have pains in your chest, you ought to see a doctor**

document [ˈdɒkjʊmənt] *noun* **(a)** piece of paper with written text; **please read this document carefully and sign at the bottom of page two (b)** separate text in a computer; **the letter was saved as a Word document**

dodge [dɒdʒ] **1** *noun (informal)* clever trick; **he told me a dodge to avoid paying on the underground 2** *verb* to get out of the way so as not to be hit; **he ran across the street, dodging the traffic**

does, doesn't [dʌz or ˈdʌznt] *see* DO

dog [dɒg] *noun* animal kept as a pet, which barks, and moves its tail from side to side when it is pleased; **can you take the dog out for a walk?; police with dogs were hunting the gang of escaped prisoners**

doll [dɒl] *noun* child's toy which looks like a baby; **Susie is upstairs playing with her dolls and teddy bears**

dollar [ˈdɒlə] *noun* **(a)** money used in the USA; **there are less than two dollars to the pound (b)** similar currency used in many other countries; **what is the price in Australian dollars?**

dolphin [ˈdɒlfɪn] *noun* sea animal like a very small whale; **dolphins followed the boat as it crossed the bay; a group of dolphins is called a 'school'**

dome [dəʊm] *noun* round roof shaped like half of a ball; **you can climb up into the dome of St Paul's Cathedral**

domino [ˈdɒmɪnəʊ] *noun* one of a set of small flat blocks used to play a game, each block being divided into two sections, with up to six dots in each section; *let's have a game of dominoes*

done [dʌn] *see* DO

donkey [ˈdɒŋki] *noun* grey farm animal with long ears, used for riding or pulling carts; *donkeys have long ears*

don't [dəʊnt] *see* DO

door [dɔː] *noun* **(a)** piece of wood, metal, etc., which closes an entrance; *he went into his bedroom and locked the door behind him* **(b)** used to show where a building is in a street; *they live a few doors away from us*

dot [dɒt] *noun* **(a)** small round spot; *a blue tie with white dots* **(b)** printing sign (.) used in decimals and email addresses; *my email address is peter@petercollin.com (say 'peter at petercollin dot com')*

double [ˈdʌbl] **1** *adjective* **(a)** twice the size; *she asked for a double portion of ice cream* **(b)** with two parts, for two people; **double bed** = bed for two people; *do you want a double bed or two single beds?*; **double room** = room for two people **2** *adverb* twice as much; *her pay is double mine* **3** *noun* **doubles** = tennis game for two people on either side **4** *verb* to multiply by two; *think of a number and then double it*

doubt [daʊt] **1** *noun* **(a)** not being sure; **to have doubts about** = to say that you are not sure about; *I have my doubts about how accurate his figures are* **(b)** **no doubt** = certainly; **there's no doubt about** = it is a certain fact; *there's no doubt about it - France is the best place for a holiday* **2** *verb* not to be sure of something; *I doubt whether he will want to go to the meeting*

doubtful [ˈdaʊtfʊl] *adjective* not sure; *I am doubtful if he will ever get better*

dough [dəʊ] *noun* mixture of water and flour for making bread, etc.; *the chef was making the dough for the pizza*

doughnut [ˈdəʊnʌt] *noun* small round or ring-shaped cake cooked by frying in oil; *as soon as you have made them, dip the doughnuts in sugar*

down [daʊn] **1** *preposition* **(a)** towards the bottom of; *he fell down the stairs and broke his leg* **(b)** away from where the person speaking is standing; *the police station is just down the street* **2** *adverb* **(a)** towards the bottom, towards a lower position; *put that box down in the corner*; *he sat down on the carpet* **(b)** (put) on paper; *did you write down the number of the car?*; *the policeman took down her address* **(c)** *(informal)* **down under** = in Australia and New Zealand **(d)** *(showing criticism)* **down with the government!**; *down with exams!*

downhill [daʊnˈhɪl] *adverb* towards the bottom of a hill; *the road goes downhill for a bit and then crosses the river*

downstairs [daʊnˈsteəz] **1** *adverb* on or to the lower part of a building; *he heard a noise in the kitchen and went downstairs to see what it was* **2** *adjective* on the ground floor of a building; *the house has a downstairs bedroom* **3** *noun* the ground floor of a building; *the downstairs of the house is larger than the upstairs*

downwards *US* **downward** [ˈdaʊnwədz] *adverb* towards the bottom; *he went to sleep face downwards on the floor*

doz [ˈdʌzən] = DOZEN

doze [dəʊz] *verb* to sleep a little, to sleep but not deeply; *she dozed off for a while after lunch*

dozen [ˈdʌzən] *noun* **(a)** twelve; *we bought two dozen eggs*; **half a dozen** = six; *she brought half a dozen apples for the children* **(b)** **dozens of** = a lot of; *dozens of people visited the exhibition*; *I've been to London dozens of times*

Dr *see* DOCTOR

draft [drɑːft] **1** *noun* rough plan of a document; *it's not the final version, it's just a draft* **2** *adjective* rough (plan, document); *she wrote out the draft letter on the back of an envelope* **3** *verb* **(a)** to draw up a rough plan of; *we drafted the details of the agreement on a piece of paper* **(b)** to ask someone to do something; *the police were drafted in to control the crowds*

drag [dræg] *verb* to pull something heavy along; *she dragged her suitcase across the platform* (NOTE: **dragging - dragged**)

drag on ['dræg 'ɒn] *verb* to go slowly; *the lesson seemed to drag on for hours*

dragon ['drægən] *noun* large animal in children's stories, which flies through the air and breathes fire; *the national animal of Wales is a red dragon*

drain [dreɪn] **1** *noun* pipe for carrying waste water away; *in the autumn the drains get blocked by leaves* **2** *verb* to remove a liquid; *boil the potatoes for ten minutes, drain and leave to cool; they dug a ditch to try to drain the field*

drainpipe ['dreɪnpaɪp] *noun* pipe on the outside of a house which takes water down to the drains; *the burglar got into the house by climbing up a drainpipe*

drama ['drɑːmə] *noun* **(a)** serious play in a theatre; *the 'Globe' has put on a new Elizabethan drama which has not been produced before; a new TV drama series about life in the Lake District;* **drama department** = department in a college which teaches theatre studies **(b)** series of serious and exciting events; *the drama of the rescue of the children by helicopter*

dramatic [drəˈmætɪk] *adjective* giving a shock; *the TV news showed dramatic pictures of the rescue of the children*

drank [dræŋk] *see* DRINK

draught *US* **draft** [drɑːft] *noun* flow of cool air into a room; *he sat in a draught and got a stiff neck*

draughts [drɑːfts] *noun* game with round black and white pieces; *would you like a game of draughts?; they sat quietly in a corner, playing draughts*

draw [drɔː] **1** *noun* **(a)** game where there is

no winner; *the game ended in a draw, 3-3* **2** *verb* **(a)** to make a picture with a pen or pencil; *he drew a picture of the house* **(b)** not to have a winner in a game; *the teams drew 2-2* **(c)** to pull open or to close; *can you draw the curtains - it's getting dark; she drew the curtains and let in the sun* (NOTE: **drawing - drew** [druː] **- has drawn** [drɔːn])

drawer ['drɔːə] *noun* part of a desk or cupboard like an open box which slides in and out and which you pull with a handle; *we keep the knives and forks in the top drawer of of the kitchen cupboard;* **a chest of drawers** = piece of bedroom furniture with several drawers for clothes

drawing ['drɔːɪŋ] *noun* picture done with a pen or pencil; *I've bought an old drawing of the church*

drawing pin ['drɔːɪŋ 'pɪn] *noun* pin with a large flat head, used for pinning papers to a wall; *give me some drawing pins so that I can pin the poster to the door; who put a drawing pin on the teacher's chair?*

drawn [drɔːn] *adjective see* DRAW

draw up ['drɔː 'ʌp] *verb* **(a)** to come close and stop; *as I was standing at the bus stop, a car drew up and asked if I wanted a lift* **(b)** to prepare and write down; *have you drawn up a list of people you want to invite?*

dread [dred] **1** *noun* great fear; *she has a dread of being touched* **2** *verb* to fear greatly; *I'm dreading taking my driving test*

dreadful ['dredful] *adjective* awful, very bad or unpleasant; *the weather has been dreadful all week; what dreadful news!*

dreadfully ['dredfəli] *adverb* awfully, extremely; *I'm dreadfully sorry, but we seem to have lost your ticket*

dream [driːm] **1** *noun* things which you think you see happening when you are asleep; *she had a dream about being chased by elephants* **2** *verb* **(a)** to think you see things happening while you are asleep; *last night I dreamt I was drowning* **(b)** to think about something, to consider doing something; *I wouldn't dream of wearing a big hat like that* (NOTE: **he dreamed** *or* **he dreamt** [dremt])

dress [dres] **1** *noun* piece of a woman's or girl's clothing, covering more or less all the body; *she was wearing a blue dress* (NOTE: plural is **dresses**) **2** *verb* **(a)** to put clothes on; *he got up, dressed and then had breakfast* **(b)** to clean and put a bandage on a wound; *the nurse will dress the cut on your knee*

dressed [drest] *adjective* wearing clothes; *I can't come down to see the visitors - I'm not dressed yet*; *he got up, got dressed and then had breakfast*; *she was dressed all in black*

dressing ['dresɪŋ] *noun* **(a)** putting on clothes; *dressing the children for school takes ages*; **dressing gown** = long light coat which you wear indoors over your pyjamas; *she ran out into the street in her dressing gown* **(b)** sauce (for salad); **French dressing** = mixture of oil and vinegar **(c)** bandage for a wound; *the patient's dressings need to be changed every two hours*

drew [dru:] *see* DRAW

dribble ['drɪbl] *verb* **(a)** to let liquid flow slowly out of your mouth; *the baby dribbled over her dress* **(b)** to kick a football along as you are running; *he dribbled the ball right down the pitch and scored a goal*

dried, drier, dries, driest [draɪd *or* 'draɪə *or* draɪz *or* 'draɪəst] *see* DRY

drill [drɪl] **1** *noun* **(a)** tool for making holes in wood, metal, etc.; *he used an electric drill to make the holes in the wall* **(b)** practice in doing something; **fire drill** = practice to escape from a burning building **2** *verb* to make holes; *he drilled two holes for the screws*

drink [drɪŋk] **1** *noun* **(a)** liquid which you swallow; *if you're thirsty, have a drink of water* **(b)** drink of alcohol; *I'll order some drinks from the bar* **2** *verb* **(a)** to swallow liquid; *he drank two glasses of water*; *do you want something to drink with your meal?* **(b)** to drink alcohol; *she doesn't drink or she*

never drinks (NOTE: **drinking - drank** [dræŋk] - **has drunk** [drʌŋk])

drink up ['drɪŋk 'ʌp] *verb* to drink all of a liquid; *drink up your orange juice*

drip [drɪp] **1** *noun* small drop of water; *there's a hole in the tent - a drip just fell on my nose* **2** *verb* to fall in drops; to let a liquid fall in drops; *the tap is dripping*; *his nose is dripping because he has a cold* (NOTE: **dripping - dripped**)

drive [draɪv] **1** *verb* **(a)** to make a car, lorry, etc., travel in a certain direction; *he can swim, but he can't drive*; *he was driving a lorry when the accident happened* **(b)** *(informal)* **to drive someone crazy** *or* **to drive someone mad** = to have an effect on someone so that they become very annoyed; *the noise is driving me crazy* (NOTE: **driving - drove** [drəʊv] - **has driven** ['drɪvn]) **2** *noun* **(a)** journey, especially in a car; *let's go for a drive into the country*; *it's a four-hour drive to the Channel ferry* **(b)** part of a computer which works a disk; *the computer has a CD drive*

drive away ['draɪv ə'weɪ] *verb* **(a)** to ride away in a motor vehicle; *the bank robbers leapt into a car and drove away at top speed* **(b)** to take someone away in a motor vehicle; *the children were driven away in a police car*

drive back ['draɪv 'bæk] *verb* to go back or to come back in a motor vehicle; *we were driving back to London after a weekend in the country*

drive off ['draɪv 'ɒf] *verb* **(a)** to ride away in a motor vehicle; *the bank robbers leapt into a car and drove off at top speed* **(b)** to force someone or something to go away; *they drove off the police with sticks and stones*

driven ['drɪvn] *see* DRIVE

driver ['draɪvə] *noun* person who drives a car, bus, etc.; *he's got a job as a bus driver;* US **driver's license** = DRIVING LICENCE

driving ['draɪvɪŋ] *noun* action of driving a motor vehicle; *she's taking driving lessons*; **driving school** = school where you can learn to drive a car, truck, etc.

driving licence *US* **driver's license** ['draɪvɪŋ 'laɪsəns or 'draɪvəz 'laɪsəns] *noun* permit which allows someone to drive a car, truck, etc.; *candidates for the job should hold a valid driving licence*

driving test ['draɪvɪŋ 'test] *noun* test which you have to pass to get a driving licence; *he's taken his driving test three times and still hasn't passed*

drizzle ['drɪzl] *verb* to rain a little; *it's drizzling outside, so you'd better wear a raincoat*

drop [drɒp] **1** *noun* small amount of liquid which falls; *add a few drops of milk to the mixture* **2** *verb* **(a)** to let something fall; *he dropped the glass and it broke* **(b)** to let someone get off a bus or car at a place; *I'll drop you at your house* (NOTE: **dropping - dropped**)

drop in ['drɒp 'ɪn] *verb* to call on someone, to visit; *drop in for a cup of tea if you're passing*

drop off ['drɒp 'ɒf] *verb* **(a)** to fall asleep; *she dropped off in front of the TV* **(b)** to drop someone off = to let someone who is a passenger in a car get out somewhere; *can you drop me off at the post office?*

drought [draʊt] *noun* long period when there is no rain and when the land is dry; *relief workers are bringing food to areas affected by drought*

drove [drəʊv] *see* DRIVE

drown [draʊn] *verb* to die in water by being unable to breathe; *the baby drowned in a shallow pool*

drug [drʌg] *noun* **(a)** medicine; *they have found a new drug for people with cancer* **(b)** substance which affects the nerves, and which can become a habit; *some of the youngsters have started taking drugs*

drum [drʌm] *noun* large round musical instrument which is hit with a stick; *he plays the drums in the band*

drunk [drʌŋk] *adjective* excited or ill because of drinking too much alcohol; *when he's drunk, he shouts at his children*

dry [draɪ] **1** *adjective* **(a)** not wet; *don't touch the door - the paint isn't dry yet*; *the soil is dry because it hasn't rained for weeks* **(b)** not sweet (wine); *a dry white wine is served with fish* (NOTE: **drier - driest**) **2** *verb* **(a)** to stop being wet; *the clothes are drying in the sun* **(b)** to wipe something until it is dry; *if I wash up, can you dry (the dishes)?*

duck [dʌk] **1** *noun* **(a)** common water bird; *let's go and feed the ducks in St James' Park* **(b)** meat of this bird; *we're having roast duck for dinner* **(c)** *(in cricket)* score of zero; *he scored a duck in his last two matches* **2** *verb* to lower your head quickly to avoid hitting something; *he ducked as he went under the low branch*

due [dju:] *adjective* **(a)** expected; *we are due to leave London Airport at 5 o'clock* **(b)** due to = because of; *the trains are late due to fog* **(c)** in due course = later; *in due course you will have to pass several exams*

dug [dʌg] *see* DIG

dull [dʌl] *adjective* **(a)** not exciting, not interesting; *what's so interesting about old churches? - I find them dull* **(b)** *(weather)* grey and gloomy; *a dull cloudy day* **(c)** *(colours)* gloomy, not bright; *they painted the sitting room a dull green* (NOTE: **duller - dullest**)

dumb [dʌm] *adjective* not able to speak; *to be struck dumb* = to be so surprised that you cannot say anything; *he was struck dumb by the news*

dummy ['dʌmi] *noun* plastic object given to a baby to suck, to prevent it crying; *the baby sat in its pram sucking a dummy* (NOTE: plural is **dummies)**

dump [dʌmp] **1** *noun* place for rubbish; *take your rubbish to the local dump* **2** *verb* **(a)** to put something heavy down on the ground; *she just dumped her suitcases in the hall* **(b)** to throw away, to get rid of; *someone has* *dumped an old supermarket trolley in the car park*

dungeon ['dʌndʒən] *noun* dark and unpleasant underground prison; *the prisoners were kept for years in the dungeons of the Tower of London*

during ['djʊərɪŋ] *preposition* while something lasts; *she went to sleep during the TV news*; *during the war people hadn't enough to eat*

dust [dʌst] **1** *noun* thin layer of dry dirt; *the room had never been cleaned - there was dust everywhere*; *a tiny bit of dust got in my eye* **2** *verb* to remove dust from something; *don't forget to dust the dining room table carefully*

dustbin ['dʌstbɪn] *noun* large container for household rubbish; *she put the rest of the dinner in the dustbin*

duster ['dʌstə] *noun* cloth for removing dust; *rub the surface down with a duster*

dusty ['dʌsti] *adjective* covered with dust; *his room is full of dusty old books* (NOTE: dustier - dustiest)

Dutch [dʌtʃ] **1** *adjective* referring to the Netherlands; *we are going on a tour to visit the Dutch bulb fields* **2** *noun* **(a)** the language spoken in the Netherlands; *you will need to practise your Dutch if you're going to live in Amsterdam* **(b) the Dutch** = the people living in the Netherlands; *the Dutch are great travellers*

duty ['dju:ti] *noun* **(a)** work which you have to do; *one of his duties is to see that the main doors are locked at night* **(b) on duty** = doing official work which you have to do in a job; *he's on duty from 9.00 to 6.00* **(c)** tax which has to be paid; **duty free** = without paying tax; *you can take a certain amount of goods into the country duty free*

duvet ['du:veɪ] *noun* bag stuffed with feathers, used as the only covering for a bed; *I prefer a duvet to blankets, because it is lighter*

dwarf [dwɔːf] *noun (in fairy stories)* very

small person, smaller than other people; *Snow White and the Seven Dwarfs* (NOTE: plural is **dwarfs** *or* **dwarves)**

dye [daɪ] **1** *noun* colour used to stain cloth; *she used red dye on the curtains* **2** *verb* to stain with a colour; *she dyed her hair green* (NOTE: do not confuse with **die)**

dying ['daɪɪŋ] *adjective* **dying for** *or* **to** = wanting something very much; *after walking in the hot sun, I'm dying for a cold drink*

Ee

E, e [iː] fifth letter of the alphabet, between D and F; *which is it - 'been' with two Es or 'bean' spelt 'EA'?*

each [iːtʃ] **1** *adjective* every person or thing; *he was holding a towel in each hand*; *each one of us has a separate office* **2** *pronoun* every person; every thing; *she gave them each twenty-five pounds*; *each of the books has three hundred pages*

each other ['iːtʃ 'ʌðə] *pronoun* the other one of two people or of two things; *the boys were shouting at each other*; *we always send each other presents on our birthdays*

eager ['iːgə] *adjective* wanting to do something very much; *the children were eager to go on holiday*

eagerly ['iːgəli] *adverb* in a way that shows that you want something very much; *the* children were eagerly waiting for the beginning of the holidays

ear [ɪə] *noun* **(a)** part of your head which you hear with; *rabbits have long ears* **(b)** being able to sense musical sound; **to play an instrument by ear** = to play without reading the printed notes of music; *she can play the piano by ear*

early [ˈɜːli] **1** *adverb* **(a)** before the usual time; *the plane arrived five minutes early* **(b)** at the beginning of a period of time; *we went out early in the evening* **2** *adjective* which happens at the beginning of a period of time or which happens before the proper time; *I caught an early flight to Paris* (NOTE: **earlier - earliest**)

earn [ɜːn] *verb* to be paid money for working; *he earns £20,000 a year*; *how much does a bus driver earn?*

earring [ˈɪərɪŋ] *noun* ring worn attached to your ear as an ornament; *he has a gold earring in his left ear*

earth [ɜːθ] *noun* **(a)** the planet on which we live; *the earth goes round the sun once in twenty-four hours* **(b)** soil, soft material made up of minerals and rotten vegetable matter, which plants grow in; *put some earth in the plant pot and then sow your seeds*

on earth [ɒn ˈɜːθ] *(used to make questions stronger)* *why on earth did you do that?*; *how on earth are we going to afford a holiday in Australia?*; *what on earth are they doing digging up the road again?*

earthquake [ˈɜːθkweɪk] *noun* shaking of the surface of the earth caused by movements of the earth's outer crust; *only a few houses were still standing after the earthquake*

earthworm [ˈɜːθwɜːm] *noun* worm, little animal which looks like a very small snake and lives in the soil; *the earthworms come to the surface when it rains*

ease [iːz] **1** *noun* **to put someone at their ease** = to make someone feel relaxed and confident; *the policewoman offered the*

children sweets to put them at their ease **2** *verb* to make less painful; *a couple of aspirins should ease the pain*

easier, easiest [ˈiːziə or ˈiːziəst] *see* EASY

easily [ˈiːzɪli] *adverb* **(a)** without any difficulty; *I passed my driving test easily* **(b)** *(to stress, before comparatives or superlatives)* a lot (compared to something else); *he is easily the tallest man in the team*; *our shop is easily the biggest in the High Street*

east [iːst] **1** *noun* **(a)** direction of where the sun rises; *the sun rises in the east and sets in the west* **(b)** part of a country which is to the east of the rest; *the east of the country is drier than the west* **2** *adjective* referring to the east; *the east coast is the coldest part of the country* **3** *adverb* towards the east; *the kitchen windows face east, so we get the morning sun*

Easter [ˈiːstə] *noun* important Christian festival (in March or April) celebrating Christ's death and return to life; *we have two weeks' holiday at Easter*; *what are you doing during the Easter holidays?*; **Easter egg** = chocolate or sugar egg eaten at Easter

eastern [ˈiːstən] *adjective* from, of or in the east; *Bulgaria is part of Eastern Europe*

easy [ˈiːzi] **1** *adjective* not difficult, not needing a lot of effort; *the driving test isn't very easy - lots of people fail it* **2** *adverb* **to take things easy** = to rest, not to do any hard work; *the doctor told him to take things easy for a time after his operation* (NOTE: **easier - easiest**)

eat [iːt] *verb* **(a)** to chew and swallow food; *I'm hungry - is there anything to eat?*; *we haven't eaten anything since breakfast*; *the children ate all the sandwiches* **(b)** to have a meal; *he was still eating his breakfast when I arrived*; *have you eaten yet?* (NOTE: **eating - ate** [et] **- has eaten** [ˈiːtn])

eat out [ˈiːt ˈaʊt] *verb* to have a meal in a restaurant, and not at home; *there's nothing in the fridge, so we're eating out tonight*

eat up ['iːt 'ʌp] *verb* to eat everything; *eat your vegetables up - they're good for you!*

echo ['ekəʊ] *noun* sound which is repeated (as when you shout in a cave, etc.); *if you go to the Whispering Gallery in the dome of St Paul's Cathedral you can hear the echo very clearly* (NOTE: plural is **echoes)**

eclipse [ɪ'klɪps] *noun* time when part of the sun or moon disappears, because either the earth's shadow passes over the moon, or the moon passes between the earth and the sun; *there will be an eclipse of the moon tonight*

edge [edʒ] *noun* **(a)** side of something flat; *she lay down on the roof and looked over the edge* **(b)** line between two quite different things; *she stood at the edge of the water and threw the stone as far as she could*

edible ['edɪbl] *adjective* which can be safely eaten; *how do you know which of these wild mushrooms are edible and which are poisonous?*

edit ['edɪt] *verb* **(a)** to be in charge of a newspaper or magazine; *he edited the local newspaper for more than twenty years* **(b)** to cut up a film or tape and stick it together in correct order to make it ready to be shown or played; *once the film has been edited it will run for about 90 minutes*

editor ['edɪtə] *noun* person in charge of a newspaper or part of a newspaper; *she is the sports editor of the local paper*

educate ['edjuːkeɪt] *verb* to teach someone; *we need to educate young people about the dangers of drugs*

education [edjuː'keɪʃn] *noun* system of teaching, or of being taught; *we spent a lot of money on his education, and he's got a job collecting household rubbish!*

eel [iːl] *noun* long thin fish which looks like a snake; *she ordered some smoked eel*

effect [ɪ'fekt] *noun* result or influence; *the cuts in spending will have a serious effect on the hospital*; *the cream has had no effect on her rash*; **with effect from** = starting from; *prices will be increased by 10% with effect from January 1st*

efficient [ɪ'fɪʃənt] *adjective* able to work well and do what is necessary without wasting time, money or effort; *he needs an efficient assistant to look after him*

efficiently [ɪ'fɪʃəntli] *adverb* in an efficient way; *the waitresses served the 250 wedding guests very efficiently*

effort ['efət] *noun* use of your mind or body to do something; *it took a lot of effort to get the piano up the stairs*; **to make an effort** = to try hard to do something; *if we make one more effort, we should get all that rubbish cleared away*

eg *or* **e.g.** ['iː'dʒiː or fɔː ig'zɑːmpl] *abbreviation meaning 'for example' some animals, eg polar bears, live in cold climates*

egg [eg] *noun* **(a)** oval object with a hard shell, produced by a female bird or reptile, from which a baby bird or reptile comes; *the owl laid three eggs in the nest*; *snakes lay their eggs in the sand* **(b)** a chicken's egg, used as food; *you need three eggs to make this cake*

eight [eɪt] **(a)** number 8; *the little girl is eight (years old); I usually have breakfast before eight (o'clock)* **(b)** crew of eight people who are rowing in a boat; *our college eight won the race* (NOTE: plural is **eights)**

eighteen [eɪ'tiːn] number 18; *there are eighteen people in our dance class; he will be eighteen (years old) next week; eighteen is the age at which young people in Britain become officially adult, and are able to vote; the train leaves at eighteen twenty (18:20);* **the eighteen hundreds** = the years between 1800 and 1899 (compare with the 'eighteenth century')

eighteenth (18th) [eɪ'tiːnθ] *adjective & noun the eighteenth of April or April the eighteenth (April 18th); today's the seventeenth, so tomorrow must be the eighteenth; it's his eighteenth birthday next* *week*; *the French King Louis XVIII (say: 'King Louis the Eighteenth')*; **the eighteenth century** = the years from 1700 to 1799 (compare with the 'eighteen hundreds')

eighth (8th) [eɪtθ] *adjective & noun the eighth of February or February the eighth (February 8th); King Henry the Eighth (Henry VIII) had six wives*; *his eighth birthday is next Monday*

eightieth (80th) [ˈeɪtiəθ] *adjective & noun granny's eightieth birthday is next week*

eighty [ˈeɪti] *number* 80; *it's about eighty miles from London to Dover*; *she's eighty (years old)*; **she's in her eighties** = she is between 80 and 89 years old; **the nineteen eighties (1980s)** = the period from 1980 to 1989

either [ˈaɪðə or ˈiːðə] **1** *adjective & pronoun* **(a)** one or the other (of two); *he has two sisters and I don't like either of them* **(b)** each of two; both; *there are trees on either side of the road* **2** *conjunction (showing one of two possible events)* **either ... or**; *either you come here or I'll come to see you* **3** *adverb (with a negative, or to make a statement stronger)* *she doesn't want to go, and I don't want to go either*; *the report wasn't on the TV news, and it wasn't on the radio either*

elastic [ɪˈlæstɪk] *adjective* which can stretch and contract; **elastic band** = rubber band which holds cards, papers, etc., together; *put an elastic band round those papers*

elbow [ˈelbəʊ] *noun* joint in the middle of your arm; *he sat with his elbows on the table*; *she nudged me with her elbow*

elect [ɪˈlekt] *verb* to choose by voting; *she was elected MP for Edinburgh*; *the American president is elected for a term of four years*

election [ɪˈlekʃən] *noun* process of choosing by voting; *local elections are being held next week*

electric [ɪˈlektrɪk] *adjective* **(a)** worked by electricity; *she gave me an electric toothbrush for Christmas* **(b)** making or carrying

electricity; *electric plugs in the USA are different from those in Britain*

electrical [ɪˈlektrɪkl] *adjective* referring to electricity; *they are trying to repair an electrical fault*

electricity [elekˈtrɪsɪti] *noun* energy used to make light, heat, or power; *the heating is run by electricity*

electronic [elekˈtrɒnɪk] *adjective* using devices which affect the electric current which passes through them; **electronic engineer** = engineer who specializes in electronic devices

electronics [elekˈtrɒnɪks] *noun* science of the movement of electricity in electronic devices; *he is studying electronics at university*

elephant [ˈelɪfənt] *noun* very large African or Indian animal, with large ears, and a long nose called a 'trunk'; *if you go to the zoo, you can have a ride on an elephant*

elevator [ˈelɪveɪtə] *noun* **(a)** *US* device for lifting people from floor to floor inside a building (British English is 'lift'); *take the elevator to the 26th floor* **(b)** **goods elevator** = device for lifting goods from floor to floor inside a building

eleven [ɪˈlevn] **(a)** number 11; *when you're eleven (years old) you will go to secondary school*; *come and see me at eleven (o'clock)*; **the eleven hundreds** = the years from 1100 to 1199 (compare with the 'eleventh century') **(b)** eleven people, as in a football team; *the England eleven (the England XI) played in the World Cup*

eleventh (11th) [ɪˈlevənθ] *adjective & noun the eleventh of June or June the eleventh (June 11th)*; *it's her eleventh birthday tomorrow*; **the eleventh century** = the years from 1000 to 1099 (compare with the 'eleven hundreds'); *the French King Louis XI (say: 'King Louis the Eleventh')*

elf [elf] *noun (in fairy stories)* little man; *he read the children a story about elves and fairies* (NOTE: plural is **elves** [elvz])

else [els] *adverb (used after pronouns)* other; *what else can I say?*; *everyone else had already left*; *who else was at the meeting?*

or else *phrase* or if not; *put a coat on to go out, or else you'll catch cold*; *we'd better get up early or else we'll miss the train*

email *or* **e-mail** ['iːmeɪl] **1** *noun* **(a)** system of sending messages from one computer to another, using telephone lines; *you can contact me by phone or email if you want*; *I'll give you my email address* **(b)** message sent by email; *I had two emails from him this morning* **2** *verb* to send a message by email; *I emailed her to tell her when we were due to arrive*

embarrass [ɪm'bærəs] *verb* to make someone feel uncomfortable by being rude, etc.; *she wanted to embarrass me in front of my friends*

embarrassed [ɪm'bærəst] *adjective* not comfortable, ashamed because you have done something wrong; *he was so embarrassed that he turned bright red*

embarrassing [ɪm'bærəsɪŋ] *adjective* that makes you feel embarrassed; *it was very embarrassing to find that my best friend was wearing exactly the same dress as me*

embryo ['embriəʊ] *noun* first state of a living animal or plant; *a human embryo* (NOTE: plural is **embryos**)

emergency [ɪ'mɜːdʒənsi] *noun* dangerous situation where decisions have to be taken quickly (such as a fire, accident, etc.); *phone for an ambulance - this is an emergency!*; **emergency exit** = door in a cinema, etc., used in case of fire; **the emergency services** = the police, fire service and ambulance service (NOTE: plural is **emergencies**)

emotion [ɪ'məʊʃn] *noun* strong feeling; *he tried to hide his emotions when he said goodbye*

empire ['empaɪə] *noun* several separate territories ruled by a central government; *we're studying the history of the British Empire*

employ [ɪm'plɔɪ] *verb* to give someone regular paid work; *he is employed by the town council to look after the town hall gardens*

employee [emplɔɪ'iː] *noun* person who is employed; *the company has decided to take on twenty new employees*

employer [ɪm'plɔɪə] *noun* person or organization that gives work to people and pays them; *the car factory is the biggest employer in the area*

employment [ɪm'plɔɪmənt] *noun* regular paid work; **full-time employment** = work for all of a working day; *he is looking for full-time employment*; **part-time employment** = work for part of a working day; *she is in part-time employment*

empty ['emti] **1** *adjective* with nothing inside; *when we opened it, the box was empty* (NOTE: **emptier - emptiest**) **2** *verb* to make something empty; *they emptied the contents of the cash box into a bag*

encourage [ɪn'kʌrɪdʒ] *verb* to help someone to do something by making them confident; *he encouraged me to apply for the job*

end [end] **1** *noun* **(a)** last part of something; *she tied the two ends of the ribbon together*; *the telephone rang and I missed the end of the TV programme*; **to come to an end** = to be finished; *the work should come to an end next month* **(b)** last part of a period of time; *can you wait until the end of the week?* **2** *verb* to be finished, to come to an end; *the film ends with a wedding*; *the game ended in a draw*

in the end *phrase* finally, at last; *in the end the shop had to call in the police*

on end *phrase* with no breaks; *they have been working for hours on end*

end up ['end 'ʌp] *verb* to finish; *they went to several clubs, and ended up getting arrested by the police in Trafalgar Square*

ending ['endɪŋ] *noun* the way a story, film, etc., finishes; *I like films which have happy* *endings*

enemy ['enəmi] *noun* country or people fighting against you in a war; *they attacked the enemy with bombs* (NOTE: plural is **enemies**)

energetic [enə'dʒetɪk] *adjective* active and lively; *my grandmother is still extraordinarily energetic*

energy ['enədʒi] *noun* **(a)** force or strength of a person; *she wasted a lot of time and energy rushing around doing the Christmas shopping* **(b)** power which makes something work; *if you reduce the room temperature to eighteen degrees, you will save energy*

engine ['endʒɪn] *noun* **(a)** machine which powers or drives something; *the lift engine has broken down again - we shall just have to walk up the stairs* **(b)** vehicle which pulls a train; *the engine broke down and the train was stuck in the tunnel*

engineer [endʒɪ'niːə] *noun* **(a)** person who looks after equipment, especially engines; *telephone engineers are trying to repair the lines* **(b)** person who designs mechanical or electric equipment, or equipment for industry; **civil engineer** = person who specializes in the construction of roads, bridges, etc.

England ['ɪŋlənd] *noun* country in the southern part of the island of Great Britain, the largest country in the United Kingdom; *how long does it take to cross from England to France?*; *the word 'England' is often used instead of Britain, and this is a mistake, as England is only one part of Great Britain* (NOTE: also the capital: **London**; people: **the English**; language: **English**)

English ['ɪŋlɪʃ] **1** *adjective* referring to England; *is the English weather really as bad as they say it is?*; **English breakfast** = cooked breakfast with bacon, eggs, sausages, etc.; **the English Channel** = the sea between England and France; *the boat only takes 50 minutes to cross the English Channel*; *'English' is often used instead of British, and this is a mistake, as England is only one part of Great Britain*

2 *noun* **(a)** language spoken in the United Kingdom, the USA, Australia, and many other countries; *we managed to make ourselves understood, even though no one in the hotel spoke English*; *several of her books have been translated into English*; *English is spoken as a first language by 415 million people in the world* **(b)** English language as a subject taught in school or university; *she's good at maths but not so good at English*; *there are twenty students in my English class* **(c) the English** = the people of England; *the English on the whole do not show their emotions*

Englishman, Englishwoman ['ɪŋlɪʃmən or 'ɪŋlɪʃwumən] *noun* person from England; *a group of young Englishwomen were helping in the relief effort in Africa* (NOTE: plural is **Englishmen, Englishwomen**)

enhance [ɪn'hɑːns] *verb* to increase the value or power of something; *he took drugs to enhance his performance as a runner*

enjoy [ɪn'dʒɔɪ] *verb* to take pleasure in doing something; *have you enjoyed the holiday so far?*; *she didn't enjoy the boat trip because she felt sick all the time*; **to enjoy yourself** = to have a good time; *are you all enjoying yourselves?*; *we enjoyed ourselves so much that we're going to the same place for our holiday next year*

enjoyment [ɪn'dʒɔɪmənt] *noun* pleasure; *the man next to me had a cough and this spoilt my enjoyment of the concert*

enormous [ɪ'nɔːməs] *adjective* very large; *he ate an enormous lunch*

enormously [ɪ'nɔːməsli] *adverb* very much; *we were enormously relieved to see her again*

enough [ɪ'nʌf] **1** *adjective* as much as is needed; *have you got enough money for your fare?* **2** *pronoun* as much of something as is needed; *I had £20 in my purse to pay the taxi, but it wasn't enough* **3** *adverb* as much as is needed; *this box isn't big enough for all these books*

enter ['entə] *verb* **(a)** to go in, to come in; *he took off his hat as he entered the church* **(b) to enter for something** = to decide to take part in a race or competition; *she has entered for the 2000 metres* **(c)** to type information on a keyboard, and put it into a computer system; *we will just enter your name and address on the computer* **(d)** key on a keyboard which you press when you have finished keying something, or when you want to start a new line; *to change a function, move to the menu and press ENTER*

entertain [entə'teɪn] *verb* **(a)** to amuse; *we hired a clown to entertain the children* **(b)** to offer meals, accommodation, a visit to the theatre, etc., to a visitor; *they're entertaining some Swedish friends this evening*

entertainment [entə'teɪnmənt] *noun* things which amuse, such as films, dances, etc.; *there's not much entertainment in the village - the nearest cinema is 25km away*

enthusiasm [ɪn'θjuːziæzəm] *noun* great interest and liking; *she showed a lot of enthusiasm for our new project*

enthusiastic [ɪnθjuːzi'æstɪk] *adjective* showing great interest and approval; *I'm very enthusiastic about his new project*

entire [ɪn'taɪə] *adjective* whole; *we spent the entire day working in the garden*

entrance ['entrəns] *noun* **(a)** door for going in; *she was sitting at the entrance to the museum*; *we will meet at the Oxford Street entrance of Selfridges* **(b)** money which you have to pay to go in; *entrance is £1.50 for adults and £1 for children*

entry ['entri] *noun* **(a)** going in; *the sign on the door said 'no entry'*; **entry charge** = price to be paid before going into an exhibition, etc.; *the entry charge is £5* **(b)** place where you go in; *the entry to the cave was blocked by rocks* **(c)** written information in a reference book, an accounts or computer system; *she looked up the entry on 'roses' in the book about garden flowers* **(d)** person who enters a competition; *there were thousands of entries for the Christmas holiday competition* (NOTE: plural is **entries**)

envelope ['envələʊp] *noun* folded paper cover for sending letters; *she wrote the address on the envelope and sealed it*

envious ['enviəs] *adjective* feeling or showing envy; *we're all envious of his new car*

environment [ɪn'vaɪərənmənt] *noun* the earth, its natural landscape and resources, seen as the place where man lives; *they are trying to protect the environment*

envy ['envi] **1** *noun* feeling that you would like to have something which someone else has; *her beautiful new car filled us all with envy* **2** *verb* to feel you would like to be someone else; *I don't envy him with a job like the one he has*

equal ['iːkwəl] **1** *adjective* exactly the same size as, with exactly the same amount as; *male and female workers must have equal pay* **2** *verb* **(a)** to be exactly the same as; *his time for the 100 metres equals the existing record* **(b)** to give a result; *equals is usually written = : 2 + 2 = 4 (say 'two plus two equals four')*

equally ['iːkwəli] *adverb* in exactly the same way; *they were both equally responsible for the accident*

equator [ɪ'kweɪtə] *noun* imaginary line running round the earth halfway between the North and South Poles; *Quito, the capital of Ecuador, lies very close to the equator*

equipment [ɪ'kwɪpmənt] *noun* all the tools, machinery, etc., which you need to do something; *he brought all his camera equipment with him*

error ['erə] *noun* mistake; *the waiter made an error in calculating the total*; **computer error** = mistake made by a computer

erupt [ɪ'rʌpt] *verb (of volcano)* to throw out hot rocks, ash, etc.; *the volcano last erupted in 1968*

escalator ['eskəleɪtə] *noun* moving stairs; *the children played a game, trying to run down the up escalator*; *one of the escalators at Holborn Station is being repaired*

escape [ɪ'skeɪp] **1** *noun* action of getting away from prison or from an awkward situation; *there were three escapes from this jail last year*; *we had a narrow escape* = we were almost killed **2** *verb* to get away from prison or from an awkward situation; *he escaped from the prison by sawing through the bars*

especially [ɪ'speʃəli] *adverb* particularly, very, more than anything else; *that black suitcase is especially heavy - what's inside it?*

essay ['eseɪ] *noun* piece of writing on a particular subject; *for our homework, we have to write an essay on pollution*

essential [ɪ'senʃl] *adjective* which is very important or which you cannot do without; *the refugees lack essential winter clothing*; *sun cream is essential in the south of Spain*

essentially [ɪ'senʃəli] *adverb* basically, for the most part; *my new job is essentially not so very different from my old one*

estate [ɪ'steɪt] *noun* **(a)** large area of land belonging to one owner; *he owns a 250-acre estate in Norfolk* **(b)** group of houses and flats, etc., on one piece of land, belonging to a local authority, and let at cheap rents; *she lives on the Bellevue estate;* **business estate** *or* **trading estate** = area of land near a town especially for factories and warehouses

estimate 1 *noun* ['estɪmət] calculation which shows the rough amount of something, or its worth or cost; *the gas bill is only an estimate*; **rough estimate** = calculation which is not exact **2** *verb* ['estɪmeɪt] to calculate approximately the cost or worth, etc., of something; *I estimate that it will cost £100,000*

etc. [et'setərə] *Latin phrase meaning 'and so on', 'and other things like this'; fruit such as oranges, bananas, etc.*

EU ['i:'ju:] = EUROPEAN UNION

euro ['jʊərəʊ] *noun* money used in the EU; *it is priced at €150 (150 euros)*

Europe ['jʊərəp] *proper noun* **(a)** the continent of Europe, the part of the world to the west of Asia, from Russia to Ireland; *Poland is in eastern Europe, and Greece, Spain and Portugal are in southern Europe* **(b)** the same area, but not including the UK; *holidays in Europe are less popular than last year*

European [jʊərə'pi:ən] *adjective* referring to Europe; *at home we always eat Asian food, not European*

European Union (EU) [jʊərə'pi:ən 'ju:nɪən] *noun* an organization which links several European countries together based on the proposal that the movement of goods, of capital, of people and of services should all be free; *European Union ministers met today in Brussels*; *the USA is increasing its trade with the European Union*

Eurostar ['jʊərəʊsta:] *noun* train going from England to France and Belgium, through the Channel Tunnel; *we took the 8.25 Eurostar to Paris*

evaluation [ɪvælju'eɪʃn] *noun (formal)* act of calculating what something is worth; *the inspectors will carry out a careful evaluation of the teacher's performance*

evaporate [ɪ'væpəreɪt] *verb (of liquid)* to be changed into gas; *water gradually evaporates from the soil*

eve [i:v] *noun* the night or day before; **Christmas Eve** = 24th December; **New Year's Eve** = 31st December

even ['i:vn] **1** *adjective* **(a) even numbers** = numbers which can be divided by 2; *on the right-hand side of the street all the houses have even numbers* **(b)** with equal scores (in a competition); *at the end of the competition three teams were even with 96 points each* **(c)** flat, level; *the road has a smooth even surface* **(d)** which does not change; *the temperature is* *an even 28° all through the day* **2** *adverb (showing surprise or making an expression stronger)* **she's fat, but her sister is even fatter**; **even worse** = worse than before; **that film was bad, but this one is even worse**

even if ['iːvn 'ɪf] *conjunction* it doesn't matter if; **we'll try and drive across the mountains, even if it's snowing**

even so ['iːvn 'səʊ] *adverb* in spite of what has happened; **it was pouring with rain, but even so they decided to go ahead with the village fair**

even though ['iːvn 'ðəʊ] *conjunction* although, in spite of the fact that; **he didn't take an umbrella, even though it was raining quite hard**

evening ['iːvnɪŋ] *noun* late part of the day, when it is getting dark; **I saw her yesterday evening**; **the accident took place at 8.30 in the evening**; **this evening** = today in the evening; **we'll all meet this evening after work**

event [ɪ'vent] *noun* **(a)** thing which happens; **a baby's first birthday is always a very happy event (b)** sporting competition; **field events** = jumping and throwing competitions; **track events** = running races

in any event *or* **at all events** *phrase* whatever may happen; **I don't know exactly what happened - in any event it doesn't matter**

eventually [ɪ'ventjuəli] *adverb* in the end; **after weeks of waiting they eventually decided to sell their cottage**

ever ['evə] *adverb* **(a)** *(used with negatives, questions)* at any time; **nothing ever happens here**; **have you ever been to Germany? (b)** *(to stress after comparatives)* **he went on playing the drums louder than ever (c)** **ever since (then)** = from that time on; **she was knocked down by a car and ever since has been afraid to go out onto the main road**

for ever [fə 'evə] *phrase* **(a)** always; **I will love you for ever and ever (b)** *(exclamation to show support for a team)* **Scotland for ever!**

evergreen ['evəgriːn] *noun* tree which keeps its leaves all winter; **holly and other evergreens can be used as decorations in winter**

every ['evri] *adjective* **(a)** each; **it rained every day during the holidays**; **every Wednesday, he goes for a swim in the local swimming pool (b)** *(showing regular periods of time or distance)* **the medicine is to be taken every four hours**; **have your car checked every 10,000 kilometres**

every other day *phrase* on one day, not on the next, but on the one after that (e.g. on Monday, Wednesday and Friday, etc.)

everybody *or* **everyone** ['evribɒdi or 'evriwʌn] *pronoun* all people, or all people involved in a particular situation; **everybody in our class is going to the party**; **if everyone is here, we can start**; **is everybody enjoying themselves?**

everything ['evriθɪŋ] *pronoun* **(a)** all things; **did you bring everything you need? (b)** things in general; **everything was dark in the street**; **everything is under control**

everywhere ['evriweə] *adverb* **(a)** in all places; **we've looked everywhere for the key and can't find it (b)** the whole place; **everywhere was white after the first snow fell**

evidence ['evidəns] *noun* facts which show that something really exists or has happened; **scientists are looking for evidence of life on Mars**; **the police couldn't find any evidence that she had stolen the money**

evident ['evidənt] *adjective* obvious; **it was quite evident that they didn't want to come with us**

evil ['iːvl] *adjective* very wicked; **she's an evil old woman**

ex- [eks] *prefix meaning* who used to be; **Tom's my ex-boyfriend**

exact [ɪg'zækt] *adjective* completely accurate, not different in any way from what is expected, what has been written, etc.; **could you repeat the exact words she said?**; **the shop assistant asked me if I had the exact**

sum, since she didn't have any change

exactly [ɪgˈzæktli] *adverb* not more, not less, not different in any way from an amount; *that comes to exactly ten dollars and fifty cents; the time is exactly 16.24*

not exactly [ˈnɒt ɪgˈzæktli] *phrase* not really; *it's not exactly the colour I wanted*

exaggerate [ɪgˈzædʒəreɪt] *verb* to make things seem worse, better, bigger, etc., than they really are; *she exaggerated the dangers involved*

exam [ɪgˈzæm] *noun* = EXAMINATION

examination [ɪgzæmɪˈneɪʃn] *noun* (a) written or spoken test; *he did badly in his English examination; the English exam was very difficult - half the students failed; she came first in the final examination for the course* (b) looking at something to see if it works properly, or if something is wrong; *he had to have an X-ray examination*

examine [ɪgˈzæmɪn] *verb* to look at something to see if it is correct or healthy, that it works properly, etc.; *the doctor examined her throat*

example [ɪgˈzɑːmpl] *noun* (a) something chosen to show something; *she brought some examples of her work to the interview* (b) **to set an example** = to do things in the right way yourself, so that other people can copy you; *she sets everyone a bad example by talking for hours to her boyfriend on the phone* (c) **for example** = as a typical case; *she is keen on getting her weight down - for example she's stopped eating bread*

exceed [ɪkˈsiːd] *verb* to go beyond; *the car was exceeding the speed limit*

excellent [ˈeksələnt] *adjective* very good; *we had an excellent meal in a Chinese restaurant*

except [ɪkˈsept] **1** *preposition* other than; *she's allowed to eat anything except fish; everyone was sick on the boat, except (for) me* **2** *conjunction* other than, apart from; *he*

doesn't do anything except sit and watch football on the TV; everything went well, except that James was sick (NOTE: do not confuse with **accept**)

exception [ɪkˈsepʃn] *noun* thing not included; *all the students failed, with one exception*

exchange [ɪksˈtʃeɪndʒ] **1** *noun* giving one thing for another; **part exchange** = giving an old machine as part of the payment for a new one; *he took my old car in part exchange* **2** *verb* (a) to give something and get something similar back; *after the game the two teams exchanged shirts* (b) **to exchange something for something else** = to give one thing and get another in return; *if the trousers are too small you can take them back and exchange them for a larger pair*

in exchange *phrase* for something else; *I gave him my mountain bike in exchange for his collection of CDs*

excited [ɪkˈsaɪtɪd] *adjective* lively and happy because you hope something will happen; *the children are excited because it's Christmas; what's everyone so excited about?*

excitement [ɪkˈsaɪtmənt] *noun* being excited; *what's all the excitement about?*

exciting [ɪkˈsaɪtɪŋ] *adjective* which gives you a particular feeling; *the news about your new job is really exciting*

exclaim [ɪkˈskleɪm] *verb* to say something loudly and suddenly; *'here it is!' she exclaimed*

exclamation mark [ekskləˈmeɪʃn ˈmɑːk] *noun* written sign (!) which shows surprise; *it's obvious that she was excited, her letter was full of exclamation marks*

excuse 1 *noun* [ɪkˈskjuːs] reason given for doing something wrong or not as expected; *his excuse for missing the party was that he forgot the date* **2** *verb* [ɪkˈskjuːz] to forgive someone for making a small mistake; *please excuse my arriving late like this*

excuse me [ɪkˈskjuːz ˈmiː] (a) *(to attract*

someone's attention) **excuse me, is this the right bus for Oxford Circus?** (b) please forgive me; *excuse me for arriving so late*

execute ['eksɪkjuːt] *verb* to kill someone who has been sentenced to death; *people who commit murder are no longer executed in this country*

exercise ['eksəsaɪz] *noun* (a) practice in using physical or mental powers; **to take exercise** = to do physical things, like walking or jogging, to keep fit; *you should take some exercise every day if you want to lose weight* (b) piece of work done to keep you fit, to practise or to help you learn; *he does his exercises every morning before breakfast; she does her piano exercises for two hours every day*; **exercise book** = book for writing out school work

exhausted [ɪg'zɔːstɪd] *adjective* tired out; *I'm exhausted after running three miles*

exhibition [eksɪ'bɪʃn] *noun* display (of works of art, flowers, etc.); *the exhibition is open from 10 a.m. to 5 p.m.; we stood in line for half an hour waiting to get into the Picasso exhibition*

exist [ɪg'zɪst] *verb* to be, to live; *when my grandmother was young colour TV didn't exist; they got lost in the jungle and managed to exist on berries and roots*

existence [ɪg'zɪstəns] *noun* (a) life, being; *is there anything which proves the existence of animals on Mars?* (b) **in existence** = which exists, which is actually here; *the original painting is no longer in existence*

exit ['egzɪt] *noun* way out of a building, an aircraft, etc.; *the customers all rushed towards the exits when the fire alarm rang*; **No Exit!** = sign showing that you must not go out this way; **emergency exit** = door used in emergency

expand [ɪk'spænd] *verb* to become bigger; *water expands when it freezes; heat caused the metal pipes to expand*

expect [ɪk'spekt] *verb* to think or hope that something is going to happen; *I expect you are tired after your long train journey; he expects me to do all the housework; we expect him to arrive at any moment*

expedition [ekspɪ'dɪʃn] *noun* journey to explore or to look for something; *he set off on an expedition to the South Pole; they went on a shopping expedition in the West End*

expensive [ɪk'spensɪv] *adjective* which costs a lot of money; *don't ask her out - she always orders the most expensive things on the menu*

experience [ɪk'spiːəriəns] *noun* (a) knowledge got by working or living in various situations; *I have no experience of travelling in the desert* (b) event that happens to someone; *you must write a book about your experiences in prison*

experiment [ɪk'sperɪmənt] *noun* scientific test; *the company has stopped carrying out experiments on live animals; we're offering our customers free samples as an experiment*

expert ['ekspɜːt] **1** *adjective* (a) knowing a lot about a subject; *she can give you expert advice on repairing gas cookers* (b) **expert at doing something** = good at doing something; *I'm not very expert at making cakes* **2** *noun* (a) person who knows a great deal about a subject; *a rose expert was the judge at the flower show* (b) person who is very good at doing something; *she's an expert at getting the children to go to bed*

explain [ɪk'spleɪn] *verb* (a) to give your reasons for something; *can you explain why the weather is cold in winter and warm in summer?* (b) to make something clear; *she explained what had happened, but the manager still thought she had tried to steal the watch*

explanation [eksplə'neɪʃn] *noun* reason for something; *the policeman asked him for an explanation of why the stolen car was in his garage*

explode [ɪk'spləud] *verb (of bombs, etc.)* to

blow up, to go off with a bang; *a bomb exploded in a crowded train*

explore [ɪk'splɔː] *verb* to travel and discover, especially places you have not visited before; *we spent our holidays exploring Holland by canal*

explosion [ɪk'spləʊʒn] *noun* bang made by blowing up bombs, petrol tanks, etc.; *several explosions were heard during the night as the army occupied the city*

explosive [ɪk'spləʊsɪv] *noun* material which can blow up with a bang; *tests revealed traces of explosive on his hands*; *the box contained explosives*

express [ɪk'spres] **1** *noun* rapid train; *we took the express from London to Glasgow* **2** *verb* to put into words or diagrams; *he expressed his thanks in a short speech*

expression [ɪk'spreʃn] *noun* **(a)** word or group of words; *'until the cows come home' is an expression which means 'for a very long time'* **(b)** look on a person's face which shows feeling; *his expression showed how miserable he was*

extension [ɪk'stenʃn] *noun* **(a)** thing added on; *we added an extension at the back of the house*; *I need an extension cable for the electric saw* **(b)** office telephone; *the manager is on extension 23*

extent [ɪk'stent] *noun* degree, size, area; *the extent of the storm damage was only revealed later*; **to some extent** *or* **to a certain extent** = partly, in some way; *to some extent, bad weather was the reason why our team lost*

extinct [ɪk'stɪŋkt] *adjective* of which all specimens are dead; *several species of birds have become extinct since 1990*

extra ['ekstrə] **1** *adjective* more than normal; additional; *we need four extra teachers for this course*; *staff get extra pay for working on Sundays* **2** *adverb* more than normal; *I need*

some extra strong string to tie the parcel

extraordinarily [ɪk'strɔːdnrəli] *adverb* extremely, very; *her action was extraordinarily brave*

extraordinary [ɪk'strɔːdnri] *adjective* marvellous, strange and unusual; *it's extraordinary weather for June*

extreme [ɪk'striːm] **1** *adjective* very great; *this engine is made to work well even in extreme cold*; **at the extreme end** = right at the end **2** *noun* something very unusual, very extraordinary; *you get extremes of temperature here - very hot summers and very cold winters*

extremely [ɪk'striːmli] *noun* very; *it was extremely hot in August*; *her brother is extremely tall*

eye [aɪ] *noun* **(a)** part of your head, used for seeing; *close your eyes and count to ten while we all hide*; **to keep an eye on something** = to watch something carefully to see that it is safe; *can you keep an eye on the house while we are away?*; **to keep an eye out for something** = to watch to see if something is near; *can you keep an eye out for the traffic warden while I go into the bank?* **(b)** small hole in the end of a needle, through which the thread goes; *I can't get the thread to go through the eye*

eyebrow ['aɪbraʊ] *noun* small line of hair above your eye; **he raised his eyebrows** = he looked surprised

eyelash ['aɪlæʃ] *noun* one of the hairs growing round the edge of the eye; *she wore false eyelashes in the film* (NOTE: plural is **eyelashes**)

eyelid ['aɪlɪd] *noun* piece of skin which covers the eye; *her eyelids began to close and soon she was fast asleep*

eyesight ['aɪsaɪt] *noun* being able to see; *he has got very good eyesight*

Ff

F, f [ef] sixth letter of the alphabet, between E and G; *'raffle' is spelt with a double F or with two Fs*

fabric ['fæbrɪk] *noun* cloth, material; *we need a strong fabric for the chairs*

face [feɪs] **1** *noun* **(a)** front part of your head; *don't forget to wash your face before you go to the party*; **face to face** = looking at each other; *he turned a corner and came face to face with a policeman* **(b)** front part of something; *she put the photograph face down on the desk* **2** *verb* **(a)** to have the face or front towards; *can everyone please face the camera?* **(b) to face something** *or* **be faced with something** = to be likely to have to deal with an unpleasant situation; **not to be able to face something** = not to want to do something which you expect will be unpleasant; *he couldn't face another meeting*; **let's face it** = we must accept it; *let's face it, she's failed her test five times and will probably never pass*

face up to ['feɪs ʌp tuː] *verb* to accept an unpleasant state of affairs and try to deal with it; *he had to face up to the fact that he wasn't fit enough to play*

fact [fækt] *noun* **(a)** thing that is true; *it's a fact that it rains a lot in the west of England* **(b) the fact of the matter is** = what is true is that; *the fact of the matter is that he isn't fit enough to play*; **as a matter of fact** = actually; *have you seen John recently? - as a matter of fact I met him yesterday*

in fact *phrase* really; *he said he was going to school but in fact he went fishing instead*

factory ['fæktri] *noun* building where things are made; *she works in a shoe factory; the*

factory makes computers (NOTE: plural is **factories**)

fade [feɪd] *verb* **(a)** to lose colour; *my jeans have faded* **(b)** to become less bright or light; *the light from the torch began to fade as the batteries ran out* **(c)** to become less noisy; *the sound of the music faded away*

Fahrenheit ['færənhaɪt] *noun* scale of temperatures where the freezing and boiling points of water are 32° and 212°; *the temperature outside was 56°F (say 'fifty-six degrees Fahrenheit'); to calculate Fahrenheit degrees as Celsius, subtract 32 and divide by 1.8, so 68°F is equal to 20°C*

fail [feɪl] *verb* **(a)** not to do something which you were trying to do; *he passed in maths, but failed his English exam* **(b)** not to do something; *she failed to stop at the red light* **(c)** not to work properly; *the brakes failed and he couldn't stop the car*

failure ['feɪljə] *noun* **(a)** breakdown or stopping; *the accident was caused by brake failure* **(b)** person or thing which does not work in a satisfactory way; *I'm no good at anything - I'm a failure*

faint [feɪnt] **1** *adjective* difficult to see or hear; *there's a faint smell of cheese; we could hear a faint noise coming from the ruins* (NOTE: **fainter - faintest**) **2** *verb* to become unconscious for a short time; *she fainted when she saw the blood*

fair [feə] **1** *adjective* **(a)** light-coloured (hair, skin); *she's dark, but her brother is fair* **(b)** right, giving someone what they deserve; *it isn't fair for him to take a day off when we have so much work to do* (NOTE: do not confuse with **fare**; note also: **fairer - fairest**) **2** *noun* group of amusements, games, food stalls, etc., set up in one place for a short time; *he went to the fair and won a prize in the shooting competition*

fairly ['feəli] *adverb* quite; *I'm fairly certain I have seen this film before; the school is fairly close to the centre of town*

fairy ['feəri] *noun* little creature who can work magic; *I believed in fairies when I was little*; **fairy godmother** = kind person who gives you magic presents; *Cinderella's fairy godmother helped her go to the ball*; **fairy story** *or* **fairy tale** = children's story about fairies, princesses, giants, etc. (NOTE: plural is **fairies**)

faith [feɪθ] *noun* **to have faith in someone or something** = to believe that someone is good and strong, or will protect you; *I don't have any faith in this new treatment*

faithful ['feɪθfʊl] *adjective* loyal, who can be trusted; *his faithful old dog sat by his bed*

faithfully ['feɪθfəli] *adverb* **Yours faithfully** = used as an ending for business letters, when addressed to no particular person

fake [feɪk] *noun* thing which is copied, not the real thing; *that picture isn't by Picasso, it's a fake*

fall [fɔːl] **1** *noun* **(a)** losing your balance; *he had a fall and hurt his back* **(b)** US **the fall** = autumn, the season of the year between summer and winter; *we go to New England in the fall to see the trees* **2** *verb* **(a)** to drop down to a lower level; *she fell down the stairs*; *he fell off the ladder*; *did he fall into the river or did someone push him?* **(b)** his **face fell** = he looked sad and disappointed (NOTE: **falling - fell** [fel] **- has fallen**)

fall asleep ['fɔːl ə'sliːp] *phrase* to go to sleep; *we all fell asleep after dinner*

fall back on ['fɔːl 'bæk ɒn] *verb* to use something which you were keeping as a reserve; *the car broke down, so we had to fall back on public transport*

fall behind [fɔːl bɪ'haɪnd] *verb* to be late in doing something; *he fell behind with his work*

fall down ['fɔːl 'daʊn] *verb* **(a)** to drop to the ground; *she fell down and hurt her knee* **(b)** to become a ruin; *the house has been empty for so long it's falling down*

fall off ['fɔːl 'ɒf] *verb* to become fewer; *the number of tourists has fallen off this summer*

fall on ['fɔːl 'ɒn] *verb* to happen or to take place; *my birthday falls on a Tuesday this year*

fall out ['fɔːl 'aʊt] *verb* to have an argument; *they fell out over the bill*

fall over ['fɔːl 'əʊvə] *verb* to fall down from being vertical; *don't put the jug on the cushion - it may fall over*

fall through ['fɔːl 'θruː] *verb* not to take place as was planned; *our planned holiday in Spain fell through*

false [fɔːls] *adjective* not real; **false teeth** = artificial teeth; **false alarm** = signal for an emergency when there isn't one; *the fire brigade has answered two false alarms today*

familiar [fə'mɪljə] *adjective* heard or seen before; *he looked round the room, and saw a couple of familiar faces*

family ['fæmɪli] *noun* **(a)** group of people who are related to each other, especially mother, father and children; *the Jones family are going on holiday to Spain*; *they have a big family - three sons and two daughters* **(b)** group of animals or plants, etc., which are closely related; *lions and tigers are members of the cat family* (NOTE: plural is **families**)

famine ['fæmɪn] *noun* very serious lack of food; *famine is to be found in some parts of Africa*

famous ['feɪməs] *adjective* who everyone knows about; *he's a famous footballer*; *this tea shop is famous for its cakes*

fan [fæn] *noun* **(a)** enthusiastic supporter of a team, pop group, etc.; *there was a crowd of fans waiting for him outside the theatre*; **a Liverpool fan** = a supporter of Liverpool football team **(b)** device for moving air to make things cooler; *we've put electric fans in the office to try to keep cool*

fancy ['fænsi] **1** *noun* **it took his fancy** = he suddenly wanted it; *the watch took her fancy, so she walked into the shop and bought it* **2** *adjective* **fancy dress** = unusual costume worn to a party **3** *verb* to like; to want to have; *I* *fancy an ice cream - any one else want one?* **4** *interjection showing surprise; fancy meeting you here!*

fantastic [fæn'tæstɪk] *adjective (informal)* wonderful, amazing; *a holiday working on fruit farms in Australia - that sounds fantastic!*; *it's fantastic being part of a TV company!*

fantasy ['fæntəsi] *noun* invented story; *her story of meeting a rich man in Paris was just fantasy* (NOTE: plural is **fantasies**)

far [fɑː] **1** *adverb* **(a)** a certain distance away; *the supermarket is not far from here*; *how far is it from Paris to London?* **(b)** much; *restaurant food is far nicer than the food at college* **2** *adjective* which is a long way away; *the shop is at the far end of the High Street* (NOTE: **far - farther** *or* **further** ['fɑːðə *or* 'fɜːðə] - **farthest** *or* **furthest** ['fɑːðəst *or* 'fɜːðəst])

far from ['fɑː 'frɒm] *adverb* not at all; *the food here is far from cheap*

by far ['baɪ 'fɑː] *adverb* very much; *a bike is by far the cheapest way to travel round London*

so far ['səʊ 'fɑː] up till now; *so far this winter I have managed not to catch flu*; *have you enjoyed your stay in England so far?*

fare [feə] *noun* price which you have to pay for a journey; *rail fares have been increased by 10%*; *if you cycle to work, you will save £5 a week on bus fares* (NOTE: do not confuse with **fair**)

farewell [feə'wel] **1** *interjection & noun (formal)* goodbye; *it's time to say farewell* **2** *adjective* at which you say goodbye; *we gave a farewell party for our neighbours who were going to live in Canada*

farm [fɑːm] *noun* land used for growing crops and keeping animals; *we're going to work on a farm during the holidays*

farmer ['fɑːmə] *noun* person who manages or owns a farm; *he is one of the biggest pig farmers in the county*

farther *or* **farthest** ['fɑːðə *or* 'fɑːðəst] *see*

FAR; *you're too close to the camera - move farther back*; *how much farther is it to the seaside?*

fascinate ['fæsɪneɪt] *verb* to interest greatly; *anything to do with stars and space travel fascinates him*

fascinating ['fæsɪneɪtɪŋ] *adjective* very interesting; *it was fascinating to hear her talk about her travels in India*

fashion ['fæʃn] *noun* **(a)** most popular style at a particular moment; *it's the fashion today to wear your hair very short*; **in fashion** = popular, following the current style; *high heels are in fashion this year*; **out of fashion** = not popular, not the current style; *red cars are out of fashion* **(b)** **after a fashion** = not very well; *he can speak French after a fashion*

fast [fɑːst] **1** *adjective* **(a)** quick; *this is the fast train to London* **(b)** *(of clock)* to show a time which is later than the correct time; *my watch is five minutes fast* (NOTE: **faster - fastest**) **2** *adverb* **(a)** quickly; *don't go so fast - you almost hit that man on the zebra crossing* **(b)** **fast asleep** = sleeping so that it is difficult to wake up; *she must have been tired - she's fast asleep already* **(c)** tight fixed; *the window was stuck fast and I couldn't open it* **3** *verb* to eat nothing for religious or health reasons; *many people fast during the period before Easter*

fasten ['fɑːsən] *verb* to close or attach securely; *please fasten your seat belts*; *my dress fastens with a zip*

fastener ['fɑːsnə] *noun* device which fastens; *I must have put on weight - I can't do the fastener up*

fat [fæt] **1** *adjective (person)* round and weighing too much; *two fat men got out of the little white car*; *you'll have to eat less - you're getting too fat* (NOTE: **fatter - fattest**) **2** *noun* **(a)** part of meat which is yellow or white; *if you don't like fat, cut it off* **(b)** **cooking fat** = white substance from animals or plants, used for cooking; *fry the onions in hot fat*

father ['fɑːðə] *noun* man who has a son or daughter; *ask your father if he will lend you his car*

Father Christmas ['fɑːðə 'krɪsməs] *noun* man in a long red coat, with a big white beard, who is supposed to bring presents to children on Christmas Day; *what did Father Christmas bring you yesterday?*

faucet ['fɔːsət] *noun US* device with a knob which, when you twist it, lets liquid come out (British English is always 'tap'); *the faucet in the bathroom is leaking*

fault [fɒlt] *noun* (a) being to blame for something which has gone wrong; *it isn't my fault if there's nothing in the fridge; it's all your fault - if you had got up earlier we would be at the seaside by now* (b) the fact that something is not working properly; *the engineers are trying to mend an electrical fault* (c) *(in tennis)* mistake in serving; *he served two double faults*

favour *US* **favor** ['feɪvə] *noun* (a) friendly act, helping someone; *can I ask a favour? will you look after my cat when I'm away?*; **to do someone a favour** = to do something to help someone (b) **to be in favour of** = to prefer; *the meeting voted in favour of the proposal*

favourite *US* **favorite** ['feɪvrɪt] **1** *adjective* which you like best; *which is your favourite TV programme?* **2** *noun* thing or person which you like best; *which ice cream is your favourite?*

fax [fæks] **1** *noun* copy of a text or picture sent by telephone; *post it to me, or send a fax* (NOTE: plural is **faxes**) **2** *verb* to send a letter or picture by telephone; *I will fax the details to you as soon as they are ready*

fear ['fɪə] **1** *noun* (a) feeling of being afraid; *she has no fear of heights* (b) *(informal)* **no fear!** = certainly not!; *go on, touch that snake - no fear!* **2** *verb* to be afraid of something; *when the little girl had not been found three days later, everyone began to fear the worst*

feast [fiːst] *noun* very large meal for a group of people; *they celebrated the king's wedding with a feast*

feat [fiːt] *noun* very difficult act; *scoring a hat trick is quite a feat*

feather ['feðə] *noun* one of many light soft parts which cover a bird's body; *a peacock has very long feathers in its tail*

February ['februəri] *noun* second month of the year, between January and March; *my birthday is in February*; *we are moving to a new flat next February*

fed [fed] *see* FEED

fed up ['fed 'ʌp] *adjective (informal)* **fed up (with)** = tired of, unhappy because you have had enough of something; *I'm fed up with always doing the washing up, why can't someone else do it for a change?*; *she went back to school last Tuesday and she's fed up already*

feed [fiːd] *verb* (a) to give food to someone, to an animal; *let's go to the park and feed the ducks* (b) to eat; *the lambs are feeding* (NOTE: feeding - fed [fed] - has fed)

feel [fiːl] *verb* (a) to touch (usually with your fingers); *feel how soft the bed is* (b) to seem soft, cold, etc., when touched; *the bed feels hard*; *the stone floor felt cold* (c) to sense something with your body or mind; *I felt the lift go down suddenly*; *they felt happy when they saw that everything was working properly* (NOTE: feeling - felt [felt] - has felt)

feel for ['fiːl 'fɔː] *verb* to have sympathy for; *I feel for him, he's lost his job and now his wife has been taken to hospital*

feel like ['fiːl 'laɪk] *verb* (a) to want to do something; *I feel like going for a swim*; *do you feel like a cup of coffee?* (b) to seem like, when touched; *it feels like plastic, not metal*

feel up to ['fiːl 'ʌp tʊ] *verb* to be strong enough to do something; *do you feel up to going for a walk round the park?*

feeling ['fiːlɪŋ] *noun* something which you sense; *I had a feeling that someone was* *following me*

feet [fiːt] *see* FOOT

fell [fel] *see* FALL

felt [felt] **1** *noun* thick material made of wool fibres pressed together; **felt pen** *or* **felt-tipped pen** = pen whose writing end is made of hard felt **2** *verb see* FEEL

female [ˈfiːmeɪl] **1** *adjective* referring to the sex which has young; *a female kitten* **2** *noun* animal, insect, bird which gives birth to young or lays eggs; *in some spiders, the female of the species is larger than the male*

feminine [ˈfemənɪn] *adjective (in grammar)* referring to words which have a particular form or behave in a different way, to show they are female; *is the French word 'table' masculine or feminine?*

fence [fens] *noun* barrier of wood or wire, used to keep people or animals in or out of a place; *the boys looked through the hole in the fence*; *the builders put up a fence round the building site*

fender [ˈfendə] *noun* US panel over the wheel of a car, which protects against splashing water and mud (British English for this is a 'wing'); *the front fender was dented in the crash*

ferocious [fəˈrəʊʃəs] *adjective* fierce and angry; *a couple of ferocious dogs leapt at him*

ferry [ˈferi] **1** *noun* boat which carries cars or trucks or people backwards and forwards across a stretch of water; *we are going to take the night ferry to Belgium*; **car ferry** = ferry which carries cars (NOTE: plural is **ferries**) **2** *verb* to take across by boat; *small boats ferried the tourists across the lake*

festival [ˈfestɪvl] *noun* **(a)** religious celebration which comes at the same time each year and usually is a public holiday; *the tour will visit Hong Kong for the Moon Festival* **(b)** entertainment which is put on at regular intervals with many different performances; *there are some excellent plays at the Edinburgh Festival this year*

fetch [fetʃ] *verb* to go and bring someone or something; *it's your turn to fetch the children from school*

fete *or* **fête** [feɪt] *noun* small public festival, usually in the open air, with stalls, shows of interesting things, and competitions; *I hope it doesn't rain for the village fête*

fever [ˈfiːvə] *noun* state when the temperature of your body is higher than normal; *you must stay in bed until the fever goes down*

few [fjuː] *adjective & noun* **(a)** not many; *she has very few friends*; **few and far between** = not very frequent; *trains are few and far between on Sundays* **(b) a few** = some, not very many; *take a few photographs and we'll choose which one is the best* (NOTE: **fewer - fewest**)

fibre US **fiber** [ˈfaɪbə] *noun* thin thread of material; *the police found fibres from the suspect's coat at the scene of the murder*

fiction [ˈfɪkʃn] *noun* novels, stories which are invented; *if you want to find Martin Amis, look in the fiction section of the library*

field [fiːld] *noun* **(a)** piece of ground on a farm, with a fence or hedge around it; *the sheep are in the field*; *he planted a field of potatoes* **(b) playing field** = piece of ground for playing a game; *the two teams ran onto the field*; **field events** = jumping and throwing competitions; *athletics is made up of both track and field events*

fierce [fɪəs] *adjective* very angry and likely to attack; *watch out - that dog looks fierce*

fiercely [ˈfɪəsli] *adverb* in a strong or violent way; *the shop was blazing fiercely when the fire brigade arrived*

fifteen [fɪfˈtiːn] **(a)** number 15; *there are fifteen players in a rugby side*; *she's fifteen (years old) the train leaves at nine fifteen (9.15)*; **the fifteen hundreds (1500s)** = the years from 1500 to 1599 (compare the 'fifteenth century') **(b)** group of fifteen people (as in a Rugby team); *the England XV (say 'the England fifteen')*

fifteenth (15th) [fɪfˈtiːnθ] *adjective & noun the fifteenth of July* or *July the fifteenth (July 15th); it will be her fifteenth birthday next week*; **the fifteenth century** = the years from 1400 to 1499 (compare the 'fifteen hundreds'); *the French King Louis XV (say: 'King Louis the Fifteenth')*

fifth (5th) [fɪfθ] **1** *adjective; the fifth of May* or *May the fifth (May 5th); it's his fifth birthday tomorrow; King Henry V (say: 'King Henry the Fifth') won the battle of Agincourt*; **the fifth century** = period from 400 to 499 AD **2** *noun* **a fifth** = 20%; *he spends a fifth of the year travelling*

fiftieth (50th) [ˈfɪftɪəθ] *adjective & noun* *she came fiftieth and last in the race; it's her fiftieth birthday on Monday*

fifty [ˈfɪfti] **(a)** number 50; *she's fifty (years old);* **she's in her fifties** = she's between 50 and 59 years old; **the (nineteen) fifties (1950s)** = the period from 1950 to 1959 **(b) fifty-fifty** = divided into two equal amounts; **to go fifty-fifty** = with each paying half of the cost; *we'll go fifty-fifty on the bill*

fight [faɪt] **1** *noun* struggle against someone or something; *he got into a fight with boys who were bigger than him* **2** *verb* to struggle against someone or something using force; *the two boys were fighting over a book* (NOTE: **fighting - fought** [fɔːt] **- has fought**)

figure [ˈfɪɡə US ˈfɪɡjə] **1** *noun* **(a)** written number (such as 35); *cheques have to be made out in both words and figures* **(b)** shape of a person; *they could see two figures hiding in the trees* **2** *verb* **(a) to figure out** = to try to think of an answer or to understand something; *try to figure out the answer yourself instead of asking the teacher* **(b)** *(informal)* to consider, to think; *we figured you'd be late because of the show*

file [faɪl] *noun* **(a)** metal tool used for making rough surfaces smooth; *use a file to round off the edges of the metal* **(b)** cardboard container for papers and documents; *when you have finished with the papers, put them back in the*

file (c) section of data on a computer; *type the name of the file and then press ENTER* **(d) in single file** = one behind the other; *the children entered the hall in single file*

fill [fɪl] *verb* **(a)** to make something full; *he filled the bottle with water* **(b) to fill a post** = to find someone to do a job; *your application arrived too late - the post has already been filled*

fill out [ˈfɪl ˈaʊt] *verb* to write in all the empty spaces on a form; *fill out the form and send it back to this address*

fill up [ˈfɪl ˈʌp] *verb* **(a)** to make something completely full; *he filled the bottle up with fresh water* **(b)** to write in all the empty spaces on a form; *fill up the form and send it back to this address*

film [fɪlm] *noun* **(a)** moving pictures shown at a cinema or on TV; *have you seen this old Laurel and Hardy film?* **(b)** roll of plastic which you put into a camera to take photographs or moving pictures; *I must buy another film before the wedding*

filthy [ˈfɪlθi] *adjective* very dirty; *where have you been playing - you're filthy!*; *don't touch that filthy old carpet* (NOTE: **filthier - filthiest**)

fin [fɪn] *noun* thin part on the body of a fish or shark which helps it to swim; *from the beach they could see a black fin in the sea*

final [ˈfaɪnəl] **1** *adjective* last, coming at the end; *the competition is in its final stages*; **final date for booking** = last date by which a booking should be made **2** *noun* last competition in a series between several teams or individuals; *I thought they would win a couple of rounds, but I never imagined they would get to the final*; **cup final** = last game in a series of football games, where the winner is given a silver cup

finally [ˈfaɪnəli] *adverb* at last, in the end; *the bus finally turned up twenty minutes late*

finance [ˈfaɪnæns] **1** *noun* money; *how are you going to get the finance to buy that car?* **2** *verb* to provide money for; *how is he going* *to finance his course at college if he doesn't have a grant?*

financial [fɪ'nænʃl] *adjective* referring to money; *I think he has financial problems*

find [faɪnd] *verb* **(a)** to discover (something hidden or lost); *I found a £2 coin behind the sofa* **(b)** to discover something which was not known before; *no one has found a cure for the common cold yet* (NOTE: **finding - found** [faʊnd])

find out ['faɪnd 'aʊt] *verb* to discover information; *the police are trying to find out why she went to Scotland*

find time ['faɪnd 'taɪm] *phrase* to do something even though you are short of time; *in the middle of the meeting he still found time to phone his girlfriend*

fine [faɪn] **1** *adjective* **(a)** good (weather); *we'll go for a walk tomorrow if it stays fine*; *let's hope it's fine for the cricket match* **(b)** well, healthy; *I was in bed with flu yesterday, but today I'm feeling fine* **(c)** good; *how are things at home? - fine!* **(d)** very thin or very small; *use a sharp pencil if you want to draw fine lines* (NOTE: **finer - finest**) **2** *noun* money which you have to pay for having done something wrong; *I had to pay a £25 fine for parking in a no parking area* **3** *verb* to make someone pay money for having done something wrong; *he was fined £25 for parking on double yellow lines*

finger ['fɪŋgə] *noun* **(a)** one of the parts at the end of your hand, but usually not including the thumb; *he wears a ring on his little finger*; *he pressed the button with his finger* **(b)** part of a glove into which a finger goes; *I must mend my glove - there's a hole in one of the fingers* **(c)** long thin piece of food; *a box of chocolate fingers*

fingernail ['fɪŋgəneɪl] *noun* hard thin part covering the end of each finger; *she painted her fingernails green*

fingerprint ['fɪŋgəprɪnt] *noun* mark left by a finger when you touch something; *the police*

found his fingerprints on the car door

finish ['fɪnɪʃ] *verb* to do something completely; to come to an end; *haven't you finished your homework yet?*; *tell me when you've finished reading the paper*; *the game will finish at about four o'clock*

finish up ['fɪnɪʃ 'ʌp] *verb* **(a)** to be in the end; *we got lost and finished up miles from where we wanted to be* **(b)** to eat something completely; *you must finish up all your vegetables*

Finland ['fɪnlənd] *noun* large country in northern Europe, between Sweden and Russia; *we like to go camping and sailing in Finland in summer* (NOTE: capital: **Helsinki**; people: **the Finns**; language: **Finnish**)

Finn [fɪn] *noun* person from Finland; *the Finns are used to cold winters*

Finnish ['fɪnɪʃ] **1** *adjective* referring to Finland; *Finnish summers can be quite hot* **2** *noun* language spoken in Finland; *I bought a Finnish phrase book before going to Helsinki*

fir [fɜː] *noun* evergreen tree with leaves shaped like needles; *fir trees are often used as Christmas trees* (NOTE: do not confuse with **fur**)

fire ['faɪə] **1** *noun* **(a)** something which is burning; **to set fire to** = to make something start burning; *his cigarette set fire to the carpet* **(b)** electric or gas machine which heats; *we have an electric fire in the living room* **2** *verb* **(a)** to shoot a gun; *the robbers fired at the police car* **(b)** to dismiss someone from a job; *she was fired for being late*

fire engine ['faɪə 'endʒɪn] *noun* large red van used by the fire services, with pumps, ladders, etc., to fight fires; *six fire engines were at the fire*

fire fighter ['faɪə 'faɪtə] *noun* person who tries to put out fires; *dozens of fire fighters tried to put out the forest fire*

fireman ['faɪəmən] *noun* man who tries to put out fires; *the firemen were fighting the fire in the town centre* (NOTE: plural is **firemen**)

fireplace ['faɪəpleɪs] *noun* hole in the wall of

a room where you can light a fire for heating; *our dog likes to lie on the carpet in front of the fireplace*

firework ['faɪəwɜːk] *noun* small cardboard tube holding chemicals which will explode when lit; *there was a big firework display on Bonfire Night*

firm [fɜːm] **1** *adjective* **(a)** solid or fixed; *make sure that the ladder is firm before you climb up* **(b)** not going to change; *be firm with the children - don't let them do what they want* (NOTE: **firmer - firmest**) **2** *noun* business or company; *the firm I work for was taken over last year*

firmly ['fɜːmli] *adverb* in a firm way; *she said firmly that she did not want to go*

first [fɜːst] **1** *adjective & noun* referring to the thing that comes before all other things; *my birthday is on the first of July (July 1st); it's our baby's first birthday on Tuesday; the bank is the first building on the left past the post office; King Charles I (say 'King Charles the First') was executed in 1649;* **the first century** = the period from the year 1 to 99 AD; **first name** = a person's Christian name or given name, as opposed to the surname or family name; *her first name is Natasha, but I don't know her surname* **2** *adverb* **(a)** at the beginning; *she came first in the exam* **(b)** before doing anything else; *wash your hands first, and then come and sit down*

at first [æt 'fɜːst] at the beginning; *at first he didn't like the work but later he got used to it*

first aid ['fɜːst 'eɪd] *noun* help given to a person who is hurt, before a doctor or ambulance arrives; *the police gave first aid to the accident victims; we keep a first aid kit in the classroom*

first-class ['fɜːst'klɑːs] *adjective* **(a)** very good; *he is a first-class tennis player* **(b)** *(post)* expensive and faster than second-class; *send the letter first-class if it is urgent*

fish [fɪʃ] **1** *noun* **(a)** animal with no legs, which lives in water and which you can usually eat; *I sat by the river all day and only caught two little fish* **(b)** **fish and chips** = traditional British food, obtained from special shops, where portions of fried fish are sold with chips; *we're having fish and chips for supper;* **fish fingers** = frozen piece of fish, shaped like a finger, fried and covered in bread crumbs; *we all love fish fingers* **2** *verb* to try to catch a fish; *we often go fishing in the lake*

fisherman ['fɪʃəmən] *noun* man who catches fish, either as his job or for sport; *fishermen are complaining that pollution is killing all the fish* (NOTE: plural is **fishermen**)

fist [fɪst] *noun* tight closed hand; *he punched her with his fist*

fit [fɪt] **1** *noun* sudden sharp attack of illness, etc.; *she had a fit of coughing and had to have a glass of water* **2** *adjective* healthy; *he isn't fit enough to go back to work* (NOTE: **fitter - fittest**) **3** *verb* to be the right size or shape; *he's grown so tall that his jackets don't fit him any more; these shoes don't fit me - they're a size too small* (NOTE: **fitting - fitted**)

five [faɪv] number 5; *she drank five cups of tea; he's five (years old) next week; the meeting has been arranged for five (o'clock)*

fix [fɪks] *verb* **(a)** to fasten or to attach; *fix one end of the rope to the tree and the other to the fence* **(b)** to arrange; *we'll try to fix a time for the meeting* **(c)** to mend; *the telephone people are coming to fix the telephone*

fixed [fɪkst] *adjective* attached firmly; *the sign is fixed to the post with big nails*

fizzy ['fɪzi] *adjective* full of little bubbles; *I don't like fizzy orange - do you have any squash?*

flag [flæg] *noun* **(a)** piece of brightly coloured material with the design of a country or club, etc., on it; *the French flag has blue, red and white stripes* **(b)** small paper badge sold in aid of a charity; *pin the flag to your coat to show that you have given something*

flake [fleɪk] *noun* **(a)** small piece of snow which falls from the sky; *snow fell in large soft flakes all night* **(b)** tiny, thin piece; *the paint came off in little flakes*

flame [fleɪm] *noun* bright tongue of fire; *flames could be seen coming out of the upstairs windows*; **in flames** = burning; *the building was already in flames when the fire engine arrived*

flannel [ˈflænl] *noun* small square of cloth for washing your face or body; *he put his flannel under the hot tap and wiped his face*

flap [flæp] **1** *noun* flat part which is attached to a main structure and which can move up and down; **cat flap** = little door in the door of a house, which allows a cat to go in or out **2** *verb* to move up and down like a bird's wing; *flags were flapping in the breeze*; *the swans stood by the edge of the water, flapping their wings* (NOTE: flapping - flapped)

flash [flæʃ] **1** *noun* **(a)** short sudden burst of light; *flashes of lightning lit up the sky with thunder in the distance* **(b)** device for making a bright light, which allows you to take photographs in the dark; *people sometimes have red eyes in photos taken with a flash* (NOTE: plural is **flashes**) **2** *verb* **(a)** to light up quickly and suddenly; *a light flashed twice as a signal* **(b)** **to flash by** *or* **to flash past** = to move or to pass by quickly; *the champion flashed past to win in record time*

flask [flɑːsk] *noun* bottle for keeping liquids hot or cold; *we've brought a flask of coffee*

flat [flæt] **1** *adjective* **(a)** level, not sloping or curved; *a house with a flat roof* **(b)** **a flat tyre** = a tyre which has lost all the air in it; *he pulled up at the side of the road to change a flat tyre* **(c)** with no electric charge left; *the car wouldn't start because the battery was flat* (NOTE: flatter - flattest) **2** *adverb* level, not sloping or curved; *lay your clothes out flat on the bed*; *he tripped over and fell flat on his face* **3** *noun* set of rooms for one family, on one floor, usually in a building with several similar sets of rooms (American English for this is an 'apartment'); *we have bought a flat in London after selling our house in the country*

flatten [ˈflætən] *verb* to make flat; *the rain flattened the corn in the fields*; *thousands of buildings were flattened in the San Francisco earthquake of 1906*

flatter [ˈflætə] *verb* to praise someone too much; *just flatter the boss a bit and he'll give you a rise*

flavour *US* **flavor** [ˈfleɪvə] **1** *noun* taste of something; *what flavours of ice cream have you got?* **2** *verb* to add things such as spices and seasoning in cooking something, to give it a special taste; *use pepper to flavour the meat*

flesh [fleʃ] *noun* **(a)** soft part of the body covering the bones; **a flesh wound** = wound which goes into the flesh but is not very deep and doesn't hit the bones or organs **(b)** soft part of a fruit; *some grapefruit have pink flesh*

flew [fluː] *see* FLY (NOTE: do not confuse with flu)

flies [flaɪz] *see* FLY

flight [flaɪt] *noun* **(a)** travel in a plane; *go to gate 25 for flight AB198 to Paris* **(b)** **flight of stairs** = set of stairs going in one direction; *go up two flights of stairs and the bathroom is the first door on the left*

fling [flɪŋ] *verb* to throw something wildly; *he flung the empty bottle into the sea*; *she flung herself into an armchair* (NOTE: flinging - flung [flʌŋ])

flipper [ˈflɪpə] *noun* **(a)** long flat piece of rubber which you can attach to your foot to help you swim faster; *she put on her flippers and mask and dived in* **(b)** flat arm or leg of a sea animal used for swimming; *the seal walked across the rock on its flippers*

float [fləʊt] **1** *noun* piece of cork, etc., attached to a fishing line, which stays on the surface of the water, with the line and hook hanging down in the water below; *if the float goes up and down in the water it means you* *have caught a fish* **2** *verb* to lie or put on the top of a liquid; *dead fish were floating in the river*; *he floated a paper boat on the lake*

flock [flɒk] **1** *noun* group of animals together, such as sheep, goats, or birds; *a flock of sheep were grazing in the field* **2** *verb* to move in large numbers; *tourists flocked to see the Changing of the Guard*

flood [flʌd] **1** *noun* large amount of water over land which is usually dry; *the floods were caused by heavy rain* **2** *verb* **(a)** to cover with water; *fields were flooded after the river burst its banks*; *he forgot to turn the tap off and flooded the bathroom* **(b)** to come in large numbers; *the office was flooded with complaints*

floor [flɔː] *noun* **(a)** part of a room on which you walk; *if there are no empty chairs left, you'll have to sit on the floor* **(b)** all the rooms on one level in a building; *the bathroom is on the ground floor*; *there is a good view of the town from the top floor*

flop [flɒp] **1** *noun (informal)* failure; *the film was a big hit in New York but was a flop in London* **2** *verb* **(a)** to fall or sit like a heavy bag; *she got back from the sales and flopped down on the sofa* **(b)** *(informal)* not to be a success; *the play was a big hit on Broadway but flopped in London* (NOTE: **flopping - flopped**)

flour [ˈflaʊə] *noun* grain crushed to powder, used for making bread, cakes, etc.; *she made the cake by mixing eggs, sugar and flour*

flourish [ˈflʌrɪʃ] *verb* **(a)** to grow well; to do well; *palm trees flourish in hot countries* **(b)** to wave something in the air; *she came in with a big smile, flourishing a cheque*

flow [fləʊ] **1** *noun* movement of liquid, air, etc.; *she tried to stop the flow of blood with a tight bandage*; *there was a steady flow of visitors to the exhibition* **2** *verb* to move along in a smooth way; *the river flows into the sea*

flower [ˈflaʊə] **1** *noun* brightly coloured part of a plant which attracts bees and then

produces fruit or seeds; *a plant with bright yellow flowers* **2** *verb* to produce flowers; *the cherry trees flowered very late this year*

flown [fləʊn] *see* FLY

flu [fluː] *noun* common illness like a bad cold, often with a high temperature; *half of our team are down with flu* (NOTE: do not confuse with **flew**)

fluid [ˈfluːɪd] *noun* liquid; *you need to drink plenty of fluids in hot weather*

flung [flʌŋ] *verb see* FLING

flute [fluːt] *noun* wind instrument held sideways, and played by blowing across a small hole near the end; *she plays the flute in the local orchestra*

fly [flaɪ] **1** *noun* small insect with two wings which lays its eggs on food; *he tried to kill the fly with a newspaper* (NOTE: plural is **flies**) **2** *verb* **(a)** to move through the air (with wings, in a plane, etc.); *I'm flying to China next week*; *some birds fly to Africa for the winter* **(b)** to make (a plane) move through the air; *the pilot flew through the storm* **(c)** to move fast; *the door flew open and two men rushed in* (NOTE: **flying - flew** [fluː] **- has flown** [fləʊn])

foam [fəʊm] *noun* mass of little bubbles; *this soap powder makes a huge amount of foam*; **foam rubber** = rubber in blocks with many little holes in it, used for chair cushions, etc.; *the sofa has foam rubber cushions*

focus [ˈfəʊkəs] **1** *noun (of a photograph)* point where the details of the photograph are clear and sharp; **in focus** = clear; **out of focus** = not clear **2** *verb* to adjust a telescope or microscope so that the image is clear (NOTE: **focusing - focused**)

fog [fɒg] *noun* thick mist which is difficult to see through; *all flights out of London Airport have been delayed by fog*; *the fog is so thick that you can hardly see ten metres in front of you*

fold [fəʊld] *verb* **(a)** to bend something so that one part is on top of another; *fold the piece of paper in half*; *he folded up the* newspaper and put it in his briefcase **(b) to fold your arms** = to cross your arms in front of your body; *he sat on the stage with his arms folded, looking annoyed*

folder ['fəʊldə] *noun* cardboard envelope for holding papers; *she took a folder from the drawer*

folk [fəʊk] *noun* **(a)** people; *they took the old folk down to the sea for a picnic* **(b) folk dance** = traditional country dance; **folk song** = traditional country song

follow ['fɒləʊ] *verb* **(a)** to come after or behind; *the group of tourists followed the guide round the town*; *what follows B in the alphabet?* **(b)** to do what someone tells you to do; *she followed the instructions on the packet of dye*

fond (of) ['fɒnd 'ɒv] *adjective*; **to be fond of something** = to like something; *I am fond of music*; *she's very fond of chocolate*

food [fuːd] *noun* things which you eat; *do you like Chinese food?*; *we went on a picnic and found that we had forgotten to bring the food*

foolish ['fuːlɪʃ] *adjective* stupid; *it was foolish of them to go into the jungle without a guide*

foot [fʊt] *noun* **(a)** end part of your leg on which you stand; *he has very big feet*; *watch out, you trod on my foot!* **(b)** bottom part, end; *there is a door at the foot of the stairs*; *there are traffic lights at the foot of the hill* **(c)** measurement of how long something is (= 12 inches or approximately 30 cm); *the table is four foot or four feet long*; *she's almost six foot tall*

on foot ['ɒn 'fʊt] *phrase* walking; *don't wait for the bus - it's quicker to go on foot*

under foot ['ʌndə 'fʊt] *phrase* on the ground; *it's very wet under foot after the rain*

football ['fʊtbɔːl] *noun* **(a)** game played between two teams with a round ball which can be kicked or headed, but not carried; *he's got a new pair of football boots*; *they went to a football match*; *the children were playing*

football in the street (b) ball used for kicking; *they were kicking a football around in the street*

footballer ['fʊtbɔːlə] *noun* person who plays football; *he's the famous United footballer*

footprint ['fʊtprɪnt] *noun* mark left by your foot on the ground; *they followed the footprints in the snow to the cave*

footstep ['fʊtstep] *noun* sound made by a foot touching the ground; *we heard soft footsteps along the corridor*

for [fɔː] *preposition* **(a)** *(showing the purpose or use of something)* *this plastic bag is for old papers*; *what's that key for?* **(b)** *(showing why something is given)* *what did you get for your birthday?*; *what shall we buy her for Christmas?* **(c)** *(showing person who gets something)* *there were no letters for you this morning*; *I'm making a cup of tea for my mother* **(d)** *(showing how long something happens)* *he has gone to France for two days*; *we've been waiting at the bus for hours* **(e)** *(showing distance)* *you can see for miles from the top of the hill* **(f)** *(showing destination)* *when is the next bus for Oxford Circus?* **(g)** in the place of someone; *can you sign this letter for me?*

for ever [fə 'evə] *phrase* **(a)** always; *I will love you for ever and ever* **(b)** *(exclamation to show support for a team)* *Scotland for ever!*

for example *or* **for instance** ['fɔː ɪɡˈzɑːmpl *or* fər ˈɪnstəns] *phrase* to mention one thing among many; *some animals, for example polar bears, are not used to hot weather*

for good [fɔː 'ɡʊd] for ever; *she left school for good when she was 16*

forbade [fəˈbæd] *verb see* FORBID

forbid [fəˈbɪd] *verb* to tell someone not to do something; *she forbade her children to go near the pub*; *smoking has been forbidden on trains* (NOTE: **forbidding - forbade** [fəˈbæd] - **forbidden** [fəˈbɪdn])

force [fɔːs] **1** *noun* **(a)** strength or power; *the* *police had to use force to push back the demonstrators*; **from force of habit** = because this is what you usually do **(b)** organized group of people; *he served in the police force for twenty years* **2** *verb* to make someone do something; *he was forced to lie down on the floor*; *you can't force me to go if I don't want to*

forecast ['fɔːkɑːst] **1** *noun* description of what you think will happen in the future; **weather forecast** = report on what sort of weather there will be in the next few days **2** *verb* to say what will happen in the future; *they are forecasting storms for the south coast*; *they forecast a rise in the number of tourists* (NOTE: **forecasting - forecast**)

forehead ['fɔːhed] *noun* part of the front of your head between the eyes and the hair; *his hair was falling down over his forehead*

foreign ['fɒrɪn] *adjective* not from your own country; *there are lots of foreign medical students at our college*; **foreign language** = language spoken by people in another country; *she speaks several foreign languages, such as German and Chinese*

forest ['fɒrɪst] *noun* large area covered with trees; *in dry weather there's a danger of forest fires*; *in winter bears come out of the forest to search for food*

forgave [fə'geɪv] *see* FORGIVE

forget [fə'get] *verb* **(a)** not to remember; *he's forgotten the name of the restaurant*; *she forgot all about her doctor's appointment*; *don't forget to lock the door* **(b)** to leave something behind; *when he left the office he forgot his car keys* (NOTE: **forgetting - forgot** [fə'gɒt] **- has forgotten** [fə'gɒtən])

forgive [fə'gɪv] *verb* to stop being angry with someone; *please forgive us for being late* (NOTE: **forgiving - forgave** [fə'geɪv] **- has forgiven**)

forgot *or* **forgotten** [fə'gɒt or fə'gɒtən] *see* FORGET

fork [fɔːk] **1** *noun* object with a handle at one end and several sharp points at the other, used for picking food up when eating; *don't try to eat Chinese food with a knife and fork*; **garden fork** = very large fork used for digging **2** *verb* **(a)** to turn off a road; *fork left at the next road junction* **(b)** to split into two parts; *the railway line forks at Crewe and one branch goes to the coast*

form [fɔːm] **1** *noun* **(a)** paper with blank spaces which you have to write in; **application form** = form which has to be filled in to apply for something; *don't forget to fill in the passport application form* **(b)** state or condition; *their team wasn't in top form and lost*; **in good form** = in a good mood, very amusing; *she's in good form today* **(c)** class (in school); *little children go into the first form*; **sixth form** = class for children who are over 16 **2** *verb* **(a)** to make; *the children formed a circle* **(b) formed of** = made of; *the committee is formed of retired teachers*

formal ['fɔːml] *adjective* **(a)** done according to certain rules; *the formal opening ceremony for the new town hall will be held next week* **(b)** (language) which is serious, which is used on special occasions

fort [fɔːt] *noun* **(a)** strong army building which can be defended against enemy attacks; *the soldiers rode out of a fort in the desert* **(b) to hold the fort** = to be in charge while someone is away; *everyone is away on holiday so I've been left holding the fort* (NOTE: do not confuse with **fought**)

forth [fɔːθ] *adverb (formal)* forwards; **back and forth** = backwards and forwards; *they went back and forth across the bridge* (NOTE: do not confuse with **fourth**)

and so forth [nd 'səʊ 'fɔːθ] *adverb* with other things; *he talked about plants: flowers, vegetables, and so forth*

fortieth (40th) ['fɔːtiəθ] *adjective & noun* *he came fortieth and last in the race*; *it's her fortieth birthday tomorrow*

fortnight ['fɔːtnaɪt] *noun* two weeks; *see you in a fortnight!*; *she's taking a fortnight's holiday*; *we will be on holiday during the last* *fortnight of July*

fortress ['fɔːtrəs] *noun* strong castle; *the king built a row of fortresses along the border* (NOTE: plural is **fortresses**)

fortunate ['fɔːtʃənət] *adjective* lucky; *we've been fortunate with the weather this year*

fortunately ['fɔːtʃənətli] *adverb* by good luck; *fortunately, he had remembered to take an umbrella*

fortune ['fɔːtjuːn] *noun* **(a)** large amount of money; *he won a fortune on the lottery* **(b)** what will happen in the future; **to tell someone's fortune** = to say what will happen to someone in the future; *she tells fortunes from cards*

forty ['fɔːti] *number* 40; *she's forty (years old);* **he's in his forties** = he's between 40 and 49 years old; **the nineteen forties (1940s)** = the period from 1940 to 1949

forward ['fɔːwəd] **1** *adverb* **(a)** in the direction that you are facing; *she took two steps forward; the policeman made a sign with his hand and the cars began to go forward* **(b) to look forward to something** = to think happily about something which is going to happen; *I'm looking forward to my holidays; he isn't looking forward to his exams* **2** *noun* player in a team whose job is to attack the other side; *the England defence came under attack from the Brazilian forwards*

forwards ['fɔːwədz] *adverb* in the direction that you are facing; *the cars were moving slowly forwards;* **backwards and forwards** = from one side to the other several times; *the policeman walked backwards and forwards in front of the bank*

fossil ['fɒsl] *noun* remains of an ancient animal or plant left in rock; *they found some fossil shells in the cliffs*

foster-parents ['fɒstə'peərənts] *noun* parents who bring up a child who is not their own; *her foster-parents brought her up as one of the family*

fought [fɔːt] *see* FIGHT

foul [faʊl] **1** *adjective* bad, unpleasant (taste, language, air, etc.); *what foul weather we're having!; the boss has been in a foul temper all day* **2** *noun* action which is against the rules of a game; *the referee gave a free kick for a foul on the goalkeeper*

found [faʊnd] *verb* **(a)** to start a business, to begin something; *the business was founded in 1900* **(b)** *see also* FIND

foundation [faʊn'deɪʃn] *noun* **foundations** = stone or concrete base below the ground on which a building is built; *the foundations of the building need to be made more solid;* **foundation course** = basic course at a university, which allows you to go on to a more advanced course

fountain ['faʊntɪn] *noun* jet of water sent into the air; *there is a statue and a fountain in the middle of the lake; on New Year's Eve people try to jump into the fountains in Trafalgar Square*

four [fɔː] **(a)** number 4; *he's four (years old); I have an appointment with the doctor at four (o'clock)* **(b)** crew of four people rowing in a boat; *our college four won the race* **(c)** *(in cricket)* score of four runs for sending the ball over the boundary; *he scored a century, including seven fours and two sixes*

fourteen [fɔː'tiːn] *number* 14; *he's fourteen (years old) next week;* **the fourteen hundreds (1400s)** = the period from 1400 to 1499 (compare with the 'fourteenth century')

fourteenth (14th) [fɔː'tiːnθ] *adjective & noun the fourteenth of July* or *July the fourteenth (July 14th); it was her fourteenth birthday yesterday;* **the fourteenth century** = the period from 1300 to 1399 (compare with the 'fourteen hundreds')

fourth (4th) [fɔːθ] *adjective; this is the fourth time he's had to go to hospital this year; it's her fourth birthday tomorrow; the fourth of October* or *October the fourth*

(October 4th); *King Charles IV (say 'King Charles the Fourth')* the fourth century = the period from 300 to 399 AD (NOTE: do not confuse with **forth**)

Fourth of July [ˈfɔːθ əv dʒʊˈlaɪ] *noun* the national day of the United States; *we're having a Fourth of July party*

fox [fɒks] *noun* clever wild animal with red fur and a thick tail; *a family of foxes live in the wood next to our house*

fraction [ˈfrækʃn] *noun* **(a)** *(in mathematics)* part of a whole number shown in figures; *1/4 and 1/2 are fractions* **(b)** small part of something; *only a fraction of the stolen money was ever found*

fracture [ˈfræktʃə] **1** *noun* break (especially in bones); *the X-ray showed up the fracture clearly* **2** *verb* to break a bone; *he fractured his leg in the accident*

fragile [ˈfrædʒaɪl] *adjective* easily broken; *be careful when packing the glasses - they're very fragile*

fragment *noun* [ˈfrægmənt] small piece; *when digging in the garden he found some fragments of pottery*

frame [freɪm] **1** *noun* border round glasses, a picture, mirror, window, etc.; *he has some new glasses with gold frames; I think the frame is worth more than the painting* **2** *verb* to put a frame round a picture; *the photograph has been framed in red*

France [frɑːns] *noun* country in Europe, south of Britain and west of Belgium and Germany; *last year we went to France on holiday; he's visiting friends in France* (NOTE: capital: **Paris**; people: **the French**; language: **French**)

fray [freɪ] *verb (of material)* to become worn so that threads are loose; *the carpet is fraying at the edges; you could see the frayed collar on his shirt*

free [friː] **1** *adjective* **(a)** not busy, not occupied; *will you be free next Tuesday?; there is a table free in the corner of the*

restaurant **(b)** not costing any money; *send in four labels cut from cereal boxes and you can get a free toy; I got a free ticket for the exhibition* **(c)** able to do what you want, not forced to do anything; *he's free to do what he wants* **(d)** not in prison, not in a cage; *lions wander free in the park*; to set free = to allow someone to leave prison, to let an animal out of a cage; *the young birds were raised in the zoo and then set free in the open* (NOTE: **freer - freest**) **2** *verb* **(a)** to release someone who is trapped, who is in prison; *it took the fire service some time to free the passengers in the bus*

freeze [friːz] *verb* **(a)** to change from liquid to solid because of the cold; *it's so cold that the lake has frozen solid* **(b)** to become very cold; *the forecast is that it will freeze tonight* **(c)** to make food very cold, so that it keeps; *we freeze a lot of vegetables from our garden* (NOTE: **froze** [frəʊz] - has **frozen**)

freezer [ˈfriːzə] *noun* refrigerator which freezes food and keeps it frozen; *put the ice cream back into the freezer before it starts to melt*

French [frentʃ] **1** *adjective* referring to France; *the French railways have a system of high speed trains covering the whole country* **2** *noun* **(a)** language spoken in France; *he speaks French very well* **(b)** the French = the people of France; *the French are famous for their wines and their cooking*

French fries [ˈfrentʃ ˈfraɪz] *noun* thin pieces of potato, shaped like sticks, fried in deep oil or fat (also called 'chips' in British English); *she ordered a hamburger and French fries*

frequent *adjective* [ˈfriːkwənt] happening often; often seen; *skin cancer is becoming more frequent; how frequent are the planes to Birmingham?*

frequently [ˈfriːkwəntli] *adverb* often; *she could frequently be seen walking her dog in the park*

fresh [freʃ] *adjective* **(a)** not used or not

dirty; **fresh air** = open air; *they were glad to come out of the tunnel into the fresh air* **(b)** made quite recently; *a basket of fresh rolls*; *let's ask for a fresh pot of coffee* **(c) fresh water** = water in rivers and lakes which contains no salt (as opposed to salt water in the sea) **(d)** not tinned or frozen; *fresh fruit salad is better than tinned; fresh vegetables are difficult to get in winter* (NOTE: fresher - freshest)

Friday ['fraɪdeɪ] *noun* the fifth day of the week, the day between Thursday and Saturday; *we had a meal together last Friday; we always go to the cinema on Friday evenings; we usually have our meetings on Fridays; the 15th is a Thursday, so the 16th must be a Friday;* **Good Friday** = the Friday before Easter Day

fridge [frɪdʒ] *noun (informal)* refrigerator, kitchen machine for keeping things cold; *shall I put the milk back in the fridge?*

fried [fraɪd] *adjective* which is cooked in a little oil or fat; *would you like a fried egg for breakfast?; we had fried rice with our sweet and sour pork*

friend [frend] *noun* person whom you know well and like; *Helen's my best friend; we're going on holiday with some friends from work;* **to make friends with someone** = to get to know and like someone; *we made friends with some French people on holiday*

friendly ['frendli] *adjective* like a friend, wanting to make friends; *don't be frightened of the dog - he's very friendly* (NOTE: friendlier - friendliest)

fries [fraɪz] *see* FRENCH, FRY

fright [fraɪt] *noun* fear; **to give someone a fright** = to make someone jump with fear; *don't creep up behind me like that - you gave me a fright!*

frightened ['fraɪtənd] *adjective* full of fear, scared; *the frightened children ran out of the building;* **frightened of something or someone** = afraid of someone or something; *don't be*

frightened of the dog - he won't hurt you

frightening ['fraɪtnɪŋ] *adjective* which makes someone afraid; *he had a frightening thought - what if no one heard his cries for help?*

frog [frɒg] *noun* small animal with long legs, which lives both on land and in water; *a little green frog hopped into the pond*

from [frɒm] *preposition* **(a)** away; *take three from four and you get one* **(b)** (showing the place where something starts or started) *he comes from Germany; we've had a letter from Uncle George* **(c)** (showing the time when something starts or started) *the hours of work are from 9.30 to 5.30; from now on I'm going to get up early* **(d)** (showing distance) *it is more than 3km from here to the railway station* **(e)** (showing difference) *his job is quite different from mine* **(f)** (showing a cause) *he died from the injuries he received in the accident*

front [frʌnt] **1** *noun* part of something which faces forward; *there is a picture of the Houses of Parliament on the front of the book; she spilt coffee down the front of her dress* **2** *adjective* which is in front; *she sat in the front seat, next to the driver*

in front of [ɪn 'frʌnt ɒv] *phrase* before something; *there are six people in front of me in the queue; you can park your car in front of the shop*

front door ['frʌnt 'dɔː] *noun* main door to a house or building; *he came to the front door when I rang the bell; she gave him a front door key*

frost [frɒst] *noun* **(a)** cold white layer on the ground, trees, etc., when the temperature is below freezing; *the garden was white with frost* **(b)** cold weather, when the temperature is below freezing; *there was a hard frost last night*

frown [fraʊn] *verb* to pull your eyebrows together because you are concentrating or worried; *he frowned as he tried to do the puzzle*

froze [frəʊz] *see* FREEZE

frozen ['frəʊzn] *adjective* **(a)** very cold; *come inside - you must be frozen out there* **(b)** at a temperature below freezing point; *we went skating on the frozen lake*; **frozen food** = food stored at a temperature below freezing point; *use frozen peas if you can't get fresh ones*; *see also* FREEZE

fruit [fruːt] *noun* part of a plant which has seeds and which is often eaten raw and is usually sweet; *I must remember to buy some fruit at the market*; **fruit salad** = pieces of different fruit, cut up and mixed together; *for pudding we had fruit salad and ice cream*

fry [fraɪ] *verb* to cook in oil or fat in a shallow pan; *fry the onions gently until they go brown*; *do you want your eggs fried or boiled?* (NOTE: **fries** [fraɪz] - **frying** - **fried** [fraɪd])

frying pan ['fraɪɪŋ pæn] *noun* shallow, open pan used for frying; *put some butter in the frying pan and fry the mushrooms*

ft = FOOT, FEET

fuel ['fjʊəl] *noun* substance (coal, gas, oil, petrol, wood, etc.) which can be burnt to give heat or power; *what fuel do you use to heat the house?*; *we ran out of fuel on the motorway*

full [fʊl] *adjective* **(a)** with as much inside as is possible; *is the box full?*; *the bag is full of potatoes*; *we couldn't get on the first bus because it was full* **(b)** complete; *write your full name and address at the top of the paper*; **he got full marks** = he got 100 out of 100 (NOTE: **fuller - fullest**)

full stop ['fʊl 'stɒp] *noun* **(a)** printed mark, a small dot (.), showing the end of a sentence or an abbreviation; *you should put a full stop after 'etc'* **(b)** complete stop; *the car slid across the road and came to a full stop when it hit a wall*

fun [fʌn] *noun* amusement; *having to stay in bed on my birthday is not much fun*; **to have fun** = to enjoy yourself; *we had a lot of fun on the river*

funds [fʌndz] *noun* money which is available for spending; *he started a course at college and then ran out of funds*

funeral ['fjuːnərəl] *noun* ceremony when a dead person is buried or burned; *the funeral will take place on Friday morning*

fungus ['fʌŋgəs] *noun* plant which has no green leaves or flowers and which lives on rotting stuff in damp places; *some fungi, such as mushrooms, can be eaten, but others are poisonous* (NOTE: plural is **fungi** ['fʌŋgaɪ])

funnel ['fʌnl] *noun* **(a)** tube with a wide mouth and narrow bottom used when pouring liquids from one container into another; *using a funnel, she poured the oil from the pan into a bottle* **(b)** chimney on a ship from which the smoke comes; *the liner sailed away, with smoke pouring out of her funnel*

funny ['fʌni] *adjective* **(a)** which makes you laugh; *he made funny faces and all the children laughed* **(b)** strange or odd; *she's been behaving in a funny way recently*; *there's a funny smell in the bathroom* (NOTE: **funnier - funniest**)

fur [fɜː] *noun* soft hair of an animal; *our cat has short white fur*; *she was wearing a fur coat* (NOTE: do not confuse with **fir**)

furious ['fjʊəriəs] *adjective* very angry; *he's furious because someone has scratched his new car*

furniture ['fɜːnɪtʃə] *noun* tables, chairs, beds, cupboards, etc.; *the burglars stole all our kitchen furniture*; *you should cover up the furniture before you start painting the ceiling*

furry ['fɜːri] *adjective* covered with fur; *a little furry caterpillar*

further ['fɜːðə] **1** *adverb* a greater distance; *can you all move further back, I can't get you in the picture*; *the police station is quite close, but the post office is further away* **2** *adjective* more; *please send me further details of holidays in Greece*; **further education** = teaching for people who have left school

furthest ['fɜːðəst] *see* FAR

fury ['fjʊəri] *noun* fierce anger; *in a fit of fury he threw the plate across the kitchen*

fuse [fjuːz] **1** *noun* small piece of wire in an electric circuit which prevents damage; *the plug has a 13-amp fuse*; *if the lights go out, the first thing to do is to check the fuses* **2** *verb* to break an electric circuit; *she fused the lights by plugging her hair drier into the wrong socket*

fuss [fʌs] **1** *noun* unnecessary excitement or complaints; **to make a fuss** *or* **to kick up a fuss about something** = to complain for a long time about something which is not important; *what's all the fuss about?*; *don't make such a fuss - it's only a little scratch* **2** *verb* **to fuss over something** = to worry about something, or to pay too much attention to something; *don't fuss - it will be all right*

future ['fjuːtʃə] **1** *noun* **(a)** time which has not yet happened; *what are his plans for the future?*; *can you imagine what London will be like in the future?* **(b)** **future (tense)** = form of a verb which shows that something will happen later; *'he will eat' and 'he is going to eat' are future forms of the verb 'to eat'* **2** *adjective* which is coming, which has not happened yet; *I try to save some money each week for future emergencies*

in future *phrase* from now on; *I must try to get to the French class on time in future*

Gg

G, g [dʒiː] seventh letter of the alphabet, between F and H; *'jogger' is spelt with two Gs*

g = GRAM

gadget ['gædʒɪt] *noun* useful tool; *I bought a gadget for taking the tops off bottles*

gain [geɪn] **1** *noun* increase in value, weight, quantity, size, etc.; **gain in experience** = getting more experience **2** *verb* **(a)** to get; *she gained some useful experience working on a farm* **(b)** *(of a clock, watch)* to move ahead of the correct time; *my watch gains five minutes a day*

galaxy ['gæləksi] *noun* huge group of stars; *there are vast numbers of galaxies in space* (NOTE: plural is **galaxies**)

gale [geɪl] *noun* very strong wind; *several trees were blown down in the gale*

galleon ['gæliən] *noun* large 16th century sailing ship; *divers found the wreck of a Spanish galleon*

gallery ['gæləri] *noun* **(a)** place where pictures and sculptures are shown to the public; *the National Gallery is in Trafalgar Square*; *the Tate Gallery has a collection of modern paintings* **(b)** **(art) gallery** = shop selling pictures or antiques; *she runs an art gallery selling pictures by local artists* **(c)** balcony inside a church, hall or theatre; **public gallery** = place in a court, meeting room, etc., where the public can sit to listen to what is being said (NOTE: plural is **galleries**)

galley ['gæli] *noun* **(a)** large ship rowed by men rowing; *Roman galleys had five sets of oars on each side* **(b)** kitchen on plane or ship; *the flight attendant will get you some water* *from the galley*

gallon [ˈgælən] *noun* measure of quantity of liquid; *a car which is cheap to run does 40 miles to the gallon*; *in Britain one gallon equals 4.55 litres, but in the USA only 3.78 litres*

gallop [ˈgæləp] **1** *noun* fast ride on a horse; *let's go for a gallop along the beach* **2** *verb* to go fast; *the soldiers galloped through the woods*

game [geɪm] *noun* **(a)** sport played according to set rules, which can be won with skill, strength or luck; *she's not very good at games* **(b)** single match between two opponents or two opposing teams; *do you want a game of snooker?*; *our team have won all their games this year* **(c)** single round in tennis, bridge, etc.; *he lost the first game, then won the next two* **(d)** Games = large organized sports competition; *the Olympic Games are held every four years*; *she won a gold medal in the Commonwealth Games*

gang [gæŋ] **1** *noun* **(a)** band of criminals, youths, etc.; *gangs of football fans wandered round the streets breaking shop windows* **(b)** group of workers; *gangs of men worked all night to repair the railway track* **2** *verb* to gang up on someone = to form a group to attack one person; *she felt as if the rest of the girls were ganging up on her*

gaol [dʒeɪl] *see* JAIL

gap [gæp] *noun* space between two things; *the sheep all rushed through the gap in the hedge*; gap year = year which a student takes off from his or her studies, between finishing school and starting at university; *she spent her gap year working in Australia*

gape [geɪp] *verb* to open your mouth wide in surprise or shock; *he gaped when he saw the bill*

garage [ˈgærɪdʒ or ˈgærɑːʒ] *noun* **(a)** small building where you can keep a car; *she drove the car out of the garage*; *don't forget to lock the garage door* **(b)** business where petrol is sold and cars are repaired or sold; *where's the nearest garage? - I need some petrol*; *I can't drive you to the station - my car is in the garage*

garbage [ˈgɑːbɪdʒ] *noun* US *(informal)* rubbish; household waste; *don't forget to put the garbage out*

garbage can [ˈgɑːbɪdʒ ˈkæn] *noun* US large plastic or metal container for household rubbish; *they come to empty the garbage cans once a week*

garden [ˈgɑːdən] *noun* **(a)** piece of ground near a house, used for growing vegetables, flowers, etc.; *we grow all the vegetables we need in the back garden*; *I keep my tools in the garden shed* **(b)** gardens = large area of garden, usually in several sections; *the hotel is surrounded by flower gardens*; *when you're in London you must visit Kew Gardens*

garlic [ˈgɑːlɪk] *noun* bulb of a plant with a strong smell, a little like an onion; *his breath smelled of garlic*

gas [gæs] *noun* **(a)** chemical substance which has no shape and which becomes liquid if it is cooled; *air is formed of several gases, but mainly oxygen* **(b)** chemical substance used for cooking or heating; *there is a smell of gas in the kitchen*; *turn the gas up - the kettle hasn't boiled yet* **(c)** US liquid used to drive a car engine (British English is 'petrol'); *we ran out of gas on the way to Detroit*

gasoline [ˈgæsəliːn] *noun* = GAS (c)

gasp [gɑːsp] **1** *noun* sudden breath showing you are surprised or hurt; *she gave a gasp when she saw the face at the window* **2** *verb* to take a short deep breath; to have difficulty in breathing; *after the race he lay on the ground gasping for breath*

gate [geɪt] *noun* **(a)** low door made of bars of wood or metal, in a wall or fence, not in a building; *shut the gate - if you leave it open the sheep will get out of the field* **(b)** door which leads to an aircraft at an airport; *flight AZ270 is now boarding at Gate 23*

gather ['gæðə] *verb* **(a)** to come together; *groups of people gathered outside the law courts* **(b)** to understand; *I gather that his father is in hospital* **(c)** to pick plants, flowers, fruit, etc.; *the children were gathering blackberries*

gave [geɪv] *see* GIVE

gaze [geɪz] *verb* to look steadily; *he stood on the cliff, gazing out to sea*

GB ['dʒiː 'biː] = GREAT BRITAIN *British cars which are travelling abroad have GB stickers*

gear ['gɪə] *noun* **(a)** equipment; *he took all his climbing gear with him* **(b)** *(of car, bicycle, etc.)* **gears** = arrangement of wheels of different sizes with teeth which link together, that control the rate at which the machine moves; **bottom gear** = the lowest gear, used when going slowly, or when climbing hills; **top gear** = the highest gear, used for fast speeds; *always use a low gear when going down steep hills*

geese [giːs] *see* GOOSE

general ['dʒenərəl] **1** *adjective* referring to everything, everybody; *there was a general feeling of excitement in the college*; **in general** = usually, in the usual way; *in general, the weather is warmer in the south*; **general election** = election where everyone can vote for a new government **2** *noun* army officer of high rank; *General Robinson is in command*

generally ['dʒenərəli] *adverb* usually, in a general way; *the college is generally closed between Christmas and the New Year*

generous ['dʒenərəs] *adjective* **(a)** willing to give money or presents gladly; *he got a generous birthday present from his aunt* **(b)** large; *a generous helping of pudding*

gentle ['dʒentl] *adjective* **(a)** soft and kind; *the nurse has gentle hands* **(b)** not very strong; *he gave the door a gentle push* **(c)** not very steep; *there is a gentle slope down to the lake* (NOTE: gentler - gentlest)

gentleman *noun (polite way of referring to a man) this gentleman is waiting to be served*; **'ladies and gentlemen'** = way of starting to talk to a group of men and women (NOTE: plural is **gentlemen)**

gently ['dʒentli] *adverb* **(a)** carefully, in a soft way; *he gently put the blanket over the baby* **(b)** not very steep; *the path rises gently to the top of the hill*

genuine ['dʒenjuɪn] *adjective* real, true; *the painting was not a genuine Picasso*

geography [dʒiː'ɒgrəfi] *noun* study of the earth's surface, weather, countries, etc.; *we're studying the geography of the Thames Valley*; *I've lost my geography book*

geranium [dʒə'reɪniəm] *noun* brightly coloured summer flower, usually red or pink; *they put pots of geraniums outside the front door*

germ [dʒɜːm] *noun* tiny thing which causes disease; *wash your hands after emptying the dustbin so you don't spread any germs*

German ['dʒɜːmən] **1** *adjective* referring to Germany; *there are three German players in the team* **2** *noun* **(a)** language spoken in Germany, Austria and parts of Switzerland and Italy; *do you know the German for 'one - two - three'?*; *'Tisch' in German means 'table'* **(b)** person from Germany; *our neighbours are Germans*

Germany ['dʒɜːməni] *proper noun* large west European country, to the east of France, and west of Poland; *last March we went to Germany*; *they used to live in Germany* (NOTE: capital: **Berlin**; people: **Germans**; language: **German)**

get [get] *verb* **(a)** to receive; *we got a letter from the bank this morning*; *he will get £10 for washing the car* **(b)** to become; *I'm getting too old to play rugby*; *he's got much fatter over the last year or so* **(c)** to have something done; *we got the car mended in time to go on holiday* **(d)** to persuade someone to do something; *she got a policeman to show* *her the way* (e) to catch (an illness); *I think I'm getting a cold*; *half the people in our class have got flu* (f) to make something become; *she's busy getting the meal ready* (g) to travel on a train, bus, etc.; *I got the 8.30 train* (NOTE: **getting - got** [gɒt] **- has got** US **gotten**)

get across ['get ə'krɒs] *verb* (a) to manage to cross; *they got across the river by boat* (b) to make someone understand; *I'm trying to get across to the students that they all have to work harder*

get along ['get ə'lɒŋ] *verb* (a) to manage; *we seem to get along very well without the telephone* (b) **to get along (with someone)** = to be friendly with someone, to work well with someone; *I don't think they get along*

get around ['get ə'raʊnd] *verb* to move from place to place; *since he had his accident he gets around on two sticks*

get at ['get 'æt] *verb* (a) to reach; *you'll need to stand on a chair to get at the box on the top shelf* (b) *(informal)* **to get at someone** = to criticize someone all the time; *she thinks she's being got at*

get away ['get ə'weɪ] *verb* (a) to escape; *the robbers got away in a stolen car* (b) **to get away with something** = not to be punished for having done something; *he was rude to the teacher but got away with it somehow*; *(formal)* **to get away with murder** = to do something really bad and still not be punished for it; *he's the teacher's favourite and she lets him get away with murder* (c) *(informal)* **get away with you!** = don't try to make me believe that!

get back ['get 'bæk] *verb* (a) to return; *they got back home very late*; *when did they get back from the cinema?* (b) to get something again which you had before; *I got my money back after I had complained to the manager*

get down ['get 'daʊn] *verb* (a) to go back down onto the ground; *the cat climbed up the tree and couldn't get down* (b) to bring down; *can you get that box on the top shelf down for me?*

get dressed ['get 'drest] *verb* to put your clothes on; *if the house catches fire, don't wait to get dressed, just jump out of a window*

get going ['get 'gəʊɪŋ] *verb (informal)* to start; *come on, let's get going!*

get in ['get 'ɪn] *verb* (a) to go inside (a car, etc.); *the burglars must have got in through the bathroom window* (b) to ask someone to come to do a job; *we'll get a builder in to mend the wall*

get into ['get 'ɪntuː] *verb* (a) to go inside (a car, etc.); *they got into the back of the car* (b) **to get into the habit of** = to start to do something in a regular way; *he got into the habit of calling his father 'the Boss'*

get off ['get 'ɒf] *verb* to come down from or out of (a vehicle, etc.); *she got off her bicycle at the red light*; *if you want the post office, you should get off at the next stop*

get on ['get 'ɒn] *verb* (a) to go inside or onto (a vehicle, etc.); *they got on the bus at the bank* (b) *(informal)* to become old; *he's getting on and can't work as hard as he used to* (c) **to get on (well)** = to do well; *she's getting on well at college* (d) **to get on with someone** = to be friendly with someone; *she doesn't get on with her new boss*

get out ['get 'aʊt] *verb* (a) to go out of something; *the bus stopped and the driver got out* (b) **to get out of the habit of doing something** = not to do something any more; *I've got out of the habit of eating meat*

get over ['get 'əʊvə] *verb* (a) to climb over; *they got over the wall into the garden* (b) to become better; *he's got over his flu*

get ready ['get 'redi] *phrase* (a) to prepare yourself for something; *how long will it take you to get ready for the wedding?* (b) to get something prepared; *we need to get the dinner ready - everyone will be arriving in 30 minutes*

get round ['get 'raʊnd] *verb* **to get round to (doing) something** = to do something at last; *he only got round to sending his Christmas cards in the week before Christmas*

get through [ˈget ˈθruː] *verb* **(a)** to go through; *the sheep got through the hole in the fence* **(b)** to be successful; *he got through all his exams*

get to [ˈget ˈtʊ] *verb* **(a)** to arrive, to reach (a place); *when does your train get to London?* **(b) to have got to** = must, to be forced to; *you've got to come*; *he's got to be at the station at 8 o'clock*

get up [ˈget ˈʌp] *verb* **(a)** to get out of bed; *it is 9.30 and John still hasn't got up* **(b)** to make someone get out of bed; *you must get everyone up by 7.30 if we are going to leave on time* **(c)** to stand up; *he got up from the table and walked out of the room*

ghost [gəʊst] *noun* image of a dead person which appears; *they say the Tower of London is haunted by the ghost of Anne Boleyn, who was executed there*

giant [ˈdʒaɪənt] **1** *noun (in children's stories)* very large man; *a story about a giant who lived in a castle at the top of a mountain* **2** *adjective* very large; *they are planning a giant party for her 18th birthday*

giddy [ˈgɪdi] *adjective* dizzy, feeling that everything is turning round; *she felt giddy and had to sit down*

gift [gɪft] *noun* present, something given to someone; *she was wrapping up gifts to put under the Christmas tree*

gigantic [dʒaɪˈgæntɪk] *adjective* very large, huge; *he was eating a gigantic sandwich*

giggle [ˈgɪgl] **1** *noun* little laugh, often showing you are embarrassed; **fit of the giggles** = attack of laughter which you cannot stop; *when the fat lady came onto the stage, I had a fit of the giggles* **2** *verb* to make a little laugh; *when he saw his mother's hat he started giggling*

ginger [ˈdʒɪndʒə] **1** *noun* plant whose root has a sharp burning taste and is used in cooking; **ginger biscuits** = hard biscuits, flavoured with ginger **2** *adjective* bright orange in colour; *a ginger cat sat outside the door in the sun*

gingerbread [ˈdʒɪndʒəbred] *noun* dark cake flavoured with ginger; **gingerbread man** = children's cake, made of gingerbread in the shape of a man

giraffe [dʒɪˈrɑːf] *noun* large African animal with a very long neck; *because of their long necks, giraffes can eat leaves from tall trees*

girl [gɜːl] *noun* female child; *they have four children - two boys and two girls*

girlfriend [ˈgɜːlfrend] *noun* girl or woman, usually young, that someone is very friendly with; *he's broken up with his girlfriend*

give [gɪv] *verb* **(a)** to send or pass something to someone as a present; *we gave her flowers for her birthday* **(b)** to pass something to someone; *give me another piece of cake* **(c)** to do something (to someone); *he gave her a kiss* **(d)** to organize; *we gave a party to celebrate her twenty-first birthday* (NOTE: **giving - gave** [geɪv] **- has given** [ˈgɪvn])

give back [ˈgɪv ˈbæk] *verb* to hand something back to someone; *give me back my watch*; *she borrowed my book and hasn't given it back*

give in [ˈgɪv ˈɪn] *verb* to agree to do something even if you didn't want to do it; *the children kept on asking their father to let them go to the cinema and in the end he gave in*

give up [ˈgɪv ˈʌp] *verb* **(a)** to stop doing something; *she's trying to give up smoking* **(b) I give up** = I don't know the answer

give way [ˈgɪv ˈweɪ] *phrase* **(a)** to let someone go first; *give way to cars at a road junction* **(b)** to collapse; *the chair gave way when he sat on it* **(c)** to stop objecting to something; *in the end father gave way and let us go camping by ourselves*

glad [glæd] *adjective* pleased; *after walking all day, she was glad to sit down*

gladly [ˈglædli] *adverb* in a pleased way, with great pleasure; *I'll gladly look after your dog while you're away*

glance [glɑːns] **1** *noun* quick look; *she took a quick glance over her shoulder* **2** *verb* to look quickly; *he glanced backwards to see who was following him*

glare [ˈgleə] **1** *noun* **(a)** very bright light; *the glare of the sun on the wet road blinded me* **(b)** fierce look; *he gave her a glare and walked on* **2** *verb* to look angrily; *she glared at me and went on reading her book*

glass [glɑːs] *noun* **(a)** material which you can see through, used to make windows, etc.; *the house has a glass roof; a car with black glass windows* **(b)** thing to drink out of, usually made of glass; *we took plastic wine glasses on the picnic; he broke two glasses when he was washing up* **(c)** liquid contained in a glass; *he was so thirsty he drank three glasses of water; she drinks a glass of milk each evening before she goes to bed* (NOTE: plural is **glasses)**

glasses [ˈglɑːsɪz] *noun* two pieces of plastic or glass in a frame which you wear in front of your eyes to help you see better; *have you seen my glasses anywhere?; she has to wear glasses to read;* **dark glasses** = glasses made of dark glass, for wearing in sunshine

glide [glaɪd] *verb* to move in a smooth way; *young people were gliding across the ice in time to the music*

glider [ˈglaɪdə] *noun* aircraft which flies without a motor; *the glider rose slowly up above the clouds*

glimpse [glɪmps] **1** *noun* brief sight; *we caught a glimpse of the princess as she drove past* **2** *verb* to catch sight of; *we only glimpsed the back of her head as she was leaving*

globe [gləʊb] *noun* **(a)** map of the world on a ball; *he spun the globe round and pointed to Canada* **(b) the globe** = the earth; *he is trying to be the first person to fly round the globe in a balloon* **(c) the Globe (Theatre)** = one of the original London theatres where Shakespeare's plays were performed, now built again; *have you seen the production of 'Henry V' at the Globe?*

gloomy [ˈgluːmi] *adjective* **(a)** miserable, unhappy; *she was gloomy about her chances of passing the exam* **(b)** dark; *a gloomy Sunday afternoon in November* (NOTE: **gloomier - gloomiest)**

glossy [ˈglɒsi] *adjective* shiny; **glossy magazines** = expensive colour magazines, printed on shiny paper (NOTE: **glossier - glossiest)**

glove [glʌv] *noun* piece of clothing worn on your hand; *she gave him a pair of gloves for his birthday*

glow [gləʊ] *verb* to shine with a red colour; *the logs glowed in the fireplace; her face glowed with pride*

glue [gluː] **1** *noun* material which sticks things together; *she spread the glue carefully onto the back of the poster; the glue on the envelope doesn't stick very well* **2** *verb* to stick things together; *he glued the label to the box*

gnaw [nɔː] *verb* to chew, to bite something again and again; *the dog was gnawing a bone*

gnome [nəʊm] *noun (in children's fairy stories)* little man with a beard and a pointed hat; **garden gnome** = little coloured statue of a gnome, used as a garden decoration

go [gəʊ] **1** *verb* **(a)** to move from one place to another; *she is going to London for the weekend; she was going downstairs when she fell; she has gone shopping* **(b)** *(of engine)* to work; *he's trying to get his motorbike to go* **(c)** to leave; *the last bus goes at half past two* **(d)** to fit; *this case won't go into the back of the car* **(e)** to be placed; *that book goes on the top shelf* **(f)** to become; *her face went red from sitting in the sun* **(g)** to happen (successfully or not); *the party went very well* **(h)** to make a sound; *do you remember the song that goes: 'there's no place like home'?* (NOTE: **going - went** [went] **- has gone** [gɒn]) **2** *noun* **(a) on the go** = always busy; *the shop is so busy before Christmas that we're on the go* *from morning till night* **(b)** try, attempt; *he won the lottery at the first go*

to be going to [biː ˈɡəʊɪŋ tuː] *phrase* **(a)** *(showing future)* *I hope it's going to be fine tomorrow*; *he's going to be a great tennis player when he's older* **(b)** to be going to do something = to be about to do something; *watch out - that tree is going to fall down!*

go ahead [ˈɡəʊ əˈhed] *verb* to start; *the project went ahead even though there were not enough staff*

go-ahead [ˈɡəʊəhed] *noun* to give something the go-ahead = to give permission for something to start; *we got the council's go-ahead to build the new supermarket*

go away [ˈɡəʊ əˈweɪ] *verb* to leave; *he went away and we never saw him again*

go back [ˈɡəʊ ˈbæk] *verb* to return; *she worked for two years and then went back to college*

go back on [ˈɡəʊ ˈbæk ɒn] *verb* not to do what has been promised; *he promised to lend me his car, and then went back on his promise*

go down [ˈɡəʊ daʊn] *verb* to go to a lower level; *be careful when going down the hill*

go down with [ˈɡəʊ daʊn ˈwɪθ] *verb* *(informal)* to catch a disease; *half the crew went down with flu*

go in [ˈɡəʊ ˈɪn] *verb* to enter; *she opened the door and went in*

go in for [ˈɡəʊ ˈɪn fɔː] *verb* to take (an examination); *she went in for her swimming test*

go into [ˈɡəʊ ˈɪntuː] *verb* **(a)** to enter; *she went into the bedroom* **(b)** to examine, to look at something carefully; *the bank wants to go into the details of his account*

go off [ˈɡəʊ ˈɒf] *verb* **(a)** to go to another place; *he went off to look for a parking space* **(b)** to start working suddenly; *the burglar alarm went off in the middle of the night* **(c)** to explode; *the bomb went off when there were still lots of people in the building*

go on [ˈɡəʊ ˈɒn] *verb* **(a)** to continue; *please*

go on, I like hearing you sing*; *they went on working in spite of the fire* **(b)** to happen; *what's been going on here?*

go out [ˈɡəʊ ˈaʊt] *verb* **(a)** to leave a building; *he forgot to lock the door when he went out* **(b)** not to be burning any more; *the fire went out and the room got cold*

go round [ˈɡəʊ ˈraʊnd] *verb* **(a)** to turn; *the wheels went round and round* **(b)** to visit; *you'll need at least two hours to go round the museum* **(c)** to be enough for; *there wasn't enough ice cream to go round all twelve of us*

go up [ˈɡəʊ ˈʌp] *verb* **(a)** to go to a higher place; *she took the lift and went up to the fourth floor* **(b)** to increase, to rise to a higher level; *the price of bread has gone up again*

go with [ˈɡəʊ ˈwɪθ] *verb* to match, to fit with; *blue shoes won't go with a green dress*; *red wine goes best with meat*

go without [ˈɡəʊ wɪˈðaʊt] *verb* not to have something which you usually have; *we have too much work, so we'll have to go without a holiday this year*

go wrong [ˈɡəʊ ˈrɒŋ] *phrase* to stop working properly; *something has gone wrong with the central heating*

goal [ɡəʊl] *noun* **(a)** *(in games)* two posts between which you have to send the ball to score a point; *he kicked and missed the goal* **(b)** *(in games)* point scored by sending the ball between the posts; *our team scored three goals* **(c)** aim; *his goal is to become a millionaire before he is thirty*

goalkeeper [ˈɡəʊlkiːpə] *noun* player who stands in front of the goal to stop the ball going in; *the goalkeeper dropped the ball and the other team scored*

goat [ɡəʊt] *noun* small farm animal with horns and a beard, giving milk and wool; *they keep a herd of goats*

God [ɡɒd] **1** *noun* the most important being, the being to whom people pray; *we pray to God that the children will be found alive* **2** *interjection* **(a)** *(showing surprise, etc.)* *God, what awful weather!*; *my God, have you seen* *how late it is?* **(b)** *(showing thanks)* **Thank God no one was hurt in the crash!**

goddess [ˈgɒdes] *noun* female god; *Diana was the goddess of hunting* (NOTE: plural is **goddesses**)

goes [gəʊz] *see* GO

gold [gəʊld] *noun* **(a)** very valuable metal with a yellow colour; *gold is worth more than silver*; *he wears a gold ring on his left ear* **(b)** **gold (medal)** = medal given to someone who finishes first in a race or competition; *England won three golds at the Olympics*

golden [ˈgəʊldən] *adjective* coloured like gold; *she has beautiful golden hair*; **golden wedding (anniversary)** = celebration when two people have been married for fifty years

goldfish [ˈgəʊldfɪʃ] *noun* small orange fish which is kept as a pet; *he won a goldfish at the fair and brought it home in a plastic bag* (NOTE: plural is **goldfish**)

golf [gɒlf] *noun* a game played on a large grass course in the open air; *in golf, you hit a small ball into 18 separate holes in the ground, using as few strokes as possible*; *he plays golf every Saturday*

golf club [ˈgɒlf ˈklʌb] *noun* **(a)** stick used to hit the ball in golf; *she put her golf clubs into the back of the car* **(b)** organization for people who play golf together; *he's joined his local golf club*

gone [gɒn] *see* GO

good [gʊd] **1** *adjective* **(a)** not bad; *we had a good breakfast and then started work* **(b)** clever; *he's good at making things out of wood* **(c)** who behaves well; *be a good girl and I'll give you a sweet*; *have you been good while we've been away?* **(d)** **a good deal of** or **a good many** = a lot of; *a good many people saw that TV programme* **(e)** **good for** = making better or healthy; *running a mile before breakfast is good for you* (NOTE: **good - better** [ˈbetə] - **best** [best]) **2** *noun* **(a)** advantage, making better; *the medicine didn't do me any good* **(b)** **for good** = for ever; *he's left the*

town for good

goodbye [gʊdˈbaɪ] *noun & interjection*; *(used when leaving someone)* **say goodbye to your teacher**; *goodbye! we'll see you again on Thursday*

good evening [ˈgʊd ˈiːvnɪŋ] *interjection (used when meeting or leaving someone in the evening)* **good evening, Mrs Smith!**

Good Friday [ˈgʊd ˈfraɪdeɪ] *noun* the Friday before Easter Day; *by tradition, hot cross buns are eaten on Good Friday*

good-looking [ˈgʊdˈlʊkɪŋ] *adjective (of a person)* pleasant to look at; *she's far better-looking than her sister*

good morning [ˈgʊd ˈmɔːnɪŋ] *interjection (used when meeting or leaving someone in the morning)* **good morning, Mr Smith!**

goodnight [gʊdˈnaɪt] *interjection (used when leaving someone late in the evening)* **goodnight, everyone! sleep well!**

goods [gʊdz] *noun* things that are produced to be sold; *the company sells goods from various European countries*; **goods train** = train for carrying goods, not passengers

goose [guːs] *noun* large bird, living near water, either wild or bred on farms; *a flock of wild geese landed in the field* (NOTE: plural is **geese** [giːs])

gossip [ˈgɒsɪp] **1** *noun* stories or news about someone, which may or may not be true; *have you heard the latest gossip about Sue?* **2** *verb* to talk about people; *they spent hours gossiping about the people working in the office*

got [gɒt] *see* GET

gotten [ˈgɒtn] *US see* GET

govern [ˈgʌvən] *verb* to rule a country; *the country is governed by three generals*

government [ˈgʌvəmənt] *noun* **(a)** people or political party which governs a country; *the government ought to do something to help poor people* **(b)** **central government** = main organization, dealing with the affairs of the whole country; **local government** =

organizations dealing with the affairs of small areas of the country, such as towns and counties

grab [græb] *verb* **(a)** to pick something up suddenly; *he grabbed his suitcase and ran to the train* **(b)** to get something quickly; *let's grab some lunch before the game starts* (NOTE: grabbing - grabbed)

graceful ['greɪsfʊl] *adjective* moving in a smooth and beautiful way; *she crossed the stage with graceful steps*

gradual ['grædjʊəl] *adjective* which changes a little at a time; *we're forecasting a gradual improvement in the weather*

gradually ['grædjʊəli] *adverb* little by little; *the snow gradually melted*

graffiti [grə'fiːti] *noun* writing on walls in public places; *they're trying to remove the graffiti from railway carriages*

grain [greɪn] *noun* **(a)** cereal crop; *the grain harvest has been good this year* **(b)** a very small piece; *a grain of sand*

gram *or* **gramme** [græm] *noun* weight equal to one thousandth of a kilogram; *you will need 250g (250 grams) of sugar*

grammar ['græmə] *noun* **(a)** rules of a language; *Russian grammar is very difficult* **(b)** book of rules of a language; *I'll look it up in my new German grammar*

grand [grænd] *adjective* **(a)** big and important; *he explained his grand plan for making a lot of money*; *we went to a very grand wedding* **(b)** final; **grand total** = the total of all the figures (NOTE: grander - grandest)

grandad ['grændæd] *noun (informal)* grandfather; *tell me a story, grandad!*

grandchild ['græntʃaɪld] *noun* child of a son or daughter; *all her six grandchildren came to her eightieth birthday party* (NOTE: plural is grandchildren ['græntʃɪldrən])

granddaughter ['grændɔːtə] *noun* daughter of a son or daughter; *my granddaughter is*

nineteen now, and at university

grandfather ['grænfɑːðə] *noun* father of your mother or father; *tomorrow is grandfather's hundredth birthday*; **a grandfather clock** = a tall clock that stands on the floor

grandma ['grænmɑː] *noun (informal)* grandmother; *how old is your grandma?*

grandmother ['grænmʌðə] *noun* mother of your mother or father; *grandmother showed me how to make bread*

grandpa ['grænpɑː] *noun (informal)* grandfather; *is grandpa coming to the party?*

grandparents ['grænpeərənts] *noun* parents of your mother or father; *my grandparents are all dead*

grandson ['grænsʌn] *noun* son of a son or daughter; *her grandson is nearly eighteen, and will be leaving school soon*

granny ['græni] *noun (informal)* grandmother; *tell me a story, granny!*; **granny flat** = small separate flat in a large house, for a relative to live in (though not necessarily a granny)

grant [grɑːnt] **1** *noun* sum of money to help; *not many students get a full grant*; *my grant only pays for a few books* **2** *verb* to agree to give something; *the government has granted them a loan at very low interest*

grape [greɪp] *noun* fruit of the vine, eaten as dessert or used to make wine; *he bought a bunch of grapes*

grapefruit ['greɪpfruːt] *noun* large yellow fruit, like an orange but not as sweet; *she asked for a glass of grapefruit juice* (NOTE: plural is grapefruit)

graph [grɑːf] *noun* chart showing figures in the form of a line; *he drew a graph to show the increase in students getting top marks*

graphics ['græfɪks] *noun* pictures on a computer screen or designed on a computer; *the graphics on this game are brilliant*

grasp [grɑːsp] *verb* **(a)** to hold tight; *she grasped the branch of the tree with both* hands **(b)** to understand; *they didn't seem to grasp my meaning*

grass [grɑːs] *noun* low green plant, which is eaten by sheep and cows in fields, or used in gardens to make lawns; *the cows are eating the fresh green grass*; *we'll sit on the grass and have our picnic*

grate [greɪt] **1** *noun* metal frame for holding coal in a fireplace; *he put some more coal in the grate* **2** *verb* to make into small pieces by rubbing against a rough surface; *sprinkle grated cheese over your pasta* (NOTE: do not confuse with **great**)

grateful [ˈgreɪtfʊl] *adjective* showing thanks for something that someone has done for you; *we are most grateful to you for your help*

grave [greɪv] **1** *noun* hole in the ground where a dead person is buried; *at the funeral, the whole family stood by the grave*; *(informal)* **to have one foot in the grave** = to be getting old **2** *adjective* quietly serious; *she looked at him with a grave expression* (NOTE: graver - gravest)

gravity [ˈgrævɪti] *noun* force which pulls things towards the ground; *apples fall to the ground because of the earth's gravity*; **centre of gravity** = the point in an object at which it will balance without falling over; *a bus has a very low centre of gravity*

gravy [ˈgreɪvi] *noun* brown sauce from meat during cooking, served with meat; *can I have some more gravy with my meat?*

gray [greɪ] *US* = GREY

graze [greɪz] **1** *noun* slight wound where the skin has been rubbed off; *he had a graze on his knee* **2** *verb* **(a)** to hurt the skin slightly; *he fell off his bicycle and grazed his knee* **(b)** to feed on grass; *the sheep were grazing in the fields*

grease [griːs] **1** *noun* thick oil; *put some grease on your back wheel* **2** *verb* to cover with oil; *don't forget to grease the wheels*

great [greɪt] *adjective* **(a)** large; *we visited the Great Wall of China*; *she was carrying a*

great big pile of sandwiches; **a great deal of** or **a great many** = a lot of; *there's a great deal of work to be done* **(b)** important or famous; *who was the greatest tennis player of all time?* **(c)** *(informal)* wonderful, very good; *what did you think of the film? - it was great!* (NOTE: do not confuse with **grate**. Note also: **greater - greatest**)

Great Britain (GB) [ˈgreɪt ˈbrɪtən] *noun* country formed of England, Scotland and Wales (which with Northern Ireland makes up the United Kingdom); *in Great Britain cars drive on the left hand side of the road* (NOTE: capital: **London**; people: **British**; language: **English**)

greatly [ˈgreɪtli] *adverb* very much; *they greatly enjoyed the birthday party*

Greece [griːs] *noun* country in southern Europe; *we go to Greece on holiday every year* (NOTE: capital: **Athens**; people: **Greeks**; language: **Greek**)

greedy [ˈgriːdi] *adjective* always wanting food; *don't be greedy - you've already had two pieces of cake* (NOTE: greedier - greediest)

Greek [griːk] **1** *adjective* referring to Greece; *he's opened a Greek restaurant near us* **2** *noun* **(a)** person from Greece; *the ancient Greeks lived many years before the Romans* **(b)** language spoken in Greece; *she bought a Greek phrase book before going on holiday*

green [griːn] **1** *adjective* **(a)** of a colour like the colour of grass; *he was wearing a bright green shirt*; *they painted the door dark green* **(b)** relating to, interested in, or concerned about the environment; *she's very worried about green problems* (NOTE: greener - greenest) **2** *noun* **(a)** colour like grass; *have you any paint of a darker green than this?* **(b)** piece of public land covered with grass in the middle of a village; *they were playing cricket on the village green* **(c) greens** = green vegetables, especially cabbage; *eat up your greens - they're good for you*

greenhouse [ˈgriːnhaʊs] *noun* glass building for growing plants; *we grow tomatoes in our greenhouse in winter*; **greenhouse effect** =

effect of gases in the earth's atmosphere which makes the climate warmer (NOTE: plural is **greenhouses** ['griːnhaʊzɪz])

greet [griːt] *verb* to meet someone and say hello; *she greeted him with a kiss*

greetings ['griːtɪŋz] *noun* good wishes; *Christmas greetings from all our family!*

grew [gruː] *see* GROW

grey *US* **gray** [greɪ] **1** *noun* colour like a mixture of black and white; *he was dressed all in grey* **2** *adjective* of a colour like a mixture of black and white; *her hair has turned quite grey* (NOTE: **greyer - greyest**)

grief [griːf] *noun* very sad feeling; *she couldn't hide her grief as they told her the news*

grill [grɪl] **1** *noun* part of a cooker where food is cooked under the heat; *cook the chops under the grill* **2** *verb* to cook under a grill; *do you want your fish grilled or fried?*

grim [grɪm] *adjective* **(a)** stern and not smiling; *the head teacher's expression was grim* **(b)** grey and unpleasant; *the town centre is really grim* (NOTE: **grimmer - grimmest**)

grin [grɪn] **1** *noun* broad smile; *she gave me a big grin* **2** *verb* to give a broad smile; *he grinned when we asked him if he liked his job* (NOTE: **grinning - grinned**)

grind [graɪnd] *verb* **(a)** to crush to powder; *a cup of fresh ground coffee* **(b)** to rub surfaces together; **to grind your teeth** = to rub your teeth together and make a noise (usually because you are annoyed); **to grind to a halt** = to stop working gradually; *the driver put on the brakes and the train ground to a halt* (NOTE: **grinding - ground** [graʊnd])

grip [grɪp] **1** *noun* firm hold; *these new tyres give a better grip on the road surface*; **to lose your grip** = not to be as much in control as before **2** *verb* **(a)** to hold tight; *she gripped the rail with both hands* **(b)** to be very interesting; *the story gripped me from the first page* (NOTE: **gripping - gripped**)

groove [gruːv] *noun* wide line cut into a surface; *the door slides along a groove in the floor*

gross [grəʊs] **1** *adjective* total, with nothing taken away; **gross income** *or* **gross salary** = salary which is paid without taking away any tax, insurance, etc. (NOTE: **grosser - grossest**) **2** *adverb* with nothing taken away; *his salary is paid gross* **3** *noun* twelve dozen (i.e. 144); *we ordered two gross of the bars of chocolate*

ground [graʊnd] **1** *noun* **(a)** soil or earth; *you should dig the ground in the autumn* **(b)** surface of the earth; *the factory was burnt to the ground*; *there were no seats, so we had to sit on the ground* **(c)** land used for a special purpose; *the fans were arriving at the local football ground* **2** *verb see* GRIND

ground floor ['graʊnd 'flɔː] *noun* floor (in a shop, block of flats, etc.) which is level with the street (in America, this is the 'first floor'); *the men's department is on the ground floor*

grounds ['graʊndz] *plural noun* **(a)** land around a big house; *the police searched the grounds of the school for the weapon* **(b)** reasons; *what grounds have you got for saying that?*

group [gruːp] *noun* **(a)** a number of people or things taken together; *groups of people gathered in the street* **(b)** way of classifying things; **blood group** = people with the same type of blood **(c)** people playing music together; *she sings the lead with a pop group*

grow [grəʊ] *verb* **(a)** to live (as a plant); *there was grass growing in the middle of the road* **(b)** to make plants grow; *we are going to grow some carrots this year* **(c)** to become taller or bigger; *he's grown a lot since I last saw him* (NOTE: **growing - grew** [gruː] - **grown** [grəʊn])

grow up ['grəʊ 'ʌp] *verb* to become an adult; *what does your son want to do when he grows up?*

grown [grəʊn] *adjective (person)* of full size; *a grown man like you shouldn't be afraid of* *a little spider*

growth [grəʊθ] *noun* increase in size, becoming bigger; *the rapid growth of the population since 1980*

grumble ['grʌmbl] *verb* **to grumble about something** = to complain about something; *he's always grumbling about the noise from the flat above*

guarantee [gærən'tiː] **1** *noun* legal document which promises that a machine is in good condition and will work without problems for a certain length of time; *the fridge is sold with a twelve-month guarantee*; **under guarantee** = covered by a guarantee; *the car is still under guarantee, so the garage will pay for the repairs* **2** *verb* to give a firm promise that something will work, that something will be done; *the product is guaranteed for twelve months*; *you can almost guarantee to have good weather in the Caribbean at this time of year*

guard [gɑːd] **1** *noun* **(a) to be on guard** *or* **to keep guard** = to be looking out for danger; *you must be on your guard against burglars at all times* **(b)** person who protects, often a soldier; *armed guards patrol the factory at night* **2** *verb* to protect; *the prisoners are closely guarded*

guardian ['gɑːdiən] *noun* person who protects, especially someone who has been appointed by a court to look after a child; *when his parents died, his uncle became his guardian*

guess [ges] **1** *noun* trying to give the right answer or figure; *at a guess, I'd say it weighs about 10 kilos* (NOTE: plural is **guesses**) **2** *verb* to try to give the right answer or figure; *I would guess it's about six o'clock*

guest [gest] *noun* **(a)** person who is asked to your home or to an event; *we had a very lively party with dozens of guests* **(b)** person staying in a hotel; **guests' lounge** = special lounge for guests in a hotel

guidance ['gaɪdəns] *noun* advice; *he asked for guidance about how to fill in the job application form*

guide [gaɪd] **1** *noun* **(a)** person who shows the way; *they used local farmers as guides through the forest*; **guide dog** = dog which has been trained to lead a blind person; *the only dogs allowed into the restaurant are guide dogs* **(b)** person who shows tourists round a place; *the guide spoke French so fast that we couldn't understand what she was saying* **(c)** book which gives information; *a guide to the butterflies of Europe* **2** *verb* to show the way; to show tourists round a place; *she guided us up the steps in the dark*; *he guided us round the castle*

guidebook ['gaɪdbʊk] *noun* book with information about a place; *the guidebook lists three hotels by the beach*

guilty ['gɪlti] *adjective* **(a)** who has committed a crime; *he was found guilty of murder* **(b)** being unhappy because you have done something wrong; *I feel very guilty about not having written to you* (NOTE: **guiltier - guiltiest**)

guinea pig ['gɪni 'pɪg] *noun* **(a)** little furry animal kept as a pet; *she keeps guinea pigs in a hutch in the garden* **(b)** person used in an experiment; *twenty people were used as guinea pigs to test the new drug*

guitar [gɪ'tɑː] *noun* musical instrument with six strings, played with the fingers; *he plays the guitar in a pop group*

gulf [gʌlf] *noun* **(a)** area of sea partly surrounded by land; *the Gulf of Mexico lies south of the United States* **(b)** *(especially)* **the Gulf** = the Persian Gulf (the sea near Iran, Iraq, Saudi Arabia, etc.); *the tanker was carrying oil from the Gulf*

gum [gʌm] **1** *noun* **(a)** glue; *she spread gum on the back of the photo and stuck it onto a sheet of paper* **(b)** flesh around the base of your teeth; *brushing your teeth every day is good for your gums* **(c)** **(chewing) gum** = sweet substance which you chew but do not swallow; *he took a piece of gum out of his* *mouth and dropped it on the pavement* **(d)** small fruit sweet which can be sucked until it melts away; *a packet of fruit gums* **2** *verb* to stick with glue; *she gummed the pictures onto a sheet of paper* (NOTE: **gumming - gummed**)

gun [gʌn] *noun* **(a)** small weapon which shoots bullets; *she grabbed his gun and shot him dead* **(b)** large weapon which shoots shells; *we heard the enemy guns firing all night* **(c)** small device which you hold in your hand to spray paint, glue, etc.; *a spray gun gives an even coat of paint*

gut [gʌt] **1** *noun* **(a)** *(informal)* the tube inside your body which passes down from the stomach and in which food is digested as it passes through; *he complained of pain in the gut* **(b)** *(informal)* **guts** = courage; *he didn't have the guts to tell the boss what he really thought* **2** *verb* to destroy the inside of a building completely; *the house was gutted by fire* (NOTE: **gutting - gutted**)

gutter ['gʌtə] *noun* **(a)** channel by the side of a road to take away rain water; *pieces of paper and leaves were blowing about in the gutter* **(b)** open pipe along the edge of a roof to catch rain water; *it rained so hard the gutters overflowed*

guy [gaɪ] **1** *noun* **(a)** *(informal)* man; *the boss is a very friendly guy*; *hey, you guys, come and look at this!*; *(in a story or film)* **bad guy** = wicked character; *the bad guy is the one with the black hat*; **good guy** = hero; *the good guys always win* **(b)** figure of a man burnt on 5th November; *the children are collecting clothes to make a guy*

Guy Fawkes Day *or* **Night** ['gaɪ 'fɔːks 'deɪ or 'naɪt] *noun* 5th November, when the attempt by Guy Fawkes to blow up the Houses of Parliament in 1605 is remembered; *Guy Fawkes Night is always a busy time for the fire brigade*; *on Guy Fawkes' day, children collect money to pay for fireworks by asking for a 'penny for the guy'*

gym *or* **gymnasium** [dʒɪm or dʒɪm'neɪziəm] *noun* **(a)** hall for indoor sports; *because it rained, we had to hold the school fair in the gym* **(b)** exercises done in a gymnasium; *I forgot my plimsolls and had to do gym in my bare feet*

Hh

H, h [eɪtʃ] eighth letter of the alphabet, between G and I; *the street sign for a hospital is a white H on a blue background*

habit ['hæbɪt] *noun* regular way of doing things; *he has the habit of going to bed at 10 o'clock and reading until midnight*; **to get into the habit of doing something** = to start to do something regularly; *she got into the habit of going for a swim every morning before breakfast*; **to get out of the habit** = to stop doing something which you used to do regularly; *he's got out of the habit of playing the piano*; **bad habit** *or* **nasty habit** = regular way of doing something which is not good or pleasant; *she has the bad habit of biting her nails*

had, hadn't [hæd or 'hædənt] *see* HAVE

hail [heɪl] **1** *noun* frozen rain; *I thought the hail was going to break the glass roof* **2** *verb* **(a)** to wave, call, etc., to make a taxi stop; *he whistled to hail a taxi* **(b)** to fall as frozen rain; *it suddenly started to hail*

hair [heə] *noun* **(a)** mass of long threads growing on your head; *she has long brown hair*; *you must get your hair cut*; **hair drier** =

electric machine for drying wet hair; *can I borrow your hair drier - my hair's wet and I'm going to be late* **(b)** one of the long threads growing on the body of a human or animal; *the cat has left hairs all over the cushion*

hairdresser ['heədresə] *noun* person who cuts and washes your hair; **the hairdresser's** = the shop where you have your hair cut, washed, etc.; *I must go to the hairdresser's before the party*

half [hɑːf] **1** *noun* **(a)** one of two parts which are the same in size; *she cut the orange in half* **(b)** *(in sport)* one of two parts of a game; *our team scored a goal in the first half* (NOTE: plural is **halves** [hɑːvz]) **2** *adjective* divided into two equal parts; **half an hour** = 30 minutes; *I'll be back in half an hour*

half past ['hɑːf 'pɑːst] *phrase* 30 minutes after an hour; *I have an appointment with the doctor at half past five (= 5.30)*

half-term ['hɑːf 'tɜːm] *noun* short holiday in the middle of a school term; *the children have a few days' holiday at half-term*; *the museums are full of children at half-term*

halfway [hɑːf'weɪ] *adverb* in the middle; *the post office is about halfway between the station and our house*

hall [hɔːl] *noun* **(a)** passage at the entrance to a house, where you can leave your coat; *don't wait in the hall, come straight into the dining room* **(b)** large room for meetings; *the children have their dinner in the school hall*; **town hall** = building where the town council meets and from where the town is governed; **village hall** = building in a village where meetings, shows, etc., can take place

hallo [hə'ləʊ] *see* HELLO

Halloween [hæləʊ'iːn] *noun* 31st October, when witches and ghosts are said to be seen; *traditionally at Halloween, there are pumpkins with faces cut into them and candles put inside them*

halt [hɔːlt] **1** *noun* complete stop; **to come to**

a halt = to come to a dead stop; *the lorry came to a halt just before the wall* **2** *verb* to stop; *the cars halted when the traffic lights went red*

halve [hɑːv] *verb* to reduce by half; *we are trying to halve the number of road accidents*

halves [hɑːvz] *see* HALF

ham [hæm] *noun* salted or smoked meat from a pig; *she cut three slices of ham*; *he bought a ham sandwich and a cup of coffee*; **ham and eggs** = fried ham with fried eggs

hamburger ['hæmbɜːgə] *noun* minced beef grilled and served in a toasted roll; *the children want hamburgers and French fries for lunch*

hammer ['hæmə] **1** *noun* tool with a heavy head for hitting nails; *she hit the nail hard with the hammer* **2** *verb* **(a)** to knock something into something with a hammer; *it took him a few minutes to hammer the nails into the post* **(b)** to hit hard, as with a hammer; *she hammered on the door with her stick*

hammock ['hæmək] *noun* bed made from a piece of strong cloth hanging between two hooks; *she spent the afternoon lying in a hammock in the shade, drinking lemonade*

hamster ['hæmstə] *noun* small furry animal, kept as a pet; *they keep the hamster in a cage in the classroom*

hand [hænd] **1** *noun* **(a)** part of the body at the end of each arm, with fingers which you use for holding things; *she was carrying a cup of tea in each hand*; **to lend a hand** *or* **to give a hand with something** = to help with something; *he gave me a hand with the washing up*; **they walked along hand in hand** = holding each other by the hand **(b)** one of the two pieces on a clock (the minute hand and the hour hand) which turn round and show the time; *the minute hand is longer than the hour hand* **2** *verb* to pass something to someone; *can you hand me that box?*

by hand ['baɪ 'hænd] *phrase* using your hands and tools but not using large machines;

he made the table by hand

hand in ['hænd 'ɪn] *verb* to give in something by hand; *please have the completed form ready to hand in at the reception desk*

hand over ['hænd 'əʊvə] *verb* to give something to someone; *she handed over all the documents to the lawyers*

handbag ['hænbæg] *noun* small bag which a woman carries to hold her money, pens, handkerchief, etc.; *a robber snatched her handbag in the street*

handicap ['hændɪkæp] *noun* something which makes you not able to do something well; *not being able to drive is a handicap in this job*

handicapped ['hændɪkæpt] **1** *adjective* not physically able to do something; *she was handicapped by not being able to speak Russian*; *a school for handicapped children* **2** *noun* **the handicapped** = people who are disabled; *there is a toilet for the handicapped on the ground floor*

handkerchief ['hæŋkətʃiːf] *noun* piece of cloth or thin paper for wiping your nose; *he wiped his eyes with his handkerchief*

handle ['hændl] **1** *noun* part of something which you hold in your hand to carry it or to use for opening, etc.; *I turned the handle but the door didn't open*; *be careful, the handle of the frying pan may be hot* **2** *verb* to move by hand; *be careful when you handle the bottles of acid*

handsome ['hænsəm] *adjective* good-looking, very good to look at; *her boyfriend is very handsome - I'm jealous!*

handwriting ['hændraɪtɪŋ] *noun* way of writing by hand; *his handwriting's so bad I can't read it*

handy ['hændi] *adjective* practical and useful; *this small case is handy when travelling*; *it's handy having the post office next door* (NOTE: **handier - handiest**)

hang [hæŋ] *verb* to attach something to something so that it does not touch the ground;

hang your coat on the hook behind the door; *he hung the painting in the hall* (NOTE: **hanging - hung** [hʌŋ])

hang around ['hæŋ ə'raʊnd] *verb* *(informal)* to wait in a certain place without doing anything much; *groups of teenagers were hanging around the bar*

hang on ['hæŋ 'ɒn] *verb* **(a)** to wait; *if you hang on a few minutes you will be able to see her* **(b)** *(while phoning)* to wait; *if you hang on a moment, Mr Smith will be off the other line soon* **(c)** **to hang on to something** = to hold something tight; *hang on to the ladder and don't look down*

hanger ['hæŋə] *noun* **coat hanger** = piece of wood, wire or plastic on which you can hang a coat, a shirt, etc.; *when I got to the hotel room, there were no hangers in the wardrobe*

happen ['hæpən] *verb* **(a)** to take place; *the accident happened at the traffic lights*; *he's late - something must have happened to him* **(b)** **what's happened to his brother?** = what is his brother doing now? **(c)** to be by chance; *the fire engine happened to be there when the fire started*; *the shop happened to be empty at the time*

happily ['hæpɪli] *adverb* in a happy way; *the children played happily in the sand for hours*

happiness ['hæpinəs] *noun* feeling of being happy; *you could see her happiness in the expression on her face*

happy ['hæpi] *adjective* **(a)** *(of people)* very pleased; *I'm so happy to hear that you are better*; *she's very happy in her job* **(b)** *(greetings)* **Happy Birthday!** *or* **many Happy Returns of the Day!** = greeting said to someone on their birthday; **Happy Christmas!** = greeting said to someone at Christmas; **Happy New Year!** = greeting said to someone at the New Year (NOTE: **happier - happiest**)

harbour *US* **harbor** ['hɑːbə] *noun* port, place where boats can come and tie up; *the ship came into harbour last night*

hard [hɑːd] **1** *adjective* **(a)** not soft; *if you have back trouble, you ought to get a hard bed* **(b)** difficult; *the exam was very hard, and most students failed* **(c)** severe; *there was a hard winter in 1962*; *(informal)* **hard luck!** = I'm sorry you didn't win (NOTE: **harder - hardest**) **2** *adverb* strongly; *he hit the nail hard*; *it's snowing very hard*

hardly ['hɑːdli] *adverb* **(a)** almost not; *we hardly slept last night*; *she hardly eats anything at all* **(b) hardly anyone** = almost no one; *hardly anyone came to the party*; **hardly ever** = almost never; *it hardly ever rains in September*

hardware ['hɑːdweə] *noun* **(a)** tools and pans used in the home; *I bought the paint in a hardware shop* **(b) computer hardware** = computers, printers, keyboards, etc. (as opposed to 'software' which is the programs)

hare ['heə] *noun* wild animal like a large rabbit; *in spring, you see hares running around in the fields*

harm [hɑːm] **1** *noun* damage; *there's no harm in having a drink of chocolate before you go to bed* **2** *verb* to damage; *walking to college every morning won't harm you*

harmless ['hɑːmləs] *adjective* which does not hurt; *are you sure this spray is harmless to animals?*; *our dog barks a lot, but really he's quite harmless*

harsh [hɑːʃ] *adjective* **(a)** severe, cruel; *the court gave him a harsh sentence* **(b)** rough; *he shouted in a harsh voice* (NOTE: **harsher - harshest**)

harvest ['hɑːvɪst] **1** *noun* picking ripe crops; *the grape harvest is in September*; *it's the best corn harvest for years* **2** *verb* to pick ripe crops; *the corn will be ready to harvest next week*

has, hasn't [hæz or 'hæzənt] *see* HAVE

hat [hæt] *noun* **(a)** piece of clothing which you wear on your head; *he's bought a fur hat for the winter* **(b) hat trick** = score of three goals, etc., by the same person in football,

three wickets taken by the same bowler in cricket, etc.; *Jones scored a hat trick*

hatch [hætʃ] *verb (of a baby bird)* to break out of the egg; *all the chicks hatched on the same day*

hate [heɪt] *verb* to dislike very strongly; *I think she hates me, but I don't know why*; *I hate getting up on cold mornings*

haul [hɔːl] *verb* to pull with difficulty; *they hauled the boat up onto the beach*; *the police hauled the body out of the water*

haunted ['hɔːntɪd] *adjective* visited by ghosts; *they live in a haunted house*; *the Tower of London is said to be haunted by the ghost of Anne Boleyn*

have [hæv] *verb* **(a)** to own or possess; *they have a new green car*; *she has long dark hair* **(b)** to take, to eat, to play, etc.; *she had her breakfast in bed*; *they had a game of tennis* **(c)** to pay someone to do something for you; *I must have my hair cut* **(d)** *(used to form the past of verbs)* *have they finished their work?*; *she has never been to Paris*; *I haven't seen him for two days* **(e)** *(greetings)* *have a nice day!*; *have a good trip!*; *have a nice party!* (NOTE: present: **I have, you have, he/she/it has, we have, they have**; short forms: **I've, you've, he's, she's, it's, we've, they've**; past: **had**)

have got ['hæv 'gɒt] *verb* **(a)** to have; *have you got a table for three, please?*; *half the people in the office have got flu* **(b)** to own or possess; *she's got a lot of money*; *they've got a new green car* **(c)** *(used with other verbs to mean 'must')* *she's got to learn to drive*; *why have you got to go so early?*

have to ['hæv 'tu] *verb (used with other verbs to mean 'must')* *he had to walk to work because he missed the bus*; *do we have to get up early?*

haven't ['hævənt] = HAVE NOT

hawk [hɔːk] *noun* large bird that catches and eats other birds or small animals; *the hawk was hovering over the motorway*

hay [heɪ] *noun* dried grass used to feed farm

animals; *we store the hay to feed to the cows in winter*

hayfever ['heɪfiːvə] *noun* running nose and eyes caused by an allergy to flowers, scent or dust; *when I have hayfever I have to stay indoors*; *the hayfever season starts in May*

he [hiː] *pronoun referring to a man or boy, and some animals; he's my brother*; *he and I met in Oxford Circus*; *don't be frightened of the dog - he won't hurt you*

head [hed] **1** *noun* **(a)** top part of the body, which contains the eyes, nose, mouth, brain, etc.; *she hit her head on the cupboard door*; **to shake your head** = to move your head from side to side to mean 'no'; *she asked him if he wanted any more coffee and he shook his head* **(b)** brain, being clever; *she has a good head for figures*; *he tried to do the sum in his head* **(c)** first place, top part; *an old lady was standing at the head of the queue* **(d)** most important person; *she's the head of the English department* **(e)** one person, when counting; **a head** *or* **per head** = for each person; *the trip costs £25.00 a head or per head* **2** *verb* **(a)** to go towards; *the car headed east along the motorway* **(b)** to be the first, to lead; *our team heads the list of champions* **(c)** to hit the a ball with your head; *he headed the ball into the goal*

head teacher ['hed 'tiːtʃə] *noun* teacher who is in charge of a school; *the head teacher plans to retire next year*

headache ['hedeɪk] *noun* pain in your head; *I must lie down, I've got a dreadful headache*; *take an aspirin if you have a headache*

headline ['hedlaɪn] *noun* **(a)** words in large letters on the front page of a newspaper; *the newspaper headline says TAXES TO GO UP* **(b) news headlines** = summary of the news on TV or radio

headphones ['hedfəʊnz] *noun* devices which you put on your ears to listen to recorded music, etc.; *please use the headphones if you want to listen to the music*

programme

headquarters (HQ) [hed'kwɔːtəz] *noun* main offices; *three people were arrested and taken to the police headquarters*

heal [hiːl] *verb* to become healthy again; *after six weeks, the cut on his knee still has not healed* (NOTE: do not confuse with **heel**)

health [helθ] *noun* being well, being free from any illness; *she's been in poor health for some time*; *smoking is bad for your health*; **health service** = service in charge of doctors, hospitals, etc.; **health warning** = warning that something may be bad for your health; *each pack of cigarettes carries a government health warning*

healthy ['helθi] *adjective* **(a)** not ill; *he's healthier than he has ever been* **(b)** which makes you well; *she's keeping to a healthy diet* (NOTE: **healthier - healthiest**)

heap [hiːp] *noun* **(a)** pile; *heaps of sand lay in the yard*; *he brushed the dead leaves into heaps* **(b)** *(informal)* **heaps of** = lots of; *apple pie with heaps of cream*; *don't rush - we've heaps of time*

hear [hɪə] *verb* **(a)** to catch sounds with your ears; *he heard footsteps behind him*; *I can hear a bird singing* **(b)** to listen to something; *I heard it on the BBC news* **(c)** to get information; *I hear he's got a new job* (NOTE: **hearing - heard** [hɜːd])

heard [hɜːd] *see* HEAR

hearing ['hɪərɪŋ] *noun* being able to hear; *bats have a very sharp sense of hearing*; **hearing aid** = electric device put in your ear to make you hear better; *she wears a little hearing aid which you can hardly see*

heart [hɑːt] *noun* **(a)** main organ in the body, which pumps blood around the body; *the doctor listened to her heart*; **heart attack** = condition where the heart suffers because of bad blood supply; *she had a heart attack but is recovering well* **(b)** centre of feelings; *my heart sank when I realized that I hadn't passed*; **to know something by heart** = to know and remember something; *I don't know his phone number by heart, so I'll just look it up for you* (c) centre, middle; *the restaurant is in the heart of the old town* (d) one of the red suits in a game of cards, shaped like a heart (the other red suit is diamonds; clubs and spades are the black suits); *my last two cards were the ten and the queen of hearts*

heat [hi:t] **1** *noun* (a) being hot; *the heat of the sun made the ice cream melt* (b) one part of a sports competition; **dead heat** = race where two runners finish equal; *the race finished in a dead heat* **2** *verb* to make hot; *can you heat the soup while I'm getting the table ready?*; *the room was heated by a small electric fire*

heather ['heðə] *noun* low plant with mainly purple or pink flowers, found on hills and mountains; *the mountains of Scotland are beautiful in autumn when the heather is in flower*

heating ['hi:tɪŋ] *noun* way of warming a house, an office, etc.; *we switch the heating off on May 1st*; **central heating** = heating of a whole house from one main heater and several radiators; *the central heating has broken down again*

heaven ['hevn] *noun* (a) place where good people are believed to go to live with God after they die; *she believes that when she dies she will go to heaven* (b) *(phrase showing surprise)* *good heavens! it's almost ten o'clock!*; **for heaven's sake** = expression showing you are annoyed, or that something is important; *what are you screaming for? - it's only a little mouse, for heaven's sake*

heavy ['hevi] *adjective* (a) which weighs a lot; *this suitcase is so heavy I can hardly lift it* (b) in large amounts; *there was a heavy fall of snow during the night*; *the radio says there is heavy traffic in the centre of town* (NOTE: heavier - heaviest)

he'd [hi:d] = HE HAD, HE WOULD

hedge [hedʒ] *noun* row of bushes planted and kept cut to form a screen around a field or garden; *the sheep got through a hole in the hedge*

hedgehog ['hedʒhɒg] *noun* small animal covered in spines; *many hedgehogs get killed by cars*

heel [hi:l] *noun* (a) the back part of your foot; *after walking all day she got a blister on her heel* (b) back part of a sock, stocking or shoe; *he's got a hole in the heel of his sock*; *she always wears shoes with high heels* (NOTE: do not confuse with **heal**)

height [haɪt] *noun* (a) measurement of how tall something is; *the height of the bridge is only 3m* (b) highest point; *it is difficult to find hotel rooms at the height of the tourist season*; *I don't like heights or I haven't got a head for heights* = my head goes round and round when I am high up on a building

held [held] *see* HOLD

helicopter ['helikɒptə] *noun* aircraft with a large propeller on top, which can rise straight up in the air; *a police helicopter flew over the crash site*

he'll [hi:l] = HE WILL

hello [hə'ləʊ] *interjection showing greetings;* *hello! Mary, I'm glad to see you*; *when you see her, say hello to her from me*

helmet ['helmət] *noun* solid hat used as a protection; *soldiers wear helmets when they are on patrol*; *you must wear a helmet when riding a motorbike*; **crash helmet** = solid hat worn by people riding motorcycles, bikes, etc.

help [help] **1** *noun* (a) something which makes it easier for you to do something; *do you need any help with moving the furniture?*; *her assistant is not much help in the office - he can't type or drive* (b) making someone safe; **to go to someone's help** = to try to rescue someone; *the rescue teams went to the help of the flood victims* **2** *verb* (a) to make it easier for someone to do something; *he helped the old lady up the steps*; *your father can help you with your homework* (b)

cannot help = not to be able to stop doing something; *he couldn't help laughing* **(c) to help yourself** = to serve yourself with food, etc.; *she helped herself to some cake*; *if you feel thirsty just help yourself to juice* **3** *interjection meaning that you are in difficulties; help! help! call the police!*; *help! I can't stop the car!*

helping ['helpɪŋ] *noun* amount of food given to someone; *children's helpings are not as large as those for adults*; **second helping** = more of the same food; *can I have a second helping of pudding, please?*

helpless ['helpləs] *adjective* not able to do anything; *he's helpless when his car breaks down*

hem [hem] *noun* the sewn edge of a skirt, tablecloth, etc.; *she was wearing a long skirt, with the hem touching the floor*

hen [hen] *noun* female chicken; *look, one of the hens has laid an egg!*

her [hɜː] **1** *object pronoun referring to a female; did you see her?*; *he told her to go away*; *that's her - the tall girl over there!* **2** *adjective referring to a female, a ship, a country; have you seen her father?*; *the dog doesn't want to eat her food*

herb [hɜːb *US* ɜːb] *noun* plant used to give flavour to food; *add some herbs to the sauce*

herd [hɜːd] *noun* a group of animals, especially cows; *herds of cows were grazing in the fields* (NOTE: do not confuse with **heard**)

here [hɪə] *adverb* **(a)** in this place; *I'll sit here in the shade and wait for you*; *here are the keys you lost* **(b)** to this place; *come here at once!*; *can you bring the chairs here, please?*; *here comes the bus!* (NOTE: do not confuse with **hear**)

hero ['hɪərəʊ] *noun* **(a)** brave man; *the heroes of the fire were the firemen who managed to rescue the children from an upstairs room* **(b)** man or boy who is the main character in a book, play, film, etc.; *the hero of the story is a little boy* (NOTE: plural is

heroes)

heroine ['herəʊɪn] *noun* **(a)** brave woman; *the heroine of the accident was a passing cyclist who pulled the children out of the burning car* **(b)** woman or girl who is the main character in a book, play, film, etc.; *the heroine of the film is a school teacher*

hers [hɜːz] *pronoun* belonging to her; *that watch is hers, not mine*; **she introduced me to a friend of hers** = to one of her friends

herself [hɜːˈself] *pronoun referring to a female subject; did your sister enjoy herself?*; *she's too young to be able to dress herself*; **by herself** = all alone, with no one else; *she lives all by herself*; *she did it all by herself*; *now she's eight, we let her go to the shops all by herself*

he's [hiːz] = HE HAS, HE IS

hesitate ['hezɪteɪt] *verb* to be slow to speak, because you can't decide; *she's hesitating about what to do next*; *he hesitated for a moment and then said 'no'*

hi [haɪ] *interjection showing greetings; Hi! I'm your tour leader*; *Hi! Mary, how are you today?*; *say hi to her from me*

hibernate ['haɪbəneɪt] *verb (of animals)* to rest during the winter, being more or less completely unconscious; *bears hibernate during the Canadian winter*

hid [hɪd] *see* HIDE

hidden ['hɪdn] *adjective* which cannot be seen; *they're digging in the grounds of the castle, looking for hidden treasure*

hide [haɪd] *verb* **(a)** to put something where no one can see it or find it; *she hid the presents in the kitchen*; *someone has hidden my car keys* **(b)** to put yourself where no one can see you or find you; *they hid in the bushes until the police car had gone past*; *quick! hide behind the door!* (NOTE: **hiding - hid** [hɪd] **- has hidden** ['hɪdn])

hiding ['haɪdɪŋ] *noun* action of putting yourself where no one can find you; *he stayed* *in hiding until the police had gone*; **hiding place** = place where you can hide

high [haɪ] **1** *adjective* **(a)** reaching far above other things; *Everest is the highest mountain in the world*; *the new building is 20 storeys high* **(b)** large in quantity; *high prices put customers off*; *gold will melt at high temperatures* **2** *adverb* above; up in the air; *the sun rose high in the sky*; *the bird flew higher and higher* (NOTE: **higher - highest**)

High Street [ˈhaɪ ˈstriːt] *noun* most important street in a village or town, where shops and banks are; *if you want the post office, go down the High Street until you come to the traffic lights*

highly [ˈhaɪli] *adverb* greatly; *the restaurant has been highly recommended*

highway [ˈhaɪweɪ] *noun* main public road; **the Highway Code** = book published by the British government containing the rules for people travelling on roads; *you need to know the Highway Code if you're taking your driving test*

hijack [ˈhaɪdʒæk] *verb* to take control of a vehicle by force; *the robbers hijacked the lorry and killed the driver*; *they hijacked an aircraft and ordered the pilot to fly to Moscow*

hill [hɪl] *noun* piece of high land, but lower than a mountain; *their house is on top of a hill*

him [hɪm] *object pronoun referring to a male*; *have you spoken to him today?*; *that's him! - the man with the beard*

himself [hɪmˈself] *pronoun referring to a male subject*; *I was served by the manager himself*; *did your brother enjoy himself?*; **all by himself** = all alone, with no one else; *he lives all by himself*; *he did it all by himself*; *now he's eight, we let him go to the shops all by himself*

Hindu [ˈhɪnduː] *noun* person who follows Hinduism, the main religion of India; *the Hindus worship several gods*

hinge [hɪndʒ] *noun* piece of metal used to

hold a door, window, lid, etc., so that it can swing open and shut; *that hinge squeaks and needs some oil*

hint [hɪnt] **1** *noun* **(a)** hidden suggestion, clue; *he didn't give a hint as to where he was going on holiday* **(b)** piece of advice; *she gave me some useful hints about painting furniture* **2** *verb* to say something in a way that makes people guess what you mean; *she hinted that her sister was going to get married*

hip [hɪp] *noun* **(a)** part of the body at the top of your thighs; *the tailor measured him round the hips* **(b)** joint where the thigh bone turns at the top of the leg; **hip replacement** = operation to replace the whole hip joint with an artificial one

hippopotamus *(informal)* **hippo** [hɪpəˈpɒtəməs or ˈhɪpəʊ] *noun* large heavy African animal which spends most of its time in water, but comes onto dry land to feed (NOTE: plurals are **hippopotamuses** *or* **hippopotami** [hɪpəˈpɒtəmaɪ] and **hippos** [ˈhɪpəʊz])

hire [ˈhaɪə] **1** *noun* paying money to rent a car, boat, piece of equipment, etc., for a period of time; **'for hire'** = sign on a taxi showing it is empty and available for hire **2** *verb* **(a)** *(someone who is borrowing it)* to pay money to use a car, boat, piece of equipment, etc., for a time; *she hired a car for the weekend* **(b)** *(someone who owns it)* **to hire out** = to allow other people to take something, use it and pay for it; *he hires out boats on the river*

his [hɪz] **1** *adjective referring to a male person or animal*; *he's lost all his money*; *our dog wants his food* **2** *pronoun* belonging to him; *that watch is his, not mine*; *he introduced me to a friend of his* = to one of his friends

historical [hɪˈstɒrɪkl] *adjective* referring to history; **historical novel** = story set in a particular period in the past

history [ˈhɪstəri] *noun* **(a)** study of the past, of past events; *he is studying Greek history*; *when the geography teacher was ill, the* *history teacher took over his class* **(b)** book which tells the story of what happened in the past; *he wrote a history of the French Revolution*

hit [hɪt] **1** *noun* very popular song, film, performer, etc.; *the song rapidly became a hit* **2** *verb* **(a)** to knock; *the car hit the tree*; *she hit him on the head with a bottle* **(b)** to realize; *it suddenly hit her that she was all alone in the forest* (NOTE: hitting - hit)

hit back [ˈhɪt ˈbæk] *verb* **(a)** to hit someone who has hit you; *he fell down before he could hit the other boy back* **(b)** to do something as a reaction to something; *he hit back at the inspectors, saying that their report was unfair*

hive [haɪv] *noun* box for bees to make a nest in; *he took the honey carefully out of the hive*

hoard [hɔːd] **1** *noun* store of food, money, etc., which has been collected; *they discovered a hoard of gold coins in the field* **2** *verb* to buy and store supplies in case of need; *squirrels hoard nuts for the winter*; *everyone has started hoarding fuel in case supplies run out*

hobby [ˈhɒbi] *noun* favourite thing which you do in your spare time; *his hobby is making model planes* (NOTE: plural is **hobbies**)

hockey [ˈhɒki] *noun* team game played on grass, where you try to hit a small ball into your opponents' goal using a long stick which is curved at the end; *he played in the hockey team at school*; **ice hockey** = form of hockey played on ice using a hard rubber disk instead of a ball; *the ice hockey final will be between Canada and Russia*

hold [həʊld] **1** *verb* **(a)** to keep tight, especially in your hand; *she was holding a gun in her left hand*; *he held the bag close to his chest* **(b)** to contain, to be large enough for something to fit inside; *the bottle holds two litres*; *will the car hold eight people?* **(c)** to make something happen; *the meeting will be held next Tuesday in the town hall* **(d)** to possess; *she holds a valid driving licence*; *he holds the record for the 2000 metres* **(e)** to

hold your breath = to keep air in your lungs to go under water, as a test or because you are afraid that something will happen; *she held her breath under water for a minute* (NOTE: holding - held [held]) **2** *noun* **(a)** action of gripping something; *keep tight hold of the bag, we don't want it stolen*; **to get hold of someone** = to find someone you need by telephone; *I tried to get hold of the doctor but he was out* **(b)** bottom part of a ship or an aircraft, in which cargo is stored; *you can't take all that luggage with you, it has to go in the hold*

hold on [ˈhəʊld ˈɒn] *verb* **(a)** to hold something tightly; *she held on to the rope with both hands*; *hold on to your purse in the crowd* **(b)** to wait; *hold on a moment, I'll get my umbrella*

hold out [ˈhəʊld ˈaʊt] *verb* **(a)** to move something towards someone; *hold out your plate to be served* **(b)** to resist against; *the castle held out for ten weeks against a huge enemy army*

hold up [ˈhəʊld ˈʌp] *verb* **(a)** to lift; *he held up his hand* **(b)** to make late; *the planes were held up by fog* **(c)** to attack and rob; *six men wearing black masks held up the security van*

hold-up [ˈhəʊldʌp] *noun* **(a)** delay, time when something is later than planned; *long hold-ups are expected because of road works on the motorway* **(b)** armed attack; *the gang carried out three hold-ups in the same day*

hole [həʊl] *noun* opening, space in something; *you've got a hole in your sock*; *rabbits live in holes in the ground*

holiday [ˈhɒlɪdeɪ] *noun* **(a)** period when you don't work, but rest, go away and enjoy yourself; *when are you planning to go on holiday?*; *we always spend our holidays in the mountains* **(b)** day on which no work is done because of laws or religious rules; *the office is closed for the Christmas holiday*; **bank holiday** = special day when most people do not go to work and the banks are closed; *New Year's Day is a bank holiday*

hollow ['hɒləʊ] *adjective* with an empty space inside; *if you tap the wall it sounds hollow*

holly ['hɒli] *noun* small evergreen tree with shiny dark green leaves with sharp spines, and bright red berries; *for the Christmas party, we decorate the house with holly and balloons*

holy ['həʊli] *adjective* blessed by God; *they went to ask a holy man his advice*

home [həʊm] **1** *noun* **(a)** place where you live; *their home is a flat in the centre of London*; **make yourself at home** = do as if you were in your own home; *he lay down on the sofa, switched on the TV, and made himself at home* **(b)** house; *they are building fifty new homes in fields near the village* **(c)** house where people are looked after; *my aunt has moved to an old people's home* **(d)** *(in sports)* **at home** = on the local sports ground (the opposite is 'away'); *our team is playing at home next Saturday* **2** *adverb* towards the place where you usually live; *we've got to go home now*; *he usually gets home by 7 o'clock*

homework ['həʊmwɜːk] *noun* work which you take home from school to do in the evening; *have you finished your maths homework?*; *I haven't any homework today, so I can watch TV*

honest ['ɒnɪst] *adjective* **(a)** who tells the truth; *he was honest with the police and told them what he had done* **(b)** (person) who can be trusted; *I wouldn't buy a car from that garage - I'm not sure they're honest*

honey ['hʌni] *noun* sweet substance produced by bees; *I like honey on toast*

honeymoon ['hʌnimuːn] *noun* holiday taken immediately after a wedding; *they went on honeymoon to Corfu*

honour *US* **honor** ['ɒnə] **1** *noun* **(a)** acting according to what you think is right; *he's a man of honour* **(b)** mark of respect; *it is an honour for me to be invited here today* **2** *verb* to respect, to pay respect to; *we honour the dead soldiers on November 11th*

hood [hʊd] *noun* **(a)** loose piece of clothing to cover your head; *he has a blue anorak with a hood* **(b)** folding roof on a car, pram, etc.; *let's put down the hood, it's very hot* **(c)** *US* metal cover for the front part of a car, covering the engine (British English for this is 'bonnet'); *he lifted the hood to see what was wrong with the motor*

hoof [huːf] *noun* hard part of the foot of a horse, cow, and many other animals (NOTE: plural is **hooves** [huːvz])

hook [hʊk] *noun* **(a)** bent piece of metal for hanging things on; *hang your coat on the hook behind the door* **(b)** very small piece of bent metal, attached to a line for catching fish; *the fish ate the worm but didn't swallow the hook*

hop [hɒp] *verb* **(a)** to jump on one leg; *he hurt his toe and had to hop around on one foot* **(b)** *(of birds, animals, etc.)* to jump with both feet together; *the bird hopped across the lawn* (NOTE: **hopping - hopped**)

hope [həʊp] **1** *noun* wanting and expecting something to happen; *they have given up all hope of rescuing any more victims from the floods* **2** *verb* **(a)** to want and expect something to happen; *we all hope our team wins*; **I hope so** = I want it to happen; **I hope not** = I don't want it to happen; *it's going to rain tomorrow, isn't it? - I hope not!* **(b)** to expect to do something; *they said that they hoped to be back home by 6 o'clock*

hopeful ['həʊpfʊl] *adjective* quite sure that something will happen; *we are hopeful that she will accept our offer*

hopeless ['həʊpləs] *adjective* **(a)** with no hope; *the library books are in a hopeless mess* **(b)** no good; *he's hopeless when it comes to mending cars*

hopped, hopping ['hɒpt or 'hɒpɪŋ] *see* HOP

horizon [hə'raɪzn] *noun* line where the earth and the sky meet; *two ships could be seen on the horizon*

horizontal [hɒrɪˈzɒntl] *adjective* flat, level with the ground; *he drew a horizontal line across the page*

horn [hɔːn] *noun* **(a)** sharp pointed bone growing out of an animal's head; *that bull's horns look very dangerous* **(b)** warning device on a car; *sound your horn when you get to the corner* **(c)** metal musical instrument which is blown into to make a note; *they played a piece for horn and orchestra*

horrible [ˈhɒrəbl] *adjective* awful, terrible; *what horrible weather we're having!*; *I had a horrible dream last night*

horrified [ˈhɒrɪfaɪd] *adjective* very frightened or shocked; *the horrified spectators watched the two planes collide at the air show*

horror [ˈhɒrə] *noun* feeling of fear or disgust; *she has a horror of spiders*; *everyone watched in horror as the two cars collided*; **horror film** = frightening film, with ghosts, dead bodies, etc.

horse [hɔːs] *noun* large animal used for riding or pulling; *she was riding a black horse*; *he's out on his horse every morning*

hose *or* **hosepipe** [həʊz *or* ˈhəʊzˈpaɪp] *noun* long tube, either rubber or plastic, for sending water; *the firemen used their hoses to put out the fire*; *that hosepipe isn't long enough to reach to the bottom of the garden*

hospital [ˈhɒspɪtəl] *noun* place where sick or hurt people are looked after; *she was taken ill at work and sent to hospital*; *he was in hospital for several days after the accident*

hot [hɒt] *adjective* **(a)** very warm; with a high temperature; *August is usually the hottest month*; *if you're too hot, take your coat off*; *I like to have a cup of hot chocolate before I go to bed* **(b)** (food) with a lot of spices; *he chose the hottest curry on the menu* (NOTE: **hotter - hottest**)

hot cross bun [ˈhɒt ˈkrɒs ˈbʌn] *noun* small spicy cake with spices inside and a sugar cross on top, eaten at Easter; *he ate two hot cross buns for breakfast*

hot dog [ˈhɒt ˈdɒg] *noun* snack made of a hot German sausage eaten in a roll of bread; *you can buy hot dogs at the food stall by the station*

hotel [həʊˈtel] *noun* building where travellers can rent a room for the night, eat in a restaurant, drink in a bar, etc.; *they are staying at the Grand Hotel*; *I'll meet you at the hotel entrance*

hour [ˈaʊə] *noun* **(a)** period of time which lasts sixty minutes; *the train journey usually takes two hours*; *it's a three-hour flight to Greece*; *the car was travelling at over 100 miles an hour*; *the hours of work are from 9.30 to 5.30*; **a quarter of an hour** = 15 minutes; **half an hour** = 30 minutes; *I'll be ready in a quarter of an hour*; *the next train will be in half an hour's time* **(b)** *(informal)* **hours** = a very long time; *we waited hours for the bus*

house **1** *noun* [haʊs] **(a)** building in which someone lives; *he has bought a house in London*; *all the houses in our street look the same* **(b)** part of the Parliament; *the British Parliament is formed of the House of Commons and the House of Lords* **(d)** bar or pub, etc.; **house wine** = special cheap wine selected by a restaurant; *we'll have a bottle of your house red, please* (NOTE: plural is **houses** [ˈhaʊzɪz]) **2** *verb* [haʊz] to provide accommodation for someone or something; *we have been asked if we can house three students for the summer term*

Houses of Parliament [ˈhaʊzɪz əv ˈpɑːləmənt] *noun* building in London where Parliament meets; *he took a picture of the Houses of Parliament*; *you can go on a tour of the Houses of Parliament*

household [ˈhaʊshəʊld] *noun* people living together in a house; *the newspaper is distributed free to every household in the town*

housework [ˈhaʊswɜːk] *noun* cleaning work in a house or flat; *I have a lot of housework to do*

hover ['hɒvə] *verb* **(a)** to hang in the air without moving forward; *flies were hovering over the surface of a pool* **(b)** to hover around = to stay near; *he was hovering round the snack bar, hoping that someone would offer him a meal*

how [haʊ] *adverb* **(a)** *(showing or asking the way in which something is done)* **can you tell me how to get to the railway station from here? (b)** *(showing or asking to what extent)* **how big is their house?; how many people are there in your family? (c)** *(showing surprise)* **how cold it is outside!**

how about? ['haʊ ə'baʊt] *phrase (informal)* would you like?; *how about a swim before breakfast?; how about a cup of coffee?*

how are you? *or* **how do you do?** ['haʊ 'ɑː juː *or* 'haʊ djə 'duː] **(a)** *(showing general greetings)* **hi Robert! how are you? (b)** *(asking the state of your health)* **the doctor asked me how I was**

how are you doing? ['haʊr juː 'duːɪŋ] *(general greeting)* **hi Kate, how're you doing?**

how come? ['haʊ 'kʌm] *(informal)* why; *how come you're late?; how come the front door was left open?*

however [haʊ'evə] *adverb* **(a)** *(form of 'how' which stresses)* **however did you manage to get in? (b)** in this case; *we don't usually go out on Saturdays - however, this Saturday we're going to a wedding*

howl [haʊl] **1** *verb* to make a long loud cry; *the wild dogs howled outside the cabin* **2** *noun* long loud cry; *howls of anger came from the disappointed fans*

HQ ['eɪtʃ 'kjuː] = HEADQUARTERS; *we had a call from HQ asking for more details*

hug [hʌg] **1** *noun* throwing your arms round someone; *she ran to the little girl and gave her a hug* **2** *verb* to throw your arms around someone; *the players hugged each other when the goal was scored* (NOTE: **hugging - hugged**)

huge [hjuːdʒ] *adjective* very large; *huge*

waves hit the ship; the concert was a huge success

hullo [hə'ləʊ] *see* HALLO, HELLO

hum [hʌm] *verb* **(a)** to make a low buzz; *bees were humming around the hive* **(b)** to sing without words; *if you don't know the words of the song, you can always hum the tune* (NOTE: **humming - hummed**)

human ['hjuːmən] **1** *adjective* referring to a person or to people; **human error** = mistake made by a person, and not by a machine; *they came to the conclusion that the accident was due to human error* **2** *noun* person, a human being; *the animals in the park are not afraid of humans*

human being ['hjuːmən 'biːɪŋ] *noun* a person; *I've been walking all day in the forest and you're the first human being I've met*

humble ['hʌmbl] *adjective* modest, not very important; *they live in a humble little house in the mountains* (NOTE: **humbler - humblest**)

humour *US* **humor** ['hjuːmə] *noun* seeing what is funny; *he has a good sense of humour*

hump [hʌmp] *noun* **(a)** raised part on the back of an animal; *some camels have one hump, others have two* **(b)** raised part of a road; *they have built humps in the road to slow down the traffic*

hundred ['hʌndrəd] **(a)** number 100; *the church is over a hundred years old; my grandfather will be 100 next month* **(b)** **hundreds of** = very many; *hundreds of people caught flu last winter*

hundredth (100th) ['hʌndrədθ] *adjective & noun* *a penny is one hundredth of a pound*

hung [hʌŋ] *see* HANG

Hungarian [hʌŋ'geəriən] **1** *adjective* referring to Hungary; *the Hungarian capital is Budapest* **2** *noun* **(a)** person from Hungary; *it has been three years since a Hungarian last won a gold medal* **(b)** language spoken in Hungary; *I am going to study in Budapest and want to take a course in Hungarian*

Hungary ['hʌŋgəri] *noun* country in central Europe, east of Austria and west of Romania; *the river Danube flows north-south through the centre of Hungary* (NOTE: capital: **Budapest**; people: **the Hungarians**; language: **Hungarian**)

hungry ['hʌŋgri] *adjective* wanting to eat; *you must be hungry after that game of football*; *I'm not very hungry - I had a big lunch* (NOTE: **hungrier - hungriest**)

hunt [hʌnt] *verb* **(a) to hunt for something** = to search for something; *we're hunting for a cheap flat*; *the police are hunting for the driver of the car* **(b)** to chase wild animals for food or sport; *our cat is not very good at hunting mice*

hunter ['hʌntə] *noun* person who hunts; *a deer hunter*; **bargain hunter** = person who looks for bargains; *bargain hunters were queuing outside Harrods on the first day of the sales*

hurricane ['hʌrɪkən] *noun* tropical storm with strong winds and rain; *the hurricane damaged properties all along the coast*

hurry ['hʌri] **1** *noun* **in a hurry** = doing things fast; *the waiters are always in a hurry*; *can't you drive any faster? - we're in a hurry to catch our plane!* **2** *verb* to go, do or make something fast; *she hurried across the room*; *you'll have to hurry if you want to catch the last post*; *there's no need to hurry - we've got plenty of time*

hurry up ['hʌri 'ʌp] *verb* to go or do something faster; *hurry up - we'll be late for the film*; *can't you get the cook to hurry up, I'm getting hungry?*

hurt [hɜːt] **1** *verb* to have pain; to give pain; *my tooth hurts*; *no one was badly hurt in the accident*; *two players got hurt in the game* (NOTE: **hurting - hurt**) **2** *noun* (informal) (children's language) place where you have a pain; *he has a hurt on his toe*

husband ['hʌzbənd] *noun* man to whom a woman is married; *her husband is Scottish*

hut [hʌt] *noun* small rough wooden house; *they found a shepherd's hut where they spent the night*

hutch [hʌtʃ] *noun* box or cage for rabbits, etc.; *she keeps a white rabbit in a hutch in the garden* (NOTE: plural is **hutches**)

hyacinth ['haɪəsɪnθ] *noun* bulb which produces spikes of bright pink, white or blue scented flowers; *she had a bowl of hyacinths by her window*

hydrogen ['haɪdrədʒən] *noun* a common gas which combines with oxygen to form water

hygiene ['haɪdʒiːn] *noun* being clean and keeping healthy conditions; *for reasons of hygiene, dogs are not allowed into the shop*

hymn [hɪm] *noun* religious song sung during a Christian religious service; *the priest asked everyone to stand for the first hymn*

hyphen ['haɪfn] *noun* printing sign (-) used to show that two words are joined or that a word has been split; *'cooperate' doesn't take a hyphen but 'first-class' does*

Ii

I, i [aɪ] ninth letter of the alphabet, between H and J; **to dot your i's and cross your t's** = to be very careful to get the final details right

I [aɪ] *pronoun used by a speaker when talking about himself or herself*; *she said, 'I can do it', and she did it*; *she and I come from the same town*

ice [aɪs] **1** *noun* water which is frozen and has become solid; *the ice on the lake is dangerous, it isn't thick enough to walk on* **2** *verb* to put icing on a cake; *a cake iced with chocolate*

ice cream [ˈaɪs ˈkriːm] *noun* frozen sweet made from cream flavoured with fruit juice or other sweet substance; *what sort of ice cream do you want - strawberry or chocolate?*

iceberg [ˈaɪsbɜːg] *noun* huge block of ice floating on the sea; *the Titanic hit an iceberg and sank*

icicle [ˈaɪsɪkl] *noun* long piece of ice hanging from a roof, etc., formed by water dripping in freezing weather; *icicles hung down from the edge of the roof*

icing [ˈaɪsɪŋ] *noun* covering of sugar with different flavours, spread over a cake or biscuits; *she made some chocolate icing for the cake*

I'd [aɪd] = I HAD, I WOULD

idea [aɪˈdɪə] *noun* **(a)** something which you think of; **to have an idea that** = to think that; *I have an idea that the buses don't run on Sundays* **(b)** plan which you make in your mind; *I've had an idea - let's all go for a picnic!*

ideal [aɪˈdɪəl] *adjective* perfect, extremely suitable; *this is the ideal site for a factory*; *the cottage is an ideal place for watching birds*

identical [aɪˈdentɪkl] *adjective* exactly the same; *the twins wore identical clothes for the party*; **identical twins** = twins who look exactly alike

idle [ˈaɪdl] *adjective* lazy (person); **he's bone idle** = he never does any work at all (NOTE: idler - idlest)

ie *or* **i.e.** [ˈaɪ ˈiː] *abbreviation meaning* 'that is'; *it's best to study Russian in a country where they speak it - i.e. Russia*

if [ɪf] *conjunction* **(a)** *(showing what might happen)* *if it freezes tonight, the pavements will be dangerous tomorrow morning* **(b)** *(asking questions)* *do you know if the plane is late?*; *I was wondering if you would like to have some tea*

if only [ˈɪf ˈəʊnli] *(exclamation showing regret)* *if only she'd told me, I could have advised her what to do*

ignorant [ˈɪgnərənt] *adjective* not knowing anything; stupid; *he left school completely ignorant of the rules of English spelling*

ignore [ɪgˈnɔː] *verb* not to notice someone or something on purpose; *she ignored the red light and just drove straight through*

ill [ɪl] *adjective* sick, not well; *if you're feeling ill you ought to see a doctor* (NOTE: ill - worse [wɜːs] - worst [wɜːst])

I'll [aɪl] = I WILL, I SHALL

illness [ˈɪlnəs] *noun* not being well; *she developed a serious illness*; *a lot of the staff are absent because of illness* (NOTE: plural is illnesses)

illustrate [ˈɪləstreɪt] *verb* to put pictures into a book; *the book is illustrated with colour photographs of birds*

illustration [ɪləˈstreɪʃn] *noun* picture in a book; *the book has 25 colour illustrations*

I'm [aɪm] = I AM

image [ˈɪmɪdʒ] *noun* **(a)** portrait; *(informal)* **he's the spitting image of his father** = he looks exactly like his father **(b)** picture produced by a lens, mirror or computer; *the mirror throws an image onto the screen*

imaginary [ɪˈmædʒɪnəri] *adjective* not real, which is imagined; *all his novels are set in an imaginary town in Central Europe*

imagination [ɪmædʒɪˈneɪʃn] *noun* being able to picture things in your mind; *she let her imagination run riot in her stories for children*

imagine [ɪˈmædʒɪn] *verb* to picture something in your mind; *imagine yourself sitting on a beach in the hot sun*; *she thought she had heard footsteps, and then decided she had imagined it*

imitate [ˈɪmɪteɪt] *verb* to copy something or

someone; to do as someone does; *he made us all laugh by imitating the head teacher*

imitation [ɪmɪˈteɪʃn] *noun* **(a)** act of imitating; *he does a very good imitation of the Prime Minister* **(b)** copy made of something; *it's not real leather, just imitation*

immediately [ɪˈmiːdɪətli] *adverb* straight away after something; *he got my letter, and wrote back immediately*

impact [ˈɪmpækt] *noun* **(a)** strong effect; *the TV programme made a strong impact on the viewers* **(b)** shock; *the car was totally crushed by the impact of the collision*

impatient [ɪmˈpeɪʃnt] *adjective* not able to wait for something, always in a hurry to do something; *we were all impatient for the film to start*

impatiently [ɪmˈpeɪʃntli] *adverb* in a hurried way, not patiently; *'can't you go any faster,' she said impatiently*

importance [ɪmˈpɔːtəns] *noun* serious effect or influence; *do not attach too much importance to what he says*

important [ɪmˈpɔːtənt] *adjective* **(a)** which matters a great deal; *it's important to be in time for the interview* **(b)** (person) in a high position; *she's an important government official*

impossible [ɪmˈpɒsəbl] *adjective* which cannot be done; *it's impossible to do all this work in two hours; getting tickets for the show is quite impossible*

impress [ɪmˈpres] *verb* to make someone admire or respect someone; *I'm impressed by your cooking; his skill with oil paints impressed her*

impression [ɪmˈpreʃn] *noun* **(a)** effect on someone's mind; *the exhibition made a strong impression on her* **(b) to be under** or **to labour under an impression** = to believe something which is quite wrong; *he was labouring under the impression that air fares were cheaper in Europe than in the USA*

impressive [ɪmˈpresɪv] *adjective* which impresses; *he had a series of impressive wins in the chess tournament*

improve [ɪmˈpruːv] *verb* **(a)** to make something better; *we are trying to improve the design of the car* **(b)** to get better; *the general manager has promised that the bus service will improve*

improvement [ɪmˈpruːvmənt] *noun* **(a)** making or becoming better; *the new software is a great improvement on the old version* **(b)** thing which is better; *they carried out some improvements to the house*

in [ɪn] *preposition & adverb* **(a)** *(showing place)* *in Japan it snows a lot during the winter; she's in the kitchen* **(b)** at home, in an office, at a station; *is the boss in?; my father usually gets in from work about 6 p.m.* **(c)** *(showing time)* *in autumn the leaves turn brown; she was born in 1996* **(d)** *(showing time in the future)* *I'll be back home in about two hours* **(e)** *(showing a state or appearance)* *he was dressed in black; she ran outside in her dressing gown*

in for [ˈɪn ˈfɔː] *adverb* **to be in for something** = to be about to get something; *I think we're in for some bad weather; she's in for a nasty shock*

in front [ˈɪn ˈfrʌnt] **1** *adverb* further forwards; *my mother sat in the back seat and I sat in front* **2** *preposition* **in front of** = placed further forwards than something; *a tall man sat in front of me and I couldn't see the screen*

inch [ɪnʃ] *noun* measure of length (= 2.54cm); *snow lay six inches deep on the ground*

incidentally [ɪnsɪˈdentəli] *adverb* by the way; *incidentally, you didn't see my watch anywhere, did you?*

include [ɪnˈkluːd] *verb* to count someone or something along with others; *there were 120 people at the wedding if you include the children; the bill does not include service*

including [ɪnˈkluːdɪŋ] *preposition* taking something together with something else; *the total comes to £25.00 including VAT*

income [ˈɪŋkʌm] *noun* money which you receive, especially as pay for your work, or as interest on savings; *their weekly income is not enough to pay the rent*; **income tax** = tax on money earned as wages or salary; *income tax is taken direct from your salary each month*

increase 1 *noun* [ˈɪŋkriːs] (**a**) process of becoming larger; *the government is proposing an increase in tax* (**b**) rise in salary; *she went to her boss and asked for an increase* **2** *verb* [ɪŋˈkriːs] (**a**) to rise, to grow, to expand; *the price of petrol has increased twice in the past year*; **to increase in price** = to become more expensive (**b**) to make something become bigger; *rail fares have been increased by 10%*

indeed [ɪnˈdiːd] *adverb (to stress)* greatly, really; *thank you very much indeed for inviting me to stay*

indefinite [ɪnˈdefɪnɪt] *adjective* **the indefinite article** = 'a' or 'an' (as opposed to the definite article 'the')

index [ˈɪndeks] *noun* (**a**) list showing the references in a book; *look up the references to London in the index* (**b**) regular report which shows rises and falls in prices, unemployment, etc.; **cost-of-living index** = way of measuring the cost of living, shown as a percentage increase on the figure for the previous year; *some pensions are linked to the cost-of-living index* (NOTE: plural in this meaning is **indexes** *or* **indices** [ˈɪndɪsiːz])

India [ˈɪndjə] *noun* large country in southern Asia, south of China and east of Pakistan; *India is the second largest country in the world* (NOTE: capital: **New Delhi**; people: **Indians**; official languages: **Hindi, English, Gujarati, Tamil,** etc.)

Indian [ˈɪndjən] **1** *adjective* (**a**) referring to India; *Indian cooking is famous for its curries*; **Indian elephant** = elephant found in India and South-East Asia, slightly smaller than the African elephant, and used as a working animal in forests (**b**) referring to one of the original peoples of America; *the traditional Indian skills of hunting and tracking*; **Indian summer** = period of hot weather in autumn; *why not take advantage of the Indian summer and visit Scotland for a weekend break?* **2** *noun* (**a**) person from India; *many Indians came to live in Britain in the 1960s* (**b**) person from one of the original American peoples; *the train of farmers' wagons was attacked by Indians*

indignant [ɪnˈdɪgnənt] *adjective* feeling offended or angry; *he was very indignant when the inspector asked him for his ticket*

individual [ɪndɪˈvɪdjuəl] **1** *noun* one single person; *we provide a service for private individuals as well as for groups* **2** *adjective* single, for one person; *each member of the group has an individual information pack*; *I want three individual portions of ice cream, please*

indoor [ˈɪndɔː] *adjective* inside a building; *our school has an indoor swimming pool*

indoors [ɪnˈdɔːz] *adverb* inside a building; *everyone ran indoors when it started to rain*

industry [ˈɪndʌstri] *noun* companies which manufacture things, or other types of commercial activity, seen as a whole; *the car industry has had a good year*; *the tourist industry brings in a lot of foreign currency* (NOTE: plural is **industries**)

infant [ˈɪnfənt] *noun (formal)* very young child; **infant school** = school for little children from 4 years old

infectious [ɪnˈfekʃəs] *adjective* (disease) which can be passed from one person to another; *this strain of flu is highly infectious*; *he's covered with red spots - do you think it is infectious?*

influence [ˈɪnfluəns] **1** *noun* being able to change someone or something; *what exactly is the influence of the moon on the tides?* **2** *verb* to make someone or something change;

she was deeply influenced by her old teacher

inform [ɪnˈfɔːm] *verb* to tell someone officially; *have you informed the police that your car has been stolen?*

informal [ɪnˈfɔːml] *adjective* **(a)** relaxed, not formal; *the guide gave us an informal talk on the history of the castle* **(b)** (type of language) used when talking to friends, but not used on formal occasions

information [ɪnfəˈmeɪʃn] *noun* facts about something; *can you send me information about holidays in Greece?*; *she couldn't give the police any information about how the accident happened*; **information technology (IT)** = computers, and forms of technology that depend on computers; *the government is determined to increase the resources for information technology in schools*

infuriate [ɪnˈfjʊərieɪt] *verb* to make someone very angry; *slow service in restaurants always infuriates him*

ingenious [ɪnˈdʒiːniəs] *adjective* very clever; *she has an ingenious scheme for winning money on the national lottery*

ingredient [ɪnˈgriːdiənt] *noun* thing which goes to make something cooked; *you can buy all the ingredients for the cake at your local supermarket*

inhabit [ɪnˈhæbɪt] *verb* to live in a place; *the island is mainly inhabited by wild goats*

inhabitant [ɪnˈhæbɪtənt] *noun* person who lives in a place; *London has over seven million inhabitants*

initials [ɪˈnɪʃlz] *noun* the first letters of a person's names; *John Smith has a bag with his initials JS on it*

injection [ɪnˈdʒekʃn] *noun* act of putting a liquid into the body with a needle to prevent a disease; *the doctor gave him a flu injection*

injure [ˈɪndʒə] *verb* to hurt in a fight or accident; *six people were injured in the car crash*

injury [ˈɪndʒəri] *noun* hurt, wound; *she*

received severe back injuries in the accident (NOTE: plural is **injuries**)

ink [ɪŋk] *noun* liquid for writing with a pen; *he signed his name in red ink*

inland [ˈɪnlænd] *adverb* to the inner part of a country, away from the coast; *if you go inland from the capital, you soon get into the forest*

inn [ɪn] *noun* small hotel; *we stayed in a little inn in the mountains*

inner [ˈɪnə] *adjective* inside; *the area code for inner London is 0207*; **inner city** = the central part of a city; *there are always traffic jams in the inner city at rush hour*; **inner tube** = thin rubber tube containing air inside a tyre

innocent [ˈɪnəsənt] *adjective* not guilty of having done something; *in English law, the person who is accused is always believed to be innocent until he or she is proved to be guilty*

input [ˈɪnpʊt] *noun* data fed into a computer; *the input from the various branches is fed into the head office computer*

inquire [ɪnˈkwaɪə] *verb* to ask questions about something; *she's inquiring about air fares to Australia*

inquiry [ɪnˈkwaɪri] *noun* **(a)** question about something; *all inquiries should be addressed to Department 27* **(b)** formal discussion about a problem; *a public inquiry will be held about plans to build the new ring road* (NOTE: plural is **inquiries**)

insect [ˈɪnsekt] *noun* small animal with six legs and a body in three parts; *a butterfly is a kind of insect*; *insects have eaten the leaves of my cabbages*

insert [ɪnˈsɜːt] *verb* to put something inside; *to get a bar of chocolate, just insert a 50p coin into the slot*

inside [ɪnˈsaɪd] **1** *adverb* indoors; *it rained all afternoon, so we just sat inside and watched TV* **2** *preposition* in; *she was sitting inside the car, reading a book*; *I've never* *been inside his flat* **3** *noun* part which is in something; *the meat isn't cooked - the inside is still quite red* **4** *adjective* which is in something; *he put his wallet into his inside pocket*

inside out ['ɪnsaɪd 'aʊt] *phrase* **(a)** turned with the inner part facing out; *he put his pyjamas on inside out* **(b) to know something inside out** = to know something very well; *she knows Central London inside out*

insist [ɪn'sɪst] *verb* to state in a firm way; *he insisted that he had never touched the car;* **to insist on something** = to state in a firm way that something must be done; *she insisted on being given a refund*

inspect [ɪn'spekt] *verb* to look at something closely; *she inspected the room to see if it had been cleaned properly*

inspector [ɪn'spektə] *noun* senior official who examines something closely; *ticket inspectors came onto the train to check that everyone had a ticket;* **police inspector** = important officer in the police force

instalment *US* **installment** [ɪn'stɔːlmənt] *noun* **(a)** payment of part of a total sum which is made regularly; *you pay £25 down and twelve instalments of £20* **(b)** part of a story or TV series which is being shown in parts; *the next instalment of the series will be shown on Monday evening*

instant ['ɪnstənt] **1** *noun* moment or second; *for an instant, he stood still and watched the policemen* **2** *adjective* happening immediately; **instant coffee** = coffee powder to which you add hot water to make a fast cup of coffee; *she made a cup of instant coffee*

instantly ['ɪnstəntli] *adverb* immediately, at once; *he got my letter, and wrote back instantly; when the plane crashed all the passengers must have died instantly*

instead (of) [ɪn'sted] *adverb* in place of; *instead of stopping when the policeman shouted, she ran away; why don't you help me clean the car, instead of sitting and*

watching TV?; we haven't any coffee - would you like some tea instead?

instruction [ɪn'strʌkʃən] *noun* **(a)** order, telling someone what to do; *the guide gave an instruction in Russian to the driver* **(b)** showing how something is to be done or used; *she gave us detailed instructions how to get to the church;* **instruction book** = book which tells you how something should be used

instructor [ɪn'strʌktə] *noun* teacher, especially of a sport; **driving instructor** = person who teaches people how to drive; **swimming instructor** = person who teaches people how to swim

instrument ['ɪnstrəmənt] *noun* **(a)** piece of equipment; *the inspectors have instruments which measure the amount of pollution* **(b)** **musical instrument** = something which is blown or hit, etc., to make a musical note; *he doesn't play the piano, the drums or any other musical instrument*

insult 1 *noun* ['ɪnsʌlt] rude word said to or about a person; *the crowd shouted insults at the police* **2** *verb* [ɪn'sʌlt] to say rude things about someone; *he was accused of insulting the head of college*

insurance [ɪn'ʃuːrəns] *noun* agreement with a company by which you are paid for loss or damage in return for regular payments of money; **car insurance** *or* **motor insurance** = agreement that an insurance company will pay money if a car is damaged or if the driver and passengers are hurt

integer ['ɪntɪdʒə] *noun* whole number, not a fraction; *integers are numbers such as 25, 1755 or -161 but not 33/4*

intelligent [ɪn'telɪdʒənt] *adjective* clever, able to understand things very well; *he's the most intelligent child in his class*

intend [ɪn'tend] *verb* **to intend to do something** = to plan to do something; *I intended to get up early but I didn't wake up till 9*

intense [ɪn'tens] *adjective* very strong or

vigorous; *we have an intense period of study before our exams*; *the intense heat melted the metal*

interest ['ɪntrəst] **1** *noun* **(a)** special attention to something; *he takes no interest in what his sister is doing* **(b)** thing which you pay attention to; *her main interest is sailing* **(c)** money (a percentage) which is paid to someone who lends money; *if you put your money in a savings account you should get 6% interest* **2** *verb* to attract someone's special attention; *the film didn't interest me at all*

interesting ['ɪntrəstɪŋ] *adjective* which attracts your attention; *she didn't find the TV programme very interesting*; *what's so interesting about old cars? - I find them dull*

interfere [ɪntə'fɪə] *verb* **to interfere in** *or* **with something** = to get in the way of something, to be involved in something in such a way that it doesn't work well; *my father is always interfering in what I'm trying to do*; *stop interfering with the TV controls*

interjection [ɪntə'dʒekʃn] *noun* exclamation, a word used to show surprise; *interjections like 'ooh' are usually followed by an exclamation mark*

international [ɪntə'næʃənəl] *adjective* **1** *adjective* between countries; *an international conference on the environment* **2** *noun* **(a)** sportsman who has played for his country's team against another country; *there are three England internationals in our local team* **(b)** game between two countries; *the Rugby international will be held next Saturday at Twickenham*

Internet ['ɪntənet] *noun* international system linking millions of computers by telephone; *he searched the Internet for information on cheap tickets to Greece*

interpret [ɪn'tɜːprət] *verb* to translate aloud what is spoken in one language into another; *the guide knows Greek, so he will interpret for us*

interrupt [ɪntə'rʌpt] *verb* to start talking when someone else is talking and so stop them continuing; *excuse me for interrupting, but have you seen the car keys anywhere?*

interval ['ɪntəvl] *noun* **(a)** short period of time between two points; *there will be sunny intervals during the morning* **(b)** period of time between two parts of a play or film; *anyone arriving late won't be allowed in until the first interval* **(c)** **at intervals** = from time to time; *at intervals he looked at his watch*

interview ['ɪntəvjuː] **1** *noun* **(a)** meeting between one or more people and a person applying for a job; *he's had six interviews, but still no job offers* **(b)** discussion (on radio, TV, in a newspaper) between an important or interesting person and a journalist; *she gave an interview to the Sunday magazine* **2** *verb* **(a)** to talk to a person applying for a job to see if he or she is suitable; *we interviewed ten candidates, but did not find anyone we liked* **(b)** to ask a famous or interesting person questions and publish them afterwards; *the journalist interviewed the Prime Minister*

into ['ɪntuː] *preposition* **(a)** *(showing movement towards the inside)* *she went into the shop*; *he fell into the lake*; *you can't get ten people into a taxi* **(b)** against, colliding with; *the bus drove into a tree* **(c)** *(showing a change)* *water turns into steam when it is heated*; **to burst into tears** = to start crying suddenly **(d)** *(showing that you are dividing)* *try to cut the cake into ten equal pieces*

introduce [ɪntrə'djuːs] *verb* to present someone to another person or to people who did not know him or her before; *he introduced me to a friend of his called Anne*

introduction [ɪntrə'dʌkʃn] *noun* **(a)** piece at the beginning of a book which explains the rest of the book; *read the introduction which gives details of how the book came to be written* **(b)** basic book about a subject; *he's the author of an introduction to mathematics*

invalid ['ɪnvəlɪd] *noun* sick or disabled person; *she's been an invalid since her* *operation*

invent [ɪnˈvent] *verb* **(a)** to make something which has never been made before; *who invented television?* **(b)** to think up an excuse; *when she asked him why he was late he invented some story about missing the bus*

invention [ɪnˈvenʃn] *noun* act of making something which has never been made before; *the invention of computers has changed the way businesses work*

inventor [ɪnˈventə] *noun* person who invents new processes or new machines; *he's the inventor of the clockwork radio*

investigate [ɪnˈvestɪgeɪt] *verb* to study or to examine something closely; *detectives are investigating the details of the case*

invisible [ɪnˈvɪzəbl] *adjective* which cannot be seen; *the message was written in invisible ink*

invitation [ɪnvɪˈteɪʃn] *noun* letter or card, asking someone to do something; *he received an invitation to his sister's wedding*

invite [ɪnˈvaɪt] *verb* to ask someone to do something, especially to come to a party, etc.; *we invited two hundred people to the party*; *he's been invited to talk to the club about his experiences in Africa*

invoice [ˈɪnvɔɪs] *noun* note sent to ask for payment for services or goods; *the salesman made out an invoice for £250*

involve [ɪnˈvɒlv] *verb* **(a)** to bring someone or something into an action, situation, crime, etc.; *the competition involves teams from ten different countries* **(b)** to make necessary; *going to Oxford Circus from here involves taking a bus and then the Underground*

Ireland [ˈaɪələnd] *noun* large island forming the western part of the British Isles, containing the Republic of Ireland and Northern Ireland; *these birds are found all over Ireland*

Ireland (the Republic of Ireland) [ˈaɪələnd] *noun* country to the west of the United Kingdom, forming the largest part of the island of Ireland, a member of the EU; *Ireland was declared a republic in 1949* (NOTE: capital: **Dublin**; people: **the Irish**; languages: **Irish, English**)

Irish [ˈaɪrɪʃ] **1** *adjective* referring to Ireland; *the Irish Sea lies between Ireland and Britain* **2** *noun* **the Irish** = people who live in Ireland; *the Irish are famous for their folk music*

iron [ˈaɪən] **1** *noun* **(a)** common grey metal; *the old gates are made of iron* **(b)** electric instrument used to make clothes smooth after washing; *your iron must be really hot to make shirts smooth* **2** *verb* to make cloth smooth, using an iron; *she was ironing a sheet when the telephone rang*

irritable [ˈɪrɪtəbl] *adjective* easily annoyed; *he was tired and irritable, and snapped at the children*

is [ɪz] *see* BE

Islam [ˈɪzlɑːm] *noun* the religion of the Muslims, founded by the prophet Muhammad

island [ˈaɪlənd] *noun* piece of land with water all round it; *they live on a little island in the middle of the river*

isn't [ˈɪznt] *see* BE

it [ɪt] *pronoun* referring to a thing **(a)** *(used to show something which has just been mentioned)* *she picked up a potato and then dropped it*; *I put my book down somewhere and now I can't find it*; *the dog's thirsty, give it something to drink* **(b)** *(referring to no particular thing)* *look! - it's snowing*; *it's miles from here to the railway station*; *it's almost impossible to get a ticket at this time of year*; *what time is it? - it's ten o'clock*

IT [ˈaɪ ˈtiː] = INFORMATION TECHNOLOGY

Italian [ɪˈtæljən] **1** *adjective* referring to Italy; *he loves Italian food like spaghetti* **2** *noun* **(a)** person from Italy; *Italians are mad about football* **(b)** language spoken in Italy; *we go to Italy on holiday every year, and the children speak quite good Italian*

italics [ɪˈtælɪks] *noun* sloping letters; *this example is printed in italics*

Italy [ˈɪtəli] *noun* country in southern Europe, south of France, Switzerland and Austria; *Italy is the home of several important football clubs* (NOTE: capital: **Rome**; people: **Italians**; language: **Italian**)

itch [ɪtʃ] **1** *noun* place on the skin where you want to scratch; *I've got an itch in the middle of my back which I just can't reach* (NOTE: plural is **itches**) **2** *verb* to make someone want to scratch; *the cream made my skin itch more than before*

item [ˈaɪtəm] *noun* thing (in a list); *I couldn't buy several items on the shopping list because the shop had run out*

it'll [ɪtl] = IT WILL

its [ɪts] *adjective referring to 'it'; I can't use my bike - its back tyre is flat* (NOTE: do not confuse with **it's**)

it's [ɪts] = IT IS, IT HAS

itself [ɪtˈself] *pronoun referring to a thing; the dog seems to have hurt itself*; **all by itself** = alone, with no one helping; *the church stands all by itself in the middle of the street; the bus started to move all by itself*

I've [aɪv] = I HAVE

ivy [ˈaɪvi] *noun* evergreen plant which climbs up walls and trees; *we've planted some ivy to climb over the old garden fence*

Jj

J, j [dʒeɪ] tenth letter of the alphabet, between I and K

jab [dʒæb] *verb* to poke with something sharp; *he jabbed the piece of meat with his fork*; *she jabbed me in the back with her umbrella* (NOTE: **jabbing - jabbed**)

jack [dʒæk] *noun* **(a)** instrument for raising something heavy, especially a car; *I used the jack to lift the car up and take the wheel off* **(b)** *(in playing cards)* the card with the face of a young man, with a value between the queen and the ten; *I won because I had the jack of hearts* **(c)** the **Union Jack** = flag of the United Kingdom

jacket [ˈdʒækɪt] *noun* short coat worn with trousers; *this orange jacket shows up in the dark when I ride my bike; take your jacket off if you are hot*; **jacket potatoes** or **potatoes in their jackets** = potatoes cooked in an oven with their skins on

jail [dʒeɪl] **1** *noun* prison; *she was sent to jail for three months* **2** *verb* to put someone in prison; *he was jailed for six years*

jam [dʒæm] **1** *noun* **(a)** sweet food made by boiling fruit and sugar together; *open another pot of blackcurrant jam*; *do you want jam or honey on your bread?* **(b)** block which happens when there are too many things in a small space; **traffic jam** = too much traffic on the roads, so that cars and trucks can't move; *the accident on Waterloo Bridge caused traffic jams all over London* **2** *verb* **(a)** *(of machine)* to stick and not to be able to move; *hold on - the paper has jammed in the printer* **(b)** to force things into a small space; *don't try to jam all those boxes into the back of the car*

(NOTE: jamming - jammed)

January [ˈdʒænjuəri] *noun* first month of the year, followed by February; *he was born on January 26th*; *we never go on holiday in January because it's too cold*

Japan [dʒəˈpæn] *noun* country in the Far East, formed of several islands to the east of China and south of Korea; *the 1998 Winter Olympics were held in Japan* (NOTE: capital: **Tokyo**; people: **the Japanese**; language: **Japanese**)

Japanese [dʒæpəˈniːz] **1** *adjective* referring to Japan; *a typical Japanese meal can include rice and raw fish* **2** *noun* **(a)** **the Japanese** = people from Japan; *the Japanese are very formal people* **(b)** language spoken in Japan; *he has lived in Japan for some time and speaks quite good Japanese*; *we bought a Japanese phrase book before we went to Japan*

jar [dʒɑː] *noun* container for jam, etc., usually made of glass; *there was some honey left in the bottom of the jar*

jaw [dʒɔː] *noun* bones in the face which hold your teeth and form your mouth; *she hit him so hard that she broke his jaw*

jealous [ˈdʒeləs] *adjective* feeling annoyed because you want something which belongs to someone else; *she was jealous of his new car*; *her new boyfriend is very handsome - I'm jealous!*

jeans [dʒiːnz] *noun* trousers made of a type of strong blue cloth; *I like wearing jeans better than wearing a skirt; he bought a new pair of jeans*

Jeep [dʒiːp] *noun* trademark for a strong small vehicle used for travelling over rough ground, used especially by the army; *the line of jeeps and tanks crossed slowly over the bridge*

jelly [ˈdʒeli] *noun* type of sweet food which wobbles, flavoured with fruit; *the children had fish fingers and chips followed by jelly and ice cream*

jelly baby [ˈdʒeli ˈbeɪbi] *noun* children's sweet made of coloured jelly, shaped like a little baby; *she gave the little girl a bag of jelly babies*

jelly bean [ˈdʒeli ˈbiːn] *noun* sweet of coloured jelly, shaped like a bean; *he keeps a jar of jelly beans on his desk*

jellyfish [ˈdʒelifɪʃ] *noun* animal with a body like jelly, which lives in the sea; *watch out when you're bathing - jellyfish can sting!* (NOTE: plural is **jellyfish**)

jerk [dʒɜːk] **1** *noun* sudden sharp pull; *he felt a jerk on the fishing line* **2** *verb* to pull something sharply; *he jerked the rope*

jersey [ˈdʒɜːzi] *noun* **(a)** pullover which fits close to your body; *after the game the players swapped jerseys with the other team* **(b)** type of cow which gives very rich milk

jet [dʒet] *noun* **(a)** long narrow stream of liquid or gas; *jets of water from the fire engines put out the flames* **(b)** aircraft with jet engines; *we live near the airport so jets fly overhead all the time*

jet engine [ˈdʒet ˈendʒɪn] *noun* engine which is worked by a jet of gas; *the two jet engines are on either side of the plane*

jewel [ˈdʒuəl] *noun* valuable stone, such as a diamond; *I'll just lock up these jewels in the safe*

jewellery *US* **jewelry** [ˈdʒuːəlri] *noun* pretty decorations to be worn, made from valuable stones, gold, silver, etc.; *the burglar stole all her jewellery*

jigsaw [ˈdʒɪgsɔː] *noun* puzzle made of pieces of wood or cardboard which are cut into strange shapes and which you have to fit together to make a picture; *I'm struggling with a 2000-piece jigsaw that my mother gave me for my birthday*

job [dʒɒb] *noun* **(a)** regular work which you get paid for; *she's got a job in the supermarket*; *he's finding it difficult getting a job because he can't drive* **(b)** piece of work; *he does all sorts of little electrical jobs around the house* **(c)** *(informal)* **it's a good**

job that = it's lucky that; *what a good job you brought your umbrella!*; *it's a good job you're not hungry, as there's nothing in the fridge* **(d)** *(informal)* difficulty; *I had a job trying to find your house*; *what a job it was getting a hotel room during August*

jog [dʒɒg] *verb* **(a)** to run at an easy pace, especially for exercise; *he jogged along the river bank for two miles* **(b)** to give a little push; *someone jogged my elbow and I spilt my drink*; *it jogged his memory* = it made him remember (NOTE: **jogging - jogged**)

join [dʒɔɪn] *verb* **(a)** to come together; *the two rivers join about four kilometres beyond the town* **(b)** to become a member of a club, group, etc.; *after university, he is going to join the police* **(c)** to do something with someone; *we're going to the cinema tonight - why don't you join us?*

joint [dʒɔɪnt] *noun* **(a)** place in your body where bones come together and can move, such as your knee or elbow; *her elbow joint hurt after the game of tennis* **(b)** large piece of meat, especially for roasting; *the joint of lamb was very tender*

joke [dʒəʊk] *noun* thing said or done to make people laugh; *she poured water down his neck as a joke*; *he told jokes all evening*

jolly ['dʒɒli] **1** *adjective* happy, pleasant, which you enjoy; *her birthday party was a very jolly affair* (NOTE: **jollier - jolliest**) **2** *adverb (informal)* very; *it's jolly hard work carrying all those boxes upstairs*

journal ['dʒɜːnl] *noun (formal)* diary; *he kept a journal during his visit to China*

journalist ['dʒɜːnəlɪst] *noun* person who writes for newspapers or reports on events for radio or TV; *the journalists asked the police inspector some very awkward questions*

journey ['dʒɜːni] *noun* travelling, usually a long distance; *they went on a train journey across China*

joy [dʒɔɪ] *noun* state of being very happy; *we all wished them great joy on their wedding day*

judge [dʒʌdʒ] **1** *noun* **(a)** person appointed to make legal decisions in a court of law; *the judge let him off with a small fine* **(b)** person who decides which is the best entry in a competition; *the three judges of the beauty contest couldn't agree* **2** *verb* to make decisions in a court of law or competition, etc.; *her painting was judged the best and she won first prize*

jug [dʒʌg] *noun* container with a handle, used for pouring liquids; *could we have another jug of water, please?*

juice [dʒuːs] *noun* liquid from fruit, vegetables, etc.; *they charged me £1 for two glasses of orange juice*; *she had a glass of carrot juice for breakfast*

juicy ['dʒuːsi] *adjective* full of juice; *these are the juiciest oranges we've had this year* (NOTE: **juicier - juiciest**)

July [dʒuˈlaɪ] *noun* seventh month of the year, between June and August; *July is always one of the busiest months for holidays*; *last July it rained a lot*

jumble sale ['dʒʌmbl 'seɪl] *noun* sale of odd items organized by a club or organization to raise money; *there will be a jumble sale at the village hall on May 2nd*

jump [dʒʌmp] **1** *noun* sudden movement off the ground and into the air; *(in sports)* **long jump** *or* **high jump** = sport where you see who can jump the furthest or highest; *she won a gold medal in the high jump* **2** *verb* **(a)** to go suddenly into the air off the ground; *quick, jump on that bus - it's going to Oxford Circus!*; *she jumped down from the chair; the horse jumped over the fence* **(b)** to make a sudden movement because you are frightened; *when they fired the gun, it made me jump*

jumper ['dʒʌmpə] *noun* warm woollen knitted pullover; *I bought a pink jumper in the sales*

junction ['dʒʌŋkʃn] *noun* place where railway lines or roads meet; *leave the motorway at Junction 5*

June [dʒuːn] *noun* sixth month of the year, between May and July; *last June we had a holiday in Canada*; *June is usually one of the hottest months here*

jungle [ˈdʒʌŋgl] *noun* thick tropical forest which is difficult to travel through; *they walked into the jungle, hoping to find rare birds*

junior [ˈdʒuːnɪə] *adjective* for younger children; **junior school** = school for children from 7 to 11 years old

junk [dʒʌŋk] *noun* **(a)** useless things, rubbish; *you should throw away all that junk you keep under your bed*; **junk food** = bad food which you can buy and which is less good for you than food made at home **(b)** large Chinese sailing boat; *Hong Kong harbour was full of junks*

just [dʒʌst] *adverb* **(a)** exactly; *is that too much sugar? - no, it's just right*; *thank you, that's just what I was looking for* **(b)** *(showing the very recent past)* *the train has just arrived from Paris*; *she had just got into her bath when the phone rang*
just as [ˈdʒʌst ˈæz] **(a)** at the same time; *just as I got into the car there was a loud bang* **(b)** in exactly the same way; *she loves her cats just as other people love their children*
just now [ˈdʒʌst ˈnaʊ] **(a)** at the present time; *we're very busy in the office just now* **(b)** a short time ago; *I saw her just now in the post office*

justice [ˈdʒʌstɪs] *noun* fair treatment in law; *justice must always be seen to be done*

justify [ˈdʒʌstɪfaɪ] *verb* to show that something is fair, to prove that something is right; *how can you justify spending all that money?*

Kk

K, k [keɪ] eleventh letter of the alphabet, between J and L; *in words like 'know' or 'knock' the K is not pronounced*

kangaroo [kæŋgəˈruː] *noun* large Australian animal, which carries the young animals in a pouch

keel [kiːl] *noun* long beam in the bottom of a ship; *the dolphins swam under the keel and came up on the other side of the ship*

keen [kiːn] *adjective* **keen on something or someone** = liking something or someone, enthusiastic about something; *he's very keen on keeping fit - he goes running every morning*; *I don't think she's very keen on her new maths teacher* (NOTE: **keener - keenest**)

keep [kiːp] *verb* **(a)** to have for a long time or for ever; *I don't want that book any more, you can keep it* **(b)** to continue to do something; *the clock kept going even after I dropped it on the floor*; *I keep going to sleep in the French class*; *the food will keep warm in the oven* **(c)** to have or put something in a particular place; *I keep my car keys in my pocket* **(d)** to make someone stay in a place or state; *it's cruel to keep animals in cages*; *I was kept late at the office* **(e)** to stay; **let's keep in touch** = we mustn't lose contact with each other; **she kept him company** = she stayed with him; **to keep an eye on** = to watch carefully; *he's keeping an eye on the shop while I'm away* **(f)** to raise animals; *she keeps a pair of goats in her back garden* (NOTE: **keeps - keeping - kept** [kept])

keep down [ˈkiːp ˈdaʊn] *verb* **(a)** to keep at a low level; *keep your voice down, the guard will hear us!* **(b)** to stay bent down and hidden; *keep down behind the wall so that they won't see us*

keep off ['kiːp 'ɒf] *verb* not to walk on; *keep off the grass!*

keep on ['kiːp 'ɒn] *verb* to continue to do something; *my computer keeps on breaking down*; *the cars kept on moving even though the road was covered with snow*

keep out ['kiːp 'aʊt] *verb* **(a)** to stop someone going in; *there were 'Keep Out!' notices round the building site* **(b)** not to get involved; *try to keep out of trouble with the police*

keep up with ['kiːp 'ʌp wɪð] *verb* to go at the same speed as; *my foot hurts, that's why I can't keep up with the others*

kennel ['kenl] *noun* small hut for a dog; *the dog spent the night in its kennel*

kept [kept] *see* KEEP

kerb [kɜːb] *noun* stone edge to a pavement; *she slipped on the edge of the kerb and twisted her ankle*

ketchup ['ketʃʌp] *noun* spiced tomato sauce, available in bottles; *do you want some ketchup with your hamburgers?*

kettle ['ketl] *noun* container with a lid and spout, used for boiling water; *each bedroom has an electric kettle, tea bags and packs of instant coffee*; **to put the kettle on** = to start heating the water in a kettle; *I've just put the kettle on so we can all have a cup of tea*; **the kettle's boiling** = the water in the kettle is boiling

key [kiː] **1** *noun* **(a)** specially shaped piece of metal used to open a lock; *I can't start the car, I've lost the key*; *where did you put the front door key?* **(b)** part of a computer, piano, etc., which you push down with your fingers; *the 'F' key always sticks*; *there are sixty-four keys on the keyboard* **2** *adjective* most important; *the key person in the team is the goalkeeper*

keyboard ['kiːbɔːd] **1** *noun* set of keys on a computer, piano, etc.; *she spilled her coffee*

on the computer keyboard **2** *verb* to put data into a computer, using a keyboard; *she was keyboarding the figures*

kg = KILOGRAM

kick [kɪk] **1** *noun* **(a)** hitting with your foot; *the goalkeeper gave the ball a kick* **(b)** *(informal)* thrill, feeling of excitement; *he gets a kick out of watching a football match on TV* **2** *verb* to hit something with your foot; *he kicked the ball into the net*; *she kicked her little brother*

kid [kɪd] **1** *noun* **(a)** *(informal)* child; *I saw your kids going off on the bus this morning*; *they've been married a few years, and have got a couple of kids*; **kid brother** = younger brother **(b)** young goat; *a mother goat and two little kids* **2** *verb* *(informal)* to make someone believe something which is not true; **I was only kidding** = I didn't mean it (NOTE: kidding - kidded)

kidnap ['kɪdnæp] *verb* to steal a child or an adult and take them away; *the millionaire's son was kidnapped and held for two weeks* (NOTE: kidnapping - kidnapped)

kill [kɪl] *verb* to make someone or something die; *the drought has killed all the crops*; *the car hit a cat and killed it*

kilo ['kiːləʊ] *noun* = KILOGRAM *I want to buy two kilos of sugar*; *these oranges cost 75p a kilo* (NOTE: plural is kilos)

kilogram ['kɪləgræm] *noun* measure of weight (= one thousand grams); *I bought a 2kg (two kilogram) bag of sugar*

kilometre US **kilometer** [kɪ'lɒmɪtə] *noun* measure of distance, one thousand metres; *the car was only doing 80 kilometres (80km) an hour when the accident occurred*; *the town is about ten kilometres from the sea*

kilt [kɪlt] *noun* skirt worn by men in Scotland, and also by women; *she wore a red kilt*; *Scottish soldiers wear kilts*

kind [kaɪnd] **1** *adjective* friendly, offering help, thinking about other people; *it's very kind of you to offer to help*; *how kind of you* *to invite him to your party!* (NOTE: **kinder - kindest**) **2** *noun* sort, type; *a butterfly is a kind of insect*; *we have several kinds of apples in our garden*

king [kɪŋ] *noun* **(a)** man who reigns over a country; *the king and queen came to visit the town*; *King Henry VIII had six wives* **(b)** main piece in chess; *she moved her knight to attack his king* **(c)** *(in cards)* the card with the face of a man with a beard; *he knew he could win because he had the king of spades*

kingdom [ˈkɪŋdʌm] *noun* **(a)** land ruled over by a king or queen; *England is part of the United Kingdom* **(b)** part of the world of nature which groups all of one type of living things; *the animal kingdom*

kingfisher [ˈkɪŋfɪʃə] *noun* small bright blue bird that dives for fish; *we saw a kingfisher down by the pond*

kiss [kɪs] **1** *noun* touching someone with your lips to show love; *she gave the baby a kiss* (NOTE: plural is **kisses**) **2** *verb* to touch someone with your lips to show that you love them; *they kissed each other goodbye*

kit [kɪt] *noun* **(a)** clothes and personal equipment, usually packed for carrying; *did you bring your tennis kit?* **(b) first aid kit** = box with bandages kept to be used in an emergency; *the doctor rushed to the scene with his first aid kit*; **repair kit** = box with tools for repairing a machine, especially for repairing a car; *there is a repair kit provided in the boot of each car*

kitchen [ˈkɪtʃən] *noun* room where you cook food; *if you're hungry, have a look in the kitchen to see if there's anything to eat*; *don't come in with dirty shoes on - I've just washed the kitchen floor*

kite [kaɪt] *noun* **(a)** toy made of light wood and paper or cloth which is flown in a strong wind on the end of a string; *the wind nearly blew the kite away* **(b)** shape in mathematics like a kite, with two short sides and two long sides, and no right angles

kitten [ˈkɪtn] *noun* baby cat; *the kittens are playing in their basket*

kiwi [ˈkiːwiː] *noun* bird which cannot fly, found in New Zealand; **kiwi fruit** = small tropical fruit, with a rough skin and green flesh; *kiwi fruit are full of vitamins*

km [kɪˈlɒmɪtəz] = KILOMETRE *the furthest distance I have travelled by train is 800km (say 'eight hundred kilometres')*; *the road crosses the railway line about 2km from here*

knee [niː] *noun* **(a)** joint in the middle of your leg, where it bends; *she sat the child on her knee*; *he was on his knees looking under the bed* **(b)** part of a pair of trousers that covers the knee; *my jeans have holes in both knees*

kneel [niːl] *verb* to go down on your knees; *everyone knelt down and the priest said a prayer* (NOTE: **kneeling - kneeled** *or* **knelt** [nelt])

knew [njuː] *see* KNOW

knickers [ˈnɪkəz] *noun* woman's or girl's underwear; *she bought a pair of blue knickers*

knife [naɪf] **1** *noun* instrument used for cutting, with a sharp metal blade fixed in a handle; *put out a knife, fork and spoon for each person*; *you need a sharp knife to cut meat* (NOTE: plural is **knives** [naɪvz]) **2** *verb* to stab someone with a knife; *he was knifed in the back during the fight* (NOTE: **knifes - knifing - knifed**)

knight [naɪt] *noun* **(a)** man honoured for services to his country (and taking the title 'Sir'); *he was made a knight* **(b)** brave soldier; *many knights were killed in the Wars of the Roses* **(c)** one of two pieces in a chess set with a horse's head; *with a clever move she took his knight*

knit [nɪt] *verb* to make a piece of clothing out of wool by using two long needles; *my mother is knitting me a pullover*; *he was wearing a blue knitted hat* (NOTE: **knitting - knitted**)

knives [naɪvz] *see* KNIFE

knob [nɒb] *noun* **(a)** round handle on a door, a chest of drawers, etc.; *to open the door, just*

turn the knob (**b**) round button which you turn on a radio, TV, etc.; *turn the knob to increase the volume*

knock [nɒk] **1** *noun* sound made by hitting something; *suddenly, there was a knock at the door* **2** *verb* to hit something; *knock twice before going in*

knock down ['nɒk 'daʊn] *verb* (**a**) to make something fall down; *they are going to knock down the old house to build a factory* (**b**) to hit on the road; *she was knocked down by a car* (**c**) to reduce a price; *they knocked the price down to £50*

knock out ['nɒk 'aʊt] *verb* to hit someone so hard that he or she is no longer conscious; *she was knocked out by a blow on the head*

knot [nɒt] *noun* (**a**) the ends of a piece of string, rope, etc., fastened together; *he's too small to be able to tie knots properly* (**b**) measure of speed used to show the speed of a ship or of the wind; *the ship was doing 22 knots when she hit the rocks*

know [nəʊ] *verb* (**a**) to have learned something, to have information about something; *do you know how to start the computer?*; *do you know the Spanish for 'one - two - three'?*; *his mother doesn't know where he is* (**b**) to have met someone; *I know your sister - we were at school together* (**c**) to have been to a place often; *I know Paris very well*; *she doesn't know Germany at all* (**d**) **you never know** = perhaps; *you never know, she may still turn up*; **as far as I know** = all I know is that; *as far as I know, he left by car at 6 p.m.* (NOTE: **knowing - knew** [njuː] **- has known** [nəʊn])

knowledge ['nɒlɪdʒ] *noun* what a particular person knows about something; **to the best of my knowledge** = as far as I know

known [nəʊn] *see* KNOW

knuckle ['nʌkl] *noun* joint in your fingers; *she hurt her knuckles when she fell*

koala [kəʊ'ɑːlə] *noun* small Australian animal which carries its young in a pouch and lives in trees; *koalas move very slowly and eat leaves*

L, l [el] twelfth letter of the alphabet, between K and M; *Louise wrote her initials 'LL' on the back of the letter*

l = LITRE

label ['leɪbl] **1** *noun* piece of paper, plastic, etc., attached to something to show the price, contents, someone's name and address, etc.; *put a luggage label on your bag if you don't want it to get lost*; **address label** = label with an address on it **2** *verb* to put a label on something; *all the goods are labelled with the correct price*

laboratory [lə'bɒrətri US 'læbrətɔːri] *noun* place where scientific experiments, testing and research are carried out; *all our products are tested in our own laboratories* (NOTE: plural is **laboratories**)

labour *US* **labor** ['leɪbə] *noun* (**a**) hard work; **to charge for materials and labour** = to charge for both the materials used in a job and also the hours of work involved (**b**) **the Labour Party** = political party, one of the main political parties in Britain, which is in favour of the state being involved in industry and welfare; *the polls showed that more people were going to vote Labour than Conservative*

lace [leɪs] *noun* **(a)** thin strip of leather, string, etc., for tying up a shoe; *she's too little to be able to do up her laces herself* **(b)** fabric with open patterns of threads like a net; *her wedding dress was trimmed with lace*

lack [læk] **1** *noun* not having enough of something; *children in the region are suffering from a lack of food* **2** *verb* not to have enough of something; *the doctors staff lack essential equipment*

ladder ['lædə] *noun* climbing device made of horizontal bars between two vertical poles; *he was climbing up a ladder to look at the roof*

ladies ['leɪdɪz] *noun (informal)* women's toilet; *the ladies is down the corridor on the right*; *see also* LADY

ladle ['leɪdl] **1** *noun* large deep spoon for serving soup; *the cook stood by the soup bowl, with her ladle in her hand* **2** *verb* **to ladle out** = to serve with a ladle; *he ladled the soup out into bowls*

lady ['leɪdi] *noun (polite way of referring to a woman)* *there are two ladies waiting to see you* (NOTE: plural is **ladies)**

ladybird *US* **ladybug** ['leɪdɪbɜːd or 'leɪdɪbʌg] *noun* small beetle, usually red with black spots; *I found a ladybird with six spots in the garden*

laid [leɪd] *see* LAY

lain [leɪn] *see* LIE

lake [leɪk] *noun* area of fresh water surrounded by land; *let's take a boat out on the lake*; **the Lake District** = area of north-west England where there are several large lakes and mountains

lamb [læm] *noun* **(a)** young sheep; *in spring, the fields are full of sheep and their tiny lambs* **(b)** meat from a lamb or sheep; *we had roast lamb and mint sauce for lunch*

lamp [læmp] *noun* device which makes light; *the camp site is lit by large electric lamps*; **street lamp** = large light in a street; **table lamp** = lamp on a table

lamppost ['læmpəʊst] *noun* tall post beside a road, holding a lamp; *the bus hit a lamppost*

land [lænd] **1** *noun* solid earth (as opposed to water); *they were glad to be back on (dry) land again after two weeks at sea*; *we bought a piece of land to build a house* **2** *verb* to arrive on the ground; *the flight from Amsterdam has landed*; *we will be landing at London Airport in five minutes*

land up ['lænd 'ʌp] *verb* to arrive finally (in a place); *we were trying to go to the town centre and landed up on the opposite side of the river*

landing ['lændɪŋ] *noun* **(a)** *(especially of aircraft)* arriving on the ground or on a surface; *strong winds meant that landing was difficult* **(b)** flat place at the top of stairs; *she was waiting for me on the landing*

landlady ['lændleɪdi] *noun* woman from whom you rent a house, room, etc.; *you must pay your rent to the landlady every month* (NOTE: plural is **landladies)**

landlord ['lændlɔːd] *noun* man or company from whom you rent a house, room, office, etc.; *the landlord refused to make any repairs to the roof*

landmark ['lændmɑːk] *noun* building or large object on land which you can see easily; *the Statue of Liberty is a famous New York landmark*

landscape ['lændskeɪp] *noun* scenery, appearance of the country; *go to the West Country if you want to see beautiful landscapes*

lane [leɪn] *noun* **(a)** narrow road, often in the country; *we drove along a country lane with hedges on both sides* **(b)** way for traffic going in a particular direction or at a certain speed; *motorways usually have three lanes on either side*; **bus lane** = part of a road where only buses may go

language ['læŋgwɪdʒ] *noun* way of speaking or writing used in a country or by a group of people; *Chinese is a very difficult* *language to learn, but it is the language spoken by most people in the world*; *I don't like travelling in places where I don't know the language*; **foreign language** = language which is not English; *he's studying Greek and Russian in the foreign languages department*

lap [læp] **1** *noun* **(a)** your body from your waist to your knees, when you are sitting; *she listened to the story, sitting in her father's lap* **(b)** one trip round a racetrack; *he's finished lap 23 - only two laps to go!* **2** *verb* **(a)** *(of animal)* to drink with its tongue; *the dog lapped the water in the pond* **(b)** to go so fast that you are one whole lap ahead of another runner in a race; *the winner had lapped three other runners* (NOTE: lapping - lapped)

large [lɑːdʒ] *adjective* very big; *she ordered a large cup of coffee*; *our house has one large bedroom and two very small ones* (NOTE: larger - largest)

larva ['lɑːvə] *noun* early stage in the life of an insect, like a fat worm; *caterpillars are the larvae of butterflies* (NOTE: plural is larvae ['lɑːviː])

laser ['leɪzə] *noun* instrument which produces a very strong beam of light; **laser printer** = office printing machine which prints using a laser beam

lasso [lə'suː] **1** *noun* rope with a loop at the end for catching cows, horses, etc.; *he caught the horse with a lasso* (NOTE: plural is lassoes) **2** *verb* to catch an animal with a lasso; *he lassoed the horse* (NOTE: lassoes - lassoing - lassoed)

last [lɑːst] **1** *adjective* **(a)** which comes at the end of a list, line or period of time; *the post office is the last building on the right*; **last thing at night** = at the very end of the day; *we always have a drink of hot milk last thing at night* **(b)** most recent; *she's been ill for the last ten days*; *the last three books I read were rubbish* **(c)** *(time)* **last night** = the evening and night of yesterday; *we had dinner together last night*; **last Tuesday** = the Tuesday before today; *I saw her last Tuesday*;

have you still got last Tuesday's newspaper? **2** *noun* thing or person coming at the end; *she was the last to arrive* **3** *adverb* **(a)** at the end; *she came last in the competition* **(b)** most recently; *when did you see her last?*; *she was looking ill when I saw her last* **4** *verb* to stay; to go on; *the fine weather won't last*; *our holidays never seem to last very long*

at last *or* **at long last** [æt 'lɑːst or æt 'lɒŋ lɑːst] in the end, after a long time; *I waited for half an hour, and at long last two buses came together*

late [leɪt] **1** *adjective* **(a)** after the usual time; after the time when it was expected; *the plane is thirty minutes late*; *it's too late to change your ticket* **(b)** at the end of a period of time; *the traffic is always bad in the late afternoon*; *he moved to London in the late 1980s* **(c)** **latest** = most recent; *have you seen his latest film?*; *he always drives the latest model car* **2** *adverb* **(a)** after the usual time; *the plane arrived late*; *I went to bed later than usual last night* **(b)** **later** = at a time after the present; after a time which has been mentioned; *can we meet later this evening?*; *we were only told later that she was very ill*; **see you later!** = I hope to see you again later today (NOTE: later - latest)

lately ['leɪtli] *adverb* during recent days or weeks; *have you seen her father lately?*

laugh [lɑːf] **1** *noun* sound you make when you think something is funny; *'that's right,' she said with a laugh* **2** *verb* to make a sound to show you think something is funny; *she fell off the ladder and everyone laughed*

laughter ['lɑːftə] *noun* sound or act of laughing; *as soon as he opened his mouth, the audience burst into laughter*

launch [lɔːntʃ] **1** *noun* type of small motor boat; *he took the launch out on the lake* (NOTE: plural is launches) **2** *verb* **(a)** to put a boat into the water, especially for the first time and with a lot of ceremony; *the Queen launched the new ship* **(b)** to give something or someone a start; *the TV ad helped to* *launch her film career*

launderette *US* **laundromat** ['lɔːndret or 'lɔːndrəmæt] *noun* shop with washing machines which anyone can pay to use; *I take my washing to the launderette once a week*

laundry ['lɔːndri] *noun* **(a)** place where clothes are washed; *the hotel's sheets and towels are sent to the laundry every day* **(b)** dirty clothes to be sent for washing; *please put any laundry into the bag provided*

lava ['lɑːvə] *noun* hot liquid rock flowing from a volcano; *the flow of lava came down the side of the mountain towards our house*

lavatory ['lævətri] *noun* **(a)** toilet, a small room for getting rid of waste matter or water from your body; *the men's lavatory is to the right*; *the lavatories are at the rear of the plane* **(b)** bowl with a seat and water system, for getting rid of waste matter from the body; *the drink was so awful that I poured it down the lavatory* (NOTE: plural is **lavatories**)

law [lɔː] *noun* **(a) the law** = the set of rules by which a country is governed; **within the law** = according to the laws of a country; **against the law** = not according to the laws of a country **(b)** one single part of the rules governing a country, usually in the form of an act of parliament; *Parliament has passed a law against the owning of guns* **(c)** general scientific rule; *you can show how the law of gravity works by throwing an apple into the air and watching it fall to the ground*

lawn [lɔːn] *noun* part of a garden covered with short grass; *he lay on his back on the lawn*

lawnmower ['lɔːnməʊə] *noun* machine for cutting grass; *the quiet of the Sunday morning was broken by the sound of electric lawnmowers in all the gardens*

lawyer ['lɔːjə] *noun* person who has studied law and can advise you on legal matters; *if you are arrested you have the right to speak to your lawyer*

lay [leɪ] *verb* **(a)** to put something down flat; *he laid the papers on the table* **(b) to lay the table** = to put knives, forks, spoons, etc., on the table ready for a meal; *the table is laid for four people* **(c)** to produce an egg; *the hens laid three eggs* **(d)** *see also* LIE (NOTE: **laying - laid**)

layer ['leɪə] *noun* flat, usually horizontal, covering of something; *she put a layer of chocolate on the cake, then one of cream*

layout ['leɪaʊt] *noun* design, especially of a building, a garden, a book, etc.; *the burglars must have had a plan of the layout of the house*

lazy ['leɪzi] *adjective* not wanting to do any work; *he is so lazy he doesn't even bother to open his mail* (NOTE: **lazier - laziest**)

lb [paʊndz] = POUND(S) *take 6lb of sugar*

lead 1 [led] *noun* **(a)** very heavy soft metal; *tie a piece of lead to your fishing line to make it sink* **(b)** black part in the middle of a pencil; *you can't draw if your lead's broken* **2** [liːd] *noun* **(a)** electric wire which joins a machine to the electricity supply; *the lead is too short to go across the room* **(b)** first place (in a race); *who's in the lead at the halfway stage?* **(c)** string or thin piece of leather to hold a dog; *all dogs must be kept on a lead in the park* **3** [liːd] *verb* **(a)** to be in first place, to have the most important place; *our side was leading at half time* **(b)** to go in front to show the way; *she led us to a room at the back of the shop* **(c)** to be in charge of; to be the main person in a group; *she is leading a group of young people on a tour of the Far East* (NOTE: **leading - led** [led])

lead up to ['liːd 'ʌp tuː] *verb* to prepare the way for something to happen; *the events which led up to the war*

leader ['liːdə] *noun* person who leads; *he is the leader of the Labour Party*

leaf [liːf] *noun* one of many flat green parts of a plant; *the leaves of most trees turn brown or red in autumn* (NOTE: plural is **leaves** [liːvz])

leaflet ['liːflət] *noun* folded sheet of paper

giving information; *we handed out leaflets at the beginning of the meeting*

league [liːg] *noun* group of sports clubs which play against each other; *he plays for a club in the southern football league*; **league table** = list of things placed in order of quality, good work, etc.; *the newspapers published the government's annual league table of schools*

leak [liːk] **1** *noun* **(a)** escape of liquid or gas, etc., through a hole; *I can smell gas - there must be a gas leak in the kitchen* **(b)** escape of secret information; *she was embarrassed by the leak of the news* **2** *verb* **(a)** *(of liquid or gas, etc.)* to flow away, to escape; *water must have been leaking through the ceiling for days* **(b)** *(of container or pipe)* to have a hole; *the kettle has started leaking* **(c)** to pass on secret information; *governments don't like their plans to be leaked to the press*

lean [liːn] **1** *adjective; (of meat)* with little fat; *a slice of lean ham* (NOTE: leaner - leanest) **2** *verb* **(a)** to keep upright by being in a sloping position; *the ladder was leaning against the shed*; *she leant her bike against the wall* **(b)** to bend over; *it's dangerous to lean out of car windows* (NOTE: leaning - leaned *or* leant [lent])

lean on ['liːn 'ɒn] *verb* **(a)** to try to influence someone; *someone must have leant on the committee to get them to agree* **(b)** to depend on someone; *if things get difficult she always has her father to lean on*

leant [lent] *see* LEAN

leap [liːp] *verb* to jump; *she leapt with joy when she heard the news* (NOTE: leaping - leaped *or* leapt [lept])

leap year ['liːp 'jɜː] *noun* every fourth year, in which February has 29 days; *the years 2008 and 2012 are both leap years*

leapt [lept] *see* LEAP

learn [lɜːn] *verb* **(a)** to find out about something, or how to do something; *he's learning to ride a bicycle*; *we learn French and German at school* **(b)** to hear (news); *her teacher learned that she was planning to*

leave the college (NOTE: learning - learnt [lɜːnt] *or* learned)

least [liːst] **1** *adjective* smallest; *this car uses by far the least petrol* **2** *pronoun* the least = the smallest amount; *out of our group she spent the least during our trip to Paris*; **to say the least** = which was more than I expected; *he was supposed to be in class so when I saw him in the supermarket I was surprised to say the least*

leather ['leðə] *noun* skin of animals used to make shoes, bags, etc.; *my shoes have leather soles*

leave [liːv] *verb* **(a)** to go away from somewhere; *Eurostar leaves Waterloo for Brussels every day at 8.25* **(b)** to forget to do something; to forget to take something with you; *I packed in a rush and left my toothbrush at home* **(c)** to allow something to stay in a certain condition; *did you leave the light on when you locked up?*; *someone left the door open and the dog got out* **(d)** to go away from someone; **leave me alone** = don't bother me **(e)** not to do something, so that someone else has to do it; *she went out leaving me to do all the washing up* (NOTE: leaving - left [left])

leave behind ['liːv bɪ'haɪnd] *verb* to forget to take something with you; not to take something with you; *he left his car keys behind in the post office*

leave out ['liːv 'aʊt] *verb* to forget something; not to put something in; *she left out the date on the cheque*

leaves [liːvz] *see* LEAF, LEAVE

led [led] *see* LEAD

ledge [ledʒ] *noun* narrow flat part which sticks out from a cliff or building; *every little ledge on the cliff is occupied by a seagull's nest*

leek [liːk] *noun* vegetable of the onion family, with a white stem and long green leaves; *a bowl of leek and potato soup* (NOTE: do not confuse with **leak**)

left [left] **1** *adjective* **(a)** not right, referring to the side of the body which usually has the hand you use less often; *I can't write with my left hand*; *the post office is on the left side of the street as you go towards the church* **(b)** still there, not used up; *after paying for the food and drink, I've still got £3 left* **2** *noun* the side towards the left; *remember to drive on the left when you are in Britain*; *the school is on the left as you go towards the town centre* **3** *adverb* towards the left; *go straight ahead and turn left at the traffic lights*

left-hand ['left'hænd] *adjective* on the left side; *the book is in the left-hand drawer of his desk*; *in England cars drive on the left-hand side of the road*

left-handed ['left'hændɪd] *adjective* using the left hand more often than the right for doing things; *she's left-handed, so we got her a left-handed cup for her birthday*

leg [leg] *noun* **(a)** part of the body with which a person or animal walks; *she fell down the steps and broke her leg;* **to pull someone's leg** = to tease someone, to play a joke on someone **(b)** one of the parts of a chair, etc., which touch the floor; *the table has four legs* **(c)** leg of an animal used for food; *roast leg of lamb*

legal ['li:gl] *adjective* **(a)** according to the law, allowed by the law; *it's legal to learn to drive at 17* **(b)** referring to the law; **to take legal advice** = to ask a lawyer to advise about a problem to do with the law

leisure ['leʒə *US* 'li:ʒə] *noun* **leisure (time)** = free time when you can do what you want; **leisure centre** = building where people can play sports, put on plays, dance, act, etc.; *she goes to dance classes at the local leisure centre*

lemon ['lemən] *noun* pale yellow fruit with a sour taste; *oranges are much sweeter than lemons*; **lemon squash** = drink made of lemon juice and water

lemonade [lemə'neɪd] *noun* drink flavoured with lemons; *can I have a glass of lemonade with ice, please?*

lend [lend] *verb* to let someone use something for a certain period of time; *he asked me if I would lend him £5 till Monday*; *I lent her my dictionary and now she won't give it back* (NOTE: **lending - lent** [lent])

length [leŋθ] *noun* **(a)** measurement of how long something is from end to end; *the table is at least twelve feet in length* **(b)** **length of time** = amount of time something takes or lasts; *can you estimate the length of time you need to do this?* **(c)** long piece of something; *we need two 3m lengths of copper pipe for the central heating system* **(d)** distance from one end to the other of a swimming pool; *he swam two lengths of the swimming pool*

lens [lenz] *noun* piece of curved glass or plastic used in spectacles, cameras, etc.; *if the sun is strong enough you can set fire to a piece of paper using a lens*; **contact lenses** = tiny lenses worn directly on your eyes instead of glasses

lent [lent] *see* LEND

less [les] **1** *adjective & pronoun* a smaller amount (of); *you will get thinner if you eat less bread*; *the total bill came to less than £10*; *she finished her homework in less than an hour* **2** *adverb* not as much; *the second film was less interesting than the first*; **less and less** = getting smaller all the time; *I enjoy my work less and less*; **more or less** = almost, not completely; *the rain has more or less stopped* **3** *preposition* minus, with a certain amount taken away; *we pay £10 an hour, less 50p for insurance*

lessen ['lesən] *verb* to become less; to make something become less; *wearing a seat belt lessens the risk of injury* (NOTE: do not confuse with **lesson**)

lesson ['lesən] *noun* **(a)** period of time in school, etc., when you are taught something; *he went to sleep during the French lesson*; *she's taking driving lessons* **(b)** something which you learn from experience and which makes you wiser; **to teach someone a lesson** = to punish someone for doing something wrong; *I locked up her bike - that will teach her a lesson*

let [let] *verb* **(a)** to allow someone to do something; *he let her borrow his car*; *will you let me see the papers?* **(b) to let someone know something** = to tell someone about something, to give someone information about something; *can you let me know when the parcel arrives?* **(c)** to allow someone to borrow a house or office for a while and pay for it; *we're letting our cottage to some friends for the weekend* (NOTE: **letting - has let**)

let go ['let 'gəʊ] *verb* to stop holding on to something; *don't let go of the driving wheel*; *she was holding on to a branch, but then had to let go*

let in ['let 'ɪn] *verb* to allow to come in; *don't let the dog in if she's wet*

let yourself in for ['let jə'self 'ɪn fɔː] *verb* to allow yourself to get involved in something difficult or unpleasant; *she didn't realize what she was letting herself in for when she said she would look after six little children*

let off ['let 'ɒf] *verb* **(a)** not to punish someone severely; *he was charged with stealing, but the judge let him off with a fine* **(b)** to make a gun, etc., fire; *they let off fireworks in the town centre*

let up ['let 'ʌp] *verb* to do less, to become less; *the rain didn't let up all day*; *she's working too hard - she ought to let up a bit*

let's [lets] *(making a suggestion that you and someone else should do something together)* *let's go to the cinema*; *don't let's leave yet* or *let's not leave yet*

letter ['letə] *noun* **(a)** piece of writing sent from one person to another to pass on information; *there were two letters for you in the post*; *don't forget to write a letter to your mother to tell her what we are doing* **(b)** one of the signs which make up the alphabet, a sign used in writing which means a certain

sound; *Z is the last letter of the alphabet*

letterbox ['letəbɒks] *noun* **(a)** box on the pavement where you post letters; *there's a letterbox at the corner of the street* **(b)** hole in a front door through which the postman pushes letters; *the Sunday paper is too big to go through our letterbox*

lettuce ['letɪs] *noun* plant with large green leaves which are used in salads; *he made a salad with lettuce, tomatoes, and cucumber*

level ['levəl] **1** *noun* position relating to height or amount; *the floods had reached a level of 5m above normal* **2** *adjective* **(a)** flat, even; *I don't think these shelves are level, they're sloping* **(b)** equal, the same; *at half-time the scores were level* **(c) level with** = at the same level as; *the floor which is level with the street is the ground floor*

lever ['liːvə] *noun* **(a)** instrument like a metal rod, which helps to lift a heavy object, or to move part of a machine, etc.; *we used a pole as a lever to lift up the block of stone* **(b) gear lever** = handle in a car which changes the gears

liable ['laɪəbl] *adjective* **(a) liable for** = responsible for something in law; *parents can be made liable for their children's debts* **(b) liable to** = likely to do something; *the trains are liable to be late*

library ['laɪbri] *noun* **(a)** place where books are kept which can be borrowed; *he forgot to take his books back to the library* **(b)** collection of books, records, etc.; *he has a big record library* (NOTE: plural is **libraries**)

licence *US* **license** ['laɪsəns] *noun* document which gives you official permission to do something; **driving licence** *US* **driver's license** = permit which allows someone to drive a car, truck, etc.; *people applying for the job hold a valid driving licence*

lick [lɪk] *verb* to stroke with your tongue; *you shouldn't lick the plate when you've finished your pudding*

lid [lɪd] *noun* covering for a container,

sometimes with a handle; *where's the lid of the black saucepan?*; *he managed to get the lid off the jam jar*

lie [laɪ] **1** *verb* **(a)** to say something which is not true; *she was lying when she said she had been at home all evening* (NOTE: in this meaning: **lying - lied**) **(b)** to be in a flat position; to be situated; *the dog spends the evening lying in front of the fire* (NOTE: in this meaning: **lying - lay** [leɪ] - **has lain** [leɪn]) **2** *noun* something which is not true; *that's a lie! - don't believe what he says*

lie down [ˈlaɪ ˈdaʊn] *verb* to put yourself in a flat position, especially on a bed; *I'll just go and lie down for five minutes*

life [laɪf] *noun* **(a)** time when you are alive; *he spent his whole life working on the farm* **(b)** being a living person; **to lose your life** = to die; *several lives were lost when the ship sank*; **she saved my life** = she saved me from dying (NOTE: plural is **lives**) **(c)** living things; **there's no sign of life in the house** = it looks as though there is no one in it

lifeboat [ˈlaɪfbəʊt] *noun* special boat used to rescue people at sea; *the lifeboat looked for the crew of the ship which had sunk*

lift [lɪft] **1** *noun* **(a)** machine which takes people up or down from one floor to another in a building (American English for this is 'elevator'); *take the lift to the tenth floor* **(b)** ride in a car offered to someone; *she gave me a lift to the station* **2** *verb* to pick something up or move it to a higher position; *my case is so heavy I can hardly lift it off the floor*; *he lifted the little girl up so that she could see the soldiers*

light [laɪt] **1** *noun* **(a)** being bright, the opposite of darkness; *I can't read the map by the light of the moon* **(b)** electric bulb which gives light; *turn the light on - I can't see to read*; *it's dangerous to ride a bicycle with no lights* **(c)** **to throw light on something** = to make something easier to understand; **to come to light** = to be discovered **2** *verb* to start to burn, to make something start to burn; *he is*

trying to get the fire to light; *can you light the candles on the birthday cake?* (NOTE: **lighting - lit** [lɪt]) **3** *adjective* **(a)** not heavy; *I can lift this box easily - it's quite light* **(b)** *(colour)* pale; *he was wearing a light green shirt* **(c)** having a lot of light so that you can see well; *it was six o'clock in the morning and just getting light* (NOTE: **lighter - lightest**)

light bulb [ˈlaɪt ˈbʌlb] *noun* glass ball which gives electric light; *you'll need a ladder to change the light bulb*

lighten [ˈlaɪtən] *verb* **(a)** to make brighter, not so dark; *you can lighten the room by painting it white* **(b)** to make lighter, not so heavy; *I'll have to lighten my suitcase - it's much too heavy to carry*

lighthouse [ˈlaɪthaʊs] *noun* tall building near the sea containing a bright light to guide ships away from rocks; *most of the lighthouses on Scottish islands are worked automatically*

lightning [ˈlaɪtnɪŋ] *noun* flash of electricity in the sky, followed by thunder; *the storm approached with thunder and lightning*

lights [laɪts] *noun* traffic lights, red, green and orange lights for making traffic stop and start; *turn left at the next set of lights*

like [laɪk] **1** *preposition* **(a)** similar to, in the same way as; *he's like his mother in many ways*; *like you, I don't get on with the new boss*; **do you feel like a cup of coffee?** = do you want a cup of coffee? **(b)** *(asking someone to describe something)* *what was the weather like when you were on holiday?* **2** *verb* **(a)** to have pleasant feelings about something or someone; *how does he like his new job?*; *in the evening, I like to sit quietly and read the newspaper* **(b)** to want; *I'd like to go to Paris next week*; *take as many apples as you like*

likely [ˈlaɪkli] *adjective* which you think is going to happen; *it's likely to snow this weekend*; *he's not likely to come to the party* (NOTE: **likelier - likeliest**)

limb [lɪm] *noun* leg or arm; *he was lucky not to break a limb in the accident*

lime [laɪm] *noun* **(a)** white substance used in making cement; *the builder brought some bags of lime* **(b)** small green tropical fruit, similar to a lemon; *you need the juice of two limes to make this recipe* **(c)** lime (tree) = large northern tree with smooth leaves; *an avenue of limes*

limit [ˈlɪmɪt] *noun* furthest point beyond which you cannot go; **speed limit** = highest speed at which you are allowed to drive; *the speed limit in towns is 30 miles per hour*; **weight limit** = heaviest weight which something can stand; *the bridge has a weight limit of 3 tonnes*

limited company (Ltd) [ˈlɪmɪtɪd ˈkʌmpəni] *noun* private company in which the shareholders are only responsible for the company's debts up to the amount of capital they have put in; *he works for Jones & Smith, Ltd*

limp [lɪmp] **1** *noun* way of walking, when one leg hurts or is shorter than the other; *he walks with a limp since his accident* **2** *verb* to walk with a limp; *after the accident she limped badly* **3** *adjective* soft, not stiff; *all we had as a salad was two limp lettuce leaves*

line [laɪn] *noun* **(a)** long thin mark; *parking isn't allowed on yellow lines* **(b)** wire along which telephone messages are sent; *the snow brought down the telephone lines* **(c)** row of people, etc.; *we had to stand in line for half an hour to get into the exhibition* **(d)** row of written or printed words; *he printed the first two lines and showed them to me* **(e)** railway line = rails on which trains run; *don't cross the line when a train might be coming* **(f)** piece of string; **fishing line** = long piece of string with a hook at the end; **washing line** = string held between two posts on which clothes are put to dry

line up [ˈlaɪn ˈʌp] *verb* to stand in a line; *line up over there if you want to take the next boat*

linen [ˈlɪnɪn] *noun* cloth made from a plant; *he bought a white linen suit*

liner [ˈlaɪnə] *noun* **(a)** thing used to put inside something; **bin liner** = plastic bag for putting inside a dustbin **(b)** large passenger ship; *they went on a cruise round the Caribbean on a Norwegian liner*

lining [ˈlaɪnɪŋ] *noun* material put on the inside of something, especially of a piece of clothing; *you'll need a coat with a warm lining if you're going to Canada in winter*

link [lɪŋk] **1** *noun* **(a)** something which connects things or places; *the Channel Tunnel provides a fast rail link between England and France* **(b)** one of the rings in a chain; *a chain with solid gold links* **2** *verb* to join together; *they linked arms and walked down the street*; *Eurostar links London and Paris or Brussels*

lion [ˈlaɪən] *noun* large wild animal of the cat family, with yellow-brown fur; *lions can be seen in African nature reserves*

lip [lɪp] *noun* one of the two parts forming the outside of the mouth; *put some cream on your lips to stop them getting cracked*

lipstick [ˈlɪpstɪk] *noun* soft coloured substance for colouring your lips; *she bought a stick of pink lipstick*

liquid [ˈlɪkwɪd] **1** *noun* substance like water, which flows easily and which is not a gas or a solid; *you will need to drink more liquids in hot weather* **2** *adjective* which is neither gas nor solid, and which flows easily; *a bottle of liquid soap*

list [lɪst] **1** *noun* number of things such as names, addresses, etc., written or said one after the other; *we've drawn up a list of people to invite to the party*; *I'll write out a list of the things I need*; **address list** *or* **mailing list** = list of names and addresses of people and companies; **shopping list** = list of things which you need to buy **2** *verb* to say or to write a number of items one after the other; *she listed the ingredients on the back of an envelope*

listen [ˈlɪsən] *verb* to pay attention to

someone who is talking or to something which you can hear; *don't make a noise - I'm trying to listen to the music*; *why don't you listen to what I tell you?*

lit [lɪt] *see* LIGHT

liter [ˈliːtə] *US* = LITRE

literacy [ˈlɪtərəsi] *noun* being able to read and write; *the school is concentrating on improving literacy*

litre *US* **liter** [ˈliːtə] *noun* measurement for liquids (almost 2 pints); *I need a 2 litre tin of blue paint*

litter [ˈlɪtə] *noun* **(a)** rubbish left on streets or in public places; *the council tries to keep the main street clear of litter* **(b)** group of young animals born at one time; *she had a litter of eight puppies*

little [ˈlɪtl] **1** *adjective* **(a)** small, not big; *they have two children - a baby boy and a little girl* **(b)** not much; *we drink very little milk*; *a TV set uses very little electricity* (NOTE: **little - less - least** [liːst]) **2** *pronoun* **a little** = a small quantity; *can I have a little more coffee please?* **3** *adverb* not much; not often; *we go to the cinema very little these days*

little by little [ˈlɪtl ˈbaɪ ˈlɪtl] *adverb* gradually, not all at once; *she's getting better little by little*

live 1 *adjective* [laɪv] **(a)** living, not dead; *there are strict rules about transporting live animals* **(b)** not recorded in advance; *a live radio show* **(c)** carrying electricity; *the boys were killed trying to jump over the live rail* **2** *adverb* [laɪv] not recorded; *the show was broadcast live* **3** *verb* [lɪv] **(a)** to have your home in a place; *they have gone to live in France* **(b)** to be alive; *King Henry VIII lived in the 16th century*

live on [ˈlɪv ˈɒn] *verb* to use food or money to stay alive; *they seem to live on bread and eggs*; *a family can't live on £50 a week*

lively [ˈlaɪvli] *adjective* very active; *it was a very lively party with a dance band and dozens of young people* (NOTE: **livelier -**

liveliest)

liver [ˈlɪvə] *noun* **(a)** large organ in the body which helps to digest food and cleans the blood; *her liver was damaged in the car crash* **(b)** animal's liver used as food; *I'll start with chicken livers and salad*

lives [lɪvz] *see* LIVE

lives [laɪvz] *see* LIFE

living [ˈlɪvɪŋ] **1** *adjective* alive; *does she have any living relatives?* **2** *noun* money that you need for your daily life; *he earns his living by selling postcards to tourists*

living room [ˈlɪvɪŋ ˈruːm] *noun (in a house or flat)* comfortable room for sitting in; *they were sitting in the living room watching TV*

lizard [ˈlɪzəd] *noun* type of small reptile with four legs and a long tail; *little lizards were running around on the walls*

llama [ˈlɑːmə] *noun* animal like a camel, with thick hair, found in South America; *Dan went for a ride on a llama when he was in Peru*

load [ləʊd] **1** *noun* **(a)** heavy objects which are carried in a truck, wagon, etc.; *the lorry delivered a load of bricks* **(b)** responsibility, thing which is difficult to live with; *that's a load off my mind* = I feel much less worried **(c)** *(informal)* **loads of** = plenty, lots of; *you don't have to rush - there's loads of time before the train leaves* **2** *verb* to put something, especially something heavy, into or on to a truck, van, etc.; *they loaded the furniture into the van*

loaf [ləʊf] *noun* large single piece of bread made separately, which you cut into slices before eating it; *he bought a loaf of bread at the corner shop* (NOTE: plural is **loaves** [ləʊvz])

loan [ləʊn] *noun* thing lent, especially a sum of money; *he bought the house with a £100,000 loan from the bank*

loaves [ləʊvz] *see* LOAF

lobster [ˈlɒbstə] *noun* shellfish with a long body, two large claws, and eight legs, used as food; *we had a bowl of lobster soup*

local [ˈləʊkəl] *adjective* referring to a place or district near where you are; *she works as a nurse in the local hospital*; *the local paper comes out on Fridays*; **local authority** = section of elected government which runs a town or district; *we complained to the local authority about the bus service*

locate [ləʊˈkeɪt] *verb* to find the position of something; *divers are trying to locate the wreck of an old Spanish galleon*

location [ləʊˈkeɪʃn] *noun* place or position; *the hotel is in a very central location*

lock [lɒk] **1** *noun* device which closes a door, safe, box, etc., so that you can only open it with a key; *she left the key in the lock, so the burglars got in easily* **2** *verb* to close a door, safe, box, etc., so that it has to be opened with a key; *we always lock the front door before we go to bed*
lock up [ˈlɒk ˈʌp] *verb* **(a)** to close a building by locking the doors; *she was locking up the shop when a customer walked in* **(b)** to put someone in prison; *they locked him up for a week*

locomotive [ləʊkəˈməʊtɪv] *noun* engine of a train; *when the line became electric they got rid of the old steam locomotives*

loft [lɒft] *noun* top part of a house right under the roof; *they have made a bedroom in their loft*

log [lɒg] *noun* thick piece of wood from a tree; *he brought in a load of logs for the fire*

lollipop [ˈlɒlɪpɒp] *noun* sweet on the end of a stick; *the little girl sat sucking a lollipop and didn't say anything*

London [ˈlʌndən] *proper noun* capital of England and the United Kingdom; *she went to the railway station to ask about cheap tickets to London*; *there is a picture of the Tower of London on the front of the book*; **the London Eye** = huge wheel on the south bank of the Thames which turns slowly, with cars (called 'pods') carrying passengers

lonely [ˈləʊnli] *adjective* **(a)** feeling sad because of being alone; *it's odd how lonely you can be in a big city full of people* **(b)** (place) with few or no people; *we spent the weekend in a lonely cottage in the Welsh hills* (NOTE: **lonelier - loneliest**)

long [lɒŋ] **1** *adjective* **(a)** not short in length; *the Nile is the longest river in the world* **(b)** not short in time; *what a long film - it lasted almost three hours* **(c)** *(showing measurement in time)* *how long is it before your holiday starts?* **(d)** *(showing measurement in length)* *the road is six miles long*; *a piece of string a metre long* **2** *adverb* **(a)** for a long time; *have you been waiting long?*; *I didn't want to wait any longer, so I set off home on foot* **(b)** **as long as** *or* **so long as** = provided that; *I like going on picnics as long as it doesn't rain* (NOTE: **longer - longest**) **3** *verb* to want something very much; *I'm longing for a cup of tea*

loo [luː] *noun (informal)* lavatory, toilet; *where's the ladies' loo?*

look [lʊk] *verb* **(a)** to turn your eyes towards something; *I want you to look carefully at this photograph*; *look in the restaurant and see if there are any tables free* **(b)** to appear to be; *is he only forty? - he looks much older than that*
look after [ˈlʊk ˈɑːftə] *verb* to take care of; *who's going to look after your dog when you're away?*
look back [ˈlʊk ˈbæk] *verb* to turn your head to see what is behind you; *he looked back and saw a police car was following him*
look for [ˈlʊk ˈfɔː] *verb* to try to find; *we looked for the watch everywhere but couldn't find it*
look forward to [ˈlʊk ˈfɔːwəd ˈtuː] *phrase* to think happily about something which is going to happen; *the whole family is looking forward to going on holiday*
look into [ˈlʊk ˈɪntʊ] *verb* to try to find out about a matter or problem; *I've asked the manager to look into the question of staff holidays*

look like ['lʊk 'laɪk] *phrase* **(a)** to be similar to; *he looks just like his father* **(b)** *(asking someone to describe something)* *what's he look like, her new boyfriend?* **(c)** to seem to be going to happen; *take an umbrella, it looks like rain*

look out ['lʊk 'aʊt] *verb* to be careful; *look out! - that car is going backwards!*

look out for ['lʊk 'aʊt fɔː] *verb* to keep looking to try to find; *I'll look out for his sister at the party*

look up ['lʊk 'ʌp] *verb* to try to find some information in a book; *I'll look up his address in the telephone book*; *look up the word in the dictionary if you don't know what it means*

loom [luːm] **1** *noun* machine on which you make cloth; *she weaves cloth on a hand loom in her cottage* **2** *verb* to appear in a threatening way; *a storm loomed on the horizon*; *a bus suddenly loomed out of the fog*

loop [luːp] *noun* circle made by a piece of thread or ribbon, etc., which crosses over itself; *to tie your laces, start by making a loop*

loose [luːs] *adjective* not attached; *the front wheel is loose and needs to be tightened* (NOTE: **looser - loosest**)

loosen ['luːsən] *verb* to make something less tight; *he loosened his laces because his shoes were tight*

lord [lɔːd] *noun* **(a)** person who rules or is above other people in society; *powerful lords forced King John to sign the Magna Carta* **(b)** *(expression of surprise or shock)* *good lord! I didn't realize it was so late!*

lorry ['lɒri] *noun* truck, a large motor vehicle for carrying goods; *they put the bricks onto his lorry* (NOTE: plural is **lorries**)

lose [luːz] *verb* **(a)** to put or drop something somewhere and not to know where it is; *I can't find my purse - I think I lost it on the train* **(b)** not to have something any longer; **to lose weight** = to get thinner; *she doesn't eat potatoes as she's trying to lose weight* **(c)** not

to win; *we lost the match 10 - 0; did you win? - no, we lost* (NOTE: **losing - lost** [lɒst])

lost [lɒst] *adjective* **to be lost** = to end up not knowing where you are; *did you bring a map - I think we're lost!*

lot [lɒt] *noun* **(a) a lot of** *or* **lots of** = a large number, a large quantity; *there's lots of time before the train leaves*; *what a lot of cars there are in the car park!* **(b) the lot** = everything; *that's the lot - there's nothing left*

lottery ['lɒtri] *noun* game in which tickets with numbers are sold with prizes given for certain numbers; **the National Lottery** = British lottery which takes place twice a week, where you try to forecast a series of numbers; *she won over £2m on the lottery*; *he buys a lottery ticket every week* (NOTE: plural is **lotteries**)

loud [laʊd] **1** *adjective* making a sound which is very easily heard; *turn down the radio - it's too loud* **2** *adverb* in a loud voice; *I can't sing any louder* (NOTE: **louder - loudest**)

loudly ['laʊdli] *adverb* in a way which is easily heard; *I wish you wouldn't talk so loudly*

loudspeaker [laʊd'spiːkə] *noun* part of a radio, TV, public address system, etc., which allows sound to be heard; *the captain called the passengers over the loudspeaker and asked them to go on deck*

lounge [laʊnʒ] *noun* comfortable room for sitting in; *let's go and watch TV in the lounge*; **departure lounge** = room at an airport where passengers wait to board their planes

love [lʌv] **1** *noun* **(a)** liking someone or something very much; *give my love to your wife*; **to be in love** = to love each other; *they seem to be very much in love* **(b)** *(in games such as tennis)* score of zero points; *she lost the first set six - love (6-0)* **2** *verb* **(a)** to have strong feelings for someone or something; *she loves little children*; *the children love their teacher* **(b)** to like something very much; *we love going on holiday by the seaside*

lovely ['lʌvli] *adjective* very pleasant; *it's a lovely warm day* (NOTE: lovelier - loveliest)

low [ləu] **1** *adjective* not high; *she hit her head on the low branch*; *we shop around to find the lowest prices* (NOTE: lower - lowest) **2** *adverb* towards the bottom; not high up; *the plane was flying too low - it hit the trees*

lower ['ləuə] **1** *adjective* which is below something else of the same sort; **lower deck** = bottom deck on a ship or bus; *they booked a cabin on the lower deck* **2** *verb* to make something go down; *they lowered the boats into the water*

loyal ['lɔɪəl] *adjective* faithful, who always supports someone or something; *dogs are very loyal to their owners*

Ltd ['lɪmɪtɪd] = LIMITED COMPANY; *she has a job at Jones & Smith, Ltd*

luck [lʌk] *noun* something, usually good, which happens to you; *the bus is empty - that's a bit of luck!*; **good luck with your driving test!** = I hope you do well in your driving test; **bad luck** = something bad which happens to you; *it was just my bad luck to have homework when everyone else went swimming*

luckily ['lʌkɪli] *adverb* which is a good thing; *it started to rain but luckily I had taken my umbrella*

lucky ['lʌki] *adjective* **(a)** having good things happening to you; *how lucky you are to be going to Spain!* **(b)** which brings luck; *15 is my lucky number* (NOTE: luckier - luckiest)

luggage ['lʌgɪdʒ] *noun* suitcases, bags, etc., for carrying your clothes when travelling; *check that you haven't left any luggage behind on the train*

lump [lʌmp] *noun* **(a)** piece of something, often with no particular shape; *he put two lumps of sugar into his cup* **(b)** hard or swollen part on the body; *she went to the doctor because she had found a lump in her throat*

lunch [lʌnʃ] *noun* meal eaten in the middle of the day; *we always have lunch at 12.30*; *we are having fish and chips for lunch* (NOTE: plural is **lunches**)

lung [lʌŋ] *noun* one of two parts in the chest which suck in air when you breathe; *the doctor listened to his chest to see if his lungs were all right*

luxury ['lʌkʃəri] *noun* **(a)** great comfort; *he lived a life of great luxury*; **luxury hotel** = a five-star hotel, a very good hotel, with very comfortable rooms and higher prices **(b)** thing which is pleasant to have, but not necessary; *she often buys little luxuries like bars of French soap* (NOTE: plural is **luxuries**)

lying ['laɪɪŋ] *see* LIE

Mm

M, m [em] thirteenth letter of the alphabet, between L and N; *'accommodation' is spelt with two Ms*

machine [mə'ʃiːn] *noun* thing which works with a motor; *the washing machine has broken and flooded the kitchen*; *there is a message on my answering machine*

machinery [mə'ʃiːnəri] *noun* many machines, taken as a group; *the factory has got rid of a lot of old machinery*

mad [mæd] *adjective* **(a)** with a serious mental illness; *he became mad and was put in a special hospital* **(b)** silly, crazy; *everyone thought he was mad to try to cross the*

Atlantic in a rowing boat; *(informal)* **mad about** = very keen on; *he's mad about doing puzzles in newspapers* **(c)** wild and annoyed; *the noise is driving her mad*; *(informal)* **like mad** = very fast; with a lot of enthusiasm; *he drove like mad and managed to get to the station in time to catch the train* **(d)** very angry; *he was hopping mad when they told him his car had been stolen* (NOTE: **madder - maddest)**

madam ['mædəm] *noun* **(a)** *(polite way of referring to a lady)* *after you, madam* **(b)** *(used when writing a letter to a lady you do not know)* ***Dear Madam***

made [meɪd] *see* MAKE

magazine [mægə'ziːn] *noun* illustrated paper which is published on the same day each week or month; *the TV magazine comes out on Fridays*

magic ['mædʒɪk] *noun* spells, tricks, etc., which do not appear to follow normal scientific rules; *he made a rabbit appear in his hat, and the children all thought it was magic*

magician [mə'dʒɪʃn] *noun* **(a)** wizard; *Merlin was the great magician in old stories* **(b)** conjuror; *they hired a magician to entertain the children at the party*

magnet ['mægnət] *noun* piece of metal which attracts iron and steel; *she has a Mickey Mouse magnet which sticks to the fridge door*

magnetic [mæg'netɪk] *adjective* which attracts metal; *iron and steel can be magnetic but paper and wood can't*

magnificent [mæg'nɪfɪsənt] *adjective* very fine, very splendid; *he lives in a magnificent 20-bedroom house by the lake*

magnifying glass ['mægnɪfaɪɪŋ 'glɑːs] *noun* lens which makes small objects appear larger; *she used a magnifying glass to read the instructions on the bottle*

magpie ['mægpaɪ] *noun* common large black and white bird; *magpies sometimes steal bright objects like bits of glass*

mail [meɪl] **1** *noun* **(a)** letters which are delivered; *the mail hasn't come yet* **(b)** service provided by the post office; *the cheque was lost in the mail* **2** *verb* to send something by post; *we mailed the cheque last Friday*

mail order [meɪl 'ɔːdə] *noun* ordering and buying by post; *I bought the sofa by mail order or from a mail-order catalogue*

mailman ['meɪlmən] *noun US* man who delivers letters (the British equivalent is a 'postman'); *the mailman's been, but he left nothing for you* (NOTE: plural is **mailmen)**

main [meɪn] **1** *adjective* most important; *the main thing is to get to work on time*; *January is the main month for skiing holidays* **2** *noun* large pipe for water, gas, etc.; *a water main burst and flooded the street*

mainly ['meɪnli] *adverb* most often; *people mainly go on holiday in the summer*; *she is mainly interested in old churches*

mains [meɪnz] *noun* electricity brought into a building; *our radio can run either on a battery or the mains*

major ['meɪdʒə] **1** *adjective* important; *cigarettes are a major cause of lung cancer* **2** *noun* officer in the army; *a major arrived in a truck with six soldiers*

make [meɪk] *verb* **(a)** to put together, to build; *these knives are made of steel* **(b)** to get ready; *do you want me to make some tea?*; *she is making a Christmas cake* **(c)** to add up to a total; *six and four makes ten* **(d)** to give someone a feeling; *the smell of coffee makes me hungry*; *the rough sea made him feel sick* **(e)** to force someone to do something; *his mother made him clean his room*; *the teacher made us all stay in after school* (NOTE: **making - made** [meɪd])

make for ['meɪk 'fɔː] *verb* to go towards; *as soon as the film started, she made straight for the exit*

make out ['meɪk 'aʊt] *verb* **(a)** to be able to see clearly; *can you make out the house in the dark?* **(b)** to claim something which is probably not true; *she tries to make out that she's very poor*

make up [ˈmeɪk ˈʌp] *verb* **(a)** to invent a story; *he said he had seen a man climbing into the house, but in fact he made the whole story up* **(b)** **to make yourself up** = to put on powder, lipstick, etc. **(c)** **to make up your mind** = to decide; *they can't make up their minds on where to go for their holiday*

makeup [ˈmeɪkʌp] *noun* face powder, lipstick, etc., which are put on your face to make it more beautiful or to change its appearance; *she wears no makeup apart from a little lipstick*; *he spent hours over his makeup for the part of the old grandfather in the school play*

male [meɪl] **1** *adjective* referring to the sex which does not give birth to young; *a male deer crossed the road in front of our car* **2** *noun* animal or insect of the sex which does not give birth to young or lay eggs; *with spiders, the female is usually bigger than the male* (NOTE: do not confuse with **mail**)

mammal [ˈmæml] *noun* type of animal which gives birth to live young and feeds them with milk; *human beings, cats, dolphins and bats are all mammals*

man [mæn] **1** *noun* male human being; *there's a young man at reception asking for Mr Smith* (NOTE: plural is **men** [men]) **2** *verb* to provide staff to work something; *she sometimes mans the front desk when everyone else is at lunch* (NOTE: **mans - manning - manned**)

manage [ˈmænɪdʒ] *verb* **(a)** to be in charge of something; *we want to appoint someone to manage the new shop* **(b)** **to manage to do something** = to succeed in doing something; *did you manage to phone the office?*; *the burglars managed to open the door of the safe*

manager [ˈmænɪdʒə] *noun* **(a)** person in charge of a department in a shop or in a business; *the bank manager wants to talk about your account*; *she's the manager of the shoe department* **(b)** person who organizes a sports team; *the club have just sacked their manager*

mane [meɪn] *noun* long hair on the neck of a lion or horse; *he clung onto the horse's mane as it raced along the edge of the sea* (NOTE: do not confuse with **main**)

mango [ˈmæŋgəʊ] *noun* large tropical fruit with yellow flesh and a big stone; *we ate fresh mangoes after our Indian meal* (NOTE: plural is **mangoes**)

manner [ˈmænə] *noun* **(a)** way of behaving; *the doctor has a very unpleasant manner* **(b)** **manners** = way of behaving in public; *it's bad manners to speak with your mouth full*

mantelpiece [ˈmæntlpiːs] *noun* shelf above a fireplace; *the clock on the mantelpiece struck twelve*

manufacture [mænjuˈfæktʃə] *verb* to make products for sale; *we no longer manufacture tractors here*

many [ˈmeni] **1** *adjective* **(a)** a large number of things or people; *many old people live on the south coast*; *she ate twice as many cakes as her sister did* **(b)** *(asking a question)* how *many times have you been to France?*; *how many passengers were there on the plane?* **(c)** **a great many** *or* **a good many** = quite a lot; *a good many people think we should build a ring road round the town*; **too many** = more than necessary; *there were too many people at the meeting and not enough chairs for all of them* (NOTE: **many - more** [mɔː] **- most** [məʊst]) **2** *pronoun* a large number of people; *many of the students know the teacher well because he used to be a student at the college himself*

map [mæp] *noun* drawing which shows a place, such as a town, a country or the world, as if it is seen from the air; *they lost their way because they'd forgotten to take a map*; *if you're going to Paris, you'll need a street map*

marathon [ˈmærəθən] *noun* long distance

race; *a marathon is run over 26 miles*; *she's training for the New York marathon*

marble ['mɑːbl] *noun* **(a)** very hard type of stone which can be polished so that it shines brightly; *the entrance hall has a marble floor* **(b)** marbles = set of small glass balls for playing with; *children were playing marbles in the school playground*

march [mɑːtʃ] **1** *noun* **(a)** walking in step by soldiers, sailors, etc.; *the soldiers were tired after their long march through the mountains* **(b)** protest march = mass of people walking to protest about something; *thousands of people took part in the protest march* **(c)** music with a regular beat for marching; **wedding march** = music which is played after a wedding; *as the bride and bridegroom came out of the church the organ played the wedding march* (NOTE: plural is **marches**) **2** *verb* **(a)** to walk in step; *we were just in time to see the soldiers march past* **(b)** to walk quickly and with a particular purpose; *she marched into the shop and asked to speak to the manager* **(c)** to walk in a protest march; *thousands of workers marched to the parliament building*

March [mɑːtʃ] *noun* third month of the year, between February and April; *her birthday is in March*; *we moved house last March*

margarine [mɑːdʒə'riːn] *noun* mixture of animal or vegetable oil which is used instead of butter; *can you tell the difference between butter and margarine?*

margin ['mɑːdʒɪn] *noun* white space at the edge of a page of writing; *write your notes in the margin*

mark [mɑːk] **1** *noun* **(a)** small spot of a different colour; *the red wine has made a mark on the tablecloth* **(b)** points given to a student; *what sort of mark did you get for your homework?*; *no one got full marks - the top mark was 8 out of 10* **(c)** printed sign; **exclamation mark** = written sign (!) which shows surprise; **question mark** = written sign (?) which shows that a question is being asked

2 *verb* **(a)** to make a mark on something; *the box is marked 'dangerous'* **(b)** to correct and give points to work; *the teacher hasn't finished marking our homework*

market ['mɑːkɪt] *noun* **(a)** place where fruit and vegetables, etc., are sold from small tables, often in the open air; *we buy all our vegetables and fish at the market*; **farmers' market** = market where local farmers sell fruit, vegetables, meat, etc., from their farms direct to the public **(b)** on the market = for sale; *their house has been on the market for three months*

marmalade ['mɑːməleɪd] *noun* jam made from oranges, lemons, grapefruit, etc.; *marmalade is eaten with toast at breakfast, and not at any other time of day*

maroon [mə'ruːn] **1** *adjective* deep purple red; *he was wearing a maroon tie* **2** *verb* to leave someone in a place from which there is no escape; *the bus broke down, leaving us all marooned miles from anywhere*

marriage ['mærɪdʒ] *noun* **(a)** being joined together as husband and wife according to the law; *a large number of marriages end in divorce* **(b)** wedding, the ceremony of being married; *they had a simple marriage, with just ten guests*

marry ['mæri] *verb* **(a)** to make two people husband and wife; *they were married in the village church* **(b)** to become the husband or wife of someone; *she married the boy next door*; *they're getting married next Saturday*

marsh [mɑːʃ] *noun* area of wet land; *ducks and geese come to the marshes during winter* (NOTE: plural is **marshes**)

marsupial [mɑː'suːpiəl] *noun* type of animal found in Australia, which carries its young in a pocket of skin in the front of its body; *kangaroos and koalas are both marsupials*

marvellous *US* **marvelous** ['mɑːvələs] *adjective* wonderful; *the children had a marvellous time at the circus*

masculine ['mæskjʊlɪn] *adjective (in*

grammar) referring to words which have a particular form to show they are male; *is the French word 'table' masculine or feminine?*

mashed potatoes ['mæʃd pə'teɪtəʊz] *noun* potatoes which have been boiled until they are soft and then crushed smooth and mixed with butter and milk; *our children prefer chips to mashed potatoes*

mask [mɑːsk] *noun* something which covers or protects your face; *the burglars wore black masks*; *he wore a mask to go diving*

mass [mæs] **1** *noun* **(a)** large number or large quantity of things; *a mass of leaves blew onto the pavement*; *I have masses of letters to write* **(b)** main Catholic religious service; *she's a strict Catholic and goes to mass every week* (NOTE: plural is **masses**) **2** *adjective* involving a large number of people; **mass meeting** = meeting where a lot of people gather together

massive ['mæsɪv] *adjective* very large; *a massive rock came rolling down the mountain*

mast [mɑːst] *noun* **(a)** tall pole on a ship which carries the sails; *the gale was so strong that it snapped the yacht's mast* **(b)** tall metal construction to carry an aerial; *they have put up a television mast on top of the hill*

mat [mæt] *noun* **(a)** small piece of carpet, etc., used as a floor covering; *wipe your shoes on the mat before you come in*; **bath mat** = small carpet which you step on to when you get out of a bath **(b)** **place mat** = small piece of cloth, wood, etc., put under a plate on a table; *the table was laid with glasses, knives and forks, and place mats*

match [mætʃ] **1** *noun* **(a)** game between two teams, etc.; *we watched the football match on TV* **(b)** small piece of wood or cardboard with a tip which catches fire when you rub it against a rough surface; *she struck a match and lit the candles on the cake* (NOTE: plural is **matches**) **2** *verb* to fit or to go with; *the yellow wallpaper doesn't match the bright green carpet*

mate [meɪt] **1** *noun* **(a)** one of a pair of people or animals, male or female, husband or wife; *some birds sing and others show off their feathers to attract a mate* **(b)** *(informal)* friend; *he's gone down to the pub with his mates*; *sorry, mate, I can't help you!*

material [mə'tɪəriəl] *noun* **(a)** something which can be used to make something; *you can buy all the materials you need in the hardware shop*; **building materials** = cement, wood, bricks, etc., used to build houses **(b)** cloth; *I bought three metres of material to make a curtain*

mathematics *or* **maths** *US* **math** [mæθə'mætɪks *or* mæθs *or* mæθ] *noun* study of numbers and measurements; *mathematics is my best subject*; *he passed in maths, but failed in English*

matter ['mætə] **1** *noun* **(a)** problem, difficulty; **what's the matter?** = what's wrong?; *there's something the matter with the engine* **(b)** concern, business; **it's a matter for the police** = it is something which we should tell the police about **2** *verb* to be important; *it doesn't matter if you're late*; *does it matter if we sit by the window?*

mattress ['mætrəs] *noun* thick pad forming the part of a bed that you lie on; *the children who didn't have beds slept on mattresses on the floor* (NOTE: plural is **mattresses**)

May [meɪ] *noun* fifth month of the year, after April and before June; *her birthday's in May*; *we went on holiday last May*

may [meɪ] *verb used with other verbs* **(a)** *(to mean it is possible)* *take your umbrella, they say it may rain* **(b)** *(to mean 'can', 'it is allowed')* *guests may park in the hotel car park free of charge* **(c)** *(asking questions in a polite way)* *may I ask you something?*

maybe ['meɪbiː] *adverb* possibly, perhaps; *maybe the next bus will be the one we want*; **maybe not** = possibly not; *are you coming? - maybe not*

mayor ['meə] *noun* person who is chosen as the official head of a town, city or local council; *the new leisure centre was opened by the mayor*

me [miː] *object pronoun used by the person who is speaking to talk about himself or herself; give me that book; she's much taller than me; who is it? - it's me!*

meadow ['medəʊ] *noun* large field of grass; *the path through the meadow leads to a little bridge over the river*

meal [miːl] *noun* occasion when people eat food at a special time; *most people have three meals a day - breakfast, lunch and dinner*

mean [miːn] **1** *adjective* **(a)** nasty or unpleasant; *he played a mean trick on his mother* **(b)** who does not like to spend money or to give something; *don't be mean - let me have another chocolate biscuit* (NOTE: **meaner - meanest**) **2** *verb* **(a)** to talk about, to refer to; *did he mean Alex when he was talking about fat children?* **(b)** to show, to represent; *when a red light comes on it means that you have to stop* **(c)** to mean to = to plan to; *I meant to phone you but I forgot* (NOTE: **meaning - meant** [ment])

meaning ['miːnɪŋ] *noun* what a word represents; *if you want to find the meaning of the word, look it up in a dictionary*

means [miːnz] *noun* **(a)** way of doing something; *the bus is the cheapest means of getting round London* **(b)** by all means = of course; *by all means use my phone if you want to* **(c)** money; *it is beyond my means* = I don't have enough money to buy it

meant [ment] *verb* to be meant to = should, ought to; *this medicine is not meant to be used by children*

meanwhile ['miːnwaɪl] *adverb* during this time; *she hid under the table - meanwhile, we were all looking for her in the garden*

measles ['miːzlz] *noun* children's disease which gives a red rash and a high temperature; *one of the children in our class has got*

measles

measure ['meʒə] **1** *noun* **(a)** thing which shows the size or quantity of something; **tape measure** = long strip of plastic marked in centimetres or inches, etc., used for measuring; *he took out a tape measure and measured the length of the table* **(b)** way of showing size; *kilos and pounds are measures of weight* **2** *verb* **(a)** to be of a certain size, length, quantity, etc.; *how much do you measure round your waist?* **(b)** to find out the length or quantity of something; *she measured the room before buying the carpet*

measurement ['meʒəmənt] *noun* quantity or size, etc., found out when you measure; *he took the measurements of the room*

meat [miːt] *noun* food from an animal or bird, not from a fish; *can I have some more meat, please?; would you like meat or fish for your main course?*

mechanical [meˈkænɪkl] *adjective* referring to machines; *engineers are trying to fix a mechanical fault;* **mechanical digger** = machine for digging large holes

medal ['medl] *noun* metal disc, usually attached to a ribbon, made to remember an important occasion or battle, or given to people who have done good things; *the old soldiers put on all their medals for the parade;* **gold medal** *or* **silver medal** *or* **bronze medal** = medal for first, second, third place in sports competitions; *she won a silver medal at the 1996 Olympics*

media ['miːdɪə] *noun* the (mass) media = means of passing information to a large number of people, such as newspapers, TV, radio; *the book attracted a lot of interest in the media*

medical ['medɪkl] *adjective* referring to medicine; *the Red Cross provided medical help;* **medical certificate** = document signed by a doctor to show that a worker has been ill

medicine ['medsɪn] *noun* **(a)** drug taken to treat a disease; *some cough medicines make* *you feel sleepy* **(b)** study of diseases and how to cure or prevent them; *he went to university to study medicine*

medium ['mi:diəm] **1** *adjective* middle, average; *he is of medium height* **2** *noun* type of paint or other materials used by an artist; *he started to experiment with different mediums, such as poster paints* (NOTE: plural is **media** *or* **mediums**)

meet [mi:t] *verb* **(a)** to come together with someone; *he met her at the railway station*; *if you don't know how to get to our house, I'll meet you at the bus stop* **(b)** to come together; *several streets meet at Piccadilly Circus* **(c)** to get to know someone; *I've never met your sister - come and meet her then!* (NOTE: **meeting - met** [met])

meeting ['mi:tɪŋ] *noun* action of coming together in a group; *the next meeting of the club will be on Tuesday*

melon ['melən] *noun* large round fruit which grows on a low plant; *to start the meal we had melon and ham*

melt [melt] *verb* to change from solid to liquid by heating; *if the sun comes out the snow will start to melt*

member ['membə] *noun* person who belongs to a group; *three members of the family are ill*; **Member of Parliament (MP)** = person elected to the House of Commons

membership ['membəʃɪp] *noun* belonging to a group; *membership of the tennis club costs £50 a year*; **membership card** = card which shows you belong to a club or to a political party; *bring your membership card with you*

memory ['memri] *noun* **(a)** *(in people)* being able to remember; *he repeated the poem from memory* **(b)** *(in computers)* part which stores information; *this computer has a much larger memory than the old one* **(c)** memories = things which you remember; *we have many happy memories of our holidays in Greece* (NOTE: the plural is **memories**)

men [men] *see* MAN; **men's toilet** *or* **men's**

room = public lavatory for men

mend [mend] *verb* to repair something which is broken or damaged; *I dropped my watch on the pavement, and I don't think it can be mended*

mental ['mentl] *adjective* referring to the mind; **mental illness** = illness which affects your mind

mention ['mentʃən] *verb* **(a)** to refer to something; *the press has not mentioned the accident* **(b)** not to mention = as well as, not forgetting; *it cost us £20 just to get into the exhibition, not to mention the cost of the meal we had in the museum restaurant*

menu ['menju:] *noun* **(a)** list of food available in a restaurant; *what's on the menu today?* **(b)** list of possible things you can do using a computer program

mercury ['mɜːkjəri] *noun* liquid metal coloured like silver, used in thermometers; *as it got hotter, the mercury rose in the thermometer*

merely ['mɪəli] *adverb* simply, only; *I'm not criticizing you - I merely said I would have done it in a different way*

meringue [mə'ræŋ] *noun* sweet baked dessert made of egg whites and sugar; **lemon meringue pie** = pie with lemon cream inside and meringue on top

merry ['meri] *adjective* happy; *a very Merry Christmas to all our friends!*

mess [mes] *noun* dirt, not being tidy; *the milk boiled over and made a mess on the floor*; *someone will have to clear up the mess after the party*

mess up ['mes 'ʌp] *verb (informal)* to ruin or to spoil; *I can't come because I've got flu - I hope it doesn't mess up your arrangements*

message ['mesɪdʒ] *noun* information which is sent; *can you give Mr Brown a message from his wife?*

messenger ['mesəndʒə] *noun* person who brings a message; *we sent the package by* *special messenger*

met [met] *see* MEET

metal ['metl] *noun* material, such as iron, copper, etc., which can carry heat and electricity and is used for making things; *these spoons are plastic but the knives are metal*; *these chairs are very heavy - they must be made of metal*

meter ['mi:tə] *noun* **(a)** device for counting how much time, water, gas, etc., has been used; *he came to read the gas meter*; **parking meter** = device into which you put money to pay to park your car for a certain time **(b)** US = METRE

method ['meθəd] *noun* way of doing something; *my grandmother showed me her method of making bread*

metre *US* **meter** ['mi:tə] *noun* **(a)** standard measurement of length (equal to 100 centimetres or approximately 39.4 inches); *the river is 50 metres across*; *the table is more than two metres long*; *the walls are two metres thick* **(b)** race over a certain distance measured in metres; *he holds the world record for the 1000 metres*

metric system ['metrɪk 'sɪstəm] *noun* system of measuring, using metres, litres and grams; *the metric system is a decimal system, using basic units multiplied or divided by hundreds, thousands, etc.*

Mexican ['meksɪkən] **1** *adjective* referring to Mexico; *the Mexican football team looks like winning*; *have you seen the photos from our Mexican holiday?* **2** *noun* person from Mexico; *many Mexicans have crossed the border to live in California*

Mexico ['meksɪkəʊ] *noun* large country in Latin America, south of the United States; *there is a long border between the USA and Mexico* (NOTE: capital: **Mexico City**; people: **Mexicans**; language: **Spanish**)

mice [maɪs] *see* MOUSE

microchip ['maɪkrəʊtʃɪp] *noun* very small piece of a mineral substance with electronic circuits printed on it; *microchips are used in computers*

microphone ['maɪkrəfəʊn] *noun* device which you speak into to send sound through the radio or TV, or to record on disk or tape; *the MP had difficulty in making himself heard without a microphone*

microscope ['maɪkrəskəʊp] *noun* instrument with lenses which makes things which are very small appear much larger; *he examined the blood sample under the microscope*

microscopic [maɪkrə'skɒpɪk] *adjective* so small as to be visible only through a microscope; *microscopic forms of life are visible in the oldest rocks*

microwave ['maɪkrəweɪv] **1** *noun* small oven which cooks very rapidly using very short electric waves; *put the dish in the microwave for three minutes* **2** *verb* to cook something in a microwave; *you can microwave those potatoes*

midday ['mɪddeɪ] *noun* twelve o'clock in the middle of the day; *he won't be back home before midday*; *we were having our midday meal when the builders arrived*

middle ['mɪdl] **1** *adjective* in the centre; halfway between two ends; *they live in the middle house of the row, the one with the green door* **2** *noun* **(a)** *(referring to space)* centre; *she was standing in the middle of the road, trying to cross*; *Chad is a country in the middle of Africa* **(b)** *(referring to time)* halfway through a period; *we were woken in the middle of the night by a dog barking*; *we were just in the middle of eating our supper when the phone rang*

midnight ['mɪdnaɪt] *noun* twelve o'clock at night; *I must go to bed - it's after midnight*

might [maɪt] *verb used with other verbs* **(a)** *(to mean it is possible)* *take an umbrella, it might rain*; *if he isn't here, he might be waiting outside* **(b)** *(to mean something should have been)* **you might have told me** = I wish you had told me; *you might have told me* *you'd invited her as well*

migrate [mai'greit] *verb* to move from one place to another with the seasons; *herds of animals migrate across the desert in search of water*

mild [maild] *adjective* **(a)** not harsh, not too bad; *he had a mild heart attack and was soon back to work again* **(b)** not severe (weather); *winters in the south of the country are usually milder than in the north* **(c)** which does not have a strong taste; *we'll choose the mildest curry on the menu* (NOTE: milder - mildest)

mile [mail] *noun* **(a)** measure of length (= 1,760 yards or 1.61 kilometres); *he thinks nothing of cycling ten miles to work every day*; *the car can't go any faster than sixty miles per hour* **(b)** miles = a very long distance; *we walked for miles and came back to the point where we started from* **(c)** *(informal)* miles = much; *it's miles too big* = it's much too big

military ['militri] *adjective* referring to the armed forces; *military service* = period of time served in the armed forces

milk [milk] *noun* white liquid produced by female animals to feed their young, especially the liquid produced by cows; *do you want milk with your coffee?*; *don't forget to buy some milk, there's none in the fridge*; *milk chocolate* = pale brown chocolate made with milk

milk shake ['milk 'ʃeik] *noun* drink made by beating milk with a sweet juice; *she drank two banana milk shakes*

mill [mil] *noun* **(a)** small machine for grinding seeds into powder; *there is a pepper mill on the table* **(b)** large machine for grinding corn into flour; *corn is fed into the mill through a little door* **(c)** large factory; *paper mill* = factory producing paper; *steel mill* = factory producing steel

millimetre *US* millimeter ['milimi:tə] *noun* one thousandth part of a metre; *one inch*

equals roughly 25 millimetres (25mm)

million ['miljən] **(a)** number 1,000,000; *the population of Great Britain is over 58 million* **(b)** millions of = a very large number of; *millions of trees are chopped down to make paper*

millionaire [miljə'neə] *noun* person who has more than a million pounds or a million dollars; *if you win the lottery you will become an instant millionaire*

mince [mins] **1** *noun* meat which has been made into very small pieces; *add the mince to the onions and fry till it is brown* **2** *verb* to grind up meat or vegetables until they are in very small pieces; *hamburgers are made of minced beef*

mince pie ['mins 'pai] *noun* small pie filled with mincemeat, eaten at Christmas; *go on, have another mince pie*

mincemeat ['minsmi:t] *noun* mixture of fat, apples, spices, dried fruit, etc., used to make mince pies

mind [maind] **1** *noun* part of the body which controls memory and thought; *I think of her all the time - I just can't get her out of my mind*; *my mind went blank as soon as I saw the exam paper*; *to make up your mind (to do something)* = to decide (to do something); *she couldn't make up her mind what to wear to the wedding*; *to change your mind* = to decide to do something different; *he was going to go by car but then changed his mind and went by bus* **2** *verb* **(a)** to be careful, to watch out; *mind the steps - they're very steep!*; *mind out !* = be careful! **(b)** to worry about; *don't mind me, I'm used to working with children*; *never mind* = don't worry; *never mind - there's another lottery draw next Saturday* **(c)** to look after something for someone, or while the owner is away; *who will be minding the house while you're on holiday?* **(d)** to be bothered or annoyed by; *there aren't enough chairs, but I don't mind standing up*

mine [main] **1** *pronoun* belonging to me; *can*

I borrow your bike, mine's been stolen? **2** *noun* **(a)** deep hole in the ground from which coal, etc., is taken out; *the coal mine has stopped working after fifty years* **(b)** sort of bomb which is hidden under the ground or under water; *it will take years to clear all the mines left during the war*

miner ['maɪnə] *noun* person who works in a mine; *twelve miners were trapped when the roof of a coal mine collapsed yesterday* (NOTE: do not confuse with **minor**)

mineral ['mɪnərəl] *noun* chemical substance which is dug out of the earth, like rock; *the company hopes to discover valuable minerals in the mountains*; **mineral water** = water which comes from a spring in the ground; *do you want orange juice or mineral water?*

minister ['mɪnɪstə] *noun* **(a)** member of a government in charge of a department; *he was the Minister of Defence in the previous government* **(b)** Protestant priest; *at the funeral, the minister spoke about the dead man*

minor ['maɪnə] *adjective* not very important; *it was just a minor injury* (NOTE: do not confuse with **miner**)

mint [mɪnt] *noun* **(a)** factory where coins are made; *the mint is preparing to make the new coins* **(b)** common herb used to give flavour to a dish; **mint sauce** = sauce made of chopped mint, served with lamb **(c)** small white sweet, tasting of peppermint; *he always keeps a packet of mints in his pocket to suck when driving*

minus ['maɪnəs] **1** *preposition* less, take away; *ten minus eight equals two (10 - 8 = 2)* **2** *noun* sign (-) meaning less; *minus 10 degrees (-10°)*

minute 1 ['mɪnɪt] *noun* **(a)** one sixtieth part of an hour; *there are sixty minutes in an hour, and sixty seconds in a minute* **(b)** very short space of time; **I won't be a minute** = I'll be very quick; *I'm just going to pop into the bank - I won't be a minute* **2** [maɪ'njuːt]

adjective very small; *a minute piece of dust must have got into the watch*

miracle ['mɪrəkl] *noun* **(a)** very lucky happening; *it was a miracle she was not killed in the accident* **(b)** marvellous event which happens apparently by the power of God; *she went to the church and was cured - it must have been a miracle*

mirror ['mɪrə] *noun* piece of glass which reflects an image; *he looked at himself in the bathroom mirror*

mischief ['mɪstʃɪf] *noun* naughty or wicked action; *the children were full of mischief last night - they just wouldn't go to bed*; **he is always getting into mischief** = he's always doing something naughty

mischievous ['mɪstʃɪvəs] *adjective* wicked or naughty; *he's a mischievous little boy - whatever is he doing now?*

miserable ['mɪzrəbl] *adjective* **(a)** sad, unhappy; *can't you cheer her up? - she's very miserable since her boyfriend left her* **(b)** bad or unpleasant (weather); *what miserable weather - will it ever stop raining?*

misery ['mɪzəri] *noun* being very unhappy; *his life at school was sheer misery*

Miss [mɪs] *noun* title given to a girl or woman who is not married; *the letter is addressed to Miss Anne Smith*

miss [mɪs] **1** *noun* not having hit something; *he scored two goals and then had two misses* (NOTE: plural is **misses**) **2** *verb* **(a)** not to hit; *she tried to shoot the rabbit but missed* **(b)** not to see, hear, notice, etc.; *I missed the article about books in yesterday's evening paper* **(c)** not to catch; *she missed the last bus and had to walk home* **(d)** to be sad because you don't do something any more, because someone is not there any more; *do you miss living by the sea?*; *I miss going on those long country walks*

miss out on ['mɪs 'aʊt ɒn] *verb (informal)* not to enjoy something because you are not there; *I missed out on the skiing trip because*

I had measles

missile [ˈmɪsaɪl *US* ˈmɪsl] *noun* **(a)** thing which is thrown to try to hit someone; *the students used stones as missiles to throw at the police* **(b)** explosive rocket which can be guided to its target; *they think the plane was hit by an enemy missile*

missing [ˈmɪsɪŋ] *adjective* lost, which is not there; *I'm looking for my missing car keys*; *they found there was a lot of money missing*

mission [ˈmɪʃn] *noun* **(a)** aim or purpose for which someone is sent; *the children were sent on a mission to find the best place for a picnic* **(b)** group of people sent somewhere with a particular aim; *a rescue mission was sent out into the mountains*

mist [mɪst] *noun* thin fog; *early morning mist covered the fields*

mistake [mɪsˈteɪk] **1** *noun* act or thought which is wrong; *she made a mistake in typing the address*; **by mistake** = wrongly; *we took the wrong bus by mistake* **2** *verb* to think wrongly; **to mistake someone for someone else** = to think someone is another person; *I mistook him for his brother* (NOTE: mistaking - mistook - mistaken)

mistletoe [ˈmɪzəltəʊ] *noun* green plant with small white berries, which grows on other plants, especially trees; *at Christmas, we decorated the house with holly and mistletoe*

mitt *or* **mitten** [mɪt or ˈmɪtn] *noun* glove without separate fingers; *she knitted a pair of woollen mittens for the baby*; **oven mitt** = thick glove for holding hot dishes

mix [mɪks] *verb* to put different things together; *she made the cake by mixing eggs and flour*; *if you mix red and blue you get purple*

mix up [ˈmɪks ˈʌp] *verb* to think someone or something is someone or something else; *I always mix her up with her sister*; *she must have got the addresses mixed up*

mixture [ˈmɪkstʃə] *noun* different things mixed together; *if the mixture is too thick, add some more water*; **cough mixture** = liquid medicine to cure a cough

mm *abbreviation for* MILLIMETRE

moan [məʊn] **1** *noun* low sound from someone who is hurt; *the rescue team could hear moans from inside the ruins* **2** *verb* to make a low sound as if you are hurt; *I could hear someone moaning in the bathroom*

mobile [ˈməʊbaɪl *US* ˈməʊbl] **1** *adjective* which can move; **mobile library** = library in a van which travels around from place to place; **mobile phone** = small telephone which you can carry around; *mobile phones won't work in the London Underground* **2** *noun* **(a)** mobile phone; *I'll call him on his mobile*; *he gave me the number of his mobile* **(b)** construction by an artist using small pieces of metal, card, etc., which when hung up moves in the slightest draught; *they bought a mobile of coloured fish to hang over the baby's cot*

model [ˈmɒdl] *noun* **(a)** small version of something larger; *he spends his time making model planes* **(b)** person who wears new clothes to show them to customers; *he used only top models to show his designs during the London Fashion Week* **(c)** particular type of car, etc., produced at a particular time; *this is last year's model*

modern [ˈmɒdən] *adjective* referring to the present time; *you expect really modern houses to have automatic gates and central heating systems*; **modern languages** = languages which are spoken today; *she's studying German and Italian in the modern languages department*

modest [ˈmɒdɪst] *adjective* not boasting; *he was very modest about his gold medal*

moist [mɔɪst] *adjective* slightly wet; *to clean the oven, just wipe with a moist cloth* (NOTE: moister - moistest)

moisture [ˈmɔɪstʃə] *noun* small drops of water in the air or on a surface; *there's a lot of moisture in the air*

mold [məʊld] *US* = MOULD

mole [məʊl] *noun* **(a)** small mammal with soft dark grey fur, which lives under the ground; *moles made little hills of soil all over the lawn* **(b)** small dark spot on the skin; *the doctor removed a mole from the back of her hand*

moment ['məʊmənt] *noun* **(a)** very short time; *can you please wait a moment - the doctor is on the phone?* **(b) at any moment** = very soon; *I expect it to rain at any moment*; **at the moment** = now; *I'm rather busy at the moment*

Monday ['mʌndeɪ] *noun* first day of the week, the day between Sunday and Tuesday; *some supermarkets are shut on Mondays*; *she had to go to the doctor last Monday*; *next Monday is a bank holiday*; *the 15th is a Sunday, so the 16th must be a Monday*

money ['mʌni] *noun* **(a)** coins or notes which are used for buying things; *how much money have you got in the bank?*; *he doesn't earn very much money* **(b)** currency used in a country; *I want to change my British pounds into Canadian money*

monitor ['mɒnɪtə] **1** *noun* screen of a computer, or a small television screen used for checking what is happening; *my computer has a colour monitor*; *a row of monitors allows the police to see everything which happens in the shopping centre* **2** *verb* to check, to watch over (the progress of something); *doctors are monitoring her heart condition*

monk [mʌŋk] *noun* man who is a member of a religious group; *the monks lived on a little island off the north coast*

monkey ['mʌŋki] *noun* a tropical animal which lives in trees and usually has a long tail; *monkeys ran up the trees looking for fruit*

monster ['mɒnstə] **1** *noun* horrible, strange and frightening animal; *the Loch Ness Monster is a large dinosaur living in the bottom of Loch Ness in Scotland* **2** *adjective* (*informal*) very large; *look at the monster cabbage Dad's grown in the garden*

month [mʌnθ] *noun* **(a)** one of the twelve parts that a year is divided into; *December is the last month of the year*; *there was a lot of hot weather last month, in fact it was hot the whole of the month*; *a month from now I'll be sitting on the beach* **(b) months** = a long time; *it's months since we went to the cinema*

monument ['mɒnjʊmənt] *noun* stone, building, statue, etc., built in memory of someone who is dead; *they put up a monument to the people from the village who died in the war*

mood [muːd] *noun* feeling in general; *wait until she's in a good mood and then ask her*; *the boss is in a terrible mood this morning*

moon [muːn] *noun* satellite in the sky which goes round the earth and shines at night; *the moon is shining very brightly tonight*; **full moon** = time when the moon is a full circle; **new moon** = time when the moon is visible as a thin curved line; (*informal*) **once in a blue moon** = very rarely; *we only go to the theatre once in a blue moon*

moonlight ['muːnlaɪt] *noun* light from the moon; *we could see the path clearly in the moonlight*

moor ['mʊə or mɔː] **1** *noun* poor land covered with heather and grass and small bushes; *the Lake District is wild country, full of moors and forests* **2** *verb* to attach a boat to something; *the boat was moored to the river bank*

moose [muːs] *noun* large deer from North America; *a herd of moose crossed the river* (NOTE: plural is **moose**)

mop [mɒp] **1** *noun* soft brush with a head made of soft string or foam rubber, used for washing floors; *I'll just pass the mop over the kitchen floor* **2** *verb* to wash with a mop; *she was mopping the kitchen floor* (NOTE: mopping - mopped)

more [mɔː] **1** *adjective* which is added; *do you want any more tea?*; *there are many more trains during the week than on Sundays*

2 *pronoun* extra thing; *is there any more of that soup?*; *there are only nine of us, we need two more to make a football team* **3** *adverb (used with adjectives to make the comparative) the dog was more frightened than I was*

more or less not completely; *the rain has more or less stopped*

not...any more no longer; *she doesn't write to me any more*

morning ['mɔːnɪŋ] *noun* first part of the day before 12 o'clock; *every morning he took his packed lunch and went off to work*; *we'll all meet for coffee on Tuesday morning*

mortar ['mɔːtə] *noun* cement mixture for holding together the bricks or stones used in building; *the wall is dangerous - you can see how the mortar is crumbling*

Moslem ['mɒzləm] *see* MUSLIM

mosque [mɒsk] *noun* building where Muslims meet for prayer; *everyone must take off their shoes before entering a mosque*

mosquito [məs'kiːtəʊ] *noun* small flying insect which sucks blood and stings; *her arms were covered with mosquito bites* (NOTE: plural is **mosquitoes)**

moss [mɒs] *noun* low green plant which grows on the ground or on stones; *the old stone wall is covered with moss*

most [məʊst] **1** *adjective* the largest number of; *most people go on holiday in the summer*; *most apples are sweet* **2** *pronoun* very large number or amount; *she spent most of the evening on the phone to her sister*; *most of the children in the group can ride bikes* **3** *adverb (making the superlative) she's the most intelligent child in the class*; *the most important thing is to be able to drive a car*

moth [mɒθ] *noun* flying insect with large wings like a butterfly, but which flies mainly at night; *moths were flying round the street light*

mother ['mʌðə] *noun* woman who has children; *he's twenty-two but still lives with his mother*; *Mother! there's someone asking*

for you on the telephone!

motion ['məʊʃn] *noun* act of moving; *the motion of the ship made him feel ill*; **in motion** = moving; *do not try to get on or off while the train is in motion*

motor ['məʊtə] *noun* **(a)** the part of a machine which makes it work; *the model plane has a tiny electric motor* **(b)** car; **motor insurance** = insurance for a car, the driver and passengers in case of accident

motorbike ['məʊtəbaɪk] *noun (informal)* motorcycle, a cycle with two wheels driven by a motor; *my brother let me sit on his new motorbike*

motorcycle ['məʊtəsaɪkl] *noun* cycle with two wheels driven by a motor; *he fell off his motorcycle as he went round the corner*

motorway ['məʊtəweɪ] *noun* road with several lanes and very few junctions, on which traffic can travel at high speeds (in Britain given numbers following the letter M); *you will get there faster if you take the motorway*; *take the M4 if you want to go to Wales*

mould *US* **mold** [məʊld] *noun* **(a)** hollow shape into which a liquid is poured, so that when the liquid becomes hard it takes that shape; *gold bars are made by pouring liquid gold into moulds*; **jelly mould** = shape for making separate jellies **(b)** grey plant which looks like powder; *throw that old bread away - it's got mould on it*

mount [maʊnt] *verb* **(a)** to climb on to something; to climb up something; *they mounted their horses and rode off*; *he mounted the stairs two at a time* **(b)** to increase; *excitement is mounting as the time for the football final approaches*

mountain ['maʊntən] *noun* very high piece of land, rising much higher than the land which surrounds it; *Everest is the highest mountain in the world*

mouse [maʊs] **1** *noun* **(a)** small animal with a long tail, often living in holes in the walls of houses; *I saw a mouse sitting in the* *middle of the kitchen floor*; *our cat is good at catching mice* (NOTE: plural is **mice** [maɪs]) **(b)** device which you hold in your hand and move across a flat surface, used to control a computer; *click twice on the mouse to start the program*

moustache *US* mustache [məˈstɑːʃ *US* ˈmʌstæʃ] *noun* hair grown on a man's upper lip; *he looks quite different now he's shaved off his moustache*

mouth [maʊθ] *noun* **(a)** opening in your face through which you take in food and drink, and which has your teeth and tongue inside; *don't talk with your mouth full*; *he sleeps with his mouth open* **(b)** wide or round entrance; *the mouth of the cave is hidden by bushes*; *New York is built on the mouth of the Hudson river* (NOTE: plural is **mouths** [maʊðz])

move [muːv] **1** *noun* change from one place to another; *it's time to make a move* = we must leave; *get a move on!* = hurry up! **2** *verb* **(a)** to change the place of something; *move the chairs to the side of the room* **(b)** to change your position; *I could hear some animal moving about outside the tent*; *the only thing moving was the tip of the cat's tail* **(c)** to leave one house, flat or office to go to another; *he got a new job and they had to move from Scotland to London*

movement [ˈmuːvmənt] *noun* moving, not being still; *there was hardly any movement in the trees*; *all you could see was a slight movement of the cat's tail*

mow [məʊ] *verb* to cut grass, hay, etc.; *I must mow the lawn while it is dry* (NOTE: mowing - mowed - has mown [məʊn])

MP [ˈem ˈpiː] *noun* = MEMBER OF PARLIAMENT *you should write to your MP if you want to complain* (NOTE: plural is **MPs** [ˈem ˈpiːz])

Mr [ˈmɪstə] *noun* title given to a man; *Mr Jones is our new sales manager*

Mrs [ˈmɪsɪz] *noun* title given to a married woman; *Mrs Jones is our school head*

Ms [mʌz or mɪz] *noun* way of referring to a woman (without showing if she is married or not); *Ms Jones deals with complaints from customers*

much [mʌtʃ] **1** *adjective* **(a)** a lot of; *how much sugar do you need?*; *I never take much money with me when I go on holiday* **(b)** *(asking the price)* *how much does it cost to go to Edinburgh?*; *how much is that book?* **2** *adverb* very; a lot; *he's feeling much better today*; *it's much less cold in the south of the country*; *a bit much* = not fair; *being told it was my fault when I wasn't even there is a bit much* (NOTE: **much - more** [mɔː] **- most** [məʊst]) **3** *pronoun* a lot; *much of the work has already been done*; *do you see much of your brother?*

mud [mʌd] *noun* very wet earth; *you need a stiff brush to get the mud off your shoes*

muddle [ˈmʌdl] **1** *noun* confused mess; *the papers were lying all over the floor in a muddle*; *there was some muddle over the tickets* **2** *verb* **to muddle (up)** = to confuse, to mix up; *don't muddle the papers - I've just put them in order*; *I always muddle him up with his brother - they are very alike*

muddy [ˈmʌdi] *adjective* covered with mud; *don't come into the kitchen with your muddy boots on* (NOTE: **muddier - muddiest**)

muffled [ˈmʌfəld] *adjective* not as loud or clear as usual because the sound has been made quieter; *muffled cries were coming from inside the cupboard*

mug [mʌg] **1** *noun* large china cup with a handle; *she passed round mugs of coffee* **2** *verb* to attack and rob someone in the street; *she was mugged as she was looking for her car keys*; *she's afraid of going out at night for fear of being mugged* (NOTE: **mugging - mugged**)

multiple [ˈmʌltɪpl] **1** *adjective* involving many people or things; **multiple crash** = crash involving several cars or lorries **2** *noun* number which contains another number several times exactly; *nine is a multiple of three*

multiplication [mʌltɪplɪˈkeɪʃn] *noun* action of multiplying; *the children are taught addition, subtraction and multiplication*; **multiplication sign** = sign (x) used to show that one number is to be multiplied by another

multiply [ˈmʌltɪplaɪ] *verb* to make a number bigger by several times; *square measurements are calculated by multiplying length by width*; *ten multiplied by five gives fifty*

mum [mʌm] *see* MUMMY

mumble [ˈmʌmbl] *verb* to speak in a low voice which is not clear; *she mumbled something about the telephone and went to the back of the shop*

mummy *or* **mum** [ˈmʌmi or mʌm] *noun* **(a)** child's name for mother; *tell your mum I want to see her*; *hello, John, is your mummy at home?* **(b)** ancient dead body which has been treated with chemicals to stop it from going rotten; *we went to see the Egyptian mummies in the British Museum* (NOTE: plural is **mummies)**

mumps [mʌmps] *noun* infectious disease where you get swellings on the sides of the neck; *she caught mumps from the children next door*; *he can't go to school - he's got mumps*

munch [mʌnʃ] *verb* to chew something that is crisp or dry (and make a noise while chewing); *he was munching a biscuit when he answered the phone*

murder [ˈmɜːdə] **1** *noun* deliberately killing someone; *the murder was committed during the night* **2** *verb* to kill someone deliberately; *he was accused of murdering a policeman*

murmur [ˈmɜːmə] **1** *noun* low sound of people talking, of water flowing, etc.; *there was a murmur of voices in the hall* **2** *verb* to speak very quietly; *she murmured something and closed her eyes*

muscle [ˈmʌsl] *noun* part of the body which makes other parts move; *he has very powerful arm muscles*

museum [mjuˈziːəm] *noun* place which you can visit to see a collection of valuable or rare objects; *the Natural History Museum is always very popular with school parties*

mushroom [ˈmʌʃruːm] *noun* round white plant which can be eaten; *do you want fried mushrooms with your steak?*

music [ˈmjuːzɪk] *noun* **(a)** sound made when you sing or play an instrument; *do you like Russian music?*; *she's taking music lessons* **(b)** written signs which you read to play an instrument; *here's some music, see if you can play it on the piano*

musical [ˈmjuːzɪkl] **1** *adjective* referring to music; *do you play any musical instrument?* **2** *noun* play with songs and popular music; *musicals such as 'Cats' and 'Evita' were playing in London for years*

musician [mjuˈzɪʃn] *noun* person who plays music as a profession; *a group of young musicians were playing in the street*

Muslim [ˈmʊzləm] **1** *adjective* following the religion of Muhammad; *he comes from a strict Muslim family* **2** *noun* person who follows the religion of Muhammad; *Islam is the religion of Muslims*

must [mʌst] *verb used with other verbs* **(a)** *(meaning it is necessary)* *you must go to bed before eleven*; *we mustn't be late or we'll miss the last bus* **(b)** *(meaning it is very likely)* *I must have left my umbrella on the train*

mustard [ˈmʌstəd] *noun* **(a)** yellow paste with a hot taste, made from mixing powdered seeds and water, eaten with meat; *would you like some mustard on your ham sandwich?* **(b)** little plant used for salads, especially together with small cress plants; *the egg sandwiches were served with mustard and cress*

mustn't [ˈmʌsnt] = MUST NOT

my [maɪ] *adjective* belonging to me; *have you seen my glasses anywhere?*; *we went skiing and I broke my leg*

myself [maɪˈself] *pronoun* referring to me; *I hurt myself climbing down the ladder*; *I enjoyed myself a lot at the party*; **all by myself** = all alone, with no one else; *I built the house all by myself*; *I don't like being all by myself in the house at night*

mysterious [mɪˈstɪəriəs] *adjective* which cannot be explained; *she died in a mysterious way*

mystery [ˈmɪstri] *noun* thing which cannot be explained; *the police finally cleared up the mystery of the missing body* (NOTE: plural is **mysteries**)

myth [mɪθ] *noun* ancient story about gods; *old plays were based on Greek myths*

Nn

N, n [en] fourteenth letter of the alphabet, between M and O; *can you think of a five-letter word beginning with N and ending in R?*

nail [neɪl] **1** *noun* **(a)** little pointed metal rod used to hold two things together; *hit the nail hard with the hammer* **(b)** hard part at the end of your fingers and toes; *she painted her nails red*; **nail file** = flat stick covered with rough paper, used to smooth your nails **2** *verb* to attach with nails; *he nailed the notice to the door*

naked [ˈneɪkɪd] *adjective* with no clothes on; *naked children were playing around in the river*

name [neɪm] **1** *noun* special way of calling someone or something; *hello! my name's James*; *what's the name of the shop next to the post office?* **2** *verb* to call someone or something by a name; *the Queen named the ship 'Britannia'*; *they have a black cat named Jonah*

nanny [ˈnæni] *noun* **(a)** girl who looks after small children in a family; *our new nanny starts work tomorrow* (NOTE: plural is **nannies**) **(b)** *(children's word)* **nanny goat** = female goat; *a nanny goat and her two kids*

nappy [ˈnæpi] *noun* cloth which is wrapped round a baby's bottom to keep it clean (American English for this is a 'diaper'); *she changed the baby's nappy*; *they bought a a pack of nappies* (NOTE: plural is **nappies**)

narrow [ˈnærəʊ] *adjective* not wide; *why is your bicycle seat so narrow?* (NOTE: **narrower - narrowest**) **2** *verb* to become less wide; *the road narrows suddenly, and there is hardly enough room for two cars to pass*

nasty [ˈnɑːsti] *adjective* unpleasant; *what a nasty smell!*; *he's going to get a nasty shock when he opens the letter* (NOTE: **nastier - nastiest**)

nation [ˈneɪʃən] *noun* **(a)** country; *the member nations of the EU* **(b)** people living in a country; *the Prime Minister spoke to the nation when war was declared*

national [ˈnæʃənl] *adjective* **(a)** belonging to a country; *the story appeared in the national newspapers*; *we're going to see a new play at the National Theatre* **(b)** **National Health Service (NHS)** = system of free doctors, nurses, hospitals, etc., run by the government; **National Insurance** = insurance run by the government which provides for state medical care, unemployment payments, etc.

native [ˈneɪtɪv] **1** *noun* **(a)** person born in a place; *he's a native of Cornwall* **(b)** flower, bird, etc., which has always existed in a place;

the oak is a native of the British Isles **2** *adjective* belonging to a country; *the elephant is native to Africa*; **native language** = language which you spoke when you were a little child; *she speaks English very well, but German is her native language*

natural ['nætʃərəl] *adjective* **(a)** ordinary, not unusual; *it's natural to be worried if your baby is ill* **(b)** coming from nature, and not made by man; **natural gas** = gas which is found in the earth and not made by men; **natural history** = study of plants, animals, etc.

naturally ['nætʃərəli] *adverb* of course; *naturally the top team beat the bottom team*

nature ['neɪtʃə] *noun* **(a)** plants and animals; *we must try to protect nature and the environment* **(b)** character of a person, thing, animal; **human nature** = the general character of people; *it's only human nature to want to get on and do better than others*

naughty ['nɔːti] *adjective (usually of a child)* behaving badly, not doing what you are told to do; *the children are very quiet - they must be doing something naughty*; *it was very naughty of you to put glue on your daddy's chair* (NOTE: **naughtier - naughtiest**)

navigate ['nævɪgeɪt] *verb* **(a)** to guide a ship or aircraft; *the pilot navigated the boat into the harbour* **(b)** to give directions to the driver of a car; *can you navigate as far as Oxford Circus? - I know my way from there*

navy ['neɪvi] **1** *noun* military force which fights battles at sea; *he left school and joined the navy*; **the Royal Navy** = British military ships and the men who serve in them **2** *adjective* **navy (blue)** = of a dark blue colour; *he's bought a navy blue pullover*

near [nɪə] *adverb, preposition & adjective* **(a)** close to, not far away from; *our house is near the post office*; *bring your chair nearer to the table*; *which is the nearest chemist's?* **(b)** soon, not far off in time; *her birthday is on December 21st - it's quite near to Christmas*

(NOTE: **nearer - nearest**)

nearly ['nɪəli] *adverb* almost; *he's nearly 18 - he'll be going to university next year*; *hurry up, it's nearly time for breakfast*

neat [niːt] *adjective* tidy, without any mess; *leave your bedroom neat and tidy*; *a shirt with a neat white collar* (NOTE: **neater - neatest**)

necessarily [nesə'serəli] *adverb* which cannot be avoided; *going to Newcastle from here necessarily means changing trains twice*

necessary ['nesesri] *adjective* which has to be done; *it is necessary to have a current passport if you are going abroad*; *are you sure all this equipment is really necessary?*

neck [nek] *noun* **(a)** part of the body which joins your head to your body; *he wore a gold chain round his neck* **(b)** part of a piece of clothing which goes round your neck; *he takes size 16 neck in shirts*

necklace ['nekləs] *noun* string of jewels, etc., which is worn round your neck; *the queen wore a necklace of diamonds*

need [niːd] *verb* **(a)** *(meaning to be necessary)* *I need someone to help me with the cooking* **(b)** *(meaning to want to use)* *we don't need all these chairs*; *will you be needing this hammer any more or can I use it?* **(c)** *(used with other verbs meaning to be necessary)* *the living room needs painting*

needle ['niːdl] *noun* **(a)** metal tool for sewing, like a long pin, with a hole at one end for the thread to go through; *this needle hasn't got a very sharp point*; **knitting needle** = thin pointed plastic or metal stick used for knitting **(b)** hollow metal tool used for injections; *it is a serious disease which is passed on by using dirty needles* **(c)** hand on a dial; *he looked at the dial and saw the needle was pointing to zero* **(d)** thin leaf of a pine tree; *the carpet was covered with needles from the Christmas tree*

needn't ['niːdnt] *verb (used with other verbs to mean 'it isn't necessary')* *she needn't come if she has a cold*; *you needn't make such a* *fuss about a little spider*

negative ['negətɪv] **1** *noun* developed film with an image where the light parts are dark and dark parts light; *don't touch the negatives with your dirty fingers* **2** *adjective* **(a)** showing that something is not there; *her blood test was negative* **(b) negative film** = film where the light parts are dark and the dark parts are light (as opposed to positive film); **negative terminal** = one of the terminals in a battery, shown by a minus (-) sign; *the brown wire should be attached to the negative terminal*

neighbour *US* **neighbor** ['neɪbə] *noun* person who lives near you, who is sitting next to you, etc.; *help yourself and then pass the plate on to your neighbour*; **next door neighbours** = people who live in the house next to yours

neighbourhood *US* **neighborhood** ['neɪbəhʊd] *noun* small area and the people who live in it; *this is a quiet neighbourhood, we don't like big parties*

neither ['neɪðə or 'niːðə] **1** *adjective & pronoun* not either of two (people, etc.); *neither of the cars passed the test*; *neither of the sisters is dark* **2** *adverb* not either; *he doesn't eat meat and neither does his wife* **3** *conjunction* **neither...nor** = not one...and not the other; *the water is neither too hot nor too cold - it's just right*

nephew ['nefjuː] *noun* son of a sister or brother; *my nephew has just finished university*

nerve [nɜːv] *noun* **(a)** one of many threads in the body which takes messages to and from the brain; *nerves are very delicate and easily damaged* **(b) to get on someone's nerves** = to annoy someone; *that buzzing noise is really getting on my nerves* **(c)** *(informal)* being too confident; *he's got a nerve to ask for another day off, when he was away all last week* **(d)** being brave; *he wanted to try jumping with a parachute but at the last minute he lost his nerve*

nervous ['nɜːvəs] *adjective* worried; *she gets nervous if she is alone in the house at night*; *he's nervous about driving in London*

nest [nest] *noun* place built by birds to lay their eggs in; *the birds built their nests among the trees*

nestle ['nesl] *verb* to settle in comfort; *the cat nestled down quietly in the cushions*

net [net] **1** *noun* **(a)** woven material with large holes between the threads; **net curtains** = light curtains made of thin material **(b)** piece of this material used for a special purpose; **a fishing net** = large net used by fishermen to catch fish; **a tennis net** = net stretched across the middle of a tennis court; *he hit the ball into the net* **(c) the Net** = INTERNET **2** *adjective* after everything else has been taken away; **net income** = money earned after tax has been paid; **net weight** = weight after taking away the weight of packaging material

Netherlands ['neðələndz] *noun* European country, to the west of Germany and north of Belgium; *Amsterdam is the largest city in the Netherlands* (NOTE: capital: **Amsterdam**; people: **the Dutch**; language: **Dutch**)

nettle ['netl] *noun* type of common weed which stings when you touch it; *he walked with bare legs through the wood and got stung by nettles*

never ['nevə] *adverb* not at any time; not ever; *I've never bought anything in that shop although I've often been inside it*; **never mind!** = don't worry, don't bother about it

new [njuː] *adjective* **(a)** made quite recently, never used before, which has just been bought; *are your shoes new?*; *she bought herself a new motorbike* **(b)** which arrived recently, fresh; *there are two new students in our class* **(c)** quite different from what was before; *they put some new wallpaper in the bedroom* (NOTE: **newer - newest**)

New Year ['njuː 'jɜː] *noun* the first few days of the year; *I started my new job in the New Year*; **Happy New Year!** = good wishes for the New Year

New Year's Day [nju: jɜːz 'deɪ] *noun* 1st January; *it's a shame you have to work on New Year's Day*

New Year's Eve [nju: jɜːz 'iːv] *noun* 31st December; *the only time my mother drinks wine is on New Year's Eve*

New York ['nju: 'jɔːk] *noun* large town on the Eastern coast of the USA; *we are due to arrive in New York at 5 o'clock*; *yesterday New York had three inches of snow*

New Zealand ['nju: 'ziːlənd] *noun* country in the Pacific Ocean, to the east of Australia; *the sheep trade is important to New Zealand* (NOTE: capital: **Wellington**; people: **New Zealanders**; language: **English**)

New Zealander ['nju: 'ziːləndə] *noun* person from New Zealand; *my sister recently married a New Zealander*

news [njuːz] *noun* spoken or written information about what has happened; *she told me all the latest news about the office*; *he was watching the 10 o'clock news on TV*; **have you heard the news?** = have you heard what has happened?

newspaper ['njuːzpeɪpə] *noun* set of loose folded sheets of printed paper, which usually is published every day, with news of what has happened (also called a 'paper'); *I buy the newspaper to read on the train every morning*; *the newspapers are full of news of the election*; **a daily newspaper** = newspaper which is published every day except Sunday

next [nekst] **1** *adjective & adverb* **(a)** coming after in time; *on Wednesday we go to Paris, and the next day we travel to Italy*; *the next time you go to the supermarket, can you get some coffee?* **(b)** nearest in place; *the ball went over the fence into the next garden* **2** *pronoun* the thing or person following; *after two buses went past full, the next was almost empty*

NHS ['en'eɪtʃ'es] = NATIONAL HEALTH SERVICE

nibble ['nɪbl] **1** *verb* to take small bites; *she*
was nibbling a biscuit **2** *noun (informal)* **nibbles** = little snacks, such as peanuts or crisps, served with drinks

nice [naɪs] *adjective* **(a)** pleasant, fine; *if the weather's nice let's have a picnic* **(b)** pleasant, polite; *that wasn't a very nice thing to say*; *try and be nice to your grandfather* (NOTE: **nicer - nicest**)

nickname ['nɪkneɪm] **1** *noun* short or informal name given to someone; *her real name's Henrietta, but everyone calls her by her nickname 'Bobbles'* **2** *verb* to give a nickname to; *he was nicknamed 'Camel' because of his big nose*

niece [niːs] *noun* daughter of a brother or sister; *my niece gave me a tie for my birthday*

night [naɪt] *noun* part of the day when it is dark; *it's dangerous to walk alone in the streets at night* (NOTE: do not confuse with **knight**)

nightmare ['naɪtmeə] *noun* dream which makes you afraid; *I had a nightmare that I was drowning*

nine [naɪn] number 9; *she's nine (years old) tomorrow*; *the shop opens at 9 o'clock*

999 ['naɪn 'naɪn 'naɪn] telephone number to call the emergency services in Britain (in America, it is 911); *the firemen came quickly when we called 999*; *the ambulance drove through the snow to answer the 999 call*

nineteen [naɪn'tiːn] number 19; *he's nineteen (years old) tomorrow*; **the nineteen fifteen train** = the train leaving at 19.15; **in the 1950s** = during the years 1950 to 1959; **the nineteen hundreds (1900s)** = the years from 1900 to 1999 (compare with the 'nineteenth century')

nineteenth (19th) [naɪn'tiːnθ] *adjective & noun* referring to nineteen; *it's his nineteenth birthday tomorrow*; *the nineteenth of August* or *August the nineteenth (August 19th)*; **the nineteenth century** = the period from 1800 to 1899 (compare with the 'nineteen hundreds')

ninetieth (90th) ['naɪntiəθ] *adjective & noun*

referring to ninety; *it will be grandfather's ninetieth birthday next month*

ninety ['naɪnti] number 90; *my old aunt will be ninety next week and her husband is ninety-two: they are both in their nineties*; **the nineteen nineties (1990s)** = the years from 1990 to 1999

ninth (9th) [naɪnθ] *adjective & noun* referring to nine; *tomorrow is his ninth birthday*; *today is the ninth of June* or *June the ninth (June 9th); King Charles IX (say: 'King Charles the Ninth') reigned in the fifteenth century*; **the ninth century** = the period from 800 to 899 AD

no [nəʊ] *adjective & adverb* **(a)** *(showing the opposite of 'yes') I asked my mother if we could borrow her car but she said 'no'; do you want another cup of coffee? - no, thank you* **(b)** not any; *there's no milk left in the fridge* **(c)** *(signs)* **no entry** = do not go in this way; **no exit** = do not go out this way; **no parking** = do not park your car here; **no smoking** = do not smoke here

nobody ['nəʊbədi] *pronoun* no one, no person; *there was nobody in the café; we met nobody on our way here;* **nobody else** = no other person

nocturnal [nɒk'tɜːnl] *adjective* referring to the night; **nocturnal animals** = animals which are active at night, and sleep during the daytime

nod [nɒd] **1** *noun* little movement of the head up and down, meaning 'yes'; *he gave me a nod as I came in* **2** *verb* to move your head slightly up and down, meaning 'yes'; *when he asked her if she understood the question, she nodded* (NOTE: **nodding - nodded**)

noise [nɔɪz] *noun* **(a)** loud or unpleasant sound; *the workmen are making such a lot of noise that we can't use the telephone* **(b)** sound in general; *is there something the matter with the washing machine - it's making a funny noise*

none [nʌn] *pronoun* **(a)** not any; *can you buy*

some milk, we've none left in the fridge? **(b)** not one; *none of my friends smokes; none of the group can speak Chinese*

nonsense ['nɒnsəns] *noun* silly ideas; *it's nonsense to expect people to pay money for that*

non-stop ['nɒnstɒp] **1** *adjective* which does not stop; *they took a non-stop train to Edinburgh* **2** *adverb* without stopping; *they worked non-stop to finish the job on time*

noon [nuːn] *noun* twelve o'clock in the middle of the day; *we'll stop for lunch at noon*

no one ['nəʊwʌn] *pronoun* nobody, no person; *you can go to the bathroom - there's no one there; we met no one we knew;* **no one else** = no other person; *no one else has a driving licence so you'll have to be the driver*

nor [nɔː] *conjunction* and not; *I never went there again, nor did my sister*

normal ['nɔːməl] *adjective* usual, what usually happens; *we hope to start our normal service again as soon as possible; look at the rain - it's just a normal British summer*

north [nɔːθ] **1** *noun* **(a)** direction to your left when you are facing the direction where the sun rises; *there will be snow in the north of the country* **(b)** part of a country which is to the north of the rest; *the north of the country is colder than the south* **2** *adjective* referring to the north; *we went on holiday to the north coast of Scotland; when the north wind blows, you can expect snow* **3** *adverb* towards the north; *go north for three miles and then you'll see the road to London*

North America ['nɔːθ ə'merɪkə] *noun* part of the American continent to the north of Mexico, formed of the USA and Canada; *he has travelled all over North America from Alaska to Florida*

north-east [nɔːθ'iːst] **1** *adverb* direction between north and east; *go north-east for three miles and then you'll come to our village; our office windows face north-east* **2**

noun part of a country to the north and east; *the North-East of England will have snow showers* **3** *adjective* between north and east; *North-East Europe is an important trading area*

North Pole [ˈnɔːθ ˈpəʊl] *noun* furthest point at the north of the earth; *not many people have been to the North Pole*

north-west [nɔːθˈwest] **1** *adverb* direction between west and north; *they were travelling north-west across the desert* **2** *noun* part of a country to the north and west; *the North-West of England is wetter than the east coast*; *we can expect rain when the wind blows from the north-west* **3** *adjective* between north and west; *North-West China has a cold dry climate*

northern [ˈnɔːðən] *adjective* from, of or in the north; *they live in the northern part of the country*

Norway [ˈnɔːweɪ] *noun* country in northern Europe, to the west of Sweden; *in northern Norway it is light almost all day long in summer* (NOTE: capital: **Oslo**; people: **Norwegians**; language: **Norwegian**)

Norwegian [nɔːˈwiːdʒən] **1** *adjective* referring to Norway; *he's a famous Norwegian author* **2** *noun* **(a)** person from Norway; *the Norwegians have a large number of fishing boats* **(b)** language spoken in Norway; *Norwegian is similar in many ways to Swedish*

nose [nəʊz] *noun* part of the head which you breathe through and smell with; *he has a cold, and his nose is red*; *dogs have wet noses*; **to blow your nose** = to clear a blocked nose by blowing down it into a handkerchief; *she has a cold and keeps sneezing and blowing her nose*

nostril [ˈnɒstrl] *noun* one of two holes in your nose, which you breathe through; *my left nostril's blocked*

not (n't) [nɒt] *adverb* **(a)** *(used with verbs to show the negative)* *she can't come*; *it isn't* there; *we couldn't go home because of the fog* **(b)** not...either = and not...also; *she doesn't eat meat, and she doesn't eat fish either* **(c)** not only...but also = not just this...but this as well; *the film wasn't only very long, but it was also very boring* **(d)** *(used to make a strong negative)* *is it going to rain? - I hope not*; *I don't like bananas - why on earth not?*

note [nəʊt] **1** *noun* **(a)** a few words in writing to remind yourself of something; *she made a note of what she needed to buy before she went to the supermarket*; *he wrote me a note to say he couldn't come* **(b)** piece of paper money (American English for this is 'bill'); *I tried to pay with a ten-pound note* **(c)** musical sound or a written sign meaning a musical sound; *he can't sing high notes* **2** *verb* to write down something in a few words; *the policeman noted all the details of the accident*

notebook [ˈnəʊtbʊk] *noun* small book for making notes; *the policeman wrote down the details in his notebook*

nothing [ˈnʌθɪŋ] *pronoun* not anything; *there's nothing interesting on TV*; *he has nothing left in the bank*; **nothing else** = no other thing; **for nothing** = free, without having to pay; *we're friends of the woman running the show and she got us in for nothing*; **it's nothing to do with you** = it doesn't concern you

notice [ˈnəʊtɪs] **1** *noun* **(a)** piece of writing giving information, usually put in a place where everyone can see it; *he pinned up a notice about the tennis match* **(b)** official warning that something has to be done, that something is going to happen; *they gave us two minutes' notice to get out of the building* **2** *verb* to see; to take note of; *I wore one blue and one white sock all day and nobody noticed*

noun [naʊn] *noun* *(in grammar)* word which can be the subject of a verb and is used to refer to a person or thing; *nouns are words such as* 'brick' and 'elephant'; **proper noun** = word which is the name of a place, a person, a building, etc.; *proper nouns are almost always written with a capital letter*

novel ['nɒvl] *noun* long story with invented characters and plot; *'Pickwick Papers' was Dickens' first major novel*

November [nə'vembə] *noun* eleventh month of the year, the month after October and before December; *she was born in November*; *we never go on holiday in November*; *November 5th is the day when people celebrate Bonfire Night with bonfires and fireworks*

now [naʊ] **1** *adverb* at this point in time; *please can we go home now?*; *now's the best time for going skiing*; *a week from now we'll be sitting on the beach*; **just now** = quite recently; *she must have gone out for a moment - she was here just now* **2** *interjection* (showing a warning) *now then, don't be rude to the teacher!*; *now, now! nobody wants to hear you crying*; *now, everyone, let's begin the meeting*

nowhere ['nəʊweə] *adverb* **(a)** not in or to any place; **nowhere else** = in no other place; *why is the piano in the kitchen? - there was nowhere else to put it* **(b) nowhere near** = not at all; *the work is nowhere near finished*

nudge [nʌdʒ] **1** *noun* little push, usually with your elbow; *she gave me a nudge to wake me up* **2** *verb* to give a little push, usually with the elbow; *he nudged me when it was my turn to speak*

nuisance ['njuːsəns] *noun* thing which annoys; *it's a nuisance the bus doesn't run on Sundays*; **to make a nuisance of yourself** = to do something annoying; *the children made a nuisance of themselves running round the restaurant and throwing bits of bread*

numb [nʌm] *adjective* which has no feeling; *the tips of his fingers went numb*

number ['nʌmbə] *noun* **(a)** figure; *13 is not a lucky number*; *they live on the opposite side*

of road at number 49; *a number 6 bus goes to Oxford Street* **(b)** quantity of people or things; *large numbers of children went to visit the dinosaur exhibition*; *there were only a small number of people at the meeting* **(c)** copy of a magazine, newspaper, etc.; *we keep back numbers of magazines for six months and then throw them away* **(d)** piece of music, song; *he sang a selection of numbers by Noel Coward*

number plate ['nʌmbə 'pleɪt] *noun* one of two plates on a car (one on the front and one on the back) which shows the individual number of the vehicle; *the thieves had changed the van's number plates*

Number Ten ['nʌmbə 'ten] *noun* No. 10 Downing Street, London, the house of the British Prime Minister; *he won the election and so has moved into Number Ten*

numeracy ['njuːmərəsi] *noun* being able to work with numbers; *staff are trying to improve the children's numeracy skills*

numerous ['njuːmərəs] *adjective* very many; *he has been out late on numerous evenings this term*

nun [nʌn] *noun* woman member of a religious order; *nuns served hot soup to the earthquake victims* (NOTE: do not confuse with **none**)

nurse [nɜːs] **1** *noun* person who looks after sick people; *she has a job as a nurse in the local hospital*; *he's training to be a nurse* **2** *verb* to look after people who are ill; *when she fell ill her daughter nursed her until she was better*

nursery ['nɜːsəri] *noun* **(a)** place where babies or young children are looked after; *my sister goes to a local nursery every day*; **nursery school** = first school for very small children **(b)** place where young plants are grown and sold; *buy some plants from the nursery* (NOTE: plural is **nurseries**)

nut [nʌt] *noun* **(a)** fruit of a tree, with a hard shell outside and a softer inside which you can eat; *he was eating a chocolate bar with nuts* **(b)** metal ring which screws onto a metal rod to hold it tight; *screw the nut on tight*

Oo

O, o   [əʊ] fifteenth letter of the alphabet, between N and P; *'cooperate' is spelt with two Os*

oak   [əʊk] *noun* **(a)** type of large tree which loses its leaves in winter; *oaks grow to be very old* **(b)** wood from this tree; *they had a big oak table in the dining room*

oar   [ɔ:] *noun* long wooden pole with a flat part at the end, used for moving a boat along; *his oar got stuck in the weeds in the river*

oasis   [əʊ'eɪsɪs] *noun* **(a)** place in the desert where there is water, and where plants grow; *after crossing the desert for days they finally arrived at an oasis* **(b)** quiet pleasant place which is different from everything else around it; *Golden Square is a peaceful oasis in the middle of London's West End* (NOTE: plural is **oases** [əʊ'eɪsi:z])

oath   [əʊθ] *noun* solemn legal promise that someone will say or write only what is true; *all the witnesses have to take an oath* (NOTE: plural is **oaths** [əʊðz])

oats   [əʊts] *noun* cereal plant of which the seeds are used as food; *oats are used to make porridge*

obedient   [ə'bi:dɪənt] *adjective* doing what your are told to do; *our old dog is very obedient - he always comes when you call him*

obey   [əʊ'beɪ] *verb* to do what someone tells you to do; *if you can't obey orders you shouldn't be a soldier*

object   **1** *noun* ['ɒbdʒekt] **(a)** thing; *they thought they saw a strange object in the sky* **(b)** *(in grammar)* noun or pronoun, which follows directly from a verb or preposition; *in the phrase 'the cat caught the mouse', the word 'mouse' is the object of the verb 'caught'* **2** *verb* [əb'dʒekt] **to object (to)** = to refuse to agree to; *I object to having to pay extra for my little suitcase; does anyone object if I have a cigarette?*

oblong   ['ɒblɒŋ] *noun* shape with two pairs of equal sides, one pair being longer than the other; *the screen is an oblong, approximately 30cm by 40cm*

observe   [əb'zɜ:v] *verb* **(a)** to watch carefully; *the police observed the car coming out of the garage* **(b)** to make a remark; *I merely observed that the bus was late as usual* **(c)** to follow or to obey (a law, rule, custom, etc.); *his family observes all the religious festivals*

obstruct   [əb'strʌkt] *verb* **(a)** to block, to stop something going through; *a large black car was obstructing the entrance* **(b)** to stop someone doing something; *he was fined for obstructing the referee*

obtain   [əb'teɪn] *verb* to get; *she obtained a copy of the exam questions*

obvious   ['ɒbvɪəs] *adjective* clear; easily seen; *it's obvious that we will have to pay for the damage*

occasion   [ə'keɪʒən] *noun* happening, time when something happens; **a special occasion** = a special event (such as a wedding, etc.); *our baby's first birthday was a special occasion*

occasional   [ə'keɪʒnəl] *adjective* happening now and then, not very often; *we make the occasional trip to London*

occasionally [əˈkeɪʒnəli] *adverb* sometimes, not very often; *occasionally he has to work late*; *we occasionally go to the cinema*

occupation [ɒkjuˈpeɪʃn] *noun* job, employment; *my Sunday afternoon occupation is washing the car*

occupied [ˈɒkjupaɪd] *adjective* **(a)** being used; *all the rooms in the hotel are occupied*; *all the toilets are occupied, so you'll have to wait* **(b)** busy; *the manager is occupied just at the moment*; *keeping a class of 30 little children occupied is difficult*

occupy [ˈɒkjuːpaɪ] *verb* **(a)** to live in or work in; *they occupy the flat on the first floor* **(b)** to be busy; *dealing with the office occupies most of my time*

occur [əˈkɜː] *verb* **(a)** to happen; *when did the accident occur?* **(b)** to come to your mind; *it has just occurred to me* = I have just thought (NOTE: **occurring - occurred**)

ocean [ˈəʊʃn] *noun* very large area of sea surrounding the continents; *ocean currents can be very dangerous*; *the five oceans are: the Atlantic, the Pacific, the Indian, the Antarctic (or Southern) and the Arctic*

o'clock [əˈklɒk] *adverb* (used with numbers to show the time) *get up - it's 7 o'clock*; *we never open the shop before 10 o'clock*; *by 2 o'clock in the morning everyone was asleep*

October [ɒkˈtəʊbə] *noun* tenth month of the year, between September and November; *do you ever go on holiday in October?*; *last October we moved to London*

octopus [ˈɒktəpəs] *noun* sea animal with eight long arms; *there's a huge octopus in the aquarium* (NOTE: plural is **octopuses**)

odd [ɒd] **1** *adjective* **(a)** strange, peculiar; *he doesn't like chocolate - really, how odd!* **(b)** **odd numbers** = numbers (like 17 or 33) which cannot be divided by two; *the buildings with odd numbers are on the opposite side of the street* **(c)** roughly, approximately; *she had twenty odd cardboard boxes to move to her*

new flat **(d)** one forming part of a group; *an* **odd shoe** = one shoe of a pair (NOTE: **odder - oddest**) **2** *noun* **odds and ends** = group of various things that have no connection with each other; *we made a meal from various odds and ends we found in the fridge*

odour *US* **odor** [ˈəʊdə] *noun (formal)* smell, scent; *I think I can smell a faint odour of cheese*

of [ɒv] *preposition* **(a)** *(showing a connection)* *where's the lid of the jam jar?*; *what are the names of Henry VIII's wives?* **(b)** *(showing a part or a quantity)* *how much of the cloth do you need?*; *half of the team are sick with flu* **(c)** *(making a description)* *the town of Edinburgh is important for its festival* **(d)** *(showing position, material, cause)* *the jumper is made of cotton*; *she died of cancer*

of course [ˈɒv ˈkɔːs] **(a)** *(used to make 'yes' or 'no' stronger)* *are you coming with us? - of course I am!*; *do you want to lose all your money? - of course not!* **(b)** naturally; *he is rich, so of course he lives in a big house*

off [ɒf] **1** *adverb & preposition* **(a)** *(showing movement or position away from a place)* *the children got off the bus*; *take your boots off before you come into the house* **(b)** away from work; *she took the week off*; *half the staff are off with flu* **(c)** not switched on; *switch the light off before you leave the office*; *is the TV off?* **2** *adjective* cancelled; *she phoned to say the party was off*

off and on [ˈɒf ənd ˈɒn] *adverb* not all the time, with breaks in between; *it's been raining off and on all afternoon*

offend [əˈfend] *verb* **(a)** to upset someone, to go against someone's feelings; *he offended the whole family by writing about them in the paper* **(b)** to commit a crime; *he was released from prison and immediately offended again*

offer [ˈɒfə] *verb* **1** *noun* thing which is proposed; *she accepted his offer of a job in Paris* **2** *verb* to say that you will give something or do something; *she offered to* drive him to the station; **to offer someone a job** = to tell someone that he can have a job in your company; *if they offer you the job, take it*

office ['ɒfɪs] *noun* room or building where you carry on a business or where you organize something; *I'll be working late at the office this evening; her office is bigger than mine*

officer ['ɒfɪsə] *noun* **(a)** person who holds an official position in the army, navy, air force, etc.; *ordinary soldiers must always salute officers* **(b) police officer** = policeman; *there are two police officers at the door*

official [ə'fɪʃl] **1** *adjective* referring to any organization, especially part of a government, etc.; *he left official papers in his car* **2** *noun* person holding a recognized position; *I'll ask an official of the social services department to help you*

officially [ə'fɪʃəli] *adverb* **(a)** in an official way; *she has been officially named as a member of the British team* **(b)** according to what is said in public; *officially, you are not supposed to go in through this door, but everyone does*

often ['ɒfən] *adverb* many times, frequently; *I often have to go to town on business; how often is there a bus to Piccadilly Circus?*; **every so often** = from time to time; *we go to the cinema every so often*

oil [ɔɪl] *noun* **(a)** thick mineral liquid found mainly underground, used as a fuel or to make something move easily; *the door squeaks - it need some oil*; *some of the beaches are covered with oil* **(b)** liquid of various kinds which flows easily, produced from plants and used in cooking; *cook the vegetables in hot oil*

ointment ['ɔɪntmənt] *noun* smooth healing cream which you spread on the skin; *rub the ointment onto your knee*

OK *or* **okay** ['əʊ'keɪ] **1** *interjection* all right, yes; *it's ten o'clock - OK, let's get going* **2** *adjective* all right; *he was off ill yesterday, but he seems to be OK now*

old [əʊld] *adjective* **(a)** not young; *she lives in an old people's home* **(b)** not new; which has been used for a long time; *put on an old shirt if you're going to wash the car*; *he got rid of his old car and bought a new one* **(c)** with a certain age; *he's six years old today*; *how old are you?* (NOTE: **older - oldest**)

olive ['ɒlɪv] *noun* small black or green fruit from which oil is made for use in cooking; *olives are grown in Mediterranean countries like Spain, Greece and Italy*; **black olives** = ripe olives; **green olives** = olives which are eaten before they are ripe; **olive oil** = oil made from olives; *put a little olive oil in the frying pan*

Olympics *or* **Olympic Games** [ə'lɪmpɪks *or* ə'lɪmpɪk 'ɡeɪmz] *noun* international athletic competition held every four years; *she broke the world record* or *she set up a new world record in the last Olympics*; *the Olympic Games were held in Sydney in 2000*

omelette *US* **omelet** ['ɒmlət] *noun* dish made of beaten eggs, cooked in a frying pan and folded over before serving, with various other things inside; *I had a cheese omelette and chips for lunch*

on [ɒn] **1** *preposition* **(a)** on the top or surface of something; *put the box down on the floor* **(b)** hanging from; *hang your coat on the hook* **(c)** (showing movement or place) *a crowd of children got on the train* **(d)** doing something; *I have to go to Germany on business*; *we're off on holiday tomorrow* **(e)** (showing time, date, day) *the shop is open on Sundays*; *we went to see my mother on her birthday* **(f)** (means of travel) *she came on her new bike* **(g)** (showing an instrument or machine) *the film was on TV last night* **2** *adverb* **(a)** being worn; *have you all got your wellingtons on?* **(b)** working; *have you put the kettle on?*; *she left all the lights on* **(c)** being shown or played; *what's on at the cinema this week?* **(d)** continuing, not stopping; *he went on playing the drums even though we asked him to stop*

on and off ['ɒn ənd 'ɒf] *adverb* not all the time; *it's been raining on and off all afternoon*

once [wʌns] **1** *adverb* (a) one time; *take the tablets once a day*; *the magazine comes out once a month* (b) at a time in the past; *he's a man I knew once when I worked in London*; *(beginning children's stories)* **once upon a time** = at a certain time in the past; *once upon a time, there was a wicked old woman* **2** *conjunction* as soon as (in the future); *once he starts talking you can't get him to stop*

one [wʌn] **1** number 1; *one plus one makes two* **2** *noun* single item; *have a chocolate - oh dear, there's only one left!* **3** *adjective & pronoun* single (thing); *which hat do you like best - the black one or the red one?*; *small cars use less petrol than big ones*

onion ['ʌnjən] *noun* vegetable with a strong smell, shaped like a round white bulb; *fry the onions in butter*; **spring onion** = young onion eaten raw in salad

only ['əʊnli] **1** *adjective* one single (thing or person); *don't break it - it's the only one I've got*; **only child** = son or daughter who has no other brothers or sisters; *she's an only child* **2** *adverb* (a) with no one or nothing else; *we've only got ten pounds between us* (b) as recently as; *we saw her only last week* **3** *conjunction* (a) but, except; *I like my sister very much, only I don't want to see her every day of the week* (b) *(phrase showing a strong wish)* *if only we had known you were in town!*

only just ['əʊnli 'dʒʌst] almost not; *we only just had enough money to pay the bill*

only too ['əʊnli 'tuː] very much; *we would be only too glad to help you if we can*

onto ['ɒntuː] *preposition* on to; *the door opens directly onto the garden*; *the sheep have strayed onto the golf course* (NOTE: also spelt **on to**)

ooh! [uː] *interjection (showing surprise or shock)* *ooh look at that spider!*

open ['əʊpən] **1** *adjective* (a) not shut; *leave the window open - it's very hot in here* (b) working, which you can go into; *is the supermarket open on Sundays?* **2** *verb* (a) to make something open; *can you open the door for me?* (b) to start doing something, to start working; *most shops open early in the morning*

opener ['əʊpnə] *noun* device which opens; *we took a tin of pineapple with us and forgot to take a tin opener*

opening ['əʊpnɪŋ] *noun* (a) action of becoming open; *the office opening times are 9.30 to 5.30* (b) hole or space; *the cows got out through an opening in the wall*

opera ['ɒprə] *noun* performance on the stage with music, in which the words are sung and not spoken; *'the Marriage of Figaro' is one of Mozart's most famous operas*

operate ['ɒpəreɪt] *verb* (a) to make something work; *he knows how to operate the machine* (b) **to operate on a patient** = to treat a patient by cutting open his or her body; *she was operated on by Mr Jones*

operation [ɒpə'reɪʃn] *noun* (a) action of operating; *the rescue operation was successful* (b) treatment when a surgeon cuts open a patient's body; *she's had three operations on her leg*

opinion [ə'pɪnjən] *noun* what someone thinks about something; *ask the lawyer for his opinion about the letter*; **in my opinion** = as I think; *in my opinion, we should wait until the weather gets warmer before we go on holiday*

opponent [ə'pəʊnənt] *noun* (a) *(in boxing, an election, etc.)* person who fights someone else; *he knocked out his last three opponents* (b) person or group which is against something; *opponents of the planned motorway are sitting on the site*

opportunity [ɒpə'tjuːnɪti] *noun* chance or situation which allows you to do something; *when you were in London, did you have an opportunity to visit St Paul's Cathedral?*

opposed to [əˈpəʊzd ˈtuː] *adjective* **(a)** not in favour of; *he is opposed to the government's plans for education* **(b)** as **opposed to** = in contrast to; *if you paint the kitchen a light colour as opposed to dark red, you will find it will look bigger*

opposite [ˈɒpəzɪt] **1** *preposition* on the other side of, facing; *I work in the offices opposite the railway station* **2** *adjective* which is on the other side; *her van was hit by a lorry going in the opposite direction* **3** *noun* something which is completely different; *'black' is the opposite of 'white'*; *what's the opposite of 'soft'?*

optician [ɒpˈtɪʃn] *noun* person who tests your eyesight, and sells glasses or contact lenses, etc.; **the optician's** = the shop and offices of an optician; *I must go to the optician's to have my eyes tested*

or [ɔː] *conjunction* **(a)** *(showing other things that can be done)* *you can come with us in the car or just take the bus*; *do you prefer tea or coffee?* **(b)** *(approximately)* *five or six people came into the shop*

or else [ˈɔː ˈels] or if not; *don't miss the bus, or else you'll have a long wait for the next one*

orange [ˈɒrɪnʒ] **1** *noun* sweet tropical fruit, coloured between red and yellow; *she had a glass of orange juice and a cup of coffee for breakfast*; **orange squash** = drink made of orange juice and water; *do you want some orange squash?* **2** *adjective* of the colour of an orange; *his new orange tie is awful*

orbit [ˈɔːbɪt] **1** *noun* curved path of something moving through space; *the satellite is in orbit round the earth* **2** *verb* to move in an orbit round something; *the satellite orbits the earth once every five hours*

orchestra [ˈɔːkəstrə] *noun* large group of musicians who play together; *she plays in the school orchestra*

order [ˈɔːdə] **1** *noun* **(a)** instruction to someone to do something; *if you can't obey*

orders you can't be a soldier **(b)** *(from a customer)* asking for something to be served or to be sent; *she gave the waitress her order* **(c)** special way of putting things; *put the invoices in order of their dates*; *the stock in the warehouse is all in the wrong order* **(d)** out of **order** = not working; *you'll have to use the stairs, the lift is out of order* **2** *verb* **(a)** to tell someone to do something; *the doctor ordered him to take four weeks' holiday* **(b)** *(of a customer)* to ask for something to be served or to be sent; *they ordered chicken and chips*

ordinary [ˈɔːdənri] *adjective* not special; *I'll wear my ordinary suit to the wedding*

organ [ˈɔːgən] *noun* **(a)** musical instrument with a keyboard and many pipes through which air is pumped to make a sound; *the organ played the 'Wedding March' as the bride and bridegroom walked out of the church* **(b)** part of the body that does a special type of work, such as the heart, liver, etc.; *he was very ill and some of his organs had stopped working*

organic [ɔːˈgænɪk] *adjective* produced without using chemicals; *organic vegetables are more expensive but are better for you*

organization [ɔːgənaɪˈzeɪʃn] *noun* official organized group; *international relief organizations are sending supplies to the flood victims*

organize [ˈɔːgənaɪz] *verb* **(a)** to arrange; *she is responsible for organizing the meeting* **(b)** to put into a special order; *we organized ourselves into two groups*

origin [ˈɒrɪdʒɪn] *noun* beginning, where something or someone comes from; **country of origin** = country where a product is manufactured or where food comes from; *there should be a label saying which is the country of origin*

original [əˈrɪdʒɪnl] *adjective* **(a)** new and different, made for the first time; *he produced some very original ideas for the design of the new town centre* **(b)** not a copy; *send a copy* *of the will but keep the original*

ornament [ˈɔːnəmənt] *noun* small thing used as decoration; *there's a row of china ornaments on the mantelpiece*

ostrich [ˈɒstrɪtʃ] *noun* very large bird which cannot fly but which can run fast, and is found in Africa; *ostrich feathers used to be popular as decoration for hats* (NOTE: plural is **ostriches)**

other [ˈʌðə] *adjective & pronoun* **(a)** different (person or thing), not the same; *we went swimming while the other children sat and watched*; *I'm fed up with Spain - can't we go to some other place next year?* **(b)** second one of two; *he has two cars - one is red, and the other one is blue* **(c)** **the other day** = a day or two ago; *I'm surprised to hear he's in hospital - I saw him only the other day and he looked perfectly well*
every other every second one; *he wrote home every other day* = on Monday, Wednesday, Friday, etc.
one after the other following in line; *all the family got colds one after the other*

otherwise [ˈʌðəwaɪz] *adverb* **(a)** in other ways; *your little boy can make a noise sometimes, but otherwise he's very good in class* **(b)** if not, or else; *are you sure you can't come on Tuesday? - otherwise I'll have to cancel my visit to the doctor*

ought [ɔːt] *verb used with other verbs* **(a)** *(to mean it would be a good thing to)* *you ought to go swimming more often*; *you ought to see the doctor if your cough doesn't get better* **(b)** *(to mean it is probable that)* *he left his office an hour ago, so he ought to be home by now*

ounce [aʊns] *noun* measure of weight (= 28 grams); *the baby weighed 6lb 3oz (six pounds three ounces); ounce is usually written 'oz' after figures: 3oz of butter*

our [aʊə] *adjective* which belongs to us; *our school is near the station; our cat is missing again* (NOTE: do not confuse with **hour)**

ours [aʊəz] *pronoun* thing or person that

belongs to us; *that house over there is ours; friends of ours told us that the restaurant was good* (NOTE: do not confuse with **hours)**

ourselves [aʊəˈselvz] *pronoun* **(a)** referring to us; *we were enjoying ourselves when the police came* **(b)** **all by ourselves** = with no one else; *we don't like being all by ourselves in the dark house*

out [aʊt] *adverb* **(a)** away from inside; *how did the rabbit get out of its cage?* **(b)** not at home; *no one answered the phone - they must all be out*

outdoor [aʊtˈdɔː] *adjective* in the open air; *the club has an outdoor swimming pool*

outdoors [aʊtˈdɔːz] *adverb* in the open air, not inside a building; *why don't we take our coffee outdoors and sit in the sun?*; *the concert will be held outdoors if the weather is good*

outer [ˈaʊtə] *adjective* on the outside; *the outer surface of the pie was hot, but the inside was still frozen*

outfit [ˈaʊtfɪt] *noun* set of clothes; *she bought a new outfit for the wedding*

outing [ˈaʊtɪŋ] *noun* short trip; *the children went on an outing to the seaside*

outline [ˈaʊtlaɪn] *noun* line showing the outer edge of something; *he drew the outline of a car on the paper*

outside [ˈaʊtsaɪd] **1** *noun* part which is not inside; *the apple was red and shiny on the outside, but it was rotten inside* **2** *adjective* which is on the outer surface; *the outside walls of the house are brick* **3** *adverb* not inside a building; *it's beautiful and warm outside in the garden* **4** *preposition* in a position which is not inside; *I left my umbrella outside the front door*

outstanding [aʊtˈstændɪŋ] *adjective* excellent; of very high quality, of a very high standard; *her performance as 'Lady Macbeth' was outstanding*

oval [ˈəʊvl] **1** *noun* long rounded shape like

an egg; *he drew an oval on the paper* **2** *adjective* with a long rounded shape like an egg; *a rugby ball isn't round, it's oval*

oven ['ʌvən] *noun* metal box with a door, which is heated for cooking; *supper is cooking in the oven*; *can you look in the oven to see if the chicken is ready?*

over ['əʊvə] **1** *preposition* **(a)** above or higher than; *we live near the airport, so planes fly over our house every minute* **(b)** on the other side, to the other side; *he threw the ball over the wall* **(c)** from the top of; *he fell over the cliff* **(d)** more than; *children over 16 years old have to pay full price* **2** *adverb* **(a)** down from being upright; *she knocked over the plant pot*; *he leaned over and picked up a coin from the floor* **(b)** more than; *children of 16 and over pay full price*; *there are special prices for groups of 30 and over* **(c)** not used, left behind; *any food left over after the meal can be given to the dog*

overall [əʊvə'ɔːl] *adjective* covering or taking in everything; *the overall outlook for the weekend weather is good*

overalls [əʊvə'ɔːlz] *noun* suit of working clothes (trousers and top) worn over normal clothes to keep them clean when you are working; *all the workers wear white overalls*

overboard ['əʊvəbɔːd] *adverb* into the water from the edge of a ship, etc.; *he fell overboard and was drowned*

overcoat ['əʊvəkəʊt] *noun* thick coat which you wear over other clothes outside; *put on your overcoat - it's just started to snow*

overflow **1** [əʊvə'fləʊ] *verb* to flow over the top; *the river overflowed its banks* **2** ['əʊvəfləʊ] *noun* pipe to take away a liquid when there is too much of it; *the overflow was blocked and water started coming through the ceiling*

overgrown [əʊvə'grəʊn] *adjective* covered with plants and weeds because it has not been looked after; *the garden is completely overgrown*

overhead [əʊvə'hed] **1** *adverb* above you, above your head; *look at that plane overhead* **2** *adjective* which is above (your head); *please put your hand luggage in the overhead racks*

overhear [əʊvə'hiə] *verb* to hear accidentally something which you are not meant to hear; *I couldn't help overhearing what you said just then* (NOTE: overheard [əʊvə'hɜːd])

overlap [əʊvə'læp] *verb* to cover part of something else; *try not to let the pieces of wallpaper overlap* (NOTE: overlapping - overlapped)

overseas [əʊvə'siːz] **1** *adverb* in a foreign country, across the sea; *he went to work overseas for some years* **2** *adjective* referring to foreign countries, across the sea; *overseas sales are important for our company*

overtake [əʊvə'teɪk] *verb* to go past someone travelling in front of you; *our bus was going so slowly that we were overtaken by cyclists* (NOTE: overtaking - overtook - has overtaken)

owe [əʊ] *verb* **(a)** to owe money to someone = to be due to pay someone money; *he still owes me the £50 he borrowed last month* **(b)** to owe something to something = to have something because of something else; *he owes his good health to taking a lot of exercise*

owing to ['əʊɪŋ 'tu] *preposition* because of; *the plane was late owing to fog*

owl [aʊl] *noun* bird with large eyes, which is mainly busy at night; *owls hunt mice and other small animals*

own [əʊn] **1** *adjective* belonging to you alone; *I have my own car - I don't need to borrow yours* **2** *noun* on my own, on his own, etc. = alone; *I'm on my own this evening - my girlfriend's gone out with her family*; *he built the house all on his own* **3** *verb* to have, to possess; *there's no sense in owning a car since there's nowhere to park*

own up ['əʊn 'ʌp] *verb* to say that you have done something wrong; *the teacher asked who had written the rude words on the blackboard* but no one would own up

owner ['əʊnə] *noun* person who owns something; *the police are trying to find the owner of the car*

oxygen ['ɒksɪdʒən] *noun* common gas which is present in the air and is essential for plant and animal life; *hydrogen combines with oxygen to form water*

oyster ['ɔɪstə] *noun* type of expensive fish with two flat shells; *you eat oysters with lemon juice, straight out of their shells*

oz [aʊns or 'aʊnsɪz] *abbreviation for* OUNCE *or* OUNCES; *according to the recipe I need 12oz flour and 5oz butter (say 'twelve ounces of flour', 'five ounces of butter')*

ozone ['əʊzəʊn] *noun* form of oxygen, which is found in the atmosphere and which is poisonous to humans; **ozone layer** = layer of ozone in the upper atmosphere, formed by the action of sunlight on oxygen, which protects against rays from the sun which might harm you

Pp

P, p [piː] **(a)** sixteenth letter of the alphabet, between O and Q; *you spell 'photo' with a PH and not an F* **(b)** letter used to show a price in pence; *this book costs 99p*; *you should get a 60p ticket from the machine*

pace [peɪs] **1** *noun* **(a)** distance covered by one step; *step three paces back* **(b)** speed at which something happens; **to keep pace with** = to keep up with; *I can't keep pace with all the work we have to do* **2** *verb* to measure by walking; *he paced out the distance between the tree and the house*

Pacific (Ocean) [pə'sɪfɪk] *noun* huge ocean between North America and Asia and South America and New Zealand; *they set out to cross the Pacific in a small boat*

pack [pæk] **1** *noun* **(a)** set of things put together in a box; *he bought a pack of chewing gum*; **a pack of cards** = set of playing cards **(b)** group of wild animals together; *a pack of wild dogs* **(c)** bag which you can carry on your back; *he carried his pack over his shoulder* **2** *verb* **(a)** to put things into a suitcase ready for travelling; *the taxi's arrived and she hasn't packed her suitcase yet*; *he packed his toothbrush at the bottom of the bag* **(b)** to put things in containers ready for sending; *the books are packed in boxes of twenty*; *fish are packed in ice* **(c)** to put a lot of people or things into something; *how can you pack ten adults into one tent?*

pack off ['pæk 'ɒf] *verb* to send someone away; *we've packed the children off to their grandparents for the summer holidays*

pack up ['pæk 'ʌp] *verb* **(a)** to put things into a box before going away; *they packed up all their equipment and left* **(b)** to stop working; *I'll pack up now and finish the job tomorrow morning*

package ['pækɪdʒ] *noun* **(a)** parcel which has been wrapped up for sending; *we mailed the package to you yesterday* **(b)** box or bag in which goods are sold; *instructions for use are printed on the package* **(c)** **package holiday** = holiday where everything (hotel, food, travel, etc.) is arranged and paid for before you leave; *they went on a package holiday to Greece*

packaging ['pækɪdʒɪŋ] *noun* paper, cardboard, etc., used to wrap goods; *the boxes are sent in plastic packaging*

packed [pækt] *adjective* **(a)** full of people; *the restaurant was packed and there were no free tables* **(b)** put in a box; **packed lunch** = sandwiches, etc., put ready in a box

packet ['pækɪt] *noun* small bag, parcel or box; *a packet of cigarettes*; *a packet of soup*

pad [pæd] **1** *noun* **(a)** soft cushion which protects; *put a pad of cotton wool on your knee* **(b)** set of sheets of paper attached together; **phone pad** = pad of paper kept by a telephone for noting messages; *I wrote down his address on the phone pad* **(c)** soft part of the sole of an animal's foot; *the poor cat has a prickle in one of her pads* **2** *verb* to walk with heavy soft feet; *the lion was padding up and down in its cage* (NOTE: **padding - padded**)

paddle ['pædl] **1** *noun* short oar used to make a canoe go; *help - I've dropped my paddle into the river* **2** *verb* **(a)** to make a canoe move forward using a paddle; *they quickly paddled across the lake* **(b)** to walk about in very shallow water; *the children were paddling in little pools*

padlock ['pædlɒk] **1** *noun* small portable lock with a hook for locking things together; *the gate is fastened with a padlock* **2** *verb* to lock with a padlock; *he padlocked his bicycle to the lamppost*

page [peɪdʒ] *noun* **(a)** a side of a sheet of paper used in a book, newspaper, etc.; *it's a short book, it only has 64 pages; look at the picture on page 6* **(b)** boy who is one of the bride's attendants at a wedding (a girl who does the same is a 'bridesmaid'); *two little page boys followed the bride into the church*

paid [peɪd] *see* PAY

pail [peɪl] *noun* bucket, round container with a handle but no lid, used mainly for liquids; *he took a pail of water to the horse*

pain [peɪn] *noun* **(a)** feeling of being hurt; *if you have a pain in your chest, you ought to see a doctor*; *I get pains in my teeth when I eat ice cream* **(b)** *(informal)* **a pain (in the neck)** = annoying person; *he's a real pain in the neck*; *she's a pain - she's always gets top marks*

painful ['peɪnfʊl] *adjective* which hurts, which causes pain; *she got a painful blow on the back of the head*

paint [peɪnt] **1** *noun* **(a)** coloured liquid which you use to give something a colour or to make a picture; *we gave the ceiling two coats of paint* **(b)** **paints** = set of tubes of paint or cubes of water paints, in a box; *she bought me a box of paints for my birthday* **2** *verb* **(a)** to cover something with paint; *they painted their front door blue*; *she painted her nails bright red* **(b)** to make a picture of something using paint; *she painted a picture of the village*; *the sky isn't easy to paint*

paintbrush ['peɪntbrʌʃ] *noun* brush used to put paint on something; *I dropped my paintbrush in the can of paint*; *he used a very fine paintbrush to paint the branches of the trees* (NOTE: plural is **paintbrushes**)

painting ['peɪntɪŋ] *noun* **(a)** action of putting on paint; *painting the kitchen always takes a long time* **(b)** picture done with paints; *do you like this painting of the old church?*

pair [peə] *noun* **(a)** two things taken together; *she gave me a pair of gloves for my birthday*; *she's bought a new pair of boots*; **these socks are a pair** = they go together **(b)** two things joined together to make a single one; *I'm looking for a clean pair of trousers*; *this pair of scissors isn't sharp*

pajamas [pə'dʒɑːməz] *US see* PYJAMAS

palace ['pæləs] *noun* large building where a king, queen, president, etc., lives; *the Queen lives in Buckingham Palace*

pale [peɪl] *adjective* **(a)** with a light colour; *what colour is your hat? - it's a pale blue* **(b)** not looking healthy, with a white face; *she's always pale and that worries me* (NOTE: **paler - palest**)

palm [pɑːm] *noun* **(a)** soft inside surface of your hand; *she held out some bits of bread in the palm of her hand and the birds came and* *ate them* **(b)** tall tropical tree with long leaves; *date palms grow in the desert*; *the boy climbed a coconut palm and brought down a nut*

pan [pæn] *noun* metal container with a handle, used for cooking; *boil the potatoes in a pan of water*; *she burnt her hand on the hot frying pan*

pancake [ˈpænkeɪk] *noun* **(a)** thin soft flat cake made of flour, milk, and eggs, cooked in a frying pan; *we ate pancakes and syrup for breakfast* **(b)** *as flat as a pancake* = very flat; *the country round Cambridge is as flat as a pancake*

Pancake Day [ˈpænkeɪk ˈdeɪ] *noun* Shrove Tuesday, the Tuesday when people start to fast before Easter; *in Britain, pancakes are eaten on Pancake Day, usually with lemon and sugar*

panda [ˈpændə] *noun* **(giant) panda** = large black and white animal found in China, which looks like a bear

pane [peɪn] *noun* sheet of glass in a window, etc.; *they threw some stones and broke three panes in the window* (NOTE: do not confuse with **pain**)

panel [ˈpænl] *noun* flat piece which forms part of something; *take off the panel at the back of the washing machine*

panic [ˈpænɪk] **1** *noun* terror, great fear; *the flooding has caused panic in towns near the river* **2** *verb* to become frightened; *don't panic, the fire engine is its way* (NOTE: **panicking - panicked**)

pant [pænt] *verb* to breathe fast; *he was red in the face and panting as he crossed the finishing line*

pantomime [ˈpæntəmaɪm] *noun* funny Christmas play for children on a traditional subject of fairy tales, with songs and dances; *we took the children to the pantomime as a Christmas treat*; *the most popular stories for pantomimes are 'Jack and the Beanstalk', 'Aladdin', 'Puss in Boots', and 'Cinderella'*

pants [pænts] *noun (informal)* **(a)** shorts worn on the lower part of your body under other clothes; *I put on clean pants and socks every morning* **(b)** trousers, clothes which cover your body from the waist down, split in two parts, one for each leg; *I need a belt to keep my pants up*

paper [ˈpeɪpə] *noun* **(a)** piece of thin material which you write on, and which is used for wrapping or to make books, newspapers, etc.; *he got a letter written on pink paper*; *there was a box of paper handkerchiefs by the bed* **(b)** newspaper, a set of loose folded sheets of printed paper, which usually is published every day, with news of what has happened; *I buy the paper to read on the train every morning*; *his photo was on the front page of today's paper*; *the Sunday papers are so big that it takes me all day to read them*; **a daily paper** = newspaper which is published every day except Sunday

parachute [ˈpærəʃuːt] **1** *noun* large piece of thin material shaped like an umbrella, with ropes attached, which allows you to float down slowly and safely from a plane; *his parachute did not open and he was killed* **2** *verb* to jump from an aircraft with a parachute; *the pilot parachuted safely from the burning plane*

parade [pəˈreɪd] *noun* series of bands, soldiers, decorated cars, etc., passing in a street; *the parade was led by a children's band*; *Independence Day is always celebrated with a military parade through the centre of the capital*

paragraph [ˈpærəɡrɑːf] *noun* section of several lines of writing, which can be made up of several sentences; *a paragraph always starts a new line, often with a small blank space at the beginning*

parallel [ˈpærəlel] **1** *adjective* (lines) which are side by side and remain the same distance apart without ever touching; *draw two parallel lines three millimetres apart*; *the road runs parallel to the railway* **2** *noun* line running round the earth at a certain distance from the North and South Poles; *the 49th parallel forms the border between the United States and Canada*

paralyzed ['pærəlaɪzd] *adjective* with muscles made so weak that they cannot work properly; *his arm was paralyzed after his stroke*

parcel ['pɑːsəl] *noun* package (to be sent by post, etc.); *the postman has brought a parcel for you*; *if you're going to the post office, can you post this parcel for me?*

pardon ['pɑːdən] **1** *noun* forgiving someone; **I beg your pardon!** = excuse me, forgive me; *I beg your pardon, I didn't hear what you said* **2** *verb* to forgive someone for having done something wrong; *pardon me for interrupting, but you're wanted on the phone*

parents ['peərənts] *noun* mother and father; *she's left college and has gone back to live with her parents*

park [pɑːk] **1** *noun* **(a)** open space with grass and trees; *Hyde Park and Regents Park are in the middle of London*; *you can ride a bicycle across the park but cars are not allowed in* **(b) car park** = area where you can leave a car when you are not using it; *he left his car in the hotel car park*; *the supermarket car park is full* **2** *verb* to leave your car in a place while you are not using it; *you can park your car in the street next to the hotel*; *you mustn't park on a double yellow line*

parking ['pɑːkɪŋ] *noun* action of leaving a car in a place; *parking is difficult in the centre of the city on Saturdays*; **No Parking** = sign showing that you must not park your car in a certain place; **parking meter** = device into which you put money to pay for parking; *US* **parking lot** = place where you can leave a car when you are not using it

parliament ['pɑːləmənt] *noun* group of people who are elected to run a country and vote laws; *Parliament has passed a law forbidding the sale of dangerous drugs*; **the**

Houses of Parliament = the building in London where Parliament meets; *he took a picture of the Houses of Parliament*

parrot ['pærət] *noun* bright coloured tropical bird with a large curved beak; *he keeps a green parrot in a cage in his sitting room*

parsley ['pɑːsli] *noun* green herb used in cooking; *sprinkle some chopped parsley on top of the fish*

parsnip ['pɑːsnɪp] *noun* plant with a long white root which is eaten as a vegetable; *roast parsnips are served with beef and potatoes*

part [pɑːt] *noun* **(a)** piece; *parts of the film were very good*; *they spend part of the year in France* **(b)** character in a play, film, etc.; *he played the part of Hamlet*

part with ['pɑːt 'wɪθ] *verb* to give or sell something to someone; *he refused to part with his old bicycle*

particle ['pɑːtɪkl] *noun* very small piece; *the inspectors found tiny particles of glass in the bread*

particular [pə'tɪkjuːlə] **1** *adjective* **(a)** special, referring to one thing or person and to no one else; *the printer works best with one particular type of paper* **(b) in particular** = especially; *fragile goods, in particular glasses, need careful packing* **2** *noun* **particulars** = details; *this sheet gives particulars of the cars we have for sale*

particularly [pə'tɪkjuːləli] *adverb* especially; *he isn't particularly worried about his exams*

partly ['pɑːtli] *adverb* not completely; *the road was partly covered with snow*

partner ['pɑːtnə] *noun* **(a)** person who plays games or dances with someone; *Sally is my usual tennis partner* **(b)** person you live with, without necessarily being married; *we invited him and his partner for supper*

party ['pɑːti] *noun* **(a)** special occasion when several people meet, usually in someone's house; *we're having a party on New Year's Eve*; *she invited twenty friends to her birthday party* **(b) political party** =

organisation of people who believe in a certain type of politics (NOTE: plural is **parties**)

pass [pɑːs] **1** *noun* season ticket on a bus or train; *I left my bus pass at home, so I had to pay for a ticket* (NOTE: plural is **passes**) **2** *verb* **(a)** to go past; *if you walk towards the bank you will pass our house on your right* **(b)** to move something towards someone; *can you pass me the salt, please?*; *he passed the ball to one of the backs* **(c)** to be successful in a test or examination; *he passed in English, but failed in French*; *she passed her driving test first time*

pass out [ˈpɑːs ˈaʊt] *verb* to become unconscious for a short time; *he passed out when he saw the blood on the floor*

pass round [ˈpɑːs raʊnd] *verb* to hand something to various people; *she passed round the box of chocolates*

passage [ˈpæsɪdʒ] *noun* **(a)** corridor; *there's an underground passage between the two railway stations* **(b)** section of a text; *I photocopied a passage from the book*

passenger [ˈpæsɪndʒə] *noun* person who is travelling in a car, bus, train, plane, etc., but who is not the driver or one of the crew; *his car's quite big - it can take three passengers on the back seat*; *the plane was carrying 104 passengers and a crew of ten*

passive [ˈpæsɪv] **1** *adjective* allowing things to happen to you and not taking any action yourself; **passive smoking** = breathing in smoke from other people's cigarettes, when you do not smoke yourself **2** *noun* form of a verb which shows that something has happened to the subject; *if you say 'the car hit him' the verb is active, but 'he was hit by the car' is passive*

passport [ˈpɑːspɔːt] *noun* official document which shows who you are and allows you to go from one country to another; *if you are going abroad you need to have a passport*

password [ˈpɑːswɜːd] *noun* secret word which you need to know to be allowed to go into a military camp or to use a computer system; *the soldiers stopped him at the gate and asked for the password*; *you need to know the password to get into the system*

past [pɑːst] **1** *preposition* **(a)** later than, after; *it's past 1 o'clock, and mother's still not come back from the shops*; *it's ten past nine (9.10) - we've missed the TV news*; *it's already half past two (2.30)* **(b)** from one side to the other in front of something; *if you go past the bank, you'll see the shop on your left*; *she walked past me without saying anything* **2** *adjective* which has passed; *he has spent the past year working in France* **3** *noun* **(a)** time before now; *in the past we always had a family party at Christmas* **(b)** past **(tense)** = form of a verb which shows that it happened before the present time; *'sang' is the past of the verb 'to sing'*

pasta [ˈpæstə] *noun* Italian food made of flour and water, cooked by boiling and eaten with oil or sauce; *spaghetti, tagliatelle, macaroni, etc., are all types of pasta*

paste [peɪst] **1** *noun* **(a)** thin liquid glue; *spread the paste carefully over the back of the wallpaper* **(b)** soft food; *mix the flour, eggs and milk to a smooth paste*; *add tomato paste to the soup* **2** *verb* to glue; *he pasted the pictures from the newspaper into a big book*

pastry [ˈpeɪstri] *noun* **(a)** mixture of flour, fat and water, used to make pies; *she was in the kitchen making pastry* **(b)** **pastries** = sweet cakes made of pastry filled with cream or fruit, etc.; **Danish pastries** = sweet pastry cakes with jam or fruit folded inside

pat [pæt] *verb* to give someone or something a little tap with your hand; *he patted his pocket to make sure that his money was still there*; **to pat someone on the back** = to praise someone (NOTE: **patting - patted**)

patch [pætʃ] *noun* **(a)** small piece of material used for covering up a hole; *his mother sewed a patch over the hole in his trousers* **(b)** small area; *they built a shed on a patch of ground by the railway line* (NOTE: plural is **patches**)

path [pɑːθ] *noun* **(a)** narrow track for walking; *there's a path across the field*; *follow the path until you get to the sea* **(b)** **bicycle path** = narrow lane for bicycles by the side of a road

patience ['peɪʃns] *noun* **(a)** being patient, being able to wait for a long time calmly; *with a little patience, you'll soon learn how to ride a bike* **(b)** card game for one person; *she sat by herself in her hotel room, playing patience*

patient ['peɪʃənt] **1** *adjective* being able to wait a long time without getting annoyed; *you must be patient - you will get served in time* **2** *noun* sick person who is in hospital or who is being treated by a doctor, dentist, etc.; *there are six other patients in the ward*; *the nurse is trying to take the patient's temperature*

patiently ['peɪʃəntli] *adverb* without getting annoyed; *they waited patiently for the bus to arrive*

patrol [pə'trəʊl] **1** *noun* **(a)** keeping guard by walking or driving up and down; *the policeman was on patrol in the centre of town when he saw some men running away from a bank* **(b)** group of people keeping guard; *each time a patrol went past we hid behind a wall* **2** *verb* to keep guard by walking or driving up and down; *armed guards are patrolling the warehouse* (NOTE: **patrolling - patrolled)**

pattern ['pætən] *noun* **(a)** design of lines, flowers, etc., repeated again and again on cloth, wallpaper, etc.; *she was wearing a coat with a pattern of black and white spots* **(b)** instructions which you follow to make something; *she followed a pattern from a magazine to knit the pullover*

pause [pɔːz] **1** *noun* short stop during a period of time; *there was a pause in the conversation* **2** *verb* to rest for a short time; to stop doing something for a short time; *she ran along the road, only pausing for a second to look at her watch*

pavement ['peɪvmənt] *noun* **(a)** hard path for pedestrians at the side of a road (in American

English, this is 'sidewalk'); *it's safer to walk on the pavement, not in the road*; *watch out! - the pavement is covered with ice* **(b)** US hard road surface

paw [pɔː] *noun* foot of an animal with claws; *the bear held the fish in its paws*

pay [peɪ] **1** *noun* wages or salary; *they're on strike for more pay*; **basic pay** = normal salary without extra payments **2** *verb* **(a)** to give money for something; *how much did you pay for your car?*; *we pay £100 a week in rent* **(b)** to give money to someone for doing something; *I paid them one pound each for washing the car* **(c)** **to pay a visit** = to visit; *we'll pay my mother a visit when we're in town* (NOTE: **paying - paid** [peɪd])

pay back ['peɪ 'bæk] *verb* to give someone money which you owe; *he borrowed ten pounds last week and hasn't paid me back*

pay up ['peɪ 'ʌp] *verb* to pay all the money which you owe; *the tourist paid up quickly when the taxi driver called the police*

payment ['peɪmənt] *noun* giving money for something; *she made a payment of £10,000 to her solicitor*; *if you fall behind with your payments, they will take the car back*

PC ['piː'siː] = PERSONAL COMPUTER, POLICE CONSTABLE

PE ['piː 'iː] = PHYSICAL EDUCATION; *she goes to a PE class every Tuesday*

pea [piː] *noun* round green seed eaten as a vegetable; *what vegetables do you want with your meat? - peas and carrots, please*

peace [piːs] *noun* **(a)** state of not being at war; *United Nations troops are trying to keep the peace in the area*; **peace process** = discussions which take place over a long time, with the aim of ending a war **(b)** being calm and quiet; *motorcycles ruin the peace and quiet of the village*

peaceful ['piːsfʊl] *adjective* calm and quiet; *we spent a peaceful afternoon by the river*

peach [piːtʃ] *noun* juicy sweet fruit, with a large stone and soft skin; *we had peaches and* *cream for dessert* (NOTE: plural is **peaches**)

peacock [ˈpiːkɒk] *noun* large bird, of which the cock has an enormous tail with brilliant blue and green feathers; *peacocks were wandering about the palace garden*

peak [piːk] *noun* **(a)** top of a mountain; *can you see that white peak in the distance? - it's Everest* **(b)** **peak period** = period of the day when most electricity is used, when most traffic is on the roads, etc. **(c)** front part of a cap which sticks out; *he wore a white cap with a dark blue peak*

peanut [ˈpiːnʌt] *noun* little round nut which grows in the ground in hard pods like peas; *I bought a packet of peanuts to eat with my beer*; **peanut butter** = paste made from crushed peanuts; *she made peanut butter sandwiches for the children*

pear [peə] *noun* fruit like a long apple, with one end fatter than the other; *when will these pears be ripe?* (NOTE: do not confuse with **pair**)

pearl [pɜːl] *noun* little round white ball found inside an oyster; *she wore a string of pearls which her grandmother had given her*

pebble [ˈpebl] *noun* small round stone; *the boys were throwing pebbles into the water*

peck [pek] **1** *noun* bite with a bird's beak; *the goose gave me a nasty peck* **2** *verb* to bite with a beak; *the birds were pecking around in the field*

peculiar [pɪˈkjuːliə] *adjective* odd, strange; *there's a peculiar smell coming from the kitchen*

pedal [ˈpedəl] **1** *noun* **(a)** lever worked by your foot; *if you want to stop the car put your foot down on the brake pedal* **(b)** flat part which you press down on with your foot to make a bicycle go forwards; *he stood up on his pedals to make the bike go up the hill* **2** *verb* to make a bicycle go by pushing on the pedals; *we had to pedal hard to get up the hill*

pedestrian [pəˈdestriən] *noun* person who walks on a pavement or along a road; *two pedestrians were injured in the accident*;

pedestrian crossing = place where pedestrians can cross a road

peel [piːl] **1** *noun* outer skin of a fruit, etc.; *throw the banana peel into the rubbish bin*; *this orange has got very thick peel* **2** *verb* to take the outer skin off a fruit or a vegetable; *he was peeling a banana*; *if the potatoes are very small you can boil them without peeling them*

peer [ˈpiə] **1** *noun* member of the House of Lords; *the peers voted on the proposed bill* **2** *verb* to look at something hard when you cannot see very well; *she peered at the screen to see if she could read the figures*

peg [peg] **1** *noun* **(a)** small wooden or metal stake or nail; *the children hang their coats on pegs in the hall* **(b)** **clothes peg** = little wooden clip, used to attach wet clothes to a washing line **2** *verb* to attach with a peg; *she pegged the washing out on the line* (NOTE: **pegging - pegged**)

pen [pen] *noun* thing for writing with which uses ink; *I've lost my red pen - can I borrow yours?*; **felt pen** = pen with a point made of hard cloth

penalty [ˈpenəlti] *noun* punishment; *the penalty for the crime is two years in prison*; *the referee gave a penalty against the England team* (NOTE: plural is **penalties**)

pence [pens] *see* PENNY

pencil [ˈpensəl] *noun* thing for writing with, made of a stick of wood, with a stick of coloured material in the middle; *exam answers must be written in ink, not in pencil*

penguin [ˈpeŋgwɪn] *noun* black and white bird found near the South Pole, which swims well but cannot fly; *penguins nest on the ice in huge numbers*

penknife [ˈpennaɪf] *noun* small pocket knife which folds up; *he was peeling an apple with his penknife* (NOTE: the plural is **penknives** [ˈpennaɪvz])

penny [ˈpeni] *noun* smallest British coin, one hundredth of a pound; *it cost £4.99, so I paid with a five-pound note and got a penny* *change*; *a cup of tea is cheap - it only costs 50 pence* (NOTE: plural is **pennies** or **pence**)

pension ['penʃn] *noun* money paid on the same date each month to someone who has retired from work; *she finds a teacher's pension quite enough to live on*; **old age pension** = money paid by the state each week or each month to old people

people ['piːpl] *noun* men, women or children taken as a group; *there were at least twenty people waiting to see the doctor*; *the people of China work very hard*

pepper ['pepə] *noun* (a) hot spice used in cooking; *add salt and pepper to taste* (b) green or red fruit used as a vegetable; *we had stuffed green peppers for lunch*

peppermint ['pepəmɪnt] *noun* (a) herb which produces an oil used in sweets, drinks and toothpaste; *I always use toothpaste that is flavoured with peppermint* (b) a sweet flavoured with peppermint; *he carried a bag of peppermints with him*

per [pɜː] *preposition* (a) out of each; **twenty per thousand** = twenty out of every thousand; *there are about six mistakes per thousand words* (b) for each; *I can't cycle any faster than fifteen miles per hour*; *potatoes cost 10p per kilo*

per cent or **percent** [pə 'sent] *noun* out of each hundred; *'per cent' is written % when used with figures;* **twenty-five per cent (25%)** = one quarter, twenty-five parts out of a total of one hundred; **fifty per cent (50%)** = half, fifty parts out of a total of one hundred; *sixty two per cent (62%) of the people voted*; *eighty per cent (80%) of the cars on the road are less than five years old*

perch [pɜːtʃ] **1** *noun* branch or ledge on which a bird sits; *the parrot flew down from his perch and landed on the back of my chair* (NOTE: plural is **perches**) **2** *verb* (a) *(of bird)* to sit; *the pigeon was perched on a high branch* (b) to be placed high up; *a castle is perched high on the side of a mountain*

perfect ['pɜːfəkt] *adjective* which is good in every way; *don't change anything - the room is perfect as it is* (b) ideal; *I was in a perfect position to see what happened*

perfectly ['pɜːfɪktli] *adverb* extremely well; *the dress fits you perfectly*; *I'm perfectly capable of finding my own way home*

perform [pə'fɔːm] *verb* to act in public; *the group will perform 'Hamlet' next week*; *the play will be performed in the village hall*

performance [pə'fɔːməns] *noun* (a) how well a machine works, a team plays, etc.; *we're looking for ways to improve our performance*; *after last night's performance I don't think the team is likely to reach the final* (b) public show; *the next performance will start at 8 o'clock*

perfume ['pɜːfjuːm] *noun* scent, a liquid which smells nice, and which is put on the skin; *do you like my new perfume?*

perhaps [pə'hæps] *adverb* possibly; *perhaps the train is late*; *is it going to be fine? - perhaps not, I can see clouds over there*

period ['pɪəriəd] *noun* (a) length of time; *the offer is open for a limited period only* (b) time during which a lesson is given in school; *we have three periods of English on Thursdays*

permanent ['pɜːmənənt] *adjective* lasting for ever; supposed to last for ever; *they are living with her parents for a few weeks - I don't think it's a permanent arrangement*

permanently ['pɜːmənəntli] *adverb* for ever; always; *the shop seems to be permanently closed*

permission [pə'mɪʃn] *noun* being allowed to do something; *he asked the manager's permission to take a day off*

permit 1 ['pɜːmɪt] *noun* paper which allows you to do something; *you have to have a permit to sell ice cream from a van*; **parking permit** = paper which allows you to park a car **2** [pə'mɪt] *verb* (a) to allow; *smoking is not permitted in London Underground stations*

(b) weather permitting = if the weather is good; *we're planning a picnic for next Saturday, weather permitting* (NOTE: permitting - permitted)

persist [pə'sɪst] *verb* to persist in doing something = to continue doing something, even though it is wrong; *he will persist in singing while he works although we've told him again and again to stop*

person ['pɜːsən] *noun* man or woman; *the police say a person or persons entered the house by the window*; **missing person** = someone who has disappeared, and no one knows where he or she is; *her name is on the police Missing Persons list*

personal ['pɜːsnəl] *adjective* belonging or referring to a particular person or people; *they lost all their personal property in the fire*; **personal computer (PC)** = small computer used by a person at home

persuade [pə'sweɪd] *verb* to get someone to do what you want by explaining or asking; *she managed to persuade her father to let her borrow his car*

pest [pest] *noun* **(a)** plant, animal, or insect that causes damage; *many farmers look on rabbits as a pest* **(b)** *(informal)* person who annoys; *that little boy is a pest - he won't stop whistling when I'm trying to work*

pet [pet] *noun* animal kept in the home to give pleasure; *the family has several pets - two cats, a dog and a white rabbit*

petal ['petl] *noun* colourful part of a flower; *daffodils have bright yellow petals*

petrol ['petrəl] *noun* liquid used as a fuel for engines (American English is 'gas'); *this car doesn't use very much petrol*; *petrol prices are lower at supermarkets*

phone [fəʊn] **1** *noun* telephone, a machine which you use to speak to someone who is some distance away; *she lifted the phone and called the ambulance* **2** *verb* to call someone using a telephone; *your mother phoned when you were out*

by phone ['baɪ 'fəʊn] using the telephone; *I booked my ticket by phone*

on the phone ['ɒn ðə 'fəʊn] speaking by telephone; *she has been on the phone all morning*

phone back ['fəʊn 'bæk] *verb* to reply by telephone; *the manager is out - can you phone back in about fifteen minutes?*

phone book ['fəʊn 'bʊk] *noun* book which gives the names of people and businesses in a town, with their addresses and phone numbers; *it's a new restaurant - it isn't in the phone book*

phone call ['fəʊn 'kɔːl] *noun* telephone call, speaking to someone by telephone; *I need to make a quick phone call before we leave*

phone number ['fəʊn 'nʌmbə] *noun* number of one particular phone; *what's the phone number of the garage?*; *if I give you my phone number promise you won't forget it*

photo ['fəʊtəʊ] *noun* photograph, a picture taken with a camera; *I've brought some holiday photos to show you* (NOTE: plural is photos)

photocopier ['fəʊtəʊkɒpiə] *noun* machine which makes photocopies; *I'll just take this down to the photocopier and make some copies*; *you can make colour photocopies on a colour photocopier*

photocopy ['fəʊtəʊkɒpi] **1** *noun* copy of a document made by photographing it; *she made six photocopies of the contract* **2** *verb* to copy something and make a print of it; *can you photocopy this letter, please?*

photograph ['fəʊtəɡrɑːf] *noun* picture taken with a camera; *I've found an old black and white photograph of my grandparents' wedding*; *you'll need two passport photographs for your bus pass*

phrase [freɪz] *noun* short sentence or group of words; *'a big green door' and 'at the bottom of the stairs' are both phrases*; **phrase book** = book of common phrases with translations; *we bought a Japanese phrase book before we went to Japan*

physical [ˈfɪzɪkl] *adjective* referring to the human body; **physical education (PE)** = time in school when students do exercises, play sports, etc.

physically [ˈfɪzɪkli] *adverb* **(a)** referring to the body; *she is physically handicapped, but manages to look after herself* **(b)** referring to the laws of nature; *it is physically impossible for a lump of lead to float*

piano [ˈpjænəʊ] *noun* large musical instrument with black and white keys which you press to make music; *he learnt to play the piano when he was at school*; *she's taking piano lessons*

pick [pɪk] **1** *noun* a large heavy tool with a curved metal head with a sharp end that you lift up and bring down to break things; *they started to smash the concrete path with picks and spades* **2** *verb* **(a)** to choose; *the captain picks the football team*; *she was picked to play a part in the TV show* **(b)** to take fruit or flowers from plants; *they've picked all the strawberries*; *don't pick the flowers in the public gardens*

pick up [ˈpɪk ˈʌp] *verb* **(a)** to lift something up which is lying on the ground; *after the picnic, remember to pick up all your litter* **(b)** to learn something easily without being taught; *she never took any piano lessons, she just picked it up* **(c)** to give someone a lift in a vehicle; *the car will pick you up from the hotel*; *can you pick us up at seven o'clock?*

pickle [ˈpɪkl] *noun* **pickle(s)** = small pieces of vegetables in a vinegar sauce; *a cheese and pickle sandwich*; *do you want pickles with your meat pie?*

picnic [ˈpɪknɪk] **1** *noun* meal eaten in the open air; *if it's fine, let's go for a picnic*; *they stopped by a wood, and had a picnic lunch* **2** *verb* to eat a picnic; *people were picnicking on the bank of the river* (NOTE: **picnicking - picnicked**)

picture [ˈpɪktʃə] *noun* drawing, painting, photo, etc., of something; *she drew a picture of the house*

pie [paɪ] *noun* **(a)** meat or fruit cooked in pastry; *for pudding, there's apple pie and ice cream*; *if we're going on a picnic, I'll buy a big pork pie* **(b)** **cottage pie** *or* **shepherd's pie** = minced meat cooked in a dish with a layer of mashed potatoes on top; **fisherman's pie** = cooked fish in a dish with potatoes on top

piece [piːs] *noun* **(a)** (small) bit of something; *'piece' is often used to show one item of something which has no plural, such as 'a piece of equipment'*; *would you like another piece of cake?*; *I need two pieces of black cloth*; *she played a piece of music by Chopin* **(b)** **pieces** = broken bits of something; *he dropped the vase and it broke to pieces*; **to take something to pieces** = to undo something to see how it works inside; *you will have to take the clock to pieces to mend it*

pierce [pɪəs] *verb* to make a hole in something; *she decided to have her ears pierced*; *use your straw to pierce the top of the carton of juice*

pig [pɪg] *noun* fat pink or black farm animal with short legs, which gives meat; *the farmer next door keeps pigs*; *fresh meat from a pig is called pork*

pigeon [ˈpɪdʒn] *noun* fat grey bird which is common in towns; *there are lots of pigeons in Trafalgar Square but you're not supposed to feed them*

pile [paɪl] **1** *noun* **(a)** heap of things on top of each other; *the waiter was carrying a pile of plates*; *the wind blew piles of dead leaves into the road* **(b)** *(informal)* **piles of** = a lot of; *there's no need to hurry, we've got piles of time* **2** *verb* **to pile (up)** = to put things on top of each other in a heap; *all the Christmas presents are piled (up) under the tree*

pill [pɪl] *noun* small round tablet of medicine; *take two pills before breakfast*

pillar [ˈpɪlə] *noun* thick column which holds up part of a building; *the roof is supported by a row of wooden pillars*

pillar box [ˈpɪlə ˈbɒks] *noun* round red

metal box into which you can post letters; *there's a pillar box at the corner of the street*

pillow ['pɪləʊ] *noun* bag full of soft material which you put your head on in bed; *I like to sleep with two pillows*

pillowcase ['pɪləʊkeɪs] *noun* cloth bag to cover a pillow with; *they put clean sheets and pillowcases on the beds every morning*

pilot ['paɪlət] *noun* (a) person who flies a plane; *passengers must not talk to the pilot* (b) person who guides boats into or out of a harbour; *ships are not allowed into the harbour without a pilot* (c) made or used as a test; *the council is running a pilot scheme for training unemployed young people*

pimple ['pɪmpl] *noun* small red bump on the surface of your skin; *you've got a pimple on your chin*

pin [pɪn] **1** *noun* (a) small thin metal stick with a round head and a sharp point, used for attaching clothes, papers, etc., together; *she fastened the ribbons to her dress with a pin* (b) **pins and needles** = sharp tickling feeling in your foot after it has lost feeling for a time; *I can't run - I've got pins and needles in my foot* **2** *verb* to attach with a pin; *she pinned up a notice about the meeting*; *he pinned her photograph on the wall* (NOTE: **pinning - pinned**)

pincers ['pɪnsəz] *noun* claws of a crab or lobster; *a crab can pinch you with its pincers*

pinch [pɪnʃ] **1** *noun* small amount of something which you hold between your first finger and thumb; *add a pinch of salt to the boiling water* (NOTE: plural is **pinches**) **2** *verb* (a) to squeeze tight, using the finger and thumb; *Ow! you're pinching me!* (b) *(informal)* to steal; *someone's pinched my bike!*

pine [paɪn] **1** *noun* (a) type of tall tree with green leaves shaped like needles, which stay on the tree all year round; *they planted a row of pines along the edge of the field* (b) wood from a pine tree; *we've bought a pine table for*

the kitchen; *there are pine cupboards in the children's bedroom* **2** *verb* **to pine for someone** = to feel sad because you do not have someone you love any more; *she's miserable because she's pining for her cat*

pineapple ['paɪnæpl] *noun* large sweet tropical fruit, with stiff leaves on top; *she cut up a pineapple to add to the fruit salad*

pink [pɪŋk] *adjective* very pale red colour; *she uses pink paper when she writes to her friends*

PIN number ['pɪn 'nʌmbə] *noun* (= PERSONAL IDENTIFICATION NUMBER) special number which is given to someone who has a credit card or cash card; *I can never remember my PIN number*

pint [paɪnt] *noun* measure for liquids (= 0.568 of a litre); *he drinks a pint of milk a day*

pipe [paɪp] *noun* (a) tube; *he's clearing a blocked pipe in the kitchen* (b) tube for smoking tobacco, with a bowl at one end in which the tobacco burns; *he only smokes a pipe, never cigarettes*

pirate ['paɪərət] *noun* sailor who attacks and robs other ships; *pirates buried treasure on the island hundreds of years ago*

pistol ['pɪstl] *noun* small gun which is held in the hand; *he pointed a pistol at the shopkeeper and asked for money*

pit [pɪt] *noun* (a) deep, dark hole in the ground; *they dug a pit to bury the rubbish* (b) mine where coal is dug; *my grandfather spent his whole life working down a pit*

pitch [pɪtʃ] **1** *noun* (a) ground on which a game is played; *I'll time you, if you run round the football pitch*; *the pitch is too wet to play on* (NOTE: plural is **pitches**) (b) high point (of anger or excitement); *excitement was at fever pitch* **2** *verb* to put up a tent; *they pitched their tent in a field by the beach*

pity ['pɪti] **1** *noun* (a) feeling of sympathy for someone who is in a difficult situation; **to take pity on someone** = to feel sorry for someone; *at last someone took pity on the old lady and* *helped her across the road* (b) it's a pity that = it is sad that; *it's a pity you weren't there to see the show*; *it's such a pity that the rain spoiled the picnic* 2 *verb* to feel sympathy for someone; *I pity the poor teachers who have to cope with children like ours*

pizza ['piːtsə] *noun* Italian dish, consisting of a flat round pie base cooked with tomatoes, onions, etc., on top; *we can pick up a pizza for supper tonight*

place [pleɪs] 1 *noun* (a) where something is, or where something happens; *here's the place where we saw the cows*; *make sure you put the book back in the right place*; all over the place = everywhere; *litter was lying all over the place outside the takeaway* (b) seat; *I'm keeping this place for my sister*; *I'm sorry, but this place has been taken*; to change places with someone = to take each other's seat; *if you can't see the screen, change places with me* (c) position (in a race); *the British runners are in the first three places* (d) to take place = to happen; *the fight took place outside the football ground*; *the film takes place in China* 2 *verb* to put; *the waitress placed the bottle on the table*; *please place the envelope in the box*

plague [pleɪg] *noun* infectious disease passed by insects from rats to humans; *thousands of people died in the Great Plague of London in 1665*

plaice [pleɪs] *noun* common flat sea fish; *we ordered plaice and chips*

plain [pleɪn] 1 *adjective* (a) easy to understand; *the instructions are written in plain English* (b) obvious; *it's perfectly plain what he wants* (c) simple, not decorated; *we put plain wallpaper in the dining room* (d) not pretty; *his two daughters are rather plain* (e) plain chocolate = dark bitter chocolate; plain yoghurt = yoghurt without any fruit flavour (NOTE: do not confuse with **plane**; also note: **plainer - plainest**) 2 *noun* flat area of country; *from the hills there is a wonderful view over the plain*

plainly ['pleɪnli] *adverb* (a) in an obvious way; *he's plainly bored by the French lesson* (b) clearly; *it is plainly visible from here*

plait [plæt] 1 *noun* long pieces of hair, woven into a long rope; *she wears her hair in a plait or in plaits* 2 *verb* to weave hair, etc., to form a plait; *my mother used to plait my hair before I went to school in the morning*

plan [plæn] 1 *noun* (a) organized way of doing things; *she drew up plans for the school trip to Germany* (b) drawing of the way something is arranged; *the fire exits are shown on the plan of the building*; town plan = map of a town; *can you find London Road on the town plan?* 2 *verb* (a) to arrange how you are going to do something; *she's busy planning her holiday in Greece* (b) to intend to do something; *we weren't planning to go on holiday this year*; *I plan to take the 5 o'clock flight to New York* (NOTE: planning - planned)

plane [pleɪn] *noun* (a) aircraft, machine which flies; *when is the next plane for Glasgow?*; *how are you getting to Paris? - we're going by plane* (b) tool with a sharp blade for making wood smooth; *he smoothed off the rough edges of the table with a plane* (c) large tree with broad leaves, often grown in towns; *the bark of plane trees comes off in large pieces*; *many London squares are planted with planes* (NOTE: do not confuse with **plain**)

planet ['plænɪt] *noun* (a) one of the bodies in space which turn round the sun; *Earth is the third planet from the Sun* (b) the planet Earth; *rising sea levels could affect the whole planet*

plank [plæŋk] *noun* long flat piece of wood used in building; *hold the plank steady while I saw it in half*

plant [plɑːnt] 1 *noun* (a) living thing which grows in the ground and has leaves, a stem and roots; *he has several rows of cabbage plants in his garden*; house plants *or* pot plants = plants which you grow in pots in the house;

will you water my house plants for me while I'm on holiday?; **plant pot** = special pot for growing plants in **(b)** large factory; *they are planning to build a car plant near the river* **2** *verb* to put a plant in the ground; *we've planted two pear trees and a peach tree in the garden*

plaster ['plɑːstə] *noun* **(a)** white mixture which is mixed with water and is used for covering the walls of houses; *the flat hasn't been decorated yet and there is still bare plaster in most of the rooms* **(b)** white paste used to make a solid cover to hold a broken arm or leg in place; *he had an accident skiing and now has his leg in plaster* **(c) sticking plaster** = sticky tape used for covering small wounds; *I put a piece of sticking plaster on my cut*

plastic ['plæstɪk] *noun* artificial material made in factories, used to make all sorts of things; *we take plastic plates when we go to the beach*; *the supermarket gives you plastic bags to put your shopping in*

Plasticine™ ['plæstɪsiːn] *noun* trademark for a type of coloured material like clay, which children use to make model figures; *the children spent the afternoon making animals out of Plasticine*

plate [pleɪt] *noun* **(a)** flat round dish for putting food on; *pass all the plates down to the end of the table*; *they passed round plates of sandwiches* **(b)** flat piece of metal, glass, etc.; *the sitting room has big plate glass windows; see also* NUMBER PLATE

platform ['plætfɔːm] *noun* **(a)** high flat floor by the side of the railway lines at a station, to help passengers get on or off the trains easily; *crowds of people were waiting on the platform*; *the train for Liverpool will leave from platform 10* **(b)** high wooden floor for people to speak from; *someone in the audience threw a tomato at one of the MPs on the platform*

play [pleɪ] **1** *noun* written text which is acted in a theatre or on TV; *did you see the play on TV last night?*; *two of Shakespeare's plays are on the list for the English exam* **2** *verb* **(a)** to take part in a game; *he plays rugby for the college*; *do you play tennis?* **(b)** *(of a game)* to take place; *cricket isn't played in the winter* **(c)** to amuse yourself; *when you've finished your homework you can go out to play*; *he doesn't like playing with other children* **(d)** to make music on a musical instrument or to put on a disk; *he can't play the piano very well*; *let me play you my new CD*

play back ['pleɪ 'bæk] *verb* to listen to something which you have just recorded on tape; *he played back the messages left on his answering machine*

player ['pleɪə] *noun* **(a)** person who plays a game; *you only need two players for chess*; *rugby players have to be strong and fit* **(b)** person who plays a musical instrument; *a famous guitar player*

playground ['pleɪgraʊnd] *noun* place at a school or in a public area, where children can play; *the little girls were playing quietly in a corner of the playground*

playing cards ['pleɪɪŋ 'kɑːdz] *noun* set of 52 pieces of card with pictures or patterns on them, used for playing various games; *he pulled out a pack of playing cards and asked me if I wanted a game*; *conjurors do tricks with playing cards*

playtime ['pleɪtaɪm] *noun* time in school when children can play; *as it was wet, the children had to stay in during playtime*

pleasant ['plezənt] *adjective* which makes you happy or satisfied; *how pleasant it is to sit here under the trees!* (NOTE: **pleasanter - pleasantest**)

please [pliːz] **1** *interjection (used to ask in a polite way)* *can you close the window, please?*; *please can I have a ham sandwich?*; *do you want some more tea? - yes, please!* **2** *verb* to make someone happy or satisfied; *we try to please our customers*; *she's not difficult to please*

pleased [pliːzd] *adjective* happy; *we're very pleased with our new house*; *I'm pleased to hear you're feeling better*

pleasure ['pleʒə] *noun* happy feeling; *it gives me great pleasure to welcome you to our house*

pleat [pliːt] *noun* ironed fold in a skirt, etc.; *her skirt has pleats*

plenty ['plenti] *noun* large quantity; *you've got plenty of time to catch the train*; *have you got enough bread? - yes, I've got plenty*

pliers ['plaɪəz] *noun* **(pair of) pliers** = tool shaped like scissors for pinching, pulling, or cutting wire; *I need a pair of pliers to pull out these rusty nails*

plimsolls ['plɪmsɒlz] *noun* canvas shoes with thin rubber soles, worn when doing exercises; *I forgot my plimsolls and had to do gym in my bare feet*

plot [plɒt] **1** *noun* **(a)** small area of land for building, for growing vegetables, etc.; *they own a plot of land next to the river*; *the plot isn't big enough to build a house on* **(b)** basic story of a book, play, film; *I won't tell you the plot of the film so as not to spoil it for you* **(c)** wicked plan; *they thought up a plot to kill the Prime Minister's wife* **2** *verb* to draw up a wicked plan; *they plotted to kidnap the President's daughter* (NOTE: **plotting - plotted**)

plough *US* **plow** [plaʊ] **1** *noun* **(a)** farm machine for digging and turning over soil; *the plough is pulled by a tractor* **(b)** **snow plough** = powerful machine with a large blade in front, used for clearing snow from streets, railway lines, etc.; *the snow ploughs were out all night clearing the main roads* **2** *verb* to turn over the soil; *some farmers still use horses to plough the fields*

pluck [plʌk] *verb* **(a)** to pull out feathers; *to pluck a chicken* **(b)** to pull and release the strings of a guitar or other musical instrument to make a sound; *he was plucking the strings of his guitar*

plug [plʌg] **1** *noun* **(a)** device with pins which go into holes and allow electric current to pass through; *the vacuum cleaner is supplied with a plug* **(b)** flat rubber disc which covers the hole for waste water in a bath or sink; *she pulled out the plug and let the dirty water drain away* **2** *verb* to block up (a hole); *we plugged the leak in the bathroom*; *he plugged his ears with cotton wool because he couldn't stand the noise* (NOTE: **plugging - plugged**)

plug in ['plʌg 'ɪn] *verb* to push an electric plug into holes and so attach a device to the electricity supply; *the computer wasn't plugged in - that's why it wouldn't work*

plum [plʌm] *noun* sweet gold, red or purple fruit with a smooth skin and a large stone; *she bought a pound of plums to make a pie*

plumber ['plʌmə] *noun* person who puts in or mends water pipes, radiators, etc.; *there's water dripping through the kitchen ceiling, we'll have to call a plumber*

plunge [plʌnʒ] *verb* **(a)** to throw yourself into water; *he plunged into the river to rescue the little boy* **(b)** to push something into something; *the country was plunged into chaos by the train strike*

plural ['plʊərəl] *adjective & noun (in grammar)* form of a word showing that there are more than one; *does 'government' take a singular or plural verb?*; *what's the plural of 'mouse'?*

plus [plʌs] **1** *preposition* **(a)** added to; *his salary plus bonuses comes to more than £25,000*; *10 + 4 = 14: 'ten plus four equals fourteen'* **(b)** more than; **houses valued at £200,000 plus** = houses valued at over £200,000 **2** *noun* **plus (sign)** = sign (+) meaning more than; *she put in a plus instead of a minus*

p.m. *US* **P.M.** ['piː 'em] *adverb* in the afternoon, after 12.00; *the exhibition is open from 10 a.m. to 5.30 p.m.*; *if you phone New York after 6 p.m. the calls are at a cheaper rate*

PO = POST OFFICE

poach [pəʊtʃ] *verb* **(a)** to cook eggs without their shells, or fish, etc., in gently boiling water; *would you like your eggs boiled or poached?*; *they served poached salmon as a first course* **(b)** to catch animals, birds or fish on someone else's land without permission; *the farmer suspected that someone was poaching his rabbits*

pocket ['pɒkɪt] *noun* one of several little bags sewn into the inside of a coat, etc., in which you can keep your money, handkerchief, keys, etc.; *she looked in all her pockets but couldn't find her keys*; *he was leaning against a fence with his hands in his pockets*; **pocket calculator** = small calculator which you can put in your pocket; **pocket money** = money which parents give to children each week; *she gets more pocket money than I do*

pod [pɒd] *noun* **(a)** long green tube in which peas or beans, etc., grow; *some peas can be eaten in their pods* **(b)** glass container with seats for travellers; *we all got into a pod on the London Eye*

poem ['pəʊɪm] *noun* piece of writing, with words carefully chosen to sound attractive, set out in short lines usually of a regular length; *he wrote a long poem about an old sailor*

poet ['pəʊɪt] *noun* person who writes poems; *the poet gives a wonderful description of a summer morning*

poetry ['pəʊɪtri] *noun* poems in general; *reading poetry makes me cry*; *he reads a lot of German poetry*

point [pɔɪnt] **1** *noun* **(a)** sharp end of something long; *the point of my pencil has broken*; *the stick has a very sharp point* **(b)** dot used to show the division between whole numbers and parts of numbers; *the answer is 5.2% (say 'five point two percent ')* **(c)** particular place; *the path went for miles through the woods and in the end we came back to the point where we started from*; *we*

had reached a point 2000m above sea level **(d)** particular moment in time; *from that point on, things began to change*; **at that point** = at that moment; *all the lights went off at that point*; **on the point of doing something** = just about to do something; *I was on the point of phoning you* **(e)** meaning or reason; *there's no point in asking him to pay - he hasn't any money*; *what's the point of doing the same thing all over again?* **(f)** score in a game; *their team scored three points*; *in rugby, a try counts as five points* **2** *verb* to aim a gun or your finger at something; to show with your finger; *the teacher is pointing at you*; *don't point that gun at me - it might go off*

pointed ['pɔɪntɪd] *adjective* with a sharp point at one end; *he was carrying a pointed stick*

poison ['pɔɪzn] **1** *noun* substance which kills or makes you ill if it is swallowed or if it gets into the blood; *there's enough poison in this bottle to kill the whole town* **2** *verb* to kill with poison; *she was accused of poisoning her husband*

poisonous ['pɔɪsənəs] *adjective* which can kill or harm with poison; *these red berries are poisonous*

poke [pəʊk] *verb* to push with your finger or with a stick; *he poked the pig with his stick*

Poland ['pəʊlənd] *noun* large country in Eastern Europe, between Germany and Russia; *Poland is an important farming country* (NOTE: capital: **Warsaw**; people: **the Poles**; language: **Polish**)

polar bear ['pəʊlə 'beə] *noun* big white bear found in areas near the North Pole; *the hunters were attacked by polar bears*

pole [pəʊl] *noun* **(a)** long rod of wood or metal; **tent pole** = pole which holds up a tent; *one of the tent poles snapped in the wind* **(b)** **North Pole** = furthest point at the north of the earth; **South Pole** = furthest point at the south of the earth

Pole [pəʊl] *noun* person from Poland; *only*

one Pope has been a Pole

police [pə'liːs] *noun* organization which controls traffic, tries to stop crime and tries to catch criminals; *the police are looking for the driver of the car; call the police - I've just seen someone drive off in my car*

police officer ['pliːs 'ɒfisə] *noun* member of the police force; *I'm a police officer, madam, please get out of the car*

policeman, policewoman ['pliːsmən or 'pliːswʊmən] *noun* ordinary member of the police; *three armed policemen went into the building; if you don't know the way, ask a policeman* (NOTE: plurals are **policemen, policewomen**)

polish ['pɒlɪʃ] **1** *noun* soft substance used to make things shiny; **floor polish** = polish used to make wooden floors shiny; **shoe polish** = wax used to make shoes shiny (NOTE: plural is **polishes**) **2** *verb* to rub something to make it shiny; *he polished his shoes until they shone*

Polish ['pəʊlɪʃ] **1** *adjective* referring to Poland; *the Polish Army joined in the military exercises* **2** *noun* language spoken in Poland; *you will need an English-Polish phrase book if you're visiting Warsaw*

polite [pə'laɪt] *adjective* not rude; *sales staff should always be polite to customers* (NOTE: **politer - politest**)

political [pə'lɪtɪkl] *adjective* referring to politics; *I don't want to get involved in a political argument*

politician [pɒlɪ'tɪʃn] *noun* person who works in politics, especially a Member of Parliament; *politicians from all parties have welcomed the report*

politics ['pɒlɪtɪks] *noun* **(a)** ideas and methods used in governing a country; *he went into politics when he left university* **(b)** study of how countries are governed; *he studied politics and social studies at university*

pollen ['pɒlən] *noun* yellow powder in a flower which touches part of a female flower and so creates seeds; *bees carry pollen from one flower to the next*; **pollen count** = number showing the amount of pollen in the air, which can cause hayfever

pollution [pə'luːʃn] *noun* action of making the environment dirty; *pollution of the atmosphere has increased over the last 50 years; it took six months to clean up the oil pollution on the beaches*

polyester [pɒlɪ'estə] *noun* type of artificial fibre used especially to make clothes; *he bought two polyester shirts in the sale*

polythene ['pɒlɪθiːn] *noun* type of strong transparent plastic used in thin sheets; *pack the sandwiches in a polythene bag*

pond [pɒnd] *noun* small lake; *children sail their boats on the pond in the park*

pony ['pəʊni] *noun* small horse; *my best friend lets me ride her pony sometimes* (NOTE: plural is **ponies**)

ponytail ['pəʊnɪteɪl] *noun* way of having your hair where the hair is tied at the back and falls loose like the tail of a pony; *she usually wears her hair in a ponytail*

pool [puːl] *noun* **(a) swimming pool** = large bath of water for swimming in; *we have a little swimming pool in the garden; he swam two lengths of the pool* **(b)** small amount of liquid; *there was a pool of blood on the pavement*

poor [pɔː] *adjective* **(a)** with little or no money; *the poorer students find it difficult to get through college if they don't have grants* **(b)** not very good; *she's been in poor health for some months* **(c)** *(showing you are sorry)* *poor old John! - he has to stay at home and finish his homework while we all go to the disco* (NOTE: **poorer - poorest**)

pop [pɒp] **1** *noun* **(a)** noise like a cork coming out of a bottle; *the balloon landed on the candles and burst with a pop* **(b) pop (music)** = modern popular music; *he spends all day listening to pop records; we went to a pop concert last night* **2** *verb* **(a)** to go quickly; *he popped into the chemist's; I'm just popping round to see Jane* **(b)** to put quickly; *pop the pie in the microwave for six minutes* (NOTE: popping - popped)

popcorn ['pɒpkɔːn] *noun* corn seed which is heated (sometimes with sugar) until it bursts, eaten as a snack; *we always buy a carton of popcorn when we go to the cinema*

Pope [pəʊp] *noun* the head of the Roman Catholic Church; *the Pope said mass in a stadium before 50,000 people*

poppy ['pɒpi] *noun* common red wild flower which often grows in fields; *she picked a bunch of poppies on her way home through the fields* (NOTE: plural is **poppies**)

popular ['pɒpjʊlə] *adjective* liked by a lot of people; *the South Coast is the most popular area for holidays*

population [pɒpjuˈleɪʃn] *noun* number of people who live in a place; *central London has a population of over three million*

pork [pɔːk] *noun* fresh meat from a pig, eaten cooked; *we're having pork for dinner tonight*; *in England, roast pork is served with apple sauce*; **pork pie** = pie with pork filling; *let's buy a pork pie to eat on the picnic*; **pork sausage** = sausage made with pork

porpoise ['pɔːpəs] *noun* sea animal similar to a dolphin, which swims in groups; *a school of porpoises followed the ship*

porridge ['pɒrɪdʒ] *noun* oats cooked in water, eaten for breakfast; *she put a bowl of porridge on the table in front of him*

port [pɔːt] *noun* (a) harbour, or town with a harbour; *the ship is due in port on Tuesday* (b) left side (when looking forward on board a ship or aircraft); *passengers sitting on the port side of the plane can see Tower Bridge as we pass over it*; *the ship turned to port to avoid the yacht*

portable ['pɔːtəbl] **1** *adjective* which can be carried; *we have a portable television which we take on holiday with us* **2** *noun* small computer which can be carried; *I type all my letters on my portable*

porter ['pɔːtə] *noun* (a) person who carries luggage for travellers at railway stations; *find a porter to help us with all this luggage* (b) person who does general work in a hospital, including moving the patients around; *the nurse asked a porter to fetch a wheelchair*

portion ['pɔːʃn] *noun* (a) part; *this is only a small portion of the fruit we picked* (b) serving of food, usually for one person; *ask the waitress if they serve children's portions*

portrait ['pɔːtreɪt] *noun* painting or photograph of a person; *he has painted a portrait of the Queen*

Portugal ['pɔːtjʊgəl] *noun* country is Southern Europe, to the west of Spain; *Portugal is a country of great travellers* (NOTE: capital: **Lisbon**; people: **the Portuguese**; language: **Portuguese**)

Portuguese [pɔːtjuˈgiːz] **1** *adjective* referring to Portugal; *a Portuguese sailor* **2** *noun* (a) person from Portugal; *she married a Portuguese*; **the Portuguese** = people from Portugal (b) language spoken in Portugal, Brazil, etc.; *I don't know the word for 'passport' in Portuguese*

posh [pɒʃ] *adjective (informal)* very smart; *I decided I had better wear my poshest dress to the wedding*; *we ate in a really posh restaurant* (NOTE: posher - poshest)

position [pəˈzɪʃən] *noun* (a) place where someone or something is; *from his position on the roof he can see the whole of the street* (b) way in which something is; *she was in a sitting position* (c) situation or state of affairs; *we found ourselves in a very awkward position*

positive ['pɒzɪtɪv] **1** *adjective* (a) certain, sure; *I'm positive I put the key in my pocket*; *are you positive he said six o'clock?* (b) *(in a test)* showing that something is there; *the cancer test was positive* (c) **positive film** = film where the light parts are light and the dark are dark (as opposed to negative film); **positive terminal** = one of the terminals in a battery, shown by a plus (+) sign; *the wire should be attached to the positive terminal*

possess [pə'zes] *verb* to own; *he lost all he possessed in the fire*

possession [pə'zeʃn] *noun* **(a)** owning something; **in someone's possession** = being held by someone **(b) possessions** = things which you own; *they lost all their possessions in the flood*

possible ['pɒsəbl] *adjective* which can be, which can happen; *that field is a possible site for the factory*; *it is possible that the plane has been delayed*

as possible [æz 'pɒsəbl] *(used to make a superlative)* *I want to go as far away as possible for my holiday*; *please do it as quickly as possible*

possibly ['pɒsəbli] *adverb* **(a)** perhaps; *in January we had possibly the most snow we have ever seen* **(b)** *(used with 'can' or 'can't' to make a phrase stronger)* *you can't possibly eat twenty-two cakes!*; *how can you possibly expect me to do all that work in one day?*

post [pəʊst] **1** *noun* **(a)** letters, etc., sent; *there were no cheques in this morning's post*; *he usually opens the post before anyone else can see it* **(b)** system of sending letters, parcels, etc.; *it is easier to send the parcel by post than to deliver it by hand* **(c)** job; *he applied for a post in the sales department* **(d)** long piece of wood, metal, etc., put in the ground; *the fence is attached to concrete posts* **2** *verb* to send a letter, parcel, etc.; *don't forget to post your Christmas cards*; *the letter should have arrived by now - we posted it ten days ago*

post office (PO) ['pəʊst 'ɒfɪs] *noun* building where you can buy stamps, send letters and parcels, pay bills, collect your pension, pay your car tax, etc.; *the main post office is in the High Street*; *post offices are shut on Sundays*

postbox ['pəʊstbɒks] *noun* box into which you can put letters, which will then be collected and sent on by the post office; *if you're going out, could you put this letter in the postbox for me?*

postcard ['pəʊstkɑːd] *noun* flat piece of card (often with a picture on one side) which you send to someone with a short message on it; *send us a postcard when you arrive in China*; *they sent me a postcard of the village where they were staying*

postcode ['pəʊstkəʊd] *noun* system of letters or numbers to show the town or street in an address, to help with the sorting of mail (the American English is 'zip code'); *my postcode is BA2 5NT*; *don't forget the postcode when writing the address on the envelope*

poster ['pəʊstə] *noun* large notice, picture or advertisement stuck on a wall; *they put up posters advertising the concert*

postman ['pəʊstmən] *noun* person who delivers letters to houses (American English is 'mailman'); *the postman comes very early - before eight o'clock* (NOTE: plural is **postmen**)

postpone [pəs'pəʊn] *verb* to put back to a later date or time; *the meeting has been postponed until next week*

pot [pɒt] *noun* glass or china container, usually without a handle; *the plant is too big - it needs a bigger pot*; *she made ten pots of strawberry jam*

potato [pə'teɪtəʊ] *noun* **(a)** common root vegetable which grows under the ground; *do you want any more potatoes?*; *we're having roast lamb and potatoes for Sunday lunch* **(b) sweet potato** = a tropical vegetable like a long red potato with sweet yellow flesh inside (NOTE: plural is **potatoes**)

pottery ['pɒtri] *noun* **(a)** pots, plates, etc., made of clay; *there's a man in the market who sells local pottery* **(b)** workshop or factory where pots are made; *I bought this vase from the pottery where it was made* (NOTE: plural in this meaning is **potteries**)

pouch [paʊtʃ] *noun* **(a)** small bag for carrying coins, etc.; *she carried the ring in a* small leather pouch round her neck **(b)** bag in the skin in front of animals such as kangaroos, where the young are carried; *the kangaroo carries its young in its pouch* (NOTE: plural is **pouches)**

pounce [paʊns] *verb* **to pounce on something** = to jump on something; *the cat was waiting in the bushes, ready to pounce on any bird that came by*

pound [paʊnd] **1** *noun* **(a)** measure of weight (about 450 grams); *she bought a pound of onions and five pounds of carrots*; *the parcel weighed 26lb (twenty-six pounds)* **(b)** money used in Britain and several other countries; *he earns more than a six pounds an hour*; *the price of the car is over £50,000 (fifty thousand pounds); he tried to pay for his bus ticket with a £20 note (twenty pound note)* **2** *verb* **(a)** to hit hard; *he pounded the table with his fist* **(b)** to smash into little pieces; *the ship was pounded to pieces by huge waves*

pour [pɔː] *verb* **(a)** to make a liquid flow; *she poured water down his neck as a joke* **(b)** to flow out or down; *clouds of smoke poured out of the house; there was a sudden bang and smoke poured out of the engine* **(c)** **to pour with rain** = to rain very hard; *it poured with rain all afternoon*

pour down ['pɔː 'daʊn] *verb* to rain very hard; *don't go out without an umbrella - it's pouring down*

powder ['paʊdə] *noun* very fine dry dust like flour; *the drug is available in the form of a white powder*; **washing powder** *or* **soap powder** = soap in powder form, used in washing machines; *can you buy some washing powder next time you go to the supermarket?*

power ['paʊwə] *noun* **(a)** driving force; *the engine is driven by steam power*; **wind power** = force of the wind (used to make a windmill go round, make a yacht go forward, etc.) **(b)** **(electric) power** = electricity used to drive machines or devices; *turn off the power*

before you try to repair the TV set **(c)** political control; *the government came to power in 1997* **(d)** important, powerful country; *China is one of the great world powers*

powerful ['paʊwəfʊl] *adjective* very strong; *this motorbike has a very powerful engine*; *she was swept away by the powerful current*

practical ['præktɪkl] *adjective* **(a)** referring to actual work; *she needs more practical experience in the job*; *he passed the practical exam but failed the written part* **(b)** which actually works; *has anyone got a more practical suggestion to make?*

practically ['præktɪkli] *adverb* almost; *practically all the students passed the test*; *his T-shirt is such a dark grey it is practically black*

practice ['præktɪs] *noun* doing something again and again until you are good at it; *she does her piano practice every morning*; *racing cars make several practice runs before each race*

practise *US* **practice** ['præktɪs] *verb* to do something again and again until you are good at it; *he's practising catching and throwing*; *she practises the piano every day*

prairie ['preəri] *noun* plains in North America, mainly covered in grass, where most of the world's grain is produced; *the road crosses the prairie, going straight for hundreds of miles*

praise [preɪz] **1** *noun* words to show that you admire someone; *the teacher was full of praise for my work* **2** *verb* to show that you approve of someone or something; *the mayor praised the firemen for their efforts in putting out the fire*

pram [præm] *noun* light carriage on wheels for pushing a baby in; *we put the baby in her pram and went off for a walk*

prawn [prɔːn] *noun* sea animal like a large shrimp; *for lunch we had grilled prawns and salad*

pray [preɪ] *verb* to speak to God, asking God for something; *farmers prayed for rain*; **to pray for someone** = to ask God to protect someone

prayer [preə] *noun* speaking to God; *she says her prayers every night before going to bed*; *in church they said prayers for the victims of the floods*

precious ['preʃəs] *adjective* (a) worth a lot of money; **precious metal** = metal, such as gold, which is worth a lot of money (b) of great value to someone; *all her precious photographs were saved from the fire*

precipice ['presɪpɪs] *noun* steep side of a mountain; *she was hanging on a rope over the edge of the precipice*

precise [prɪ'saɪs] *adjective* exact; *we need to know the precise measurements of the box*

precisely [prɪ'saɪsli] *adverb* exactly; *the train arrived at 12.00 precisely*

predict [prɪ'dɪkt] *verb* to tell what you think will happen in the future; *the weather forecast predicted rain*

prefer [prɪ'fɜː] *verb* **to prefer something to something** = to like (to do) something better than something else; *I prefer butter to margarine*; *I'd prefer not to go to Germany this summer* (NOTE: **preferring - preferred**)

prefix ['priːfɪks] *noun* part of a word which is put in front of another word to form a new word; *the prefix 'anti-' is very common* (NOTE: plural is **prefixes**)

pregnant ['pregnənt] *adjective (of a woman)* carrying a child inside your body before it is born; *don't lift heavy weights when you're pregnant*

prehistoric [priːhɪ'stɒrɪk] *adjective* referring to the time before there was a written history; *prehistoric people used sharp stones as knives*

preparations [prepə'reɪʃnz] *noun* things done to get something ready; *we've finished our preparations and now we're ready to start*

prepare [prɪ'peə] *verb* (a) to get something ready; *we have prepared the hall for the school play* (b) to get ready for something; *he is preparing for his exam*

prepared [prɪ'peəd] *adjective* (a) ready; *be prepared, you may have quite a shock when you meet her* (b) **prepared to do something** = willing to do something; *they are prepared to go to live in Australia if necessary*

preposition [prepə'zɪʃn] *noun* word used with a noun or pronoun as its object to show place or time; *prepositions like 'by' and 'near' are very common, as in 'he was knocked down by a motorbike' or 'she was sitting near me'*

present 1 *noun* ['prezənt] (a) thing which you give to someone as a gift; *I got a watch as a Christmas present*; *how many birthday presents did you get?* (b) the time we are in now; *the novel is set in the present*; **at present** = now (c) form of a verb showing that the action is happening now; *the present of the verb 'to go' is 'he goes' or 'he is going'* **2** *adjective* ['prezənt] being there when something happens; *how many people were present at the meeting?* **3** *verb* [prɪ'zent] (a) to give as a formal gift; *when he retired after thirty years, the firm presented him with a large clock* (b) to introduce a show on TV, etc.; *she presents a TV programme on cooking*

presently ['prezəntli] *adverb* (a) soon; *he'll be making a speech presently* (b) US now, at the present time; *he's presently working for a chemical company*

preserve [prɪ'zɜːv] *verb* (a) to look after and keep in the same state; *we are trying to preserve the wild flowers in our area* (b) to treat something so that is does not rot; *spray the fence to preserve it; meat can be preserved in salt*

president ['prezɪdənt] *noun* head of a republic; *President Bush was elected in 2000; the French President came on an official visit*

press [pres] **1** *noun* newspapers and magazines; *the election was reported in the British press*; *there has been no mention of the problem in the press* **2** *verb* to push (such as a button to call something); *press 12 for room service*

pressure ['preʃə] *noun* **(a)** force of something which is pushing or squeezing; *there is not enough pressure in your tyres* **(b)** something which forces you to do something; *pressure from farmers forced the minister to change his mind*; **to put pressure on someone to do something** = to try to force someone to do something

pretend [prɪ'tend] *verb* to make someone believe you are something else, so as to trick them; *he got into the house by pretending to be a gas engineer*

pretty ['prɪti] **1** *adjective* pleasant to look at; *her daughters are very pretty*; *what a pretty little house!* **2** *adverb* (informal) quite; *you did pretty well, considering it's was the first time you had played snooker*

prevent [prɪ'vent] *verb* **(a)** to stop something happening; *we must try to prevent pollution of the atmosphere* **(b)** **to prevent someone from doing something** = to stop someone doing something; *we can't do much to prevent the river from flooding*

previous ['pri:viəs] *adjective* which happened earlier; *the letter was sent to my previous address*; *I had spent the previous day getting to know my way round the town*

previously ['pri:viəsli] *adverb* before; *this is my first visit to Paris by train - previously I've always gone by plane*

prey [preɪ] *noun* animal eaten by another animal; *mice and small birds are the favourite prey of owls*; **birds of prey** = birds which eat other birds or small animals (NOTE: do not confuse with **pray**)

price [praɪs] *noun* money which you have to pay to buy something; *the price of petrol is going up*; *there has been a sharp increase in house prices during the first six months of the year*

prick [prɪk] *verb* to jab with something sharp; *she pricked her finger when she was picking the roses*

prickle ['prɪkl] *noun* sharp point on a plant or animal; *be careful of the prickles when you're picking blackberries*

pride [praɪd] *noun* **(a)** pleasure in what you have done or in something which belongs to you; *he takes great pride in his garden* **(b)** feeling that you are better or more important than you really are; *his pride would not let him admit that he had made a mistake*

priest [pri:st] *noun* person who has been blessed to serve God, to carry out formal religious duties, etc.; *they were married by the local priest*

primary school ['praɪməri 'sku:l] *noun* school for children up to the age of eleven; *John is still at primary school*; *her mother is a primary school teacher*

prime [praɪm] **1** *adjective* most important; *the prime suspect in the case is the dead girl's boyfriend* **2** *noun* period when you are at your best; **past your prime** = no longer at your best; *at 35, she's past her prime as a tennis player*

Prime Minister ['praɪm 'mɪnɪstə] *noun* head of the government in Britain and other countries; *the Prime Minister will speak on TV at 6 o'clock tonight*

primrose ['prɪmrəʊz] *noun* small pale yellow spring flower; *primroses flower in early spring*

prince [prɪns] *noun* son of a king or queen; *the wicked witch changed the prince into a frog*

princess [prɪn'ses] *noun* daughter of a king or queen; wife of a prince; *once upon a time a beautiful princess lived in a castle by the edge of the forest*

principal ['prɪnsɪpl] **1** *adjective* main, most important; *the country's principal products* *are paper and wood* **2** *noun* head (of a school, a college); *the principal wants to see you in her office* (NOTE: do not confuse with **principle**)

principle ['prɪnsɪpl] *noun* law; general rule; *it is a principle of the British system of justice that a person is innocent until he is proved guilty*; **in principle** = in agreement with the general rule; *in principle, the results should be the same every time you do the experiment*; **on principle** = because of what you believe; *she refuses to eat meat on principle* (NOTE: do not confuse with **principal**)

print [prɪnt] **1** *noun* **(a)** picture or photograph which has been printed; *I'm going to have some more prints made of this photo* **(b)** letters marked on paper; *the instructions are written in very small print* **2** *verb* **(a)** to mark letters or pictures on paper by a machine, and so produce a book, poster, newspaper, etc.; *the book is printed directly from a computer disk*; *we had five hundred copies of the leaflet printed* **(b)** to write using only capital letters; *print your name in the space below*
print out ['prɪnt 'aut] *verb* to print information from a computer on a printer; *she printed out three copies of the letter*

printer ['prɪntə] *noun* **(a)** person or company that prints books, newspapers, etc.; *the book has gone to the printer, and we should have copies next week* **(b)** machine which prints; **laser printer** = office printing machine which prints using a laser beam

printout ['prɪntaut] *noun* printed information from a computer; *the travel agent gave me a printout of flight details and hotel reservations*

prison ['prɪzn] *noun* building where people are kept when they are being punished for a crime; *the judge sent him to prison for five years*; *the prisoners managed to escape from prison by digging a tunnel*

prisoner ['prɪznə] *noun* person who is in prison; *the prisoners were taken away in a police van*

private ['praɪvət] *adjective* **(a)** which belongs to one person, not to everyone; **private property** = property which belongs to a person, not to the public; *you can't park here - this is private property* **(b)** which refers to one particular person and should kept secret from others; *this is a private discussion between me and my lawyer*; **in private** = away from other people; *she asked to see the teacher in private*

prize [praɪz] *noun* something given to a winner; *he won first prize in the music competition*; *she answered all the questions correctly and claimed the prize*

probable ['prɒbəbl] *adjective* likely; *it's probable that the ship sank in a storm*

probably ['prɒbəbli] *adverb* likely to happen; *we're probably going to France for our holidays*

problem ['prɒbləm] *noun* **(a)** something which is difficult to answer; *half the students couldn't do all the problems in the maths test* **(b) no problem!** = don't worry, it isn't difficult

proceed [prə'siːd] *verb* **(a)** to go further; *he proceeded down the High Street towards the river* **(b)** to do something after something else; *the students then proceeded to shout and throw bottles at passing cars*

process ['prəuses] **1** *noun* **(a)** method of making something; *a new process for getting oil from coal* (NOTE: plural is **processes**) **(b) in the process of doing something** = while doing something; *she interrupted me while I was in the process of writing a letter* **2** *verb* **(a)** to manufacture goods from raw materials; *the iron is processed to make steel* **(b)** to deal with a claim, bill, etc., in the usual routine way; *orders are processed in our warehouse*

procession [prə'seʃn] *noun* group of people (with a band, etc.) walking in line; *the procession will march down Whitehall to the Houses of Parliament*; **in procession** = in a line as part of a ceremony; *the people who* *have received their degrees will walk in procession through the university grounds*

produce 1 *noun* ['prɒdjuːs] things grown on the land; *vegetables and other garden produce* (NOTE: do not confuse with **product**) 2 *verb* [prə'djuːs] **(a)** to show or bring out; *he produced a bundle of notes from his inside pocket* **(b)** to make; *the factory produces cars and trucks* **(c)** to grow crops, to give birth to young, etc.; *the region produces enough rice to supply the needs of the whole country* **(d)** to put on a play, a film, etc.; *she is producing 'Hamlet' for the local drama club*

producer [prə'djuːsə] *noun* person who puts on a play or a film; *she's the producer of the play now showing at the local theatre*

product ['prɒdʌkt] *noun* **(a)** thing which is manufactured; *how did you come to learn about our products?* (NOTE: do not confuse with **produce**) **(b)** *(in mathematics)* number which is the result when numbers are multiplied; *the product of 4 times 10 is 40*

production [prə'dʌkʃn] *noun* **(a)** the making of something; *we are trying to step up production* **(b)** putting on a play or film; *the film is currently in production at Teddington Studios* **(c)** particular version of a play; *have you seen the production of 'Henry V' at the Globe Theatre?*

profession [prə'feʃn] *noun* work which needs special training, skill or knowledge; *judges are members of the legal profession*

professional [prə'feʃnəl] **1** *adjective* referring to a profession; **professional qualifications** = documents showing that someone has finished a course of study which allows him or her to work in one of the professions; *he got a job as a solicitor even though he had no professional qualifications* **2** *noun* sportsman who is paid to play; *he turned professional last year*

profit ['prɒfɪt] *noun* money you gain from selling something which is more than the money you paid for it; *he bought the car last*

week and sold it today at a profit of £1000; **to make a profit** = to have more money as a result of a deal

program ['prəʊɡræm] **1** *noun* instructions given to a computer; *I'm running a word processing progam* **2** *verb* to give instructions to a computer; *the computer is programmed to print labels* (NOTE: **programming - programmed**)

programme *US* **program** ['prəʊɡræm *US* 'prəʊɡrəm] *noun* **(a)** TV or radio show; *we watched a programme on life in South-East Asia*; *there's a football programme after the news* **(b)** paper sold to people in a theatre or at a football match, etc., which gives information about the show, the teams, etc.; *the programme gives a list of the actors*

progress **1** *noun* ['prəʊɡres] **(a)** movement forwards; *we are making good progress towards finishing the house* **(b)** **in progress** = which is happening or being done; *the meeting is still in progress* **2** *verb* [prə'ɡres] to advance; *work on the new road is progressing slowly*

project **1** ['prɒdʒekt] *noun* work planned and written by students on their own; *her project is to write the history of her village* **2** [prə'dʒekt] *verb* to send a picture onto a screen; *the teacher projected slides of his visit to Africa*

projector [prə'dʒektə] *noun* machine which sends pictures onto a screen; *the projector broke down so we couldn't see the end of the film*

promise ['prɒmɪs] **1** *noun* saying that you will definitely do something; *you made a promise not to tell anyone else and now you've told my mother!*; **to go back on a promise** *or* **to break a promise** = not to do what you said you would do; *he broke his promise to take her to Mexico on holiday*; **to keep a promise** = to do what you said you would do; *she kept her promise to write to him every day* **2** *verb* to say that you will definitely do something; *they promised to be* back for supper; *promise you will bring the book back when you have finished with it*

prompt [prɒmpt] **1** *adjective* done immediately; *thank you for your prompt reply to my letter* (NOTE: **prompter - promptest**) **2** *verb* to tell an actor words which he has forgotten; *he had to be prompted in the middle of a long speech*

pronoun ['prəʊnaʊn] *noun* word used instead of a noun, such as 'I', 'you', 'he', 'she' and 'it'; *there are three pronouns in the sentence 'she gave it to me'*

pronounce [prə'naʊns] *verb* **(a)** to speak sounds which form a word; *how do you pronounce 'Paris' in French?* **(b)** to state officially; *he was pronounced dead on arrival at hospital*

pronunciation [prənʌnsi'eɪʃn] *noun* way of speaking words; *you should try to improve your pronunciation by living in the country for a time*

proof [pruːf] *noun* thing which proves or which shows that something is true; *the police have no proof that he committed the murder*

prop [prɒp] **1** *noun* support, something which holds something up; *I used a piece of wood as a prop to keep the window open* **2** *verb* to support; *he propped up the table with a pile of books*; *she propped the door open with a brick* (NOTE: **propping - propped**)

propeller [prə'pelə] *noun* set of blades which turns rapidly to drive a boat or an aircraft; *he fell overboard and was killed by the propeller*

proper ['prɒpə] *adjective* right and correct; *this is the proper way to use a knife and fork*; *the parcel wasn't delivered because it didn't have the proper address*

properly ['prɒpəli] *adverb* correctly; *the accident happened because the garage hadn't fitted the wheel properly*

property ['prɒpəti] *noun* **(a)** things that belong to someone; *the hotel guests lost all their property in the fire*; *the management is*

not responsible for property left in the restaurant* **(b)** buildings and land; *the family owns property in West London*; *we have several properties for sale in the centre of town*

proportion [prə'pɔːʃn] *noun* **(a)** the amount of one thing compared to the amount of something else; *the proportions of sugar and flour should one cup of sugar to two cups of flour* **(b) proportions** = the relative height, length of a building, picture, etc.; *the picture looks odd, the artist seems to have got the proportions of the people wrong*

proposal [prə'pəʊzl] *noun* suggestion, plan which has been suggested; *the head teacher made a proposal to build a new laboratory*

propose [prə'pəʊz] *verb* **(a)** to suggest, to make a suggestion; *I propose that we all go for a swim* **(b) to propose to do something** = to say that you intend to do something; *they propose to pay back the money at £20 a month*

prosecute ['prɒsɪkjuːt] *verb* to bring someone to court to answer a criminal charge; *people found stealing from the shop will be prosecuted*

protect [prə'tekt] *verb* to keep someone or something safe from dirt, germs, or harm; *the injection is supposed to protect you against flu*; *a police guard protected the Prime Minister*

protection [prə'tekʃn] *noun* shelter, being protected; *the trees give some protection from the rain*; **police protection** = being protected by the police

protein ['prəʊtiːn] *noun* compound which is an essential part of living cells, which you need to get from food you eat to keep your body working properly; *the doctor told her she needed more protein in her diet*; *meat, eggs and fish contain a lot of protein*

protest **1** *noun* ['prəʊtest] statement to show that you think something is wrong; *the new motorway went ahead in spite of the protests* of local people **2** verb [prə'test] **to protest against something** = to say that you do not approve of something; *everyone has protested against the increase in bus fares*

proud [praud] *adjective* **proud of something** = showing pleasure in what you have done or in something which belongs to you; *you must be very proud of your children*; *he is proud to have served in the navy* (NOTE: **prouder - proudest)**

proudly ['praudli] *adverb* with pride; *she proudly showed me her new car*

prove [pruːv] *verb* **(a)** to show that something is true; *the police think he stole the car but they can't prove it* **(b)** to prove to be something = to actually be something when it happens; *the weather for the holiday weekend proved to be even hotter than was expected*

proverb ['prɒvɜːb] *noun* saying which teaches you something; *'the early bird catches the worm' is a proverb meaning that if you decide quickly, you will succeed*

provide [prə'vaɪd] *verb* to give something when it is needed; *medical help was provided by the Red Cross*

provided (that) *or* **providing** [prə'vaɪdɪd ðæt *or* prə'vaɪdɪŋ] *conjunction* on condition that; as long as; *it's nice to go on a picnic provided it doesn't rain*; *you can all come to watch the rehearsal providing you don't make any noise*

prune [pruːn] **1** *noun* dried plum; *he had a bowl of stewed prunes for breakfast* **2** *verb* to cut back a tree or bush, to keep it in good shape; *that bush is blocking the window - it needs pruning*

PTO [piːtiː'əʊ] *short for* 'please turn over', letters written at the bottom of a page, showing that there is something written on the other side

pub [pʌb] *noun (informal)* place where you can buy beer and other types of alcohol, as well as snacks, meals, etc.; *I happened to meet him at the pub*

public ['pʌblɪk] **1** *adjective* which is used by, or applies to people in general; **public gardens** = place in a town where there are flowers and trees and grass, where people can walk around and enjoy themselves; **public holiday** = holiday for everyone, when everyone can rest and enjoy themselves instead of working; *most of the shops are shut today because it's a public holiday*; **public opinion** = general feeling held by most of the public; **public transport** = transport (such as buses, trains) which can be used by anyone; *its quicker to go into central London by public transport than by car* **2** *noun* **(a)** people in general; *the public have the right to know what is going on* **(b) in public** = in the open; in front of everyone; *this is the first time he has appeared in public since his accident*

publish ['pʌblɪʃ] *verb* to bring out a book, a newspaper or magazine for sale; *the company publishes six magazines for the business market*; *we publish dictionaries for students*

publisher ['pʌblɪʃə] *noun* person who produces books or newspapers for sale; *I'm trying to find a publisher for my book of poems*

pudding ['pʊdɪŋ] *noun* **(a)** dessert, the sweet course at the end of the meal; *I'll have some ice cream for my pudding* **(b)** sweet food which has been cooked or boiled; *we had Christmas pudding on Christmas day*

puddle ['pʌdl] *noun* small pool of water, such as a pool on the pavement left after rain; *I stepped into a puddle and got my shoes wet*

pull [pʊl] *verb* to move something towards you or behind you; *pull the door to open it, don't push*; *she pulled some envelopes out of her bag*

pull in *or* **into** ['pʊl 'ɪn *or* 'ɪntʊ] *verb* to drive close to the side of the road and stop; *all the cars pulled into the side of the road when they heard the fire engine coming*

pull off ['pʊl 'ɒf] *verb* to take off a piece of clothing by pulling; *he sat down and pulled off his dirty boots*

pull out ['pʊl 'aʊt] *verb* **(a)** to pull something out of something; *they used a rope to pull the car out of the river* **(b)** to drive a car away from the side of the road; *don't pull out into the main road until you can see that there is nothing coming*

pull over ['pʊl 'əʊvə] *verb* to drive a car towards the side of the road; *the police car signalled to him to pull over*

pull up ['pʊl 'ʌp] *verb* **(a)** to bring something closer; *pull your chair up to the window* **(b)** to stop a car, etc.; *a car pulled up and the driver asked me if I wanted a lift*

pulley ['pʊli] *noun* apparatus for lifting heavy weights with a rope that runs round several wheels; *we arranged a pulley to raise the beams to roof level*

pullover ['pʊləʊvə] *noun* piece of clothing made of wool, which covers the top part of your body, and which you pull over your head to put it on; *he was wearing his new red pullover*

pulse [pʌls] *noun* **(a)** regular beat of your heart; *you can feel my pulse if you put your finger on my wrist* **(b)** dried seed of peas or beans; *pulses are used a lot in Mexican cooking*

pump [pʌmp] **1** *noun* machine for forcing liquid or air into or out of something; **bicycle pump** = small hand pump for blowing up bicycle tyres **2** *verb* to force in something, such as liquid or air, with a pump; *your back tyre needs pumping up*; *the heart pumps blood round the body*

pumpkin ['pʌmpkɪn] *noun* large round orange vegetable; *pumpkin pie is a favourite American dish*; *hollow pumpkins are used as decorations for Halloween (31st October)*

punch [pʌnʃ] **1** *noun* **(a)** blow with the fist; *she landed two punches on his head* **(b)** metal tool for making holes; *the holes in the belt are made with a punch* (NOTE: plural is **punches**) **2** *verb* **(a)** to hit someone with your fist; *he punched me on the nose* **(b)** to make holes in

something with a punch; *the conductor punched my ticket*

punctual ['pʌŋktʃuəl] *adjective* on time; *he was punctual for his appointment with the dentist*

punctuation [pʌŋktʃu'eɪʃn] *noun* dividing up groups of words using special printed signs; **punctuation marks** = symbols used in writing, such as full stop, comma, dash, etc., to show how a sentence is split up; *the sentence reads 'Charles I walked and talked half an hour after he was dead' - there must be some punctuation missing*

puncture ['pʌŋktʃə] **1** *noun* hole in a tyre; *I've got a puncture in my back tyre* **2** *verb* to make a small hole in something; *the tyre had been punctured by a nail*

punish ['pʌnɪʃ] *verb* to make someone suffer because of something he has done; *the simplest way to punish them will be to make them pay for the damage they caused*

punishment ['pʌnɪʃmənt] *noun* action taken to punish someone; *as a punishment, you'll wash the kitchen floor*

pupil ['pjuːpl] *noun* **(a)** child at a school; *there are twenty-five pupils in the class* **(b)** black hole in the central part of the eye, through which the light passes; *the pupil of the eye grows larger when there is less light*

puppet ['pʌpɪt] *noun* doll which moves, used to give a show; **glove puppet** = doll which fits over your hand; **string puppet** = puppet which works by strings attached to its arms and legs

puppy ['pʌpi] *noun* baby dog; *our dog has had four puppies* (NOTE: plural is **puppies**)

purchase ['pɜːtʃəs] **1** *noun* thing which has been bought; **to make a purchase** = to buy something; *we didn't make many purchases on our trip to Oxford Street* **2** *verb* to buy; *they purchased their car in France and brought it back to the UK*

pure ['pjʊə] *adjective* **(a)** very clean; not mixed with other things; *her pullover is 100% pure wool*; *they drank from the pure* *mountain streams* (b) total, complete; *it was by pure good luck that I happened to find it* (NOTE: **purer - purest**)

purple ['pɜːpl] *adjective* (colour) mixing red and blue; *the sky turned purple as night approached*

purpose ['pɜːpəs] *noun* what is planned; *the purpose of the meeting is to arrange the school open day*

on purpose *phrase* in a way which was planned; *don't be cross - he didn't do it on purpose*; *she pushed him into the swimming pool on purpose*

purse [pɜːs] *noun* small bag for carrying money; *I know I had my purse in my pocket when I left home*; *she put her ticket in her purse so that she wouldn't forget where it was*

pursue [pə'sjuː] *verb* to chase someone or something; *the police pursued the stolen car across London*

push [pʊʃ] **1** *noun* action of making something move forward; *can you give the car a push? - it won't start* **2** *verb* (a) to make something move away from you or in front of you; *we'll have to push the car to get it to start*; *the piano is too heavy to lift, so we'll have to push it into the next room* (b) to press with your finger; *push the right-hand button to start the computer*

pushchair ['pʊʃtʃeə] *noun* light folding carriage for pushing a child in; *she pushed the pushchair across the busy road*

puss *or* **pussy** *or* **pussycat** [pʊs *or* 'pʊsi *or* 'pʊsikæt] *noun* children's names for a cat; *a big black pussy came to meet us*; *you mustn't pull pussy's tail* (NOTE: plural is **pussies**)

put [pʊt] *verb* to place; *did you remember to put the milk in the fridge?*; *where do you want me to put this book?* (NOTE: **putting - put - has put**)

put back ['pʊt 'bæk] *verb* to put something where it was before; *did you put the milk back in the fridge?*

put down ['pʊt 'daʊn] *verb* (a) to place something lower down onto a surface; *he put his suitcase down on the floor beside him* (b) to make a deposit; *he put £500 down on a new motorbike*

put in ['pʊt 'ɪn] *verb* (a) to place inside; *I forgot to put in my pyjamas when I packed the case* (b) to put in, to fix; *the first thing we have to do with the cottage is to put in central heating*

put off ['pʊt 'ɒf] *verb* (a) to arrange for something to take place later; *we have put the meeting off until next month* (b) to bother someone so that he can't do things properly; *stop making that strange noise, it's putting me off my work* (c) to say or do something to make someone decide not to do something; *reading about conditions in chicken farms put me off eating eggs*

put on ['pʊt 'ɒn] *verb* (a) to place something on top of something, on a surface; *put the lid on the saucepan* (b) to dress yourself in a certain piece of clothing; *put your gloves on, it's cold outside* (c) to switch on; *can you put the light on, it's getting dark?*

put out ['pʊt 'aʊt] *verb* (a) to place outside; *did you remember to put the cat out?* (b) to switch off; *he put the light out and went to bed*

put up ['pʊt 'ʌp] *verb* (a) to attach to a wall, to attach high up; *they are putting up Christmas decorations all along Regent Street* (b) to build something so that it is upright; *they put up a wooden shed in their garden* (c) to increase, to make higher; *the shop has put up all its prices by 5%* (d) to give someone a place to sleep in your house; *we've missed the last train, can you put us up for the night?*

put up with ['pʊt 'ʌp wɪθ] *verb* to accept someone or something even if they are unpleasant; *how can you put up with the smell of the pig farm next door?*

puzzle ['pʌzl] **1** *noun* game where you have to find the answer to a problem; *I can't do the* *puzzle in today's paper* **2** *verb* to be difficult to understand; *it puzzles me how the robbers managed to get away*

pyjamas *US* **pajamas** [pɪˈdʒɑːməz] *noun* light shirt and trousers which you wear in bed; *I bought two pairs of pyjamas in the sale*; *when fire broke out in the hotel, the guests ran into the street in their pyjamas*

pyramid [ˈpɪrəmɪd] *noun* shape with a square base and four sides rising to meet at a point; **the Pyramids** = huge stone buildings, built as temples or places for the dead by the Ancient Egyptians and Central Americans; *we went to Egypt mainly to see the Pyramids*

Qq

Q, q [kjuː] seventeenth letter of the alphabet, between P and R; *a 'Q' is always followed by the letter 'U'*

qualifications [kwɒlɪfɪˈkeɪʃnz] *noun* proof that you have completed a specialized course of study; *does she have the right qualifications for the job?*; **professional qualifications** = proof that you have got a diploma for a particular type of skilled work

qualify [ˈkwɒlɪfaɪ] *verb* **to qualify as** = to get a certificate which allows you to do a certain type of work; *he has qualified as an engineer*; *she's a qualified doctor*; *all our staff are highly qualified*

quality [ˈkwɒlɪti] *noun* **(a)** how good

something is; *we want to measure the air quality in the centre of town*; *the carpet is expensive because it is of very good quality* **(b)** a typical part of a person's character; *she has many qualities, but unfortunately is extremely lazy* (NOTE: plural is **qualities**)

quantity [ˈkwɒntɪti] *noun* amount; **a quantity of** = a lot of; *the police found a quantity of stolen jewels* (NOTE: plural is **quantities**)

quarrel [ˈkwɒrəl] **1** *noun* angry argument; *they have had a quarrel and aren't speaking to each other* **2** *verb* **to quarrel about** or **over something** = to argue angrily about something; *they're always quarrelling over money*

quarry [ˈkwɒri] *noun* place where stone, etc., is dug out of the ground; *if you hear an explosion, it is because they're working in the quarry* (NOTE: plural is **quarries**)

quarter [ˈkwɔːtə] *noun* **(a)** one of four parts, a fourth or 25%; *she cut the pear into quarters*; *he paid only a quarter of the normal fare because he works for the airline* **(b) three quarters** = three out of four parts or 75%; *three quarters of the flats are empty* **(c) a quarter of an hour** = 15 minutes; **it's (a) quarter to three** = it's 2.45; **at a quarter past eight** = at 8.15 **(d)** *US* 25 cent coin; *do you have a quarter for the machine?*

quarter-final [ˈkwɔːtəˈfaɪnəl] *noun (in sport)* one of four matches in a competition, the winners of which go into the semi-finals; *Ireland got through to the quarter-finals of the World Cup*

quay [kiː] *noun* place where ships tie up to load or unload; *we went down to the quay to watch the fishing boats unload* (NOTE: do not confuse with **key**)

queen [kwiːn] *noun* **(a)** wife of a king; *King Charles I's queen was the daughter of the King of France* **(b)** woman ruler of a country; *the Queen sometimes lives in Windsor Castle* **(c)** second most important piece in chess, after the king; *in three moves he had captured my*

queen (d) *(in playing cards)* the card with the face of a woman, with a value between the king and the jack; *he had the queen of spades*

queer ['kwɪə] *adjective* odd or strange; *there's something very queer about the message*; *isn't it queer that she hasn't phoned back?* (NOTE: **queerer - queerest**)

query ['kwɪəri] **1** *noun* question; *she had a mass of queries about her tax form* (NOTE: plural is **queries**) **2** *verb* to ask a question about something; *the head teacher queried the cost of the Christmas party*

question ['kwestʃən] **1** *noun* **(a)** words which need an answer; *some of the questions in the exam were too difficult* **(b)** problem or matter; *the question is, who can we get to run the shop when we're on holiday?* **2** *verb* to ask questions; *the police questioned the driver for four hours*

question mark ['kwestʃən 'mɑːk] *noun* sign (?) used in writing to show that a question is being asked; *there should be a question mark at the end of that sentence*

questionnaire [kwestʃə'neə] *noun* printed list of questions given to people to answer; *we sent out a questionnaire to ask people what they thought of the new toothpaste*

queue [kjuː] **1** *noun* line of people, cars, etc., waiting one behind the other for something; *there was a queue of people waiting to get into the exhibition*; **to form a queue** = to stand in line; *please form a queue to the left of the door*; **to jump the queue** = to go in front of other people standing in a queue; *are you trying to jump the queue? - go to the back!* **2** *verb* **to queue (up)** = to stand in a line waiting for something; *we queued for hours to get the theatre tickets* (NOTE: **queuing - queued**)

quick [kwɪk] *adjective* fast; *I'm trying to work out the quickest way to get to the Tower of London*; *we had a quick lunch and then went off for a walk* (NOTE: **quicker - quickest**)

quickly ['kwɪkli] *adverb* rapidly, without taking much time; *he ate his supper very*

quickly because he wanted to watch the football on TV

quiet ['kwaɪət] *adjective* **(a)** without any noise; *can't you make the children keep quiet - I'm trying to work!*; *the hotel said that the rooms were quiet, but ours looked out over a busy main road* **(b)** with no great excitement; *we live in a quiet little village* (NOTE: **quieter - quietest**)

quietly ['kwaɪətli] *adverb* without making any noise; *the burglar climbed quietly up to the window*

quit [kwɪt] *verb* **(a)** *(informal)* to leave a job, a house, etc.; *I'm fed up with my job, I'm thinking of quitting* **(b)** *(informal)* to stop doing something; *will you quit bothering me!*; *he quit smoking* (NOTE: **quitting - quit** *or* **quitted**)

quite [kwaɪt] *adverb* **(a)** more or less; *it's quite a long play* **(b)** completely; *you're quite mad to go walking in that snow*; *the work is not quite finished yet* **(c)** **quite a few** *or* **quite a lot** = several, many; *quite a few people on the boat were sick*

quiz [kwɪz] *noun* game where you are asked a series of questions; **quiz show** = TV or radio programme where people are asked a series of questions (NOTE: plural is **quizzes**)

quotation [kwəʊ'teɪʃn] *noun* words quoted; *the article ended with a quotation from Shakespeare*; **quotation marks** = inverted commas (« «), printed or written marks showing that a quotation starts or finishes; *that part of the sentence should be in quotation marks*

quote [kwəʊt] **1** *noun* quotation, words quoted; *I need a good quote from his speech to put into my project* **2** *verb* **(a)** to repeat a number as a reference; *in reply please quote this number* **(b)** to repeat what someone has said or written; *he started his speech by quoting lines from 'Hamlet'*

Rr

R, r [ɑː] eighteenth letter of the alphabet, between Q and S; *there are three Rs in 'referred'*

rabbit [ˈræbɪt] *noun* common wild animal with grey fur, long ears and a short white tail; *the rabbit ran down its hole*

race [reɪs] **1** *noun* **(a)** competition to see which person, horse, car, etc., is the fastest; *she was second in the 200 metres race; the bicycle race goes round the whole country* **(b)** large group of people with similar skin colour, hair, etc.; **race relations** = relations between different groups of races in the same country **2** *verb* **(a)** to run, ride, etc., to see who is the fastest; *I'll race you to see who gets to school first* **(b)** to run fast; *we saw the bus coming and raced to the bus stop*

rack [ræk] *noun* frame which holds things such as luggage; **luggage rack** = space for bags above the seats in a plane, train, etc.; *please place all hand luggage in the overhead luggage racks*

racket [ˈrækɪt] *noun* **(a)** light frame with a handle and tight strings, used for hitting the ball in games; **tennis racket** = racket used to play tennis; *she bought a new racket at the start of the summer season* **(b)** loud noise; *stop that racket at once!*

radar [ˈreɪdɑː] *noun* system for finding objects such as ships or aircraft, and working out where they are from radio signals; *the plane's radar picked up another plane coming too close*

radiator [ˈreɪdɪeɪtə] *noun* **(a)** metal panel filled with hot water for heating; *when we arrived at the hotel our room was cold, so we* switched the radiators on **(b)** metal panel filled with cold water to keep a car engine cool; *the radiator froze and the car wouldn't start*

radio [ˈreɪdiəʊ] *noun* **(a)** way of sending out and receiving messages using air waves; *we always listen to BBC radio when we're on holiday* **(b)** piece of equipment which sends out and receives messages using air waves; *turn on the radio - it's time for the weather forecast; I heard the news on the car radio*

radish [ˈrædɪʃ] *noun* small red root vegetable, eaten raw in salads; *we started with a bowl of radishes and butter* (NOTE: plural is radishes)

radius [ˈreɪdiəs] *noun* **(a)** line from the centre of a circle to the outside edge; *we were asked to measure the radius of the circle* **(b)** distance in any direction from a particular central point; *people within a radius of twenty miles heard the explosion* (NOTE: the plural is radii [ˈreɪdɪaɪ])

raffle [ˈræfl] **1** *noun* lottery where you buy a ticket with a number on it, in the hope of winning a prize; *she won a bottle of perfume in a raffle* **2** *verb* to give a prize in a raffle where people buy tickets and hope to win the prize; *they raffled a car for charity*

raft [rɑːft] *noun* boat made of pieces of wood tied together to form a flat surface; *they took their raft all the way down the Amazon*

rag [ræg] *noun* **(a)** piece of torn cloth; *he used an old rag to clean his motorbike* **(b)** **rags** = old torn clothes; *the children were dressed in rags*

rage [reɪdʒ] **1** *noun* violent anger; **to fly into a rage** = to get very angry suddenly; *when he phoned her she flew into a rage* **2** *verb* to be violent; *the storm raged all night*

ragged [ˈrægɪd] *adjective* torn (clothes); *old photographs of London streets show poor children standing in ragged clothes*

raid [reɪd] **1** *noun* sudden attack; *police carried out a series of raids on addresses in*

London; **air raid** = sudden attack by planes **2** *verb* to make a sudden attack on a place; *the police raided the club*

rail [reɪl] *noun* **(a)** straight metal or wooden bar; *hold on to the rail as you go down the stairs*; *there is a heated towel rail in the bathroom* **(b)** one of two parallel metal bars on which trains run; *don't try to cross the rails - it's dangerous* **(c)** the railway, a system of travel using trains; *six million office workers travel to work by rail each day*; *rail travellers are complaining about rising fares*

railings ['reɪlɪŋz] *noun* metal bars used as a fence; *don't put your hand through the railings round the lion's cage*

railway *US* **railroad** ['reɪlweɪ or 'reɪlrəʊd] *noun* way of travelling which uses trains to carry passengers and goods; *the railway station is in the centre of town*

rain [reɪn] **1** *noun* drops of water which fall from the clouds; *the ground is very dry - we've had no rain for days*; *yesterday we had 3cm of rain* **2** *verb* to fall as drops of water from the clouds; *as soon as we sat down on the grass and took out the sandwiches it started to rain*; *it rained all day, so we couldn't visit the gardens* (NOTE: do not confuse with **reign, rein**)

rain forest ['reɪn 'fɒrɪst] *noun* thick forest which grows in tropical regions where there is a lot of rain; *tropical rain forests contain over half of all the world's animals and plants*

rainbow ['reɪnbəʊ] *noun* arch of colours which shines in the sky when it is sunny and raining at the same time; *the colours of the rainbow are: red, orange, yellow, green, blue, indigo (dark blue) and violet*

raincoat ['reɪnkəʊt] *noun* coat which keeps off water, which you wear when it is raining; *take a raincoat with you if you think it's going to rain*

raise [reɪz] *verb* **(a)** to make something higher; *the newspaper headline says TAXES TO BE RAISED*; *air fares will be raised on*

June 1st **(b)** to mention a subject which could be discussed; *no one raised the subject of the money he owed us* **(c)** to obtain money; *the hospital is trying to raise £2m to finance its building programme*

raisin ['reɪzn] *noun* dried grape; *can you buy some raisins for the Christmas pudding?*

rake [reɪk] **1** *noun* garden tool with a long handle and metal teeth, used for smoothing earth or for pulling dead leaves together **2** *verb* **(a)** to smooth loose soil with a rake; *she raked the vegetable bed before sowing her carrots* **(b)** to pull dead leaves together with a rake; *he raked the leaves from under the trees*

rally ['ræli] *noun* large meeting of people; *we are holding a rally to protest against the job cuts* (NOTE: plural is **rallies**)

ram [ræm] **1** *noun* male sheep; *we keep the rams separate from the females* **2** *verb* **(a)** to hit another ship, car, etc., hard; *the car rammed into the side of the lorry* **(b)** to push something hard; *he rammed the envelope into his pocket* (NOTE: **ramming - rammed**)

Ramadan ['ræmədæn] *noun* Muslim religious festival, the ninth month of the Muslim year, during which you are not allowed to eat or drink during the daytime

ramp [ræmp] *noun* slightly sloping surface joining two different levels; *they have built a ramp so that wheelchairs can get into the library*

ran [ræn] *see* RUN

ranch [rɑːntʃ] *noun* farm where horses or cattle are reared; *the cowboys returned to the ranch each evening* (NOTE: plural is **ranches**)

rang [ræŋ] *see* RING

range [reɪndʒ] **1** *noun* **(a)** choice or series of colours, etc., available; *we have a range of holidays at all prices* **(b)** distance which you can go; distance over which you can see or hear; *the police said the man had been shot at close range* **(c)** series of buildings or mountains in line; *they looked out at the vast mountain range from the plane window* **2**

verb **to range from** = to spread; *the sizes range from small to extra large*; *holidays range in price from £150 to £350 per person*

rank [rænk] *noun* **(a)** position in the army; *after ten years he had reached the rank of sergeant* **(b) taxi rank** = place where taxis wait in line; *there's a taxi rank is just outside the station*

rap [ræp] **1** *noun* form of West Indian poetry and music where someone speaks words rapidly; *the club played rap all evening* **2** *verb* to give a sharp tap; *he rapped on the door with a stick, but no one heard him* (NOTE: **rapping - rapped**)

rapid ['ræpɪd] *adjective* fast; *we heard rapid footsteps on the stairs*

rapidly ['ræpɪdli] *adverb* quickly; *the new shop rapidly increased sales*

rare [reə] *adjective* not usual, not common; *it's very rare to meet someone who speaks perfect Chinese*; *this lake is the breeding ground of a rare type of frog* (NOTE: **rarer - rarest)**

rarely ['reəli] *adverb* not often, hardly ever; *I rarely buy a Sunday newspaper*

rash [ræʃ] **1** *noun* mass of red spots on the skin, which stays for a time and then disappears; *she had a rash on her arms* (NOTE: plural is **rashes**) **2** *adjective* not careful; done without thinking; *it was a bit rash of him to suggest that he would pay for everyone* (NOTE: **rasher - rashest)**

rasher ['ræʃə] *noun* slice of bacon; *two rashers of bacon and a sausage, please!*

raspberry ['rɑːzbri] *noun* common red soft fruit which grows on tall plants; *they picked raspberries and ate them for tea*

rat [ræt] *noun* common small grey animal with a long tail, living in basements, refuse dumps, on ships, etc.; *rats live in the drains in the city*

rate [reɪt] *noun* **(a)** number shown as a proportion of another; **birth rate** = number of children born per 1,000 of the population; *the national birth rate fell in the second half of the 20th century*; **death rate** = number of deaths per 1,000 of population; *the death rate from flu rose suddenly during the winter* **(b)** how frequently something is done; *his heart was beating at a rate of only 59 per minute* **(c)** level of payment; *their rate of pay is lower than ours* **(d)** speed; *at the rate he's travelling, he'll be there before us*

at any rate *phrase* whatever happens; *the taxi cost more than I expected, but at any rate we got to the airport on time*

rather ['rɑːðə] *adverb* **(a)** quite; *her dress is a rather pretty shade of blue* **(b) would rather** = would prefer; *we'd rather stay in the office than go to the party*

rattle ['rætl] **1** *noun* toy which makes a loud noise when waved; *the baby threw its rattle out of the cot* **2** *verb* to make a repeated banging noise; *the wind made the windows rattle*

ravine [rə'viːn] *noun* deep narrow valley; *the car crashed through the fence and ended up at the bottom of a ravine*

raw [rɔː] *adjective* **(a)** not cooked; *don't be silly - you can't eat raw potatoes!* **(b) raw materials** = substances in their natural state which have not yet been made into manufactured goods (such as wool, wood, sand, etc.); *what raw materials are needed for making soap?*

ray [reɪ] *noun* beam of light; *a ray of sunshine lit up the gloomy room*

razor ['reɪzə] *noun* knife with a very sharp blade for shaving; *he was shaving with his electric razor*

Rd [rəʊd] *short for* ROAD; *their address is 1 Cambridge Rd*

reach [riːtʃ] **1** *noun* how far you can stretch out your hand; *keep the medicine bottle out of the reach of the children* **2** *verb* **(a)** to stretch out your hand to; *she reached across the table and took some meat from my plate* **(b)** to arrive at a place; *we were held up by fog and only reached home at midnight* **(c)** to get to a certain level; *the water has reached the top of the dam*

react [ri'ækt] *verb* to do or to say something in reply to words or an action; *how did he react when you told him the news?*

reaction [ri'ækʃn] *noun* thing done or said in reply; *his first reaction to the news was to burst into laughter*

read [ri:d] *verb* **(a)** to look at and understand written words; *she was reading a book when I saw her; what are you reading at the moment?* **(b)** to speak aloud from something which is written; *she read a story to the children last night* (NOTE: **reading - read** [red])

read aloud *or* **read out** ['ri:d ə'laud *or* 'ri:d 'aut] *verb* to speak the words you are reading; *she read the letter aloud to the family*

reading ['ri:dɪŋ] *noun* **(a)** act of looking at and understanding written words; *reading and writing should be taught to children early*; **reading glasses** = glasses that help you to read things which are close **(b)** speaking aloud from something which is written; *they gave a poetry reading in the book shop*

ready ['redi] *adjective* **(a)** prepared to do something; *hold on - I'll be ready in two minutes*; *are all the children ready to go to school?* **(b)** fit to be used or eaten; *don't sit down yet - the meal isn't ready* (NOTE: **readier - readiest)**

real ['rɪəl] *adjective* **(a)** not a copy, not artificial; *is that watch real gold?; that plastic apple looks very real* **(b)** *(used to stress)* *that car is a real bargain at £300* **(c)** which exists; *have you ever seen a real live tiger?*

realize ['ri:əlaɪz] *verb* to get to a point where you understand clearly; *she didn't realize what she was letting herself in for when she said she would look after the children; we soon realized we were on the wrong road*

really ['rɪəli] *adverb* **(a)** in fact; *she's not really French, is she?; the building really*

belongs to my father **(b)** *(used to show surprise) it's really time you had your hair cut*

rear ['rɪə] **1** *noun* part at the back; *the rear of the car was damaged in the accident* **2** *adjective* at the back; *the children sat in the rear seats in the car* **3** *verb* **(a)** to breed animals; *they stopped rearing pigs because of the smell* **(b)** to rise up, to lift up; *the walls of the castle reared up before them*

reason ['ri:sən] **1** *noun* **(a)** thing which explains why something has happened; *the airline gave no reason for the plane's late arrival* **(b)** being able to make sensible decisions; *she wouldn't listen to reason*; **within reason** = to a sensible degree, in a sensible way; *the children get £5 pocket money each week, and they can spend it as they like, within reason* **2** *verb* to think or to plan carefully; *he reasoned that any work is better than no work, so he took the job*

reasonable ['ri:zənəbl] *adjective* **(a)** not expensive; *the restaurant offers good food at reasonable prices* **(b)** sensible, showing sense; *the manager of the shop was very reasonable when she tried to explain that she had left all her money at home*

rebel **1** *noun* ['rebəl] person who fights against a government or against people who are in authority; *the rebels ran away to the mountains after the army captured their headquarters* **2** *verb* [rɪ'bel] to fight against someone or something; *the ordinary people rebelled against the military government* (NOTE: **rebelling - rebelled)**

recall [rɪ'kɔ:l] *verb* to remember; *I don't recall having met her before*

receive [rɪ'si:v] *verb* **(a)** to get something which has been sent; *we received a parcel from Aunt Jane this morning; the staff have not received any wages for six months* **(b)** to greet or to welcome a visitor; *the group of parents was received by the head teacher*

recent ['ri:sənt] *adjective* new, which took

place not very long ago; *we will mail you our most recent catalogue*

recently ['riːsəntli] *adverb* only a short time ago; *I've seen him quite a lot recently*

reception [rɪ'sepʃn] *noun* **(a)** welcome; *you should have seen the reception the fans gave to their team* **(b)** *(at a hotel)* place where guests register; *let's meet at reception at 9.00 am tomorrow*; **reception desk** = desk where visitors check in; *please leave your key at the reception desk when you go out* **(c)** *(at an office)* place where visitors register and say who they have come to see; *there's a parcel waiting for you in reception* **(d)** big party held to welcome special guests; *they held a reception for the president*; **wedding reception** = party held after a wedding; *will you be going to Anne and John's wedding reception?* **(e)** quality of the sound on a radio or the sound and picture on a TV screen; *perhaps you'd get better reception if you moved the TV to another room*

recipe ['resɪpi] *noun* instructions for cooking food; *I copied the recipe for onion soup from the newspaper*; **recipe book** = book of recipes; *if you're not sure how long to cook your turkey, look it up in the recipe book*

recite [rɪ'saɪt] *verb* to say a poem, etc., aloud in public; *the author will recite two of his poems this evening*

reckon ['rekn] *verb* **(a)** to calculate, to estimate; *we reckon the costs to be about £25,000* **(b)** to think; *I reckon we'll be there before lunch*

recognize ['rekəgnaɪz] *verb* **(a)** to know someone or something because you have seen him or it before; *he'd changed so much since I last saw him that I hardly recognized him*; *do you recognize the handwriting on the letter?* **(b)** to approve of something or someone officially; *he has a certificate from a recognized language school*

recommend [rekə'mend] *verb* **(a)** to suggest that someone should do something; *the doctor*

recommended that I should see an eye specialist **(b)** to praise something or someone; *she was highly recommended by her boss*

record 1 *noun* ['rekɔːd] **(a)** success in sport which is better than any other; *she holds the world record for the 100 metres*; *he broke the world record at the last Olympics* **(b)** written evidence of something which has happened; *we have no record of the sale* **(c)** flat, round piece of black plastic on which sound is stored; *she bought me an old Elvis Presley record for Christmas* **2** *verb* [rɪ'kɔːd] **(a)** to report; to make a note; **recorded delivery** = mail service where the person receiving the parcel, letter, etc., must sign a paper to show that it has been delivered; *it is safer to send the parcel by recorded delivery* **(b)** to fix sounds on a film or tape; *the police recorded the whole conversation on video*

recorder [rɪ'kɔːdə] *noun* small wooden musical instrument which you play by blowing; *most children learn to play the recorder at school*

recover [rɪ'kʌvə] *verb* **to recover from an illness** = to get well again after an illness; *she is still recovering from flu*

recreation [rekrɪ'eɪʃn] *noun* pleasant activity for your spare time; *doesn't he have any recreations other than watching TV?*

rectangle ['rektæŋgl] *noun* shape with four sides and right angles at the corners, with two sets of long and short sides; *if all four sides are the same size it isn't a rectangle, it's a square*

recycle [riː'saɪkl] *verb* to process waste material so that it can be used again; *glass and newspapers are the main items for recycling*

red [red] *adjective* **(a)** coloured like the colour of blood; *she turned bright red when we asked her what had happened to the money*; *don't start yet - the traffic lights are still red* **(b) red hair** = hair which is a red or orange colour; *all their children have red hair* (NOTE: **redder - reddest**) **2** *noun (informal)* red wine; *a glass of the house red, please*

Red Cross ['red 'krɒs] *noun* international organization which provides emergency medical help, and also relief to victims of floods, etc.; *Red Cross officials have been sent to the refugee camps*

reduce [rɪ'djuːs] *verb* to make smaller or less; *you must reduce speed when approaching traffic lights*; *there are reduced prices for groups of 30 and over*

reed [riːd] *noun* tall thick grass growing in wet places; *reeds grow by the edge of rivers or lakes* (NOTE: do not confuse with **read**)

reef [riːf] *noun* long line of rocks just above or beneath the surface of the sea; *the Great Barrier Reef is off the north-east coast of Australia*

reel [riːl] *noun* (a) round object used for winding thread, wire or film round; *she put a new reel of cotton on the sewing machine* (b) wild Scottish dance; *some of the guests started to dance reels*

refer to [rɪ'fɜː tʊ] *verb* (a) to mention something; *do you think he was referring to me when he talked about fat people?* (b) to look into something for information; *he referred to his diary to see if he had a free afternoon* (NOTE: **referring - referred**)

referee [refə'riː] *noun (in sports)* person who is in charge of a game, making sure that it is played according to the rules; *the referee sent several players off*; *referees are in charge of most sports, such as football, rugby or boxing, but not tennis and cricket*

reference ['refrəns] *noun* direction for further information; **reference book** = book, such as a dictionary, where you can look for information; **reference library** = library with reference books, where you can look for information but cannot take the books away from the library

refill **1** *noun* ['riːfɪl] container with a fresh quantity of liquid; *dishwasher soap is sold in handy refill packs* **2** *verb* [riː'fɪl] to fill again;

we stopped twice to refill the car on the way to Scotland

reflect [rɪ'flekt] *verb* to send back light, heat, an image, etc.; *white surfaces reflect light better than dark ones*; *a photograph of white mountains reflected in a clear blue lake*

reflection [rɪ'flekʃn] *noun* (a) sending back of light or heat; *you should wear dark glasses because of the reflection of the sun on the snow* (b) image reflected in a mirror, in water, etc.; *she saw her reflection in the shop window and smiled*

refreshing [rɪ'freʃɪŋ] *adjective* which makes something fresh again; *a refreshing shower of rain made the air cool*

refreshments [rɪ'freʃmənts] *noun* food and drink; *light refreshments will be served after the concert*

refrigerator [rɪ'frɪdʒəreɪtə] *noun* electric kitchen cabinet for keeping food and drink cold (often called a 'fridge'); *there's some cold orange juice in the refrigerator*; *milk will keep for several days in a refrigerator*

refugee [refjuˈdʒiː] *noun* person who has left his or her country because of war, religious differences, etc.; *at the beginning of the war, thousands of refugees crossed the border*

refuse **1** *noun* ['refjuːs] rubbish, things which are not wanted; *refuse collection on our road is on Thursdays* **2** *verb* [rɪ'fjuːz] (a) to say that you will not do something; *his father refused to lend him any more money* (b) not to do something; *once again this morning the car refused to start*

regard [rɪ'gɑːd] **1** *noun* **regards** = best wishes; *please give my regards to your mother* **2** *verb* to **regard someone or something as** = to consider someone or something to be; *the police are regarding the case as attempted murder*

region ['riːdʒən] *noun* (a) large area; **the London region** = the area around London (b) **in the region of** = about or approximately; *he is earning a salary in the region of £25,000*;

the house was sold for a price in the region of £200,000

register ['redʒɪstə] **1** *noun* **(a)** list of names; *she ticked his name on the register* **(b)** book in which you sign your name; *please sign the hotel register when you check in* **2** *verb* **(a)** to write a name officially in a list; *babies have to be registered as soon as they are born*; **to register at a hotel** = to write your name and address when you arrive at the hotel **(b)** to put a letter into the special care of the post office; *she registered the letter, but it still got lost*

regret [rɪ'gret] *verb* to be sorry that something has happened; *we regret the delay in the arrival of our flight from Amsterdam*; *we regret to inform you that the tour has been cancelled* (NOTE: **regretting - regretted**)

regular ['regjuːlə] *adjective* **(a)** done at the same time each day; *his regular train is the 12.45*; *the regular flight to Athens leaves at 06.00* **(b)** ordinary, standard; *the regular price is £1.25, but we are offering them at 99p*

rehearsal [rɪ'hɜːsəl] *noun* practice of a play or concert, etc., before the first public performance; *the director insisted on extra rehearsals because some of the actors didn't know their words*

reign [reɪn] **1** *noun* period when a king or queen rules; *during the reign of Elizabeth I* **2** *verb* to rule; *Queen Victoria reigned between 1837 and 1901* (NOTE: do not confuse with **rain, rein**)

rein [reɪn] *noun* leather strap which a person holds to control a horse; *he pulled hard on the reins to try to make the horse stop* (NOTE: do not confuse with **rain, reign**)

reindeer ['reɪndɪə] *noun* type of large deer which lives in the northern parts of Europe; *besides Finland, in which other countries can you find reindeer?*; *according to tradition, on Christmas Eve Father Christmas arrives in a sleigh pulled by reindeer* (NOTE: plural is **reindeer**)

related (to) [rɪ'leɪtɪd 'tuː] *adjective* **(a)**

belonging to the same family; *are you related to the Smith family in London Road?* **(b)** linked; *a disease which is related to the weak condition of the heart muscle*

relating to [rɪ'leɪtɪŋ 'tuː] *adverb* referring to, connected with; *the solicitor sent us documents relating to the sale*; *civil law is law relating to individual people and their rights*

relation [rɪ'leɪʃn] *noun* **(a)** member of a family; *all my relations live in Canada* **(b) relations** = links (with other people); *we try to keep good relations with our customers*

relative ['relətɪv] **1** *noun* person who is related to someone; member of a family; *we have several relatives living in Canada* **2** *adjective (in grammar)* **relative pronoun** = pronoun, such as 'who' or 'which', which connects two clauses

relatively ['relətɪvli] *adverb* more or less; *the children have been relatively free from colds this winter*

relax [rɪ'læks] *verb* to rest from work; *they spent the first week of their holiday relaxing on the beach*; *just lie back and relax - the injection won't hurt*

relay race ['riːleɪ 'reɪs] *noun* race for teams in which one runner passes a stick to another who then runs on; *they won the 400m relay*

release [rɪ'liːs] *verb* **(a)** to set free; *six prisoners were released from prison* **(b)** to make public; *the government has released figures about the number of people out of work*

reliable [rɪ'laɪəbl] *adjective* which can be relied on, which can be trusted; *it is a very reliable car*

relief [rɪ'liːf] *noun* **(a)** reducing worry or pain; *he breathed a sigh of relief when the police car went past without stopping* **(b)** help in the form of food, money, etc.; *the Red Cross is organizing relief for the flood victims*

relieved [rɪ'liːvd] *adjective* glad to be rid of a problem; *she was relieved to find that she did* not owe him any money after all

religion [rɪˈlɪdʒən] *noun* belief in gods or in one God; *it is against our religion to eat meat on Fridays*

religious [rɪˈlɪdʒəs] *adjective* referring to religion; *there is a period of religious study every morning*

reluctant [rɪˈlʌktənt] *adjective* not eager to, not willing to; *she was reluctant to go into the swimming pool because the water looked cold*

reluctantly [rɪˈlʌktəntli] *adverb* not eagerly; *he reluctantly agreed to do the work*

rely (on) [rɪˈlaɪ ɒn] *verb* to depend on; *I'm relying on you to tell me how to get to the house*

remain [rɪˈmeɪn] *verb* (a) to stay; *we expect it will remain fine for the rest of the week* (b) to be left; *after the earthquake only one house remained standing*

remainder [rɪˈmeɪndə] *noun* what is left after everything else has gone; *what shall we do for the remainder of the holidays?*

remains [rɪˈmeɪnz] *noun* things left over or left behind; *the police found the house empty but the remains of a meal were left on the table*

remark [rɪˈmɑːk] *noun* words which show what you feel about something; *she made some remarks about the dirty plates in the restaurant*

remarkable [rɪˈmɑːkəbl] *adjective* very unusual, which you might notice; *it's remarkable to have have such warm weather in January*

remarkably [rɪˈmɑːkəbli] *adverb* in a very unusual way; *remarkably, the bank didn't ask for the money to be paid back*

remedy [ˈremədi] *noun* thing which may cure; *it's an old remedy for colds* (NOTE: plural is **remedies**)

remember [rɪˈmembə] *verb* (a) to bring back into your mind something which you have seen or heard before; *do you remember the day when we got lost in the fog?*; *she can't remember where she put her umbrella* (b) to do something which you said you would do; *did you remember to switch off the kitchen light?*

remind [rɪˈmaɪnd] *verb* (a) to make someone remember something; *remind me to buy the plane tickets today* (b) **to remind someone of** = to make someone think of something; *she reminds me of her mother*

remote [rɪˈməʊt] *adjective* (a) far away; *the hotel is in a remote mountain village* (b) slight, not very strong; *there's a remote chance that the train will be on time* (NOTE: remoter - remotest)

remote control *noun* device which controls a model plane, TV, etc., by radio signals; *has anyone seen the TV remote control?*

removal [rɪˈmuːvəl] *noun* (a) taking something away; *the council is responsible for the removal of household rubbish* (b) moving to a new home, new office, etc.; **removal men** = workers who move furniture from one house to another; **removal van** = van which takes your furniture from one house to another; *today's the day we move - the removal van is already here*

remove [rɪˈmuːv] *verb* to take away; *the waitress removed the dirty plates and brought us some tea*

rent [rent] **1** *noun* money paid to live in a flat, house, to use an office, etc.; *rents are high in the centre of the town* **2** *verb* (a) to pay money to use a house, flat, car, etc.; *they rented a cottage by the beach for three weeks* (b) **to rent (out)** = to let someone use a house, office, flat, etc., for money; *we rented (out) a room in our house to some American students*

repair [rɪˈpeə] **1** *noun* mending something which is broken or has been damaged; *during the school holidays they will be carrying out repairs to the heating system* **2** *verb* to mend, to make something work which is broken or damaged; *I dropped my watch on the pavement, and I don't think it can be repaired*

repeat [rɪ'piːt] **1** *verb* to say something again; *could you repeat what you just said?*; *he repeated the address so that the policeman could write it down* **2** *noun* performance (of a play, TV show) which is done a second time; *during the summer the TV only seems to show repeats*

replace [riː'pleɪs] *verb* **(a)** to put something back where it was before; *please replace the books correctly on the shelves* **(b)** to replace something with something else = to put something in the place of something else; *the washing machine needs replacing*; *(in computers)* **search and replace** = looking for words or phrases and replacing them automatically with other words or phrases

replacement [rɪ'pleɪsmənt] *noun* **(a)** replacing something with something else; **hip replacement** = operation to replace the whole hip joint with an artificial one; *old people sometimes need to have hip replacements* **(b)** thing or person who is used to replace something; *we bought a new electric motor as a replacement for the old one*; *our secretary leaves us next week, so we are advertising for a replacement*

reply [rɪ'plaɪ] **1** *noun* answer; *I asked him what he was doing but got no reply*; *we had six replies to our advertisement* (NOTE: plural is **replies**) **2** *verb* to answer; *he never replies to my letters*; *we wrote last week, but he hasn't replied yet*

report [rɪ'pɔːt] **1** *noun* description of what has happened or what will happen; *we read the reports of the accident in the newspaper* **2** *verb* **(a)** to tell someone what happened; *she reported that some money had been stolen from her bedroom* **(b)** to present yourself officially; *candidates should report to this office at 9.00*

reporter [rɪ'pɔːtə] *noun* journalist who writes reports of events for a newspaper or for a radio or TV news programme; *the BBC sent reporters to report on the floods*; *he works as a reporter for a local newspaper*

represent [reprɪ'zent] *verb* **(a)** to speak or act on behalf of someone or of a group of people; *he asked his solicitor to represent him at the meeting* **(b)** to show, to be a symbol of; *the dark green on the map represents woods*

representative [reprɪ'zentətɪv] **1** *adjective* typical; *the sample wasn't representative of the whole load* **2** *noun* **(a)** person who represents, who speaks on behalf of someone else; *he asked his solicitor to act as his representative* **(b)** *(in the United States)* the **House of Representatives** = the lower house of Congress

reptile ['reptaɪl] *noun* animal with cold blood, which lays eggs; *frogs and snakes are reptiles*

republic [rɪ'pʌblɪk] *noun* country governed by elected representatives headed by a president; *France and Germany are republics, but Spain and the UK are not*

reputation [repjʊ'teɪʃn] *noun* what people think about someone; *he has a reputation for being difficult to deal with*; *the cook has a reputation for often losing his temper*

request [rɪ'kwest] **1** *noun* asking for something in a polite way; *your request will be dealt with as soon as possible*; **request stop** = bus stop where buses stop only if you signal to them **2** *verb* to ask for something in a polite way; *guests are requested to leave their keys at reception*

require [rɪ'kwaɪə] *verb* to need; *writing computer programs requires special skills*

rescue ['reskjuː] **1** *noun* action of saving; *mountain rescue teams tried to reach the children*; *rescue parties were sent out immediately after the plane came down in the jungle* **2** *verb* to save someone from a dangerous situation; *the helicopter rescued the crew of the sinking ship*; *when the river flooded, the party of tourists had to be rescued by boat*

research [rɪˈsɜːtʃ] **1** *noun* scientific study, which tries to find out facts; *the company is carrying out research to find a cure for colds* **2** *verb* to study, to try to find out facts; *research your subject thoroughly before you start writing about it*

resent [rɪˈzent] *verb* to feel annoyed because of something you do not like; *she resents having to look after her brother's parrot*

reservation [rezəˈveɪʃn] *noun* booking of a seat, table, etc.; *I want to make a reservation on the train to Plymouth tomorrow evening*; **(room) reservations** = department in a hotel which deals with bookings for rooms; *can you put me through to reservations?*

reserve [rɪˈzɜːv] **1** *noun* **(a)** *(in sport)* extra player who can play if someone drops out of the team; *one of the players was hurt so a reserve was called up* **(b)** **nature reserve** = area of land where animals and plants are protected; *we often go to a nature reserve in Suffolk to watch birds and walk by the sea* **2** *verb* **(a)** to book a seat or a table; *I want to reserve a table for four people*; *can you reserve two seats for me for the evening performance?* **(b)** to keep back for a special use, or to use later; *don't read this book now, reserve it for your holidays*

reservoir [ˈrezəvwɑː] *noun* large artificial lake where drinking water is kept for pumping to a city; *there has been very little rain this year and the reservoirs are only half full*

resign [rɪˈzaɪn] *verb* **(a)** to give up a job; *he resigned with effect from July 1st* **(b)** to **resign yourself to something** = to accept something which you don't like; *I have to resign myself to never being rich*

resist [rɪˈzɪst] *verb* to fight against something, not to give in to something; *he resisted all attempts to make him move to a smaller flat*; *the soldiers resisted the enemy attacks for two weeks*

resolve [rɪˈzɒlv] *verb* to decide firmly to do something; *we all resolved to work harder in future*

resources [rɪˈsɔːsɪz] *noun* supply of what is needed or used; **financial resources** = supply of money for something; **natural resources** = raw materials which come from nature, such as minerals, oil, wood; *the country is rich in natural resources*

respect [rɪˈspekt] **1** *noun* **(a)** liking and admiring someone; *no one deserves more respect than her mother* **(b)** **respects** = polite good wishes; *my father sends you his respects* **2** *verb* to admire or to honour someone; *everyone respected her for what she did*

respectable [rɪˈspektəbl] *adjective* considered by people to be good, proper, and worth respecting; *she's marrying a very respectable young engineer*

respond [rɪˈspɒnd] *verb* **(a)** to give a reply; *we sent him a letter, but he didn't respond* **(b)** to show a positive reaction to; *I hope the public will respond to our new advertisement*

responsibility [rɪspɒnsɪˈbɪlɪti] *noun* being in a position where you look after or deal with something; *the management accepts no responsibility for customers' property*; **he has taken on a lot of responsibility** = he has agreed to be responsible for many things

responsible [rɪˈspɒnsɪbl] *adjective* **(a)** **responsible for** = causing; *the fog was responsible for the accident* **(b)** looking after something, and so likely to be blamed if it gets lost, damaged, etc.; *we hold customers responsible for any items which are broken*

rest [rest] **1** *noun* **(a)** being quiet and peaceful, being asleep, doing nothing; *all you need is a good night's rest and you'll be fine again tomorrow*; *I'm having a nice rest after working hard all week* **(b)** what is left; *here are the twins, but where are the rest of the children?*; *I drank most of the milk and the cat drank the rest* **2** *verb* **(a)** to be quiet and peaceful; *don't disturb your father - he's resting* **(b)** to lean something against something; *she rested her bike against the* *wall*

restaurant ['restərɒnt] *noun* place where you can buy and eat a meal; *let's go to the Italian restaurant in the High Street*

restful ['restfʊl] *adjective* which makes you feel calm and relaxed; *after struggling through the crowds we were glad to get back to the restful calm of the hotel*

restless ['restləs] *adjective* not relaxed, always moving about; *the children were restless and I sent them out to play*

restore [rɪˈstɔː] *verb* to repair, to make something like new again; *the old castle has been restored and is now open to the public*

result [rɪˈzʌlt] **1** *noun* **(a)** something which happens because of something else; *what was the result of the police investigation?*; **as a result (of)** = because of; *there was a traffic jam and as a result, she missed her plane* **(b)** final score in a game, final marks in an exam, etc.; *she isn't pleased with her exam results*; *he listened to the football results on the radio* **2** *verb* **to result in** = to produce as an effect; *reducing prices resulted in increased sales*

résumé ['rezuːmeɪ] *noun* **(a)** short piece which sums up the main points of a discussion, of a book, etc.; *a brief résumé of the contents of the book is all I need* **(b)** US summary of the details of a person's life, especially details of your education and previous jobs; *attach a résumé to your application form* (NOTE: British English is **curriculum vitae** *or* **CV**)

retire [rɪˈtaɪə] *verb* to stop work and take a pension; *he will retire from his job as manager next April*; *when he retired, the firm presented him with a watch*; *I enjoy my work and I don't want to retire*

retreat [rɪˈtriːt] **1** *noun* pulling back an army from a battle; *the French army's retreat from Moscow*; *(informal)* **to beat a retreat** = to go backwards; *he went into the ladies' toilet by mistake and had to beat a rapid retreat* **2** *verb* to go back from a battle; *Napoleon retreated from Moscow in 1812*

return [rɪˈtɜːn] **1** *noun* **(a)** going back, coming back to a place; **return ticket** *or* **a return** = ticket which allows you to go to one place and come back; *I want two returns to Edinburgh* **(b)** key on a keyboard which you press when you have finished keying something, or when you want to start a new line; *to change to a different function, move to the menu and press return* **(c)** **Many Happy Returns of the Day** = greetings said to someone on his or her birthday **2** *verb* **(a)** to come back or to go back; *when she returned from lunch she found two messages waiting for her* **(b)** to give back or to send back; *I must return these books to the library*

reveal [rɪˈviːl] *verb* to show something which was hidden; *the X-ray revealed a broken bone*

revenge [rɪˈvenʒ] *noun* punishing someone for harm he has caused you; *they attacked the police station in revenge for the arrest of three members of the gang*

reverse [rɪˈvɜːs] **1** *adjective* opposite; **in reverse order** = backwards; *they called out the names of the winners in reverse order* **2** *noun* **(a)** opposite side; *didn't you read what was on the reverse of the label?* **(b)** car gear which makes you go backwards; *put the car into reverse and back very slowly into the garage* **3** *verb* **(a)** to make a car go backwards; *be careful not to reverse into that tree* **(b)** to put a series of things into the opposite order; *she set out the books with the biggest on the left and smallest on the right, and then decided to reverse them*

revise [rɪˈvaɪz] *verb* **(a)** to study a lesson again; *there isn't enough time to revise before the exam*; *I'm revising for my history test* **(b)** to change, to make something correct; *these figures will have to be revised, there seems to be a mistake*

revision [rɪˈvɪʒən] *noun* action of revising; *have you started doing your revision yet?*

revolting [rɪˈvəʊltɪŋ] *adjective* which disgusts you, which makes you feel ill; *look at the state of the kitchen - it's revolting!*

revolution [revəˈluːʃn] *noun* **(a)** armed rising against a government; *he led a revolution against the last president, but it failed* **(b)** change in the way things are done; *the technological revolution* = the change to using computers in business and industry

revolver [rɪˈvɒlvə] *noun* small hand gun which turns after each shot is fired, so that another shot can be fired quickly; *British policemen do not usually carry revolvers*

reward [rɪˈwɔːd] *noun* money given to someone as a gift for finding something, or for information about something; *she got a £25 reward when she took the purse she had found to the police station*

rhinoceros [raɪˈnɒsərəs] *noun* large Asian or African animal with a thick skin and one or two horns on its head; *look out - that rhinoceros is going to charge!* (NOTE: plural is **rhinoceroses**)

rhubarb [ˈruːbɑːb] *noun* plant of which the thick red leaf stalks are cooked and eaten as a dessert; *we're having rhubarb tart for pudding*

rhyme [raɪm] **1** *noun* **(a)** way in which some words end in the same sound; *can you think of a rhyme for 'taught'?* **(b)** little piece of poetry; **nursery rhyme** = little piece of poetry for children; *the children sang nursery rhymes and danced in a ring* **2** *verb* **to rhyme with** = to end with the same sound as another word; *'Mr' rhymes with 'sister'*

rhythm [ˈrɪðəm] *noun* strong regular beat in music, poetry, etc.; *they stamped their feet to the rhythm of the music*

rib [rɪb] *noun* one of the curved bones which protect your chest; *he fell while skiing and broke two ribs*

ribbon [ˈrɪbn] *noun* long thin strip of material for tying things or used as decoration; *she tied the parcel up with red ribbon*

rice [raɪs] *noun* very common food, the seeds of a tropical plant which grows in wet soil; *she only had a bowl of rice for her evening meal*;

rice pudding = a pudding made of rice, milk and sugar, cooked together

rich [rɪtʃ] *adjective* **(a)** who has a lot of money; *if only we were rich, then we could buy a bigger house* **(b) rich in** = containing a lot of; *these tablets are rich in vitamin B* **(c)** made with a lot of cream, butter, etc.; *this cream cake is too rich for me* (NOTE: **richer - richest**)

rid [rɪd] *phrase* **to get rid of something** = to throw something away; *do you want to get rid of that old chair?*; *she doesn't seem able to get rid of her cold* (NOTE: **getting rid - got rid**)

ridden [ˈrɪdən] *see* RIDE

riddle [ˈrɪdl] *noun* puzzling question to which you have to find the answer; *here's a riddle for you: 'what's black and white and red all over?'* (the answer is 'a book' if you say 'read' instead of 'red')

ride [raɪd] **1** *noun* pleasant trip on a horse, on a bike, in a car, etc.; *does anyone want to come for a bike ride?*; *the station is only a short bus ride from the college* **2** *verb* to go on a horse, on a bike, etc.; *he rode his bike across the road without looking*; *my little sister is learning to ride, but she's frightened of big horses* (NOTE: **rides - riding - rode** [rəʊd] - **has ridden** [ˈrɪdən])

ridiculous [rɪˈdɪkjʊləs] *adjective* silly, which everyone should laugh at; *it's ridiculous to tell everyone to wear their blazers when it's so hot*

rifle [ˈraɪfl] *noun* gun with a long barrel; *soldiers with rifles were on the roofs surrounding the ministry*

right [raɪt] **1** *adjective* **(a)** not wrong, correct; *you're right - the number 8 bus doesn't go to Marble Arch*; *she gave the right answer every time*; *is this the right train for Manchester?*; *is that the right time?* **(b)** not left, referring to the hand which most people use to write with; *outside Britain, cars drive on the right side of the road*; *the keys are in the top right drawer of my desk* **2** *noun* **(a)** the side opposite to the left; *when driving in France remember to keep to the right*; *when you get to the next junction, turn to the right* **(b)** being allowed by law to do or to have something; *the manager has no right to read my letters* **(c)** **rights** = what you should be allowed to do or to have; *they are working for women's rights*; *the rights of ordinary working people are being ignored* **3** *adverb* **(a)** straight; *to get to the police station, keep right on to the end of the road*; *go right along to the end of the corridor, you'll see my office in front of you* **(b)** exactly; *the phone rang right in the middle of the TV programme*; *she stood right in front of the TV and no one could see the screen* **(c)** towards the right-hand side; *to get to the station, turn right at the traffic lights*; *children should be taught to look right and left before crossing the road* **4** *interjection* agreed, OK; *right, so we'll all meet again at 7 o'clock?*

right angle ['raɪt 'æŋgl] *noun* angle of 90°; *the four sides of a square all meet at right angles*

right-hand ['raɪt 'hænd] *adjective* on the right side; *look in the right-hand drawer of my desk*; *in Germany cars drive on the right-hand side of the road*; **right-hand man** = main assistant; *he's my right-hand man, I couldn't do without him*

right-handed ['raɪt 'hændɪd] *adjective* using the right hand more often than the left for things like writing and eating; *she's right-handed*

rigid ['rɪdʒɪd] *adjective* stiff, which doesn't bend; *a concrete post is too rigid, you will need something which will bend*

rim [rɪm] *noun* **(a)** edge of something round, like a wheel or a cup; *the rim of the glass is chipped* **(b)** frame of spectacles; *he wears glasses with steel rims*

rind [raɪnd] *noun* skin on fruit, bacon or cheese; *add the grated rind of a lemon*; *can you eat the rind of this cheese?*

ring [rɪŋ] **1** *noun* **(a)** round shape of metal,

etc.; *she has a gold ring in her nose*; *he wears a ring on his little finger*; **wedding ring** = ring which is put on your fourth finger during the wedding ceremony **(b)** circle of people or things; *the teacher asked the children to sit in a ring round her* **(c)** noise of an electric bell; *there was a ring at the door* **(d)** space where a show takes place, where a boxing match is held, etc.; *everyone shouted when the clowns ran into the ring*; *the champion climbed into the ring* **2** *verb* **(a)** to make a sound with a bell; *if you ring your bicycle bell people will get out of the way* **(b)** to telephone; *he rang me to say he would be late*; *don't ring tomorrow afternoon - I won't be at home* **(c)** **to ring a bell** = to remind someone of something; *does the name Arbuthnot ring any bells?* (NOTE: **ringing - rang** [ræŋ] **- has rung** [rʌŋ])

ring road ['rɪŋ 'rəʊd] *noun* road which goes right round a town; *instead of driving through the town centre, it will be quicker to take the ring road*

ring up ['rɪŋ 'ʌp] *verb* to make a telephone call; *I rang up the doctor to say I was going to be late*

rink [rɪŋk] *noun* **ice rink** *or* **skating rink** = large area for ice skating, playing ice hockey, etc.; *in the evening we all went to the local rink*

rinse [rɪns] **1** *noun* washing something in clean water to get rid of soap; *give your shirt a good rinse* **2** *verb* to put things covered with soap or dirty things into clean water to remove the soap or the dirt; *rinse the dishes before drying them*

riot ['raɪət] **1** *noun* wild fighting by a crowd of people; **to run riot** = to get out of control; *after the match, the fans ran riot and the police had to be called in* **2** *verb* to take part in a riot; to get out of control; *angry fans rioted when they heard the decision of the referee*

rip [rɪp] *verb* to tear, to pull roughly; *she ripped open the parcel to see what he had given her*; *the old bathroom is being ripped* out and new units put in (NOTE: ripping - ripped)

ripe [raɪp] *adjective* ready to eat or to be harvested; *don't eat that apple - it isn't ripe yet* (NOTE: **riper - ripest**)

ripple ['rɪpl] *noun* little wave; *even a little stone thrown into the water will make ripples*

rise [raɪz] **1** *noun* movement or slope upwards; **pay rise** = increase in salary; *he's had two rises this year* **2** *verb* to go up; *the sun always rises in the east*; *the road rises gently for a few miles* (NOTE: **rising - rose** [rəʊz] **- has risen** ['rɪzn])

risk [rɪsk] **1** *noun* **(a)** possible bad result; *there is not much risk of rain in August; at the risk of looking silly, I'm going to ask her to come out with me* **(b) to take a risk** = to do something which may make you lose money or suffer harm; *drive slowly, we're in no hurry and there's no need to take any risks* **2** *verb* to do something which may possibly harm you; *the fireman risked his life to save her*; *you risk going blind if you look at the sun*

risky ['rɪski] *adjective* which is dangerous; *there is ice on the road, driving will be very risky* (NOTE: **riskier - riskiest**)

rival ['raɪvl] **1** *adjective* competing, who competes; *Simon and I are friends but we play for rival teams* **2** *noun* person who competes; company which competes; *we keep our prices low to compete with our biggest rival*

river ['rɪvə] *noun* large mass of fresh water which runs across the land and goes into the sea or into a lake; *London is on the River Thames*; *the river is very deep here, so it's dangerous to swim in it*

road [rəʊd] *noun* **(a)** hard way used by cars, trucks, etc., to travel along; *the road to York goes directly north from London; children are taught to look both ways before crossing the road; what is your address? - 26 London Road* **(b) on the road** = travelling; *we were on the road for thirteen hours before we*

finally reached the hotel (NOTE: usualy written **Rd** in names of roads)

roam [rəʊm] *verb* to wander about without any particular destination; *angry fans roamed around the streets smashing windows*

roar [rɔː] *verb* to make a loud noise; *he roared with laughter at the film; the lion roared and then ran towards us*

roast [rəʊst] **1** *verb* to cook over a fire or in an oven; *if you want your meat well cooked, roast it for two hours* **2** *adjective* which has been roasted; *we had roast chicken for dinner*; **roast potato** = potato baked in fat in an oven; *serve the meat with roast potatoes and green vegetables*

rob [rɒb] *verb* to attack and steal from someone; *a gang robbed our local bank last night; the old lady was robbed of all her savings* (NOTE: **robbing - robbed**)

robber ['rɒbə] *noun* person who attacks and steals from someone; *robbers attacked the bank in broad daylight*

robin ['rɒbɪn] *noun* common small brown bird with a red patch on its breast; *every time I work in the garden, a robin comes and sits on the fence*

robot ['rəʊbɒt] *noun* machine which is programmed to work like a person automatically; *these cars are made by robots*

rock [rɒk] **1** *noun* **(a)** very hard material, found in the ground; *the house is built on solid rock* **(b)** large stone, large piece of stone; *the ship was breaking up on the rocks* **(c)** hard pink sweet stuff, shaped like a stick, often with the name of a town printed in it, bought mainly by tourists; *a stick of Brighton rock* **(d)** music with a strong rhythm; *rock (music) is the only music he listens to* **2** *verb* to move from side to side; to make something move from side to side; *the little boats rocked as the ferry passed; the explosion rocked the town*

rocket ['rɒkɪt] *noun* **(a)** type of firework which flies up into the sky; *we stood in the square and watched the rockets lighting up* the sky **(b)** **space rocket** = large device which is fired into space, carrying satellites, etc.; *the Americans are sending a rocket to Mars*

rod [rɒd] *noun* long stick; *you need a stiff rod to hold the plants upright*; **fishing rod** = long stick with a line attached, used for fishing

rode [rəʊd] *see* RIDE

rodent ['rəʊdənt] *noun* type of small animal which chews and gnaws; *mice and rats are probably the best known rodents*; *did you know that squirrels are also rodents?*

role [rəʊl] *noun* part played by someone, in a play or film; *he plays the role of the king* (NOTE: do not confuse with **roll**)

roll [rəʊl] **1** *noun* **(a)** tube of something which has been turned over and over on itself; *a roll of toilet paper* or *a toilet roll* **(b)** very small loaf of bread for one person, sometimes cut in half and used to make a sandwich; *will a bowl of soup and a roll and butter be enough for you?*; **cheese roll** or **ham roll** = roll with cheese or ham in it **(d) sausage roll** = small pastry with sausage meat inside (NOTE: do not confuse with **role**) **2** *verb* **(a)** to make something go forward by turning it over and over; *he rolled the ball to the other player* **(b)** to go forward by turning over and over; *the coin rolled under the piano* **(c)** to make something move on wheels; *the desk is on wheels, so you can just roll it into another room* **(d)** to turn something flat over and over; *he rolled the poster into a tube*

roller ['rəʊlə] *noun* **(a)** heavy round object which rolls, such as one used for making lawns or cricket pitches flat; *they used the roller just before the match started* **(b)** plastic tube used for rolling your hair into curls; *she isn't ready yet - her hair is still in rollers*

rollerblades ['rəʊləbleɪdz] *noun* trademark for a type of roller-skate, with a series of little wheels in line; *the young man on rollerblades zoomed past us at great speed*

roller-skate ['rəʊləskeɪt] *noun* boot with wheels which you wear to glide along fast; *I*

have some roller-skates but I'd love to have rollerblades

roof [ruːf] *noun* **(a)** part of a building, etc., which covers it and protects it; *she lives in a little white cottage with a red roof* **(b)** top of the inside of the mouth; *I burnt the roof of my mouth drinking hot soup* **(c)** top of a car, bus, lorry, etc.; *we had to put the cases on the roof of the car*

room [ruːm] *noun* **(a)** part of a building, divided from other parts by walls; *the flat has six rooms, plus kitchen and bathroom*; **dining room** = room where you eat **(b)** bedroom in a hotel; *your room is 316 - here's your key*; *his room is just opposite mine*; **room service** = arrangement in a hotel where food or drink can be served in a guest's bedroom; *if you call room service, you can get sandwiches brought up to your room* **(c)** space for something; *the table is too big - it takes up a lot of room*; *there isn't enough room in the car for six people*; *we can't have a piano in our flat - there just isn't enough room*; **to make room for** = to squeeze together to make more space for; *there's no way we can make room for two more passengers*

roost [ruːst] **1** *noun* perch where a bird sleeps; *the owl has its roost in an old oak tree* **2** *verb* to perch asleep; *six chickens were roosting in the shed*

rooster ['ruːstə] *noun* male chicken; *we were woken by the rooster on our neighbour's farm*

root [ruːt] *noun* **(a)** part of a plant which goes down into the ground, and which takes energy from the soil; *the little plant has very delicate roots*; **root crops** or **root vegetables** = vegetables which are grown for their roots which are eaten, such as carrots, etc.; *you can't grow root crops in this kind of soil* **(b)** part of a hair or a tooth which goes down into the skin; *he pulled her hair out by the roots* (NOTE: do not confuse with **route**)

rope [rəʊp] **1** *noun* very thick string made of several pieces of thinner string twisted together; *you'll need a rope to pull the car out of the ditch*; *the burglar climbed down from the balcony on a rope* **2** *verb* **(a)** to tie together with a rope; *we roped the sofa onto the roof of the car* **(b)** **to rope off** = to stop people going into a place by putting a rope around it; *that section has been roped off - you need a special ticket to get in*

rose [rəʊz] **1** *noun* common flower with spines on the stem and a strong scent; *he gave her a bunch of red roses*; *these roses have a beautiful scent* **2** *verb see* RISE

rot [rɒt] *verb* to decay, to go bad; *the wooden fence is not very old but it has already started to rot* (NOTE: **rotting - rotted**)

rotate [rəʊ'teɪt] *verb* to turn round a central point like a wheel; *rotate the knob to the right to increase the volume*

rotten ['rɒtən] *adjective* **(a)** decayed; *the apple looked nice on the outside, but inside it was rotten* **(b)** *(informal)* miserable; *we had rotten weather on holiday*; **to feel rotten** = to feel ill, upset; *today I feel really rotten, I think I've got flu*

rough [rʌf] *adjective* **(a)** not smooth; *the sea's rough today - I hope I won't be sick* **(b)** not very accurate; *I made some rough calculations on the back of an envelope* **(c)** not finished; *he made a rough draft of the new design* **(d)** not gentle; *don't be rough when you're playing with the puppy* (NOTE: **rougher - roughest**)

roughly ['rʌfli] *adverb* **(a)** approximately, more or less; *there were roughly one hundred people in the audience* **(b)** in a rough way; *the removal men threw the boxes roughly into the back of their van*

round [raʊnd] **1** *adjective* **(a)** with a shape like a circle; *in Chinese restaurants, you often sit at round tables* **(b)** with a shape like a globe; *soccer is played with a round ball, while a Rugby ball is oval* **2** *adverb & preposition* **(a)** in a circle; *the wheels of the lorry went round and round*; *the Earth goes*

round the Sun **(b)** towards the back; *she turned round when he tapped her on the shoulder*; *he ran down the street and disappeared round a corner* **(c)** from one person to another; *can you pass the plate of cakes round, please?* **(d)** in various places, here and there; *they spent the afternoon going round the town* **3** *noun* **(a)** **a round of toast** = piece or pieces of toast made from one slice of bread; **a round of sandwiches** = two or four sandwiches made from two slices of bread **(b)** part of a competition, boxing match, etc.; *if you answer all the questions correctly, you go on to the next round*

round down ['raʊnd 'daʊn] *verb* to reduce to the nearest full figure; *the figures have been rounded down to the nearest pound*

round up ['raʊnd 'ʌp] *verb* **(a)** to gather people or animals together; *the police rounded up about fifty suspects and took them off in vans* **(b)** to increase to the nearest full figure; *the figures have been rounded up to the nearest pound*

roundabout ['raʊndəbaʊt] *noun* **(a)** place where several roads meet, and traffic has to move in a circle; *when you get to the next roundabout, turn right* **(b)** *(in a children's playground)* heavy wheel which turns, and which children ride on; *the children all ran to get on the roundabout* **(c)** *(in a fair)* large amusement machine, which turns round and plays music, usually with horses to sit on which move up and down; *let's go for a ride on the roundabout*

rounders ['raʊndəz] *noun* team game similar to baseball, played with a bat and ball, where the person batting has to run round the pitch to score; *the children were playing rounders in the park*

route [ruːt *US also* raʊt] *noun* way you take to get to a place; *we still have to decide which route we will take*; **bus route** = usual way which a bus follows; *the cinema is not on the bus route, we'll have to go there by car* (NOTE: do not confuse with **root**)

routine [ruː'tiːn] **1** *noun* normal, regular way of doing things; *children don't like their routine to be changed*; *having a cup of coffee while reading the newspaper is part of his morning routine* **2** *adjective* normal, which happens at a regular time; *we're making a routine check of the central heating system*

row **1** *noun* **(a)** [rəʊ] line of things, side by side or one after the other; *he has a row of cabbages in the garden*; *I want two seats in the front row* **(b)** [raʊ] loud noise; *stop making that dreadful row!* **(c)** [raʊ] serious argument; *they had a row about who was responsible for the accident* **2** *verb* [rəʊ] to make a boat go forward by using oars or long blades; *she rowed across the lake*

royal ['rɔɪəl] *adjective* referring to a king or queen; **the Royal Family** = family of a king or queen

rub [rʌb] *verb* to move something across the surface of something else; *he rubbed his hands together to get them warm*; *the cat rubbed herself against my legs* (NOTE: **rubbing - rubbed**)

rub out ['rʌb 'aʊt] *verb* to remove a pencil mark with a rubber; *the note is written in pencil so you can rub it out easily*

rubber ['rʌbə] *noun* **(a)** elastic material made from juice from a tropical tree; *car tyres are made of rubber* **(b)** piece of rubber used for removing pencil marks; *he used a rubber to try to rub out what he had written*

rubbish ['rʌbɪʃ] *noun* **(a)** waste, things which are no use and are thrown away; *we had to step over heaps of rubbish to get to the restaurant*; **rubbish bin** = container for putting rubbish; *throw all those old cans into the rubbish bin* **(b)** nonsense, something which has no value; *he's talking rubbish, don't listen to him*

rudder ['rʌdə] *noun* flat vertical part at the stern of a boat or on the tail of an aircraft, used for steering; *after the rudder broke off they had to use an oar to steer with*

rude [ruːd] *adjective* not polite, likely to offend; *don't point at people - it's rude*; *the teacher asked who had written rude words on the board* (NOTE: **ruder - rudest**)

rudely ['ruːdli] *adverb* in a rude way; *she told him rudely what he could do with his money*

rug [rʌg] *noun* **(a)** small carpet; *this beautiful rug comes from the Middle East* **(b)** thick blanket, especially one used when travelling; *we spread rugs on the grass to have our picnic*

rugby ['rʌgbi] *noun* type of football played with an oval ball which is thrown as well as kicked; *we lost our two latest rugby matches*; *did you watch the rugby international on TV?*

ruin ['ruːɪn] **1** *noun* **(a)** remains of an old building with no roof, fallen walls, etc.; *the house was a total ruin when I bought it* **(b)** **ruins** = remains of old buildings with no roofs, fallen walls, etc.; *in the afternoon we visited the castle ruins;* **in ruins** = wrecked; *the town was in ruins after the war* **2** *verb* to wreck or to spoil completely; *our holiday was ruined by the weather*

rule [ruːl] **1** *noun* statement of what you should or should not do; *there are no rules that forbid parking here at night*; *according to the rules, your ticket must be paid for two weeks in advance* **2** *verb* **(a)** to govern or to control; *the country is ruled by army generals* **(b)** to draw a straight line using a ruler; *he ruled three lines across the paper*

as a rule *phrase* usually; *as a rule, we go to bed early*

ruler ['ruːlə] *noun* **(a)** long piece of wood or plastic with measurements marked on it, used for measuring and drawing straight lines; *you need a ruler to draw a rectangle* **(b)** person who governs; *he's the ruler of a small African state*

run [rʌn] **1** *noun* **(a)** going quickly on foot as a sport; *I always go for a run before breakfast* **(b)** score in cricket; *he made 45 runs before* *he was out* **2** *verb* **(a)** to go quickly on foot; *when she heard the telephone, she ran upstairs*; *children must be taught not to run across the road*; *she's running in the 200 metre race* **(b)** *(of buses, trains, etc.)* to be working; *all trains are running late because of the accident*; *this bus doesn't run on Sundays* **(c)** *(of machines)* to work; *he left his car in the street with the engine running* **(d)** to direct, to organize a business, a club, etc.; *I want someone to run the shop for me when I'm away on holiday* **(e)** to drive by car; *let me run you to the station* **(f)** *(of liquid)* to flow, to move along easily; *the river runs past our house* (NOTE: **running - ran** [ræn] **- has run**)

run away ['rʌn ə'weɪ] *verb* to escape, to go away fast; *they were running away from the police*; *she ran away from school when she was 16*

run into ['rʌn 'ɪntʊ] *verb* **(a)** to go into a place fast; *she ran into the street, shouting 'Fire!'* **(b)** to go fast and hit something (usually in a vehicle); *the bus turned the corner too fast and ran into a parked van* **(c)** to amount to; *costs have run into thousands of pounds* **(d)** to find someone by chance; *I ran into him in a café on the South Bank*

run out of ['rʌn 'aʊt 'ɒv] *verb* to have nothing left of something; *the car ran out of petrol on the motorway*

run over ['rʌn 'əʊvə] *verb* to knock someone down by hitting them with a vehicle; *she was run over by a taxi*

rung [rʌŋ] **1** *noun* one of the bars on a ladder; *if you stand on the top rung you can climb onto the roof* **2** *verb see* RING

runner ['rʌnə] *noun* person or horse running in a race; *there are 30,000 runners in the London Marathon*

running ['rʌnɪŋ] **1** *adjective* **(a)** which runs; **running water** = water which is available in a house through water pipes and taps; *there is hot and cold running water in all the bedrooms* **(b)** **for three days running** = one day after another for three days **2** *noun* action

of managing; *he leaves the running of the shop to his son*

runway ['rʌnweɪ] *noun* track on which planes land and take off at an airport; *the plane went out onto the runway and then stopped for half an hour*

rush [rʌʃ] **1** *noun* fast movement; *when the film ended there was a rush for the exits* **2** *verb* to hurry, to go forward fast; *the ambulance rushed to the accident*

rush hour ['rʌʃ 'aʊə] *noun* time of day when traffic is bad, when trains are full, etc.; *don't travel during the rush hour if you want to avoid the traffic*

Russia ['rʌʃə] *proper noun* large country in Eastern Europe, covering also a large part of Asia up to the Pacific Ocean; *have you ever been to Russia?*; *he went on a journey across Russia* (NOTE: capital: **Moscow**; people: **Russians**; language: **Russian**)

Russian ['rʌʃn] **1** *adjective* referring to Russia; *she speaks English with a Russian accent*; *Russian winters can be extremely cold* **2** *noun* **(a)** person from Russia; *are there any Russians in the group?* **(b)** language spoken in Russia; *we'll start the Russian lesson by learning the alphabet*; *I can read Russian but I can't speak it*

rust [rʌst] **1** *noun* orange layer which forms on metal left in damp air; *the underneath of the car is showing signs of rust* **2** *verb* to form rust; *don't leave the hammer outside in the rain - it will rust*

rustle ['rʌsl] *verb* to make a soft dry noise; *don't rustle the newspaper when the radio is on, I can't hear the news*

rusty ['rʌsti] *adjective* covered with rust; *she tried to cut the string with a pair of rusty old scissors* (NOTE: **rustier - rustiest**)

rut [rʌt] *noun* deep track made in soft earth by the wheels of vehicles; *the wheels of the car were stuck in deep ruts*

Ss

S, s [es] nineteenth letter of the alphabet, between R and T; *'she sells sea shells on the sea shore'* - *how many Ss are there in that?*

sack [sæk] **1** *noun* **(a)** large bag made of strong cloth or paper, used for carrying heavy things; *he hurt his back lifting up a sack of potatoes* **(b)** *(informal)* **to get** *or* **to be given the sack** = to be dismissed from a job; *you'll get the sack if you are rude to the boss* **2** *verb (informal)* to dismiss someone from a job; *he was sacked because he was always late for work*

sad [sæd] *adjective* not happy, miserable; *he's sad because the holidays have come to an end*; *she felt sad watching the boat sail away*; *it's sad that her father can't come to see her* (NOTE: **sadder - saddest**)

saddle ['sædl] **1** *noun* seat on a bicycle, motorbike or horse; *my old saddle was very comfortable but this new one is harder* **2** *verb* **to saddle someone with** = to give someone a difficult job; *he got saddled with the job of sorting out the rubbish*

sadly ['sædli] *adverb* **(a)** in a sad way; *after the funeral we walked sadly back to the empty house*; *she stared sadly out of the window at the rain* **(b)** unfortunately; *sadly, John couldn't join us for my birthday party*

safari [sə'fɑːri] *noun* expedition to photograph or kill wild animals in Africa; *he went on a safari holiday in Kenya*; **safari park** = park where large wild animals are free to run about, and visitors drive around in their cars to look at them

safe [seɪf] **1** *adjective* **(a)** not in danger, not likely to be hurt; *all the children are safe, but the school was burnt down*; *it isn't safe to go into the centre of town alone at night* **(b) safe and sound** = without being hurt or damaged; *we all arrived back home safe and sound* (NOTE: **safer - safest**) **2** *noun* strong box for keeping documents, money, jewels, etc., in; *the burglars managed to open the safe*

safely ['seɪfli] *adverb* without being hurt; *the rescue services managed to get all the passengers safely off the burning train*; *'drive safely!' she said as she waved goodbye*

safety ['seɪfti] *noun* **(a)** being safe; *I am worried about the safety of air travel*; **safety belt** = belt which you wear in a plane to stop you being hurt if there is an accident; **safety helmet** = solid hat worn by construction workers, etc.; **safety pin** = pin whose point fits into a little cover when it is fastened, and so can't hurt anyone **(b)** place where you are safe; *the firemen brought the children to safety out of the burning building*

said [sed] *see* SAY

sail [seɪl] **1** *noun* piece of cloth which catches the wind and drives a boat along; *they pulled up the sail and set out across the Channel*; *a group of little boats with blue sails* (NOTE: do not confuse with **sale**) **2** *verb* **(a)** to travel on water; *the ship was sailing towards the rocks* **(b)** to travel in a sailing boat; *she was the first woman to sail alone round the world* **(c)** to leave harbour; *the ferry sails at 12.00*

sailing ['seɪlɪŋ] *noun* sport of going in a sailing boat; *we have booked to go on a sailing holiday in the Mediterranean*; **sailing boat** *US* **sailboat** = boat (such as a yacht) which mainly uses sails to travel; *two sailing boats sank in the race*

sailor ['seɪlə] *noun* person who works on a ship; *the sailors were washing down the deck of the ship*

sake [seɪk] *noun* **(a) for the sake of something** *or* **for something's sake** = for certain reasons, because of something; *the robbers attacked the old lady, just for the* *sake of a few pence*; **for the sake of someone** *or* **for someone's sake** = because you want to help someone or to please someone; *will you come to the meeting for my sake?* **(b)** *(exclamation)* **for heaven's sake** *or* **for goodness' sake** = expressions showing you are annoyed, or that something is important; *what are you screaming for? - it's only a little mouse, for heaven's sake*; *for goodness' sake try to be quiet, we don't want the guards to hear us!*

salad ['sæləd] *noun* cold food, such as cold fish or meat served with cold vegetables; *I found some chicken, tomatoes and lettuce in the fridge, and made myself a chicken salad sandwich*; **fruit salad** = pieces of fresh fruit, mixed and served cold

salary ['sæləri] *noun* payment for work, received each month; *I expect a salary increase next month*; **starting salary** = amount of pay an employee gets when starting work with a company (NOTE: plural is **salaries)**

sale [seɪl] *noun* **(a)** act of selling, act of giving an item in exchange for money; *the shop only opened this morning and we've just made our first sale* **(b)** time when things are sold at cheaper prices; *I bought these plates for £1 in a sale* (NOTE: do not confuse with **sail)**

for sale ready to be sold; *these items are not for sale to the general public*; *I noticed there was a 'for sale' sign outside her house*

on sale ready to be sold in a shop; *you will find local cheeses on sale in the market*

sales [seɪlz] *noun* **(a)** time when many shops sell goods at low prices; *the sales start on Saturday*; *I bought these shirts in the January sales* **(b)** money which a business receives from selling things; *the shop has sales of over £250,000 each year*

salmon ['sæmən] *noun* large fish with silver skin and pink flesh; *we had grilled salmon and new potatoes* (NOTE: plural is **salmon)**

salt [sɒlt] *noun* white substance used to make food taste better (used especially with meat,

fish and vegetables); *there's too much salt in this soup*; *you don't need to put any salt on your fish*

salute [sə'luːt] **1** *noun* movement to show respect, etc., especially putting your right hand up to touch the peak of your cap; **to take the salute** = to be the person who is saluted by soldiers on parade; *the general took the salute as the soldiers marched past* **2** *verb* to give a salute to someone; *ordinary soldiers must salute their officers*

same [seɪm] *adjective & pronoun* **(a)** being, looking, sounding, etc., exactly alike; *you must get very bored doing the same work every day*; *she was wearing the same dress as me* **(b)** showing that two or more things share one thing; *they all live in the same street*; *I go to the same school as she does*

sample ['sɑːmpl] **1** *noun* a small part which is used to show what the whole is like; *try a sample of the local cheese* **2** *verb* to try something by taking a small amount; *would you like to sample the cheese?*

sand [sænd] *noun* mass of tiny bits of rock, found on beaches, in the desert, etc.; *we walked along a beach of fine white sand*; **sand castle** = little castle of sand made by children on a beach; *the children built sand castles on the beach with their buckets*

sandal ['sændl] *noun* light open shoe worn in the summer; *he was wearing a pair of brown sandals and shorts*

sandwich ['sændwɪʃ] *noun* snack made with two slices of bread with meat, salad, etc., between them; *she ordered a cheese sandwich and a cup of coffee*; *what sort of sandwiches do you want for your lunch?* (NOTE: plural is **sandwiches)**

sang [sæŋ] *see* SING

sank [sæŋk] *see* SINK

sardine [sɑː'diːn] *noun* small fish which can be eaten fresh, and is also bought in tins; *we had grilled sardines in a little restaurant which looked over the harbour*; **packed**

(together) like sardines = standing or sitting very close together

sat [sæt] *see* SIT

satchel ['sætʃəl] *noun* small leather or canvas bag worn on your shoulders, used mainly by children going to school; *a line of children walked past, each carrying a neat little satchel*

satellite ['sætəlaɪt] *noun* **(a)** device that goes round the earth, receiving and sending signals, pictures and data; *the signals are sent by satellite all round the world*; **satellite dish** = device, shaped like a large saucer, used to receive broadcasts from satellites; **satellite TV** = television system, where pictures are sent via a satellite; *we watched the programme on satellite TV* **(b)** body in space which goes round a planet; *the Moon is the only satellite of the Earth*

satisfactory [sætɪs'fæktəri] *adjective* quite good; *John's French and English are satisfactory but he's weak in maths and sciences*

satisfy ['sætɪsfaɪ] *verb* to make someone pleased with what he has bought, with the service he has received; *when we've finished painting the kitchen, I hope you'll be satisfied with the result*; **satisfied customer** = customer who has got what he or she wanted

Saturday ['sætədeɪ] *noun* sixth day of the week, the day between Friday and Sunday; *he works in a shop, so Saturday is a normal working day for him*; *the 15th is a Saturday, so the 16th must be a Sunday*; *we arranged to meet up at the cinema next Saturday evening*

sauce [sɔːs] *noun* liquid with a particular taste, poured over food; *she asked for ice cream with chocolate sauce*; *the waitress put a bottle of tomato sauce on the table*; *we had roast duck and orange sauce for dinner*

saucepan ['sɔːspæn] *noun* deep metal cooking pan with a lid and a long handle; *watch the saucepan - I don't want the milk to boil over*

saucer ['sɔːsə] *noun* shallow dish which a cup stands in; *where are the cups and saucers? - they're in the cupboard*

sausage ['sɒsɪdʒ] *noun* tube full of minced and seasoned meat, eaten hot; *you can't possibly eat all those sausages!*

save [seɪv] *verb* **(a)** to stop someone or something from being hurt or killed; *the firemen saved six people from the burning house*; *how many passengers were saved when the ferry sank?*; *we managed to save most of the paintings from the fire* **(b)** to put money to one side so that you can use it later; *I'm saving to buy a car*; *if you save £10 a week, you'll have £520 at the end of a year* **(c)** not to waste (time, money, etc.); *by cycling to work, he saves £25 a week in bus fares*; *she took the parcel herself so as to save the cost of the stamps* **(d)** to store data on a computer disk; *don't forget to save your files when you have finished keyboarding them*

savings ['seɪvɪŋz] *noun* money which you have saved; *she spent all her savings on a round the world trip*

saw [sɔː] **1** *noun* tool with a long metal blade with teeth along its edge, used for cutting; *he was cutting logs with a saw* **2** *verb* **(a)** to cut with a saw; *that piece of wood is too long - you will need to saw it in half* (NOTE: sawing - sawed - has sawn [sɔːn] **(b)** *see also* SEE

say [seɪ] *verb* **(a)** to speak words; *don't forget to say 'thank you' after the party*; *the weather forecast said it was going to rain and it did* **(b)** to give information in writing; *the letter says that we owe the bank £200*; *the notice says that you are not allowed to walk on the grass* (NOTE: says [sez] - saying - said [sed] - has said)

saying ['seɪɪŋ] *noun* phrase which is often used; *my mother was fond of old sayings like 'red sky at night - sailor's delight'*

scaffolding ['skæfəldɪŋ] *noun* construction of poles and planks which makes a series of platforms for workmen to stand on while building a house; *they put up scaffolding round the building*

scale [skeɪl] *noun* **(a)** proportion used to show a large object in a smaller form; *map with a scale of 1 to 100,000* **(b)** measuring system which is divided into various levels; *the Richter scale is used to measure earthquakes*

scales [skeɪlz] *noun* **(a)** small machine for weighing; *she put two bananas on the scales*; *the bathroom scales must be wrong - I'm heavier than I was yesterday* **(b)** thin pieces protecting the skin of fish; *don't forget to scrape the scales off the sardines before you grill them*

scar [skɑː] *noun* mark left on the skin after a wound has healed; *he still has the scars of his operation*

scarce [skeəs] *adjective* of which there is not very much, not enough for what is needed; *fresh vegetables are scarce in winter* (NOTE: scarcer - scarcest)

scare [skeə] *verb* to make someone afraid; *the thought of travelling alone across Africa scares me*; **to scare away** = to make something so afraid that it goes away; *the cat has scared all the birds away from the garden*

scarecrow [ˈskeəkrəʊ] *noun* figure made to look like a person dressed in old clothes, put up in a field to scare the birds; *look at the scarecrow with his black coat and funny hat!*

scared [skeəd] *adjective* frightened; *don't be scared - the snake is harmless*

scarf [skɑːf] *noun* long piece of cloth which is worn round your neck to keep you warm; *the students were wearing college scarves* (NOTE: plural is **scarves** [skɑːvz])

scatter [ˈskætə] *verb* **(a)** to throw in various places; *the children scattered flowers all over the path* **(b)** to run in different directions; *when the police arrived, the crowd scattered*

scene [siːn] *noun* **(a)** place where something has happened; *the fire brigade were on the scene very quickly*; *it took the ambulance ten*

minutes to get to the scene of the accident* **(b)** short part of a play or film; *did you like the scene where he is trying to climb up the skyscraper?* **(c)** view; *he took a photo of the scene from the hotel window*

scenery [ˈsiːnri] *noun* **(a)** features of the countryside; *the beautiful scenery of the Lake District* **(b)** painted cloth background used to imitate real buildings, rooms, landscapes, etc., on the stage in a theatre; *in between the acts all the scenery has to be changed*

scent [sent] *noun* **(a)** pleasant smell of something which you can recognize; *the scent of roses in the cottage garden* **(b)** perfume, a liquid which smells nice, and which is put on the skin; *that new scent of yours makes me sneeze* **(c)** smell given off by animals, either pleasant or unpleasant; **on the scent of** = following a trail left by; *the dogs followed the scent of the robbers* (NOTE: do not confuse with cent, sent)

scheme [skiːm] *noun* plan or arrangement for making something work; *he has thought up some scheme for making money very quickly*

school [skuːl] *noun* **(a)** place where students, usually children, are taught; *our little boy is four, so he'll be going to school this year*; *when he was sixteen, he left school and joined the army*; **school year** = period which starts in September and finishes in July **(b)** section of a college or university; *the school of medicine is one of the largest in the country* **(c)** group of swimming animals; *a school of porpoises followed our boat*

science [ˈsaɪəns] *noun* study of natural physical things and the way they work, based on looking and testing to discover facts; *he's quite good at languages, but science is his best subject*; *we have a new science teacher this term*

scientific [saɪənˈtɪfɪk] *adjective* referring to science; *hundreds of people are employed in scientific research*

scientist ['saɪəntɪst] *noun* person who specializes in a science, often doing research; *scientists have not yet found a cure for the common cold*

scissors ['sɪzəz] *noun* tool for cutting paper, cloth, etc., made of two blades attached in the middle, with handles with holes for the thumb and fingers; *these scissors aren't very sharp*; *have you got a pair of scissors I can borrow?*; **nail scissors** = special small curved scissors for cutting your nails

scoop [skuːp] **1** *noun* **(a)** deep round spoon with a short handle, for serving ice cream, etc.; *wash the scoop after you have used it* **(b)** portion of ice cream, etc.; *I'll have one scoop of strawberry and one scoop of chocolate, please* **2** *verb* to lift up several things together; *he scooped all the newspapers off the floor*

scooter ['skuːtə] *noun* **(a)** small type of motorbike with a curving shield in front of the seat and a platform for the feet; *she goes to work on her scooter* **(b)** child's vehicle with two wheels, with a long steering handle, which you push along with one foot; *the children all got little scooters for Christmas*

score [skɔː] **1** *noun* **(a)** number of goals or points made in a match; *the final score in the rugby match was 22 - 10* **(b)** **scores of** = very many; *scores of people stayed at home during the train strike*; *I must have seen that film scores of times* **2** *verb* to make a goal or point in a match; *they scored three goals in the first twenty minutes*

Scot [skɒt] *noun* person from Scotland; *is she English? - no, she's a Scot*

Scotch [skɒtʃ] *adjective* referring to Scotland; **Scotch eggs** = hard boiled eggs covered with minced meat and bread crumbs; **Scotch whisky** = whisky made in Scotland

Scotland ['skɒtlənd] *noun* country to the north of England, forming part of the United Kingdom; *he was brought up in Scotland*; *Scotland's most famous product is whisky* (NOTE: capital: **Edinburgh**; people: **the Scots**)

Scottish ['skɒtɪʃ] *adjective* referring to Scotland; *the beautiful Scottish mountains turn purple in autumn*

scramble ['skræmbl] *verb* **(a)** to hurry, on your hands and knees if necessary; *he scrambled over the wall* **(b) scrambled eggs** = eggs mixed together and stirred as they are cooked in butter; *he had scrambled eggs on toast for breakfast*

scrap [skræp] **1** *noun* **(a)** waste materials; *to sell a car for scrap*; **scrap heap** = heap of rubbish; *that car's only good for the scrap heap* **(b)** little piece; *they found a scrap of paper in his coat pocket* **2** *verb* **(a)** to throw away as useless; *they had to scrap 10,000 spare parts because each one had a fault* **(b)** to give up, to stop working on a plan; *we've scrapped our plan to go to Greece* (NOTE: **scrapping - scrapped**)

scrape [skreɪp] *verb* **(a)** to scratch with a hard object which is pulled across a surface; *he fell off his bike and scraped his knee on the pavement* **(b)** to remove something from the surface of something; *she scraped the paint off the door*; *he scraped the porridge off the bottom of the pan*

scratch [skrætʃ] **1** *noun* **(a)** long wound on the skin; *put some antiseptic on the scratches on your leg* **(b)** long mark made by a sharp point; *I will never be able to cover up the scratches on the car door* (NOTE: plural is **scratches**) **2** *verb* **(a)** to rub a part of the body with your fingernails; *he scratched his head as he wondered what to do next*; *stop scratching - it will make your rash worse!* **(b)** to make a long wound on the skin; *his legs were scratched by the bushes along the path* **(c)** to make a mark with a sharp point; *I must paint the car where it has been scratched*

scream [skriːm] **1** *noun* loud cry of pain; *you could hear the screams of people inside the burning building* **2** *verb* to make loud cries; *people on the third floor were screaming for help*

screen [skriːn] **1** *noun* **(a)** flat panel which

acts as protection against draughts, fire, noise, etc.; *the nurse asked me to go behind a screen to take off my clothes* **(b)** flat glass surface on which a picture is shown; *I'll call the information up on the screen*; *our new TV has a very large screen* **(c)** flat white surface for projecting films or pictures; *they've opened a new cinema with four screens* **2** *verb* **(a)** to show a film in a cinema or on TV; *tonight's film will be screened half an hour later than advertised* **(b) to screen people for a disease** = to examine a lot of people to see if they have a disease; *all children in the area should be screened for cancer*

screw [skruː] **1** *noun* metal pin with a groove winding round it, which you twist to make it go into a hard surface; *I need some longer screws to go through this thick piece of wood* **2** *verb* **(a)** to attach with screws; *the picture was screwed to the wall* **(b)** to attach by twisting; *he filled up the bottle and screwed on the top*

screwdriver [ˈskruːdraɪvə] *noun* tool with a long handle and special end which is used for turning screws; *she tightened up the screws with a screwdriver*

scribble [ˈskrɪbl] *verb* **(a)** to make marks which don't have any meaning; *the kids have scribbled all over their bedroom walls* **(b)** to write badly in a hurry; *she scribbled a few notes in the train*

scrub [skrʌb] *verb* to clean by rubbing with soap and a brush; *scrub your fingernails to get rid of the dirt* (NOTE: **scrubbing - scrubbed**)

sculptor [ˈskʌlptə] *noun* person who makes figures or shapes out of clay, wood, metal or stone; *we visited the sculptor's studio and watched him working on his next statue*

sculpture [ˈskʌlptʃə] *noun* figure carved out of stone or wood, etc., or made out of metal or clay; *there is a sculpture of King Charles in the centre of the square*

sea [siː] *noun* area of salt water between continents or islands, but not as large as an ocean; *swimming in the sea is more exciting than swimming in a river*; *the sea's too rough for the ferries to operate*

seagull [ˈsiːgʌl] *noun* white bird that lives near the sea; *the ferry was followed by seagulls looking for food*; *we were woken by the cries of seagulls in the harbour*

seal [siːl] **1** *noun* large animal with short fur, which eats fish, living mainly near to or in the sea; *seals lay sunning themselves on the rocks* **2** *verb* to close something tight; *a box carefully sealed with sticky tape*; **sealed envelope** = envelope where the flap has been stuck down to close it

search [sɜːtʃ] **1** *noun* action of trying to find something; *they carried out a search for the missing children*; *I did a quick search on the Internet for references to Penang* (NOTE: plural is **searches**) **2** *verb* **(a)** to look very carefully to try to find something; *the police searched the house from top to bottom but still couldn't find any weapons* **(b)** *(computers)* **search and replace** = looking for words or phrases and replacing them automatically with other words or phrases

seaside [ˈsiːdsaɪd] *noun* land by the edge of the sea; *we always take the children to the seaside in August*; *seaside towns are empty in the winter*

season [ˈsiːzən] **1** *noun* **(a)** one of four parts of a year; *the four seasons are spring, summer, autumn, and winter* **(b)** part of the year when something usually happens; *the football season lasts from September to May*; *London is very crowded during the school holiday season* **2** *verb* to add herbs, spices, etc., to food; *the meat is seasoned with mint*

seat [siːt] **1** *noun* chair, something which you sit on; *he was sitting in the driver's seat*; *all the seats on the bus were taken so I had to stand*; **seat belt** = belt which you wear in a car or plane to stop you being hurt if there is an accident; *the only person who survived the crash had been wearing a seat belt*; *in*

Britain, the driver and front-seat passenger in a car have to wear seat belts **2** *verb* to have enough seats for; *the bus seats sixty*

seaweed ['si:wi:d] *noun* plant which grows in the sea; *the rocks are covered with seaweed*

second ['sekənd] **1** *noun* **(a)** one of sixty parts which make up a minute; *they said that the bomb would go off in twenty seconds* **(b)** very short time; *wait here - I'll be back in a second* **(c)** something or someone that comes after the first thing or person; *today is the second of March*; *the Great Fire of London took place when Charles the Second (Charles II) was king* **2** *adjective* **(a)** coming after the first and before the third; *February is the second month of the year*; *B is the second letter in the alphabet*; **the second century** = the period from 100AD to 199 **(b)** *(followed by a superlative)* only one other is more; *this is the second longest bridge in the world*

second-class ['sekənd 'klɑ:s] *adjective & adverb* **(a)** *(of travel, hotels, etc.)* less expensive and less comfortable than first-class; *I find second-class hotels are perfectly comfortable* **(b)** *(of mail service)* less expensive and slower than first-class; *send the letter second-class if it is not urgent*

secondary ['sekəndri] *adjective* which is not the most important, and comes after the first (or primary); **secondary school** = school for children after the age of 11 or 12

secret ['si:krət] **1** *adjective* hidden, not known by other people; *there is a secret door into the tower* **2** *noun* thing which is not known or which is kept hidden; *if I tell you a secret will you promise not to repeat it to anyone?*; **to keep a secret** = not to tell someone something which you know and no one else does

secretary ['sekrətri] *noun* person who writes letters, answers the phone, files documents, etc., for someone; *his secretary phoned to say he would be late* (NOTE: plural is **secretaries**)

section ['sekʃn] *noun* part of something which, when joined to other parts, goes to make up a whole; *I read it in the financial section of a newspaper*; *he works in a completely different section of the building from me*

secure [sɪ'kju:ə] *adjective* **(a)** firmly fixed; *don't step on that ladder, it's not secure* **(b)** **secure job** = job which you are sure to keep for a long time

securely [sɪ'kju:əli] *adverb* in a secure way; *she tied the dog securely to a fence*

see [si:] *verb* **(a)** to use your eyes to notice; *can you see that tree in the distance?*; *they say that eating carrots helps you to see in the dark* **(b)** to watch a film, etc.; *I don't want to go to the cinema this week, I've seen that film twice already* **(c)** to understand; *I can't see why you need to borrow so much money*; *I see - they want me to help them* **(d)** to visit a lawyer, doctor, etc.; *if your tooth hurts you should see a dentist* (NOTE: **sees - seeing - saw** [sɔ:] **- has seen** [si:n])

see off ['si: 'ɒf] *verb* to go to the airport or station with someone who is leaving on a journey; *the whole family went to see her off at the airport*

see through ['si: 'θru:] *verb* to see from one side of something to the other; *I can't see through the windscreen - it's so dirty*

see to ['si: 'tu:] *verb* to arrange, to make sure that something is done; *can you see to it that the children are in bed by nine o'clock?*

seed [si:d] *noun* **(a)** part of a plant which is formed after the flowers die and from which a new plant will grow; *sow the seeds in fine earth*; *she bought a packet of parsley seed*; *can you eat melon seeds?* **(b)** *(in tennis)* player selected as one of the best players in a series of games; *she's the top women's seed*

seek [si:k] *verb (formal)* to look for; *the police are seeking a group of teenagers who were in the area when the attack took place* (NOTE: **seeking - sought** [sɔ:t] **- has sought**)

seem [si:m] *verb* to look as if; *she seems to like her new job*; *everyone seemed to be* having a good time at the party; *it seemed strange to us that no one answered the phone*

seen [si:n] *see* SEE

seesaw ['si:sɔ:] *noun* plank with seats at each end, balanced in the middle, so that when one end goes down the other goes up; *the seesaw won't work properly because you're heavier than me*

seize [si:z] *verb* to grab something and hold it tight; *she seized the bag of sweets in both hands and would not let go*

seldom ['seldəm] *adverb* not often; *I seldom get invited to parties*

select [sɪ'lekt] *verb* to choose carefully; *he was selected for the England team; selected items are reduced by 25%*

selection [sɪ'lekʃn] *noun* (a) range; *we have a huge selection of hats to choose from* (b) thing which has (or things which have) been chosen; *here is a selection of French cheeses*

self [self] *noun* your own person or character; *she's not her usual happy self today - I think she's worrying about something*

selfish ['selfɪʃ] *adjective* doing things only for yourself and not for other people; *don't be so selfish - pass the box of chocolates round*

sell [sel] *verb* to give something to someone for money; *he sold his house to my father; we managed to sell the car for £500* (NOTE: do not confuse with **cell**. Note also: **selling - sold** [səʊld])

semicolon ['semikəʊlən] *noun* punctuation mark (;) used to separate two parts of a sentence, and also used to show a pause; *you can put a semicolon when you want to show a break in a sentence*

semi-detached house [semidɪ'tætʃt 'haʊs] *noun* house which is joined to another similar house on one side, but is not joined to a house on the other; *a street of 1930s semi-detached houses*

semi-final ['semi'faɪnəl] *noun* one of the last two matches in a competition, the winners of which go into the final game; *the two semi-finals will be held on the same day*

senate ['senət] *noun* upper house of the parliament in some countries, such as the United States; *she was first elected to the Senate in 1990*

send [send] *verb* (a) to make someone or something go from one place to another; *my mother sent me to the shops to buy some bread; I was sent home from school because I had a headache* (b) to use the mail services; *send me a postcard when you get to Russia; send the letter airmail if you want it to arrive next week* (NOTE: **sending - sent** [sent])

send for ['send 'fɔ:] *verb* to ask someone to come; *he collapsed and we sent for the doctor*

senior ['si:njə] *adjective* (a) older; *the senior members of the family sat together*; **senior citizen** = old retired person (b) more important in rank, etc.; **senior manager** = manager who has a higher rank than other managers

sensation [sen'seɪʃn] *noun* (a) general feeling; *I felt a curious sensation as if I had been in the room before* (b) physical feeling; *she had a burning sensation in her arm* (c) thing or person that causes great excitement; *the new ballet was the sensation of the season*

sense [sens] *noun* (a) one of the five ways in which you notice something (sight, hearing, smell, taste, touch); *dogs have a good sense of smell* (b) being sensible; *in the end, someone showed some sense and tried to open a window*

make sense *verb* (a) to be understood; *the message doesn't make sense* (b) to be a good idea; *it makes sense to put a little money into your savings account every week*

sensible ['sensɪbl] *adjective* showing good sense; *staying indoors was the sensible thing to do*

sensitive ['sensɪtɪv] *adjective* (a) with keen feelings, easily hurt; *some people are extremely sensitive to criticism; if you have very sensitive skin use plenty of sun cream*

(b) which measures very accurately; *we need a more sensitive thermometer*

sent [sent] *see* SEND

sentence ['sentəns] **1** *noun* **(a)** words put together to make a complete statement, usually ending in a full stop; *I don't understand the second sentence in your letter* **(b)** decision by a court to punish someone; *he was given a six-month prison sentence* **2** *verb* to give someone an official legal punishment; *she was sentenced to three weeks in prison*

separate 1 *adjective* ['sepərət] not together, not attached to something; *the house has one bathroom with a separate toilet* **2** *verb* ['sepəreɪt] **(a)** to divide; *the teacher separated the class into two groups* **(b)** to keep apart; *the police tried to separate the two gangs*

September [sep'tembə] *noun* ninth month of the year, between August and October; *the weather is usually good in September*; *her birthday is in September*; *we always try to take a short holiday in September*

sequence ['siːkwəns] *noun* series of things which happen or follow one after the other; *we're trying to work out the sequence of events which led to the accident*

sergeant ['sɑːdʒənt] *noun* rank in the army or the police; *a police sergeant arrested him*; *Sergeant Jones drilled the new soldiers*

serial ['sɪəriəl] **1** *adjective* in a series; **serial killer** = person who has committed several murders, one after the other **2** *noun* radio or TV play which is presented in several instalments; *an Australian police serial* (NOTE: do not confuse with **cereal**)

series ['siːriz] *noun* **(a)** group of things which come one after the other in order; *we had a series of phone calls from the bank* **(b)** TV or radio programmes which are broadcast at the same time each week; *there's a new wildlife series starting this week* (NOTE: plural is **series**)

serious ['sɪəriəs] *adjective* **(a)** not funny; not a joke; *stop laughing - it's a very serious*

problem **(b)** important and possibly dangerous; *there was a serious accident on the motorway*; *the storm caused serious damage* **(c)** carefully planned; *he is making serious attempts to find another job*

seriously ['sɪəriəsli] *adverb* **(a)** in a serious way; *you should laugh more - don't always take things so seriously* **(b)** badly; *her mother is seriously ill*

servant ['sɜːvənt] *noun* person who is paid to work for a family; *they employ two servants in their London home*

serve [sɜːv] *verb* **(a)** to give food or drink to someone; *she served the soup in small bowls*; *take a plate and serve yourself from the dishes on the table* **(b)** to bring food or drink to someone at table; *which waitress is serving this table?*; *I can't serve six tables at once* **(c)** to go with a dish, etc.; *fish is served with a white sauce*; *you should serve red wine with meat* **(d)** to help a customer in a shop, etc.; *the manager served me himself*; *I waited ten minutes before being served* **(e)** *(in games like tennis)* to start a game by hitting the ball; *she is serving to win the match*

service ['sɜːvɪs] **1** *noun* **(a)** time when you work for a company, or organization, or in the armed forces; *she did six years' service in the police* **(b)** serving or helping someone in a shop or restaurant; *the food is good here, but the service is very slow*; **room service** = arrangement in a hotel for food or drink to be served in your bedroom **(c)** regular check of a machine; *the car has had its 20,000-kilometre service* **(d)** group of people working together; **the civil service** = the organization which runs a country, and its staff; **the health service** = doctors, nurses, hospitals, etc., all taken as a group; *we have the best health service in the world* **(e)** providing something which the public needs; *our train service to London is very reliable*; *the mail service is not very efficient* **(f)** religious ceremony; *my mother never misses the nine o'clock service on Sundays* **(g)** *(in tennis)* action of hitting the ball first; *she has a very powerful service* **2** *verb* to keep a machine in good working order; *the car needs to be serviced every six months*

serviette [sɜːviˈet] *noun* square piece of cloth or paper used to protect clothes and wipe your mouth at meals; *he tucked a large white serviette into his collar before starting to eat spaghetti*

session [ˈseʃn] *noun* time when something is taking place; **practice session** = time when a tennis player, etc., practises; **training session** = time when you are training

set [set] **1** *noun* **(a)** group of things which go together, which are used together or which are sold together; *he carries a set of tools in the back of his car*; *the six chairs are sold as a set*; *a tea set* = cups, saucers, plates, teapot, etc., **(b) TV set** = piece of electrical equipment which shows TV pictures; *they have bought a new 20-inch colour set* **2** *verb* **(a)** to put in a special place; **to set the table** = to put the knives, forks, plates, glasses, cups, etc., in their right places on the table **(b)** to fix; *when we go to France we have to set our watches to French time* **(c)** to become solid; *don't walk on the path until the concrete has set* **(d)** to make something happen; *he went to sleep smoking a cigarette and set the house on fire*; *all the prisoners were set free* **(e)** to go down; *the sun rises in the east and sets in the west*

set off [ˈset ˈɒf] *verb* **(a)** to begin a trip; *we're setting off for Germany tomorrow* **(b)** to start something working; *if you touch the wire it will set off the alarm*

set out [ˈset ˈaʊt] *verb* to begin a journey; *we set out to cross the mountains at 7.30*

settee [səˈtiː] *noun* sofa, a long seat with a soft back where several people can sit; *I just want to lie down on the settee and read a book*

setting [ˈsetɪŋ] *noun* background for a story; *the setting for the story is Hong Kong in 1935*

settle [ˈsetl] *verb* **(a)** to arrange, to agree; to end (an argument); *well, I'm glad everything's settled at last* **(b)** to place yourself in a comfortable position; *she switched on the television and settled in her favourite armchair* **(c)** to fall to the ground, to the bottom and stay there; *it snowed, but the snow didn't settle*

settle down [ˈsetl ˈdaʊn] *verb* **(a)** to place yourself in a comfortable position; *after dinner, she likes to settle down in a comfortable chair with a good book* **(b)** to change to a calmer way of life without many changes of house or much travelling; *she had lots of boyfriends, and then got married and settled down in Surrey*

seven [ˈsevən] number 7; *she's seven (years old) next week*; *the train is supposed to leave at seven (o'clock)*

seventeen [sevənˈtiːn] number 17; *he will be seventeen (years old) next month*; *the train leaves at seventeen sixteen (17.16)*; **the seventeen hundreds (1700s)** = the years from 1700 to 1799 (compare with the 'seventeenth century')

seventeenth (17th) [sevənˈtiːnθ] *adjective & noun today is October the seventeenth or the seventeenth of October (October 17th); Q is the seventeenth letter of the alphabet; it's his seventeenth birthday next week*; **the seventeenth century** = the years from 1600 to 1699 (compare with the 'seventeen hundreds')

seventh (7th) [ˈsevənθ] *adjective & noun his office is on the seventh floor; what is the seventh letter of the alphabet?; the seventh of July or July the seventh (July 7th); Henry the Seventh (Henry VII)*

seventieth (70th) [ˈsevəntiəθ] *adjective & noun don't forget tomorrow is your grandmother's seventieth birthday*

seventy [ˈsevənti] number 70; *she will be seventy (years old) on Tuesday*; *that shirt cost him more than seventy dollars*; *she's in her seventies* = she is between 70 and 79 years old; **the nineteen seventies (1970s)** = the years from 1970 to 1979

several ['sevrəl] *adjective & pronoun* more than a few, but not a large number; *several buildings were damaged in the storm; I've met her several times; several of the students are going to Italy*

severe [sə'vɪə] *adjective* **(a)** very strict, not kind; *he was very severe with any child who did not behave* **(b)** *(illness, weather, etc.)* very bad; *the severe weather has closed several main roads; she had a severe attack of flu* (NOTE: **severer - severest**)

sew [səʊ] *verb* to attach, make or mend by using a needle and thread; *the button's come off my shirt - can you sew it back on?* (NOTE: do not confuse with **sow**; note also: **sewing - sewed - sewn** [səʊn])

sewer ['suə] *noun* large pipe which takes waste water and refuse away from a building; *the main sewer runs underneath the road*

sewing machine ['səʊɪŋ mə'ʃiːn] *noun* machine which sews; *did you use a sewing machine to make your dress?*

sex [seks] *noun* one of two groups (male and female) into which animals and plants can be divided; *they've had a baby, but I don't know what sex it is;* **the opposite sex** = people of the other sex to yours (ie, men to women, women to men)

shabby ['ʃæbi] *adjective* poor, worn (clothes); *he wore a shabby coat with two buttons missing* (NOTE: **shabbier - shabbiest**)

shade [ʃeɪd] **1** *noun* **(a)** how dark or light a colour is; *her hat is a light shade of green* **(b)** dark place which is not in the sunlight; *the sun's so hot that we'll have to sit in the shade* **(c)** bright coloured cover put over a lamp; *I don't like the bright orange shade you bought* **2** *verb* to protect something from sunlight; *she shaded her eyes against the sun; the old birch tree shades that corner of the garden*

shadow ['ʃædəʊ] *noun* dark place behind an object where light is cut off by the object; *in the evening, the trees threw long shadows across the lawn; she saw his shadow move down the hall*

shaft [ʃɑːft] *noun* **(a)** long handle of a spade, etc.; *the shaft of the spade was so rotten that it snapped in two* **(b)** thin beam of light; *tiny particles of dust dancing in a shaft of sunlight* **(c)** deep hole or big tube; *the air shaft had become blocked;* **lift shaft** = tube inside a building in which a lift moves up and down

shake [ʃeɪk] **1** *verb* to move something from side to side or up and down; *shake the bottle before pouring;* **to shake your head** = to move your head from side to side to mean 'no'; *when I asked my dad if I could borrow the car he just shook his head* (NOTE: **shaking - shook** [ʃʊk] **- has shaken**) **2** *noun* **milk shake** = drink made by mixing milk and sweet juice; *he drank two chocolate milk shakes*

shake hands ['ʃeɪk 'hændz] *verb* **to shake hands** or **to shake someone's hand** = to hold someone's hand to show you are pleased to meet them or to show that an agreement has been reached; *he shook hands with me; the visitors shook hands and the meeting started*

shall [ʃæl] *verb used with other verbs* **(a)** *(to make the future)* *we shall be out on Saturday evening; tomorrow we shan't be home until after 10 o'clock* **(b)** *(to show a suggestion)* *shall I phone them?*

shallow ['ʃæləʊ] *adjective* not deep, not far from top to bottom; *children were playing in the shallow end of the pool; the river is so shallow in summer that you can walk across it* (NOTE: **shallower - shallowest**)

shame [ʃeɪm] *noun* **(a)** feeling caused by having done something which you should not have done; *to my shame, I did nothing to help* **(b)** **what a shame!** = how sad; *what a shame you couldn't come to the party!; it's a shame to have to go to work on such a beautiful sunny day*

shampoo [ʃæm'puː] **1** *noun* **(a)** liquid soap for washing hair, carpets, cars, etc.; *there are little bottles of shampoo in the bathroom* **(b)**

action of washing the hair; *she went to the hairdresser's for a shampoo* **2** *verb* to wash your hair, a carpet, a car, etc., with liquid soap; *the hairdresser shampooed her hair, and then cut it* (NOTE: **shampooing - shampooed**)

shan't [ʃɑːnt] = SHALL NOT

shape [ʃeɪp] *noun* form of how something looks; *she's got a ring in the shape of a letter S*

share [ˈʃeə] **1** *noun* part of something that is divided between two or more people; *did he get his share of the prize?* **2** *verb* **(a)** to divide up something among several people; *let's share the bill* **(b) to share something with someone** = to allow someone to use something which you also use; *he doesn't like sharing his toys with other children* **(c)** to use something which someone else also uses; *we shared a taxi to the airport*

shark [ʃɑːk] *noun* large dangerous fish which can kill people; *the guards shouted when a shark was spotted in the water*

sharp [ʃɑːp] **1** *adjective* **(a)** with a good edge for cutting or pushing in; *the beach is covered with sharp stones*; *this knife is useless - it isn't sharp enough* **(b)** sudden, great or severe; *the road makes a sharp right-hand bend*; *we had a sharp frost last night* **(c)** bitter; *lemons have a very sharp taste* **(d)** very keen and sensitive; *he's pretty sharp at spotting mistakes* (NOTE: **sharper - sharpest**) **2** *adverb* **(a)** exactly; *the coach will leave the hotel at 7.30 sharp* **(b)** suddenly, making a tight turn; *the road turned sharp right*

sharpen [ˈʃɑːpən] *verb* to make something sharp; *I must sharpen my pencil*

shave [ʃeɪv] **1** *noun* act of cutting off the hair on your face; *he went to have a shave at the men's hairdresser's next to the hotel* **2** *verb* **(a)** to cut off the hair on your face; *he cut himself shaving* **(b)** to cut off the hair on your head or legs, etc.; *I didn't recognize him with his head shaved*

she [ʃiː] *pronoun referring to a female*

person, a female animal, and sometimes to cars, ships and countries; *she's my sister*; *she and I are going on holiday to France together*; *she's a sweet little cat, but she's no good at catching mice*

shears [ˈʃɪəz] *noun* very large scissors, used for gardening, cutting wool off sheep, etc.; *he's cutting the hedge with the shears*

shed [ʃed] **1** *noun* small wooden building; *she's in the garden shed putting flowers into pots* **2** *verb* **(a)** to lose something which you are carrying or wearing; *in autumn, the trees shed their leaves as soon as the weather turns cold* **(b)** to let blood, tears, etc., flow; *she shed tears when her hamster died* (NOTE: **shedding - shed**)

she'd [ʃiːd] = SHE HAD, SHE WOULD

sheep [ʃiːp] *noun* common farm animal, which gives wool and meat; *a flock of sheep*; *the sheep are in the field*

sheer [ˈʃɪə] **1** *adjective* **(a)** complete; *it was sheer bad luck that a policeman happened to walk past just as she threw a brick through the shop window* **(b)** very steep; *there are sheer cliffs all along the coast*

sheet [ʃiːt] *noun* **(a)** large piece of thin cloth which is put over a bed (you put two of them on a bed, one to lie on, and one to cover you); *she changed the sheets on the bed* **(b)** large flat piece of paper, cardboard, metal, ice, etc.; *can you give me another sheet of paper?*

shelf [ʃelf] *noun* flat piece of wood attached to a wall or in a cupboard on which things can be put; *he put up some shelves in the kitchen*; *can you reach me down the box from the top shelf?* (NOTE: plural is **shelves** [ʃelvz])

shell [ʃel] *noun* **(a)** hard outside part covering some animals; *the children spent hours collecting shells on the beach* **(b)** hard outside part of an egg or a nut; *I found a big piece of shell in my scrambled eggs* **(c)** metal tube like a small bomb, which is fired from a gun; *a shell landed on the president's palace*

she'll [ʃiːl] = SHE WILL

shelter [ˈʃeltə] **1** *noun* **(a)** thing which protects; *we stood in the shelter of a tree waiting for the rain to stop*; **to take shelter** = to go somewhere for protection; *when the soldiers started to shoot we all took shelter behind a wall* **(b)** construction where you can go for protection; **bus shelter** = little building with a roof where you can wait for a bus **2** *verb* to go somewhere for protection; *sheep were sheltering from the snow beside the hedge*

shelves [ʃelvz] *noun see* SHELF

shepherd [ˈʃepəd] *noun* man who looks after sheep; **shepherd's pie** = minced meat cooked in a dish with a layer of mashed potatoes on top (also called 'cottage pie')

sheriff [ˈʃerɪf] *noun* American county police officer; *the sheriff of Orange County*

she's [ʃiːz] = SHE HAS, SHE IS

shield [ʃiːld] **1** *noun* large piece of flat material held in one hand, carried by soldiers, policemen, etc., to protect themselves; *the policemen were bent down behind their plastic shields* **2** *verb* to protect from danger, from attack; *he tried to shield her from the wind*

shift [ʃɪft] **1** *verb* to move; to change position or direction; *we've shifted the television from the kitchen into the dining room* **2** *noun* period of time during which one group of workers works before being replaced by another group; *the night shift starts at 10.00 p.m.*

shin [ʃɪn] *noun* front part of your leg below the knee; *he scraped his shin climbing over the wall*

shine [ʃaɪn] *verb* **(a)** to be bright with light; *the sun is shining and they say it'll be hot today*; *she polished the table until it shone*; *why do cats' eyes shine in the dark?* **(b)** to make light fall on something; *he shone his torch into the well* (NOTE: **shining - shone** [ʃɒn])

shiny [ˈʃaɪni] *adjective* which shines; *the book has a shiny cover*; *he drove up in his*

new and very shiny car (NOTE: **shinier - shiniest**)

ship [ʃɪp] **1** *noun* large boat for carrying passengers and cargo on the sea; *she's a fine ship*; *the first time we went to the United States, we went by ship* **2** *verb* to send goods (or people) but not always on a ship; *we ship goods all over the country* (NOTE: **shipping - shipped**)

shirt [ʃɜːt] *noun* light piece of clothing which you wear on the top part of your body under a pullover or jacket; *the teacher wore a blue suit and a white shirt*; *it's so hot that the workers in the fields have taken their shirts off*

shiver [ˈʃɪvə] *verb* to tremble with cold, fear, etc.; *he was coughing and shivering, so the doctor told him to stay in bed*

shock [ʃɒk] **1** *noun* **(a)** sudden, usually unpleasant, surprise; *it gave me quite a shock when you walked in*; *he'll get a nasty shock when he hears the news* **(b)** **electric shock** = sudden pain when an electric current goes through your body; *I got a shock when I touched the back of the TV set* **2** *verb* to give someone a sudden unpleasant surprise; *the conditions in the hospital shocked the inspectors*

shocking [ˈʃɒkɪŋ] *adjective* very unpleasant, which gives a sudden surprise; *it is shocking that no one offered to help*

shoe [ʃuː] *noun* piece of clothing which is worn on your foot; *she's bought a new pair of shoes*; *he put his shoes on and went out*

shone [ʃɒn] *see* SHINE

shook [ʃʊk] *see* SHAKE

shoot [ʃuːt] **1** *noun* little new growth of a plant, growing from a seed or from a branch; *one or two green shoots are already showing where I sowed my lettuces* **2** *verb* **(a)** to fire a gun; *soldiers were shooting into the woods* **(b)** to hit or kill by firing a gun; *one of the robbers was shot by a policeman when he tried to run away* **(c)** to go very fast; *when the* *bell rang she shot down the stairs* **(d)** to aim a ball at the goal; *he shot, but the ball bounced off the post* (NOTE: **shoots - shooting - shot** [ʃɒt])

shop [ʃɒp] **1** *noun* **(a)** place where you can buy things; *quite a few shops are open on Sundays*; *the sweet shop is opposite the fire station*; *the shop assistant was no help when I bought my camera - he didn't know how it worked* **2** *verb* to look for and buy things in shops; *she's out shopping for his birthday present*; *they went shopping in Oxford Street* (NOTE: **shopping - shopped**)

shopkeeper [ˈʃɒpkiːpə] *noun* person who owns a shop; *naturally the small shopkeepers were annoyed when the supermarket opened in the High Street*

shopping [ˈʃɒpɪŋ] *noun* **(a)** buying things in a shop; *we do all our shopping at the weekend*; **shopping bag** = bag for carrying your shopping in **(b)** things which you have bought in a shop; *put all your shopping on the table*

shore [ʃɔː] *noun* land at the edge of the sea or a lake; *she stood on the shore waving as the boat sailed away*

short [ʃɔːt] *adjective* **(a)** *(size, length)* not long; *have you got a short piece of wire?* **(b)** *(distance)* not far; *she only lives a short distance away* **(c)** *(period of time)* not long; *we had a short holiday in June* **(d)** *(height)* not tall; *he is only 1m 40 - much shorter than his brother* **(e)** **short for** = written or spoken with fewer letters than usual; *Ltd is short for Limited* (NOTE: **shorter - shortest**)

shorts [ʃɔːts] *noun* short trousers for men or women, that come down to above the knees; *he was wearing a pair of green running shorts*

shot [ʃɒt] **1** *noun* **(a)** action of shooting; the sound of shooting; *the police fired two shots at the car*; *a neighbour said she'd heard a shot* **(b)** kick to try to score a goal; *he kicked but his shot was stopped by the goalkeeper* **2** *verb see* SHOOT

should [ʃʊd] *verb used with other verbs* **(a)** *(used in giving advice or warnings, saying what is the best thing to do)* *you should go to the doctor if your cough gets worse*; *she shouldn't eat so much if she's trying to lose weight* **(b)** *(used to say what you expect to happen)* *if you leave now you should be there by 4 o'clock* **(c)** *(past of 'shall')* *I suggested we should go to an Indian restaurant*

shoulder [ˈʃəʊldə] *noun* **(a)** part of the body at the top of the arm; *look over your shoulder, he's just behind you* **(b)** part of a piece of clothing which covers the top of the arm; *a captain has three stars on his shoulders*

shout [ʃaʊt] **1** *noun* loud cry; *she gave a shout and dived into the water* **2** *verb* to make a loud cry, to speak very loudly; *I had to shout to the waitress to get served*

shove [ʃʌv] **1** *noun* sudden push; *she gave the car a shove and it started to roll down the hill* **2** *verb* to push roughly; *he shoved the papers into his pocket*; *stop shoving - there's no more room on the bus*

shovel [ˈʃʌvl] **1** *noun* wide spade with a round blade; *the workmen picked up shovels and started to clear the pile of sand* **2** *verb* to lift up with a shovel; *they were shovelling sand into the truck*

show [ʃəʊ] **1** *noun* **(a)** exhibition, things which are displayed for people to look at; *she has entered her two cats for the local cat show* **(b)** something which is on at a theatre; *the show starts at 7.30, so let's have dinner early* **2** *verb* **(a)** to let someone see something; *he wanted to show me his holiday photos*; *you don't have to show your passport when you're travelling in Europe* **(b)** to point something out to someone; *show me where the accident happened*; *he asked me to show him the way to the railway station* **(c)** to be seen, to be obvious; *her rash has almost disappeared and hardly shows at all* (NOTE: **showing - showed - has shown** [ʃəʊn])

show off [ˈʃəʊ ˈɒf] *verb* **(a)** to show how you think you are much better than other people; *don't watch her dancing about like that - she's just showing off* (b) to display something you are proud of; *he drove past with the radio on very loud, showing off his new car*

show over or **show round** [ˈʃəʊ ˈəʊvə or ˈʃəʊ ˈraʊnd] *verb* to lead a visitor round a place; *he showed the students round his laboratory*

show up [ˈʃəʊ ˈʌp] *verb (informal)* to come; *we invited all our friends to the picnic but it rained and only five of them showed up*

shower [ˈʃaʊə] *noun* (a) short fall of rain, snow, etc.; *in April there's usually a mixture of sunshine and showers* (b) device in a bathroom for sending out a spray of water to wash your whole body; **shower curtain** = curtain around a shower to prevent the water going everywhere (c) bath taken in a spray of water from over your head; *she went up to her room and had a shower*

shown [ʃəʊn] *see* SHOW

shrank [ʃræŋk] *see* SHRINK

shred [ʃred] **1** *noun* strip torn off something; *she tore his newspaper to shreds* **2** *verb* (a) to tear (paper) into thin strips, which can then be thrown away or used as packing material; *they sent a pile of old documents to be shredded* (b) to cut into very thin strips; *add a cup of shredded carrot* (NOTE: **shredding - shredded**)

shrimp [ʃrɪmp] *noun* little sea animal with many legs and a tail; *the children spent the afternoon fishing for shrimps in the rock pools*

shrink [ʃrɪŋk] *verb* to get smaller; *my shirt has shrunk in the wash* (NOTE: **shrank** [ʃræŋk] - **shrunk** [ʃrʌŋk])

shrivel [ˈʃrɪvl] *verb* to make or become dry and wrinkled; *you should water that plant - it's leaves are starting to shrivel*

shrug [ʃrʌg] *verb* **to shrug your shoulders** = to move your shoulders up to show you are not sure, not interested, etc.; *when I asked him what he thought about it all, he just shrugged*

his shoulders and walked off (NOTE: shrugging - shrugged)

shrunk [ʃrʌŋk] *see* SHRINK

shuffle [ˈʃʌfl] *verb* (a) to walk dragging your feet along the ground; *he shuffled into the room in his slippers* (b) to mix the playing cards before starting a game; *she shuffled and dealt us five cards each*

shut [ʃʌt] **1** *adjective* closed, not open; *some shops are shut on Sundays, but most big stores are open*; *we tried to get into the museum but it was shut* **2** *verb* (a) to close something which is open; *can you please shut the window - it's getting cold in here* (b) to close for business; *the restaurant shuts at midnight* (NOTE: **shutting - shut**)

shut in [ˈʃʌt ˈɪn] *verb* to lock inside; *the door closed suddenly and we were shut in*

shut out [ˈʃʌt ˈaʊt] *verb* (a) to lock outside; *I was shut out of the house because I'd left my keys inside* (b) to stop light getting inside; to stop people seeing a view; *those thick curtains should shut out the light*

shut up [ˈʃʌt ˈʌp] *verb* (a) to close something inside; *I hate being shut up indoors on a sunny day* (b) *(informal)* to stop talking; *tell those children to shut up - I'm trying to work*

shutter [ˈʃʌtə] *noun* (a) folding wooden or metal cover for a window; *close the shutters if the sunlight is too bright* (b) *(in a camera)* part which opens and closes very rapidly to allow the light to go on to the film; *he released the shutter and took the picture*

shy [ʃaɪ] *adjective* nervous and afraid to do something; *he's so shy he sat in the back row and didn't speak to anyone*

sick [sɪk] *adjective* (a) ill, not well; *he's been sick for months*; *we have five staff off sick* (b) **to be sick** = to bring up partly digested food from your stomach into your mouth; *the last time I ate mushrooms I was sick all night*; **to feel sick** = to want to bring food up from the stomach into the mouth;

when I got up this morning I felt sick and went back to bed (c) **to be sick (and tired) of** = to have had too much of; *I'm sick of listening to all his complaints*

side [saɪd] **1** *noun* **(a)** one of the four parts which with the top and bottom make a solid object such as a box; *stand the box upright - don't turn it onto its side* **(b)** one of the two parts which with the front and back make a building; *the garage is attached to the side of the house* **(c)** one of the surfaces of something flat; *please write on both sides of the paper* **(d)** one of the edges of something; *our office is on the opposite side of the street to the bank*; *London Airport is on the west side of the city* **(e)** one of two parts separated by something; *in England cars drive on the left-hand side of the road* **(f)** sports team; *the local side was beaten 2 - 0* **(g)** part of the body between the top of the legs and the shoulder; *I can't sleep when I'm lying on my right side* **2** *adjective* which is at the side; *there is a side entrance to the shop*; **side road** = small road leading off a larger road

sideboard [ˈsaɪdbɔːd] *noun* large piece of furniture for holding plates, glasses, etc., made like a table with a cupboard underneath; *there was a bowl of fruit on the sideboard*

sidewalk [ˈsaɪdwɔːk] *noun US* hard path for pedestrians at the side of a road; *he stepped off the sidewalk and was hit by a bus*

sideways [ˈsaɪdweɪz] *adverb* **(a)** to the side; *take a step sideways and you will be able to see the castle* **(b)** from the side; *if you look at the post sideways you'll see how bent it is*

sigh [saɪ] **1** *noun* long deep breath, showing how sad you are; *she gave a deep sigh and put the phone down* **2** *verb* to breathe deeply showing you are sad, relieved, etc.; *he sighed and wrote out another cheque*

sight [saɪt] *noun* **(a)** one of the five senses, being able to see; *my grandfather's sight isn't very good any more* **(b)** thing you see, view; *he can't stand the sight of blood*; *the fog cleared and the mountains came into sight*;

they waved until the boat was out of sight **(c)** something (especially something famous) which you ought to see; *the guidebook lists the main tourist sights in Beijing*

sign [saɪn] **1** *noun* **(a)** movement of the hand which means something; *he made a sign to us to sit down* **(b)** drawing, notice, etc., which advertises something; *the shop has a big sign outside it saying 'for sale'; a 'no smoking' sign hung on the wall* **(c)** panel by the side of a road, giving instructions or warnings; *go straight on until you come to a sign pointing left, marked 'to the sea'* **(d)** something which shows something; *he should have arrived by now, but there's no sign of him* **(e)** printed character; *the pound sign (£) is only used with figures* **2** *verb* to write your name in a special way on a document to show that you have written it or that you have approved it; *the letter is signed by the head of college; a cheque is useless if it has not been signed*

signal [ˈsɪgnl] **1** *noun* **(a)** sign or movement which tells someone to do something; *I'll give you a signal to start playing 'Happy Birthday'* **(b)** device used to tell someone to do something; *the signal was at red so the train had to stop* **2** *verb* to make signs to tell someone to do something; *the driver signalled to show that he was turning right*

signature [ˈsɪgnətʃə] *noun* name written in a special way by someone to show that a document is genuine or has been accepted; *her signature doesn't look like her name at all*

silence [ˈsaɪləns] *noun* quiet, no noise; *I love the silence of the countryside at night*; *the crowd of tourists waited in silence in the church*

silent [ˈsaɪlənt] *adjective* not talking, not making any noise; *he kept silent for the whole meeting*; *this new washing machine is almost silent*

silk [sɪlk] *noun* cloth made from threads produced by caterpillars living in trees; *she was wearing a beautiful silk scarf*; *I bought some blue silk to make a dress*

silly ['sɪli] *adjective* stupid, not thinking; *don't be silly - you can't go to the party dressed like that!*; *she asked a lot of silly questions* (NOTE: sillier - silliest)

silver ['sɪlvə] **1** *noun* **(a)** precious white metal; *gold is worth more than silver* **(b) silver paper** = thin sheet of shiny metal which looks like silver, used for wrapping food in; *chocolate bars are wrapped in silver paper* **(c) silver (medal)** = medal given to someone who finishes in second place in a race or competition; *England won ten silver medals at the Olympics* **(d) silver wedding** = celebration when two people have been married for twenty-five years **2** *adjective* of a shiny white colour, like silver; *the car has been sprayed with silver paint*; *she wore silver shoes to match her handbag*

similar ['sɪmɪlə] *adjective* very alike but not quite the same; *the two cars are very similar in appearance*

simple ['sɪmpl] *adjective* **(a)** easy; *the machine is very simple to use*; *it turned out to be a simple job to open the safe* **(b)** ordinary, not very special, not complicated; *they had a simple meal of bread and soup* (NOTE: simpler - simplest)

simple interest ['sɪmpl 'ɪntrəst] *noun* interest calculated on the capital only, and not added to it (as opposed to 'compound interest')

simply ['sɪmpli] *adverb* **(a)** in a simple way; *he described very simply how the accident had happened* **(b)** only; *he did it simply to annoy everyone* **(c)** (to stress) *it's simply terrible - what shall we do?*

since [sɪns] **1** *preposition* during the period after; *she's been here since Monday*; *we've been working non-stop since four o'clock* **2** *conjunction* **(a)** during the period after; *since we got to the hotel, it has rained every day* **(b)** because; *since it's such a fine day, let's go for a walk* **3** *adverb* during the period until now; *she phoned on Sunday and we haven't heard from her since*

sincere [sɪn'sɪə] *adjective* which you really mean; *we send you our sincere best wishes for a very happy anniversary*

sincerely [sɪn'sɪəli] *adverb* really, truly; *he sincerely believes that if he phones her she will come immediately*; **Yours sincerely** US **Sincerely yours** = used as an ending to a letter addressed to a particular person

sing [sɪŋ] *verb* to make music with your voice; *she was singing as she worked*; *please sing another song*; *the birds were singing in the garden* (NOTE: singing - sang [sæŋ] - has sung [sʌŋ])

single ['sɪŋgl] **1** *adjective* **(a)** one alone; *there wasn't a single person I knew at the party* **(b)** for one person only; *have you got a single room for two nights, please?* **(c)** not married; *she's twenty-nine and still single* **(d) single ticket** = ticket for a journey in one direction only; *two single tickets cost more than a return* **(e) in single figures** = less than ten; *pay rises were over 20% but now are down to single figures* **2** *noun* **(a)** ticket for one journey; *two singles to Oxford Circus, please* **(b) singles** = tennis game played between two people; *the men's singles champion*

singular ['sɪŋgjʊlə] **1** *adjective* showing that there is only one thing or person; *'she' is a singular pronoun* **2** *noun* form of a word showing that there is only one; *'child' is the singular, and 'children' is the plural*

sink [sɪŋk] **1** *noun* fixed washbasin for washing dishes, etc., in a kitchen; *the sink was piled high with dirty dishes* **2** *verb* **(a)** to go down to the bottom (of water, mud, etc.); *the ferry sank in 30m of water* **(b)** to drop down suddenly; *she was so tired that she just sank into an armchair and closed her eyes* (NOTE: sinking - sank [sæŋk] - sunk [sʌŋk])

sip [sɪp] **1** *noun* little drink; *she took a sip of water, and went on talking* **2** *verb* to drink taking only a small amount of liquid at a time; *the girl was sipping her drink quietly* (NOTE: sipping - sipped)

sir [sɜː] *noun* **(a)** *(usually used by someone serving in a shop or restaurant)* polite way of referring to a man; *please come this way, sir* **(b)** *(in letters)* **Dear Sir** = polite way of addressing a man you do not know; **Dear Sirs** = polite way of addressing a company **(c)** title given to a knight (used with his Christian name); *good morning, Sir George*

siren ['saɪrən] *noun* device which makes a loud warning signal; *a police car raced past with its siren howling*

sister ['sɪstə] *noun* girl or woman who has the same father and mother as someone else; *my younger sister Louise works in a bank*

sit [sɪt] *verb* **(a)** to rest your bottom on something; *mother was sitting in bed eating her breakfast*; *there were no seats left, so we had to sit on the floor* **(b)** *(of bird)* to rest; *the pigeon always comes and sits on the fence when I'm sowing seeds* (NOTE: **sits - sitting - sat** [sæt] **- has sat**)

sit down ['sɪt 'daʊn] *verb* to sit on a seat; *come and sit down next to me*

sit up ['sɪt 'ʌp] *verb* **(a)** to sit with your back straight; *sit up straight!* **(b)** to move from a lying to a sitting position; *he sat up in bed to eat his breakfast* **(c)** to stay up without going to bed; *we sat up playing cards until 2 a.m.*

site [saɪt] *noun* **(a)** place where something is or will be; *this is the site for the new factory*; **camp site** = place where you can put up your tent **(b)** place where something happened, where something once existed; *we visited the site of the Battle of Hastings*

sitting room ['sɪtɪŋ 'ruːm] *noun* lounge, comfortable room for sitting in; *we spent the evening in the sitting room watching TV*

situation [sɪtjuːˈeɪʃn] *noun* **(a)** position, way in which someone is placed; *I wonder how she got herself into this situation* **(b)** place where something is; *the hotel is in a very pleasant situation by the sea*

six [sɪks] **(a)** number 6; *he's six (years old); there are only six chocolates left in the box -*

who's eaten the rest? **(b)** *(in cricket)* score of six runs made by sending the ball over the boundary without touching the ground; *he scored a century, including four fours and two sixes*

sixteen [sɪksˈtiːn] number 16; *he'll be sixteen next month*; *the train leaves at seventeen sixteen (17.16);* **the sixteen hundreds (1600s)** = the years from 1600 to 1699 (compare with the 'sixteenth century')

sixteenth (16th) [sɪksˈtiːnθ] *adjective & noun* *she came sixteenth in the race; her sixteenth birthday is on Tuesday; King Louis XVI ('King Louis the Sixteenth') was executed during the French Revolution;* **the sixteenth century** = the years from 1500 to 1599 (compare with the 'sixteen hundreds')

sixth (6th) [sɪksθ] *adjective & noun* *his office is on the sixth floor; what is the sixth letter of the alphabet?; tomorrow is her sixth birthday; King Edward VI ('King Edward the Sixth') was Henry VIII's son;* **sixth form** = top class in a school, with students between 16 and 18 years old

sixtieth (60th) ['sɪkstɪəθ] *adjective & noun* referring to sixty; *he was sixtieth out of 120 people who entered the race; a minute is a sixtieth of an hour and a second is a sixtieth of a minute*

sixty ['sɪksti] number 60; *she's sixty (years old); the table cost more than sixty pounds (£60); she's in her sixties* = she's between 60 and 69 years old; **the (nineteen) sixties (1960s)** = the years from 1960 to 1969

size [saɪz] *noun* measurements of something, of how big something is; *their garage is about the same size as our house; he takes size ten in shoes*

sizzle ['sɪzl] *verb* to make a sound like food cooking in oil or fat; *the sausages were sizzling in the pan*

skate [skeɪt] **1** *noun* **a pair of skates** = a pair of boots with sharp blades attached underneath for sliding on ice **2** *verb* to move on ice wearing skates; *she skated across the frozen lake*

skateboard [ˈskeɪtbɔːd] *noun* board with two pairs of wheels underneath, which you stand on to move about; *put your knee pads on if you're going out on your skateboard*

skeleton [ˈskelɪtn] *noun* all the bones which make up a body; *they found the skeleton of a rabbit in the garden shed*

sketch [sketʃ] **1** *noun* quick rough drawing; *he made a sketch of the church* (NOTE: plural is **sketches**) **2** *verb* to make a quick rough drawing of something; *she was sketching the old church*

ski [skiː] **1** *noun* one of two long flat pieces of wood, etc., which are attached to your boots for sliding over snow; *someone stole my new pair of skis*; **ski boots** = boots to wear when skiing **2** *verb* to travel on skis; *we skied down to the bottom of the slope* (NOTE: **skis - skiing - skied**)

skid [skɪd] **1** *noun* sideways slide in a vehicle; *the car went into a skid and hit a lamppost* **2** *verb* to slide sideways in a vehicle suddenly because the wheels do not grip the surface; *if you brake too hard on ice you're likely to skid* (NOTE: **skidding - skidded**)

skiing [ˈskiːɪŋ] *noun* the sport of sliding on skis; *we go skiing every winter*; *she broke her arm on a skiing holiday*

skilful *US* **skillful** [ˈskɪlfʊl] *adjective* showing a lot of skill; *he's a very skilful artist*

skill [skɪl] *noun* being able to do something well; *painting portraits needs a lot of skill*

skim [skɪm] *verb* **(a)** to remove things floating on a liquid; *skim the soup to remove the fat on the surface* **(b)** to dash over the surface of something; *flies skimmed across the surface of the lake*; **to skim through a book** = to read a book quickly (NOTE: **skimming - skimmed**)

skin [skɪn] *noun* **(a)** outer surface of the body; *the baby's skin is very smooth* **(b)** outer surface of a fruit or vegetable; *this orange has a very thick skin*; *you can cook these new potatoes with their skins on*

skinny [ˈskɪni] *adjective (informal)* very thin; *a tall skinny guy walked in* (NOTE: **skinnier - skinniest**)

skip [skɪp] **1** *noun* large metal container for rubbish; *the builders filled the skip with old bricks and stones* **2** *verb* **(a)** to run along sometimes hopping and sometimes jumping; *the children skipped happily down the lane* **(b)** to jump over a rope which you turn over your head; *the boys played football and the girls were skipping* **(c)** to miss part of something; *I'm not hungry, I'll skip the pudding* (NOTE: **skipping - skipped**)

skipper [ˈskɪpə] *noun* **(a)** captain of a ship; *I told the skipper that there was water in the ship's engine room* **(b)** captain of a team; *he's the youngest skipper ever of the national rugby team*

skirt [skɜːt] *noun* piece of clothing worn by women covering the lower part of the body from the waist down; *she started wearing a skirt to work, but the boss told her she could wear jeans if she liked*

skull [skʌl] *noun* the bones which form the head, protecting the brain inside; *the X-ray showed he had a fracture of the skull*

sky [skaɪ] *noun* space above the earth which is blue during the day and where the moon and stars appear at night; *what makes the sky blue?*; *it's going to be a beautiful day - there's not a cloud in the sky*

skyscraper [ˈskaɪskreɪpə] *noun* very tall building; *they're planning to build a 80-storey skyscraper near the park*

slab [slæb] *noun* flat square block of stone, etc.; *a slab of concrete fell from the building*

slack [slæk] *adjective* **(a)** not tight; *the ropes are slack - pull on them to make them tight* **(b)** not busy; *business is slack at the end of the week* (NOTE: **slacker - slackest**)

slam [slæm] *verb* to bang a door to make it shut; *when he saw me, he slammed the door* *in my face* (NOTE: **slamming - slammed**)

slang [slæŋ] *noun* popular words or phrases used by certain groups of people but which are not used in correct style; *'banger' is slang for a sausage*

slant [slɑːnt] **1** *noun* slope; *the garden is on a slant, which makes cutting the lawn difficult* **2** *verb* to slope; *the path slants down the side of the hill*

slap [slæp] **1** *noun* blow given with your hand flat; *she gave him a slap in the face* **2** *verb* **(a)** to hit with your hand flat; *she slapped his face* **(b)** to tap in a friendly way; *they all slapped him on the back to congratulate him* (NOTE: **slapping - slapped**)

slate [sleɪt] *noun* **(a)** dark blue or grey stone which splits easily into thin sheets; *slate is used for making roofs* **(b)** thin piece of this stone used to cover a roof; *the slates were already piled up ready to be fixed on the roof*

sledge *US* **sled** [sledʒ] *noun* small vehicle with long strips of wood or metal underneath, for sliding fast over snow; *children dragged their sledges to the top of the hill*

sleek [sliːk] *adjective* smooth, shiny, which is looked after very well; *after dinner we walked across the sleek lawns to the river* (NOTE: **sleeker - sleekest**)

sleep [sliːp] **1** *noun* rest (usually at night) with your eyes closed, and when you are not conscious of what is happening; *I need eight hours' sleep a night*; *try to get a good night's sleep - there's a lot of work to be done tomorrow*; **to go to sleep** *or* **to get to sleep** = to start sleeping; *don't make all that noise - Daddy's trying to get to sleep* **2** *verb* to be asleep, to rest with your eyes closed not knowing what is happening around you; *she never sleeps for more than six hours each night*; *he slept through the whole of the TV news* (NOTE: **sleeps - sleeping - slept** [slept])

sleepy ['sliːpi] *adjective* feeling ready to go to sleep; *sitting in front of the TV made him sleepier and sleepier*; *if you feel sleepy, don't*

try to drive the car (NOTE: **sleepier - sleepiest**)

sleet [sliːt] *noun* snow mixed with rain; *the temperature fell and the rain turned to sleet*

sleeve [sliːv] *noun* part of a piece of clothing which covers your arm; *he was wearing a blue shirt with short sleeves*

sleigh [sleɪ] *noun* large sledge pulled by horses or reindeer; *at the ski village you can go out for sleigh rides*

slept [slept] *see* SLEEP

slice [slaɪs] **1** *noun* thin piece cut off something to eat; *can you cut some more slices of bread?*; *have a slice of chocolate cake* **2** *verb* to cut into slices; *she stood at the table slicing the chicken for lunch*; **sliced bread** = loaf of bread which has already been cut into slices before you buy it

slid [slɪd] *see* SLIDE

slide [slaɪd] **1** *noun* **(a)** metal or plastic structure for children to go down lying or sitting; *there are swings and a slide in the local playground* **(b)** small piece of film which can be projected on a screen; *she put the screen up and showed us the slides of her last trip* **2** *verb* to move without difficulty over an even surface; *the drawer slides in and out easily*; *the children were sliding on the ice when it broke* (NOTE: **sliding - slid** [slɪd])

slight [slaɪt] *adjective* not very big; *all you could see was a slight movement of the cat's tail*; *she wasn't the slightest bit nervous* (NOTE: **slighter - slightest**)

slightly ['slaɪtli] *adverb* not very much; *he was only slightly hurt in the car crash*

slim [slɪm] **1** *adjective* thin, not fat; *how do you manage to stay so slim?* (NOTE: **slimmer - slimmest**) **2** *verb* to diet in order to become thin; *she started slimming before her summer holidays* (NOTE: **slimming - slimmed**)

slime [slaɪm] *noun* slippery substance, which forms in ponds or on hard damp surfaces; *is there anything which will get this green slime off the path?*

slimy ['slaɪmi] *adjective* unpleasant and slippery; *what's this slimy mess at the bottom of the fridge?* (NOTE: slimier - slimiest)

sling [slɪŋ] **1** *noun* (a) type of leather loop, used for throwing stones; *David threw a stone with his sling, and killed Goliath* (b) bandage attached round your neck, used to support an injured arm; *he's going around with his arm in a sling* **2** *verb* to hold up or to put something to hang; *he slung his jacket over the back of his chair; she slung her bag over her shoulder* (NOTE: slinging - slung [slʌŋ])

slip [slɪp] **1** *noun* small piece of paper; *as she opened the book a slip of paper fell out* **2** *verb* (a) to slide (and fall) by mistake; *he slipped on the snow and dropped all his shopping* (b) to push something without being seen; *he slipped the keys into his pocket* (c) to go quickly; *I'll just slip down to the Post Office with this letter* (NOTE: slipping - slipped)

slippers ['slɪpəz] *noun* light comfortable shoes worn indoors; *he ran out into the street in his slippers*

slippery ['slɪpri] *adjective* so smooth that you can easily slip and fall; *watch out! the path's slippery*

slit [slɪt] **1** *noun* long cut or narrow opening; *she peered through a slit in the curtains* **2** *verb* to make a slit; *he slit open the envelope with a knife* (NOTE: slitting - slit)

slope [sləʊp] **1** *noun* surface or piece of ground which is not level, and rises or falls; *the land rises in a gentle slope to the church; they stopped halfway down the slope* **2** *verb* to go upwards or downwards; *the path slopes upwards*

slot [slɒt] **1** *noun* long thin hole; *a coin has got stuck in the slot of the parking meter* **2** *verb* to slot into = to fit into a slot; *the car radio slots easily into the space next to the clock* (NOTE: slotting - slotted)

slow [sləʊ] *adjective* (a) not fast; *luckily, the car was only going at a slow speed* (b) showing a time which is earlier than the right time; *the school clock is four minutes slow* (NOTE: slower - slowest)

slow down ['sləʊ 'daʊn] *verb* (a) to go more slowly; *the van had to slow down as it came to the traffic lights* (b) to make something go more slowly; *the snow slowed the traffic down on the motorway*

slowly ['sləʊli] *adverb* not fast; *luckily, the car was going very slowly when it hit the fence*

slug [slʌg] *noun* common garden animal like a snail with no shell; *slugs have eaten all my lettuces*

sly [slaɪ] *adjective* cunning and slightly dishonest; *the sly old girl - she never told me she had won the lottery*

smack [smæk] **1** *noun* hitting someone with your hand flat as a punishment; *if you pull the cat's tail you'll get a smack* **2** *verb* to punish someone by hitting with your hand flat; *she smacked the little girl for being rude*

small [smɔːl] *adjective* little, not big; *small cars use less petrol than large ones; these trousers are already too small for him; he's too small to ride a bike* (NOTE: smaller - smallest)

smart [smɑːt] **1** *adjective* (a) well-dressed; *he looked very smart in his uniform* (b) clever; *it was smart of her to note the car's number plate* (NOTE: smarter - smartest) **2** *verb* to hurt with a burning feeling; *the place where I burnt my hand is still smarting*

smash [smæʃ] *verb* (a) to break into pieces with a loud noise; *he dropped the plate and it smashed to pieces* (b) to break something to pieces; *demonstrators smashed the windows of police cars* (c) to break a record, to do better than a record; *six records were smashed at the Olympics* (d) to go with a lot of violence; *the crowd smashed through the railings* (NOTE: smashing - smashed)

smell [smel] **1** *noun* (a) one of the five senses, which you can feel through your nose; *these dogs have a very keen sense of smell* (b) something which you can sense with your nose; *I love the smell of coffee coming from the restaurant*; *he can't stand the smell of fried onions*; *there's a funny smell in the shed* **2** *verb* **(a)** to notice the smell of something; *can you smell gas?*; *I can smell fish and chips!* **(b)** to make a smell; *what's for dinner? - it smells very good!* **(c)** to bring your nose close to something to smell it; *she bent down to smell the roses* (NOTE: **smelling - smelled** *or* **smelt** [smelt])

smile [smaɪl] **1** *noun* way of showing that you are pleased, by turning your mouth up at the corners; *the dentist gave me a friendly smile* **2** *verb* to show that you are pleased by turning your mouth up at the corners; *everyone smile please - I'm taking a picture!*

smoke [sməuk] **1** *noun* white, grey or black cloud, given off by something that is burning; *the restaurant was full of cigarette smoke*; *clouds of smoke were pouring out of the upstairs windows* **2** *verb* **(a)** to breathe in smoke (from a cigarette, pipe, etc.); *she doesn't smoke much - only one or two cigarettes a day* **(b)** to give off smoke; *two days after the fire, the ruins of the factory were still smoking*

smooth [smu:ð] *adjective* **(a)** with an even surface; *the smooth surface of a polished table*; *velvet has a smooth side and a rough side* **(b)** with no sudden movements; *the plane made a very smooth landing* (NOTE: **smoother - smoothest**)

smother ['smʌðə] *verb* **(a)** to kill someone by stopping them from breathing; *they took the kittens away from the cat and smothered them* **(b)** to cover; *a chocolate cake simply smothered in cream*

smudge [smʌdʒ] **1** *noun* dirty mark; *there is a smudge on the top corner of the photograph* **2** *verb* to make a dirty mark, such as by rubbing ink which is not dry; *don't touch the paint until it's dry, otherwise you'll smudge it*

smug [smʌg] *adjective* happy with what you

have done; *he accepted his prize with a smug look on his face*

smuggle ['smʌgl] *verb* **(a)** to take goods into a country against the law; *they tried to smuggle cigarettes into the country* **(b)** to take something into or out of a place against the law; *the knives were smuggled into the prison by a someone visiting a prisoner*

snack [snæk] *noun* a light meal, a small amount of food; *we didn't have time to stop for a proper lunch, so we just had a snack on the motorway*

snag [snæg] *noun* little problem, thing which prevents you from doing something; *we've run into a snag: there are no flights to the island on Sundays*

snail [sneɪl] *noun* common little animal which lives in a shell and moves very slowly; *snails have eaten all the lettuces in the garden*

snake [sneɪk] *noun* long reptile which has no legs and moves along the ground by moving from side to side; *is this snake safe to handle?*; **snakes and ladders** = children's game, played with dice, in which landing on a ladder moves you forward and landing on a snake moves you back

snap [snæp] **1** *noun* **(a)** photograph taken quickly; *she showed me some old snaps of the house* **(b)** card game where you shout 'snap' if two similar cards are played at the same time; *do you want a game of snap?* **2** *adjective* sudden; **a snap decision** = a decision taken in a hurry; *they carried out a snap check of the passengers' luggage* **3** *verb* **(a)** to say something in a sharp angry tone; *he was tired after a long day in the office, and snapped at the children* **(b)** to break suddenly with a dry noise; *the branches snapped as he walked through the wood* (NOTE: **snapping - snapped**)

snarl [snɑ:l] **1** *noun* angry sound made by a wild animal; *as she opened the door of the cage she heard a snarl* **2** *verb* to make an angry sound; *the tiger snarled as he* *approached its cage*

snatch [snætʃ] *verb* to grab something quickly; *I didn't have time for a proper meal, but I snatched a sandwich*

sneak [sni:k] *verb* to go quietly without being seen; *she sneaked into the room*; **to sneak up on someone** = to creep up behind someone without being noticed

sneer ['snɪə] **1** *noun* unpleasant smile; *he held the axe in his hand and looked at her with a sneer* **2** *verb* to give someone a nasty smile or to speak in a way that shows that you don't approve; *he sneered at her attempts to speak French*

sneeze [sni:z] **1** *noun* automatic action to blow air suddenly out through your mouth and nose because the inside of your nose tickles; *coughs and sneezes spread diseases* **2** *verb* to make a sneeze; *the smell of roses makes me sneeze*; *he has hayfever and can't stop sneezing*

sniff [snɪf] **1** *noun* breathing in air through your nose; *the dog gave a sniff at the plate before licking it* **2** *verb* to breathe in air through your nose; *he sniffed and said 'I can smell fish and chips'*; *(informal)* **it's not to be sniffed at** = you should not refuse it; *a free ticket with Air Canada is not to be sniffed at*

snooker ['snu:kə] *noun* game for two players, played on a table with twenty-two balls of various colours; *would you like a game of snooker?*; *he's the world snooker champion*

snore [snɔ:] **1** *noun* loud noise in your nose and throat made by breathing air when you are asleep; *his snores kept her awake* **2** *verb* to make a snore; *I can't get to sleep because my husband snores*

snow [snəʊ] **1** *noun* water which falls as light white ice crystals in cold weather; *a metre of snow fell during the night*; *the highest mountains are always covered with snow* **2** *verb* to fall as snow; *look - it's started to snow!*; *it snowed all day, and the streets*

were blocked

snowball ['snəʊbɔ:l] *noun* ball of snow; *they were throwing snowballs at passing cars*

snowdrop ['snəʊdrɒp] *noun* bulb with little white flowers in the early spring; *we went for a walk to look at the snowdrops*

snowflake ['snəʊfleɪk] *noun* small piece of snow formed of a number of ice crystals; *large snowflakes soon covered the path*

snowman ['snəʊmæn] *noun* model of a man made of snow; *the children made a snowman in the school playground* (NOTE: plural is **snowmen**)

snug [snʌg] *adjective* warm, comfortable, out of the cold; *here we are, sitting by the fire, warm and snug*

snuggle ['snʌgl] *verb* to curl yourself up to be warm; *they snuggled under their blankets*

so [səʊ] **1** *adverb* **(a)** *(showing how much)* *it's so cold that the lake is covered with ice*; *the soup was so hot that I couldn't eat it* **(b)** also; *the children all caught flu, and so did their teacher* **(c)** *(showing that the answer is 'yes')* *does this train go to London? - I think so*; *will you be coming to the party? - I hope so!* **2** *conjunction* **(a)** and this is the reason why; *it was snowing hard so we couldn't go for a walk* **(b)** **so that** = in order that; *people riding bikes wear orange coats so that drivers can see them easily*

so far ['səʊ 'fɑ:] *adverb* until now; *he said he would lend me his book but so far he hasn't*

so what [səʊ 'wɒt] *phrase* what does it matter; *so what if I don't get through the exam, I can always take it again*

soak [səʊk] *verb* **(a)** to put something in a liquid for a time; *dry beans should be soaked in cold water for 24 hours* **(b)** to get or to make very wet; *I forgot my umbrella and got soaked* **(c)** **to soak up** = to absorb liquid; *the pudding has soaked up all the juice*

soap [səʊp] *noun* substance which you wash with, made from oils and with a pleasant smell; *there's no soap left in the bathroom*; *I've put a new bar of soap in the kitchen*

soar [sɔː] *verb* **(a)** to fly high up into the sky; *the rocket went soaring into the night sky* **(b)** to go up very quickly; *food prices soared during the cold weather* (NOTE: do not confuse with **sore**)

sob [sɒb] *verb* to cry, taking short breaths; *she lay sobbing on the bed* (NOTE: **sobbing - sobbed**)

soccer ['sɒkə] *noun* football; *he played soccer at school and then joined his local team*; *they went to a soccer match last Saturday*

social ['səʊʃl] *adjective* referring to people as a group; *this part of the town has very serious social problems*; **social services** = state services to help people with family problems; *the children are being looked after by social services*

society [sə'saɪəti] *noun* **(a)** a large group of people, usually all the people living in a country, considered together as a group; *we live in a free society* **(b)** club, group of people who have the same interests; *he belongs to the local drama society* (NOTE: plural is **societies**)

sock [sɒk] *noun* piece of clothing worn on your foot inside a shoe; *I've just bought a new pair of socks*; **knee socks** = long socks which go up as far as your knees

socket ['sɒkɪt] *noun* **electric socket** = device in a wall with holes into which a plug can be fitted; *this plug doesn't fit that socket*; **light socket** = part of a lamp where the bulb is fitted

sofa ['səʊfə] *noun* long comfortable seat with a soft back; *he went to sleep on the sofa*

soft [sɒft] *adjective* **(a)** not hard, which moves easily when pressed; *there are big soft armchairs in the hotel lounge* **(b)** not loud; *soft music was playing in the background* **(c)** not bright; *soft lights make a room look warm* (NOTE: **softer - softest**)

software ['sɒftweə] *noun* computer programs (as opposed to 'hardware', which is the machine itself); *what software do you use?*

soggy ['sɒgi] *adjective* wet and soft; *if you put tomato sandwiches into plastic bags they will go soggy* (NOTE: **soggier - soggiest**)

soil [sɔɪl] *noun* earth in which plants grow; *put some soil in the plant pot and then sow your flower seeds*

solar ['səʊlə] *adjective* referring to the sun; **solar energy** *or* **solar power** = electricity produced from the sun's rays; *our heating runs on solar power*; **solar system** = the sun and the planets which turn round it; *there are nine planets in the solar system*

sold [səʊld] *see* SELL

soldier ['səʊldʒə] *noun* person serving in the army; *here's a photograph of my father when he was a soldier*; *we were just in time to see the soldiers march past*

sole [səʊl] **1** *noun* **(a)** the underneath side of your foot; *he tickled the soles of her feet* **(b)** main underneath part of a shoe, but not the heel; *these shoes need mending - I've got holes in both soles* **(c)** small flat white sea fish; *he ordered grilled sole* (NOTE: do not confuse with **soul**) **2** *adjective* only; *she was the sole person to survive the crash*

solemn ['sɒləm] *adjective* **(a)** serious, when it would be wrong to laugh; *at the most solemn moment of the ceremony someone's mobile phone rang* **(b)** that should be treated as very serious; *he made a solemn promise never to smoke again*

solicitor [sə'lɪsɪtə] *noun* qualified lawyer who gives advice to members of the public and acts for them in legal matters; *I went to see my solicitor about making a will*

solid ['sɒlɪd] *adjective* **(a)** hard, not liquid; *the water in the tank had frozen solid* **(b)** firm, strong; *is the table solid enough to stand on?* **(c)** not hollow; *cricket is played with a solid ball* **(d)** made only of one material; *the box is made of solid silver*

solo ['səʊləʊ] **1** *noun* piece of music played or sung by one person alone; *she played a* *violin solo* (NOTE: plural is **solos**) **2** *adjective* done by one person alone; *she gave a solo performance in the Albert Hall*; *he crashed on his first solo flight*

solution [sə'luːʃn] *noun* (a) answer to a problem; *we think we have found a solution to the problem of where to stay on holiday* (b) mixture of a solid substance in a liquid; *wash your eye in a weak salt solution*

solve [sɒlv] *verb* to find an answer to; *he tried to solve the puzzle*

some [sʌm] *adjective & pronoun* (a) a certain number of; *some young drivers drive much too fast*; *some books were damaged in the fire*; *can you cut some more slices of bread?* (b) a certain amount of; *can you buy some bread when you go to town?* (c) *(followed by a singular noun)* referring to a person or thing which you do not know; *some man just knocked on the door and tried to sell me a magazine* (d) *(referring to a period of time or a distance)* quite a lot; *don't wait for me, I may be some time*

somebody *or* **someone** ['sʌmbədi *or* 'sʌmwɒn] *pronoun* a certain person; *I know someone who can fix your car*; **somebody else** *or* **someone else** = some other person, a different person; *she was ill, so someone else used her ticket*

somehow ['sʌmhaʊ] *adverb* by some means, although you don't know how; *somehow we must get back home by 6 o'clock*

someone ['sʌmwɒn] *see* SOMEBODY

somersault ['sʌməsɒlt] *noun* rolling over and over, head first; *he did a couple of somersaults on the mat*

something ['sʌmθɪŋ] *pronoun* (a) a certain thing; *there's something soft at the bottom of the bag*; *something's gone wrong with the TV* (b) important thing; *come in and sit down, I've got something to tell you*

sometimes ['sʌmtaɪmz] *adverb* occasionally, at various times; *sometimes the car starts easily, and sometimes it won't start*

at all

somewhere ['sʌmweə] *adverb* (a) in or at a place; *I left my umbrella somewhere when I was in London*; *let's go somewhere else, this café is full* (b) **somewhere around** *or* **somewhere between** *or* **somewhere in the region of** = approximately; *somewhere between 50 and 60 people turned up for the dance*

son [sʌn] *noun* male child of a father or mother; *they have a large family - two sons and four daughters*; *our son Nicholas goes to the local school*

song [sɒŋ] *noun* (a) words which are sung; *she was singing a song in the bath* (b) special sound made by a bird; *I'm sure that's the song of a blackbird - look, it's over there!*

soon [suːn] *adverb* (a) in a short time from now; *don't worry, we'll soon be in Oxford* (b) **as soon as** = immediately; *please phone me as soon as you get home*; *as soon as I put the phone down it rang again* (NOTE: **sooner - soonest**)

sooner ['suːnə] *adverb* (a) **sooner or later** = at some time in the future; *she drives so fast that sooner or later she'll have an accident* (b) **the sooner the better** = it would be better to do it as soon as possible; *she should go to see a lawyer, and the sooner the better*

sore [sɔː] *adjective* rough and sensitive; painful; **sore throat** = throat which is red and hurts when you swallow or speak; *she's got a sore throat and has lost her voice* (NOTE: do not confuse with **soar**. Note also: **sorer - sorest**)

sorry ['sɒri] **1** *adjective* **to be sorry** = to be sad about; *I'm sorry I can't stay for dinner*; *he trod on my foot and didn't say he was sorry*; **to feel sorry for someone** = to show sympathy for someone who has problems; to pity someone; *we all feel sorry for her - her family is always criticizing her* (NOTE: **sorrier - sorriest**) **2** *interjection (used to excuse yourself)* sorry! *I didn't see that table had been reserved*

sort [sɔːt] **1** *noun* **(a)** type, kind; *what sorts of ice cream have you got?*; *do you like this sort of TV show?*; **all sorts of** = many different types of; *there were all sorts of people at the meeting* **(b)** *(informal)* **sort of** = rather, more or less; *she was sort of expecting your phone call* **2** *verb* to arrange in order or groups; *the apples are sorted according to size before being packed*

sought [sɔːt] *see* SEEK

soul [səʊl] *noun* the spirit in a person, the part which is believed by some people to go on existing after a person dies; *do you believe your soul lives on when your body dies?* (NOTE: do not confuse with **sole)**

sound [saʊnd] **1** *noun* noise, something which you can hear; *I thought I heard the sound of guns*; *please can you turn down the sound on the TV when I'm on the phone?* **2** *verb* **(a)** to make a noise; *they sounded the alarm after two prisoners escaped* **(b)** to seem; *it sounds as if he's made a mistake*; **that sounds strange** = it seems strange to me **3** *adjective* sensible, which can be trusted; *he gave us some very sound advice* (NOTE: **sounder - soundest) 4** *adverb* deeply; *the children were sound asleep when the police came*

soup [suːp] *noun* liquid food which you eat hot from a bowl at the beginning of a meal, usually made from meat, fish or vegetables; *we started the meal with chicken soup; a bowl of hot soup is always a good idea on a cold day*

sour [saʊə] *adjective* **(a)** with a sharp bitter taste; *if the lemonade is too sour, add some sugar* **(b)** **sour milk** = milk which has gone bad (NOTE: **sourer - sourest)**

source [sɔːs] *noun* place where something comes from; *I think the source of the problem is one of your teeth which needs filling*; *the source of the river is in the mountains*

south [saʊθ] **1** *noun* **(a)** direction looking towards the sun at the middle of the day, direction to your left when you are facing the direction where the sun sets; *the city is to the south of the mountain range*; *the wind is blowing from the south* **(b)** part of a country to the south of the rest; *the south of the country is warmer than the north* **2** *adjective* referring to the south; *the south coast is popular for holidays* **3** *adverb* towards the south; *many birds fly south for the winter*; *the river flows south into the Mediterranean*

south-east [saʊθˈiːst] **1** *adverb* direction between south and east; *go south-east for three miles and then you'll come to our village*; *our office windows face south-east* **2** *noun* part of a country to the south and east; *house prices are higher in the south-east than anywhere else in England* **3** *adjective* between south and east; *South-East Asia is an important trading area*

South Pole [ˈsaʊθ ˈpəʊl] *noun* furthest point at the south of the earth; *they were trying to reach the South Pole on foot*

south-west [saʊθˈwest] **1** *adverb* direction between south and west; *we need to head south-west for two miles* **2** *noun* part of a country between south and west; *Arizona is in the south-west of the United States* **3** *adjective* between south and west; *the south-west coast is popular for holidays*

southern [ˈsʌðən] *adjective* referring to the south; *the southern part of the country is warmer than the north*

souvenir [suːvəˈniːə] *noun* thing bought which reminds you of the place where you bought it; *I bought a scarf as a souvenir of Scotland*; **souvenir shop** = shop which sells souvenirs; *there are several souvenir shops down by the sea*

sow 1 *verb* [səʊ] to put seeds into soil so that they send out shoots and become plants; *peas and beans should be sown in April* (NOTE: do not confuse with **sew**; note also: **sowing - sowed - has sown** [səʊn]) **2** *noun* [saʊ] female pig; *our sow has had eight little pigs*

soya *or* **soy** [ˈsɔɪə *or* sɔɪ] *noun* plant which

produces beans which have a high protein and fat content; **soya sauce** or **soy sauce** = dark sauce with a salt flavour, made from soya beans; *Chinese dishes are often seasoned with soya sauce*

space [speɪs] *noun* **(a)** empty place between other things; *there's a space to put a table in the corner over there*; *write your name and reference number in the space at the top of the paper* **(b)** area which is available for something; *this table takes up too much space* **(c)** (outer) space = area beyond the earth's atmosphere; *could someone be sending messages from outer space?* **(d)** in a short space of time = in a little time; *in a very short space of time the burglars had filled their pockets with jewels*

spade [speɪd] *noun* **(a)** common gardening tool with a wide square blade at the end of a long handle, used for digging; *he handed me the spade and told me to start digging* **(b)** small tool, used by children to play in sand; *the children took their buckets and spades to the beach* **(c)** spades = one of the black suits in a pack of cards (the other black suit is clubs; hearts and diamonds are the red suits); *my last two cards were the ten and the king of spades*

spaghetti [spəˈgeti] *noun* long thin strips of pasta, cooked and eaten with a sauce; *we had spaghetti with tomato sauce*

Spain [speɪn] *noun* country in southern Europe, to the south of France and the east of Portugal; *lots of people go to Spain for their holidays*; *we are going to Spain next July* (NOTE: capital: **Madrid**; people: **the Spanish** or **Spaniards**; language: **Spanish**)

span [spæn] **1** *noun* width of a bird's wings, of an arch, etc.; *each section of the bridge has a span of fifty feet* **2** *verb* to stretch across space or time; *the new bridge will span the river near the railway station* (NOTE: spanning - spanned)

Spanish [ˈspænɪʃ] **1** *adjective* referring to Spain; *I want to change my pounds into Spanish money* **2** *noun* language spoken in Spain and many countries of Latin America; *he's studying French and Spanish as part of his business course*

spanner [ˈspænə] *noun* metal tool with an opening which fits round a nut and which can be twisted to undo the nut or tighten it; *I need a smaller spanner to tighten this little nut*

spare [speə] **1** *adjective* extra, not being used; *I always take a spare pair of shoes when I travel*; *have you got a spare red pen I could borrow?*; **spare time** = time when you are not at work; *he built a model aeroplane in his spare time*; **spare wheel** = fifth wheel carried in a car to replace one that has a puncture; *when he took it out, he found the spare wheel had a puncture too* **2** *noun* spares = pieces used to mend broken parts of a car, etc.; *it's difficult to get spares for the car because they don't make this model any more* **3** *verb* (asking someone if they can do without something) *if you have a moment to spare, can you clean the car?*; *can you spare 50p for a cup of tea?*

spark [spɑːk] *noun* little flash of fire or of light; *sparks flew as the train went over the junction*

sparkle [ˈspɑːkl] *verb* to shine brightly; *her jewels sparkled in the light of the candles*; *his eyes sparkled when he heard how much money he would get*

sparkler [ˈspɑːklə] *noun* type of little firework which you can hold in your hand and which sends out bright sparks; *children love holding sparklers*

sparrow [ˈspærəʊ] *noun* common small brown and grey bird; *a flock of sparrows came down onto our lawn*

speak [spiːk] *verb* **(a)** to say words, to talk; *he was speaking to the postman when I saw him*; *have you spoken to the head teacher yet?* **(b)** to be able to say things in (a foreign language); *we need someone who can speak Russian*; *he speaks English with an American accent* (NOTE: speaking - spoke [spəʊk] **- has spoken** ['spəʊkn])

speak up ['spiːk 'ʌp] *verb* to speak louder; to say what you have to say in a louder voice; *can you speak up please - we can't hear you at the back!*

spear ['spɪə] **1** *noun* long pointed throwing stick, used as a weapon; *in some Pacific islands, they kill fish with spears* **2** *verb* to push something sharp into something to catch it; *she managed to spear a sausage on the barbecue with her fork*

special ['speʃəl] **1** *adjective* **(a)** referring to something or someone who is not ordinary but has a particular importance or use; *this is a special day for me - it's my twenty-fifth birthday* **(b) nothing special** = very ordinary; *did anything happen at college today? - no, nothing special* **2** *noun* particular dish on a menu; **today's special** = special dish prepared for the day and not listed in the printed menu

specialist ['speʃəlɪst] *noun* **(a)** person who knows a lot about something; *you should go to a tax specialist for advice* **(b)** doctor who specializes in a certain branch of medicine; *he was referred to a heart specialist*

specialize ['speʃəlaɪz] *verb* **to specialize in something** = to study one particular subject; to produce one thing in particular; *at university, she specialized in Roman history; the company specializes in electronic components*

species ['spiːʃɪz] *noun* group of living things, such as animals or plants, which can breed with each other; *several species of butterfly are likely to disappear as the weather becomes warmer* (NOTE: plural is **species**)

specimen ['spesɪmən] *noun* example of a particular kind of creature or thing; *he has some very rare specimens in his butterfly collection*

spectacles ['spektəklz] *noun* glasses, two pieces of plastic or glass in a frame which you wear in front of your eyes to help you see better; *have you seen my spectacles*

anywhere?; *she has to wear spectacles to read*

spectator ['spekteɪtə] *noun* person who watches a football match, a horse show, etc.; *thousands of spectators watched the Wimbledon tennis final*

sped [sped] *see* SPEED

speech [spiːtʃ] *noun* **(a)** talk given to an audience; *he made a funny speech at the wedding*; **speech day** = day when children at school are given prizes for good work, etc. (NOTE: plural is **speeches**) **(b)** speaking, making sounds with the voice which can be understood; *after his accident he lost the power of speech*

speed [spiːd] **1** *noun* rate at which something moves or is done; *the coach was travelling at a high speed when it crashed*; *the train travels at speeds of over 150 km per hour*; **speed limit** = fastest speed at which cars are allowed to go by law; *the speed limit in towns is 30 miles per hour* **2** *verb* **(a)** to move quickly; *the ball sped across the ice* **(b)** to go too fast; *he was arrested for speeding in the centre of town* (NOTE: **speeding - sped** [sped] *or* **speeded - has sped**)

spell [spel] **1** *noun* **(a)** short period; *there was a spell of cold weather over the weekend* **(b)** words which the person speaking hopes will have a magic effect; *her wicked sister's spell made the princess sleep for ever* **2** *verb* to write or say correctly the letters that make a word; *how do you spell your surname?*; *I spelt the name of the town wrong on the envelope* (NOTE: **spelling - spelled** *or* **spelt** [spelt])

spelling ['spelɪŋ] *noun* correct way in which words are spelt; *she writes interesting letters but her spelling is awful*

spend [spend] *verb* **(a)** to pay money; *why does he spend so much money on CDs?* **(b)** to use time doing something; *don't spend too long on your homework*; *why don't you come and spend the weekend with us?* (NOTE: **spending - spent** [spent])

sphere ['sfɪə] *noun* object which is perfectly

round like a ball; *the earth is not quite a perfect sphere*

spice [spaɪs] *noun* substance made from the roots, flowers, seeds or leaves of plants, etc., used to flavour food; *you need lots of spices for Indian cooking*

spider [ˈspaɪdə] *noun* small animal with eight legs, which makes a web and eats insects; *it is fascinating to watch a spider making its web*; *help! there's a big black spider in the bath*

spike [spaɪk] *noun* piece of metal with a sharp point at one end; *the wall was topped with a row of metal spikes*

spill [spɪl] *verb* to pour liquid, powder, etc., out of a container by mistake; *that glass is too full - you'll spill it*; *he spilt soup down the front of his shirt* (NOTE: **spilling - spilled** *or* **spilt** [spɪlt])

spin [spɪn] *verb* **(a)** to move round and round very fast; *the earth is spinning in space* **(b)** to make something turn round and round; *the washing machine spins the clothes to get the water out of them* **(c)** to twist raw wool, cotton, etc., to form a thread; *she was spinning wool by the door of the cottage* **(d)** *(of a spider)* to make a web; *the spider has spun a web between the two posts* (NOTE: **spinning - spun** [spʌn])

spin out [ˈspɪn ˈaʊt] *verb* to make something last as long as possible; *I managed to spin out one cup of coffee to last a whole hour*

spinach [ˈspɪnɪtʃ] *noun* plant with green leaves eaten raw as salad or cooked as a vegetable; *we had chicken, potatoes and spinach*

spine [spaɪn] *noun* **(a)** a series of small bones which link together to form your back; *he injured his spine playing rugby* **(b)** sharp part like a pin, on a plant, animal, fish, etc.; *some animals have dangerous spines*; *did you know that lemon trees had spines?* **(c)** back edge of a book, usually with the title printed

on it; *the title and the author's name are printed in gold letters on the spine*

spiral [ˈspaɪrəl] **1** *noun* shape which is twisted round and round like a spring; *he drew a spiral on the sheet of paper* **2** *adjective* which twists round and round; *a spiral staircase leads to the top of the tower*

spirit [ˈspɪrɪt] *noun* **(a)** feelings which are typical of a particular occasion; **Christmas spirit** = excitement and friendly feelings which are supposed to exist at Christmas **(b)** **the spirits of the dead** = the ghosts of dead people; **evil spirit** = wicked ghost which harms people **(c)** mood; **in high spirits** = in a very excited mood; *she's been in high spirits since she passed her test*

spite [spaɪt] **1** *noun* **in spite of** = although something happened or was done; *we all enjoyed ourselves, in spite of the awful weather* **2** *verb* to annoy someone on purpose; *he did it simply to spite his sister*

spiteful [ˈspaɪtfʊl] *adjective* full of a nasty feelings against someone; *he made several spiteful remarks about his teacher*

splash [splæʃ] **1** *noun* sound when something falls into a liquid or when a liquid hits something hard; *she fell into the swimming pool with a loud splash* **2** *verb* **(a)** *(of liquid)* to make a noise when something is dropped into it or when it hits something; *the rain splashed against the windows* **(b)** to make someone wet by sending liquid on to him or her; *the car drove past through a puddle and splashed my trousers* **(c)** to move through water, making a noise; *the little children were splashing about in the pools of water*

splendid [ˈsplendɪd] *adjective* very good; *after a splendid lunch we all had a short sleep*; *it was splendid to see all our old friends again*

splinter [ˈsplɪntə] **1** *noun* tiny thin piece of wood or metal which can get under your skin; *can you try and get this splinter out of my* *thumb for me?* **2** *verb* to split into thin pointed pieces; *the wooden door splintered as the firemen hit it with their axes*

split [splɪt] **1** *verb* **(a)** to divide something into parts; *he split the log into small pieces; we must try to split up the class into groups of three or four* **(b)** to divide or to come apart; *my trousers were so tight that they split when I bent down* (NOTE: **splitting - split**) **2** *noun* **banana split** = dessert made of a banana cut in half, whipped cream, ice cream, chocolate sauce and nuts, usually served in a long dish

spoil [spɔɪl] *verb* **(a)** to ruin something which was good; *we had such bad weather that our camping holiday was spoilt* **(b)** to be too kind to a child, so that he or she becomes badly behaved; *grandparents are allowed to spoil their grandchildren a little* (NOTE: **spoiling - spoilt** [spɔɪlt] or **spoiled**)

spoke [spəʊk] **1** *noun* rod which connects the centre of a wheel to the outside edge; *the wheel isn't turning straight because one of the spokes is bent* **2** *verb see* SPEAK

spoken ['spəʊkən] *see* SPEAK

sponge [spʌnʒ] **1** *noun* **(a)** block of soft material full of small holes, which soaks up water and is used for washing; *I use a large sponge to wash the car* **(b) sponge cake** = light soft cake; **sponge pudding** = light soft pudding **2** *verb* to wipe clean with a sponge; *he sponged the kitchen table*

spoon [spuːn] *noun* tool with a handle at one end and a small bowl at the other, used for eating liquids and soft food, or for stirring food which is being cooked; *use a spoon to eat your pudding; we need a big spoon to serve the soup;* **coffee spoon** = little spoon used for stirring coffee; **soup spoon** = special larger spoon for eating soup

sport [spɔːt] *noun* **(a)** all games taken together; *do you like watching the sports programmes on TV?* **(b)** game which you play; *the only sport I play is tennis; she doesn't play any sport at all*

sportsman, sportswoman ['spɔːtsmən or spɔːtswʊmən] *noun* person who plays a sport; *she's an Olympic sportswoman* (NOTE: plurals are **sportsmen, sportswomen**)

spot [spɒt] **1** *noun* **(a)** particular place; *this is a good spot for a picnic;* **on the spot** = at a particular place where something happens; *a doctor happened to be on the spot when the accident took place* **(b)** round coloured mark; *he wore a blue tie with white spots* **(c)** small round mark or bump on the skin; *she suddenly was covered in spots after eating fish* **2** *verb* to notice; *the teacher didn't spot the mistake; did you spot the number of the car?* (NOTE: **spotting - spotted**)

spotless ['spɒtləs] *adjective* very clean; *her kitchen is absolutely spotless*

spout [spaʊt] *noun* tube which sticks out of a container, shaped for pouring liquids; *you can fill the kettle through the spout*

sprain [spreɪn] *verb* to twist a joint, such as your ankle, so that it hurts when you use it; *she sprained her ankle jumping over the fence; he sprained his wrist and can't play tennis tomorrow*

sprang [spræŋ] *see* SPRING

sprawl [sprɔːl] *verb* to lie with your arms and legs spread out; *he sprawled in his armchair and turned on the TV*

spray [spreɪ] **1** *noun* mass of tiny drops of liquid; *the waves crashed against the sea wall sending spray over the road; we used a spray to kill the flies* **2** *verb* to send out liquid in fine drops; *they sprayed the room to get rid of the insects*

spread [spred] **1** *noun* **(a)** soft paste of meat, fish or cheese; *as snacks, they offered us crackers with cheese spread* **(b)** action of moving over a wide area; *doctors are trying to check the spread of the disease* **2** *verb* **(a)** to arrange over a wide area; *spread the paper flat on the floor* **(b)** to move over a wide area; *the fire started in the top floor and soon spread to the roof; the disease has spread to the main* *towns* **(c)** to cover with a layer of something; *she spread a white cloth over the table*; *he was spreading butter on a piece of bread* (NOTE: **spreading - spread**)

spring [sprɪŋ] **1** *noun* **(a)** season of the year between winter and summer; *in spring all the trees start to grow new leaves*; *you should come to England in April and see the beautiful spring flowers!* **(b)** wire which is twisted round and round and which goes back to its original shape after you have pulled it or pushed it; *the bed is so old the springs have burst through the mattress* **(c)** strong pieces of special metal which absorb energy and allow a vehicle to travel easily over bumps; *the springs in the car are starting to squeak* **(d)** place where a stream of water rushes out of the ground; *the town of Bath was built in Roman times around hot springs* **2** *verb* to move up suddenly; *he sprang out of bed when he heard the clock strike* (NOTE: **springing - sprang** [spræŋ] **- has sprung** [sprʌŋ])

sprinkle ['sprɪŋkl] *verb* to scatter around; *she sprinkled the top of the pie with sugar*

sprint [sprɪnt] *verb* to run very fast over a short distance; *I had to sprint to catch the bus*

sprout [spraʊt] **1** *noun* new shoot of a plant; **Brussels sprouts** = shoots which look like tiny cabbages **2** *verb* to produce new shoots; *throw those old potatoes away, they're starting to sprout*

sprung [sprʌŋ] *see* SPRING

spun [spʌn] *see* SPIN

spurt [spɜ:t] **1** *noun* sudden rush, sudden effort; *he put on a spurt and won the race* **2** *verb* **(a) to spurt out** = to come out in a strong jet; *oil spurted out of the burst pipe* **(b)** to run fast suddenly; *he spurted past two runners and came in first*

spy [spaɪ] **1** *noun* person who tries to find out secret information about the enemy, a gang, a rival firm; *he was arrested as a spy* (NOTE: plural is **spies**) **2** *verb* **to spy on someone** = to watch someone in secret, to find out what he is

planning to do; *we discovered that our neighbours had been spying on us*; **to spy for someone** = to find out secret information and pass it back to someone; *he was accused of spying for the Americans*

square [skweə] **1** *noun* **(a)** shape with four equal sides and four corners with right angles; *graph paper is drawn with a series of small squares* **(b)** open space in a town, with big buildings all round; *the hotel is in the main square of the town, opposite the town hall*; *tourists like feeding the pigeons in Trafalgar Square* **(c)** *(mathematics)* result when a number is multiplied by itself; *9 is the square of 3* **2** *adjective* **(a)** shaped like a square, with four equal sides and four corners with right angles; *you can't fit six people round a small square table* **(b)** multiplied by itself; **square metre** = area of one metre multiplied by one metre; *the room is 5m by 9m, so its area is 45 square metres (45m²)*

squash [skwɒʃ] **1** *verb* to crush, to squeeze; *hundreds of people were squashed into the train*; *he sat on my hat and squashed it flat* **2** *noun* **(a)** a situation where a lot of people are crowded in a small space; *it's rather a squash with twenty people in the room* **(b)** drink made of fruit juice to which water is added; *do you want some orange squash?*

squat [skwɒt] *verb* to crouch down, sitting on your heels; *she squatted on the floor, trying to clean the carpet* (NOTE: **squatting - squatted**)

squeak [skwi:k] *verb* to make a high little noise like that of a mouse or a rusty door; *that door squeaks - it needs some oil*

squeal [skwi:l] **1** *noun* loud high noise; *the children let out squeals of delight when they saw the presents under the Christmas tree* **2** *verb* to make a loud high noise; *she squealed when she heard she had won first prize*

squeeze [skwi:z] *verb* **(a)** to press on something; to press or crush a fruit, a tube, etc., to get something out of it; *she squeezed my arm gently*; *she squeezed some toothpaste onto her brush* **(b)** to crush, to force into a small space; *you can't squeeze six people into that little car*; *more people tried to squeeze on the train even though it was full already*

squirrel ['skwɪrəl] *noun* common small wild mammal with a large tail, living in trees and eating fruit and nuts; *the squirrel sat up on a branch nibbling a nut*

squirt [skwɜːt] *verb* to send out a thin jet of liquid; *don't squirt so much washing-up liquid into the bowl*; *she squeezed the tube and masses of toothpaste squirted out*

St [striːt] *short for* STREET; *our address is Great Peter St*

stab [stæb] *verb* to wound someone by jabbing with a sharp knife; *he was stabbed in the chest* (NOTE: **stabbing - stabbed**)

stable ['steɪbl] **1** *noun* building for keeping a horse; *she enjoys working in the stables because she loves horses* **2** *adjective* which does not change; *the hospital said his condition was stable*

stack [stæk] **1** *noun* pile of things one on top of the other; *there was a stack of dirty plates by the sink* **2** *verb* to pile things on top of each other; *she stacked up the dirty plates*

stadium ['steɪdiəm] *noun* large building where people watch sport, with seats arranged around a field; *our sports stadium was packed with spectators* (NOTE: plural is **stadiums** *or* **stadia**)

staff [stɑːf] *noun* **(a)** all the people who work in a company, school, college, or other organization; *she's on the school staff*; *a quarter of our staff are ill*; *three members of staff are away sick* **(b)** *(formal)* long stick; *the police attacked the demonstrators and beat them with staffs*

stage [steɪdʒ] **1** *noun* **(a)** raised floor in a theatre where the actors perform; *the pop group came onto the stage and started to sing* **(b)** one of several points in the way something develops; *the different stages of a production process* **(c)** section of a long journey; *stage one of the tour takes us from Paris to*

Bordeaux **2** *verb* to put on, to arrange a play, a show, a musical, etc.; *the exhibition is being staged in the college library*

stagger ['stægə] *verb* **(a)** not to walk steadily, almost falling down; *she managed to stagger across the road and into the police station* **(b)** to be staggered = to be enormously surprised; *I was staggered at the amount they charged for cleaning the car*

stain [steɪn] **1** *noun* mark which is difficult to remove, such as ink or blood; *there was a round stain on the table where he had put his wine glass* **2** *verb* to make a mark of a different colour on something; *the tablecloth was stained with coffee*

stair [steə] *noun* one of a set of steps which go up or down inside a building; *the little boy was sitting on the bottom stair*; *you have to go up three flights of stairs to get to his bedroom*; *he slipped and fell down the stairs*

staircase ['steəkeɪs] *noun* set of stairs which go from one floor in a building to another; *a spiral staircase leads to the top of the tower*

stake [steɪk] *noun* strong pointed piece of wood or metal, pushed into the ground to mark something, or to hold something up; *they hammered stakes into the ground to put up a wire fence*; *the young apple trees are attached to stakes* (NOTE: do not confuse with **steak**)

stale [steɪl] *adjective* no longer fresh; *if you don't eat the cakes soon they'll go stale*; *nobody likes the smell of stale tobacco smoke* (NOTE: **staler - stalest**)

stalk [stɔːk] **1** *noun* **(a)** stem of a plant which holds a leaf, a flower, a fruit, etc.; *roses with very long stalks are more expensive*; *cherries are often attached to stalks in pairs* **2** *verb* **(a)** to walk in a stiff, proud or angry way; *she stalked into the room looking very annoyed* **(b)** to follow someone or something in secret in order to catch them; *journalists from popular newspapers stalked the film star*

stall [stɔːl] *noun* **(a)** small wooden stand in a market, where you sell goods; *we wandered*

round the market looking at the fruit stalls
(b) stalls = seats on the ground floor in a
theatre or cinema; *seats in the stalls are
expensive, let's get tickets for upstairs* **(c)**
separate section for one animal in a stable;
*each horse has its own stall with its name on
it*

stammer ['stæmə] *verb* to hesitate and repeat
sounds when speaking; *she rushed into the
police station and stammered 'he's - he's -
he's after me, he's got - got - a knife'*

stamp [stæmp] **1** *noun* **(a)** little piece of
paper with a price printed on it which you
stick on a letter, postcard, etc., to show that
you have paid for it to be sent by post; *you
need a 27p stamp for that letter*; *she forgot to
put a stamp on the letter before she posted it*
(b) special mark made on something; *the
officer looked at the stamps in my passport* **2**
verb **(a)** to mark something with a stamp; *they
stamped my passport when I entered the
country* **(b)** to walk in a heavy way, banging
your feet on the ground; *she stamped her feet
to keep warm*

stand [stænd] **1** *verb* **(a)** to be upright on
your feet, the opposite of sitting or lying
down; *she stood on a chair to reach the top
shelf*; *if there are no seats left, we'll have to
stand* **(b)** to be upright; *only a few houses
were still standing after the earthquake* **(c)** to
put up with; *the office is filthy - I don't know
how you can stand working here* (NOTE:
standing - stood [stʊd]) **2** *noun* something
which holds something up; *the pot of flowers
fell off its stand*; *display stand* = special set
of shelves for showing goods for sale

stand for ['stænd 'fɔː] *verb* to represent, to
have a meaning; *what do the letters BBC
stand for?*

stand out ['stænd 'aʊt] *verb* to be easily
seen; *their house stands out because it is
painted pink*; *her red hair makes her stand
out in a crowd*

stand up ['stænd 'ʌp] *verb* to get up from
sitting; *he stood up to offer his seat to the*

old lady

standard ['stændəd] **1** *noun* **(a)** the level of
quality something has; *the standard of service
in this restaurant is very high* **(b)** excellent
quality which is set as a target; *she has set a
standard which it will be difficult to match*
(c) large official flag; *the royal standard flies
over Buckingham Palace* **2** *adjective* **(a)**
usual, normal; *the standard rate of income tax
is 20p in the pound* **(b)** on a tall pole;
standard lamp = room lamp on a tall pole
standing on the floor

stank [stæŋk] *see* STINK

staple ['steɪpl] **1** *noun* piece of wire which is
pushed through papers and bent over to hold
them together; *he used his scissors to take the
staples out of the papers* **2** *verb* to fasten
papers together with a staple or with staples;
staple your cheque to the order form

stapler ['steɪplə] *noun* little device used to
attach papers together with staples; *the stapler
has run out of staples*

star [stɑː] **1** *noun* **(a)** bright object which can
be seen in the sky at night like a very small
bright light; *on a clear night you can see
thousands of stars* **(b)** famous person who is
very well known to the public; *who is your
favourite film star?*; *look - that's the Chelsea
football star!* **(c)** shape that has several points
like a star; *draw a big star and colour it red* **2**
verb to appear as a main character in a film or
play; *she starred in 'Gone with the Wind'*
(NOTE: starring - starred)

stare [steə] *verb* to look at someone or
something for a long time; *she stared sadly
out of the window at the rain*

starfish ['stɑːfɪʃ] *noun* flat sea animal, with
five arms branching like a star from a central
body; *the children found a starfish on the
beach and brought it back home in a bucket*
(NOTE: plural is starfish)

starling ['stɑːlɪŋ] *noun* common bird with
dark feathers with a green shine on them; *a
flock of starlings were pecking about on*

the grass

start [stɑːt] **1** *verb* **(a)** to begin to do something; *the babies all started crying at the same time*; *he started to eat his dinner before the rest of the family*; *when you learn Russian, you have to start by learning the alphabet* **(b)** *(of a machine)* to begin to work; *the car won't start - the battery must be flat* **(c)** to make something begin to work; *it is difficult to start the car in cold weather* **(d)** to make something begin; *the police think that the fire was started deliberately* **(e)** to begin to exist, to make a business begin to work; *we started a gardening club* **2** *noun* the beginning of something; *building the house took only six months from start to finish*

start off [ˈstɑːt ˈɒf] *verb* **(a)** to begin; *we'll start off with soup and then have a meat dish* **(b)** to leave on a journey; *you can start off now, and I'll follow when I'm ready*

startle [ˈstɑːtl] *verb* to make someone suddenly surprised; *I'm sorry, I didn't mean to startle you*

starve [stɑːv] *verb* not to have enough food; *many people starved to death in the desert*

state [steɪt] **1** *noun* **(a)** condition (often a bad condition), the way something or someone is; *the children are in a state of excitement*; *the students left the flat in a terrible state*; *look at the state of your trousers* **(b)** condition where you are depressed, worried, etc.; *she's in such a state that I don't want to leave her alone* **(c)** government of a country; *we all pay taxes to the state* **(d)** one part of a country; *New South Wales has the largest population of all the Australian states* **(e)** the States = THE UNITED STATES OF AMERICA **2** *verb* to give information clearly; *please state your name and address*

statement [ˈsteɪtmənt] *noun* **(a)** clearly written or spoken description of what happened; *she made a statement to the police* **(b)** bank statement = written document from a bank showing how much money there is in an account

station [ˈsteɪʃn] *noun* **(a)** place where trains stop, where passengers get on or off, etc.; *the train leaves the Central Station at 14.15*; *this is a fast train - it doesn't stop at every station* **(b)** bus station *or* coach station = place where coaches or buses begin or end their journeys; *coaches leave Victoria Coach Station for all parts of the country*; underground station *or* tube station = place where underground trains stop, where passengers get on or off; *there's an underground station just a few minutes' walk away* **(c)** large main building for a service; *the fire station is just down the road from us*; *he was arrested and taken to the local police station*

stationary [ˈsteɪʃnəri] *adjective* not moving, standing still; *traffic is stationary for six kilometres on the motorway* (NOTE: do not confuse with **stationery**)

stationery [ˈsteɪʃnəri] *noun* materials used when writing, such as paper, envelopes, pens, ink, etc.; *we bought some envelopes and other office stationery* (NOTE: no plural; do not confuse with **stationary**)

statue [ˈstætʃuː] *noun* figure of a person or animal carved from stone, made from metal, etc.; *the statue of King John is in the centre of the square*

stay [steɪ] **1** *verb* **(a)** to remain, not to change; *the temperature stayed below zero all day* **(b)** to stop in a place; *they came for lunch and stayed until after midnight* **(c)** to stop in a place as a visitor; *they stayed two nights in Edinburgh on their tour of Scotland*; *where will you be staying when you're in New York?* **2** *noun* time during which you visit a place; *my sister's here for a short stay*; *did you enjoy your stay in London?*

stay put [ˈsteɪ ˈpʊt] *phrase* to stay where you are, not to move; *stay put! - I'll go and get a doctor*

stay up [ˈsteɪ ˈʌp] *verb* not to go to bed; *we stayed up late to see the New Year in*; *little children are not supposed to stay up until midnight watching TV*

steadily ['stedɪli] *adverb* in a regular or continuous way; *things have been steadily going from bad to worse*

steady ['stedi] *adjective* **(a)** firm, not moving or shaking; *he put a piece of paper under the table leg to keep it steady* **(b)** continuing in a regular way; *the car was doing a steady seventy miles an hour* (NOTE: **steadier - steadiest**)

steak [steɪk] *noun* **(a)** thick slice of beef; *he ordered steak and chips* **(b)** thick slice of a big fish; *a grilled salmon steak for me, please!* (NOTE: do not confuse with **stake**)

steal [stiːl] *verb* **(a)** to take something which does not belong to you; *someone tried to steal my handbag; she owned up to having stolen the jewels* **(b)** to move quietly; *he stole into the office and tried to find the safe* (NOTE: **stealing - stole** [stəʊl] **- stolen** ['stəʊlən] ; do not confuse with **steel**)

steam [stiːm] *noun* hot water vapour which comes off hot or boiling water; *clouds of steam were coming out of the kitchen*

steel [stiːl] *noun* strong metal made from iron; *steel knives are best for the kitchen because they are so sharp*; **steel band** = band which plays West Indian music on steel drums of different sizes which make different notes (NOTE: do not confuse with **steal**)

steep [stiːp] *adjective* which rises or falls at a sharp angle; *the car climbed the steep hill with some difficulty; the steps up the church tower are steeper than our stairs at home* (NOTE: **steeper - steepest**)

steer ['stɪə] *verb* to make a car, a ship, etc., go in a certain direction; *she steered the car off the road and into a ditch; the pilot steered the ship into harbour*

steering wheel ['stɪːrɪŋ 'wiːl] *noun* wheel which is turned by the driver to make a vehicle go in a certain direction; *in British cars the steering wheel is on the right-hand side of the car*

stem [stem] *noun* **(a)** stalk, the tall thin part of a plant which holds a leaf, a flower, a fruit, etc.; *cut the stems before you put the flowers in water* **(b)** main part of a plant or small tree; *a standard rose bush has a tall stem*

stencil ['stensl] *noun* sheet of cardboard or metal with a pattern cut out of it, so that if you place it on a surface and paint over it, the pattern will be made on the surface; *she decorated the bathroom with stencils of fish*

step [step] **1** *noun* **(a)** movement of your foot when walking; *he took his first steps on his first birthday; take a step sideways and you will be able to see the castle* **(b)** regular movement of feet at the same time as other people; **in step** = moving your feet at the same rate as everybody else; **out of step** = moving your feet at a different rate from everybody else; *I tried to keep in step with him as we walked along* **(c)** one stair, which goes up or down; *there are two steps down into the kitchen; I counted 75 steps to the top of the tower* **(d)** one thing which is done or has to be done, followed by other things; *the first step is to find out how much money has been stolen* **2** *verb* to move forwards, backwards, etc., on foot; *she stepped off the bus into a pool of water; don't step back, there's someone behind you* (NOTE: **stepping - has stepped**)

stereo ['steriəʊ] *noun* machine which produces sound through two different loudspeakers or headphones; *I bought a new pair of loudspeakers for my stereo*; **car stereo** = system in a car which produces sound in stereo

stern [stɜːn] **1** *adjective* serious and strict; *the judge gave a stern warning to all criminals* (NOTE: **sterner - sternest**) **2** *noun* back part of a ship (the front part is the 'bow'); *the stern of the ship was damaged*

stew [stjuː] **1** *noun* meal of meat and vegetables cooked together for a long time; *this lamb stew is a French recipe* **2** *verb* to cook for a long time in liquid; *stew the apples until they are completely soft*

stick [stɪk] **1** *verb* **(a)** to glue, to attach with glue; *can you stick the pieces of the cup together again?*; *she stuck the stamp on the letter* **(b)** to be fixed or not to be able to move; *the door sticks - you need to push it hard to open it* **(c)** to push something into something; *he stuck his hand into the hole*; *she stuck a needle into her finger* **(d)** to stay in a place; *stick close to your mother and you won't get lost* **(e)** *(informal)* to bear, to put up with; *I don't know how she can stick working in that office* (NOTE: **sticking - stuck** [stʌk]) **2** *noun* **(a)** thin piece of wood, thin branch of a tree; *he pushed the stick into the ground*; *let's collect some dry sticks to make a fire*; **walking stick** = strong piece of wood with a handle used as a support when walking; *since she had the accident she gets around on two sticks* **(b)** anything long and thin; *a stick of chewing gum*

sticker [ˈstɪkə] *noun* small piece of paper or plastic which you can stick on something to show a price, as a decoration or to advertise something; *she stuck stickers all over the doors of her wardrobe*

sticking plaster [ˈstɪkɪŋ ˈplɑːstə] *noun* small strip of cloth which can be stuck to the skin to cover a wound (often called by a trademark such as 'Elastoplast', or 'BandAid' in American English); *I want a piece of sticking plaster to put on my heel*

sticky [ˈstɪki] *adjective* **(a)** covered with something which sticks like glue; *after making jam my fingers were all sticky* **(b)** with glue on one side so that it sticks easily; **sticky tape** = plastic strip with glue on one side, used to stick things together, etc.; *she did the parcel up carefully with sticky tape* (NOTE: **stickier - stickiest)**

stiff [stɪf] *adjective* **(a)** which does not move or bend easily; *the lock is very stiff - I can't turn the key*; *she felt stiff all over after running in the marathon* **(b)** hard; *you need a stiff brush to get the mud off your shoes* (NOTE: **stiffer - stiffest)**

stile [staɪl] *noun* steps which allow people,

but not animals, to get over a wall or fence; *the path led across the field to a stile*

still [stɪl] **1** *adjective* not moving; *stand still while I take the photo* **2** *adverb* **(a)** continuing until now; which continued until then; *I thought he had left, but I see he's still there* **(b)** in spite of everything; *it wasn't sunny for the picnic - still, it didn't rain*

sting [stɪŋ] **1** *noun* wound made by an insect or plant; *bee stings can be very painful* **2** *verb* **(a)** to wound with an insect's or plant's sting; *I've been stung by a wasp*; *she walked through the wood and got stung by nettles* **(b)** to give a burning feeling; *the antiseptic may sting a little at first* (NOTE: **stinging - stung** [stʌŋ])

stink [stɪŋk] **1** *noun* very nasty smell; *there's a terrible stink in the downstairs toilet* **2** *verb* to make a nasty smell; *the kitchen stinks of gas* (NOTE: **stank** [stæŋk] - **stunk** [stʌŋk])

stir [stɜː] *verb* **(a)** to move and mix a liquid or something which is cooking; *he was stirring the sugar into his coffee*; *keep stirring the sauce, or it will stick to the bottom of the pan* **(b)** to move about; *I didn't stir from my desk all day* (NOTE: **stirring - stirred)**

stitch [stɪtʃ] **1** *noun* **(a)** little loop of thread made with a needle in sewing or with knitting needles when knitting; *she used very small stitches to make the baby's clothes* **(b)** small loop of thread used by a surgeon to attach the sides of a wound together to help it to heal; *she had three stitches in her arm*; *come back in ten days' time to have the stitches removed* **(c)** sharp pain in the side of your body after you have been running; *I can't go any further - I've got a stitch* (NOTE: plural is **stitches) 2** *verb* to attach with a needle and thread; *she stitched the badge to his jacket*

stock [stɒk] **1** *noun* supply of goods for sale; **in stock** = available in the shop or warehouse; **out of stock** = not available in the shop or warehouse; *we are out of stock of this item* or *this item is out of stock* **2** *verb* to keep goods for sale in a warehouse or shop; *we try to stock* *the most popular colours*

stocking ['stɒkɪŋ] *noun* long light piece of women's clothing which covers all the leg and your foot; *she was wearing black shoes and stockings*; *the robbers wore stockings over their faces*

stole [stəʊl] *see* STEAL

stolen ['stəʊlən] *adjective* which has been taken away without permission; *the police are trying to find the stolen jewels*; *see also* STEAL

stomach ['stʌmək] *noun* (a) part of the inside of the body shaped like a bag, into which food passes after being swallowed; *I don't want anything to eat - I have a pain in my stomach* (b) the middle of the front of your body; *he crept under the fence on his stomach*

stone [stəʊn] *noun* (a) very hard material, found in the ground, used for building; *all the houses in the town are built in the local grey stone*; *stone floors can be very cold* (b) small piece of stone; *the beach isn't good for bathing as it's covered with very sharp stones* (c) British measure of weight (= 14 pounds or 6.35 kilograms); *she's trying to lose weight and so far has lost a stone and a half*; *he weighs twelve stone ten (i.e. 12 stone 10 pounds)* (d) single hard seed inside a fruit; *count the cherry stones on the side of your plate*

stony ['stəʊni] *adjective* made of lots of stones; *they walked carefully across the stony beach* (NOTE: **stonier - stoniest**)

stood [stʊd] *see* STAND

stool [stuːl] *noun* small seat with no back; *when the little girl sat on the piano stool her feet didn't touch the floor*

stoop [stuːp] *verb* to bend forward; *she stooped and picked something up off the carpet*

stop [stɒp] **1** *noun* (a) end of something, especially of movement; *the police want to put a stop to car crimes*; **to come to a stop** =

to stop moving; *the car rolled on without the driver, and finally came to a stop at the bottom of the hill* (b) place where you break a journey; *we'll make a stop at the next village* (c) place where a bus or tram lets passengers get on or off; *we have been waiting at the bus stop for twenty minutes*; *there are six stops between here and Marble Arch* (d) **full stop** = printed mark like a small dot, showing the end of a sentence or an abbreviation; *when reading, you should take a breath when you come to a full stop* **2** *verb* (a) not to move any more; *the motorcycle didn't stop at the red lights*; *this train stops at all stations to London Waterloo* (b) to make something not move any more; *the policeman stopped the traffic to let the lorry back out of the garage* (c) not to do something any more; *the church clock has stopped at 4.15*; *at last it stopped raining and we could go out* (d) **to stop someone or something doing something** = to make someone or something not do something any more; *can't you stop the children making such a noise?* (e) to stay as a visitor in a place; *they stopped for a few days in Paris*; *I expect to stop in Rome for the weekend* (NOTE: **stopping - stopped**)

stopper ['stɒpə] *noun* piece of glass, wood, etc., put into the mouth of a bottle or jar to close it; *put the stopper back in the jar*

store [stɔː] **1** *noun* big shop; *you can buy shoes in any of the big stores in town* **2** *verb* to keep something to use later; *we store the apples in the garden shed*

storey *US* **story** ['stɔːri] *noun* whole floor in a building; *the upper storeys of the hotel caught fire*

storm [stɔːm] *noun* high wind and very bad weather; *how many trees were blown down in last night's storm?*; *March and October are the worst months for storms*

stormy ['stɔːmi] *adjective* when there are storms; *they are forecasting stormy weather for the weekend* (NOTE: **stormier - stormiest**)

story ['stɔːri] *noun* (a) description that tells

about things that did not really happen but are invented by an author; *she writes children's stories about animals* (b) description that tells what really happened; *she told her story to the journalist* (NOTE: plural is **stories**)

stout [staʊt] *adjective* (a) quite fat; *the stout man had difficulty going up the stairs* (b) *(of material)* strong or thick; *take a few sheets of stout paper*; *find a stout branch to stand on* (NOTE: **stouter - stoutest**)

stove [stəʊv] *noun* machine for heating or cooking; *the shed is heated by an oil stove*; *the milk boiled over and made a mess on the kitchen stove*

straight [streɪt] **1** *adjective* (a) not curved; *Edgware Road is a long straight street*; *use a ruler to draw a straight line* (b) not sloping; *the shelf should be perfectly straight but it slopes slightly to the left* (NOTE: **straighter - straightest**) **2** *adverb* (a) going in a straight line, not curving; *the road goes straight across the plain for two hundred kilometres*; **to go straight on** *or* **to keep straight on** = to continue along this road without turning off it; *go straight on past the road junction and then turn left* (b) immediately, at once; *if there is a problem, you should go straight to the manager*

straight away [ˈstreɪt əˈweɪ] *adverb* at once, immediately; *I need a lot of money straight away*

straighten [ˈstreɪtn] *verb* to make straight; *he straightened his tie and went into the interview*

strain [streɪn] **1** *noun* (a) nervous stress; *can she stand the strain of working in that office?* (b) variety, breed; *they are trying to find a cure for a new strain of the flu virus* **2** *verb* (a) to injure part of your body by pulling too hard; *he strained a muscle in his back* (b) to make great efforts to do something; *they strained to lift the piano into the van* (c) to separate solid bits from a liquid; *boil the peas for ten minutes and then strain them*

strange [streɪnʒ] *adjective* (a) not usual; *something is the matter with the engine - it's making a strange noise*; *it felt strange to be sitting in school on a Saturday afternoon* (b) which you have never seen before or where you have never been before; *I find it difficult getting to sleep in a strange room* (NOTE: **stranger - strangest**)

stranger [ˈstreɪnʒə] *noun* (a) person you have never met before; *children are told not to accept lifts from strangers* (b) person in a place where he has never been before; *I can't tell you how to get to the post office - I'm a stranger here myself*

strap [stræp] **1** *noun* long flat piece of material used to attach something; *can you do up the strap of my satchel for me?* **2** *verb* to fasten something with a strap; *the patient was strapped to a stretcher*; *make sure the baby is strapped into her seat* (NOTE: **strapping - strapped**)

straw [strɔː] *noun* (a) thin plastic tube for sucking up liquids; *she was drinking orange juice through a straw* (b) dry stalks and bits of plants left after the harvest; *you've been lying on the ground - you've got bits of straw in your hair*

strawberry [ˈstrɔːbri] *noun* common soft red summer fruit growing on low plants; *I picked some strawberries for dessert*; *she put a pot of strawberry jam on the table* (NOTE: plural is **strawberries**)

stray [streɪ] **1** *adjective* which is wandering away from home; *we found a stray cat and brought it home* **2** *verb* to wander away; *the sheep have strayed onto the golf course*

stream [striːm] *noun* (a) little river; *can you jump across that stream?* (b) things which go past all the time; *crossing the road is difficult because of the stream of traffic*; *we had a stream of customers on the first day of the sale*

street [striːt] *noun* (a) road in a town, usually with shops or houses on each side; *it is difficult to park in our street on Saturday* *mornings*; *the school is in the next street*; **street map** *or* **street plan** = diagram showing the streets of a town, with their names; *you will need a street map to get round New York* **(b)** *(used with names)* *Oxford Street, Bond Street and Regent Street are the main shopping areas in London*; **High Street** = the main shopping street in a town; *his shop is on the High Street*

strength [strenθ] *noun* being strong; *you should test the strength of the rope before you start climbing*

stress [stres] **1** *noun* nervous strain; *she has difficulty coping with the stress at work* **2** *verb* to show how important something is; *I must stress how important it is to keep the plan secret*

stretch [stretʃ] **1** *noun* **(a)** long piece of land, road, etc.; *for long stretches of the road, all you see are trees*; *stretches of the river are so dirty that bathing there is dangerous* **(b)** long period of time; *at a stretch* = without a break; *he played the piano for two hours at a stretch* (NOTE: plural is **stretches**) **2** *verb* **(a)** to spread out for a great distance; *the line of cars stretched for three miles from the accident*; *the queue stretched from the door of the cinema right round the corner* **(b)** to push out your arms or legs as far as they can; *the cat woke up and stretched* **(c)** to pull something so that it becomes loose; *these trousers are not supposed to stretch*

stretcher ['stretʃə] *noun* folding bed with handles, on which an injured person can be carried by two people; *the rescue team brought him down the mountain, strapped to a stretcher*

strict [strikt] *adjective* **(a)** which must be obeyed; *I gave strict instructions that no one was to be allowed in* **(b)** insisting that rules are obeyed; *our parents are very strict with us about staying up late* (NOTE: **stricter - strictest**)

stride [straid] **1** *noun* long step; *he took three strides to cross the room* **2** *verb* to walk with long steps; *she strode into the room carrying*

an axe (NOTE: **striding - strode** [strəud])

strike [straik] **1** *noun* stopping of work by workers; *they all voted in favour of a strike*; **to go on strike** = to stop work; *the workers went on strike for more money* **2** *verb* **(a)** to refuse to go on working until you get what you want; *the workers are striking in protest against bad working conditions* **(b)** to hit something against something hard; *she struck a match and lit the fire* **(c)** *(of a clock)* to ring to mark an time; *the church clock had just struck one when she heard a noise outside her bedroom door* **(d)** to come to someone's mind; *it suddenly struck me that I had seen him somewhere before*; **it strikes me that** = I think that (NOTE: **striking - struck** [strʌk])

string [strin] *noun* **(a)** strong thin thread used for tying up parcels, etc.; *she bought a ball of string* **(b)** long series of things; *I had a string of phone calls this morning* **(c)** thread on a musical instrument which makes a note when you hit it; *he was playing the violin when one of the strings broke*; **string instruments** = instruments (like violins) which have strings

strip [strip] **1** *noun* long narrow piece of cloth, paper, etc.; *he tore the paper into strips*; *houses are to be built along the strip of land near the church* **2** *verb* to take off your clothes; *strip to the waist for your chest X-ray*; *he stripped down to his underwear* (NOTE: **stripping - stripped**)

stripe [straip] *noun* line of colour; *he has an umbrella with red, white and blue stripes*

strode [strəud] *see* STRIDE

stroke [strəuk] **1** *noun* **(a)** becoming unconscious suddenly because of blood in the brain; *she had a stroke and died* **(b)** act of hitting something, such as a ball; *it took him three strokes to get the ball into the hole* **(c)** style of swimming; *she won the 200m breast stroke* **(d)** person rowing who sits at the back of the boat and sets the pace for the rest of the crew **2** *verb* to run your hands gently over; *she was stroking the cat as it sat in her lap*

strong [strɒŋ] *adjective* **(a)** (person) with a lot of strength; *she's not strong enough to carry that box* **(b)** which has a lot of force or strength; *the wind was so strong that it blew some tiles off the roof* **(c)** with a powerful smell, taste, etc.; *you need a cup of strong black coffee to wake you up*; *there was a strong smell of gas in the kitchen* (NOTE: stronger - strongest)

struck [strʌk] *see* STRIKE

structure [ˈstrʌktʃə] *noun* a building; *several structures were damaged in the earthquake*

struggle [ˈstrʌgl] **1** *noun* fight; *after a short struggle the burglar was arrested* **2** *verb* **(a)** to fight with someone; *two men were struggling on the floor* **(b)** to try hard to do something difficult; *she's struggling with her maths homework*

stubborn [ˈstʌbən] *adjective* not willing to change your mind; *he's so stubborn - he only does what he wants to do*

stuck [stʌk] *see* STICK

student [ˈstjuːdənt] *noun* person who is studying at a college or university; *two students had to sit the exam again*; **students' union** = building where university students meet to drink, eat, see films, etc.

studio [ˈstjuːdiəʊ] *noun* **(a)** place where films, broadcasts, etc., are made; *the TV series was made at Teddington Studios* **(b)** very small flat for one person, usually one room with a small kitchen and bathroom; *you can rent a studio with a view of the sea for £300 a week in high season* **(c)** room where an artist works; *she uses this room as a studio because of the good light* (NOTE: plural is studios)

study [ˈstʌdi] **1** *noun* room in which someone reads, writes, works, etc.; *when he says he is going to his study to read, it usually means he's going to have little sleep* **2** *verb* **(a)** to learn about a subject at college or university; *he is studying medicine because he wants to be a doctor* **(b)** to look at something carefully; *she was studying the guidebook*

stuff [stʌf] **1** *noun* **(a)** substance, especially something unpleasant; *you've got some black stuff stuck to your shoe* **(b)** things, equipment; *dump all your stuff in the living room*; *take all that stuff and put it in the dustbin* **2** *verb* **(a)** to push something into something to fill it; *he stuffed his pockets full of sweets for the children* **(b)** to put chopped onions, chopped meat, etc., inside meat or vegetables before cooking; *we had roast lamb stuffed with mushrooms*

stuffy [ˈstʌfi] *adjective* without any fresh air; *can't you open a window, it's so stuffy in here*; *I dislike travelling into town every day on stuffy underground trains* (NOTE: stuffier - stuffiest)

stumble [ˈstʌmbl] *verb* to hit your foot against something and almost fall; *he stumbled as he tried to get down the stairs in the dark*

stump [stʌmp] *noun* **(a)** short piece of something left sticking up, such as the trunk of a tree that has been cut down; *after cutting down the trees, we need to get rid of the stumps* **(b)** one of the three sticks placed in the ground as a target in cricket; *the ball hit the stumps and the last man was out*

stun [stʌn] *verb* **(a)** to knock someone out, to make someone unconscious by hitting him on the head; *the blow to his head stunned him* **(b)** to shock someone completely; *she was stunned when he told her that he was already married* (NOTE: stunning - stunned)

stung [stʌŋ] *see* STING

stunk [stʌŋk] *see* STINK

stupid [ˈstjuːpɪd] *adjective* **(a)** not very intelligent; *what a stupid idea!* **(b)** not showing any sense; *it was stupid of her not to wear a helmet when riding her scooter*

sturdy [ˈstɜːdi] *adjective* strong, with good muscles; *she has two sturdy little boys* (NOTE: sturdier - sturdiest)

stutter ['stʌtə] **1** *noun* speech problem where you repeat the sound at the beginning of a word several times; *he is trying to cure his stutter* **2** *verb* to repeat the same sounds when speaking; *he stuttered badly when making his speech*

style [staɪl] *noun* way of doing something, especially way of designing, drawing, writing, etc.; *that style of shoes was in fashion in the 1940s*

sub- [sʌb] *prefix meaning* below, under

subject ['sʌbdʒɪkt] *noun* **(a)** thing which you are talking about or writing about; *the newspaper has a special number on the subject of pollution* **(b)** something which you are studying at school or college; *maths is his weakest subject; you can take up to five subjects at 'A' Level* **(c)** to be the subject of = to be the person or thing talked about or studied; *the subject of our talk today will be the artist Turner* **(d)** *(grammar)* noun or pronoun which comes before a verb and shows the person or thing that does the action expressed by the verb; *in the sentence 'the cat sat on the mat' the word 'cat' is the subject of the verb 'sat'* **(e)** person who is born in a country, or who has the right to live in a country; *she is a British subject*

submarine [sʌbmə'riːn] *noun* special type of ship which can travel under water; *the submarine dived before she was spotted by enemy aircraft*

substance ['sʌbstəns] *noun* solid or liquid material, especially one used in chemistry; *a secret substance is added to the paint to give it its yellow colour*

subtract [sʌb'trækt] *verb* to take one number away from another; *subtract 10 from 33 and you get 23; subtracting is usually shown by the minus sign (-)*

subtraction [sʌb'trækʃn] *noun* act of subtracting one figure from another; *he tried to do the subtraction in his head*

suburb ['sʌbɜːb] *noun* area of houses on the edge of a town; *he lives in a quiet suburb of Boston*; **the suburbs** = area all round a town where a lot of people live

subway ['sʌbweɪ] *noun* **(a)** underground passage along which people can walk (as under a busy road); *there's a subway from the bus station to the shopping centre* **(b)** US underground railway system (similar to the London Underground); *it will be quicker to take the subway to Grand Central Station*

succeed [sʌk'siːd] *verb* **(a)** to do well; *his business has succeeded more than he had expected* **(b)** **to succeed in doing something** = to do what you have been trying to do; *she succeeded in passing her driving test*

success [sʌk'ses] *noun* **(a)** doing something which you have been trying to do; *she's been looking for a job in a library, but without any success so far* **(b)** doing something well; *her photo was in all the newspapers after her success in the Olympics* (NOTE: plural is **successes**)

successful [sʌk'sesfʊl] *adjective* who or which does well; *he's a successful architect*

such [sʌtʃ] *adjective* **(a)** **no such** = not existing; *there is no such day as April 31st; someone was asking for Mr Simpson but there is no such person working here* **(b)** **such as** = like; *some shops such as food stores are open on Sundays* **(c)** so much; *there was such a crowd at the party that there weren't enough chairs for everyone; few people can afford to drive such large cars*

suck [sʌk] *verb* **(a)** to hold something with your mouth and pull at it (with your tongue); *the baby didn't stop sucking his thumb until he was six* **(b)** to have something in your mouth which makes your mouth produce water; *he bought a bag of sweets to suck in the car* **(c)** to pull liquid into your mouth; *she sucked the orange juice through a straw*

sudden ['sʌdən] *adjective* **(a)** which happens very quickly or unexpectedly; *the bus came to a sudden stop* **(b)** **all of a sudden** =

suddenly, quickly, giving you a shock; *all of a sudden the room went dark*

suddenly ['sʌdənli] *adverb* quickly and giving you a shock; *the car in front stopped suddenly and I ran into the back of it*

suffer ['sʌfə] *verb* to receive an injury; *he suffered serious injuries in the accident*; **to suffer from** = to have an illness; *she suffers from constant headaches*

sufficient [sə'fiʃənt] *adjective (formal)* enough, as much as is needed; *allow yourself sufficient time to get to the airport*

suffix ['sʌfiks] *noun* letters added to the end of a word to make another word; *the suffix '-ly' can be added to an adjective to form an adverb such as 'quickly' or 'suddenly'* (NOTE: plural is **suffixes**)

sugar ['ʃʊgə] *noun* substance that you use to make food sweet; *how much sugar do you take in your tea?*; *can you pass me the sugar, please?*

suggest [sə'dʒest] *verb* to mention an idea to see what other people think of it; *I suggest that we should stop for coffee*; *what do you suggest we do now?*

suggestion [sə'dʒestʃn] *noun* idea that you mention for people to think about; *whose suggestion was it that we should go out in a boat?*

suit [suːt] **1** *noun* **(a)** set of pieces of clothing made of the same cloth and worn together, such as a jacket and trousers or skirt; *a dark grey suit will be just right for the interview* **(b)** one of the four sets of cards with the same symbol in a pack of cards; *clubs and spades are the two black suits and hearts and diamonds are the two red suits* **2** *verb* **(a)** to look good when worn by someone; *green usually suits people with red hair* **(b)** to be convenient; *Thursday at 11 o'clock will suit me fine*

suitable ['suːtəbl] *adjective* which fits or which is convenient; *the most suitable place to meet will be under the big clock at*

Waterloo Station

suitcase ['suːtkeɪs] *noun* box with a handle which you carry your clothes in when you are travelling; *I never pack my suitcase until the last minute*

sulk [sʌlk] *verb* to show you are annoyed by not saying anything; *they're sulking because we didn't invite them*

sultana [sʌl'tɑːnə] *noun* type of pale raisin with no seeds; *we will need sultanas for the Christmas cake*

sum [sʌm] *noun* **(a)** quantity of money; *he only paid a small sum for the car*; *a large sum of money was stolen from his safe* **(b)** simple problem in maths; *she tried to do the sum in her head* **(c)** total of two or more figures added together; *the sum of 250 and 350 is 600*

summary ['sʌməri] *noun* short description of what has been said or written, or of what happened, without giving all the details; *here's a summary of the book in case you don't have time to read it* (NOTE: plural is **summaries**)

summer ['sʌmə] *noun* hottest time of the year, the season between spring and autumn; *next summer we are going to Greece*; *the summer in Australia is at the same time as our winter here in England*; **the summer holidays** = period during the summer when children do not go to school; holidays taken during the period from June to September; *the weather was awful during our summer holidays*

summit ['sʌmit] *noun* **(a)** top of a mountain; *it took us three hour's hard climbing to reach the summit* **(b)** meeting of government leaders to discuss international problems; *the question was discussed at the last European summit*

sun [sʌn] *noun* **(a)** very bright star round which the earth travels and which gives us light and heat; *the sun was just rising when I got up*; *I'll try taking a photograph now that the sun's come out* **(b)** light from the sun; *I'd prefer a table out of the sun*; *she spent her* *whole holiday just sitting in the sun*

sunburnt [ˈsʌnbɜːnt] *adjective* made brown or red by the sun; *I stayed on the beach too long and got sunburnt*

Sunday [ˈsʌndi] *noun* the seventh day of the week, the day between Saturday and Monday; *last Sunday we went on a picnic*; *many shops are now open on Sundays*; *the 15th is a Saturday, so the 16th must be a Sunday*

sunflower [ˈsʌnflaʊə] *noun* very large yellow flower on a very tall stem; *the children are having a competition to see who can grow the tallest sunflower*

sung [sʌŋ] *see* SING

sunglasses [ˈsʌnɡlɑːsɪz] *noun* dark glasses worn to protect your eyes from the sun; *I always wear sunglasses when I'm driving*

sunk [sʌŋk] *see* SINK

sunlight [ˈsʌnlaɪt] *noun* light which comes from the sun; *sunlight was pouring into the room*

sunny [ˈsʌni] *adjective* **(a)** with the sun shining; *another sunny day!*; *they forecast that it will be sunny this afternoon* **(b)** where the sun often shines; *their sitting room is bright and sunny, but the dining room is dark* (NOTE: **sunnier - sunniest**)

sunrise [ˈsʌnraɪz] *noun* time when the sun comes up in the morning; *we get up at sunrise to milk the cows*

sunset [ˈsʌnset] *noun* time when the sun goes down in the evening; *at sunset, bats come out and fly around*

sunshine [ˈsʌnʃaɪn] *noun* pleasant light from the sun; *the west coast of France has more than 250 days of sunshine per year*

super [ˈsuːpə] *adjective (informal)* very good; *we had a super time in Greece*

superlative [suːˈpɜːlətɪv] *noun* form of an adjective showing the highest level when compared with another; *'biggest' is the superlative of 'big'; you can also form superlatives by adding phrases like 'as*

possible': 'as big as possible'

supermarket [ˈsuːpəmɑːkɪt] *noun* large store selling mainly food and household goods, where customers serve themselves and pay at a checkout; *we do all our shopping in the local supermarket*

supper [ˈsʌpə] *noun* light meal which you eat in the evening; *what do you want for your supper?*; **to have supper** = to eat an evening meal; *we usually have supper at about 7 o'clock*; *come and have some supper with us tomorrow evening*

supply [səˈplaɪ] **1** *noun* stock of something which is needed; *the government has sent medical supplies to the disaster area*; **in short supply** = not available in large enough quantities to meet the demand; *fresh vegetables are in short supply during the winter* **2** *verb* to provide something which is needed; *he was asked to supply a specimen of his signature; the local farm supplies the college with milk and cheese*

support [səˈpɔːt] **1** *noun* **(a)** thing which stops something from falling; *they had to build wooden supports to hold up the wall* **(b)** financial help, money; *we have had no financial support from the bank* **2** *verb* **(a)** to hold something up to stop it falling down; *the roof is supported on ten huge pillars* **(b)** to provide money to help; *we hope the banks will support us during the next few months* **(c)** to encourage; *which football team do you support?*

supporter [səˈpɔːtə] *noun* person who encourages a football team; *he's a Liverpool supporter*

suppose [sʌˈpəʊz] *verb* **(a)** to think something is probable; *I suppose you've heard the news?*; *what do you suppose they're talking about?*; *I don't suppose many people will come* **(b)** *(showing doubt)* what happens if?; *suppose it rains tomorrow, do you still want to go for a walk?*

sure [ʃʊə] **1** *adjective* **(a)** certain; *is he sure* he can borrow his mother's car?*; *I'm sure I left my car keys in my coat pocket*; *it's sure to be cold in Russia in December* **(b) sure of yourself** = confident that what you do is right; *he's only just started to drive, so he's still not very sure of himself* (NOTE: **surer - surest**) **2** *adverb* **(a)** *(meaning yes)* **can I borrow your car? - sure, go ahead!* **(b) sure enough** = as was expected; *no one thought he would pass his exams and sure enough he failed*

surf [sɜːf] **1** *noun* white waves breaking along a shore; *the surf is too rough for children to bathe* **2** *verb* **(a)** to ride on breaking waves on a board; *it's too dangerous to go surfing today* **(b) to surf the Internet** *or* **to surf the Net** = to explore websites looking at the pages in no particular order

surface ['sɜːfɪs] **1** *noun* top part of something; *when it rains, water collects on the surface of the road*; *he stayed a long time under water before coming back to the surface* **2** *verb* to come up to the surface; *the bird dived and then surfaced a few metres further on*

surgeon ['sɜːdʒən] *noun* doctor who does operations; *she has been sent to see an eye surgeon*

surgery ['sɜːdʒəri] *noun* **(a)** treatment of disease which requires an operation to cut into or remove part of your body; *the patient will need surgery* **(b)** room where a doctor or dentist sees and examines patients; *I phoned the doctor's surgery to make an appointment* (NOTE: plural is **surgeries**)

surname ['sɜːneɪm] *noun* name of someone's family, shared by all people in the family; *her first name is Anne, but I don't know her surname*; *Smith is the commonest surname in the London telephone book*

surprise [sə'praɪz] **1** *noun* **(a)** feeling when something happens which you did not expect to happen; *to his great surprise, a lot of people bought his book*; *what a surprise to find that we were at school together!* **(b)** something that was not expected to happen;

they baked a cake for her birthday as a surprise **2** *verb* to make someone astonished; *what surprises me is that she left without saying goodbye*

surrender [sə'rendə] **1** *noun* giving in to an enemy because you have lost; *the surrender of the enemy generals led to the end of the war* **2** *verb* to give in to an enemy because you have lost; *our soldiers were surrounded by the enemy and were forced to surrender*

surround [sə'raʊnd] *verb* to be all round someone or something; *the Prime Minister has surrounded himself with a group of friends from his time at university*; *their house is outside the town, surrounded by fields*

surroundings [sə'raʊndɪŋz] *noun* area around a person or place; *the surroundings of the hotel are very peaceful*

survey **1** *noun* ['sɜːveɪ] **(a)** investigating something by asking people questions; *we carried out a survey among our customers* **(b)** careful examination of a building to see if it is in good enough condition; *they asked for a survey of the house before buying it* **2** *verb* [sə'veɪ] **(a)** to ask people questions to get information about a subject; *roughly half the people we surveyed were in favour of the scheme* **(b)** to make a survey of a building; *the insurance company asked experts to survey the damage caused by the fire*

survive [sə'vaɪv] *verb* to continue to be alive after an accident, etc.; *it was such a terrible crash, it was miracle that anyone survived*

suspect **1** *adjective* ['sʌspekt] which might be dangerous; *don't open that box - it looks suspect to me* **2** *noun* ['sʌspekt] person who is thought to have committed a crime; *the police arrested several suspects for questioning* **3** *verb* [sə'spekt] **to suspect someone of doing something** = to think that someone may have done something wrong; *I suspect him of being involved in the attack on the bank*

suspense [sə'spens] *noun* waiting

impatiently for something to happen or for someone to do something; *friends and relatives of the passengers waited in suspense at the airport for news of the plane*

suspicious [səˈspɪʃəs] *adjective* **(a)** which seems to be wrong, dangerous or connected with a crime; *the police found a suspicious package on the station platform* **(b) suspicious of** = not trusting; *I'm suspicious of people who want me to lend them money*

swallow [ˈswɒləʊ] **1** *verb* to make food or liquid pass down your throat from your mouth to the stomach; *he swallowed a glass of water and went on running* **2** *noun* common bird with pointed wings and tail, which flies fast; *there are several swallows' nests under the roof*

swam [swæm] *see* SWIM

swamp [swɒmp] **1** *noun* area of land that is always wet, and the plants that grow in it; *you can't build on that land - it's a swamp* **2** *verb* to cover something with water; *the waves nearly swamped our little boat*; **swamped with** = having so much, that it is impossible to deal with it all; *the surgery has been swamped with calls from angry patients*

swan [swɒn] *noun* large white water bird with a long curved neck; *there are many swans on the River Thames near Windsor*

swap *or* **swop** [swɒp] *verb* to exchange something for something else; *can I swap my tickets for next Friday's show?*; *let's swap places, so that I can talk to Susan* (NOTE: **swapping** *or* **swopping** - **swapped** *or* **swopped**)

swarm [swɔːm] *noun* large group of insects, etc., flying around together; *a swarm of flies buzzed around the meat*

sway [sweɪ] *verb* to move gently from side to side; *the palm trees swayed in the breeze*

swear [ˈsweə] *verb* **(a)** to make a solemn public promise; *the witnesses swore to tell the truth* **(b)** *(informal)* **I could have sworn** = I was completely sure; *I could have sworn I put my keys in my coat pocket* **(c)** to shout rude

words; *they were shouting and swearing at the police* (NOTE: **swearing - swore** [swɔː] - **sworn** [swɔːn])

sweat [swet] **1** *noun* drops of salt liquid which come through your skin when you are hot; *after working in the field all day he was covered in sweat* **2** *verb* to produce sweat; *he ran up the hill, sweating and red in the face*

sweater [ˈswetə] *noun* knitted pullover with long sleeves; *you'll need a sweater in the evenings, even in the desert*

sweatshirt [ˈswetʃɜːt] *noun* thick cotton shirt with no buttons, but with long sleeves; *a sweatshirt is comfortable if the evening is cool*

Swede [swiːd] *noun* person from Sweden; *the Swedes have a very high standard of living*

Sweden [ˈswiːdən] *noun* country in northern Europe, between Norway and Finland; *we went for a camping holiday in Sweden*; *summer evenings in Sweden can be quite cool* (NOTE: capital: **Stockholm**; people: **the Swedes**; language: **Swedish**)

Swedish [ˈswiːdɪʃ] **1** *adjective* coming from Sweden; referring to Sweden; *Swedish roads do not have as much traffic as ours* **2** *noun* language spoken in Sweden; *can you translate this letter into Swedish, please?*

sweep [swiːp] *verb* **(a)** to clear up dust, dirt, etc., from the floor with a brush; *have you swept the kitchen floor yet?* **(b)** to move rapidly; **to sweep past** = to go past quickly; *the president's car swept past the crowd of demonstrators* **(c) to sweep something away** = to carry something rapidly away; *she was swept away by the powerful current* (NOTE: **sweeping - swept** [swept])

sweet [swiːt] **1** *adjective* **(a)** tasting like sugar, and neither sour nor bitter; *these apples are sweeter than those green ones*; **to have a sweet tooth** = to like sweet food **(b)** nice, pleasant; *it was sweet of her to send me flowers* (NOTE: **sweeter - sweetest**) **2** *noun* **(a)**

small piece of sweet food, made with sugar; *he likes to suck sweets when he is driving*; **cough sweets** = sweet pills which you suck to cure a cough **(b)** last course in a meal, sweet food eaten at the end of a meal; *don't bring the coffee, we haven't had our sweet yet*; **sweet trolley** = trolley with different sweet dishes, brought to your table in a restaurant for you to choose from

swell [swel] *verb* **to swell (up)** = to become larger or to increase in size; *she was bitten by an insect and her hand swelled (up)* (NOTE: **swelling - swollen** ['swələn] **- swelled**)

swelling ['swelɪŋ] *noun* part of the body which has swollen up; *he had a swelling on his neck and went to see the doctor*

swept [swept] *see* SWEEP

swerve [swɜːv] *verb* to move suddenly to one side; *she had to swerve to avoid the bicycle*

swift [swɪft] **1** *adjective* rapid; *their phone call brought a swift reaction from the police* (NOTE: **swifter - swiftest**) **2** *noun* little bird like a swallow but with shorter wings and tail, which flies very fast; *swifts were darting about high overhead*

swim [swɪm] **1** *noun* moving in the water, using your arms and legs to push you along; *what about a swim before breakfast?* **2** *verb* to move in the water using your arms and legs to push you along; *she can't swim, but she's taking swimming lessons*; *he swam four lengths of the pool before breakfast* (NOTE: **swimming - swam**) [swæm] **- has swum** [swʌm])

swimming ['swɪmɪŋ] *noun* action of swimming; **swimming costume** = clothes worn by women when swimming; *we forgot to bring our swimming costumes*; **swimming pool** = large pool for swimming; *the school has an indoor swimming pool*

swing [swɪŋ] **1** *noun* seat held by ropes or chains, on which you can sit and move backwards and forwards; *she sat on the swing and ate an apple* **2** *verb* **(a)** to move from side to side or forwards and backwards, while

hanging from a central point; *a window swung open and a man looked out* **(b)** to change direction; *the car swung off the road into the hotel car park* (NOTE: **swinging - swung** [swʌŋ])

Swiss [swɪs] **1** *adjective* **(a)** referring to Switzerland; *we eat a lot of Swiss cheese* **(b)** **Swiss roll** = cake made by rolling up a thin sheet of cake covered with jam or cream **2** *noun* **the Swiss** = people from Switzerland; *the Swiss celebrate their national day on August 1st*

switch [swɪtʃ] **1** *noun* button that you push up or down to stop or start something electric; *there is a light switch by the bed* (NOTE: plural is **switches**) **2** *verb* **(a)** to do something quite different suddenly; *we decided to switch from gas to electricity* **(b)** to change; *he switched flights in Montreal and went on to Calgary*

switch off ['swɪtʃ 'ɒf] *verb* to make an electrical device stop; *don't forget to switch off the TV before you go to bed*; *she forgot to switch her car lights off*

switch on ['swɪtʃ 'ɒn] *verb* to make an electrical device start; *can you switch the radio on - it's time for the evening news*

Switzerland ['swɪtzələænd] *noun* European country, south of Germany, east of France and north of Italy; *many people go on skiing holidays in Switzerland* (NOTE: capital: **Berne**; people: **the Swiss**; languages: **French, German, Italian**)

swollen ['swəʊlən] *adjective* much bigger than usual; *she can't walk fast with her swollen ankles*

swoop [swuːp] *verb* to come down rapidly to make a sudden attack; *the planes swooped down low over the enemy camp*

swop [swɒp] *noun & verb see* SWAP

sword [sɔːd] *noun* weapon with a handle and a long sharp blade; *he rushed onto the stage waving a sword*

swore, sworn [swɔː or swɔːn] *see* SWEAR

swum [swʌm] *see* SWIM

swung [swʌŋ] *see* SWING

syllable ['sɪləbl] *noun* a whole word or part of a word which has one single sound; *there a three syllables in the word 'sympathy'*

symbol ['sɪmbl] *noun* sign, letter, picture or shape which means something or shows something; *the olive branch is a symbol of peace*; *Pb is the chemical symbol for lead*

sympathy ['sɪmpəθi] *noun* feeling of understanding for someone else's problems, or after someone's death; *we received many messages of sympathy when grandmother died*; *he had no sympathy for his secretary who complained of having too much work*

syrup ['sɪrəp] *noun* sweet liquid; *to make syrup, dissolve sugar in a cup of boiling water*

system ['sɪstəm] *noun* **(a)** group of things which work together; *the French railway system is very efficient* **(b)** way in which things are organized; *I've got my own system for dealing with household bills*

Tt

T, t [tiː] twentieth letter of the alphabet, between S and U; *don't forget - you spell 'attach' with two Ts*

table ['teɪbl] *noun* **(a)** piece of furniture with a flat top and legs, used to eat at, work at, etc.; *we had breakfast sitting round the kitchen table*; *she says she booked a table for six people for 12.30* **(b)** list of figures, facts, or information set out in columns; **table of contents** = list of contents in a book **(c)** list of numbers to learn by heart how each number is multiplied; *he's learnt his nine times table*; *children sometimes learn their multiplication tables by heart, saying: 'three threes are nine, four threes are twelve, five threes are fifteen', etc.*

table tennis ['teɪbl 'tenɪs] *noun* game similar to tennis, but played on a large table with a net across the centre, with small round bats and a very light white ball; *do you want a game of table tennis?*

tablecloth ['teɪblklɒθ] *noun* cloth which covers a table during a meal; *put a clean tablecloth on the table*

tablet ['tæblət] *noun* small round pill taken as medicine; *take two tablets before meals*

tackle ['tækl] **1** *noun* equipment; *he brought all his fishing tackle with him* **2** *verb* **(a)** to try to deal with a problem or job; *you start cleaning the dining room and I'll tackle the washing up* **(b)** *(in football, etc.)* to try to get the ball from a player; *he was tackled before he could score*

tail [teɪl] *noun* **(a)** long thin part at the end of an animal's body, which can move; *all you could see was a slight movement of the cat's tail*; *peacocks have huge tails* **(b)** end or back part of something; *the tail of the queue stretched round the corner and into the next street*; *they say it is safer to sit near the tail of an aircraft* (NOTE: do not confuse with **tale**)

take [teɪk] *verb* **(a)** to lift and move something; *she took the pot of jam down from the shelf* **(b)** to carry something to another place; *can you take this cheque to the bank for me, please?* **(c)** to go with someone or something to another place; *he's taking the children to school*; *they took the car to the garage* **(d)** to steal; *someone's taken my watch* **(e)** to go away with something which someone else was using; *someone has taken* the newspaper I was reading; *who's taken my cup of coffee?* (f) to use or occupy; *sorry, all these seats are taken* (g) to do a test; *she had to take her driving test three times before she finally passed* (h) to accept; *if they offer you the job, take it immediately* (i) to do certain actions; *we took our holiday in September this year*; *he took a photograph of the Tower of London*; *she needs to take a rest* (j) to need; *it took three strong men to move the piano*; *it took them two days to get to London* (NOTE: **taking - took** [tʊk] **- has taken** [ˈteɪkn])

take away [ˈteɪk əˈweɪ] *verb* (a) to remove something or someone; *take those scissors away from little Nicky - he could cut himself* (b) to subtract one number from another; *ten take away four equals six (10 - 4 = 6)*

take off [ˈteɪk ˈɒf] *verb* (a) to remove, especially your clothes; *take your dirty boots off before you come into the kitchen* (b) to remove or to take away; *he took £25 off the price* (c) *(of plane)* to leave the ground; *the plane took off at 4.30*

take over [ˈteɪk ˈəʊvə] *verb* (a) to start to do something in place of someone else; *when our history teacher was ill, the English teacher had to take over his classes* (b) to buy a business; *the company was taken over by a big group last month*

take up [ˈteɪk ˈʌp] *verb* (a) to occupy or to fill a space; *this sofa takes up too much room* (b) to remove something which was down; *you will need to take up the carpets if you want to polish the floor underneath*

takeaway [ˈteɪkəweɪ] *noun & adjective* (a) shop where you can buy cooked food to eat somewhere else; *there's an Indian takeaway round the corner* (b) hot meal which you buy to eat back home; *we had a Chinese takeaway*

talcum powder [ˈtælkʌm ˈpaʊdə] *noun* soft powder with a pleasant scent, used to make the skin softer or to reduce rubbing; *she put some talcum powder between her toes*

tale [teɪl] *noun* story; *a tale of a princess and her wicked sisters*; **old wives' tale** = old, and

often silly, idea; *eating carrots won't make you see in the dark - that's just an old wives' tale* (NOTE: do not confuse with **tail**)

talent [ˈtælənt] *noun* natural ability or skill; *she has a talent for painting portraits*

talk [tɔːk] **1** *noun* (a) conversation, discussion; *I had a long talk with my father about what I should study at university* (b) formal speech about a subject; *he gave a short talk about the history of the town* **2** *verb* to say things, to speak; *the guide was talking French to the group of tourists*

talk over [ˈtɔːk ˈəʊvə] *verb* to discuss; *we've talked it over and decided not to leave*

talkative [ˈtɔːkətɪv] *adjective* who likes to talk a lot or to gossip; *our new neighbours are not very talkative*

tall [tɔːl] *adjective* high, usually higher than normal; *the bank building is the tallest building in London*; *can you see those tall trees over there?*; *his brother is over six feet tall* (NOTE: **taller - tallest**)

tame [teɪm] *adjective* (animal) which is not wild, which can be approached by human beings; *don't be afraid of that fox - he's perfectly tame*

tan [tæn] **1** *noun* brown colour of the skin after being in the sun; *she got a tan from spending each day on the beach* **2** *verb* to get brown from being in the sun; *she tans easily - just half an hour in the sun and she's quite brown* (NOTE: **tanning - tanned**)

tangerine [ˈtændʒəˈriːn] *noun* small orange with soft skin which peels easily; *there was a bowl of tangerines on the table*

tangle [ˈtæŋgl] **1** *noun* mass of threads, string, hair, etc., all mixed together; *the tangle of bushes in the back garden needs clearing* **2** *verb* to get things mixed together in knots; *her hair is so tangled that you can't comb it*

tank [tæŋk] *noun* (a) large container for liquids; *how much oil is left in the tank?*; **petrol tank** = container in a car, truck, etc., for holding petrol (b) heavy army vehicle with caterpillar tracks and powerful guns; *tanks rolled along the main streets of the town*

tanker ['tæŋkə] *noun* ship or truck for carrying liquids, especially oil; *an oil tanker ran onto the rocks in the storm*; *a petrol tanker broke down on the motorway*

tap [tæp] **1** *noun* device with a knob which, when you twist it, lets liquid or gas come out; *he washed his hands under the tap in the kitchen*; *she forgot to turn the gas tap off* **2** *verb* to hit something gently; *she tapped him on the knee with her finger*; *a policeman tapped him on the shoulder and arrested him* (NOTE: **tapping - tapped**)

tape [teɪp] **1** *noun* (a) long narrow strip of cloth, plastic, etc.; **tape measure** = long strip of plastic marked in centimetres or inches, etc., used for measuring; *he took out a tape measure and measured the length of the table* (b) **magnetic tape** = special plastic tape on which sounds and pictures can be recorded **2** *verb* to record something on magnetic tape or on video; *the whole conversation was taped by the police*; *I didn't see the programme because I was at work, but I've taped it*

tar [tɑ:] *noun* sticky black substance which comes from coal and is used for covering roads; *they were spreading tar and sand on the road*

target ['tɑ:gɪt] *noun* (a) object which you aim at with a gun, etc.; *his last shot missed the target altogether* (b) point which you try to reach; **to set targets** = to fix quantities which workers have to produce

tart [tɑ:t] **1** *noun* small pastry dish filled with sweet food; *an apple tart* **2** *adjective* bitter (taste); *the pie tastes tart - you didn't put enough sugar in* (NOTE: **tarter - tartest**)

tartan ['tɑ:tən] *noun* cloth woven into a special Scottish pattern; *she wore a tartan kilt*; *my Scottish grandmother gave me a tartan rug*

task [tɑ:sk] *noun* job of work which has to be done; *there are many tasks which need to be done in the garden*

taste [teɪst] **1** *noun* (a) one of the five senses, by which you can tell differences between things you eat, using your tongue; *I've got a cold, so I've lost all sense of taste* (b) flavour of something that you eat or drink; *the pudding has a funny taste*; *this milk shake has no taste at all* **2** *verb* (a) to notice the taste of something with your tongue; *can you taste the onions in this soup?*; *she's got a cold so she can't taste anything* (b) to have a certain taste; *this cake tastes of soap*; *the pudding tastes very good* (c) to try something to see if you like it; *she asked if she could taste the cheese before buying it*

tasty ['teɪsti] *adjective* with an especially pleasant taste; *I liked that pie - it was very tasty* (NOTE: **tastier - tastiest**)

taught [tɔ:t] *see* TEACH

tax [tæks] *noun* money taken by the government from incomes, sales, etc., to pay for government services; *the government is planning to introduce a tax on food* (NOTE: plural is **taxes**)

taxi ['tæksi] *noun* car which you can hire with a driver; *can you call a taxi to take me to the airport?*; **taxi driver** = person who drives a taxi; *the taxi driver helped me with my luggage*

tea [ti:] *noun* (a) drink made from hot water which has been poured onto the dried leaves of a tropical plant; *can I have another cup of tea?*; *I don't like tea - can I have coffee instead?* (b) the dried leaves of a tropical plant used to make a warm drink; *we've run out of tea, can you buy some at the supermarket?* (c) a cup of tea; *can we have two teas and two cakes, please?* (d) afternoon meal at which you drink tea and eat bread, cake, etc.; *why don't you come for tea tomorrow?*; *the children have had their tea*

teabag ['ti:bæg] *noun* small paper bag with

tea in it which you put into the pot with hot water; *I don't like weak tea - put another teabag in the pot*

teach [tiːtʃ] *verb* to give lessons, to show someone how to do something; *she taught me how to drive*; *he teaches maths in the local school* (NOTE: **teaching - taught** [tɔːt])

teacher [ˈtiːtʃə] *noun* person who teaches, especially in a school; *Mr Jones is our maths teacher*; *the French teacher is ill today*

team [tiːm] **1** *noun* group of people who play a game together; *there are eleven people in a football team and fifteen in a rugby team* **(b)** group of people who work together; *in this job you have to be able to work as a member of a team*

teapot [ˈtiːpɒt] *noun* pot which is used for making tea; *put two teabags into the teapot and add boiling water*

tear **1** [tɪə] *noun* **(a)** drop of salt water which forms in your eye when you cry; *tears were running down her cheeks*; **she burst into tears** = she suddenly started crying **2** [teə] *verb* **(a)** to make a hole in something by pulling; *he tore his trousers climbing over the fence* **(b)** to pull something into bits; *he tore the letter in half* (NOTE: **tearing - tore** [tɔː] **- torn** [tɔːn])

tease [tiːz] *verb* to say or do something to annoy someone on purpose; *he teased her about her thick glasses*; *stop teasing that poor cat*

teaspoon [ˈtiːspuːn] *noun* small spoon for stirring tea or other liquid; *can you bring me a teaspoon, please?*

teatime [ˈtiːtaɪm] *noun* time when tea is served (between 4 and 5.30 p.m.); *hurry up, it'll soon be teatime!*; *the children's TV programmes are on at teatime*

technology [tekˈnɒlədʒi] *noun* use or study of manufacturing or scientific skills; *we already have the technology to make this machine*; *the government has promised to give more money to research in science and technology*

teddy (bear) [ˈtedi ˈbeə] *noun* child's toy bear; *she won't go to bed without her teddy bear* (NOTE: the plural is **teddies**)

teenager [ˈtiːneɪdʒə] *noun* young person aged between 13 and 19; *most of the people who come to the club are teenagers*

teeshirt [ˈtiːʃɜːt] *noun* light shirt with no buttons or collar, usually with short sleeves; *when last seen, she was wearing jeans and a teeshirt*

teeth [tiːθ] *see* TOOTH

telephone [ˈtelɪfəʊn] **1** *noun* machine which you use to speak to someone who is some distance away; *can't someone answer the telephone - it's been ringing and ringing*; *she lifted the telephone and called the ambulance* **2** *verb* to call someone using a telephone; *your sister telephoned when you were out*

on the telephone [ˈɒn ðə ˈtelɪfəʊn] speaking by telephone; *don't make such a noise - Daddy's on the telephone*

telescope [ˈtelɪskəʊp] *noun* tube with a set of lenses for looking at objects which are very far away; *with a telescope you can see the stars very clearly*

television (TV) [telɪˈvɪʒən] *noun* **(a)** sound and pictures which are sent through the air or along cables and appear on a special machine; *we don't watch television every night - some nights we go to the club* **(b)** piece of electrical equipment which shows television pictures; *we can't watch anything - our television has broken down*

tell [tel] *verb* **(a)** to say something to someone, for example a story or a joke; *she told me a long story about how she got lost in London* **(b)** to give information to someone; *the policeman told them how to get to the post office* **(c) to tell someone to do something** = to give someone instructions; *the teacher told the children to stand in a line* **(d)** to notice; *you can tell he is embarrassed when his face goes red* **(e) to tell the time** = to be able to read the time from a clock; *he's only three, but he can already tell the time* (NOTE: **telling - told** [təʊld])

temper ['tempə] *noun* general mood of someone; **to lose your temper** = to become angry; *he lost his temper when he found his car had been stolen*

temperature ['temprətʃə] *noun* **(a)** heat measured in degrees; *the temperature of water in the swimming pool is 25°; I can't start the car when the temperature is below zero* **(b)** illness where your body is hotter than normal; *the doctor says she's got a temperature and has to stay in bed*

temple ['templ] *noun* building for worship, usually Hindu or Buddhist, or ancient Greek or Roman, but not Christian or Muslim; *we visited the Greek temples on the islands*

temporary ['temprəri] *adjective* which only lasts a short time; *she has a temporary job with a building company; we usually hire about twenty temporary staff during the Christmas period*

tempt [temt] *verb* to try to persuade someone to do something, especially something pleasant or wrong; *can I tempt you to have another cream cake?; they tried to tempt him to leave his job and work for them*

ten [ten] **(a)** number 10; *in the market they're selling ten oranges for two dollars; she's ten (years old) next week* **(b)** *(informal)* **ten to one** = very likely; *ten to one he finds out about the payment*

tend [tend] *verb* **(a) to tend to do something** = to be likely to do something; *she tends to get angry very easily* **(b)** to look after something; *his job is to tend the flower beds in front of the town hall*

tender ['tendə] **1** *adjective* **(a)** (food) which is easy to cut or chew; *a plate of tender young beans;* **tender meat** = which can be chewed or cut easily (as opposed to tough meat); *the meat was so tender, you hardly needed a knife to cut it* **(b)** showing love; *the plants*

need a lot of tender loving care **2** *noun* offer to do something at a certain price; **to put in a tender for a job** = to offer to do work at a certain price

tennis ['tenɪs] *noun* game for two or four players who hit a ball backwards and forwards over a net; *he's joined the local tennis club; would you like a game of tennis?*

tense [tens] **1** *adjective* nervous and worried; *I always get tense before going to a job interview* (NOTE: **tenser - tensest**) **2** *noun* *(grammar)* form of a verb which shows the time when the action takes place; *'he will eat' and 'he is going to eat' are forms of the future tense of the verb 'to eat'; 'sang' is the past tense of the verb 'to sing'*

tent [tent] *noun* shelter made of cloth, held up by poles and attached to the ground with ropes; *we went camping in the Alps and took our tent in the back of the car; the flower show was held in a tent in the grounds of the castle*

tenth (10th) [tenθ] *adjective & noun* the *tenth of April* or *April the tenth (April 10th); that's the tenth phone call I've had this morning; King Charles X ('King Charles the Tenth') was King of France;* **the tenth century** = the period from 900 to 999

term [tɜːm] *noun* **(a)** one of the parts of a school or university year; *a school year has three terms: autumn, spring and summer; cricket is played during the summer term only* **(b) terms** = conditions which are agreed before something else is done; *we bought the shop on very good terms*

terminal ['tɜːmɪnəl] *noun* **(a)** building at an airport where planes arrive or depart; *the flight will depart from Terminal 2* **(b)** connecting point in an electric circuit; *a positive terminal is shown by a plus sign* **(c)** **computer terminal** = computer keyboard and monitor which are linked to a system

terrace ['terəs] *noun* **(a)** flat area with a stone or tiled floor, which is raised above another area; *the guests had drinks on the terrace before going into dinner* **(b)** row of similar houses connected together; *they live in an early nineteenth century terrace in Islington* **(c) terraces** = rows of wide steps in a football stadium on which the spectators stand; *the terraces were packed with Liverpool fans*

terrible ['terɪbl] *adjective* very bad; *there was a terrible storm last night; it must have been terrible to be in the car when it fell into the river*

terrific [tə'rɪfɪk] *adjective* **(a)** wonderful; *we had a terrific time at the party* **(b)** very big or loud; *there was a terrific bang and the whole building collapsed*

terrify ['terɪfaɪ] *verb* to make someone very frightened; *the sound of thunder terrifies me*

territory ['terɪtri] *noun* **(a)** large stretch of land; land which belongs to a country; *they occupied all the territory on the east bank of the river* **(b)** area which an animal or bird thinks belongs only to it; *animals often fight to defend their territories* (NOTE: plural is **territories**)

terror ['terə] *noun* great fear; *they live in constant terror of enemy attacks*

test [test] **1** *noun* **(a)** examination to see if you know something, etc.; *we had an English test yesterday; she passed her driving test* **(b)** examination to see if something is working well; *the doctor will do a blood test* **2** *verb* **(a)** to examine to see if you can do something, etc.; *the teacher tested me in spoken German* **(b)** to examine to see if everything is working well; *he has to have his eyes tested*

text [tekst] *noun* main written section of a book, not the notes, index, pictures, etc.; *it's a book for little children, with lots of pictures and very little text*

textbook ['tekstbʊk] *noun* book which students use to learn the subject they are studying; *we've been recommended to buy this English textbook*

text message ['tekst 'mesɪdʒ] *noun* message

sent by telephone, using short forms of words, which appear on the screen of a mobile phone; *he sent me a text message asking me to meet him at the club tonight*

than [ðæn or ðən] **1** *conjunction (used to show something which is being compared with something else)* *it's hotter this week than it was last week* **2** *preposition (used to link two things that are being compared)* *his car is bigger than mine*

thank [θæŋk] *verb* **(a)** to show you are grateful to someone for doing something for you; *don't forget to thank Aunt Anne for her present* **(b) thank goodness!** *or* **thank God!** *or* **thank heavens!** = expressions used to show relief; *thank goodness it didn't rain for the school sports day!; thank God the ambulance came quickly!*

thank you ['θæŋk juː] *interjection showing that you are grateful;* *thank you very much for your letter of the 15th; did you remember to say thank you to your grandmother for the present?; would you like another piece of cake? - no thank you, I've had enough*

thanks [θæŋks] **1** *noun showing that you are grateful;* *many thanks for your letter of the 15th* **2** *interjection showing you are grateful;* *do you want some more tea? - no thanks, I've had two cups already*

thanks to ['θæŋks 'tuː] *preposition* because of, as a result of; *thanks to our map we found his house without any difficulty*

that [ðæt] **1** *adjective (used to show something which is further away)* *can you see that white house over there?; do you remember the name of that awful hotel in Brighton?* (NOTE: the plural is **those**) **2** *pronoun* *that's the book I was talking about* **3** *relative pronoun* *there's the suitcase that you left on the train!* **4** *conjunction* **(a)** *(after verbs)* *they told me that the manager was out; I'm glad that the weather turned out fine* **(b)** *(after 'so' or 'such')* *it rained so hard that the street was like a river*

thatched [θætʃt] *adjective* covered with a

straw roof; *he lives in a little thatched cottage*

thaw [θɔː] **1** *verb* **(a)** to melt; *the ice is thawing on the village pond* **(b)** to warm something which is frozen; *can you thaw the frozen peas?* **2** *noun* warm weather which makes snow and ice melt; *the thaw came early this year*

the [ðə or ðɪ] *article* **(a)** *(meaning something in particular)* *that's the cat from next door* **(b)** *(used with something of which only one exists)* *the sun came up over the hills* **(c)** *(meaning something in general)* *the streets are crowded in the middle of the day*; *many people were out of work during the 1990s* **(d)** [ðiː] *(meaning something very special)* *it's the shop for men's clothes* **(e)** *(used to compare)* *the more he eats the thinner he seems to get*

theatre *US* **theater** [ˈθɪətə] *noun* building in which plays are shown; *I'm trying to get tickets for the theatre tonight*; *what is the play at the local theatre this week?*

their [ðeə] *adjective* belonging to them, referring to them; *after the film, we went to their house for supper* (NOTE: do not confuse with **there, they're**)

theirs [ðeəz] *pronoun* the one that belongs to them; *the girls wanted to borrow my car - theirs wouldn't start*

them [ðem] *object pronoun (referring to a people or things which have been mentioned before)* *there's a group of people waiting outside - tell them to come in*

theme [θiːm] *noun* main idea; *the theme of the exhibition is 'Europe in the twenty-first century'*

themselves [ðəmˈselvz] *pronoun* **(a)** *(referring to the people or things that are the subject of the verb)* *cats always spend a lot of time cleaning themselves* **(b)** by themselves = all alone; *the girls were all by themselves in the tent*; *they did it all by themselves*

then [ðen] *adverb* **(a)** at that time in the past or future; *he had been very busy up till then* **(b)** after that, next; *we all sat down, and then*

after a few minutes the waiter brought us the menu

there [ðeə] **1** *adverb* **(a)** in or to that place; *have you ever been to China? - yes, I went there last month* **(b)** *(used when giving something to someone)* *there you are: two fish and chips and a pot of tea* (NOTE: do not confuse with **their, they're**) **2** *pronoun (used usually with the verb to 'be')*; *there's a little door leading into the garden*; *there's someone at the door asking for you*; *were there a lot of people at the cinema?*

therefore [ˈðeəfɔː] *adverb* for this reason; *the children are all over ten and therefore can be left to look after themselves*

thermometer [θəˈmɒmɪtə] *noun* instrument for measuring temperature; *put the thermometer in your mouth - I want to take your temperature*

these [ðiːz] *see* THIS

they [ðeɪ] *pronoun* **(a)** *(referring to people or things)* *where do you keep the spoons? - they're in the right-hand drawer*; *the children played in the sun and they all got red* **(b)** *(referring to people in general)* *they say it's going to be fine this weekend*

they'd [ðeɪd] = THEY HAD, THEY WOULD

they'll [ðeɪl] = THEY WILL

they're [ðeə] = THEY ARE (NOTE: do not confuse with **their, there**)

they've [ðeɪv] = THEY HAVE

thick [θɪk] **1** *adjective* **(a)** bigger than usual when measured from side to side, not thin; *he cut a slice of bread which was so thick it wouldn't go into the toaster*; *the walls of the castle are three metres thick* **(b)** close together; *they tried to make their way through thick jungle*; *the field was covered with thick grass* **(c)** *(of liquids)* which cannot flow easily; *if the paint is too thick add some water* (NOTE: **thicker - thickest**)

thief [θiːf] *noun* person who steals; *the police*

are certain they will catch the thief (NOTE: plural is **thieves** [θiːvz])

thigh [θaɪ] *noun* top part of the leg between your knee and your hip; *the water wasn't very deep, it only came up to my thighs*

thin [θɪn] *adjective* **(a)** not fat; *he's too thin - he should eat more* **(b)** not thick; *the book is printed on very thin paper* **(c)** *(of liquid)* which flows easily, which has too much water; *all we had for lunch was a bowl of thin soup* **(d)** which you can see through; *a thin mist covered the valley* (NOTE: **thinner - thinnest**)

thing [θɪŋ] *noun* **(a)** something which is not living, which is not a plant or animal; *what do you use that big blue thing for?* **(b)** something in general; *the first thing to do is to call an ambulance*; **a good thing** = something lucky; *it's a good thing there was no policeman on duty at the door* **(c) things** = clothes, equipment; *did you bring your tennis things?* **(d) things** = general situation; *he always takes things too seriously*; *how are things going at college?*

think [θɪŋk] *verb* **(a)** to use your mind; *we never think about what people might say, we always do what we think is right* **(b)** to have an opinion; *I think London is a nicer town to live in than Frankfurt*; *everyone thinks we're mad to go on holiday in December* **(c)** to make a plan to do something; *we're thinking of going to Greece in June* (NOTE: **thinking - thought** [θɔːt])

think about ['θɪŋk ə'baʊt] *verb* **(a)** to have someone or something in your mind; *all she thinks about is food* **(b)** to have an opinion about something; *what do you think about Dad's idea of selling the house?*

think of ['θɪŋk 'ɒv] *verb* **(a)** to consider a plan in your mind; *we are thinking of going to Greece on holiday* **(b)** to have an opinion about something; *she asked him what he thought of her idea*; **to tell someone what you think of something** = to criticize something; *he went up to her and told her exactly what he thought of her stupid idea*

think up ['θɪŋk 'ʌp] *verb* to invent a plan or new idea; *he thought up a mad plan for making lots of money*

third (3rd) [θɜːd] **1** *adjective* **(a)** referring to three; *she came third in the race*; *the cake shop is the third shop on the right*; *it will be her third birthday next Friday*; **the third century** = the period from 200 to 299; *King Henry III ('King Henry the Third') reigned for a long time* **(b)** *(followed by a superlative)* only two others are more; *this is the third longest bridge in the world* **2** *noun* one part out of three equal parts; *a third of the staff work in the warehouse*

thirsty ['θɜːsti] *adjective* feeling that you want to drink; *it's so hot here that it makes me thirsty* (NOTE: **thirstier - thirstiest**)

thirteen [θɜː'tiːn] number 13; *he's only thirteen (years old), but he can drive a car*; *she'll be thirteen next Monday*; **the thirteen hundreds (1300s)** = the period from 1300 to 1399 (compare with the 'thirteenth century')

thirteenth (13th) [θɜː'tiːnθ] *adjective & noun* *it's her thirteenth birthday on Monday*; *King Louis XIII ('King Louis the Thirteenth') was the father of Louis XIV*; **Friday the thirteenth (Friday 13th)** = day which many people think is unlucky; **the thirteenth century** = the period from 1200 to 1399 (compare with the 'thirteen hundreds')

thirtieth (30th) ['θɜːtɪəθ] *adjective & noun* referring to thirty; *he came thirtieth out of thirty-five in the race*; *it was his thirtieth birthday last week*

thirty ['θɜːti] number 30; *he's thirty (years old); she must have more than thirty pairs of shoes*; *she and her partner are both in their* **thirties** = they are both aged between 30 and 39 years old; **the (nineteen) thirties (1930s)** = the period from 1930 to 1939

this [ðɪs] *adjective & pronoun* **(a)** *(used to show something which is nearer - in contrast to 'that')* *this is the shop which was mentioned in the paper* (NOTE: plural is **these**)

(b) *(used to refer to a part of today, or some time close to now)* **I saw him on the train this morning; I expect to hear from him this week; they're going to Spain this summer**

thistle ['θɪsl] *noun* large wild plant with purple flowers, and leaves with prickles; *he sat down on a patch of thistles and jumped up again*

thorn [θɔːn] *noun* sharp point on a plant; *most roses have sharp thorns*

thorough ['θʌrə] *adjective* **(a)** very careful and detailed; *the police carried out a thorough search of the woods* **(b)** complete; *they made a thorough mess of the job*

thoroughly ['θʌrəli] *adverb* **(a)** in a complete and careful way; *we searched the garden thoroughly but couldn't find his red ball* **(b)** completely; *I'm thoroughly fed up with the whole business*

those [ðəʊz] *see* THAT

though [ðəʊ] *adverb & conjunction* **(a)** **(even) though** = in spite of the fact that; *he didn't wear a coat, even though it was snowing; we don't have any plants inside the house, though most people do* **(b)** **as though** = as if; *his voice sounded strange over the telephone, as though he was standing in a cave; it looks as though the house is empty*

thought [θɔːt] **1** *noun* idea which you have when thinking; *he had an awful thought - suppose he had left the bathroom taps running?* **2** *verb see* THINK

thoughtful ['θɔːtfʊl] *adjective* **(a)** thinking deeply; *he looked thoughtful, and I wondered if there was something wrong* **(b)** kind, thinking about what other people want; *it was very thoughtful of you to come to see me in hospital*

thousand ['θaʊzənd] *number* 1000; *we paid two hundred thousand pounds (£200,000) for the house; thousands of people had their holidays spoilt by the storm*

thread [θred] **1** *noun* long piece of cotton, silk, etc.; *a spider spins a thread to make its web; wait a moment, there's a white thread showing on your coat* **2** *verb* to put a piece of cotton through the little hole in a needle; *can you thread this needle for me?*

threat [θret] *noun* warning that you are going to do something unpleasant, especially if someone doesn't do what you want; *he's been making threats against her and the children;* **death threat** = warning to someone that he or she will be killed

threaten ['θretn] *verb* to warn that you are going to do something unpleasant, especially if someone doesn't do what you want; *she threatened to call the police*

three [θriː] *number* 3; *she's only three (years old), so she can't read yet; three men walked into the bank and pulled out guns*

three-quarters [θriːˈkwɔːtəz] *noun* three fourths, 75%; *about three-quarters of the class are away from school with colds;* **three-quarters of an hour** = forty-five minutes; *we had to wait for three-quarters of an hour for a bus*

threw [θruː] *see* THROW (NOTE: do not confuse with **through**)

thrill [θrɪl] **1** *noun* feeling of great excitement; *it gave me a thrill to see you all again after so many years* **2** *verb* to make someone very excited; *we were thrilled to get your letter*

thrilling ['θrɪlɪŋ] *adjective* which makes you very excited; *it was thrilling to arrive in New York for the first time*

throat [θrəʊt] *noun* **(a)** tube which goes from the back of your mouth down the inside of your neck; *she got a fish bone stuck in her throat;* **sore throat** = throat which is red and hurts when you swallow or speak; *she's got a sore throat and has lost her voice* **(b)** your neck, especially the front part; *he put his hands round her throat and pressed hard*

through [θruː] **1** *preposition* **(a)** across the inside of something; going in at one side and coming out of the other; *she looked through* the open door; the street goes straight through the centre of the town (b) during a period of time; they insisted on talking all through the film 2 adverb going in at one side and coming out of the other side; someone left the gate open and all the sheep got through (NOTE: do not confuse with threw)

throughout [θruː'aʊt] preposition & adverb everywhere, all through; throughout the country floods are causing problems on the roads; heavy snow fell throughout the night

throw [θrəʊ] verb to send something through the air; how far can he throw a cricket ball?; she threw the letter into the waste paper basket (NOTE: throwing - threw [θruː] - has thrown [θrəʊn]) 2 noun act of throwing; her throw beat the world record

throw away ['θrəʊ ə'weɪ] verb to get rid of something which you don't need any more; don't throw away those old newspapers - they may come in useful

throw out ['θrəʊ 'aʊt] verb (a) to push someone outside; when they started to fight, they were thrown out of the restaurant (b) to get rid of something which you don't need; I'm throwing out this old chair

throw up ['θrəʊ 'ʌp] verb (informal) to be sick, to bring up partly digested food from your stomach into your mouth; the cat threw up all over the sofa

thrown [θrəʊn] see THROW

thrush [θrʌʃ] noun brown bird with brown spots on its light-coloured breast; thrushes sing beautifully (NOTE: plural is thrushes)

thrust [θrʌst] verb to push something suddenly and hard; he thrust the newspaper into his pocket (NOTE: thrusting - thrust)

thud [θʌd] 1 noun dull, heavy noise; his head hit the ground with a thud 2 verb to make a dull noise; a stone thudded into the wall behind him (NOTE: thudding - thudded)

thumb [θʌm] noun short thick finger which is slightly apart from the other four fingers on each hand; the baby was sucking its thumb

thump [θʌmp] 1 noun dull noise; there was a thump from upstairs as if someone had fallen out of bed 2 verb (informal) to hit someone or something hard with your fist; he rushed up to the policeman and started thumping him on the chest

thunder ['θʌndə] 1 noun loud noise in the air following a flash of lightning; a storm accompanied by thunder and lightning 2 verb (a) to make a loud noise in the air following lightning; it thundered during the night (b) to make a loud noise like thunder; lorries thundered past on the motorway

thunderstorm ['θʌndəstɔːm] noun storm with rain, thunder and lightning; don't shelter under a tree during a thunderstorm, you may be struck by lightning

Thursday ['θɜːzdeɪ] noun day between Wednesday and Friday, the fourth day of the week; last Thursday was Christmas Day; shall we arrange to meet next Thursday?; we usually have our meetings on Thursdays; the 15th is a Wednesday, so the 16th must be a Thursday

tick [tɪk] 1 noun (a) mark written to show that something is correct; put a tick in the box marked 'R' (b) sound made every second by a clock; the only sound we could hear in the room was the tick of the grandfather clock 2 verb (a) to mark with a tick to show that you approve; tick the box marked 'I' if you require an invoice (b) to make a regular little noise; all you could hear was the clock ticking in the corner of the library

ticket ['tɪkɪt] noun (a) piece of paper or card which allows you to travel; they won't let you get on to Eurostar without a ticket; we've lost our plane tickets - how can we get to Chicago?; season ticket = ticket which can be used for any number of journeys over a period (usually one, three, six or twelve months) (b) piece of paper which allows you to go into a cinema, an exhibition, etc.; can I have three tickets for the 8.30 show please? (c) parking ticket = paper which you get when you leave a car parked wrongly, telling you that you will have to pay a fine; *if you leave your car on the yellow line you'll get a ticket!*

ticket office ['tɪkɪt 'ɒfɪs] *noun* office where tickets can be bought (either for travel or for theatres or cinemas, etc.); *there was a long queue at the ticket office*; *if the ticket office is shut you can buy a ticket on the train*

tickle ['tɪkl] *verb* to touch someone in a sensitive part of the body to make them laugh; *she tickled his toes and he started to laugh*

tide [taɪd] *noun* regular rising and falling movement of the sea; *the tide came in and cut off the children on the rocks*; *the tide is out, so we can walk across the sand*; *high tide is at 6.05 p.m. today*

tidy ['taɪdi] **1** *adjective* neat, in order; *she put her clothes in a tidy pile* (NOTE: tidier - tidiest) **2** *verb* **to tidy (up)** = to make everything completely tidy; *he tidied his room before he went to school*

tie [taɪ] **1** *noun* **(a)** long piece of coloured cloth which men wear round their necks under the collar of their shirts; *he's wearing a blue tie with red stripes*; *they won't let you into the restaurant if you haven't got a tie on* **(b)** result in a competition or election where both sides have the same score; *the result was a tie and the vote had to be taken again*; **there was a tie for second place** = two people were equal second **2** *verb* **(a)** to attach with string, rope, etc.; *the parcel was tied with a little piece of string* **(b)** to have the same score as another team in a competition; *they tied for second place*

tiger ['taɪɡə] *noun* large wild animal of the cat family living mainly in India and China; it is yellow with black stripes; *I bet you wouldn't dare put your hand into the cage and stroke that tiger*

tight [taɪt] **1** *adjective* **(a)** fitting too closely; *these shoes hurt - they're too tight* **(b)** holding firmly; *keep a tight hold of the bag, we don't want it stolen* (NOTE: tighter - tightest) **2** *adverb* **(a)** closely, firmly (shut); *make sure* *the windows are shut tight* **(b) to hold tight** = to hold something firmly; *hold tight - we're about to take off*

tighten ['taɪtn] *verb* to make tight; to become tight; *I tightened the straps on my bag*; **to tighten your belt** = to be ready to spend less, eat less, etc.; *the government warned that we must tighten our belts*

tights [taɪts] *noun* piece of clothing made of thin material, covering your hips, and your legs and feet, worn by girls, women, etc.; *look - you've got a hole in your tights!*

tile [taɪl] **1** *noun* **(a)** flat piece of baked clay used as a covering for floors, walls or roofs; *the floor is covered with red tiles* **(b)** similar piece of another kind of material used to cover a floor, etc.; **carpet tiles** = square pieces of carpet which can be put down on the floor like tiles **2** *verb* to cover the surface of a roof, a floor or a wall with tiles; *a white-tiled bathroom always looks clean*

till [tɪl] **1** *preposition & conjunction* until, up to the time when; *I don't expect him to be home till after nine o'clock* **2** *noun* drawer for keeping cash in a shop; *there was not much money in the till at the end of the day*

tilt [tɪlt] *verb* **(a)** to slope; *the shelf is tilting to the right* **(b)** to put something in a sloping position; *he tilted the tray and all the glasses fell over*

timber ['tɪmbə] *noun* wood cut ready for building; *these trees are being grown to provide timber for houses*; *the roof was built with timbers from old ships*

time [taɪm] **1** *noun* **(a)** particular point in the day shown in hours and minutes; *what time is it? or what's the time?*; *can you tell me the time please?* **(b)** hour at which something usually happens; *the closing time for the office is 5.30*; *is it time for the children to go to bed?* **(c)** amount of hours, days, weeks, etc.; *there's no need to hurry - we've got plenty of time*; *do you have time for a cup of coffee?* **(d)** certain period; *we haven't been to France* for a long time (e) particular moment when something happens; *by the time the ambulance arrived the man had died*; *you can't do two things at the same time* (f) period when things are pleasant or bad; *everyone had a good time at the party* (g) one of several moments or periods when something happens; *I've seen that James Bond film on TV four times already* (h) rhythm of a piece of music; *he tapped his foot in time to the music* 2 *verb* to count in hours, minutes and seconds; *I timed him as he ran round the track*

in time ['ɪn 'taɪm] *phrase* not late; *they drove fast and got to the station just in time to catch the train*; *we got to Buckingham Palace in time to see the Changing of the Guard*

on time ['ɒn 'taɪm] *phrase* happening at the expected time; *the plane arrived on time*; *you will have to hurry if you want to get to the wedding on time*

times [taɪmz] *noun* multiplied by; *six times twenty is one hundred and twenty*; *this book is three times as expensive as that one*

timetable ['taɪmteɪbl] *noun* printed list which shows the times of classes in school, of trains leaving, etc.; *we have two English lessons on the timetable today*; *according to the timetable, there should be a train to London at 10.22*

tin [tɪn] *noun* (a) metal container in which food, etc., is sold and can be kept for a long time; *she bought three tins of cat food*; *we'll need a tin of white paint for the ceiling* (b) any metal box; *keep the biscuits in a tin or they'll go soft* (c) soft metal with a colour like silver; *there have been tin mines in Cornwall since Roman times*

tin opener ['tɪn 'əupnə] *noun* device for opening tins of food; *we took several tins of soup with us when we went camping, but forgot the tin opener!*

tingle ['tɪŋgl] 1 *noun* sharp feeling like prickles; *it didn't hurt, I just felt a tingle in my leg* 2 *verb* to have a sharp feeling like prickles; *it will tingle when I put the antiseptic on your cut*

tinkle ['tɪŋkl] 1 *noun* noise like the ringing of a little bell; *the gentle tinkle of cow bells in the mountain fields* 2 *verb* to make a little ringing noise; *the little bell tinkled as she went into the shop*

tinned [tɪnd] *adjective* preserved and sold in a tin; *I like tinned pineapple better than fresh*

tiny ['taɪni] *adjective* very small; *she lives in a tiny village in the Welsh mountains* (NOTE: tinier - tiniest)

tip [tɪp] 1 *noun* (a) end of something long; *she touched the snake with the tips of her fingers* (b) money given to someone who has provided a service; *the service hasn't been very good - should we leave a tip for the waiter?* (c) advice on something which could be useful; *she gave me a tip about a cheap restaurant just round the corner from the hotel* (d) place where household rubbish is taken to be thrown away; *I must take these bags of rubbish to the tip* 2 *verb* (a) to pour something out; *he picked up the box and tipped the contents out onto the floor* (b) to give money to someone who has helped you; *I tipped the waiter £1* (NOTE: tipping - tipped)

tiptoe ['tɪptəu] 1 *noun* on tiptoe = on your toes, with your heels in the air; *by standing on tiptoe he could just see into the window* 2 *verb* to walk quietly on tiptoe; *she tiptoed into the room and looked at the baby*

tired ['taɪəd] *adjective* (a) feeling sleepy; *I'm tired - I think I'll go to bed* (b) feeling that you need rest; *we're all tired after a long day at the office* (c) to be (sick and) tired of something = to be bored with something, to have had too much of something; *they're tired of always having to do all the washing up*; *can't we do something else - I'm getting tired of visiting museums*

tired out ['taɪəd 'aut] *adjective* feeling very sleepy, feeling that you must have a rest; *they were tired out after their long walk*; *come and sit down - you must be tired out*

tissue [ˈtɪʃuː] *noun* **(a)** soft paper handkerchief; *there is a box of tissues beside the bed* **(b) tissue paper** = thin soft paper used for wrapping glass and other delicate objects; *wrap the glasses in tissue paper before you put them away in the box*

title [ˈtaɪtl] *noun* **(a)** name of a book, play, painting, film, etc.; *he's almost finished writing the play but hasn't found a title for it yet* **(b)** word (such as Dr, Mr, Professor, Lord, Sir, Lady, etc.) put in front of a name to show an honour or degree

to [tuː] **1** *preposition* **(a)** *(showing direction or place)* *they went to the police station*; *do you know the way to the beach?* **(b)** *(showing a period of time)* *the office is open from 9.30 to 5.30, Monday to Friday* **(c)** *(showing time in minutes before an hour)* *get up - it's five to seven (6:55)*; *the train leaves at a quarter to eight (7:45)* **(d)** *(showing person or animal that receives something)* *take the book back to the library*; *pass the salt to your grandfather* **(e)** *(showing connection)* *in this class there are 28 children to one teacher* **(f)** *(showing that you are comparing)* *do you prefer butter to margarine?* **2** *(used before a verb)* **(a)** *(following another verb)* *did you remember to switch off the light?*; *the burglar tried to run away* **(b)** *(showing purpose)* *the doctor left half an hour ago to go to the hospital* **(c)** *(used after adjectives)* *I'd be glad to help*; *is the water safe to drink?* **(d)** *(used after comparing)* *she was too tired to do anything except sit down* **(e)** *(used after nouns)* *this is the best way to do it*

toad [təʊd] *noun* animal like a large frog, which lives mainly on land; *toads have to cross the road to get to their pond*

toadstool [ˈtəʊdstuːl] *noun* fungus shaped like a mushroom, but usually poisonous and not edible; *he picked a big red toadstool and brought it into the kitchen*

toast [təʊst] *noun* slices of bread which have been cooked at a high temperature until they are brown; *can you make some more toast?*; *she asked for scrambled eggs on toast*

tobacco [təˈbækəʊ] *noun* dried leaves of a plant used to make cigarettes and cigars, and for smoking in pipes; *he bought some pipe tobacco*; *tobacco causes lung cancer*

today [təˈdeɪ] **1** *noun* this day; *what's the date today?*; *there's a story in today's newspaper about a fire in our road* **2** *adverb* on this day; *he said he wanted to see me today, but he hasn't come yet*

toddler [ˈtɒdlə] *noun* little child who has just learnt to walk; *he's been fascinated by cars ever since he was a toddler*

toe [təʊ] *noun* one of the five parts like fingers at the end of the foot; *she trod on my toe and didn't say she was sorry*; **big toe** = the largest of the five toes (NOTE: do not confuse with **tow**)

toffee [ˈtɒfi] *noun* sticky sweet made with sugar and butter; *he went to the sweet shop and bought a bag of toffees*

together [təˈgeðə] *adverb* **(a)** doing something with someone else or in a group; *tell the children to stay together or they'll get lost* **(b)** joined with something else, or with each other; *tie the sticks together with string*

toilet [ˈtɔɪlət] *noun* **(a)** bowl with a seat on which you sit to get rid of waste matter from your body; *there is a shower and toilet in the bathroom*; *the children all want to go to the toilet at the same time* **(b)** room with this toilet bowl in it; *the ladies' toilet is at the end of the corridor*

told [təʊld] *see* TELL

tomato [təˈmɑːtəʊ US təˈmeɪtəʊ] *noun* small, round red fruit used in salads and cooking; *tomatoes cost 30p per kilo*; **tomato sauce** = sauce made with tomatoes and herbs; *do you want tomato sauce with your fish and chips?* (NOTE: plural is **tomatoes**)

tomorrow [təˈmɒrəʊ] **1** *adverb* referring to the day after today; *I mustn't forget I have a dentist's appointment tomorrow morning* **2** *noun* the day after today; *today's Monday, so* *tomorrow must be Tuesday*; *we're going to Paris the day after tomorrow*

ton [tʌn] *noun* very heavy measure of weight; *a ship carrying 1000 tons of coal*

tone [təʊn] *noun* way of saying something, or of writing something, which shows a particular feeling; *his tone showed he was angry*; *she said hello in a friendly tone of voice*

tongue [tʌŋ] *noun* (a) soft part inside your mouth, which can move and is used for tasting, swallowing and speaking; *the soup was so hot it burnt my tongue* (b) language; **mother tongue** *or* **native tongue** = language which you spoke when you were a little child; *she speaks English very well, but German is her mother tongue*

tongue-twister [ˈtʌŋtwɪstə] *noun* phrase (like 'red lorry, yellow lorry') which is difficult to say quickly

tonight [təˈnaɪt] *adverb & noun* the night or the evening of today; *I'll be at home from eight o'clock tonight*; *I don't suppose there's anything interesting on TV tonight*

tonne [tʌn] *noun* measure of weight equal to one thousand kilograms; *they harvested over twenty tonnes of apples*

too [tuː] *adverb* (a) more than necessary; *there are too many people to fit into the lift*; *I think we bought too much bread* (b) *(often at the end of a clause)* also; *she had some coffee and I had some too*

took [tʊk] *see* TAKE

tool [tuːl] *noun* instrument which you hold in your hand to do certain work, such as a hammer, spade, etc.; *I always keep a set of tools in the car*

tooth [tuːθ] *noun* (a) one of a set of hard white objects in your mouth which you use to bite or chew food; *children must learn to clean their teeth twice a day* (b) one of the row of pointed pieces on a saw, comb, zip, etc.; *throw that comb away, half its teeth are broken* (NOTE: plural is **teeth** [tiːθ])

toothbrush [ˈtuːθbrʌʃ] *noun* small brush which you use to clean your teeth; *I forgot to pack my toothbrush*; *she gave him an electric toothbrush for his birthday* (NOTE: the plural is **toothbrushes**)

toothpaste [ˈtuːθpeɪst] *noun* soft substance which you spread on a toothbrush and then use to clean your teeth; *she squeezed some toothpaste onto her brush*

top [tɒp] **1** *noun* (a) highest place, highest point of something; *he climbed to the top of the stairs and sat down*; *the bird is sitting on the top of the apple tree* (b) flat upper surface of something; *do not put coffee cups on the top of the computer; the car has a black top* (c) cover for a jar, bottle, etc.; *take the top off the jar, and see what's inside* **2** *adjective* (a) in the highest place; *the restaurant is on the top floor of the building*; *jams and marmalades are on the top shelf* (b) best; *she's one of the world's top tennis players*

on top *phrase* on; *a birthday cake with sugar and fruit on top*

on top of *phrase* (a) on; *there is a roof garden on top of the hotel* (b) in addition to; *on top of all my college work, I have to clean the house and look after the baby*

topic [ˈtɒpɪk] *noun* subject which you write or talk about; *can we move on to another topic?*

topple over [ˈtɒpl ˈəʊvə] *verb* to fall down; *the bottle toppled over and smashed onto the floor*

torch [tɔːtʃ] *noun* small portable electric lamp; *take a torch if you're going into the cave* (NOTE: plural is **torches**)

tore [tɔː] *see* TEAR

torn [tɔːn] *see* TEAR

tornado [tɔːˈneɪdəʊ] *noun* violent storm with a whirlwind; *a tornado struck the southern coast* (NOTE: plural is **tornadoes**)

tortoise [ˈtɔːtəs] *noun* reptile covered with a hard shell, which moves very slowly and can live to be very old; *the giant tortoises of the Galapagos Islands*

toss [tɒs] *verb* to throw something up into the air, or to someone; *she tossed me her car keys*; **let's toss for it** = let's throw a coin in the air and the person who guesses right starts to play first or has first choice

total ['təʊtəl] **1** *adjective* complete, whole; *the expedition was a total failure*; *the total bill came to over £400,000* **2** *noun* whole amount; *the total comes to more than £1,000*

touch [tʌtʃ] **1** *noun* **(a)** one of the five senses, the sense of feeling with the fingers; *blind people have a very strong sense of touch* **(b)** contact, the passing of news and information; **to get in touch with someone** = to contact someone **(c)** gentle physical contact; *I felt a light touch on my hand* **(d)** very small amount; *he added a few touches of paint to the picture*; *there's a touch of frost in the air this morning* **2** *verb* **(a)** to feel with your fingers; *don't touch that cake - it's for your mother* **(b)** to be so close to something that you press against it; *his feet don't touch the floor when he sits on a big chair*; *the tables are so close together that they are almost touching*

tough [tʌf] *adjective* **(a)** difficult to chew or to cut (the opposite is 'tender'); *my meat's a bit tough - what's yours like?* **(b)** difficult (the opposite is 'easy'); *the final exam is extremely tough* (NOTE: **tougher - toughest**)

tour [tuːə] **1** *noun* holiday journey to various places coming back in the end to the place you started from; *there are so many tours to choose from - I can't decide which one to go on*; *she took us on a tour round the old castle* **2** *verb* to go on holiday, visiting various places; *they toured the south of France*

tourist ['tuːrɪst] *noun* person who goes on holiday to visit places; *the tourists were talking German*; *Trafalgar Square is always full of tourists*

tow [təʊ] *verb* to pull a vehicle or a ship which cannot move by itself; *the motorways were crowded with cars towing caravans*; *they towed the ship into port* (NOTE: do not confuse with **toe**)

towards *US also* **toward** [tə'wɔːdz] *preposition* **(a)** in the direction of; *the crowd ran towards the police station*; *the bus was travelling south, towards London* **(b)** near (in time); *can we meet towards the end of next week?* **(c)** as part of the money to pay for something; *he gave me £100 towards the cost of the air fare*

towel ['taʊəl] *noun* large piece of soft cloth for drying; *there's only one towel in the bathroom*; **bath towel** = very large towel for drying yourself after having a bath; **tea towel** = cloth which you use for drying plates, dishes, etc.

tower ['taʊə] *noun* very tall building; *the castle has thick walls and four square towers*; **the Tower of London** = big castle in London, built by William the Conqueror; *there is a picture of the Tower of London on the front of the book*

town [taʊn] *noun* place, much larger than a village, where many people live and work, with houses, shops, offices, factories, etc.; *there's no shop in our village, so we do our shopping in the nearest town*

toy [tɔɪ] *noun* thing for children to play with; *she won't let me play with any of her toys*

trace [treɪs] **1** *noun* something which shows that something existed; *the police found traces of blood in the kitchen;* **without trace** = leaving nothing behind; *the car seems to have vanished without trace* **2** *verb* **(a)** to find where someone or something is; *the police traced him to Dover* **(b)** to copy a drawing, etc., by placing a sheet of transparent paper over it and drawing on it; *she traced the map and put it into her project on the history of the village*

track [træk] **1** *noun* **(a)** rough path; *we followed a track through the forest* **(b)** path for races; *the horses raced round the track*; **track events** = running competitions; *athletics is made up of both track and field events* **(c)**

line of parallel rails for trains; *the trains will be late because of repairs to the track* **2** *verb* to follow someone or an animal; *the police tracked the gang to a flat in south London*

tracksuit ['træksu:t] *noun* pair of matching trousers and top, in warm material, worn when practising sports; *the runners were warming up in their tracksuits*

tractor ['træktə] *noun* heavy vehicle with large back wheels, used for work on farms; *we got a tractor to pull the car out of the ditch*

trade [treɪd] **1** *noun* business of buying and selling; *Britain's trade with the rest of Europe is up by 10%* **2** *verb* to buy and sell, to carry on a business; *the company has stopped trading*; *they trade in tobacco*

trademark ['treɪdmɑːk] *noun* particular name, design, etc., which has been registered by a company and which cannot be used by anyone else; *Acme is a registered trademark*

tradition [trə'dɪʃn] *noun* beliefs, customs and stories which are passed from parents to children; *according to local tradition, a witch used to live where the two roads meet*

traditional [trə'dɪʃnəl] *adjective* according to tradition; *on Easter Day it is traditional to give children chocolate eggs*

traffic ['træfɪk] *noun* cars, lorries, buses, etc., which are travelling on a street or road; *I leave the office early on Fridays because there is so much traffic leaving London*; *the lights turned green and the traffic moved forward*

traffic jam ['træfɪk 'dʒæm] *noun* situation where cars, lorries, etc., cannot move forward on a road because there is too much traffic; *there are traffic jams on the roads out of London every Friday evening*

traffic lights ['træfɪk 'laɪts] *noun* red, green and orange lights for making the traffic stop and start; *to get to the police station, you have to turn left at the next traffic lights*

traffic warden ['træfɪk 'wɔːdən] *noun* person whose job it is to give parking tickets to cars that are parked wrongly; *move your car*

- there's a traffic warden coming

tragedy ['trædʒədi] *noun* **(a)** serious play, film, or novel which ends sadly; *Shakespeare's tragedy 'King Lear' is playing at the National Theatre* **(b)** very unhappy event; *tragedy struck the family when their mother was killed in a car crash* (NOTE: plural is **tragedies**)

tragic ['trædʒɪk] *adjective* very sad; *a tragic accident on the motorway*

trail [treɪl] **1** *noun* **(a)** tracks left by an animal, by a criminal, etc.; *we followed the trail of the bear through the forest*; *the burglars left in a red sports car, and a police car was soon on their trail* **(b)** path or track; *keep to the trail otherwise you will get lost*; **mountain trail** = path through mountains **2** *verb* **(a)** to follow the tracks left by an animal or a person; *the police trailed the group across Europe* **(b) to trail behind** = to follow slowly after someone; *she came third, trailing a long way behind the first two runners*

trailer ['treɪlə] *noun* **(a)** small goods vehicle pulled behind a car; *we carried all our camping gear in the trailer* **(b)** parts of a full-length film shown as an advertisement for it; *we saw the trailer last week, and it put me off the film*

train [treɪn] **1** *noun* engine pulling a group of wagons or carriages on the railway; *hundreds of people go to work every day by train*; *the next train to London will be in two minutes* **2** *verb* **(a)** to teach someone or an animal how to do something; *she's being trained to be a bus driver*; *guide dogs are trained to lead blind people* **(b)** to become fit by practising for a sport; *he's training for the 100 metres*; *she's training for the Olympics*

trainer ['treɪnə] *noun* **(a)** person who trains a sportsman or a team; *his trainer says he's in good condition for the race* **(b) trainers** = light sports shoes for running; *she needs a new pair of trainers for school*; *he comes to work every morning in trainers*

tram [træm] *noun* public transport vehicle, which runs on rails laid in the street; *you can take the tram from the station to the city centre*

transfer [trænsˈfɜː] *verb* **(a)** to move something or someone to another place; *she transferred her passport from her handbag to her jacket pocket*; *he's been transferred to our New York office* **(b)** to change from one type of travel to another; *when you get to London airport, you have to transfer onto another flight* (NOTE: **transferring - transferred**)

transform [trænzˈfɔːm] *verb* to change the appearance of someone or something completely; *the frog was transformed into a handsome prince*

transistor [trænˈzɪstə] *noun* device which can control the flow of electric current in a circuit; **transistor (radio)** = small pocket radio which uses transistors

translate [trænzˈleɪt] *verb* to put words into another language; *he asked his secretary to translate the letter from the German agent*; *she translates mainly from Spanish into English, not from English into Spanish*

translation [trænzˈleɪʃn] *noun* text which has been translated; *I read Tolstoy's 'War and Peace' in translation*

transparent [trænzˈpeərənt] *adjective* which you can see through; *the meat is wrapped in transparent plastic film*

transplant **1** *noun* [ˈtrɑːnsplɑːnt] act of taking part of one person's body (such as the heart) and putting it into another person; *he had a heart transplant* **2** *verb* [trænsˈplɑːnt] to put part of one person's body into the body of another person; *they transplanted an organ from his brother*

transport **1** *noun* [ˈtrænspɔːt] moving of goods or people in vehicles; *air transport is the quickest way to travel from one country to another*; **public transport** = transport (such as buses, trains) which can be used by anyone; *how can we get to Kew Gardens by public*

transport? **2** *verb* [trænˈspɔːt] to move goods or people from one place to another in a vehicle; *the company transports millions of tons of goods by rail each year*

trap [træp] **1** *noun* something made to catch an animal; *there is a mouse in the kitchen so we will put down a trap* **2** *verb* to catch or hold; *several people were trapped in the wrecked train* (NOTE: **trapping - trapped**)

trap door [ˈtræp ˈdɔː] *noun* door in a floor or in a ceiling; *there's a trap door leading to the roof*

trapeze [træˈpiːz] *noun* bar which hangs from ropes, and which acrobats use in a circus; *she performs dangerous acts on the trapeze without using a safety net*

travel [ˈtrævəl] **1** *noun* action of moving from place to place; *air travel is the only really fast method of going from one country to another* **2** *verb* to move from place to place; *she travels fifty miles to go to work every day by car*; *he has travelled across the United States several times on his motorbike*

traveller US **traveler** [ˈtrævlə] *noun* person who travels; *travellers to France are facing delays because of the dock strike*

traveller's cheque US **traveler's check** [ˈtrævləz ˈtʃek] *noun* cheque which you buy at a bank before you travel and which you can then use in a foreign country; *most shops in the USA accept traveller's cheques*

tray [treɪ] *noun* flat board for carrying food, glasses, cups and saucers, etc.; *she bumped into a waitress who was carrying a tray of glasses*

treacherous [ˈtretʃrəs] *adverb* **(a)** dangerous; *ice is making the roads very treacherous* **(b)** not to be trusted; *he was shot by a treacherous bodyguard*

tread [tred] **1** *noun* top part of a stair or step, the part which you stand on; *the carpet on the bottom tread is loose* **2** *verb* to step, to walk; *she trod on my toe and didn't say she was sorry*; *watch where you're treading - there's* *broken glass on the floor* (NOTE: **treading - trod** [trɒd] **- has trodden** ['trɒdən])

treasure ['treʒə] *noun* jewels, gold, or other valuable things; *the school party is going to see the treasures in the British Museum*; **buried treasure** = gold, silver, etc., which someone has hidden; **treasure hunt** = game where clues lead you from place to place until you come to a hidden prize; *they organized a treasure hunt for the children's party*

treat [triːt] **1** *noun* special thing which gives pleasure; *it's always a treat to sit down quietly at home after a hard day working in the shop*; *as a treat the children were taken to Disneyland* **2** *verb* **(a)** to deal with someone; *if you treat students well they will do well in their exams* **(b) to treat someone to something** = to give someone a special meal or outing as a gift; *come along - I'll treat you all to ice creams!* **(c)** to look after a sick or injured person; *after the accident some of the passengers had to be treated in hospital for cuts and bruises*

treatment ['triːtmənt] *noun* **(a)** way of behaving towards something or someone; *we got very good treatment when we visited China* **(b)** way of looking after a sick or injured person; *he is having a course of heat treatment*

tree [triː] *noun* very large plant, with a thick trunk, branches and leaves; *the cat climbed up an apple tree and couldn't get down*; *in autumn, the leaves on the trees in the park turn brown and red*

tremble ['trembl] *verb* to shake because you are cold or afraid; *she was trembling with cold*; *I tremble at the thought of how much the party will cost*

tremendous [trɪ'mendəs] *adjective* enormous, very big; *there was a tremendous explosion and all the lights went out*; *there's tremendous excitement here in Trafalgar Square as we wait for the election result*

trend [trend] *noun* general tendency; *there is a trend away from science subjects to arts and commerce*

trial ['traɪəl] *noun* **(a)** court case held before a judge; *the trial will be heard next week*; *he's on trial for robbing a bank* **(b)** act of testing something; *the new model is going through its final trials*; **trial period** = time when a customer can use a product before deciding to buy it

triangle ['traɪæŋgl] *noun* shape with three sides and three angles; *the end of the roof is shaped like a triangle*

tribe [traɪb] *noun* group of families of the same race, with the same language and customs; *she went to South America to study the jungle tribes*

trick [trɪk] **1** *noun* clever action to confuse someone; *the record of a barking dog is just a trick to make burglars think there is a dog in the house*; *he amused the children with some card tricks* **2** *verb* to deceive, to confuse someone; *we've been tricked, there's nothing in the box*; *they tricked the old lady out of all her savings*

trickle ['trɪkl] *verb* to flow gently; *water trickled out of the cave*

tricycle ['traɪsɪkl] *noun* vehicle like a bicycle with three wheels, two at the back and one at the front; *a tricycle is best for little children because you can't fall off*

tried, tries [traɪd or traɪz] *see* TRY

trifle ['traɪfl] *noun* pudding made of cake or biscuits with jelly, jam, fruit, wine and cream; *do you want chocolate pudding or trifle for dessert?*

trigger ['trɪgə] *noun* little lever which you pull to fire a gun; *he pointed the gun at her and pulled the trigger*

trim [trɪm] **1** *adjective* **(a)** tidy, cut short; *he always keeps his beard trim* **(b)** slim and fit; *she keeps herself trim by going for a long walk every day* (NOTE: **trimmer - trimmest**) **2** *verb* **(a)** to cut something to make it tidy; *he was trimming the hedge in front of the house*

(b) to decorate (clothes); *she wore a white blazer trimmed with blue* (NOTE: trimming - trimmed)

trip [trɪp] **1** *noun* short journey; *our trip to Paris was cancelled*; *we're going on a trip to the seaside*; **coach trip** = short journey by coach **2** *verb* to catch your foot in something so that you stagger and fall down; *she tripped as she was coming out of the kitchen with a tray of food* (NOTE: tripping - tripped)

trip over ['trɪp 'əʊvə] *verb* to catch your foot in something so that you stagger and fall; *she was running away from him when she tripped over and fell down*

trip up ['trɪp 'ʌp] *verb* **to trip someone up** = to make someone fall down; *she put her foot out and deliberately tripped the waiter up*

triumph ['traɪəmf] **1** *noun* great victory, great success; *they scored a triumph in their game against the French* **2** *verb* to win a victory, to achieve something; *she triumphed in the 800 metres*

triumphant [traɪ'ʌmfənt] *adjective* happy because you have won; *he gave a triumphant wave as he crossed the finishing line*

trod, trodden [trɒd or 'trɒdn] *see* TREAD

trolley ['trɒli] *noun* small cart on wheels; *they put the piano onto a trolley to move it out of the house*; **luggage trolley** = small cart with wheels, for carrying luggage at an airport or railway station; **supermarket trolley** = small cart with wheels for pushing round a supermarket

troop [truːp] **1** *noun* **(a) troops** = soldiers; *enemy troops occupied the town* **(b)** large group of people; *she took a troop of children from her school to visit the museum* **2** *verb* to go all together in a group; *the students trooped into the hall*

tropic ['trɒpɪk] *noun* **(a)** imaginary line running round the earth between a pole and the equator; *there are two tropics: the Tropic of Cancer in the north and the Tropic of Capricorn in the south* **(b) the tropics** = the

hot parts of the world lying between the Tropic of Cancer and the Tropic of Capricorn; *he lived in the tropics for ten years*

tropical ['trɒpɪkl] *adjective* referring to hot countries; *in tropical countries it is always hot*; *she grows tropical plants in her greenhouse*

trot ['trɒt] **1** *noun* action of running with short regular steps; *let's start today's exercises with a short trot round the football field* **2** *verb* to run with short regular steps; *she trotted down the path to meet us* (NOTE: trotting - trotted)

trouble ['trʌbl] **1** *noun* **(a)** problems, things which make you worry; *the trouble with old cars is that sometimes they don't start*; *looking after your cat is no trouble - I like animals* **(b) to get into trouble** = to start to have problems; *he and his friends got into trouble with the police* **(c) to take the trouble to** = to make an extra effort and do something; *if you had taken the trouble to look at the train timetable, you would have seen that there aren't any trains on Sundays*; **to take trouble over something** = to do something carefully and well; *they took a lot of trouble over the Christmas decorations* **2** *verb* to make someone worried; *I can see that there's something troubling him but I don't know what it is*

trough [trɒf] *noun* long narrow open container for food or water for farm animals; *the pigs were eating at the trough*

trousers ['traʊzəz] *noun* clothes which cover your body from the waist down, with two parts, one for each leg; *he tore his trousers climbing over the fence*; *she bought two pairs of trousers in the sale*

trout [traʊt] *noun* type of fish living in fresh water; *we had grilled trout with potatoes and beans* (NOTE: plural is trout)

trowel ['traʊəl] *noun* hand tool, like a large spoon, used in the garden; *she made holes with a trowel before planting her bulbs*

truant ['truːənt] *noun* **to play truant** = not to go to school when you should be there; *the* *boys played truant and went fishing*

truck [trʌk] *noun* lorry, a goods vehicle for carrying heavy loads; *trucks thundered past the house all night*; **truck driver** = person who drives a truck; *a truck driver gave us a lift into town*

trudge [trʌdʒ] **1** *noun* long hard walk; *it was a long trudge through the mud back to the camp* **2** *verb* to walk slowly with heavy footsteps; *he missed the bus and had to trudge down to the village to buy some milk*

true [tru:] *adjective* correct, right; *what he says is simply not true*; *it's quite true that she comes from Scotland*

truly ['tru:li] *adverb* **(a)** really; *I'm truly grateful for all your help* **(b) Yours truly** *US* **Truly yours** = words written at the end of a slightly formal letter

trumpet ['trʌmpɪt] *noun* brass musical instrument which is played by blowing; *he plays the trumpet in the school orchestra*; *she practises the trumpet in the evenings*

trunk [trʌŋk] *noun* **(a)** thick stem of a tree; *he measured round the trunk of the old oak tree to see how big it was* **(b)** an elephant's long nose; *the elephant picked up the apple with its trunk* **(c)** large box for storing or sending clothes, etc.; *he kept his old clothes in a trunk in the loft* **(d) swimming trunks** = short trousers worn by men and boys when swimming

trust [trʌst] *verb* **(a)** to be sure of someone, to be confident that someone is reliable; *can we trust the guide to get us back to the camp site?* **(b) to trust someone with something** = to give something to someone to look after; *can she be trusted with all that cash?* **(c)** *(informal)* **trust you to** = it is typical of you to; *trust them to forget to bring any money!*

truth [tru:θ] *noun* thing which is true, a true story; *do you think he is telling the truth?*; *I don't think there is any truth in his story*

truthful ['tru:θful] *adjective* **(a)** who always tells the truth; *she's a very truthful child* **(b)**

giving true facts; *to be truthful, I'm not quite sure where we are*

try [traɪ] **1** *verb* **(a)** to make an effort to do something; *the burglar tried to climb up the tree*; *don't try to ride a motorbike if you've never ridden one before* **(b)** to test something, to see if it is good; *you must try one of my mother's cakes*; *I tried the new toothpaste and I didn't like the taste* **2** *noun* goal scored in rugby; *they scored two tries* (NOTE: plural is **tries**)

T-shirt ['ti:ʃɜ:t] *see* TEESHIRT

tube [tju:b] *noun* **(a)** long pipe for carrying liquids or gas; *he was lying in a hospital bed with tubes coming out of his nose and mouth* **(b)** soft container with a screw top, which contains paste, etc.; *I forgot to pack a tube of toothpaste*; *I need a tube of glue to mend the cup* **(c)** *(in London)* the underground railway system; *it's quicker to take the tube to Oxford Circus than to go by bus*

tuck in ['tʌk 'ɪn] *verb* to fold something around and push the ends in; *she tucked the blanket in around the baby* or *she tucked the baby in*; *he tucked his trousers into his boots*

tuck up ['tʌk 'ʌp] *verb* **to tuck someone up in bed** = to push the edge of the sheets and blankets around someone to keep them warm; *by eight o'clock the children were all tucked up in bed*

Tuesday ['tju:zdeɪ] *noun* day between Monday and Wednesday, the second day of the week; *I saw him in the college last Tuesday*; *shall we meet next Tuesday evening?*; *we usually have our meetings on Tuesdays*; *the 15th is a Monday, so the 16th must be a Tuesday*

tug [tʌg] **1** *verb* to pull hard; *he tugged on the rope and a bell rang* (NOTE: **tugging - tugged**) **2** *noun* powerful boat which pulls other boats; *two tugs helped the ship get into the harbour*

tug-of-war [tʌgəv'wɔ:] *noun* competition in which two teams pull against each other on a rope; *there will be a tug-of-war between teams from the two villages*

tulip [ˈtjuːlɪp] *noun* common spring bulb with brilliant flowers shaped like cups; *we went to Holland to see the tulip fields in flower*

tumble [ˈtʌmbl] *verb* to fall; *he tumbled down the stairs head first*

tuna [ˈtjuːnə] *noun* very large sea fish used for food; *a tuna salad* (NOTE: plural is **tuna**)

tune [tjuːn] *noun* series of musical notes which have a pattern which you can recognize; *he wrote some of the tunes for the musical*; *she walked away whistling a little tune*

tunnel [ˈtʌnl] *noun* long passage under the ground; *the Channel Tunnel links Britain to France*; *they are digging a new tunnel for the underground railway*

Turkey [ˈtɜːki] *noun* country in the eastern Mediterranean, south of the Black Sea; *Turkey lies partly in Europe and partly in Asia*; *we're going sailing off the coast of Turkey this summer* (NOTE: capital: **Ankara**; people: **the Turks**; language: **Turkish**)

turkey [ˈtɜːki] *noun* large farm bird, similar to a chicken but much bigger, often eaten at Christmas; *we had roast turkey and potatoes*

turn [tɜːn] **1** *noun* **(a)** change of direction, especially of a vehicle; *the bus made a sudden turn to the left* **(b)** road which leaves another road; *take the next turn on the right* **(c)** time when you can do something after other people; *you have to wait for your turn to see the doctor*; *it's my turn on the piano now*; **to take turns** *or* **to take it in turns** = to do something one after the other, to help each other; *they took it in turns to push the car* **2** *verb* **(a)** to go round in a circle; *the wheels of the train started to turn slowly* **(b)** to make something go round; *turn the handle to the right to open the safe* **(c)** to change direction, to go in another direction; *turn left at the next traffic lights*; *the car turned the corner too fast and hit a tree* **(d)** to move your head or body so that you face in another direction; *can*

everyone turn to look at the camera, please **(e)** to change into something different; *the leaves of the trees turn red or brown in the autumn*

turn back [ˈtɜːn ˈbæk] *verb* to go back in the opposite direction; *the path was full of mud so we turned back and went home*

turn down [ˈtɜːn ˈdaʊn] *verb* to refuse something which is offered; *she has turned down a job in the town hall*

turn into [ˈtɜːn ˈɪntʊ] *verb* **(a)** to change to become something different; *the wicked queen turned the prince into a frog* **(b)** to change direction and go into something; *we went down the main road for a short way and then turned into a little lane on the left*

turn off [ˈtɜːn ˈɒf] *verb* **(a)** to switch off; *don't forget to turn the TV off when you go to bed*; *turn the lights off - father's going to show his holiday films* **(b)** to leave a road you are travelling on; *you can turn off the High Street into one of the car parks*

turn on [ˈtɜːn ˈɒn] *verb* to switch on; *can you turn on the light - it's getting dark*; *turn the TV on - it's time for the news*

turn over [ˈtɜːn ˈəʊvə] *verb* to roll over; *the lorry went round the corner too fast and turned over*

turn round [ˈtɜːn ˈraʊnd] *verb* to move your head or body so that you face in another direction; *she turned round to see who was following her*

turn up [ˈtɜːn ˈʌp] *verb* **(a)** to arrive; *he turned up unexpectedly just as I was leaving the school* **(b)** to be found; *the police searched everywhere, and the little girl finally turned up in Edinburgh*; *the keys turned up in my coat pocket* **(c)** to make louder, stronger; *can you turn up the radio - I can't hear it*; *turn the gas up, the potatoes aren't cooked yet*

turning [ˈtɜːnɪŋ] *noun* road which goes away from another road; *take the next turning to the right*

turtle [ˈtɜːtl] *noun* sea animal with a hard

shell, similar to a tortoise; *turtles come up onto the beach to lay their eggs*

TV ['tiː 'viː] *noun* television; *they watch TV every night*; *the TV news is usually at ten o'clock*; *the daughter of a friend of mine was on TV last night*

twelfth (12th) [twelfθ] *adjective & noun* he *came twelfth out of two hundred in the competition*; *it's her twelfth birthday next week*; *King Louis XII ('King Louis the Twelfth') was King of France at the same time as Henry VII was King of England*; the **twelfth century** = the period from 1100 to 1199 (compare with the 'twelve hundreds')

twelve [twelv] number 12; *she's twelve (years old) tomorrow*; *come round for a cup of coffee at twelve o'clock*; *there are twelve months in a year*; the **twelve hundreds** = the period from 1200 to 1299 (compare with the 'twelfth century')

twentieth (20th) ['twentɪəθ] *adjective & noun it's her twentieth birthday on Wednesday*; the **twentieth century** = the period from 1900 to 1999

twenty ['twenti] number 20; *she's twenty (years old) next week*; **he's in his twenties** = he is between 20 and 29 years old; the **(nineteen) twenties (1920s)** = the years from 1920 to 1929; the **twenty-first century** = the period from the year 2000 to 2099

twice [twaɪs] *adverb* two times; *turn it off - I've seen that programme twice already*; *twice two is four, twice four is eight*

twig [twɪg] *noun* little branch of a tree; *there is a bud at the end of each twig*

twilight ['twaɪlaɪt] *noun* time when it is getting dark, between sunset and night; *the twilight hours are dangerous for drivers*

twin [twɪn] *adjective & noun* (a) one of two children born at the same time to the same mother; *he and his twin brother* (b) **twin beds** = two single beds placed in a bedroom

twinkle ['twɪŋkl] *verb (of stars, eyes)* to shine with a little moving light; *we could see the* lights of the harbour twinkling in the distance

twirl [twɜːl] *verb* to twist something round in your hand; *I wish I could twirl a stick like she does*

twist [twɪst] *verb* **(a)** to turn in different directions; *twist the cap of the bottle to take it off* **(b)** to wind something round something; *she twisted the string round a piece of stick* **(c)** to bend a joint in your body in the wrong way; *she twisted her ankle running to catch the bus*

two [tuː] number 2; *there are only two peppermints left in the box*; *his son's only two (years old), so he can't read yet*; *she didn't come home until after two (o'clock)* **one or two** = some, a few; *only one or two people came to the exhibition*

tying ['taɪɪŋ] *see* TIE

type [taɪp] **1** *noun* sort or kind; *a sole is a type of fish* **2** *verb* to write with a typewriter; *please type your letters - your writing's so bad I can't read it*

typewriter ['taɪpraɪtə] *noun* machine which prints letters or figures on a piece of paper when keys are pressed; *he wrote all his poems on his old typewriter*

typhoon [taɪ'fuːn] *noun* the name for a violent tropical storm in the Far East (in the Caribbean it is called a 'hurricane'); *the typhoon caused a lot of damage along the coast*

typical ['tɪpɪkl] *adjective* normal, as you would expect; *describe a typical day at school*; *he's definitely not a typical bank manager*

tyre *US* **tire** [taɪə] *noun* ring made of hard rubber, which is put round a wheel and which is filled with air; *check the pressure in the tyres before starting a journey*; **flat tyre** = a tyre which has lost all the air in it; *my bike got a flat tyre and I had to walk home*

Uu

U, u [ju:] twenty-first letter of the alphabet, between T and V; *the letter 'Q' is always followed by a 'U'*

ugly [ˈʌgli] *adjective* not beautiful, not pleasant to look at; *what an ugly pattern!*; *the part of the town round the railway station is even uglier than the rest* (NOTE: uglier - ugliest)

UK [ˈjuː ˈkeɪ] *abbreviation for* United Kingdom; *lots of tourists come to the UK every summer*

umbrella [ʌmˈbrelə] *noun* frame covered with cloth which you hold over your head to keep off the rain; *as it was starting to rain, he opened his umbrella*

unable [ʌnˈeɪbl] *adjective* not able (to do something); *she was unable to come to the party*

unbearable [ʌnˈbeərəbl] *adjective* which you cannot stand; *old people find this heat unbearable*; *the noise was unbearable and no one could work*

unbelievable [ʌnbɪˈliːvəbl] *adjective* which is difficult to believe; *it's unbelievable that she didn't know that the drugs were hidden in her suitcase*

unbreakable [ʌnˈbreɪkəbl] *adjective* which cannot be broken; *the windows are made of unbreakable glass*

uncertain [ʌnˈsɜːtən] *adjective* not sure; *she is uncertain as to what she should do next*

uncle [ˈʌŋkl] *noun* brother of your father or mother; husband of an aunt; *he was brought up by his uncle in Scotland*; *we had a surprise visitor last night - old Uncle Charles*

uncomfortable [ʌnˈkʌmftəbl] *adjective* not comfortable, not soft and relaxing; *what a very uncomfortable bed!*; *plastic seats are very uncomfortable in hot weather*

uncommon [ʌnˈkɒmən] *adjective* strange or not usual; *it's a very uncommon bird in the north of Scotland*

unconscious [ʌnˈkɒnʃəs] *adjective* not conscious, not aware of what is happening; *she was unconscious for two days after the accident*

under [ˈʌndə] *preposition* **(a)** in or to a place where something else is on top; *we all hid under the table*; *my pen rolled under the sofa* **(b)** less than a number; *the train goes to Paris in under three hours*

underclothes [ˈʌndəkləʊðz] *noun* underwear, clothes which you wear next to the skin, under other clothes; *he ran out of the house in his underclothes*

underground [ˈʌndəgraʊnd] **1** *adverb* under the ground; *worms live all their life underground* **2** *adjective* under the ground; *the hotel has an underground car park* **3** *noun* railway in a town, which runs under the ground (in American English, this is a 'subway'); *thousands of people use the underground to go to work*; *take the underground to go to Oxford Circus*

underline [ˈʌndəlaɪn] *verb* to write a line under a word, a figure; *he wrote 'Hamlet' on the board and then underlined it in red*

underneath [ʌndəˈniːθ] **1** *preposition* under; *can you lie down and see if my pen is underneath the sofa?* **2** *adverb* under; *he put the box of books down on the kitchen table and my sandwiches were underneath!*

understand [ʌndəˈstænd] *verb* **(a)** to know what something means; *he didn't understand what I was saying*; *I hardly speak any Japanese, but I managed to make myself understood* **(b)** to have sympathy for someone; *she's a good teacher - she really understands children* **(c)** to know why something happens or how something works; *I can easily understand why he is so annoyed* (NOTE: understanding - understood [ʌndə'stʊd])

underwear ['ʌndəweə] *noun* clothes worn next to your skin under other clothes; *he ran out of the house in his underwear; it's December, so I'd better get out my winter underwear*

undid [ʌn'dɪd] *see* UNDO

undo [ʌn'duː] *verb* to make something loose, which is tied or buttoned; *undo your top button if your collar is too tight; wait a moment, my shoe has come undone* (NOTE: undid [ʌn'dɪd] - has undone [ʌn'dʌn])

undress [ʌn'dres] *verb* to take your clothes off; *the doctor asked the patient to get undressed; he undressed and got into the bath*

uneasy [ʌn'iːzi] *adjective* nervous and worried; *I'm rather uneasy about lending her so much money* (NOTE: uneasier - uneasiest)

unemployed [ʌnɪm'plɔɪd] *adjective* without a job; *unemployed teenagers can apply for training grants*

unemployment [ʌnɪm'plɔɪmənt] *noun* lack of jobs; **unemployment is falling** = there are fewer people without jobs

uneven [ʌn'iːvn] *adjective* not smooth, not flat; *don't try to put your tent up where the ground is uneven*

unexpected [ʌnɪk'spektɪd] *adjective* which is surprising and not what was expected; *we had an unexpected visit from the police*

unexpectedly [ʌnɪk'spektɪdli] *adverb* in an unexpected way; *just as the party was starting his mother walked in unexpectedly*

unfair [ʌn'feə] *adjective* not right, not fair; *it's unfair to expect her to do all the housework while her sisters don't do anything to help*

unfortunate [ʌn'fɔːtʃənət] *adjective* which makes you sad; *it was very unfortunate that she couldn't come to see us*

unfortunately [ʌn'fɔːtʃənətli] *adverb* which you wish was not true; *unfortunately the train was so late that she missed the wedding*

unfriendly [ʌn'frendli] *adjective* not like a friend; *he answered in such an unfriendly way that I wondered what I had done to make him annoyed*

ungrateful [ʌn'greɪtfʊl] *adjective* not grateful; *he's an ungrateful boy - he never thanked me for his Christmas present*

unhappily [ʌn'hæpɪli] *adverb* in a sad way; *she sat staring unhappily out of the window*

unhappy [ʌn'hæpi] *adjective* sad, not happy; *she looked very unhappy when she came out of the hospital* (NOTE: unhappier - unhappiest)

unhealthy [ʌn'helθi] *adjective* not healthy; which does not make you healthy; *sitting around smoking and not doing any sport is very unhealthy; those children have a very unhealthy diet* (NOTE: unhealthier - unhealthiest)

uniform ['juːnɪfɔːm] *noun* special clothes worn by all members of an organization or group; *what colour is her school uniform?; the hotel staff all wear yellow uniforms;* **in uniform** = wearing a uniform; *the policeman was not in uniform at the time*

union ['juːniən] *noun* organization which represents workers; *the staff are all members of a union*

Union Jack ['juːniən 'dʒæk] *noun* national flag of the United Kingdom (also called the Union Flag); *the streets were decorated with Union Jacks*

unique [ju'niːk] *adjective* quite different from everything else, the only one that exists; *the stamp is unique, and so is worth a great deal*

unit ['juːnɪt] *noun* **(a)** one part of something larger; *if you pass three units of the course you can move to the next level* **(b)** one piece of furniture, such as a cupboard, or set of shelves, etc., which can be matched with others; *the kitchen is designed as a basic set of units with more units which can be added* *later* (c) amount used to measure something; *kilos and pounds are units of weight* (d) number one; *63 has six tens and three units*

unite [juːˈnaɪt] *verb* to join together into a single organization; *the staff united in asking for better working conditions*

United Kingdom (UK) [juːˈnaɪtɪd ˈkɪŋdəm] *noun* independent European country, formed of England, Wales, Scotland and Northern Ireland; *he came to the United Kingdom to study*; *does she have a UK passport?*; *French citizens do not need work permits to work in the United Kingdom* (NOTE: capital: **London**; people: **British**; language: **English**)

United States of America (USA) [juːˈnaɪtɪd ˈsteɪts ʌv əˈmerɪkə] *noun* independent country, a federation of states (originally thirteen, now fifty) in North America, south of Canada and north of Mexico; *she lives in the United States with her husband and two sons*; *as a student, I worked in the USA during my summer holidays* (NOTE: capital: **Washington DC**; people: **Americans**; language: **English**)

universal [juːnɪˈvɜːsəl] *adjective* which refers to everyone; *there is a universal hope for peace in the region*

universe [ˈjuːnɪvɜːs] *noun* all space and everything that exists in it, including the earth, the planets and the stars; *scientists believe the universe started as an explosion*

university [juːnɪˈvɜːsɪti] *noun* place where people study after leaving school, which gives degrees to successful students, and where a wide range of subjects are taught; *you need to do well at school to be able to go to university*; *my sister is at university* (NOTE: plural is **universities**)

unkind [ʌnˈkaɪnd] *adjective* cruel, not kind; *it was unkind of him to keep mentioning how fat she was* (NOTE: **unkinder - unkindest**)

unless [ʌnˈles] *conjunction* if not; except if; *unless you start at once you will miss the beginning of the show*; *don't come unless you*

really want to

unlike [ˈʌnlaɪk] *adjective & preposition* (a) completely different from; *he's quite unlike his brother* (b) not normal, not typical; **it is unlike him to be rude** = he is not usually rude

unlikely [ʌnˈlaɪkli] *adjective* (a) not likely; *it's unlikely that many people will come to the party* (b) (story) which is probably not true; *he told some unlikely story about how his homework had been eaten by his dog*

unload [ʌnˈləʊd] *verb* to remove a load from a vehicle; *we need a trolley to unload the lorry*; *they unloaded the ship in Hamburg*

unlock [ʌnˈlɒk] *verb* to open something which was locked; *I can't unlock the car door, I think I've got the wrong key*

unluckily [ʌnˈlʌkɪli] *adverb* with bad luck; *unluckily a police car came past just as he was climbing out of the window*

unlucky [ʌnˈlʌki] *adjective* not lucky, which brings bad luck; *many people think Friday 13th is unlucky*; *they say it's unlucky to walk under a ladder*

unnecessary [ʌnˈnesəsəri] *adjective* which is not needed, which does not have to be done; *it is unnecessary for you to wear a suit to the party*; *he makes too many unnecessary phone calls*

unpack [ʌnˈpæk] *verb* to take things out of the boxes or cases in which they were carried; *I've just come back from Canada and I'm still unpacking*

unpleasant [ʌnˈplezənt] *adjective* not nice, not pleasant; *there's a very unpleasant smell in the kitchen*; *the boss is a very unpleasant man and shouts at us all the time*

unselfish [ʌnˈselfɪʃ] *adjective* thinking only of other people; *she was praised for her unselfish work for poor families*

untidy [ʌnˈtaɪdi] *adjective* not tidy; *his bedroom is untidier than ever* (NOTE: **untidier - untidiest**)

untie [ʌnˈtaɪ] *verb* to undo something which

is tied with a knot; *someone untied our rowing boat and it floated away down the river*

until [ʌn'tɪl] **1** *conjunction* up to the time when; *he blew his whistle until the police came* **2** *preposition* up to the time when; *I don't expect to be back until after ten o'clock*

untrue [ʌn'truː] *adjective* not true, false; *his story was quite untrue - the jewels were not hidden in a teddy bear*

unusual [ʌn'juːʒuəl] *adjective* strange, not normal; *it is unusual to have rain at this time of year*

unwell [ʌn'wel] *adjective* sick, ill, not well; *she felt unwell and had to go home*

up [ʌp] **1** *adverb* **(a)** in or to a high place; *what's the cat doing up there on the cupboard?* **(b)** to a higher position; *his temperature went up suddenly*; *the price of petrol seems to go up every week* **(c)** not in bed; *the children were still up when they should have been in bed*; *he got up at six because he had an early train to catch* **(d)** *(informal)* happening in an unpleasant or dangerous way; **what's up?** = what's the matter?; *what's up with the cat? - it won't eat anything* **2** *preposition* **(a)** in or to a high place; *they ran up the stairs*; *she doesn't like going up ladders* **(b)** further along; *go up the street to the traffic lights and then turn right*

up to date *or* **up-to-date** ['ʌp tə' deɪt] **1** *adverb* modern, with the latest information; *I keep myself up to date by reading the newspaper every day* **2** *adjective* with very recent information; *do you have an up-to-date timetable?*

upper ['ʌpə] *adjective* higher or further up; *the upper slopes of the mountain are covered in snow*; **the upper deck** = the top deck in a bus; *let's go onto the upper deck - you can see London much better from there*

upright ['ʌpraɪt] *adjective* standing straight up; *she picked up the bottle and placed it upright on the table*

upset [ʌp'set] **1** *adjective* very worried, unhappy, anxious; *she gets upset if he comes home late* **2** *verb* **(a)** to knock over; *he upset all the coffee cups* **(b)** to make someone worried or unhappy; *don't upset your mother by telling her you're planning to go to live in Russia*

upside down ['ʌpsaɪd 'daun] *adverb* with the top underneath; *don't turn the box upside down - all the papers will fall out*

upstairs [ʌp'steəz] **1** *adverb* on or to the upper part of a building, bus, etc.; *let's go upstairs onto the top deck - you can see London much better from there* **2** *adjective* on the upper floors of a building; *we have an upstairs kitchen*

upwards *US* **upward** ['ʌpwədz] *adverb* towards the top; *the path went upwards for a mile*

urge [ɜːdʒ] **1** *noun* strong wish to do something; *she felt an urge to punch him on the nose* **2** *verb* **(a)** to advise someone in very strong terms to do something; *he urged her to do what her father said* **(b)** **to urge someone on** = to encourage someone to do better, to do more; *the runners were urged on by the crowd*

urgent ['ɜːdʒənt] *adjective* which is important and needs to be done quickly; *she had an urgent operation*

us [ʌs] *object pronoun (meaning me and other people) mother gave us each 50p to buy ice cream*; *who's there? - it's us!*

US *or* **USA** ['juːes *or* 'juːes'eɪ] *see* UNITED STATES; *they're thinking of going to the US on holiday next year*; *we spent three weeks travelling in the USA*

use 1 *verb* [juːz] **(a)** to take a machine, a tool, etc., and do something with it; *did you use a sewing machine to make your curtains?*; *do you know how to use a computer?* **(b)** to take something for a purpose; *she used the money she had saved to pay for a trip to Greece*; *I don't use the underground much because I* *can walk to the office* **(c)** to take a substance and do something with it; *we don't use the tap water for drinking* **2** *noun* [juːs] **(a)** being useful; *what's the use of telling the children to shut up - they never do what I say*; *it's no use just waiting and hoping that someone will give you a job* **(b) to make use of something** = to use something; *you should make more use of your bicycle*

used to   [ˈjuːzd ˈtuː] *phrase* **(a) to be used to something** *or* **to doing something** = not to worry about doing something, because you do it often; *farmers are used to getting up early*; *I'm not used to eating such a large meal in the middle of the day* **(b) to get used to something** *or* **to doing something** = to do something often or for a period of time, so that it is not a worry any more; *she'll soon get used to her new job* **(c)** *(showing that something happened often in the past)* *there used to be lots of small shops in the village until the supermarket was built*; *when we were children, we used to go to France every year for our holidays*

useful   [ˈjuːsfʊl] *adjective* who or which can help you do something; *I find these scissors very useful for opening letters*; **to make yourself useful** = to do something to help

useless   [ˈjuːsləs] *adjective* which is not useful, which doesn't help; *these scissors are useless - they won't cut anything*

usual   [ˈjuːʒʊəl] *adjective* **(a)** which is done or used often; *she took her usual bus to the college*; *we'll meet at the usual time, usual place* **(b) as usual** = as is normal, in the normal way; *as usual, it rained for the school sports day*

usually   [ˈjuːʒəli] *adverb* very often, frequently; *we usually have sandwiches for lunch*; *the bus is usually full on Friday evenings*

Vv

V, v   [viː] twenty-second letter of the alphabet, between U and W; *I know his name's Stephen but I don't know if it is spelt with a 'PH' or a 'V' (Stephen or Steven)*

vacant   [ˈveɪkənt] *adjective* empty, available for you to use; *there are six rooms vacant in the new hotel wing*; *is the toilet vacant yet?*

vacation   [vəˈkeɪʃn] *noun (especially US)* holiday; *the family went on vacation in Canada*; **vacation job** = job taken by a student during the vacation to earn money to help pay for the costs of a university or college course

vaccination   [væksɪˈneɪʃn] *noun* action of giving someone an injection to protect him or her against an illness; *he had a vaccination against the disease before he went abroad*

vacuum cleaner   [ˈvækjuəm ˈkliːnə] *noun* machine which cleans by sucking up dust; *our cat hides under the bed when she hears the vacuum cleaner*

vague   [veɪg] *adjective* not clear, with no precise details; *he's got a vague idea of what he wants to do after university*; *we've made some vague plans to go to Greece in August* (NOTE: **vaguer - vaguest**)

vain   [veɪn] *adjective* **(a) in vain** = without any success; *we waited in vain for a bus and had to walk home* **(b)** very proud of your appearance, clothes, achievements, etc.; *he's very vain, and spends all his time combing his hair* (NOTE: do not confuse with **vein**; note: **vainer - vainest**)

Valentine   [ˈvæləntaɪn] *noun* card sent to someone you love on Valentine's Day; **Valentine's Day** = 14th February, day when people send cards and flowers to people they love; *he sent her a Valentine's card*

valid ['vælɪd] *adjective* which is legal and can be used for a time; *travellers must have a valid ticket before boarding the train; I have a season ticket which is valid for one year*

valley ['væli] *noun* long piece of low land through which a river runs; *a lot of computer companies are based in the Thames Valley*

valuable ['væljuːbl] *adjective* **(a)** worth a lot of money; *the burglars stole everything that was valuable* **(b)** useful, which helps; *she gave me some very valuable advice*

value ['væljuː] **1** *noun* **(a)** amount of money which something is worth; *houses have fallen in value in some parts of the country* **(b)** being useful, giving help; *his advice was of no practical value at all* **2** *verb* to give a value to something, to say what something is worth; *these houses are valued at more than £200,000*

value added tax (VAT) ['væljuː 'ædɪd tæks] *see* VAT

van [væn] *noun* small vehicle for carrying goods by road; *our van will call this afternoon to pick up the goods*

vandal ['vændl] *noun* person who destroys property, especially public property, because they like doing that; *vandals have pulled the telephones out of the callboxes by the station*

vanish ['vænɪʃ] *verb* to disappear suddenly; *the rabbit vanished down a hole*

vapour *US* **vapor** ['veɪpə] *noun* substance which you can see in the form of mist or a gas, usually caused by heating; *you can see water vapour rising from the swimming pool in cold weather*

variety [və'raɪəti] *noun* **(a) a variety of** = a lot of different sorts of things or people; *she's had a variety of boyfriends; we couldn't go on holiday this year for a variety of reasons* **(b)** different type of plant or animal; *do you have this new variety of rose?*

various ['veəriəs] *adjective* of different sorts or types; *the shop sells goods from various*

countries; *various people have told me that I should see that film*

vary ['veəri] *verb* **(a)** to be different; *prices of flats vary from a few thousand pounds to millions* **(b)** to change what you do often; *try to vary your diet as much as possible*

vase [vɑːz] *noun* jar for keeping cut flowers in water; *she put the flowers into a vase*

vast [vɑːst] *adjective* enormous, very large; *a vast oil tanker suddenly appeared out of the fog*

VAT [væt or viːeɪ'tiː] *abbreviation for* Value Added Tax, a tax which is calculated on the value of goods or services sold; *the invoice includes VAT at 17.5%; in Britain there is no VAT on books*

vegetable ['vedʒɪtəbl] *noun* plant grown to be eaten, but not usually sweet; *we grow potatoes, carrots and other sorts of vegetables in the garden; what vegetables do you want with your meat? - beans and carrots, please*

vegetarian [vedʒɪ'teəriən] **1** *noun* person who eats only fruit, vegetables, bread, etc., but does not eat meat or fish; *our children are all vegetarians* **2** *adjective* not containing meat; *she asked for the vegetarian menu*

vehicle ['viːɪkl] *noun* car, truck, bus, etc., a machine which carries passengers or goods; *goods vehicles can park at the back of the building; motor vehicles are not allowed on this mountain path*

vein [veɪn] *noun* small tube in the body which takes blood back to the heart (as opposed to an artery which carries blood from the heart round the body); *the veins in her legs are swollen* (NOTE: do not confuse with **vain**)

velvet ['velvət] *noun* cloth made from silk, with a soft surface like fur on one side; *she wore a velvet jacket*

verb [vɜːb] *noun (grammar)* word which shows an action, being or feeling, etc.; *in the sentence 'she hit him with her fist' the word 'hit' is a verb*

verdict ['vɜːdɪkt] *noun* decision of a judge or court whether someone is guilty or not; *the verdict of the court was guilty*

verse [vɜːs] *noun* **(a)** group of lines which form a part of a song or poem; *we sang all the verses of the college song* **(b)** poetry, writing which has a certain rhythm and sometimes rhymes; *he published a several books of verse*

version ['vɜːʃn] *noun* **(a)** description of what happened as seen by one person; *the victim told her version of events to the reporters* **(b)** type of a work of art, model of car, etc.; *this is the film version of the novel*

vertical ['vɜːtɪkl] *adjective* rising straight up; *he drew a few vertical lines to represent trees*; *we looked at the vertical cliff and wondered how to climb it*

very ['veri] *adverb (used to make an adjective or adverb stronger) it's very hot in the car*; *the time seemed to go very quickly when we were on holiday*

very many ['veri 'meni] *adjective* a lot of; *very many small birds failed to survive the winter*; **not very many** = not a lot of; *there weren't very many visitors at the exhibition*

very much ['veri 'mʌtʃ] **1** *adverb* greatly, a lot; *the children like fish fingers very much* **2** *adjective* **not very much** = not a lot of; *they haven't got very much money*

vest [vest] *noun* **(a)** light piece of underwear for the top half of the body; *he wears a thick vest in winter*; *if you don't have a clean vest, wear a T-shirt instead* **(b)** US short coat with buttons and without any sleeves, which is worn over a shirt and under a jacket; *he wore a pale gray vest with a black jacket* (NOTE: British English is **waistcoat)**

vet [vet] *noun* doctor who looks after sick animals; *we have to take the cat to the vet*

via ['vaɪə] *preposition* through; *we went to France via the Channel Tunnel*

vicious ['vɪʃəs] *adjective* cruel and wicked; *the gang carried out a vicious attack on an old lady*

victim ['vɪktɪm] *noun* person who is attacked, who has been in an accident; *the victims of the train crash were taken to the local hospital*; *earthquake victims were housed in tents*

victory ['vɪktri] *noun* winning of a battle, a fight, a game, etc.; *they won a clear victory in the general election*; *the American victory in the Olympics* (NOTE: plural is **victories)**

video ['vɪdiəʊ] **1** *noun* **(a)** machine which records TV programmes; *don't forget to set the video for 8 p.m. before you go out* **(b)** film which you can view on a television; *she borrowed the video from the public library* **(c)** magnetic tape on which you can record TV programmes, films, etc., for playing back on a television set; *she bought a box of blank videos* **2** *verb* to record pictures, a TV programme or film, etc., on tape; *I didn't see the programme because I was at work, but I've videoed it*

view [vjuː] *noun* **(a)** what you can see from a certain place; *you can get a good view of the sea from the top of the tower*; *I asked for a room with a sea view and got one looking out over the railway station* **(b)** what you think about something; *his view is that the college needs more sports equipment* **(c)** **in view of** = because of; *in view of the stormy weather, we decided not to go sailing*

village ['vɪlɪdʒ] *noun* small group of houses in the country, like a little town, with a church, and usually some shops and small businesses; *the village shop sells just about everything we need*; *they are closing the village school because there aren't enough children*

vine [vaɪn] *noun* climbing plant which produces grapes; *the slopes of the hills along the river are covered with vines*

vinegar ['vɪnɪgə] *noun* liquid with a sharp taste, made from sour wine, used in cooking; *French dressing is a mixture of oil and vinegar*

violence ['vaɪələns] *noun* rough action which

is intended to hurt someone; *the game was spoilt by violence on the field*

violent ['vaɪələnt] *adjective* **(a)** very strong; *a violent storm blew all night*; *a violent earthquake damaged the city* **(b)** using force to hurt people; *the game of football was very violent - several players were hurt*

violet ['vaɪələt] *noun* **(a)** small wild plant with blue or purple flowers which have a strong scent; *we picked a bunch of violets in the woods* **(b)** blue or purple colour; *she was wearing a violet dress*

violin [vaɪə'lɪn] *noun* string instrument played with a bow; *everyone listened to him playing the violin*

virtual ['vɜːtʃuəl] *adjective* almost, nearly; *the builders turned the house a virtual rubbish dump*; **virtual reality** = computer pictures that are so real that you feel you are really there

virus ['vaɪrəs] *noun* **(a)** tiny germ which can only develop in other cells and often destroys them; *scientists have discovered a new flu virus* **(b)** hidden computer program, which destroys files; *you must check the program for viruses*

visible ['vɪzɪbl] *adjective* which can be seen; *the damage caused by the storm was clearly visible in the streets of the town*

visibly ['vɪzɪbli] *adverb* in a way which everyone can see; *she was visibly annoyed by the television cameras outside her house*

vision ['vɪʒn] *noun* **(a)** eyesight, being able to see; *many people's vision begins to get worse after the age of 50* **(b)** thing which you imagine; *he had visions of himself stuck in London with no passport and no money*

visit ['vɪzɪt] **1** *noun* short stay with someone, short stay in a town or a country; *we will be making a visit to London next week*; **to pay a visit to** = to go and see; *we will pay my sister a visit on her birthday* **2** *verb* to stay a short time with someone, to stay a short time in a town or country, to go to see something; *I am on my*

way to visit my mother in hospital; *he spent a week in Scotland, visiting museums in Edinburgh and Glasgow*

visitor ['vɪzɪtə] *noun* person who comes to visit; *how many visitors come to the museum each year?*; *we had a surprise visitor yesterday - Auntie Mary!*

vitae ['viːtaɪ] *see* CURRICULUM VITAE

vital ['vaɪtl] *adjective* very important; *it is vital that the criminal should be caught before he commits another crime*

vitamin ['vɪtəmɪn] *noun* essential substance found in food which you need for growth and health; *make sure your diet contains enough vitamins*

vivid ['vɪvɪd] *adjective* **(a)** very bright; *a painting of vivid yellow sunflowers* **(b)** very lively, very like real life; *I had a really vivid dream last night*

vocabulary [və'kæbjʊləri] *noun* **(a)** words used by a person or group of persons; *he's only three but his vocabulary is already quite large* **(b)** printed list of words; *there is a German-English vocabulary at the back of the book* (NOTE: plural is **vocabularies**)

voice [vɔɪs] *noun* sound made when you speak or sing; *I didn't recognize his voice over the telephone*; **to lose your voice** = not to be able to speak; *she's got a sore throat and has lost her voice*

volcano [vɒl'keɪnəʊ] *noun* mountain with a hole on the top through which red hot rocks, ash and gas can come out; *volcanoes are popular tourist attractions and one of the best-known ones in Europe is Vesuvius* (NOTE: plural is **volcanoes**)

volume ['vɒljuːm] *noun* **(a)** one book, especially one in a series; *can you pass me the third volume of the history of England?* **(b)** amount of sound; *can you turn down the volume on the radio?* **(c)** amount which is contained inside something; *you calculate volume by multiplying length and height and breadth*

voluntary ['vɒləntri] *adjective* **(a)** done because you want to do it, and without being paid; *many retired people do voluntary work* **(b)** done without being forced; *he made a voluntary contribution to the collection*

volunteer [vɒlən'tɪə] **1** *noun* person who offers to do something without being paid or being forced to do it; *the school relies on volunteers to help with the library* **2** *verb* to offer to do something without being paid or being forced to do it; *will anyone volunteer for the job of washing up?*

vote [vəʊt] **1** *noun* marking a paper, holding up your hand, etc., to show your choice; *how many votes did Mr Smith get?* **2** *verb* to mark a paper, to hold up your hand, etc., to show what you choose; *half of the group voted to go up the mountain*; *I vote we go for a picnic*

voucher ['vaʊtʃə] *noun* paper which is given instead of money; *with every £20 of purchases, the customer gets a cash voucher to the value of £2*; **gift voucher** = card which you give as a present and which must be exchanged in a certain store for goods

vowel ['vaʊəl] *noun* one of the five letters (a, e, i. o, u) which represent sounds made without using your teeth, tongue or lips (the letters representing sounds which are not vowels are 'consonants'); *'b' and 't' are consonants, while 'e' and 'i' are vowels*

voyage ['vɔɪɪdʒ] *noun* long journey, especially by ship; *the voyages of Sir Francis Drake*

Ww

W, w ['dʌbljuː] twenty-third letter of the alphabet, between V and X; *'one' is pronounced as if it starts with a W*

wade [weɪd] *verb* to walk through water or mud; *to explore the cave we had to wade across a river*

wag [wæg] *verb* to move from side to side or up and down; *the dog ran up to him, wagging its tail* (NOTE: **wagging - wagged**)

wage *or* **wages** [weɪdʒ *or* 'weɪdʒɪz] *noun* money paid to someone for work done; *her wages are £500 a week*; *she is earning a good wage in the pizza restaurant*

wagon ['wægn] *noun* railway truck used for carrying heavy loads; *the wagons of coal are leaving the mine*

waist [weɪst] *noun* **(a)** narrower part of your body between the bottom of your chest and your hips; *she measures 32 inches round the waist* **(b)** part of a piece of clothing such as a skirt, trousers or dress, that goes round the middle of your body; *the waist of these trousers is very tight* (NOTE: do not confuse with **waste)**

waistcoat ['weɪskəʊt] *noun* short coat with buttons and without any sleeves, which is worn over a shirt and under a jacket (American English is 'vest'); *he wore a bright silk waistcoat to the wedding*

wait [weɪt] **1** *verb* to stay where you are, and not do anything until something happens or someone comes; *wait here while I call an ambulance*; *they had been waiting for half an hour in the rain before the bus finally arrived*; **to keep someone waiting** = to make someone wait because you are late; *the boss* *doesn't like being kept waiting*; *sorry to have kept you waiting!* **2** *noun* time spent waiting until something happens or arrives; *you've just missed the bus - you'll have a very long wait for the next one* (NOTE: do not confuse with **weight**)

waiter ['weɪtə] *noun* man who brings food and drink to customers in a restaurant; *the waiter still hasn't brought us the first course*

waitress ['weɪtrəs] *noun* woman who brings food and drink to customers in a restaurant; *the waitress brought us the menu* (NOTE: plural is **waitresses**)

wake [weɪk] *verb* **(a)** to stop someone's sleep; *she was woken by the telephone*; *I banged on her door, but I can't wake her* **(b)** to stop sleeping; *he woke suddenly, feeling drops of water falling on his head* (NOTE: **waking - woke** [wəʊk] - **has woken**)

wake up ['weɪk 'ʌp] *verb* **(a)** to stop someone's sleep; *he was woken up by the sound of the dog barking* **(b)** to stop sleeping; *she woke up in the middle of the night, thinking she had heard a noise*; *come on, wake up! it's past ten o'clock*

Wales [weɪlz] *noun* country to the west of England, forming part of the United Kingdom; *there are some high mountains in North Wales* (NOTE: capital: **Cardiff**; people: the **Welsh**; languages: **Welsh, English**)

walk [wɔ:k] **1** *verb* to go on foot; *the baby is almost a year old, and is just starting to walk*; *she was walking along the high street on her way to the bank* **2** *noun* **(a)** pleasant journey on foot; *let's all go for a walk in the park* **(b)** going on foot; *it's only a short walk from here to the beach*

wall [wɔ:l] *noun* bricks, stones, etc., built up to make one of the sides of a building, of a room or to go round a space; *the walls of the restaurant are decorated with pictures of film stars*; *the garden is surrounded by an old stone wall*

wallet ['wɒlɪt] *noun* small flat leather case for credit cards and notes, carried in your pocket; *someone stole my wallet in the crowd*

wallpaper ['wɔ:lpeɪpə] *noun* paper with different patterns on it, covering the walls of a room; *the wallpaper is light green to match the carpet*

walnut ['wɒlnʌt] *noun* hard round nut with a wrinkled inside part; *he cracked the walnuts with his hammer*; *a scoop of toffee and walnut ice cream*

wand [wɒnd] *noun* thin stick used to make magic; *the fairy waved her magic wand and the pumpkin turned into a coach*

wander ['wɒndə] *verb* to walk around in no particular direction; *they wandered round the town in the rain*; *two of the group of tourists wandered off into the market*

want [wɒnt] *verb* **(a)** to hope that you will do something, that something will happen, or that you will get something; *she wants a new car for her birthday*; *where do you want to go for your holidays?*; *he wants to be a teacher* **(b)** to ask someone to do something; *the head of college wants me to go and see him* **(c)** to need; *the kitchen ceiling wants painting*

war [wɔ:] *noun* fighting between countries; *millions of soldiers and ordinary citizens were killed during the war*; **civil war** = situation inside a country where groups of armed people fight against each other or against the government

ward [wɔ:d] *noun* room or set of rooms in a hospital, with beds for patients; *the children's ward is at the end of the corridor*; *she was taken into the accident and emergency ward*

warden ['wɔ:dən] *noun* **(a)** person who looks after or guards something; **forest warden** = person who looks after a forest **(b)** person whose job it is to give parking tickets to cars that are parked wrongly; *move your car - there's a warden coming*

wardrobe ['wɔ:drəʊb] *noun* tall cupboard in which you hang your clothes; *he moved the wardrobe from the landing into the bedroom*

warehouse [ˈweəhaʊs] *noun* large building where goods are stored; *our products are sent from the central warehouse to shops all over the country*

warm [wɔːm] *adjective* **(a)** quite hot; *the temperature is below freezing outside but it's nice and warm in the house*; *the children tried to keep warm by playing football*; *are you warm enough, or do you want another blanket?* **(b)** pleasant and friendly; *we had a warm welcome from our friends* (NOTE: **warmer - warmest**) **2** *verb* to make hotter; *come and warm your hands by the fire*

warmth [wɔːmθ] *noun* being or feeling warm; *it was cold and wet outside, and he looked forward to getting back to the warmth of his house*

warn [wɔːn] *verb* **(a)** to inform someone of a possible danger; *we were warned to boil all drinking water*; *the guide warned us that there might be snakes in the ruins* **(b)** to inform someone in advance; *the weather forecast has warned of storms in the English Channel tomorrow*

warning [ˈwɔːnɪŋ] **1** *noun* **(a)** information about a possible danger; *he shouted a warning to the children*; *each packet of cigarettes has a government health warning printed on it* **(b) without warning** = unexpectedly; *the car in front braked without warning and I ran into it* **2** *adjective* which informs about a danger; *red warning flags are raised if the sea is dangerous*

was [wɒz] *see* BE

wash [wɒʃ] *verb* to clean something using water; *cooks should always wash their hands before touching food!*; *I must wash the car before we go to the wedding*

wash up [ˈwɒʃ ˈʌp] *verb* to clean dirty cups, plates, knives, forks, etc., with water; *it took us hours to wash up after the party*; *my brother's washing up, while I'm sitting watching the TV*

washbasin [ˈwɒʃbeɪsn] *noun* container, with taps, for holding water for washing your hands and face, usually attached to the wall of a bathroom; *each bedroom in the hotel has a washbasin*

washing [ˈwɒʃɪŋ] *noun* clothes which have been washed, or which are ready to be washed; *put the washing in the washing machine*; *she hung out her washing to dry*

washing machine [ˈwɒʃɪŋ məˈʃiːn] *noun* machine for washing clothes; *he took the clothes out of the washing machine and hung them up to dry*

washing up [ˈwɒʃɪŋ ˈʌp] *noun* cleaning of dirty dishes, glasses, knives and forks, etc., with water; *can someone help with the washing up?*; *it took us hours to do the washing up after the party*; **washing-up liquid** = liquid soap used for washing dirty dishes

wasn't [wɒznt] *see* BE

wasp [wɒsp] *noun* insect with black and yellow stripes, which can sting; *wasps buzzed around the kitchen as she was making jam*

waste [weɪst] **1** *noun* **(a)** unnecessary use of time or money; *that computer is a waste of money - there are plenty of cheaper models* **(b)** rubbish, things which are no use and are thrown away; *put all your waste in the rubbish bin* (NOTE: do not confuse with **waist**) **2** *verb* to use more of something than you need; *don't waste time putting your shoes on - jump out of the window now*; *we turned off all the heating so as not to waste energy* **3** *adjective* useless, ready to be thrown away; *we have heaps of waste paper to take to the dump*

watch [wɒtʃ] **1** *noun* **(a)** device like a little clock which you wear on your wrist; *what time is it? - my watch has stopped* (NOTE: plural in this meaning is **watches**) **(b)** looking at something carefully; *visitors should be on the watch for car thieves*; **to keep watch** = to be on duty; *I'll keep watch if you want to have some sleep* **2** *verb* **(a)** to look at and notice something; *did you watch the TV news last night?* **(b)** to look at something carefully to make sure that nothing happens; *can you watch the baby while I'm at the hairdresser's?*

watch out ['wɒtʃ 'aʊt] *verb* **(a)** to be careful; *watch out! there's a car coming!* **(b) to watch out for** = to be careful to avoid; *you have to watch out for children playing in the road*

water ['wɔːtə] **1** *noun* common liquid which forms rain, rivers, lakes, the sea, etc., and which you drink and use in cooking; *can I have a glass of water please?*; *cook the vegetables in boiling water*; *you are advised to drink only bottled water* **2** *verb* to pour water on the soil round a plant to make it grow; *because it is hot we need to water the garden every day*; *she was watering her pots of flowers*

waterfall ['wɔːtəfɔːl] *noun* place where a stream falls down rocks; *let's climb up to the waterfall and picnic there*; *the biggest waterfall in the world is Niagara*

watering can ['wɔːtrɪŋ 'kæn] *noun* container similar to a bucket, with a long spout, used for giving water to plants, etc.; *he filled the watering can and watered the pots on the balcony*

waterproof ['wɔːtəpruːf] *adjective* which will not let water through; *these boots aren't waterproof - my socks are soaking wet*

watertight ['wɔːtətaɪt] *adjective* made so that water cannot get in or out; *the food has to be kept in watertight containers*

wave [weɪv] **1** *noun* **(a)** moving line of water on the surface of the sea, a lake or a river; *waves were breaking on the rocks*; *watch out for big waves on the beach* **(b)** regular curve on the surface of hair; *his hair has a natural wave* **(c)** sudden increase in something; **heat wave** = sudden spell of hot weather **2** *verb* **(a)** to move up and down in the wind; *the flags were waving outside the town hall* **(b)** to make an up and down movement of your hand (usually when saying goodbye); *they waved goodbye as the boat left the harbour*; **to wave**

to someone = to signal to someone by moving your hand up and down; *when I saw him I waved to him to cross the road*

wax [wæks] *noun* solid substance made from fat or oil, used for making candles, polish, etc.; *she brought a tin of wax and started to polish the furniture*

way [weɪ] *noun* **(a)** path or road which goes somewhere; *I'll walk the first part of the way home with you* **(b)** correct path or road to go somewhere; *do you know the way to the post office?*; *they lost their way and had to ask for directions* **(c) to make your way** = to go to (a place) with some difficulty; *can you make your way to passport control?*; *he made his way to the tourist information office* **(d)** particular direction from here; *this is a one-way street*; *this way please, everybody!* **(e)** means of doing something; *my mother showed me her way to make marmalade*; *he thought of a way of making money quickly* **(f)** distance; *the bank is quite a long way away from here* **(g)** space where someone wants to be or which someone wants to use; *get out of my way - I'm in a hurry*; *it's best to keep out of the way of the police for a moment*

by the way ['baɪ ðə 'weɪ] *(used to introduce something which is not very important or to change the subject which is being talked about)* *by the way, have you seen my keys anywhere?*

on the way ['ɒn ðə 'weɪ] during a journey; *I'll stop at the post office on my way to the restaurant*; *she's on her way to the office*

way in ['weɪ 'ɪn] *noun* entrance; *this is the way in to the theatre*

way out ['weɪ 'aʊt] *noun* exit; *he couldn't find the way out of the cinema in the dark*

way up ['weɪ 'ʌp] *noun* way in which something stands; *keep the jar the right way up or the jam will spill out*

we [wiː] *pronoun (used by someone speaking or writing to refer to himself or herself and others)* *they said we could go into the exhibition*; *we were not allowed into the* *restaurant in jeans*

weak [wi:k] *adjective* **(a)** not strong; *after his illness he is still very weak*; *I don't like weak tea - put another teabag in the pot* **(b)** not good at, not having knowledge or skill; *French is his weakest subject* (NOTE: do not confuse with **week**; note: **weaker - weakest**)

wealth [welθ] *noun* a large amount of money; *his wealth came from his grandfather's mining company*

wealthy ['welθi] *adjective* very rich (person); *50% of the land is in the hands of the ten wealthiest families* (NOTE: **wealthier - wealthiest**)

weapon ['wepən] *noun* object such as a gun or sword, which you fight with; *the crowd used iron bars as weapons*

wear [weə] *verb* **(a)** to have (especially a piece of clothing) on your body; *when last seen, he was wearing a blue raincoat* **(b)** to become damaged or thin through being used; *I've worn a hole in the heel of my sock* (NOTE: **wearing - wore** [wɔ:] **- has worn** [wɔ:n])

wear out ['weə 'aut] *verb* **(a)** to use something so much that it is broken and useless; *walking across the USA, he wore out three pairs of boots* **(b)** to become useless because of being used too much; *the engine wore out and had to be replaced* **(c) to wear yourself out** = to become very tired through doing something; *she wore herself out looking after the old lady*

weary ['wiəri] *adjective* very tired; *we were all weary after a day spent walking round London* (NOTE: **wearier - weariest**)

weather ['weðə] *noun* conditions outside, i.e., if it is raining, hot, cold, windy, sunny, etc.; *what's the weather going to be like today?*; *the weather in Iceland is usually colder than here*; *rain every day - just normal English summer weather!* (NOTE: do not confuse with **whether**)

weave [wi:v] *verb* **(a)** to make cloth by putting threads under and over each other; *the cloth is woven from the wool of local sheep* **(b)** to make something by a similar method, but using straw, etc.; *she learnt how to weave baskets* (NOTE: **wove** [wəuv] **- has woven** [wəuvn])

web [web] *noun* **(a)** net made by spiders to catch flies; *in autumn the garden is full of spiders' webs* **(b)** *(Internet)* **the Web** = the World Wide Web, the thousands of websites and web pages in the Internet which people can visit; **web page** = single page of text and pictures, forming part of a website

website ['websait] *noun* collection of pages on the web which have been produced by one company or person and are linked together

we'd [wi:d] = WE HAD, WE WOULD

wedding ['wedɪŋ] *noun* ceremony when two people become officially man and wife; *don't count on having fine weather for your wedding*; *this Saturday I'm going to John and Mary's wedding*; **wedding anniversary** = date which is the date of a wedding in the past; *don't tell me that you remembered our wedding anniversary!*; **wedding cake** = special cake made with dried fruit, covered with icing, eaten at a wedding reception; *did you get a piece of wedding cake?*; **wedding ring** = ring which is put on the fourth finger during the wedding ceremony

wedge [wedʒ] **1** *noun* solid piece of wood, metal, rubber, etc., that has a V-shape; *put a wedge under the door to hold it open* **2** *verb* to put a wedge under something fix it firmly open or shut; *she wedged the door open with a piece of wood*; **to become wedged** *or* **to get wedged** = to become tight stuck; *the little boy got his head wedged between the railings*

Wednesday ['wenzdi] *noun* day between Tuesday and Thursday, the third day of the week; *she came for tea last Wednesday*; *Wednesdays are always busy days for us*; *can we meet next Wednesday afternoon?*; *the 15th is a Tuesday, so the 16th must be a Wednesday*

weed [wi:d] **1** *noun* wild plant that is

growing where you do not want it in a garden; *weeds grew all over his strawberry beds while he was on holiday* 2 *verb* to pull out plants which you do not want from a garden; *she spent all afternoon weeding the vegetable garden*

week [wiːk] *noun* period of seven days, usually from Monday to Sunday; *there are 52 weeks in the year*; *I go to the cinema at least once a week* (NOTE: do not confuse with **weak**)

weekend ['wiːkend] *noun* Saturday and Sunday, or the period from Friday evening to Sunday evening; *we're going to Brighton for the weekend*; **long weekend** = weekend, including Friday night and Sunday night; *we took a long weekend in Paris*

weigh [weɪ] *verb* (a) to use scales or a weighing machine to measure how heavy something is; *can you weigh this parcel for me?*; *I weighed myself this morning*; **weighing machine** = device for weighing someone or something; *she put the bag of sweets on the weighing machine* (b) to have a certain weight; *the packet weighs twenty-five grams*; *how much do you weigh?*

weight [weɪt] *noun* (a) how heavy something is; *what's the heaviest weight of parcel that the post office will accept?* (b) how heavy a person is; **to lose weight** = to get thinner; **to put on weight** = to get fatter; *she's put on a lot of weight since her holiday* (c) something which is heavy; *if you lift heavy weights like big stones, you can hurt your back* (NOTE: do not confuse with **wait**)

weird ['wɪəd] *adjective* strange, different from what is normal; *I don't like her new boyfriend - he's really weird* (NOTE: **weirder - weirdest**)

welcome ['welkʌm] 1 *adjective* (a) met or accepted with pleasure; *after a game of rugby a hot shower was very welcome* (b) (informal) (as a reply to 'thank you') *thanks for carrying the bags for me - you're welcome!* 2 *verb* (a) to greet someone in a friendly way; *the staff welcomed the new waitress to the café* (b) to

be glad to hear news; *I would welcome any suggestions as to how to stop the water coming through the roof* 3 *noun* action of greeting someone; **a warm welcome** = a friendly welcome; *the French family gave me a warm welcome*

welfare ['welfeə] *noun* providing comfort and happiness to people; *the club looks after the welfare of the old people in the town*

we'll [wiːl] = WE WILL

well [wel] 1 *adverb* in a good way; *he doesn't speak Russian very well*; *you should go to the Tower of London - it's well worth a visit* 2 *adjective* healthy; *she's looking well after her holiday!*; *my mother's not very well today - she's had to stay off work* 3 *interjection* (which starts a sentence, and often has no meaning) *well, I'll show you round the house first* 4 *noun* very deep hole dug in the ground with water or oil at the bottom; *we pump water from the well in our garden*

as well ['æz 'wel] also; *when my aunt comes to stay she brings her two cats and the dog as well*; *you can't eat fish and chips and a meat pie as well!*; **as well as** = not only, but also; *some newspaper shops sell food as well as newspapers*

well done ['wel 'dʌn] *interjection (showing congratulations) well done, the England team!*; *well done to all of you who passed the exam!*

well-paid ['wel'peɪd] *adjective* earning a good salary; *what I want is not just a well-paid job but one that is interesting*

wellingtons *(informal)* **wellies** ['welɪŋtənz or 'welɪz] *noun* long rubber boots which go almost up to your knees, often coloured green; *put your wellies on - it's pouring down*

Welsh [welʃ] 1 *adjective* referring to Wales; *we will be going climbing in the Welsh mountains at Easter* 2 *noun* (a) **the Welsh** = the people of Wales; *the Welsh love singing* (b) language spoken in Wales; *Welsh is used in schools in many parts of Wales*

went [went] *see* GO

wept [wept] *see* WEEP

were, weren't [wɜː or wɜːnt] *see* BE

we're [ˈwiːə] = WE ARE

west [west] **1** *noun* **(a)** direction of where the sun sets; *the sun sets in the west and rises in the east* **(b)** part of a country which is to the west of the rest; *the west of the country is wetter than the east* **2** *adjective* referring to the west; *she lives on the west coast of the United States*; *the west part of the town is near the river* **3** *adverb* towards the west; *go west for about ten kilometres, and then you'll come to the national park*; *their house has a garden that faces west*

West End [ˈwest ˈend] *noun* part of London, where the main shopping area is found; *crowds go shopping in the West End on Sunday afternoons*

western [ˈwestən] **1** *adjective* from, to or in the west; *Great Britain is part of Western Europe*; *the western part of Canada has wonderful mountains* **2** *noun* film about cowboys; *she likes watching old westerns on TV*

wet [wet] *adjective* **(a)** covered in water or other liquid; *she forgot her umbrella and got wet walking back from the shops* **(b)** when it is raining; *the summer months are the wettest part of the year* **(c)** not yet dry; *don't touch the door - the paint's still wet* (NOTE: **wetter - wettest**)

we've [wiːv] = WE HAVE

whale [weɪl] *noun* very large animal that lives in the sea; *you can take a boat out into the harbour to see the whales*

what [wɒt] **1** *adjective (asking a question) what time is it?*; *what type of food does he like best?* **2** *pronoun* **(a)** the thing which; *did you see what was in the box?*; *what we like to do most on holiday is just to sit on the beach* **(b)** *(asking a question) what's the correct time?*; *what did he give you for your birthday?*; *what's the Spanish for 'table'?* **3**

adverb (showing surprise) what beautiful weather! **4** *interjection (showing surprise) what! did you hear what he said?*

what about [wɒt əˈbaʊt] *phrase (showing a suggestion) what about having something to eat?*

what for [ˈwɒt ˈfɔː] *phrase* **(a)** why; *what are they all shouting for?*; *what did he phone the police for?* **(b)** for what use; *what's this red button for?*

whatever [wɒtˈevə] *pronoun (form of 'what' which stresses)* **(a)** it doesn't matter what; *you can have whatever you like for Christmas*; *she always does whatever she feels like doing* **(b)** *(in questions)* what, why; *whatever made him do that?*

wheat [wiːt] *noun* cereal plant of which the seeds are used to make flour; *my mother uses wheat flour to make bread*

wheel [wiːl] **1** *noun* **(a)** round piece which turns round a central point and on which a bicycle, a car, etc., runs; *the front wheel and the back wheel of the motorbike were both damaged in the accident*; *we got a flat tyre so I had to get out to change the wheel* **(b)** any similar round thing for turning; *the steering wheel is on the right-hand side of the car in British cars* **2** *verb* to push something along that has wheels; *he wheeled his motorbike into the garage*; *she was wheeling her bike along the pavement*

wheelbarrow [ˈwiːlbærəʊ] *noun* small cart with one wheel in front, and two handles, used to carry heavy loads; *he filled the wheelbarrow with soil and wheeled it to the end of the garden*

wheelchair [ˈwiːltʃeə] *noun* chair on wheels which people who cannot walk use to move around; *she has been in a wheelchair since her accident*

when [wen] **1** *adverb (asking a question)* at what time; *when is the last train for Paris?*; *I asked her when her friend was leaving* **2** *conjunction* **(a)** at the time that; *when you go* *on holiday, leave your key with me so that I can feed your cat*; *let me know when you're ready to go* **(b)** after; *wash up the plates when you've finished your breakfast* **(c)** even if; *the sales assistant said the car was worth £5000 when he really knew it was worth only half that*

whenever [wen'evə] *adverb* at any time that; *come for tea whenever you like*

where [weə] *adverb* **(a)** *(asking a question)* in what place, to what place; *where did I put my glasses?*; *where are you going for your holiday?* **(b)** *(showing place)* in a place in which; *stay where you are and don't move*

wherever [weə'evə] *adverb* **(a)** to or in any place; *you can sit wherever you want* **(b)** *(form of 'where' which stresses)* *wherever did you get that hat?*

whether ['weðə] *conjunction* **(a)** *(showing doubt, or not having reached a decision)* if; *do you know whether they're coming?*; *I can't make up my mind whether to go on holiday now or later* **(b)** *(applying to either of two things)* both; *it doesn't matter whether you're tall or short* (NOTE: do not confuse with **weather**)

which [wɪtʃ] *adjective & pronoun* **(a)** *(asking a question)* what person or thing; *which dress are you wearing to the wedding?*; *which boy threw that stone?* **(b)** *(only used with things, not people)* that; *the French restaurant which is next door to the post office*

while [waɪl] **1** *noun* some time; *it's a while since I've seen him*; **a little while** = a short period of time; *do you mind waiting a little while until a table is free?*; **quite a while** = a longer period of time; *he changed jobs quite a while ago*; **once in a while** = from time to time, but not often; *it's nice to go to have an Indian meal once in a while* **2** *conjunction* **(a)** when, at the time that; *while we were on holiday someone broke into our house*; *shall I clean the kitchen while you're having a bath?* **(b)** *(showing difference)* *he likes meat, while his sister is a vegetarian*

whine [waɪn] *verb* **(a)** to make a loud high noise; *you can hear the engines of the racing cars whining in the background* **(b)** to complain with a loud high sound; *the dogs whined when we locked them up in the kitchen* (NOTE: do not confuse with **wine**)

whip [wɪp] **1** *noun* long, thin piece of leather with a handle, used to hit animals to make them do what you want; *he used his whip to make his horse run faster* **2** *verb* **(a)** to hit someone or an animal with a whip; *he whipped the horse to make it go faster* **(b)** to beat cream, eggs, etc., until they are thick; *whip the eggs and milk together*; *a chocolate cake covered with whipped cream* (NOTE: whipping - whipped)

whirl [wɜːl] *verb* to turn round quickly, to spin; *the children's paper windmills whirled in the wind*

whirlpool ['wɜːlpuːl] *noun* stream of water that turns round and round very fast; *be careful, there are whirlpools in the river*

whirlwind ['wɜːlwɪnd] *noun* column of air that turns round and round very fast; *whirlwinds come in the summer months and cause a huge amount of damage*

whisk [wɪsk] **1** *noun* kitchen tool used for whipping cream, eggs, etc.; *where's the whisk, I want to beat some eggs?* **2** *verb* **(a)** to move something very fast; *she whisked the plate of cakes away before I could take one* **(b)** to beat cream, eggs, etc., very quickly; *next, whisk the mixture until it is smooth and has no lumps*

whiskers ['wɪskəz] *noun* moustache and beard on the side of an animal's or a man's face; *it's not only cats that have whiskers, rabbits have them too*; *that's a family portrait - my great-grandfather's the one with the black hat and whiskers*

whiskey ['wɪski] *noun* Irish or American whisky

whisky ['wɪski] *noun* alcohol made in Scotland from grain; *the factory produces* *thousands of bottles of whisky every year*

whisper ['wɪspə] **1** *noun* quiet voice, words spoken very quietly; *she spoke in a whisper* **2** *verb* to speak very quietly, to make a very quiet sound; *he whispered instructions to the other members of the gang*

whistle ['wɪsl] **1** *noun* **(a)** high sound made by blowing through your lips when they are almost closed; *we heard a whistle and saw a dog running across the field* **(b)** small metal instrument which makes a high sound when you blow through it; *the referee blew his whistle to stop the match* **2** *verb* **(a)** to blow through your lips to make a high sound; *they marched along, whistling a happy tune* **(b)** to make a high sound using a small metal instrument; *the referee whistled to stop the match*

white [waɪt] **1** *adjective* of a colour like snow or milk; *white cars always look dirty*; *her hair is now completely white*; **white coffee** = coffee with milk added; **white wine** = wine which is clear or slightly yellow (NOTE: **whiter - whitest**) **2** *noun* **(a)** person whose skin is pale **(b)** white part of something; *the white of an egg* **(d)** *(informal)* white wine; *a glass of the house white, please*

White House ['waɪt 'haʊs] *noun* building in Washington where the President of the USA lives and works; *the President invited the Prime Minister to lunch at the White House*

who [hu:] *pronoun* **(a)** *(asking a question)* which person or persons; *who was it who phoned?*; *who are you talking to?* **(b)** the person or the people that; *anyone who didn't get tickets early won't be able to get in*; *do you remember the girl who used to work here as a waitress?* (NOTE: sometimes written **whom** when used as an object)

whoever [hu:'evə] *pronoun (form of 'who' which stresses)* no matter who, anyone who; *whoever finds the umbrella can keep it*

whole [həʊl] **1** *adjective* all of something; *she must have been hungry - she ate a whole apple pie*; *the whole country was covered with*

snow **2** *noun* all, everything; *she stayed in bed the whole of Sunday morning and read the newspapers*; *did you watch the whole of the programme?* (NOTE: do not confuse with **hole**) **3** *adverb* in one piece; *the penguin swallowed the fish whole*

whom [hu:m] *see* WHO

whooping cough ['hu:pɪŋ 'kɒf] *noun* infectious disease which affects the lungs, common in children, and sometimes very serious; *she caught whooping cough from her brother*

who's [hu:z] = WHO IS, WHO HAS

whose [hu:z] *pronoun* **(a)** *(asking a question)* belonging to which person; *whose book is this?*; *whose money was stolen?* **(b)** belonging to which person; *the family whose car was stolen*; *the man whose hat you borrowed* (NOTE: do not confuse with **who's**)

why [waɪ] *adverb (asking a question)* for what reason; *why did you phone me in the middle of the TV film?*; *I asked the guard why the train was late*

wicked ['wɪkɪd] *adjective* very bad; *it was wicked of them to steal the birds' eggs*

wide [waɪd] **1** *adjective* **(a)** measured from side to side; *the table is three feet wide*; *the river is not very wide at this point* **(b)** very large; *the shop carries a wide range of British cheeses* (NOTE: **wider - widest**) **2** *adverb* as far as possible, as much as possible; *she opened her eyes wide*; *the door was wide open so we just walked in*; **wide awake** = very much awake; *at eleven o'clock the baby was still wide awake*

widow ['wɪdəʊ] *noun* woman whose husband has died and who has not married again; *she was left a widow when she was still quite young*

widower ['wɪdəʊə] *noun* man whose wife has died and who has not married again; *she married a widower aged 62*

width [wɪdθ] *noun* **(a)** measurement of something from one side to another; *I need to* *know the width of the sofa* **(b)** distance from one side to another of a swimming pool; *she swam three widths easily*

wife [waɪf] *noun* woman who is married to a man; *I know Mr Jones quite well but I've never met his wife* (NOTE: plural is **wives** [waɪvz])

wig [wɪg] *noun* false hair worn on your head; *she wore a green wig for the party*; *in the film, he wears a grey wig to make him look older*

wigwam ['wɪgwæm] *noun* tent used by American Indians

wild [waɪld] **1** *adjective* **(a)** living in nature, not in a zoo; *wild dogs wander over parts of Australia*; **wild animals** = animals which are living in natural surroundings, as opposed to pets or farm animals; *we watched a TV programme on wild animals in Africa*; **wild flower** = flower which grows naturally, not a garden plant; *the book is full of pictures of wild flowers* **(b)** *(informal)* very angry; very excited; *the fans went wild at the end of the match* **(c)** not thinking carefully; *she made a wild guess but it was wrong* **2** *adverb* **(a)** free, without any fences or cages; *in this zoo, animals can roam wild in the fields* **(b)** without any control; *the crowds were running wild through the centre of the town*

wilderness ['wɪldənəs] *noun* wild country or desert, which has no people living in it; *he spent years exploring the Arctic wilderness*

wildlife ['waɪldlaɪf] *noun* birds, plants and animals living free in nature; *they spent the summer studying the wildlife in the national park*

will [wɪl] **1** *verb used with other verbs* **(a)** *(to form the future)* *the party will start soon*; *if you ask her to play the piano, she'll say 'no'* **(b)** *(polite way of asking someone to do something)* *will someone close the curtains?* **(c)** *(showing that you are keen to do something)* *don't call a taxi - I'll take you home* **2** *noun* **(a)** what you want to do; **against your will** = without your agreement; *he was*

forced to pay the money against his will **(b)** legal document by which a person gives instructions as to what should happen to his or her property after he or she dies; *according to her will, all her property is left to her children*

willing ['wɪlɪŋ] *adjective* eager to help; *is there anyone who is willing to drive the bus?*; *I need two willing volunteers to wash the car*

willow ['wɪləʊ] *noun* tree with long thin branches often found near rivers; *she sat under an old willow, watching the river flow past*; **weeping willow** = type of large willow tree with long hanging branches

win [wɪn] *verb* **(a)** to beat someone in a game; to be first in a race; *I expect our team will win tomorrow*; *she won the race easily* **(b)** to get (a prize, etc.); *she won first prize in the art competition*; *he won two million pounds on the lottery* (NOTE: **winning - won** [wʌn])

wind 1 [wɪnd] *noun* **(a)** air which moves fast outdoors; *the wind blew two trees down in the park* **(b)** **wind instruments** = musical instruments which you have to blow to make a note; *he doesn't play any wind instrument, just the piano* **2** [waɪnd] *verb* **(a)** to turn a key, etc., to make a machine work; *I have to wind up the clock twice a week* **(b)** to twist round and round; *he wound the towel round his waist*; *the road winds round the hills* (NOTE: **winding - wound** [waʊnd])

wind up ['waɪnd 'ʌp] *verb* **(a)** to turn a key to make a machine work; *did you remember to wind the clock up?* **(b)** to turn a handle to make something go up; *wind up your window if it starts to rain* **(c)** to end up, to be in the end; *we looked for a hotel and wound up in one by the railway station*

windmill ['wɪnmɪl] *noun* **(a)** mill for grinding flour, driven by sails which turn when the wind blows; *they live in an old windmill by the sea* **(b)** little toy made of folded paper, which turns in the wind; *the children all had little paper windmills*

window ['wɪndəʊ] *noun* opening in a wall,

door, etc., which is filled with glass; *it's dangerous to lean out of car windows*; *the burglar must have got in through the bathroom window*

windscreen *US* **windshield** ['wɪnskriːn or 'wɪnʃiːld] *noun* glass window in the front of a car, bus, truck, etc.; *the windscreen broke when a stone hit it*; *I can't see through the windscreen - it's raining so hard*

windy ['wɪndi] *adjective* when a strong wind is blowing; *we have a lot of windy weather in March* (NOTE: windier - windiest)

wine [waɪn] *noun* alcohol made from grapes; *we had a glass of French red wine*; *should we have some white wine with the fish?*

wing [wɪŋ] *noun* (a) one of the two parts of the body which a bird or butterfly, etc., uses to fly; *a brown butterfly with white spots on its wings*; *which part of the chicken do you prefer, a leg or a wing?* (b) one of the two flat parts sticking from the side of an aircraft, which hold the aircraft in the air; *I had a seat by the wing, so could not see much out of the window* (c) part of a large building which leads off to the side of the main building, often built as an extension; *they are building a new wing for the hospital*

wink [wɪŋk] **1** *verb* to shut and open one eye quickly, as a signal; *she winked at him to try to tell him that everything was going well* **2** *noun* opening and shutting one eye quickly; *she gave him a wink to show that she had seen him take the last piece of cake*

winner ['wɪnə] *noun* person who wins; *he was the winner of the 1000 metres*; *the winner of the race gets a silver cup*

winter ['wɪntə] *noun* the coldest part of the year, the season between autumn and spring; *it's too cold in the winter to do any work in the garden*; **winter sports** = sports which are done in the winter, such as skiing, skating, etc.

wipe [waɪp] *verb* to clean or dry with a cloth; *wipe your shoes with a cloth before you polish them*; *here's a tissue to wipe your nose*

wire ['waɪə] *noun* (a) thin piece of metal or metal thread; *he used bits of wire to attach the apple tree to the wall* (b) thin metal thread along which electricity flows, usually covered with coloured plastic; *the wires seem to be all right, so there must be a problem with the dishwasher itself*

wise [waɪz] *adjective* intelligent and sensible; *I don't think it's wise to keep all your money in a pot under your bed*; *it was a wise decision to cancel the trip* (NOTE: wiser - wisest)

wish [wɪʃ] **1** *noun* (a) what you want to happen; **to make a wish** = to think of something you would like to have or to see happen; *close your eyes and make a wish*; *make a wish when you blow out the candles on your birthday cake* (b) greetings ; *please give my good wishes to your family* (NOTE: plural is **wishes**) **2** *verb* (a) to want something (which is almost impossible to have); *I wish we didn't have to go to work on Christmas Day*; *I wish my birthday wasn't in June when I'm taking exams* (b) to want something to happen; *she sometimes wished she could live in the country* (c) to hope something good will happen; *she wished him good luck in his interview*; *he wished me a Happy New Year*

witch [wɪtʃ] *noun (in children's stories)* wicked woman believed to have magic powers; *the wicked witch turned the prince into a frog* (NOTE: plural is **witches**)

with [wɪθ or wɪð] *preposition* (a) *(showing things or people that are together)* *my sister is staying with us for a few days* (b) *(showing something which you have)* *do you know the girl with blue eyes who is in my Spanish class?* (c) *(showing something which is used)* *he was cutting up wood with a saw*; *since his accident he walks with a stick* (d) because of; *half the people in the office are ill with flu*

within [wɪ'ðɪn] *preposition (in space or time)* in; *the house is within easy reach of the station*; **within sight** = able to be seen; *we are almost there, the house is within sight*

without [wɪˈðaʊt] *preposition* **(a)** not with; *they came on a walking holiday without any boots*; *she managed to live for a few days without any food*; *he was stuck in Germany without any money* **(b)** not doing something; *they lived in the hut in the forest without seeing anybody for weeks*

witness [ˈwɪtnəs] **1** *noun* **(a)** person who has seen something happen or who is there when something happens; *the witness happened to be outside the house when the fire started* **(b)** person who is there when someone signs a document; *the contract has to be signed in front of two witnesses* (NOTE: plural is **witnesses**) **2** *verb* **(a)** to be there when something happens, and see it happening; *did anyone witness the accident?* **(b)** to sign a document to show that you guarantee that the other signatures on it are genuine; *one of his friends witnessed his signature*

wives [waɪvz] *see* WIFE

wizard [ˈwɪzəd] *noun* man who is believed to have magic powers; *the wizard made the frog change into a prince*

wobble [ˈwɒbl] *verb* to move from side to side; *if you move the bowl the jelly will wobble*; *don't wobble the table when I'm pouring coffee*

woke *or* **woken** [wəʊk *or* ˈwəʊkn] *see* WAKE

wolf [wʊlf] *noun* wild animal like a large dog, usually living in a large group in cold northern forests; **a pack of wolves** = group of wolves living together (NOTE: plural is **wolves**)

woman [ˈwʊmən] *noun* adult female person; *there were two young women at the table next to ours*; *there are more and more women bus drivers* (NOTE: plural is **women** [ˈwɪmɪn])

won [wʌn] *see* WIN

wonder [ˈwʌndə] **1** *verb* **(a)** to want to know something; *if you don't phone, your parents will start wondering what has happened* **(b)** to think about something; *he's wondering what to do next* **(c)** *(asking a question in a polite way)* *we were wondering if you would like to come to see us on Saturday* **2** *noun* feeling of surprise at something strange; *the little girl stared at the elephant in wonder*; **no wonder** = it doesn't surprise me; *it's no wonder you had difficulty in getting tickets for the show with so many tourists in London*

wonderful [ˈwʌndəful] *adjective* very good, splendid; *they had a wonderful holiday by a lake in Sweden*; *the weather was wonderful for the whole holiday*

won't [wəʊnt] *see* WILL NOT

wood [wʊd] *noun* **(a)** hard material which comes from a tree; *the kitchen table is made of wood*; *she picked up a piece of wood and put it on the fire* **(b)** many trees growing together; *the path goes straight through the wood*; *their house is on the edge of the wood* **(c)** **woods** = area of land covered in trees; *they walked through the woods to the lake* (NOTE: do not confuse with **would**)

wooden [ˈwʊdən] *adjective* made out of wood; *she used a wooden spoon to stir the soup*; *in the market we bought little wooden dolls for the children*

woodpecker [ˈwʊdpekə] *noun* bird with a long sharp beak which makes holes in trees to find insects under the bark; *she heard the woodpecker hammering and then saw it in the tree*

woodwork [ˈwʊdwɜːk] *noun* **(a)** the art of working with wood; *woodwork classes were the ones I liked best at school* **(b)** parts of a building which are made of wood; *all the woodwork will be painted white*

wool [wʊl] *noun* **(a)** long threads of twisted hair, used to make clothes or carpets, etc.; *the carpet is made of wool*; *I need an extra ball of wool to finish this pullover* **(b)** hair growing on a sheep; *the wool is cut from sheep in early summer*

woollen *US* **woolen** [ˈwʊlən] *adjective* made of wool; *she was wearing a red woollen jumper*

woolly ['wʊli] *adjective* **(a)** made out of wool; *she wore a woolly hat* **(b)** looking like wool; *little woolly clouds floated past in the sky* (NOTE: **woollier - woolliest**)

word [wɜːd] *noun* **(a)** separate piece of language, either written or spoken; *this sentence has five words*; *he always has difficulty in spelling words like 'through'* **(b)** something spoken; *she passed me in the street but didn't say a word*; **to have a word with** = to speak to; *I had a word with the waitress about the bill* **(c)** promise which you have made; **to keep your word** = to do what you promised to do; **to take someone's word for it** = to accept what someone says as being true; *OK, I'll take your word for it* **(d) in other words** = which means, that is to say; *it's seven o'clock - in other words, time for dinner*; *we're going on holiday next month, in other words our flat will be empty for about four weeks*

wore ['wɔː] *see* WEAR

work [wɜːk] **1** *noun* **(a)** something done using your strength or your brain; *there's too much work for one person*; *cooking meals for two hundred children every day is hard work* **(b)** job done at regular times to earn money; *he goes to work every day on his bicycle*; *her work involves a lot of travelling* **(c)** book, painting, etc., done by an artist; *we are studying the complete works of Shakespeare* **2** *verb* **(a)** to use your strength or brain to do something; *I can't work in the garden if it's raining*; *he's working hard at school* **(b)** to have a job; *she works in an office in London*; *he used to work in his father's shop* **(c)** *(of machine)* to run; *the computers aren't working because of a power cut* **(d)** to make a machine run; *do you know how to work the washing machine?* **(e)** to be successful; *his plan worked well*

work out ['wɜːk 'aʊt] *verb* **(a)** to calculate; *I'm trying to work out how much it will all cost* **(b)** to succeed; *everything worked out quite well in the end* **(c)** to do exercises; *he*

works out every morning in the gym

worker ['wɜːkə] *noun* **(a)** person who works in a certain way; *he's a fast worker* **(b)** person who works, especially in a certain job; *office workers usually work from 9.30 to 5.30*

workman ['wɜːkmən] *noun* man who works with his hands; *two workmen came to mend the gas boiler* (NOTE: plural is **workmen**)

works [wɜːks] *noun* **(a)** factory; *the steel works will be closed next week for the Christmas holidays* **(b) road works** = repairs to a road

workshop ['wɜːkʃɒp] *noun* very small factory where things are made or repaired; *he runs a workshop for repairing bicycles*

world [wɜːld] *noun* **(a)** the earth on which we live; *he has to travel all over the world on business* **(b) out of this world** = magnificent; *the scenery in the Alps is out of this world*

worm [wɜːm] *noun* small animal which has no bones or legs and lives in the soil; *birds were on the grass looking for worms*

worn [wɔːn] *see* WEAR

worn out ['wɔːn 'aʊt] *adjective* very tired; *he was worn out after the game of rugby*; *she came home worn out after a busy day at college*

worried ['wʌrɪd] *adjective* anxious, feeling that something bad has happened; *I'm worried that we may run out of petrol*; *she had a worried expression on her face*

worry ['wʌri] *verb* to be anxious because of something; *I worry when the children stay out late*; *don't worry, we'll be back on time*

worse [wɜːs] *adjective* **(a)** less good (as compared to something else); *it rained for the first week of our holidays, and the second week was even worse* **(b)** more ill; *he's much worse since he started taking the medicine*

worship ['wɜːʃɪp] *verb* **(a)** to praise and respect God; *the ancient peoples worshipped stone statues of their gods* **(b)** to take part in a church service; *they worship every Sunday in* the local church (c) to praise and love someone very much; *she absolutely worships her boyfriend* (NOTE: **worshipping - worshipped**)

worst [wɜːst] **1** *adjective* worse than anything else; *this is the worst summer for fifty years*; *I think this is the worst film he's ever made* **2** *noun* very bad thing; *the worst of the bad weather is past now*

worth [wɜːθ] *adjective* **(a) to be worth** = to have a certain value or price; *this ring's worth a lot of money*; *the house is worth more than £250,000* **(b) to be worth doing something** = to be a good idea to do something; *it's worth taking a map with you, as you may get lost in the little streets*; *the old castle is well worth visiting*

would [wʊd] *verb used with other verbs* **(a)** *(polite way of asking someone to do something)* *would you like some more tea?* **(b)** *(past of 'will')* *he said he would be here for lunch* **(c)** *(past of 'will', showing something which often happens)* *my son forgot my birthday again this year - he would!* **(d)** *(following a condition)* *I would've done it if you had asked me to*; *if she were still alive, my grandmother would be a hundred years old today*

would rather ['wʊd 'rɑːðə] *verb* to prefer; *I would rather live in London than anywhere else*; *are you all going to pay? - we'd rather not*

wound 1 [wuːnd] *noun* cut made on someone's body, usually in fighting; *he was admitted to hospital with a knife wound in his chest* **2** [wuːnd] *verb* to hurt someone badly in a fight, a war; *two of the gang were wounded in the bank raid* **3** [waʊnd] *see* WIND

wove, woven [wəʊv or 'wəʊvn] *see* WEAVE

wrap (up) [ræp] *verb* **(a)** to cover something all over; *we're wrapping up the Christmas presents for the children*; *if you're cold, wrap yourself up in your blanket* **(b)** to wear warm clothes; *wrap up if you're going for a walk in*

the snow **(c) to wrap round** = to put right round something; *she wrapped her arms around the little boy* (NOTE: **wrapping - wrapped** [ræpt])

wrapping ['ræpɪŋ] *noun* paper, cardboard, plastic, etc., used to wrap something up; *the children pulled the wrapping off their presents*; **wrapping paper** = brightly coloured paper used to wrap presents; *I bought two rolls of Christmas wrapping paper*

wreck [rek] **1** *noun* **(a)** ship which has been sunk or badly damaged; *the wreck of the 'Mary Rose' was found in the sea near Southampton* **(b)** anything which has been damaged and cannot be used; *the police towed away the wreck of the car* **2** *verb* to damage something very badly; *the ship was wrecked on the rocks in the storm*

wrestle ['resl] *verb* to fight with someone to try to throw him to the ground; *the President's guards wrestled with the demonstrators*

wriggle ['rɪgl] *verb* to twist from side to side; *the baby wriggled in her father's arms*; *the worm wriggled back into the soil*

wring [rɪŋ] *verb* to twist something, especially to get water out of it; *he wrung out his shirt before hanging it up to dry* (NOTE: do not confuse with **ring**; note: **wringing - wrung** [rʌŋ])

wrinkle ['rɪŋkl] *noun* **(a)** fold in the skin; *she has wrinkles round her eyes* **(b)** line or crease in cloth, etc.; *he tried to iron out the wrinkles in his trousers*

wrinkled ['rɪŋkld] *adjective* full of lines or creases; *he was wearing a wrinkled old shirt*

wrist [rɪst] *noun* joint between the arm and the hand; *he sprained his wrist and can't play tennis tomorrow*

write [raɪt] *verb* **(a)** to put words or numbers on paper, etc., with a pen, computer, etc.; *she wrote the address on the back of an envelope*; *someone wrote 'teacher go home' on the blackboard*; *he wrote a book on keeping tropical fish* **(b)** to write a letter and send it to someone; *she writes to me twice a week*; *don't forget to write as soon as you get to your hotel* (NOTE: **writing - wrote** [rəʊt] **- has written** ['rɪtn])

write down ['raɪt 'daʊn] *verb* to write on paper, etc.; *she wrote down the number of the car*

writing ['raɪtɪŋ] *noun* **(a)** something which is written; *put everything in writing, then you have a record of what has been done* **(b)** way in which you write words by hand; *his writing's so bad I can't read it*

written ['rɪtn] *adjective* which has been put in writing; *he had a written reply from the Prime Minister's office*

wrong [rɒŋ] **1** *adjective* **(a)** not correct; *he gave three wrong answers and failed the test*; *you've come to the wrong house - there's no one called Jones living here* **(b)** not working properly; *there is something wrong with the television* **(c)** bad; *it's wrong to talk like that about your teacher*; *cheating in exams is wrong* **2** *adverb* badly; *everything went wrong yesterday*; *she spelt my name wrong*

wrongly ['rɒŋli] *adverb* not correctly; *she added up the bill wrongly*; *the teacher spelt my name wrongly*

wrote [rəʊt] *see* WRITE

wrung [rʌŋ] *see* WRING

X, x [eks] **(a)** twenty-fourth letter of the alphabet, between W and Y; *not many words begin with an X* **(b)** *(sign showing that something is multiplied)* *3 x 3 = 9 (say 'three times three equals nine')* **(c)** *(sign showing size)* *the table top is 24 x 36cm (say 'twenty-four by thirty-six centimetres')*

X-ray ['eksreɪ] **1** *noun* **(a)** ray which goes through your body, and allows the bones and organs inside to be seen; *an X-ray examination showed the key was inside the baby's stomach* **(b)** photograph taken with X-rays; *the X-ray showed that the bone was broken in two places*; *they will take an X-ray of his leg* **2** *verb* to take an X-ray photograph of someone; *there are six patients waiting to be X-rayed*

Y, y [waɪ] twenty-fifth letter of the alphabet, between X and Z; *names beginning with Y come almost at the end of the telephone book*

yacht [jɒt] *noun* **(a)** sailing boat, used for pleasure and sport; **yacht club** = private club for people who sail yachts **(b)** large expensive motor boat; *she spent her holiday on a yacht in the Mediterranean*

yard [jɑːd] *noun* **(a)** measurement of length, 36 inches (= 0.914 metres); *the police station is only yards away from where the fight took place* **(b)** area of concrete at the back or side of a house; *we keep our bikes in the yard* **(c)** large area where stores are kept outside, where lorries can pick up or put down loads; *he went to the builder's yard to buy some bricks*

yarn [jɑːn] *noun* long piece of wool used in knitting or weaving; *she sells yarn from the wool of her sheep*

yawn [jɔːn] *verb* to open your mouth wide when feeling sleepy, and to breathe in and out deeply; *half the people in the audience started yawning*

year [jɜː] *noun* **(a)** period of time, lasting twelve months, from January 1st to December 31st; *Columbus discovered America in the year 1492*; *great celebrations took place in the year 2000*; *last year we did not have any holiday* **(b)** a period of twelve months from a particular time; *he died two hundred years ago today*; *she'll be eleven years old tomorrow* **(c)** **years** = a long time; *I haven't seen him for years*

yeast [jiːst] *noun* living fungus used to make bread and alcohol; *yeast is a good source of Vitamin B*

yell [jel] **1** *verb* to shout very loudly; *the policeman yelled to her to get out of the way* **2** *noun* loud shout; *he gave a yell and everyone came running to see what he had found*

yellow ['jeləʊ] *adjective* of a colour like that of the sun or of gold; *his new car is bright yellow* (NOTE: **yellower - yellowest**)

yellow line ['jeləʊ 'laɪn] *noun* line painted along the side of a street, showing that you are not allowed to park; *he got a ticket for parking on a double yellow line*

yellow pages ['jeləʊ 'peɪdʒɪz] *noun* section of a telephone book printed on yellow paper, which lists businesses under various categories, such as computer shops, newspaper shops, etc.; *he looked up 'airlines' in the yellow pages*

yelp [jelp] *verb (usually of animals)* to give a short cry of pain or excitement; *the dogs were yelping in the back of the car*

yes [jes] *adverb (word showing that you agree, accept, etc., the opposite of 'no')* *they asked her if she wanted to come and she said 'yes'*; *anyone want more coffee? - yes, please*; *you don't like living in London? - yes I do!*

yesterday ['jestədeɪ] *adverb & noun* the day before today; *yesterday was March 1st so today must be the 2nd*; *she came to see us yesterday evening*

yet [jet] **1** *adverb* **(a)** already, until now ; *don't throw the newspaper away - I haven't read it yet* **(b)** *(to stress)* *she ate yet another piece of cake* **2** *conjunction* but, still; *he's very small and yet he can kick a ball a long way*

yew [juː] *noun* large evergreen tree with flat green needles and poisonous red berries; *you often find yews growing near churches* (NOTE: do not confuse with **you**)

yoghurt *or* **yogurt** ['jɒgət] *noun* milk which has become slightly sour after bacteria are added, often flavoured with fruit; *a pot of strawberry yoghurt*; **plain yoghurt** = white yoghurt without any special flavour

yolk [jəʊk] *noun* yellow part inside an egg; *in my boiled egg, the yolk was soft and the white was hard*; *beat the yolks of three eggs and add sugar*

you [juː] *pronoun* **(a)** *(referring to someone being spoken to)* *are you ready?*; *you look tired, you should rest a bit*; *hello, how are you?* **(b)** *(referring to anybody)* *you never know when you might need a pair of scissors* (NOTE: do not confuse with **yew**)

you'd [juːd] = YOU HAD, YOU WOULD

you'll [juːl] = YOU WILL

young [jʌŋ] **1** *adjective* not old; *she's very young, she's only six*; *my little brother's much younger than me* (NOTE: **younger - youngest**) **2** *noun* young animals or birds; *animals fight to protect their young*

youngster ['jʌŋstə] *noun* young person; *the factory has taken on four youngsters straight from school*

your [jɔː] *adjective* belonging to you; *I hope you didn't forget to bring your toothbrush*

you're [jʊə or jɔː] = YOU ARE

yours [jɔːz] *pronoun* belonging to you; *my car's in the garage, can I borrow yours?*

yourself *or* **yourselves** [jɔːˈself or jɔːˈselvz] *pronoun* **(a)** *(referring to 'you' as a subject)* *watch out for the broken glass - you might hurt yourself*; *I hope you are all going to enjoy yourselves* **(b) by yourself** *or* **by yourselves** = alone, with no one to help you; *will you be all by yourselves at Christmas?*; *did you find your way back to the hotel all by yourself?*

youth [juːθ] *noun* **(a)** young man; *gangs of youths were causing trouble in the village* **(b)** period when you are young, especially the time between being a child and being an adult; *in his youth he did a lot of swimming*

you've [juːv] = YOU HAVE

Zz

Z, z [zed *US* ziː] last and twenty-sixth letter of the alphabet; *he can say his alphabet from A to Z*

zap [zæp] *verb (informal)* **(a)** *(on a computer)* to hit, to kill; *he zapped all the monsters and got to the end of the game* **(b)** to shut down the television using the remote control (NOTE: **zapping - zapped**)

zebra ['zebrə or ziːbrə] *noun* **(a)** African animal like a horse, with black and white stripes; *zebras' stripes help them hide in the long grass* **(b) zebra crossing** = place marked with black and white lines where you can walk across a road; *it's safer to use a zebra crossing when you're crossing a main road*

zero ['zɪərəʊ] *noun* **(a)** number 0; *to make an international call, you dial zero zero (00), followed by the number of the country* **(b)** freezing point of water on a thermometer; *the temperature stayed below zero for days* **(c)** score of no points; *they lost ten - zero* (NOTE: plural is **zeros**)

zigzag ['zɪgzæg] *adjective & noun* (line) which turns one way, then the opposite way; *there are zigzag lines painted at pedestrian crossings to show that cars must not park there*

zip *or* **zipper** [zɪp or 'zɪpə] **1** *noun* sliding device for closing openings on trousers, dresses, bags, etc., consisting of two rows of teeth which lock together; *the zip of my coat is broken*; *can you do up the zip at the back of my dress?* **2** *verb* **to zip up** = to close something using a zip; *she zipped up her coat*; *he zipped up his bag* (NOTE: **zipping - zipped**)

zip code ['zɪp 'kəʊd] *noun US* system of

letters or numbers to show the town or street in an address, to help with the sorting of mail (the British English is 'postcode'); *don't forget the zip code - it's the most important part of the address*

zipper ['zɪpə] *see* ZIP

zone [zəʊn] *noun* area or part which is different from others, or which has something special; *you can't park here, it's a no-parking zone*; **pedestrian zone** = part of a town where cars are not allowed; *the town centre has been made into a pedestrian zone*

zoo [zu:] *noun* place where wild animals are kept, and where people can go to see them; *we went to the zoo to see the lions and elephants*

zoom [zu:m] *verb* **(a)** to go very fast; *cars were zooming past me on the motorway* **(b) to zoom in on something** = to focus a camera lens so that it makes a distant object seem to come closer; *he zoomed in on the yacht*